Family Therapy for Adc
Weight Disorders

Family-based treatment (FBT) for eating disorders is an outpatient therapy in which parents are utilized as the primary resource in treatment. The therapist supports the parents to do the work nurses would have done if the patient were hospitalized to an inpatient-refeeding unit, and are eventually tasked with encouraging the patient to resume normal adolescent development. In recent years many new adaptations of the FBT intervention have been developed for addressing the needs of special populations. This informative new volume chronicles these novel applications of FBT in a series of chapters authored by the leading clinicians and investigators who are pioneering each adaptation.

Katharine L. Loeb, PhD is Associate Professor of Psychology in the PhD Program in Clinical Psychology at Fairleigh Dickinson University. She was the Founding Director of the Eating and Weight Disorders Program at the Icahn School of Medicine at Mount Sinai, where she maintains an Adjunct Associate Professor of Psychiatry appointment. She has published extensively in the field of eating disorders. Her research involves improving case identification of and parenting capacities in managing child and adolescent eating disorders, and systems-level strategies, including applied behavioral economics, for pediatric overweight and obesity.

Daniel Le Grange, PhD is Benioff UCSF Professor in Children's Health in the Department of Psychiatry and Department of Pediatrics, Joint Director of the Eating Disorders Program at the University of California, San Francisco and Emeritus Professor at The University of Chicago. His research focuses mostly on treatments for adolescents with eating disorders, and he has written extensively on psychosocial treatments for this patient population. In 2013 he received the UCSF Presidential Chair Award, and in 2014 Dr Le Grange received the Leadership in Research Award from the International Academy of Eating Disorders.

James Lock, MD, PhD is Professor of Child Psychiatry and Pediatrics in the Department of Psychiatry and Behavioral Sciences at Stanford University School of Medicine where he also serves as Director of the Eating Disorders Program for Children and Adolescents at Lucile Packard Children's Hospital and Clinics. His research focuses on integrating treatment research with neuroscience in eating disorders. He was awarded the Price Family Foundation Award for Research Excellence in 2010 and the Leadership award from the International Academy of Eating Disorders in 2014.

Family Therapy for Adolescent Eating and Weight Disorders

New Applications

Edited by Katharine L. Loeb, Daniel Le Grange, and James Lock

Routledge
Taylor & Francis Group

NEW YORK AND LONDON

First published 2015
by Routledge
711 Third Avenue, New York, NY 10017

and by Routledge
27 Church Road, Hove, East Sussex BN3 2FA

Routledge is an imprint of the Taylor & Francis Group, an informa business

Library of Congress Cataloging in Publication Data
A catalog record for this book has been requested.

ISBN: 978-0-415-71473-0 (hbk)
ISBN: 978-0-415-71474-7 (pbk)
ISBN: 978-1-315-88244-4 (ebk)

Typeset in Sabon
by CodeMantra

Printed and bound in the United States of America by Publishers Graphics, LLC on sustainably sourced paper.

Contents

About the Editors

Katharine L. Loeb, PhD, is Associate Professor of Psychology in the PhD Program in Clinical Psychology at Fairleigh Dickinson University. She was the Founding Director of the Eating and Weight Disorders Program at the Icahn School of Medicine at Mount Sinai, where she maintains an Adjunct Associate Professor of Psychiatry appointment. She has published extensively in the field of eating disorders. Her research involves improving case identification of and parenting capacities in managing child and adolescent eating disorders, and systems-level strategies, including applied behavioral economics, for pediatric overweight and obesity.

Daniel Le Grange, PhD, is Benioff UCSF Professor in Children's Health in the Department of Psychiatry and Department of Pediatrics, Joint Director of the Eating Disorders Program at the University of California, San Francisco and Emeritus Professor at The University of Chicago. His research focuses mostly on treatments for adolescents with eating disorders, and he has written extensively on psychosocial treatments for this patient population. In 2013 he received the UCSF Presidential Chair Award, and in 2014 Dr Le Grange received the Leadership in Research Award from the International Academy of Eating Disorders.

James Lock, MD, PhD, is professor of Child Psychiatry and Pediatrics in the Department of Psychiatry and Behavioral Sciences at Stanford University School of Medicine where he also serves as director of the Eating Disorders Program for Children and Adolescents. His research focuses on integrating treatment research with neuroscience in eating disorders. He was awarded the Price Family Foundation Award for Research Excellence in 2010 and the Leadership award from the International Academy of Eating Disorders in 2014.

About the Contributors

Erin C. Accurso, PhD, is a postdoctoral fellow with the Midwest Regional Postdoctoral Training Grant in Eating Disorders Research at the University of Chicago. She received her BA in psychology from Dartmouth College and her PhD in clinical psychology from the San Diego State University/University of California, San Diego Joint Doctoral Program in Clinical Psychology. Her research interests include treatments for eating disorders and overweight in youth and also dissemination and implementation of evidence-based practices in the community.

Kristen E. Anderson, LCSW, is the co-director and a therapist at the University of Chicago Eating Disorders Program. Kristen's clinical and research interests include family-based treatment and the use of innovative technological approaches to treatment.

Vandana Aspen, PhD, is a postdoctoral fellow in the Department of Psychiatry and Behavioral Sciences at Stanford University, Stanford (UCSD), California.

Terri Bacow, PhD, is the director of Clinical Services at the Eating and Weight Disorders Program at the Mount Sinai School of Medicine. A graduate of Boston University, she is a practicing clinical psychologist who specializes in treating anxiety, mood, and eating disorders across the age spectrum using cognitive-behavioral and family-based treatment methods. Her research interests include investigating factors that contribute to the effectiveness of eating disorders treatment in youth.

Kelly Bhatnagar, PhD, is the site and research manager for the Emily Program–Cleveland. She has extensive training in empirically supported treatments, including FBT, DBT, and CBT. She is FBT-certified through the Training Institute for Child and Adolescent Eating Disorders and a member of the Research-Practice Committee for AED. Her research/clinical interests include integrating FBT with DBT to treat multi-diagnostic youth with eating disorders. Dr. Bhatnagar has published in peer-reviewed journals and invited book chapters. She has presented her work at national and international conferences.

Kerri Boutelle, PhD, is a professor of pediatrics and psychiatry at UCSD. She is the director of the Center for Healthy Eating and Activity Research (CHEAR) at UCSD, which has been continually funded by NIH for the past 12 years. Dr. Boutelle has a bachelor's degree in food science, a doctorate in clinical psychology, completed her clinical internship at the University of Mississippi Medical Center, and completed her postdoctoral fellowship in epidemiology at the University of Minnesota.

Danielle Colborn, PhD, is a clinical psychologist specializing in the treatment of eating disorders and adolescents. She works at Stanford University as a clinical instructor and sees patients in private practice. Dr. Colborn supervises doctoral trainees and is involved in community outreach to educate the public and medical providers about the identification and prevention of eating disorders in youth. Dr. Colborn has research interest in eating disorder treatment, neurocognition in adolescent anorexia and bulimia, and pediatric obesity.

Jennifer L. Couturier, MD, is a child and adolescent psychiatrist and the medical co-director of the Pediatric Eating Disorders Program at McMaster Children's Hospital. She is also an associate professor within the Departments of Psychiatry and Behavioural Neurosciences, Pediatrics, and Clinical Epidemiology and Biostatistics at McMaster University. Dr. Couturier completed a postdoctoral research fellowship at Stanford University. Her research focuses on psychotherapy for eating disorders, with a special interest in family therapy approaches and implementation science.

Katherine Craigen, PhD, graduated with her doctorate in clinical psychology from Fairleigh Dickinson University. She is currently a post doctoral fellow in the Eating and Weight Disorders Program at the Icahn School of Medicine at Mount Sinai in New York, NY.

Alison Darcy, PhD, is an instructor in child and adolescent psychiatry at Stanford University School of Medicine. Dr. Darcy's research is centered around the intersection of psychiatry and technology and innovation in treatment. She has developed novel methods of disseminating family-based treatment and clinical training using emerging technologies.

Gina Dimitropoulos, MSW, PhD, is a clinician scientist and the family therapy leader of the Eating Disorder Program at the University Health

Network in Toronto and is cross-appointed at the Hospital for Sick Children. Her research focuses on evaluation of various family-based treatments, including family-based treatment for transition age youth with anorexia nervosa, multi-family therapy and single-family therapy for adults with eating disorders.

Elizabeth Dodge, MSc, CQSW, is a family and systemic psychotherapist who has worked as a clinician, trainer, and researcher in eating disorders in London and more recently in New Zealand. She is currently based in London and involved in clinical practice and training.

Angela Celio Doyle, PhD, is co-director of the Eating Disorders Center at the Evidence Based Treatment Centers of Seattle and a clinical instructor of psychology at the University of Washington. Dr. Doyle received her bachelor and master's degrees from Stanford University and earned her doctorate in clinical psychology from the SDSU/UCSD Joint Doctoral Program. More recently, Dr. Doyle was on faculty at the University of Chicago in the Department of Psychiatry and Behavioral Neuroscience.

Peter M. Doyle, PhD, is co-director of the Eating Disorders Center at EBTCS in Seattle, Washington, as well as a clinical faculty member in the Department of Psychology at the University of Washington. In addition to his clinical work with adults and adolescents with a range of eating and body image issues, he and the other directors at EBTCS are pioneering the integration of clinical research in private practice.

Ivan Eisler, PhD, is emeritus professor of family psychology and family therapy at Kings College, London, and joint head of the Child and Adolescent Eating Disorders Service at the Maudsley Hospital in London. For many years, he has been developing and evaluating psychotherapies for anorexia and bulimia nervosa as well as treatments for depression, substance misuse, self-harm, and chronic illness. He and his colleagues developed an eating disorders-focused family therapy that is widely accepted as leading evidence-based treatment for adolescent anorexia nervosa and have also pioneered an innovative intensive multiple-family therapy version of this treatment

Kathleen Kara Fitzpatrick, PhD, has worked in the Eating Disorders Clinic at Stanford for nine years. She specializes in neuropsychological assessment of eating disorders and evaluation of treatments for children and adolescents. Her current research interests focus on the development of Cognitive Remediation Therapy (CRT), which utilizes neuropsychological components to address cognitive and behavioral difficulties associated with eating disorders. In addition to working as a therapist on research treatment studies, she also provides supervision to therapists on different treatment modalities.

Sarah E. Forsberg, PsyD, is a clinical instructor in the department of Psychiatry and Behavioral Sciences at Stanford University where she provides evidence-based treatments for eating disorders. Her clinical and research interests include the development, dissemination, and training practices surrounding family-based treatments for childhood eating disorders. Her recent work focuses on the therapeutic alliance and treatment fidelity within the context of family-based treatment for adolescent anorexia nervosa.

Rebecca Greif, PsyD, is a clinical psychologist and assistant clinical professor at the Mount Sinai Eating and Weight Disorders Program in New York City. Dr. Greif specializes in the treatment of children and adults with anxiety and eating disorders. Dr. Greif's research interests focus on the advancement and dissemination of evidence-based psychological treatments for these populations.

Lisa Hail, MA, is a PhD candidate at Fairleigh Dickinson University. Her research focus is on the treatment of eating disorders, particularly with co-morbid substance use disorders, and on the role of body image in treatment outcome.

Brooke Halpert, PhD, CPsych, is a licensed Clinical and Health Psychologist. She is a postdoctoral fellow with the Eating Disorders Program at the Hospital for Sick Children in Toronto, Canada. In addition, she works with the Sick Kids Team Obesity Management Program and will soon join the Eating Disorders Team at McMaster Children's Hospital. Dr. Halpert has a long-standing interest in child and adolescent development; her early research focused on factors associated with the quality of parent-child interactions in preschoolers and young children.

Tom Hildebrandt, PsyD, is the director of the Eating and Weight Disorders Program at Mount Sinai and assistant professor of psychiatry at the Icahn School of Medicine at Mount Sinai. He completed his graduate training at Rutgers University and his postdoctoral fellowship in Eating Disorders at the Icahn School of Medicine at Mount Sinai. He currently oversees the development and execution of both the clinical and research programs.

Roslyn Binford Hopf, PhD, is an individual and family-based treatment therapist in Koenigstein, Germany. She received her doctorate in clinical psychology from the University of Minnesota and completed her clinical internship and postdoctoral fellowship at the University of

Chicago. She was an Alexander von Humboldt Research Fellow at the Center for Psychotherapy Research at the University Hospital Heidelberg, Germany.

Renee Rienecke Hoste, PhD, is director of Clinical Services and Research of the University of Michigan Comprehensive Eating Disorders Program and an assistant professor of psychiatry. Dr. Hoste received her PhD from Northwestern University and completed her clinical psychology internship and postdoctoral fellowship at the University of Chicago. Her research interests include the role of expressed emotion in treatment outcome for adolescent eating disorders and the impact of the family on treatment outcome.

Elizabeth Hughes, PhD, is a research fellow at the Royal Children's Hospital and University of Melbourne, Australia. She received her PhD in psychology from Monash University. She holds honorary research fellow positions with the Murdoch Children's Research Institute and the School of Psychological Sciences at Monash University. Dr. Hughes' research focuses on the treatment of eating disorders in adolescents, particularly family-based treatment for anorexia nervosa. Her research interests also include co-morbidity in eating disorders, emotion regulation, and family systems.

Prof. Dr. Corinna Jacobi is a Professor of Clinical Psychology and Psychotherapy TU Dresden and holds the Chair "Eating and Associated Disorders". She is also the director of an outpatient unit for eating disorders associated with TU Dresden and a licensed psychotherapist in behavior therapy. Her research focus is on basic and treatment-related research on eating disorders including meta-analyses on eating disorder risk factors and treatment outcomes, as well as randomized controlled intervention trials (prevention and treatment). In close and long-standing collaboration with researchers from Stanford University she has developed and evaluated several Internet-based interventions for the prevention of eating disorders and of relapses following inpatient treatment. She has been a member of the guideline group for the development for evidence-based guidelines for ED in Germany and was awarded the "Christina Barz-Research Award" in 1997.

Megan Jones, PsyD, is a Clinical Assistant Professor in the Department of Psychiatry and Behavioral Sciences at Stanford University School of Medicine. She is the Chief Medical Officer at Lantern and Visiting Scientist at the Medical University of Vienna. Her research focuses on digital health, eating disorders prevention, and dissemination of online interventions. Dr. Jones has a clinical specialization in eating disorders and child and adolescent psychology.

Walter H. Kaye, MD, is a professor of psychiatry at the University of California San Diego and director of the Eating Disorders Research and Treatment Program. His current research is focused on exploring the relationship between brain and behavior using brain imaging and investigating new treatments in anorexia and bulimia nervosa. Dr. Kaye has an international reputation in the field of eating disorders and is the author of more than 300 articles and publications.

Melissa S. Kimber, MSW, is a PhD candidate in the Health Research Methodology Program within the Department of Clinical Epidemiology and Biostatistics at McMaster University in Ontario, Canada. Ms. Kimber's work focuses on adolescent eating disorders and body image dissatisfaction and the extent to which their putative risk and protective factors vary for immigrant and non-immigrant adolescents. Ms. Kimber has a keen interest in the extent to which evidence-based treatments are implemented and adapted by mental health service providers.

Stephanie Knatz, PhD, is a clinical psychologist and program director for the Intensive Family Treatment (IFT) Program at the University of California, San Diego Eating Disorder Treatment and Research Center. In addition to serving as lead therapist, Dr. Knatz was involved in developing the clinical content for the program alongside leading experts of family-based treatment and multi-family models of care. In addition to her clinical work, Dr. Knatz also conducts treatment research focused on developing and testing clinical applications of neurobiology in eating disorders.

Enrica Marzola, MD, is a psychiatrist who earned her MD from the University of Turin, Italy, where she completed also her residency in psychiatry. Since 2008, Dr. Marzola has been working with patients affected by eating disorders and their families. Dr. Marzola is now a PhD student in neuroscience; during her PhD, she visited the Eating Disorders Center for Treatment and Research of the University of California–San Diego, participating in research projects on Intensive Family Therapy.

Christian Pariseau, MD, is a clinical assistant professor of pediatric, adolescent, and young adult medicine, and medical co-director of the Comprehensive Eating Disorders Program at the University of Michigan.

Amy Parter, BA, is a PhD candidate in clinical psychology at Fairleigh Dickinson University. She works under the research advisement of Dr. Katharine Loeb. Her research focus is the treatment of adolescent eating disorders.

Susan M. Sawyer, MBBS, MD, FRACP, FSAHM, holds the chair of adolescent health at the University of Melbourne within the Department of Paediatrics. A pediatrician by training, she is director of the Centre for Adolescent Health at the Royal Children's Hospital Melbourne and a research fellow at the Murdoch Children's Research Institute.

Mima Simic, MD, MRCPsych, is a joint head of the CAMHS National and Specialist Child and Adolescent Eating Disorders Service (CAEDS) and consultant child and adolescent psychiatrist for the adolescent DBT Service at the Maudsley Hospital, London. For more than 25 years, her clinical work has been focused on development of new treatments for children and adolescents with eating disorders or self-harm. Her main research interest involves testing the efficacy of treatments in eating disorders.

Corinne Sweeney is a doctoral candidate in clinical psychology at Fairleigh Dickinson University. She earned her MA in psychology from New York University and her BA from Wake Forest University. Corinne's research interests and clinical work center on identification of child and adolescent eating disorders and supporting families and children confronted with medical illness.

C. Barr Taylor, MD, is a professor of psychiatry (emeritus, active) at Stanford Medical School. He attended Columbia College as an undergraduate, completed his medical training at the University of Utah and his residency in Psychiatry at the University of Utah and Stanford Medical Center. His research focus is on using technology to prevent and treat eating disorders and other mental health problems. He has published seven professional books and more than 300 academic articles.

Andrew Wallis, MFT a clinical specialist social worker and family therapist. He is currently co-head of the Eating Disorders Service at Sydney Children's Hospital Network, a tertiary service in Sydney, Australia, and deputy head of Adolescent Medicine at the Children's Hospital, Westmead. In 2003, family-based treatment was implemented as the primary mode of outpatient care. Mr. Wallis has been a central figure in the development of family therapy for eating disorders in Australasia, providing training, supervision, and consultation to numerous eating disorder teams nationally and internationally.

Lucene Wisniewski, PhD, FAED, is chief clinical officer of the Emily Program and is an adjunct assistant professor of Psychological Sciences at Case Western Reserve University. From 2006–14, she served as clinical director and co-founder of the Cleveland Center for Eating Disorders. Dr. Wisniewski has been elected fellow and has served on the board of directors and as the co-chair of the Borderline Personality Disorder special interest group of the Academy for Eating Disorders (AED).

Blake Woodside, MD, is the director of the inpatient eating disorders program at the Toronto General Hospital and professor in the department of psychiatry at the University of Toronto. His specialty in psychiatry is the treatment of eating disorders in adults. He is a clinical member and approved supervisor for the American Association of Marriage and Family Therapy.

Nancy Zucker is an Associate Professor in the Department of Psychiatry and Behavioral Sciences at Duke University School of Medicine and in the Department of Psychology and Neuroscience at Duke University. She is the Director of the Duke Center for Eating Disorders. She studies how people learn to decipher their body signals (often referred to as interoceptive signals) and use that information to make decisions and develop a sense of self-knowledge and awareness. She uses what she learns to develop interventions across the lifespan that help individuals and dyads improve their sensing and understanding of themselves and others.

Chapter 1

Introduction

The Role of the Family in Eating Disorders

*Katharine L. Loeb, Daniel Le Grange,
and James Lock*

The role of the family in understanding the psychopathology of eating disorders, particularly anorexia nervosa (AN), and by extension in interventions developed to ameliorate these pernicious syndromes, has been a topic of controversy since AN was first identified in the nineteenth century. As with many mental disorders in the history of psychiatry and psychology, eating disorders have fallen prey at times to the seductive, clinically face-valid (Bulik, 2005) parent-blaming attributions that have ultimately been disproved in other cases of severe psychopathology, such as schizophrenia and autism. The conceptualization of AN as a radical, maladaptive, unconscious ploy for autonomy and self-determination in the context of enmeshed family dynamics has historically led to clinical recommendations for minimal or no parental involvement in the recovery process; in its most extreme form, this strategy is known as a "parentectomy." In the late twentieth century, however, a new, innovative family-based intervention took form at the Maudsley Hospital in the United Kingdom that defied this clinical lore in its agnostic stance concerning the etiology of eating disorders; in its content and structure by enlisting parents as agents of change in their child's renourishment and symptom resolution; in its focus on family strengths over vulnerabilities; in its target of treatment as the externalized illness, not systems-level or individual pathology; and most importantly, in its promising early results for young patients (Russell, Szmukler, Dare, & Eisler, 1987). Beyond these factors, its relative success in achieving and/or maintaining weight restoration on an outpatient basis was remarkable for a disorder that typically required intensive hospitalization. This maverick treatment, an amalgam of established models and techniques of family therapy and pragmatic, disorder-specific methods, has over time and across continents since been subjected to academic research in the form of randomized controlled trials and case series, to media scrutiny, and to partnership with parent and patient advocacy efforts. In light of its explicit agenda of blame reduction toward parents as a clinical tactic, it has also prompted great debate about eating disorders research and clinical priorities, particularly the nature and degree of focus on familial factors (Strober & Johnson, 2012). Notably, an appreciation of the strengths (and limitations) of family-based treatment for child and adolescent eating disorders is fully compatible with caution in not throwing the proverbial "baby out with the bathwater" and ignoring the import of genetics, of epigenetics, and of passive gene–environment correlations, such as a genetically influenced family environment, in the development of eating disorders (Bulik, Reba, Siega-Riz, & Reichborn-Kjennerud, 2005; Le Grange, Lock, Loeb, & Nicholls, 2010; Strober, Peris, & Steiger, 2014). In particular, understanding such risk factors can have significant implications for the development of targeted interventions to *prevent* the onset of AN and bulimia nervosa in vulnerable individuals (Striegel-Moore & Bulik, 2007), the ultimate goal of our field.

As this family-based treatment (FBT) generated professional and public attention, two published manuals (Le Grange & Lock, 2007; Lock & Le Grange, 2013), a collection of studies in support of its utility (Couturier, Kimber, & Szatmari, 2013), and an established training institute for dissemination, it simultaneously inspired a number of creative modifications and adaptations for different patient populations, psychiatric comorbidities, and treatment settings. In a prime example of the cyclical and synergistic relationship between science and practice, the realities of clinical challenges have driven new FBT formats, applications, and research endeavors; at the same time, efficacy and other FBT study findings have yielded a paradigm shift in treatment selection in the clinical realm for youth with eating disorders. That all this occurred in a relatively accelerated timeline for a newer psychological intervention speaks to the sense of urgency in the field to thwart the default trajectory of AN as a chronic disorder with a high risk of mortality (Crow et al., 2009; Papadopoulos, Ekbom, Brandt, & Ekselius, 2009). This book was thus inspired by the growing professional, collaborative network of researchers and clinicians sharing ideas, protocols, observations, and preliminary results, and the need for their cutting-edge work to be made available as a resource in a single volume. The adaptations and new applications described in this book therefore vary in their stages of development and testing.

The book begins with the voice of Ivan Eisler and colleagues from the Maudsley Hospital on the origins of FBT, its roots in family therapy, the essence of the approach, and its evolution since the first published study. As a "parent" of family therapy for adolescent AN, Eisler provides a unique and important perspective that sets the tone and frame for the chapters that follow. Specifically, Andrew Wallis, Elizabeth Dodge, and he speak to the core elements of the treatment model and the imperative to favor fidelity to its principles over rigid manual adherence in achieving optimal outcomes, particularly with complex cases.

Part I

The section that follows contains six adaptations of FBT relevant for the original target population of children and adolescents with AN. In Chapter 1,

Fitzpatrick and colleagues describe how behaviors during the family meal contribute to recovery. The family meal is seen by some as a controversial intervention, especially as its role in outcome is unclear. This chapter provides clinicians with a comprehensive overview of how changing mealtime behaviors can enhance FBT treatment. Next, Hughes and colleagues describe a "parent only" version of FBT building on the research framework of the effectiveness of separated family therapy. The approach described focuses expressly on helping parents change their behaviors and interventions to promote weight restoration without the direct input of the adolescent. Knatz and colleagues describe a five-day intensive program for families based on the principles of FBT. Included in this five-day intensive program are assessment, multi-family groups, individual family sessions, and parent training programs. Models like these facilitate rapid training in FBT, a valuable option for families from geographical areas in which there are no FBT providers. In their chapter, Hildebrandt, Bacow, and Greif describe how FBT can be conceptualized and adapted as an exposure-based intervention, illustrating this through both research and clinical materials. Additional information about the potential role of multi-family groups (MFG) in the treatment of eating disorders in youth, Eisler and Simic describe the evolution and refinement of MFGs in the United Kingdom, Canada, Germany, and the Czech Republic. On a related theme, Binford and colleagues describe the important role that parent support groups can have to encourage and facilitate change in families who are involved in FBT.

Part II

This section contains seven chapters applying FBT principles and strategies to specialty populations in eating and weight disorders. In the first two of these chapters, Katharine Loeb and her colleagues provide a detailed description of the adaptation of FBT for two rather different clinical populations; FBT for prodromal AN as well as a transdevelopmental approach of FBT for child and adolescent overweight and obesity. These chapters extend from protocols developed in two recently completed randomized clinical trials. In the only chapter that focuses on a nonadolescent population, Gina Dimitropoulos and her colleagues highlight their Toronto-based reworking of FBT for emerging adults with AN (i.e., persons older than age eighteen making the transition to adult clinical services). DSM-5 has introduced Avoidant Restrictive Food Intake Disorder, and Kara Fitzpatrick and colleagues embark on this novel road to provide an understanding of how FBT strategies may operate and change to support families facing food neophobias. In another unique reworking of FBT, Danielle Colborn and Kara Fitzpatrick outline the therapeutic steps for families whose overweight adolescent is to embark on a surgical intervention for weight loss. The final two chapters of Part II focus on the challenges of affect dysregulation in adolescents diagnosed with an eating disorder. Kelly Bhatnagar and Lucene Wisniewski, experts in dialectical behavior therapy, highlight how the techniques from this therapeutic approach may be integrated with or work adjunctively to FBT. In the final chapter here, Nancy Zucker more broadly expands on the topic of emotional experience and regulation in eating disorders, explicating its theory, evidence, and translational application to family treatment.

Part III

Part III addresses the challenges and solutions in the dissemination and implementation of FBT. Although research supports the effectiveness of FBT, a variety of difficulties arise when applying the approach practically in real-world settings. Woodside and colleagues describe how the principles of FBT can be utilized in complex settings, such as hospitals and day programs, while in contrast, Doyle and colleagues describe how FBT can be effectively and efficiently implemented in a specialty eating disorder outpatient practice. Jones, Jacobi, and Taylor describe the development, content, and utility of a Web-based prevention program for parents whose children are at risk for developing AN. More general challenges related to implementation of FBT are illustrated by Kimber and Couturier, including training, fidelity to the treatment approach, as well as the impact of clinical practice and support services. Finally, Fitzpatrick and colleagues describe the specific challenges in describing, assessing, and maintaining fidelity to FBT. This important chapter reconciles the multiple challenges of supporting the dissemination of an effective intervention while minimizing therapist drift from aspects of the treatment that may represent its active mechanisms and maximizing the potency of each therapeutic maneuver.

Future Directions

This edited volume very aptly demonstrates a tremendous spirit for innovation in the treatment of adolescents with eating and weight disorders. Our hope is that many young sufferers and their families will benefit from these various reworkings of the original family therapy for adolescent AN spearheaded by Ivan Eisler and his colleagues in London. Much of the work described here is in the process of examination in more formal, systematic research designs. Not to discount the tremendous value of this compilation of rich and informative clinical material, it is fair to suggest that each one of these adaptations should stand the scrutiny of rigorous tests of its efficacy. Although several of these adaptations are the result of such scientific endeavors, we hope that this book inspires additional treatment research to in turn inform best practices for eating and weight disorders.

References

Bulik, C. M. (2005). Exploring the gene-environment nexus in eating disorders. *Journal of Psychiatry and Neuroscience*, 30, 335–339.

Bulik, C. M., Reba, L., Siega-Riz, A. M., & Reichborn-Kjennerud, T. (2005). Anorexia nervosa: definition, epidemiology, and cycle of risk. *International Journal of Eating Disorders, 37*, S2–S9.

Couturier, J., Kimber, M., & Szatmari, P. (2013). Efficacy of family-based treatment for adolescents with eating disorders: A systematic review and meta-analysis. *International Journal of Eating Disorders, 46*(1), 3–11.

Crow, S. J., Peterson, C. B., Swanson, S. A., Raymond, N. C., Specker, S., Eckert, E. D., & Mitchell, J. E. (2009). Increased mortality in bulimia nervosa and other eating disorders. *The American Journal of Psychiatry, 166*(12), 1342–1346.

Le Grange, D. & Lock, J. (2007). *Treatment bulimia in adolescents: A family-based approach.* New York: Guilford Press.

Le Grange, D., Lock, J., Loeb, K., & Nicholls, D. (2010). Academy for Eating Disorders position paper: The role of the family in eating disorders. *International Journal of Eating Disorders, 43*(1), 1–5.

Lock, J., & Le Grange, D. (2013). *Treatment manual for anorexia nervosa: A family-based approach* (2nd ed.). New York: Guilford Press.

Papadopoulos, F. C., Ekbom, A., Brandt, L., & Ekselius, L. (2009). Excess mortality, causes of death and prognostic factors in anorexia nervosa. *The British Journal of Psychiatry, 194*(1), 10–17.

Russell, G. F. M., Szmukler, G. I., Dare, C., & Eisler, I. (1987). An evaluation of family therapy in anorexia nervosa and bulimia nervosa. *Archives of General Psychiatry, 44*, 1047–1056.

Striegel-Moore, R. H., & Bulik, C. M. (2007). Risk factors for eating disorders. *American Psychologist, 62*, 181–198.

Strober, M., & Johnson, C. (2012). The need for complex ideas in anorexia nervosa: Why biology, environment, and psyche all matter, why therapists make mistakes, and why clinical benchmarks are needed for managing weight correction. *International Journal of Eating Disorders, 45*(2), 155–178.

Strober, M., Peris, T., & Steiger, H. (2014). The plasticity of development: How knowledge of epigenetics may advance understanding of eating disorders. *International Journal of Eating Disorders, 47*(7), 696–704.

Chapter 2

What's New Is Old and What's Old Is New

The Origins and Evolution of Eating Disorders Family Therapy

Ivan Eisler, Andrew Wallis, and Elizabeth Dodge

Any historical account has to choose a focal point in time that marks the start of its "history," a time point that is inevitably somewhat arbitrary. We start our account of the development of eating disorder focused family therapy (sometimes described as "Family-Based Treatment" or the "Maudsley model"[1]) with the series of studies undertaken from the 1980s onwards at the Maudsley Hospital/Institute of Psychiatry in London. These not only had a major influence on the treatment of adolescents, and to some extent adult eating disorders, but also on the changes in family therapy beliefs around the family being a resource in treatment rather than a dysfunctional system to be treated. More than thirty years have passed since the first Maudsley trial, and there have been significant developments regarding thinking about the etiology (Jacobi et al., 2004; Keel & Forney, 2013; Konstantellou, Campbell, & Eisler, 2012) and treatment of eating disorders (Eisler, 2005; Eisler, Lock, & Le Grange, 2010), the development of the evidence base for the effectiveness of family therapy (Couturier, Kimber, & Szatmari, 2013; Downs & Blow, 2013), the importance of the context in which the treatment is delivered (House et al., 2012), and, of course, the cultural and social contexts in which the families, patients, clinicians, and researchers live and work. Most of the story concerns the developments in the family therapy for adolescent anorexia nervosa (FT-AN), which is the focus of this chapter.

---

1 In recent years the acronym FBT has started to be used widely to refer either to the Lock and Le Grange (2013) treatment manual or more generically to what we describe here as eating disorder focused family therapy. The term FBT has several disadvantages. In addition to the ambiguity of whether it is referring to the Lock and Le Grange manual (or studies using the manual) or to other works which have not used the manual or used a different manual, it is sometimes (mis)understood as implying that it is an atheoretical treatment, disconnecting the approach from the conceptual frame of systemic family therapy. Outside of the field of eating disorders, FBT is also used to mean a multimodal treatment (including individual, family, and wider systems work with a central focus on the family). We have therefore used the term FT-AN throughout the chapter.

This chapter sets out to summarize the developments in FT-AN since the first trial, the broader themes in family therapy that were influential, and the core concepts that have been and continue to influence family therapy practice in eating disorders across the world. Future challenges and the different expressions of practice are highlighted with the unifying theme that parents are the key resource in the young person's life and therefore need to be mobilized and strengthened to take leadership over the illness in order to restore the young person's health, well-being, and psychosocial development.

Family Therapy of the Time—The Origins of Family Therapy for Anorexia Nervosa

Influential Developments in Family Therapy

The original Maudsley trials were conducted in London in the 1980s during a time of formative theoretical and model development in family therapy, and they drew heavily on the developments that had occurred since the early 1950s. The major shifts in family therapy are noted here and form a foundation for appreciating the development of family therapy for anorexia nervosa.

The early family therapists developed an understanding of problems as interpersonal rather than intrapersonal and therefore developed interventions that addressed relationships between people, with a primary focus on the family context. Problem explanations became circular rather than linear, placing an emphasis on mutual influence in the family system. Problems were seen as occurring within the context of interactional patterns of behaviors or beliefs, and maintaining homeostasis within the family system (Jackson, 1956). These developments drew on a range of theoretical ideas including General Systems Theory (von Bertalanffy, 1968), cybernetic principles (Bateson, 1972; 1979), and social psychological research of small social groups (Parsons & Bales, 1955), and these developments were a counterpoint to the dominant focus of the day on psychodynamic explanations for behavior.

In the 1960s, significant research efforts were made to develop methods to capture the minutiae of the family processes that were thought to underpin the problems that individuals presented with (in those days frequently referred to as the identified patient to emphasize that the individual was simply the "carrier of the family disturbance") (Eisler, Dare, & Szmukler, 1988; Riskin & Faunce, 1972).

As these ideas took hold, a number of influential models of family therapy emerged by the 1970s such as Structural (Minuchin, 1974), Strategic (Haley, 1976; Madanes, 1981), Brief Therapy (Watzlawick, Weakland, & Fisch, 1974), Milan Systems Therapy (Selvini Palazzoli, 1978), and Behavioral (Patterson, 1971), as well as models based on the transgenerational ideas of Bowen (1978), and the intergenerational patterns of invisible loyalties (Boszormony-Nagy & Spark, 1973). A number of these models influenced the development of FT-AN as practiced at the Maudsley Hospital. While each model subscribed to systems theory as a unifying philosophy, they were differentiated by different concepts of change and the different role that a therapist had in the process (Frosh, 1991). These theoretical developments sparked a marked increase in the development of family therapy in Child and Adolescent Mental Health services (formerly Child Guidance Clinics) particularly in the United Kingdom in the late 1970s and early 1980s, with the development of family therapy trainings and journals focused specifically on family interventions.

Theoretical developments continued in the 1980s with constructivist ideas (Dell, 1985; Maturana & Varela, 1987), which emphasize the unique perspective that each individual has in construing reality of the outside world, and social constructionist theories (Berger & Luckman, 1966; Gergen, 1985), which highlight the way meaning is shaped by language in social interactions within families but also in the context of wider social systems influenced by culture, history, and society at large. A key theoretical shift with significant practical implications was the recognition that the therapist should be considered part of the system rather than being able to independently intervene in the system from the outside (Hoffman, 1985; 1990). This was coupled with feminist critiques (Goldner, 1985; Hare-Mustin, 1986; Luepnitz, 1988) of earlier concepts of mutual influence and therapist neutrality as they ignored notions of power and therefore failed to take into account personal responsibility for abuse and violence.

These influences had a theoretical and practical impact on managing the therapeutic relationship and developments in therapeutic technique, including a more sophisticated use of questions to elicit change (Eisler, 2002; Tomm, 1987a; 1987b; 1988) and the use of narrative techniques to deconstruct and externalize problems and make available positive beliefs, stories, and resources (White, 1995; White & Epston, 1990). Careful consideration was given to the process of interaction between the therapist, the team, and the family and how to conduct this interaction in a manner that increased collaboration and addressed the issue of therapist power. These considerations included inviting families to observe and comment to team reflections (Andersen, 1987; 1995), a range of techniques that involved the use of client 'expertise' as part of the team (Sparks, 1997; White, 2000), and a general emphasis on families being mobilized as a resource rather than needing to be 'fixed' (Flaskas, 2002; Hoffman, 1998; Pocock, 1995). The overwhelming message was that families are the solution and not the problem. In many ways the current prominent carer movements (Alexander & Treasure, 2012) that promote family approaches in eating disorder treatment has its beginnings in these changes.

While these developments have been described generally, the treatment of anorexia nervosa has been prominent in the application of many of these ideas, with structural family therapy (Minuchin et al., 1975), the early work of the Milan group (Selvini-Palazzoli et al., 1978), strategic therapy (Haley, 1963; 1976; Watzlawick, Weakland, & Fisch, 1974), and narrative therapy (Epston, Morris, & Maisel, 1995; White, 1986), all models taking a particular interest in developing treatment strategies for eating disorders. Central to each model are certain notions about the family's role or position in the etiology of the problem, and these theoretical models have contributed in powerful ways to how families are viewed when anorexia nervosa develops.

The Family and Anorexia Nervosa

The role of the family has been discussed as either being part of the etiology of anorexia nervosa or, at the very least, a rather pernicious influence on treatment from the time of Gull (1874), Lasegue (1873), and Marcé (1860). For example, Gull (1874) observed, "I have remarked that these willful patients are often allowed to drift their own way into a state of extreme exhaustion, when it might have been prevented by placing them under different moral conditions. The patients should be fed at regular intervals and surrounded by persons who would have moral control over them; relatives and friends being generally the worst attendants."

A number of influential clinicians from the psychodynamic tradition, in addition to focusing on the internal world of the sufferer, have viewed the family as a dysfunctional system (Waller, Kaufman, & Deutsch, 1940), both connected to the development of the eating disorder and a required target of treatment. Hilde Bruch (1973) emphasized the role of the mother–infant relationship in which the mother's strong need to look after the child leads her to anticipate the child's needs and to attempt to meet these needs before the infant can experience them herself. Because of this the child never fully develops a clear awareness of her needs, giving her a sense of over-dependence and of pervasive ineffectiveness. In addition to individual psychotherapy, Bruch (1974) advocated "… successful treatment must always involve resolution of underlying family problems."

Selvini-Palazzoli, who developed the Milan model of family therapy (1974), observed rigidity in family functioning and, like Bruch (1973), saw the young person striving to protect herself from an overly intrusive mother. Initially, from a strategic perspective, White (1983) described rigidity of beliefs across several generations where daughters were constrained into particular roles and then become vulnerable to developing anorexia nervosa. Later, he challenged the notion of diagnosis, focusing on encouraging the sufferers (and their families) to develop narratives less dominated by pathology, encouraging the technique of externalizing the illness as a means for the sufferer to challenge its control (White, 1988/89; White & Epston, 1990).

Arguably the most influential perspective came from structural family therapy which hypothesized that particular family dynamics were required for the development of anorexia nervosa, termed the "psychosomatic family" (Minuchin, Rosman, & Baker, 1978). Minuchin et al. (1975) described the families as having three distinct features. First, the child had a physiological vulnerability predisposing her to the development of a psychosomatic problem. Second, the child's family had four specific transactional characteristics: enmeshment, overprotectiveness, rigidity, and lack of conflict resolution. Third, the child played a key role in the family's pattern of conflict avoidance (often seen to be leading to cross generational alliances), which was an important source of reinforcement for his/her symptoms.

Early treatment interventions (exemplified best by the family lunch session) focused on three areas of family change: (1) changing the perception of the child's role/position from a "sick" helpless victim of an illness to a family member caught up in a conflict with the family with anorexia seen as an expression of interpersonal family conflict rather than an attribute of the patient alone, (2) reframing of anorexia as an interpersonal problem, and (3) blocking the use of the eating behavior as a conflict detouring device (Rosman, Minuchin, & Liebman, 1975).

The particular therapeutic interventions used to achieve this varied depending on the assessment of the specific nature of the family dynamics, but interventions would typically include as a key aim to clarify boundaries between the family subsystems. With younger patients, this might include an initial strong focus on the child's refusal to eat and encouraging the parents to take strong parental action. With the older adolescent, the therapist might start in a similar way by highlighting the child's resistance to get her to eat but then shift the focus to other areas of family conflict. While the overt intervention here is apparently quite different, the underlying rationale was the same, i.e., to block the role of the symptom as a mediator of family patterns of conflict avoidance maintaining the eating disorder. In accordance with the structural model (Minuchin, 1974), the therapist functioned to assist the family to achieve a more normative structure with clear boundaries between the parental (executive) subsystem and the children with sufficient flexibility to offer a supportive environment for appropriate individuation.

Family Therapy in the Early Maudsley Studies

Motivation for the first trial came from several factors. In 1975 a cohort of in-patients from the Maudsley Hospital over two decades were followed up with the conclusion that no additional therapies provided in the course of treatment were of particular benefit. The study also found evidence that major disturbance in the families, including psychiatric illness, serious disharmony, and an inability for the patient to separate, contributed to poor prognosis (Morgan & Russell, 1975). This contrasted with a family therapy case series from Philadelphia of 53 patients, 86 percent of whom were recovered at follow-up (Minuchin, Rosman, & Baker, 1978).

The first study (Russell et al., 1987) compared four subgroups of participants all admitted to in-patient treatment and discharged at around 90 percent expected body weight for height. Family therapy was compared to individual supportive therapy, and the subgroups were divided into adolescents with a short duration of illness (< 3 years); adolescents with a longer duration of illness (> 3 years); adult onset anorexia, and those with bulimia nervosa. The main finding, maintained at 5 years (Eisler et al., 1997) was that family therapy was effective for the adolescents with short duration of illness.

Key Principles and Treatment Phases

The family therapy adopted in the first trial reflects the models prevalent at the time: the structural technique of strengthening the parental subsystem by mobilizing the parents to work together to take action (Minuchin et al., 1975), the etiological agnosticism of strategic family therapy (Watzlawick, Weakland, & Fisch, 1974), and the therapeutic neutrality of the Milan School (Selvini Palazzoli et al., 1980). The therapy was drawn from the practice in the Children's Department at the Maudsley Hospital and adapted to the needs of the trial patients and differed depending on the age of the patient (Dare, 1983). The family was seen as a resource to be mobilized to help the starving adolescent, and the therapist remained neutral to the etiology of the anorexia. At this point remaining neutral to etiology was primarily strategic and coherent with family therapy of the time, as was the notion that the re-structuring of family relationships would allow for age-appropriate separation and individuation.

The therapy is described as having three clear stages (Dare et al., 1990). The first stage, beginning usually with the family meal, focused on the eating disorder where the parents' were jointly invited to take a stance as to feeding their daughter. With the younger groups, the therapist assumed that the parents would initially take charge of their child's eating. With the adult patients, they could decide either to control their daughter's eating or adopt a consistent attitude that she should take responsibility herself. Emphasis was placed on creating a strong therapeutic relationship through the process of engagement and joining by the therapists. Influenced by the evidence that a high level of expressed emotion was linked to drop out from treatment (Szmukler et al., 1985) and often driven by guilt, particular attention was paid to the subtleties of criticism. Any raising of anxiety for the purposes of engagement needed to avoid increasing guilt, so showing positive regard for the parents' efforts and sympathy for the adolescents' predicament was crucial. As a part of this process, attention was drawn to the effects of starvation (Keys, Brozek, & Henschel, 1950) and the toxic and addictive quality of its nature (Szmukler & Tantam, 1984), which took over control of the adolescent.

The second phase began when the parents' management of the eating disorder resulted in a steady weight gain. The therapist and the family then worked together to address a return to a more normal family life, with the main focus remaining on addressing the eating disorder. The third phase began when the daughter's weight was largely under control and responsibility for appropriate eating was gradually returned to her. Therapy could then focus on other family concerns—the main focus for the adolescents being increased autonomy with a view to leaving home and the subsequent impact on the parents' relationship. With adult children, the focus was on establishing healthy adult relationships with the parents without anorexia as a form of communication.

A major factor in this first trial was that patients commenced therapy following weight restoration in a hospital setting rather than commencing treatment in a state of starvation (as was the more common practice with patients seen in the outpatient Children's Department). So unless there was rapid weight loss on discharge, the therapists did not have the therapeutic leverage of the urgency of weight restoration. The other key difference was that as the family meal session was conducted for research purposes to investigate processes of family functioning in both arms of the trial (Eisler et al., 1985), the therapists were instructed to confine themselves to making social contact with the family and to ask relatively neutral questions about their customary eating habits and how these had been affected by the patient's illness. For those families randomized to family therapy, the final part of the session included an intervention from the therapist inviting the parents to encourage their daughter to have "one more mouthful," but this intervention was generally brief and the therapist was not expected to persist as would have been the case in the outpatient context. In many instances, it was only once weight loss following discharge from hospital occurred that parents were encouraged to take a strong stance around preventing further weight loss and facilitating a reorganization of relationships so that separation and individuation could occur (Dare, 1990).

The alternate models of working for older and younger patients are clearly differentiated, though in both instances the parents are addressed as the responsible executive subsystems (Minuchin, 1974). The parents are challenged to override their child's overwhelming fear of eating—the one thing in her life that she believes that she can control. Appropriate separation from their child is expressed through acting on their fears for her life rather than being controlled by her terror when faced with food. The family therapy with the older patients involved encouraging the parents to agree on a consistent stance in regards to the eating disordered behaviors, encouraging their adult child to take more responsibility for herself.

It is noteworthy that in the early descriptions of therapy, less emphasis is placed on the technique of "externalization" of the eating disorder as drawn from the narrative therapies (White, 1983; 1988/89). Externalization has become a major feature of later practice (Eisler, Lock, & Le Grange, 2010; Lock et al., 2001; Lock & Le Grange, 2013). Although the early emphasis on the addictive quality of starvation that took over control of the adolescent can itself be seen as a form of externalization (Dare et al., 1990), this has a different quality from the externalization of the narrative therapists and provides an example of how the therapy evolved over the course of the trials (Colahan & Senior, 1995; Dare et al., 1995).

The findings of the first trial formed the basis for two further randomized controlled trials (RCTs) for adolescents with anorexia nervosa—a pilot study (Le Grange et al., 1992a) and a larger trial (Eisler et al., 2000; 2007). In the first trial, it had been noted that a higher level of parental criticism (assessed by the measure expressed emotion [EE]) (Leff & Vaughn, 1985) of the child with anorexia impacted on the process of the therapy (Szmukler et al., 1985). In families where a member has an eating disorder, the levels of EE are generally quite low compared, for example, to families with a member having schizophrenia; the number of critical comments is small and hostility rare (Hodes et al., 1999; Le brange et al., 1992a). Both studies compared two forms of family therapy: Conjoint Family Therapy, involving the whole family, and Separated Family Therapy, where the adolescent was seen separately from the parents by the same therapist. The pilot study found no significant difference between the groups overall, but participants from high EE families did better in Separated Family Therapy (Le Grange et al., 1992b). In the second, larger study, again, there were no overall differences between the groups except where there was a higher level of parental criticism; the Separated Family Therapy group achieved a better outcome and this was maintained at a 5-year follow-up (Eisler et al., 2000; Eisler et al., 2007). The conjoint treatment was more effective in bringing about individual psychological change.

The Early U.S. Studies 2010

Taking place at the same time as the Maudsley studies, showing similarities and differences, was the work of Arthur Robin (Robin et al., 1999; Robin & Le Grange, 2010; Robin, Segal, & Moye, 1995). This included an RCT where 37 adolescents with anorexia nervosa were randomized to either Behavioral Family Systems Therapy (BFST) or Ego Orientated Individual Therapy (EOIT). BFST used a modification of a manualized family behavioral treatment for adolescent behavior problems (Robin & Foster, 1989) and was very similar to the treatment used at the Maudsley. It used a structured, parent-implemented behavioral weight gain program in the initial phase of treatment. This was followed by systemic family therapy interventions targeting family structure and family communication combined with cognitive restructuring techniques directed at anorexia distorted thinking regarding weight and shape. The EOIT was an active, specific therapy targeting adolescent development that included separate parental sessions bimonthly to support the parents. There were also additional sessions with the dietician for the adolescent. BFST was significantly more effective with 67 percent reaching target weight at follow-up and 80 percent regaining menstruation. At the 1-year follow-up, 75 percent had reached target weight and 85 percent were menstruating. The number of sessions and length of treatment were longer than the Maudsley studies and subsequent RCTs in the United States.

The Impact of the Research Studies on Clinical Practice

The role of research in informing clinical practice is all too often seen in an oversimplified way as being primarily a matter of implementing the evidence of well-conducted RCTs. While many have cautioned against the reduction of the notion of evidence-based practice to the identification and dissemination of evidence-based treatments (Kazdin, 2008; Rawlins, 2008; Sackett et al., 1996), the actual way in which research can shape practice is seldom described.

Challenges to Theory

The Maudsley studies created a number of challenges both to the conceptual understanding of family therapy for eating disorders and to its application in practice. Although the main finding from the Russell et al. (1987) study supported the efficacy of family therapy, there were a number of aspects of the study that did not readily fit the theoretical conceptualization of the "psychosomatic family," which up until then offered the strongest theoretical frame for practice. For instance, there was nothing in the theory that would have predicted a differential response to adolescent compared to adult onset of the illness or families with someone suffering from anorexia nervosa rather than bulimia nervosa (Russell et al., 1987). Similarly, the findings that seeing the whole family together was no more effective than seeing the parents and adolescent separately (Eisler et al., 2000; Le Grange et al., 1992a) did not fit well with the notion of a treatment that aimed to target systemic family processes and restructure family organization. The role of criticism in relation to treatment engagement (Szmukler et al., 1985) and outcome (Eisler et al., 2000; Le Grange et al., 1992b) also raised questions about one of the central tenets of the psychosomatic family model around conflict avoidance.

None of these findings disproved the theory, but they opened up discussions as to whether alternative conceptualizations might be a better fit and strengthened the doubts about notions of family etiology of eating disorders which subsequent reviews of the literature on family functioning in eating disorders showed to be well founded (Eisler, 1995). The need to develop an understanding of the impact of high EE, and in particular the dynamics of criticism in the family, led to a study that showed that self-blame was frequently a driver of criticism (particularly for mothers) (Besharat, Eisler, & Dare, 2001) and significantly altered practice, particularly around how best to engage such families.

Challenges to Practice

There are many ways in which delivering treatment in the context of a research study challenges therapists. They have to conform to a study protocol and/or a treatment manual, have their treatment regularly monitored, and may have to make decisions that do not concur with their own clinical judgement. This may include issues of frequency and length of treatment, who attends sessions, as well as what happens during sessions or, in the case of eating disorders, how often a patient should be weighed and by whom. Clinicians often see these constraints as something that can potentially undermine the integrity and clinical validity of evidence-based treatments and may question whether the findings from RCTs are generalizable to everyday practice (see Kazdin, 2008, for a thoughtful discussion of these issues). However, such constraints can also be valuable because they force therapists into unaccustomed territories and force them to reevaluate some of their preconceived ideas.

In the Maudsley studies, therapists were challenged to establish new ways of working that are considered now to be commonplace—for example, weighing the patient, a feature of all the trial therapies, and working with the weight chart with the family. Therapists had to move from talking about the meaning of food to talking about eating and feeding—a bringing together of body and mind in the therapy room—food and weight previously being matters for nurses or dieticians.

Unlike later trials in the United States (Lock & Le Grange, 2013), in the Maudsley studies the same therapists undertook both treatments. In the 1980s, influenced particularly by the work of Bruch (1982), there was broad consensus that severely underweight patients generally are unable to engage in meaningful psychotherapy (Garner, 1985). It was through their experience of their individual work that the therapists were challenged to find ways of engaging with emaciated adolescents, an experience that enhanced their work when working with the whole family (Colahan, 1995; Dare et al., 1995) and highlighted the importance of emphasizing warmth and positive regard to an often uncommunicative adolescent (Dare et al., 1990).

Other discomforts that led to positive learning points were having to manage endings in a time-limited therapy, or (in the separated family therapy) not having siblings involved, or not being able to observe and intervene in the process of family interaction and having to address the often very different accounts from the adolescent and the parents while maintaining appropriate boundaries around the sessions. The recognition that families in the separated family therapy found their own solutions that fitted with their preferred interactional style, which may or may not have included avoiding conflict, was unexpected and raised important questions about the nature of change mechanisms in the treatments. The style of therapeutic interactions that therapists developed in the piloting of the separated family therapy (Le Grange et al., 1992b) turned out to be more distinct than had been initially anticipated, and it eventually changed the style of work with whole families as well.

Perhaps the most obvious example of the effect of the Maudsley studies on practice was not having the possibility of a family meal. In the separated sessions, the therapists could talk about what happened at home around meals but were unable to observe or interact during a whole family meal situation. At the time, the whole family meal sessions were often quite challenging and stressful (for both families and therapists), but this was seen both as a potentially life-saving intervention and a way of addressing the underlying conflict avoiding transactional family style that was thought to be maintaining the illness. However, once the validity of the "psychosomatic family model" itself started to be questioned (Dare et al., 1994), it became more difficult to justify using an intervention that could lead to overt conflict and high levels of distress. For a period, the Maudsley team stopped using the family meal as a regular intervention in their routine clinical practice. The meal was only reintroduced after the team started working with multi-family groups (Dare & Eisler, 2000; see also Simic & Eisler, 2014, this volume) where joint meals were an important component of the treatment and feedback from families confirmed their value. Important also were conversations with researchers from the United States and Australia who had continued to use the family meal in their studies but had modified it so that it was less confrontational than had sometimes been the case in the early work at the Maudsley.

Family Therapy for Its Time—New Directions for Family Therapy for Anorexia Nervosa

A number of broad influences set the scene for FT-AN to shift in two very different, but in some ways also complementary, directions by the early 2000s. The first was a trend towards greater integration and greater openness to ideas from across the family therapy field as well as from outside it (Gurman & Fraenkel, 2002; Lebow, 1997). The shift towards therapy integration has been strongly influenced by research on common factors in psychotherapy, which has shown that specific therapy models account for a relatively small amount of outcome variance (Assay & Lambert, 1999) and emphasizes therapeutic flexibility and tailoring treatments to individual needs and specific client or family contexts (Miller & Duncan, 2000). The second trend has been the growing acceptance that clinical practice needs to reflect empirical research evidence, requiring clinicians to be knowledgeable about research findings and to implement the findings in their practice. This is often seen as requiring greater specificity in what treatments are offered determined by the best available outcome research, an expectation that clinicians follow agreed guidelines which draw on such research, and an adherence to the evidence-based treatments to ensure that they are delivered in accord with the research studies. While there is an obvious tension between the two trends, they are not necessarily opposites.

Integrating Models for Specific Problems

Within the family therapy field, a number of models were developed to treat specific problems such as conduct disorder, substance abuse, and depression (Alexander & Parsons, 1982; Diamond & Josephson, 2005; Diamond & Siqueland, 2001; Diamond, Siqueland, & Diamond, 2003; Henggeler, 1999; Liddle et al., 1991), which took as their starting point the need to integrate different theoretical models while at the same time undertaking formal empirical evaluations. The trend also occurred generally in psychotherapy, including cognitive behavioral therapy (CBT) and psychodynamic therapy (e.g., Becker & Zayfert, 2001; Jones, Sellwood, & McGovern, 2005; Murphy, Russell, & Waller, 2005; Roemer & Orsillo, 2002). What all of these approaches have in common is that they integrated principles from several general therapeutic models in relation to the treatment of a specific problem. The evaluation of these approaches generally required that they be operationally described in a treatment manual. FT-AN, as developed at the Maudsley, was an early example of this process with the combination of structural, strategic, systemic, and narrative techniques applied in a focused way to the treatment of anorexia nervosa. The development of multi-family therapy for anorexia nervosa (Dare & Eisler, 2000) was part of the same trend of bringing together elements of systemic therapy, group therapy, psychodynamic concepts, and more recently, also CBT and dialectical behavioral therapy (DBT) interventions. Within the family therapy field, these developments happened alongside theoretical developments that were for a period ambivalent about empirical research

Evidence-Based Treatments and Evidence-Based Practice in Family Therapy

Throughout its history, the family therapy field has always included clinicians with a strong interest in research, although for the field as a whole this interest has waxed and waned. The 1980s and 1990s were a period when interest in research was perhaps at its lowest, as noted by an editorial in the *Journal of Marital and Family Therapy* (Gurman, 1986). The early Maudsley studies were important in continuing to develop research within a field that was increasingly becoming skeptical about the scientific method in favor of spontaneous responses to individual families.

The reservations about research were partly based on the usual fear of clinicians that the relational focus of family therapy and the uniqueness of individual clinical encounters would be corrupted by the necessary processes and techniques demanded by the rigors of research (Hayes & Nelson, 1981). Reservations also were based partly on the wish to define the field as being conceptually distinct by claiming that systemic theory and post-modern philosophical positions, such as social constructionism and constructivism, while driving a lot of the most creative developments in the field, were incompatible with the positivist tenets of empirical science (Goldberg & David, 1991; Larner, 2004; Liddle, 1991).

While many clinicians and theorists remain skeptical, continuing to reject positivist methods of generating evidence (Speedy, 2004), the debate in the field shifted clearly towards *how* to implement research on family therapy rather than whether it was appropriate (Crane & Hafen, 2002; Eisler & Dare, 1992; Pote et al., 2003). At the same time, the broader areas of medicine and psychology were embracing evidence-based practice (EBP) as the combination of best available evidence with clinical expertise and patient values (Sackett et al., 2000), part of which is to develop evidence-based treatments (EBT) (sometimes also described as empirically supported or validated treatments) (American Psychological Association, 2006). There is an important distinction between the concepts with EBT referring to treatments for a specific problem evaluated in efficacy studies and EBP encompassing the broader concept described above. The broader EBP draws on a range of relevant evidence including, for instance, research on the therapeutic relationship, research on cultural factors that might impact treatment, client motivation research, service context research, research on treatment adherence, dissemination research, etc., as well as clinical judgement and patient preferences. The evaluation of EBT is undoubtedly a key element of the development of EBP, but as Kazdin (2008) has pointed out, a lack of understanding of the distinction between the two concepts is also an important barrier to the dissemination of effective evidence-based practice.

The development of FT-AN has been imbedded in these broader movements. By the 1990s, there was growing acknowledgement that family therapy was a potential EBT for adolescent anorexia nervosa (Carr, 2000; Kaplan, 2002; Pike, 1998; Pinsof & Wynne, 1995; NICE, 2004; American Psychiatric Association, 2006). There were two barriers to this process. First, in the original Maudsley trials, treatment fidelity depended on the effectiveness of supervision, but by the 2000s this was no longer considered adequate for psychotherapy RCTs (Lock & Le Grange, 2001a; Nathan & Gorman, 1998). Second, with the exception of the Robin et al. (1994; 1999) work, the evaluation of the efficacy of family therapy for eating disorders was largely confined to the Maudsley group, where most of the studies were relatively small and lacked replication.

Treatment Manuals, Their Role in Research and Clinical Practice

Treatment manuals undoubtedly have a key role in the development and evaluation of EBT, and many have argued that they also have an important role in training and disseminating good practice (e.g., Kendall et al., 1999; Wilson, 1997). There are, of course, many who are strongly critical of the use of manuals as being too prescriptive, ignoring the specific needs of individual patients, and precluding flexibility and creativity on the part of the therapists (Seligman, 1995; Strupp & Anderson, 1997). Other critics point out that as specific treatment models account for a very small proportion of outcome variance, the whole notion of evidence-based treatments becomes questionable (Messer & Wampold, 2002). Manuals, of course, vary considerably, with some providing great detail of what therapists should do in each session and others offering broader guidelines with considerable flexibility as to which interventions are used at different points and how decisions about their use should be made. Manuals also vary greatly in the scope of their theoretical perspective, again ranging from a very strictly defined single theoretical model to those offering an integrative model drawing on a range of theories. From a research point of view, manuals are used to allow for a clear comparison between treatments and to be able to assess if the therapists deliver the treatment as intended (Luborsky & DeRubeis, 1984). More recently, Carroll & Nuro (2002) have argued that manuals need to differ depending on their purpose, with different types of manuals needed at an early stage of development of a treatment than would be the case for a large efficacy RCT or a dissemination and implementation study of a well-developed treatment, which may need to allow for the treatment being used with a range of more complex presentations.

Treatment manuals can be important for other reasons as well. The actual process of writing a manual is important in that it requires the authors to describe clearly both the therapeutic techniques and their conceptual underpinning in a way that helps crystalize the ideas that, in the context of normal clinical practice, may otherwise remain more abstract and less clearly defined. A well written manual that is able to operationalize in clear language the main concepts and therapeutic techniques that are used in a particular approach can also have a significant impact on the understanding of the treatment by those who have not been trained in the specific therapeutic modality and are less familiar with the detailed concepts (and jargon) associated with the therapeutic approach, helping to demystify it and make it more accessible.

The *Treatment Manual for Anorexia Nervosa* developed by Lock and Le Grange (Lock et al., 2001; Lock & Le Grange, 2013) is an excellent example of this. The manual was written with the explicit aim of operationalizing the FT-AN approach that had been used in the Maudsley studies and has had a significant impact on the field. Until this point, being a member of the original team, or at least having a good understanding of the field of family therapy, was a prerequisite for understanding the intricacies of the approach in clinical practice. Aside from the obvious implications for research, the manual in many ways has brought the issue of EBP to the fore in the treatment of eating disorders for children and adolescents, including the prerequisite training required to deliver the treatment.

The growing familiarity with the basic concepts and main techniques of FT-AN, which the manual has helped to promote, is not without its problems. Some have argued that it could promote uncritical application of the treatment with complex cases by clinicians with limited expertise (Strober, 2014; see also reply by Lock & Le Grange, 2014). This, of course, tends to be true of most treatments that get to be widely used. As Shafran et al. (2009) have pointed out in relation to the use of CBT, clinical practice is often so far removed from the form of the evaluated CBT that the results in routine practice are disappointingly poor. There is similar evidence of variable levels of adherence to central aspects of the manual for FT-AN, even among therapists who described themselves as committed to the approach, in many instances omitting central treatment components such as weighing the patient (Couturier et al., 2013; Kosmerly, Waller, & Robinson, 2014; Wallace & von Ranson, 2012). However, while there is a useful debate to be had about how best to disseminate good evidence-based practice, there is little doubt that the publication of the Lock and Le Grange manual (Lock et al., 2001; Lock & Le Grange, 2013) was an important factor in opening up the field in accepting the potential value of FT-AN, broadening the empirical investigations in this area, and playing a significant role in disseminating family oriented practice.

Treatment Manuals and Evidence-Based Practice

Being clear about the distinction between EBT and EBP has key implications for how we think about the use of treatment manuals outside of the research setting. From the narrower point of view of EBT, it is argued that the most appropriate way of disseminating the treatment is to ensure that the treatment should be delivered as widely as possible, adhering as much as is practicable to the manual that had been used for the efficacy research. For many (e.g., Shafran et al., 2009), this is the most logical conclusion: if the treatment has been shown in trials to work in a particular format, then it should be delivered in exactly that format. Others have argued (e.g., Beutler, 2002) that, in clinical practice, manuals need to be applied more flexibly since they are only one component of good, evidence informed, practice. Flexible application is necessary not only to attend to the important issues of client/family values, but also to the individual variability in clinical need that the existing research has not addressed. Flexible application also can take into account the huge body of additional research that has bearing on treatment outcome. For instance, research on the role of treatment adherence has shown that there is a complex relationship between adherence, competence, treatment fidelity, and outcome. It is beyond the scope of this chapter to address this in detail, but in brief the evidence suggests that the relationship between adherence and outcome is not linear but, in general, curvilinear, with very high and very low adherence associated with worse outcome (Webb et al., 2010). There is also evidence that a number of common factor variables (therapeutic alliance, therapist experience, client motivation) moderate the role of adherence (McHugh, Murray, & Barlow, 2009). Thus, for instance, if the therapeutic alliance is poor, maintaining strict adherence to a treatment manual has the opposite of the desired effect (Castonguay et al., 2006).

Research on adherence in the treatment of eating disorders is still fairly limited at present, but it is consistent with the more general research described above, suggesting that strict adherence to manuals does not in itself result in good treatment outcome (Ellison et al., 2012; Loeb et al., 2005). While we need to be mindful of the limitations of applying the notion of EBT too narrowly, it is important to not confuse the need for flexibility in applying EBT with poor adherence due to lack of understanding of the model, poor training, or lack of appropriate supervision. The eating disorder (ED) field is also some way behind the broader field of psychotherapy research in addressing questions of the most effective ways of disseminating treatments to a range of clinical contexts (Chorpita & Regan, 2009; Kazak et al., 2010; McHugh & Barlow, 2010; Schoenwald & Hoagwood, 2001).

Treatment Manuals Used in the Evaluation of Anorexia Nervosa

A number of family therapy manuals have been used in outcome research for adolescent ED at different centres. Two of these are generic family therapy manuals with no specific focus on managing the eating disorder (Godart et al., 2007; Lock et al., 2012, Pote et al., 2003), two are specific for adolescent bulimia nervosa (Le Grange et al., 2007; Schmidt et al., 2007), and three are specific for the treatment of adolescent anorexia nervosa. These three are the Lock and Le Grange (2013) manual, the manual used in Robin et al. (1999) (Robin & Siegel, unpublished; for a description see also Robin & Le Grange, 2013), and the Maudsley service model manual (Eisler et al., 2012), which includes treatment manuals for single and multi-family therapy for anorexia nervosa. The similarities and differences between these three manuals are of interest as they highlight the key areas of consensus but also show some of the variability of treatment approach that are worthy of future investigation. All three manuals share the following:

a. Focusing on working *with* the family to help their child recover, coupled with a strong message that the family is not seen as the cause of the problem.
b. Expecting the parents to take a lead in managing their child's eating in the early stages of treatment while emphasizing the temporary nature of this role.
c. Separating the eating disorder from the child. All three manuals provide specific strategies to achieve this. Robin/Siegel and Lock/Le Grange use physical illness analogies that have to be managed by parents. Lock/Le Grange also uses visual representation of how an illness obscures the healthy child. Eisler and colleagues describe a range of narrative externalizing conversation techniques that implies anorexia is a separate entity (*"When did you first begin to realize that anorexia was taking over your daughter;" "Has anorexia persuaded you that your friends are not that important anymore?"*) and also place an emphasis on using psychoeducation about the effects of starvation as a way of externalizing the illness.
d. Shifting of focus on adolescent and family developmental life cycle issues in the later stages of treatment.

All three manuals describe the treatment as occurring in phases, although the description of the phases (and their number) varies. Thus Robin/Siegel describes three phases (assessment, weight gain, and weight maintenance), Lock/Le Grange also describe three phases (weight restoration, transitioning control of eating to the adolescent, and adolescent issues), and Eisler and colleagues describe four phases (engagement and development of the therapeutic alliance, helping families manage the eating disorder, exploring issues of individual and family development, and ending treatment and discussion of future plans and discharge). In reality, the phases are fairly similar and address the different issues in a comparable sequence, with the differences being more one of emphasis. This highlights, on the one hand, the degree of arbitrariness when describing treatment phases; they should not be taken in any way as absolutes and should not, outside of a research context, be seen as prescribing how long different stages of treatment last. On the other hand, they also illustrate the importance of transition points in treatment, such as handing back to the adolescent, moving the focus of treatment away from eating and weight, or addressing ending treatment issues.

There are other differences between the manuals that are of interest. Robin/Siegel do not use a family meal in the early stages of treatment but use structured behavioral techniques to manage the adolescent's eating and provide parents with clear dietetic advice. Lock/Le Grange recommend a family meal as a routine intervention at Session 2. They generally avoid giving explicit dietetic advice to parents and explore with parents what they have tried and what might need modifying. Eisler and colleagues also recommend a family meal early in treatment (although as described earlier, the Maudsley team went through a phase of skepticism about its utility) but also describe other possibilities of using food as part of treatment (e.g., a mini-meal challenge used with very ill young people as part of an assessment if out-patient treatment is possible). Similar to Robin/Siegel, they also provide dietetic advice and written meal plans if parents feel that it would be helpful. Unlike Robin/Siegel, who use a dietician throughout but alongside the treatment, they would not generally recommend separate consultations with a dietician but incorporate such advice into the family therapy sessions, either by the therapist or on occasions inviting the dietician to join in the family therapy session, for example, towards the end of treatment to help the young person think through how she is going to get back to normal eating. Robin/Siegel routinely use cognitive restructuring techniques, including behavioral experiments, to address eating disorder cognitions in the later stages of treatment, which neither of the other two manuals describes.

Conceptually, all three manuals are very similar, but they are also sufficiently different to raise important questions about the detailed aspects of how the treatments are delivered. It is unknown to what extent the differences are simply a reflection of the different context and different time when the manuals were written and how much they represent differences that might have an impact on treatment.

Broadening of the Research on the Treatment of Adolescent Eating Disorders

While up until the 1990s family therapy outcome research for adolescent eating disorders was largely confined to one center, since then there has been a steady growth both in the number of studies and centers involved in such research.

Developments in the United States

The first major U.S. trial (Stanford) compared dose of treatment—10 sessions over 6 months compared with 20 sessions over 12 months of FT-AN. Eighty-six subjects were randomized to one of the two groups. At the end of treatment, no overall difference between the groups was found, with 67 percent reaching a body mass index (BMI) of 20 or more and scores on the Eating Disorder Examination (EDE) within 2 standard deviations (SD) of the norm (Lock et al., 2005). These results were maintained at four years (Lock, Couturier, & Agras, 2006).

The second trial was a multi-site trial (Stanford and Chicago) (Lock et al., 2010) with 121 anorexia nervosa adolescents, which compared FT-AN with adolescent-focused therapy (AFT) (Fitzpatrick et al., 2010; previously described by Robin et al., 1999 as EOIT). FT-AN was superior to AFT in terms of weight gain and eating related psychopathology. At the end of treatment, recovery rates—defined as > 95% expected body weight (EBW) and eating disorder examination (EDE) within 1 SD of community norms—were higher for FT-AN but did not reach statistical significance, although at six months and one year the FT-AN was superior. Partial remission (EBW > 85%) was superior to AFT at the end of treatment but not at follow-up. Rates of hospitalization during treatment and relapse rates from full remission between end of treatment and follow-up were lower for family therapy (Lock et al., 2010).

A moderator analysis of the dose trial (Lock et al., 2005) found that participants with more severe eating disorder related obsessive-compulsive disorder (OCD) and those from divorced or single-parent families did better in the longer treatment arm. Similarly, OCD and eating disorder psychopathology were moderators in the second trial with those patients benefiting more from the FT-AN than AFT (Le Grange et al., 2012). Finally, an important finding has been that early weight gain is predictive of overall response, suggesting that when FT-AN works, it works fast (Doyle et al., 2010; Le Grange et al., 2014; Lock et al., 2006).

Developments in Australia

Over the last 10 or so years, FT-AN has been widely disseminated in Australia due in large part to the availability of a manual (Lock & Le Grange, 2013) but more significantly due to clinicians having the opportunity to be trained and supervised. An initial training occurred in 2003 at The Children's Hospital at Westmead, a specialist eating disorder service in Sydney. Subsequent to this training, opportunities to practice were provided by The Children's Hospital at Westmead (Wallis et al., 2007), both locally and interstate. Since then, a number of major centers have developed FT-AN capabilities. The availability of the manual together with specialist training and supervision has allowed the Royal Children's Hospital in Melbourne to develop their own research program in FT-AN (Hughes et al., 2014a; 2014b).

These developments highlight the importance of context for treatment dissemination and the development of clinical research to inform practice. The team has been careful to maintain fidelity to the core tenets and structure of the manualized Lock/Le Grange approach, but implementation and practice has been strengthened by the team's previous broader family therapy experiences with a strong emphasis on interviewing technique and practices from more recent family therapy theory (Rhodes & Wallis, 2009; Murray, Wallis, & Rhodes, 2012). An integration of a strong pediatric and psychiatric partnership with therapists created systemic change in the medical environment, with therapists, medical teams, and managers benefiting from and appreciating each other's professional contribution (Hughes et al., 2014a; Rhodes & Madden, 2005; Wallis et al., 2007)—indispensable ingredients for successful implementation as recent research has demonstrated (Couturier et al., 2013; 2014).

The initial focus of implementation was to investigate the impact of providing FT-AN as a follow-up to hospital admission on the demand for readmissions. This simple change resulted in readmission rates being halved (Wallis et al., 2007). A recently completed RCT ($n = 82$) investigated the optimal length of hospital admission in combination with follow-up FT-AN for medically unstable patients, demonstrating that brief hospitalization was effective when followed by FT-AN (Madden et al., 2014). The integration of broader family therapy and other evidence-based approaches has been an area of interest to improve outcomes. For example, parent-to-parent consultations were developed and influenced by narrative therapy and multi-family therapy. This was tested in a small RCT ($n = 20$) that demonstrated a small but significant increase in the rate of weight restoration for the group who received the additional intervention, and qualitatively, parents acknowledged it as a useful practice (Rhodes et al., 2008; Rhodes, Brown, & Madden, 2009). More recent work has described intensive family admissions that integrate systemic practices, such as the reflecting team for complex presentations (Wallis et al., 2013), the development of other approaches to address poor progress and complexity (Wallis et al., submitted), and a second Australian RCT comparing two forms of FT-AN, i.e., conjoint family therapy and parent-focused therapy (see Hughes et al., 2014b).

Developments in the United Kingdom since the Original Trials

Developments in the treatment of child and adolescent eating disorders from 2000 on reflect both the changes in family therapy as well as the development in thinking around service development. The work of the Maudsley team has focused on three main areas—multi-family therapies for anorexia nervosa (AN) and bulimia nervosa (BN), single-family therapy (FT-AN), and service organization roles in delivering effective treatments.

Challenges from the earlier studies described above led to a reevaluation of the theoretical framework informing FT-AN. Maintenance factors rather than explanatory models of etiology were being seen as more helpful in the development of treatments (Treasure & Schmidt, 2005), and the Maudsley team was also influenced by observations of the ways that families accommodate physical illness (Rolland, 1994; 1999; Steinglass, 1998). The impact of anorexia on family life was observed to create major changes for all families whatever their previous pattern of functioning (Nielsen & Bará-Carril, 2003). The development of a theory of clinical practice emerged, which has become a major influence on the way the service has developed. As the family reorganizes around the eating disorder, their ability to use adaptive mechanisms of functioning to maintain stability, adapt to appropriate life cycle changes, and meet individual members' needs appropriately is challenged. Patterns observed included the central role of the eating problems in family life; the narrowing of the time focus to the here and now; the inflexibility in daily life patterns; the amplification of aspects of family functioning; the diminishing ability to meet family life-cycle needs, and the loss of a sense of agency (helplessness) (Eisler, 2005). It was noted that developing family interactional patterns may have a role in maintaining the illness either through reinforcing problem behaviors and/or interfering with effective adaptive family mechanisms such as positive parenting (Eisler, Lock, & Le Grange, 2010).

It is beyond the scope of this chapter to describe in detail the way that the changes in the conceptualization have influenced clinical practice, but an example will illustrate these developments. A key shift has arisen out of a change in understanding what enables parents to manage their child's eating. Earlier theoretical accounts emphasized the issue of control, parental sense of empowerment, and the executive function of the parental dyad. This did not take into account the position of the young person who has to accept (often not very explicitly and sometimes only grudgingly) that this is right for them. For this to happen, the meaning of parents managing the eating needs to change from "parents are in control" to "parents are being caring." This shift in conceptualization has a number of implications for how the treatment is discussed, expressing sympathy with the young person's predicament while stressing that the parents have no alternative other than to be firm around eating because they care too much to do otherwise. There are also implications for how the family meal session is presented and conducted, with the focus being on strengthening the therapeutic alliance and information and validating the experience of the family rather than creating a scenario where the parents win the battle and enforce eating (Eisler et al., 2012). This requires that there is a strong emphasis on the development of a good therapeutic alliance with the young person from the start of treatment, as well as with the parents and the family as a whole.

A particular feature of the therapeutic relationship in the early stage is to create a situation where the family can be reassured by the expertise of therapist and team. The therapeutic engagement of the adolescent and family is with a particular clinician, but in another sense, it is also with the entire multidisciplinary team. Determining the medical and risk assessment to ensure physical safety, providing psychoeducation about the effects of starvation, or giving nutritional advice all contribute to the shaping of the therapeutic relationship. This relationship contributes to the creation of an environment where the family feels supported and has a sufficient sense of safety to be able to accept responsibility to look for alternative ways of managing the problem within the family. This can lead to a sense of dependency on the team by the parents, but it also can help them feel looked after and contribute to the adolescent similarly feeling cared for. On one level, this giving of advice can be at odds with the notion of collaboration as practiced by systemic family therapists and is an example of the specificity of this particular form of family therapy for eating disorders, which might not be replicated with another condition (Eisler, 2013). Therapists, of course, need to be aware of the pitfalls of dependency and the risks of being in expert positions and should make clear that this relationship is temporary, just as it has to be clear that the parents managing their child's eating should be a transient affair. Indeed, in the early stages of treatment (particularly if the child is severely ill), there are important parallel processes among the dependency of the child on the parents, the parents on the therapist, and the therapist on the team. The often quoted maxim that FT-AN therapists "are expert in eating disorders but not in the particular family" can be understood here as having a temporal aspect. Initially the therapist (and team) act from an expert position, providing advice, support, coaching, etc., when the child is severely ill, but as time goes on, their expertise should be set to the side and the therapeutic relationship should become more equal (Eisler et al., 2012).

A key development for the Maudsley team was the introduction of multi-family therapy as a part of the outpatient program (Dare & Eisler, 2000; Eisler, 2005; Eisler, Lock, & Le Grange, 2010; Fairbairn, Simic, & Eisler, 2011; Salaminiou et al., 2014; Simic & Eisler, this volume; Voriadaki et al., 2015). A multicenter trial has shown added benefits of combining multi-family therapy with FT-AN (Eisler et al. in preparation), and the new treatment has attracted considerable interest and become part of developments in other services (Fleminger, 2005; Hollesen, Clausen, & Rokkedal, 2013; Mehl et al., 2013; Rhodes et al., 2008; Robinson et al., 2013; Rockwell et al., 2011; Scholz & Asen, 2001; Scholz et al., 2005). Training in multi-family groups has been offered across the United Kingdom and in many areas of the world (Fairbairn & Eisler, 2007). The experience of involvement in multi-family therapy has not only contributed to the evidence base but has also influenced the understanding of the practice of single-family therapy as it has evolved over the years.

The discussion of the history of FT-AN would be incomplete without considering the context in which the treatments are delivered, as the service setting is itself a powerful nonspecific factor influencing treatment outcome. A recent naturalistic study in London (House et al., 2012) found major differences for young people with an eating disorder between different areas of London depending on whether the available treatment care pathway included direct access to a specialist community-based eating disorders service or if initial referral from primary care went to a generic child and adolescent mental health service. Case identification was two to three times higher in specialist compared to nonspecialist areas. The rate of hospital admissions during the first 12 months following referral was two and a half times higher for those who started their treatment in a nonspecialist service. The study also showed that in nonspecialist contexts, 20 percent of patients were referred on immediately following initial assessment, and of the remainder, only 40 percent received care from the same team over time, while for those starting treatment in a specialist service, 80 percent required no further referral. While some of the differences (e.g., in the reduced need for hospitalization) might be in part due to the use of good EBT, other factors such as specialist expertise and confidence, availability of a multidisciplinary team that is able to manage complex cases from the start, and family and referrer expectations clearly play a key role.

What's New Is Old—Future Directions

The story of FT-AN to date has been one of evolution, and this will continue as clinicians and researchers implement treatment in their own settings. Below we address a number of future directions for family therapy in the treatment of eating disorders. This is essential given that not all patients respond to the treatment, particularly if they have significant comorbidities or live in difficult family contexts, and even those who do respond, and return to a healthy weight and normal eating, will often continue to be troubled by eating disorder cognitions for a number of years.

Enhancement and Process of Therapy

While it is beyond the scope of this chapter to describe the specific barriers families may experience in overcoming an eating disorder, a modicum of clinical experience will identify that some parents and young people find it hard to progress in the FT-AN model and that the conflict created by the eating disorder is distressing (Robin, Siegel, & Moye, 1995). The development of enhancements that integrate into the model and target specific deficits, such as emotional dysregulation; common comorbid conditions; and common trait characteristics, such as perfectionism, inflexibility, and low tolerance to distress, are important areas to investigate to improve outcome (Federici & Wisniewski, 2012; Haynos & Fruzzetti, 2011; Tchanturia & Lock, 2011). Parents seeing their offspring struggle in these areas may find it harder to remain focused on re-feeding early in treatment. Addressing these problems may help maintain parental response and efficacy, improving the likelihood of good treatment outcome (Ellison et al., 2012; Robinson et al., 2013). The small group of families that are difficult to engage in treatment early on may require modification of FT-AN that focuses on possible barriers to engagement, such as insecure attachment, raised expressed emotion, or high levels of self-blame (Besharat, Eisler, & Dare, 2001; Le Grange et al., 2011). In the later stages of treatment, comorbid conditions such as anxiety, that may have been supressed by starvation, may re-emerge and hamper further progress. Developing targeted interventions either as modifications of FT-AN or as adjunctive treatments are areas for future investigations. Likewise, parents often experience similar trait characteristics to their child

(Woodside et al., 2002), and improving the way FT-AN can respond to this may be important.

The central tenets of FT-AN after 25 plus years of research remain stable and related to outcome (Ellison et al., 2012), but further investigation about the process of therapy is an underexplored area. The activity of the family in therapy has recently been observed early in treatment (Darcy et al., 2013) with the meal session a recent focus (Godfrey et al., 2014; White et al., 2014), but therapists learning how to adjust and respond better during therapy is an underutilized area and one likely related to outcome (Webb, DeRubeis, & Barber, 2010). By this we do not mean the broader concept of therapeutic alliance that develops in FT-AN (Forsberg et al., 2013; Lo Tempio et al., 2013; Pereira, Lock, & Oggins, 2006) but the therapist activity in the room, the questions they ask, and what they emphasize or don't emphasize (Miller et al., 2013).

Context and Dissemination

In everyday clinical practice there is always a need to balance context, complexity, and fidelity to established empirically evaluated treatments. Implementing research findings, however, needs to take into account the broadest range of evidence rather than assume that training a sufficient number of individuals in "manualized" EBT will achieve the desired end. Best clinical practice requires general as well as specialist expertise, which will allow the best EBT to be delivered in a flexible way that meets the needs of specific individuals and families, without undermining essential treatment components. By definition, a manual cannot respond to every circumstance, but it can provide an anchor for ideas, values, and key directives. This is what was originally intended by the term evidence-based practice: the combination of the best available evidence with clinical expertise and patient values (Sackett et al., 2000).

There is good evidence that service context may be at least as important, if not more so, than the availability of particular treatments (House et al., 2012). The two, of course, are not in opposition. The evidence that easily accessible, specialist community-based treatments provide the best context for identifying and effectively treating young people with eating disorders, while at the same time significantly reducing unnecessary and costly residential treatments, suggests clearly that the most effective way of improving treatment provisions is by developing such specialist teams and ensuring that they receive expert training in the best evidence-based treatments.

Conclusion

Anyone observing family therapy for eating disorders today who attempted to make comparisons with similar treatments in the 1970s and 1980s could be forgiven if they concluded that the treatments look very similar and that nothing much has changed. In reality, family therapy for eating disorders has moved forward considerably. This advance is reflected not just in the developments in family therapy itself but also in research in the field of eating disorders as a whole, in development of specialist services worldwide, and in the wider context of societal changes including public awareness of eating disorders and parenting practices. While the treatments may look similar, our conceptual understanding of them has changed radically and continues to evolve, leading to new applications and creative modifications as this volume so amply demonstrates.

References

Alexander, J., & Treasure, J. (Eds.) (2012). *A Collaborative Approach to Eating Disorders*. New York: Routledge.

Alexander, J., & Parsons, B. V. (1982). *Functional Family Therapy*. California: Brooks/Cole Publishing Company.

American Psychiatric Association (2006). Treatment of patients with eating disorders, American Psychiatric Association. *The American journal of psychiatry, 163*(7 Suppl), 4.

American Psychological Association (2006). Evidence-based practice in psychology. *American Psychologist, 61*, 271–285.

Andersen, T. (1987). The reflecting team: Dialogue and meta-dialogue in clinical work. *Family Process, 26*, 415–428.

Andersen, T. (1995). Reflecting processes: Acts of informing and forming: You can borrow my eyes, but you must not take them away from me. In S. Friedman (Ed.) *The reflecting team in action: Collaborative practice in family therapy* (pp. 11–37). New York: The Guilford Press.

Asen, E., & Scholz, M. (2010). *Multi-Family therapy: Concepts and techniques*. London/New York: Routledge.

Assay, T. P., & Lambert, M. J. (1999). The empirical case for the common factors in therapy: Quantitative findings. In M. A. Hubble, B. L. Duncan, & S. D. Miller (Eds.), *The heart and soul of change* (pp. 23–55). Washington, DC: American Psychological Association.

Bateson, G. (1972). *Steps to an ecology of mind: Mind and nature*. New York: Ballantine Books.

Bateson, G. (1979). *Mind and nature: A necessary unity*. New York: Ballantine Books.

Becker, C. B., & Zayfert, C. (2001). Integrating DBT-based techniques and concepts to facilitate exposure treatment for PTSD. *Cognitive and Behavioral Practice, 8*(2), 107–122.

Berger, P., & Luckman, T. (1966). *The social construction of reality: A treatise in the sociology of knowledge*. Garden City, NY: Doubleday.

Besharat, M. A., Eisler, I., & Dare, C. (2001). The Self- and Other-Blame Scale (SOBS). The background and presentation of a new instrument for measuring blame in families. *Journal of Family Therapy, 23*, 208–223.

Beutler, L. E. (2002), It isn't the size, but the fit. *Clinical Psychology: Science and Practice, 9*, 434–438.

Boszormenyi-Nagy, I., & Spark, G. M. (1973). *Invisible loyalties: Reciprocity in intergenerational family therapy*. Hagerstown, MD: Harper & Row.

Bowen, M. (1978). *Family therapy in clinical practice*. New York: Jason Aronson.

Bruch, H. (1973). *Eating disorders: Obesity, anorexia nervosa, and the person within*. New York: Basic Books.

Bruch, H. (1974). *The golden cage*. Cambridge, MA: Harvard University Press.

Bruch, H. (1982). Anorexia nervosa: Therapy and theory. *American Journal of Psychiatry, 139*(12), 1531–1538.

Carr, A. (2000). *Family therapy: Concepts, process and practice* (2nd ed.), Chichester: John Wiley & Sons.

Carroll, K. M., & Nuro, K. F. (2002). One size cannot fit all: A stage model for psychotherapy manual development. *Clinical Psychology: Science and Practice, 9*, 396–406.

Castonguay, L. G., Constantino, M. J., & Holtforth, M. G. (2006). The working alliance: Where are we and where should we go? *Psychotherapy: Theory, Research, Practice, Training, 43*, 271.

Chorpita, B. F., & Regan, J. (2009). Dissemination of effective mental health procedures: Maximising the return on a significant investment. *Behaviour Research and Therapy, 47*, 990–993.

Colahan, M. (1995). Being a therapist in eating disorder treatment trials: Constraints and creativity. *Journal of Family Therapy, 17*, 79–96.

Colahan, M., & Senior, R. (1995). Family patterns in eating disorders: Going round in circles, getting nowhere faster. In G. I. Szmukler, C. Dare, & J. Treasure (Eds.), *Handbook of eating disorders: Theory, treatment and research*. (pp. 243–257), London: Wiley.

Couturier, J., Isserlin, L., & Lock, J. (2010). Family-based treatment for adolescents with anorexia nervosa: A dissemination study. *Eating Disorders, 18*, 199–209.

Couturier, J., Kimber, M., & Szatmari, P. (2013). Efficacy of family-based treatment for adolescents with eating disorders: A systematic review and meta-analysis. *International Journal of Eating Disorders, 46*, 3–11.

Couturier, J., Kimber, M., Jack, S., Niccols, A., Van Blyderveen, S., & McVey, G. (2013). Understanding the uptake of family based treatment for adolescents with anorexia nervosa: Therapist perspectives. *International Journal of Eating Disorders, 46*, 177–188.

Couturier, J., Kimber, M., Jack, S., Niccols, A., Van Blyderveen, S., & McVey, G. (2014). Using a knowledge transfer framework to identify factors facilitating implementation of family-based treatment. *International Journal of Eating Disorders, 47*, 410–417.

Crane, D. R., & Hafen Jr., M. (2002), Meeting the needs of evidence-based practice in family therapy: Developing the scientist-practitioner model. *Journal of Family Therapy, 24*, 113–124.

Darcy, A. M., Bryson, W. S., Agras, W. S., Fitzpatrick, K. K., Le Grange, D., & Lock, J. (2013). Do in-vivo behaviors predict early response in family-based treatment for anorexia nervosa? *Behaviour Research Therapy, 51*, 762–766.

Dare, C. (1983). Family therapy for families containing an anorectic youngster. In G. J. Bargman (Ed.), *Understanding anorexia nervosa and bulimia*. Columbus, OH: Ross.

Dare, C. (1990). Symptoms and systems: An exploration with anorexia nervosa. *Journal of Family Therapy, II*, 21–34.

Dare, C., & Eisler, I. (1995). Family therapy. In G. I. Szmukler, C. Dare, & J. Treasure (Eds.), *Eating Disorders: Handbook of Theory, Treatment and Research* (pp. 333–349). London: Wiley.

Dare, C., Eisler, I., Colahan, M., Crowther, C., Senior, R., & Asen, E. (1995). The listening heart and the chi square: Clinical and empirical perceptions in the family therapy of anorexia nervosa. *Journal of Family Therapy, 17,* 31–57.

Dare, C., Eisler, I., Russell, G. F. M., & Szmukler, G. I. (1990). The clinical and theoretical impact of a controlled trial of family therapy in anorexia nervosa. *Journal of Marital and Family Therapy, 16,* 39–57.

Dare. C., Le Grange, D., Eisler, I., & Rutherford, J. (1994). Redefining the psychosomatic family. *International Journal of Eating Disorders, 16,* 211–225.

Dare, C., & Eisler, I. (2000). A multi-family group day treatment programme for adolescent eating disorder. *European Eating Disorders Review, 8,* 4–18.

Dell, P. F. (1985). Understanding Bateson and Maturana: Towards a biological foundation of the social sciences. *Journal of Marital and Family Therapy, 11,* 1–20.

Diamond, G., & Josephson, A. (2005). Family-based treatment research: A 10-year update. *Journal of American Academy Child and Adolescent Psychiatry, 44,* 872–87.

Diamond, G., & Siqueland, L. (2001). Current status of family intervention science. *Child and Adolescent Psychiatric Clinics of North America, 10,* 641–661.

Diamond, G. S., Siqueland, L., & Diamond, G. M. (2003). Attachment-based family therapy for depressed adolescents: Programmatic treatment development. *Clinical Child and Family Psychology Review, 6,* 107–127.

Downs, K. J., & Blow, A. J. (2013). A substantive and methodological review of family-based treatment for eating disorders: The last 25 years of research. *Journal of Family Therapy, 35,* S1, 3–28.

Doyle, P., Le Grange, D., Loeb, K., Celio Doyle, A., & Crosby, R. D. (2010). Early response to family-based treatment for adolescent anorexia nervosa. *International Journal of Eating Disorders, 43,* 659–662.

Eisler, I. (1995). Family models of eating disorders. In G. Szmukler, C. Dare, & J. Treasure (Eds.), *Handbook of eating disorders: Theory, treatment and research* (pp. 155–176). Chichester: John Wiley & Sons.

Eisler I. (2002). Family interviewing. Issues of theory and practice. In Rutter M., & Taylor E. (Eds.), *Child and adolescent psychiatry: Modern approaches* (4th ed.). Oxford: Blackwells.

Eisler, I. (2005). The empirical and theoretical base of family therapy and multiple family day therapy for adolescent anorexia nervosa. *Journal of Family Therapy, 27,* 104–131.

Eisler, I. (2013). Family therapy for adolescent eating disorders: A special form of therapy or family therapy with a specific focus. *Journal of Family Therapy, 35,* 1–2.

Eisler, I., & Dare, C. (1992). You can't teach an old dog new tricks: Teaching research to family therapy trainees. *Journal of Family Psychology, 5,* 418–431

Eisler, I., Dare, C., Hodes, M., Russell, G., Dodge, E., & Le Grange, D. (2000). Family therapy for adolescent anorexia nervosa: The results of a controlled comparison of two family interventions. *Journal of Child Psychology and Psychiatry and Allied Disciplines, 41,* 727–736.

Eisler, I., Dare, C., Russell, G. F. M., Szmukler, G. I., Dodge, E., & Le Grange, D. (1997). Family and individual therapy for anorexia nervosa: A 5-year follow-up. *Archives of General Psychiatry, 54,* 1025–1030.

Eisler, I., Dare, C., & Szmukler, G. I. (1988). What's happened to family interaction research? An historical account and a family systems viewpoint. *Journal of Marital and Family Therapy, 14*, 45–61.

Eisler, I., Lock, J., & Le Grange, D. (2010). Family based treatments for adolescents with anorexia nervosa: Single-family and multi-family approaches. In C. M. Grilo, & J. E. Mitchell (Eds.), *The treatment of eating disorders: A clinical handbook* (pp. 150–174) New York: The Guildford Press.

Eisler, I., Simic, M., Russell, G. F. M., & Dare, C. (2007). A randomized controlled treatment trial of two forms of family therapy in adolescent anorexia nervosa: A five-year follow-up. *Journal of Child Psychology and Psychiatry and Allied Disciplines, 48*, 552–560.

Eisler, I., Szmukler, G. I., & Dare, C. (1985). Systematic observation and clinical insight—Are they compatible? An experiment in recognizing family interactions. *Psychological Medicine, 15*, 173–188.

Eisler, I., Simic, M., & team (2012). Maudsley service model for the management of child and adolescent eating disorders. Unpublished manuscript. Child and Adolescent Eating Disorders Service, South London & Maudsley NHS Foundation Trust.

Eisler et al. A multi-centre randomised trail of single and multi-family therapy for adolescent anorexia nervosa (in preparation).

Ellison, R., Rhodes, P., Madden, S., Miskovic, J., Wallis, A., Kohn, M., & Touyz, S. (2012). Essential components of the Maudsley model of family-based treatment for anorexia nervosa. *International Journal of Eating Disorders, 45*, 609–614.

Epston, D., Morris, F., & Maisel, R. (1995). A narrative approach to so-called anorexia/bulimia. *Journal of Feminist Family Therapy, 7*, 69–96.

Fairbairn, P., & Eisler, I. (2007). Intensive multiple family day treatment: Clinical and training perspectives. In S. Cook, & A. Almosnino (Eds.), *Therapies Multifamiliales Des Groupes Comme Agents Therapeutiques (Multiple Family Therapy: Groups as Therapeutic Agents)*.

Fairbairn, P., Simic, M., & Eisler, I. (2011). Multifamily therapy for adolescent anorexia nervosa. In D. Le Grange, & J. Lock (Eds.), *Eating Disorders in Children and Adolescents: A Clinical Handbook*, (pp. 243–261), New York: The Guilford Press.

Federici, A., & Wisniewski, L. (2012). Integrating dialectical behaviour therapy and family-based treatment for multidiagnostic adolescent patients. *A collaborative approach to eating disorders* (pp. 177–88). New York, NY: Routledge/Taylor & Francis Group.

Fitzpatrick, K. K., Moye, A., Hoste, R., Lock, J., & Le Grange, D. (2010). Adolescent focused psychotherapy for adolescent anorexia nervosa. *Journal of Contemporary Psychotherapy, 40*, 31–39.

Flaskas, C. (2002). *Family Therapy Beyond Postmodernism*. Sussex: Brunner Routledge.

Fleminger, S. (2005). A model for the treatment of eating disorders of adolescents in a specialized centre in The Netherlands. *Journal of Family Therapy, 27*, 147–157.

Forsberg, S., Lotempio, E., Bryson, S., Fitzpatrick, K. K., Le Grange, D., & Lock, J. (2013). Therapeutic alliance in two treatments for adolescent anorexia nervosa. *International Journal of Eating Disorders, 46*, 34–38.

Frosh, S. (1991). The semantics of therapeutic change. *Journal of Family Therapy, 13*, 171–186.

Garner, D. M. (1985). Individual psychotherapy for anorexia nervosa. *Journal of Psychiatric Research*, 19, 423–433.

Gergen, K. J. (1985). The social constructionist movement in modern psychology. *American Psychologist, 40*, 266.

Godart, N. T., Perdereau, F., Rein, Z., Berthoz, S., Wallier, J., Jeammet, P. H., & Flament, M. F. (2007) Comorbidity studies of eating disorders and mood disorders. Critical review of the literature. *Journal of Affective Disorders, 97*, 37–49.

Godfrey, K., Rhodes, P., Miskovic-Wheatley, J., Wallis, A., Clarke, S., Kohn, M., Touyz, S., & Madden, S. *Just one more bite: A qualitative analysis of the family meal in family-based treatment for anorexia nervosa. European Eating Disorders Review, 23, 77–85.*

Goldberg, D., & David, A. S. (1991). Family therapy and the glamour of science. *Journal of Family Therapy, 13*, 17–30.

Goldner, V. (1985). Feminism and family therapy. *Family Process, 24*, 31–7.

Gull, W. (1874). Anorexia nervosa (apepsia hysteria, anorexia hysteria). *Transactions of the Clinical Society of London, 7*, 222–228.

Gurman, A. S. (1986). Editorial Report: 1985. *Journal of Marital and Family Therapy, 12*(2), 221–222.

Gurman, A. S., & Fraenkel, P. (2002). The history of couple therapy: A millennial review. *Family Process, 41*, 199–260.

Haley, J. (1963). *Strategies of psychotherapy*. New York: Grune & Stratton.

Haley, J. (1976). *Leaving home: The therapy of disturbed young people*. New York: McGraw-Hill.

Halmi, K. A. (2013). Perplexities of treatment resistence in eating disorders. *BMC Psychiatry, 13*, 292.

Hare-Mustin, R. (1986). The problem of gender in family therapy theory. *Family Process, 26*, 15–27.

Hayes, S. C., & Nelson, R. O. (1981). Clinically relevant research: Requirements, problems, and solutions. *Behavioral Assessment, 3*, 209–215.

Haynos, A. F., & Fruzzetti, A. E. (2011). Anorexia nervosa as a disorder of emotion dysregulation: Evidence and treatment implications. *Clinical Psychology: Science and Practice, 18*, 183–202.

Henggeler, S. W. (1999). Multi-systemic therapy: An overview of clinical procedures, outcomes, and policy implications. *Child Psychology and Psychiatry Review, 4*, 2–10.

Hodes, M., Dare, C., Dodge, E., & Eisler, I. (1999). The assessment of expressed emotion in a standardised family interview. *Journal of Child Psychology and Psychiatry and Allied Disciplines, 40*, 617–625.

Hoffman, L. (1985). Beyond power and control: Towards a "second order" family systems therapy. *Family Systems Medicine, 3*, 381–396.

Hoffman, L. (1990). Constructing realities: An art of lenses. *Family Process, 29*, 1–12.

Hoffman, L. (1998). Setting aside the model in family therapy. *Journal of Marital and Family Therapy, 24*, 145–156.

Hollesen, A., Clausen, L., & Rokkedal, K. (2013). Multiple family therapy for adolescents with anorexia nervosa: A pilot study of eating disorder symptoms and interpersonal functioning. *Journal of Family Therapy, 35*, 53–67.

House, J., Schmidt, U., Craig, M., Landau, S., Simic, M., Nicholls, D., Hugo, P., Berelowitz, M., & Eisler, I. (2012). Comparison of specialist and non-specialist care pathways for adolescents with anorexia nervosa and related eating disorders. *International Journal of Eating Disorders, 45*, 949–956.

Hughes, E. K., Le Grange, D., Court, A., Yeo, M., Campbell, S., Whitelaw, M., Atkins, L., & Sawyer, S. M. (2014a). Implementation of family-based treatment for adolescents with anorexia nervosa. *Journal of Pediatric Health Care, 28*, 322–330.

Hughes, E. K., Le Grange, D., Court, A., Yeo, M. S. M., Campbell, S., Allan, E., Crosby, R. D., Loeb, K. L., & Sawyer, S. M. (2014b). Parent focused treatment for adolescent anorexia nervosa: A study protocol of a randomised controlled trial. *BMC Psychiatry, 14*, 105.

Jackson, D. D. (1956). The question of family homeostasis. *The Psychiatric Quarterly. Supplement, 31*, 79–90.

Jacobi, C., Hayward, C., de Zwaan, M., Kraemer, H. C., & Agras, W. S. (2004). Coming to terms with risk factors for eating disorders: Application of risk terminology and suggestions for a general taxonomy. *Psychology Bulletin, 130*, 19–65.

Jones, S. H., Sellwood, W., & McGovern, J. (2005). Psychological therapies for bipolar disorder: The role of model-driven approaches to therapy integration. *Bipolar Disorders, 7*, 22–32.

Kaplan, A. S. (2002). Psychological treatments for anorexia nervosa: A review of published studies and promising new directions. *Canadian Journal of Psychiatry, 47*, 235–242.

Kaye, W. (2008). Neurobiology of anorexia and bulimia nervosa purdue ingestive behavior research center symposium influences on eating and body weight over the lifespan: Children and adolescents. *Physiology and Behavior, 94*, 121–135.

Kazak, A. E., Hoagwood, K., Weisz, J. R., Hood, K., Kratochwill, T. R., Vargas, L. A., & Banez, G. A. (2010). A meta-systems approach to evidence-based practice for children and adolescents. *American Psychologist, 65*(2), 85.

Kazdin, A. E. (2008). Evidence-based treatment and practice: New opportunities to bridge clinical research and practice, enhance the knowledge base, and improve patient care. *American Psychologist, 63*, 146–159.

Keel, P. K., & Forney, K. J. (2013). Psychosocial risk factors for eating disorders. *International Journal of Eating Disorder, 46*, 433–439.

Kendall, P. C., Chu, B., Gifford, A., Hayes, C., & Nauta, M. (1999). Breathing life into a manual: Flexibility and creativity with manual-based treatments. *Cognitive and Behavioral Practice, 5*, 177–198.

Keys, A., Brozek, J., & Henschel, A. (1950). *The biology of human starvation*. Minneapolis: University of Minnesota Press.

Konstantellou, A., Campbell, M., & Eisler, I. (2012). The family context: cause, effect or resource? In J. Alexander, & J. Treasure (Eds.), *Collaborative Approach to Eating Disorders* (pp. 5–18). London: Routledge.

Kosmerly, S., Waller, G., & Robinson, A. L. (2014). Clinician adherence to guidelines in the delivery of family-based therapy for eating disorders. *International Journal of Eating Disorders*.

Krautter, T., & Lock, J. (2004). Is manualized family-based treatment for adolescent anorexia nervosa acceptable to patients? Patient satisfaction at the end of treatment. *Journal of Family Therapy, 26*, 66–82.

Larner, G. (2004). Family therapy and the politics of evidence. *Journal of Family Therapy, 26,* 17–39.

Lasègue, On hysterical anorexia. *Medical Times and Gazette* (September 6, 1873), pp. 265–266, Original French report in *Archives Générales de Médicine* (April 1873), in Brumberg, *Fasting Girls,* p. 129.

Le Grange, D., Accurso, E., Lock, J., Agras, W. S., & Bryson, S. W. (2014). Early weight gain predicts outcome in two treatments for adolescent anorexia nervosa. *International Journal of Eating Disorders, 47,* 124–129.

Le Grange, D., Crosby, R. D., Rathouz, P. J., & Leventhal, B. L. (2007). A randomised controlled comparison of family-based treatment and supportive psychotherapy for adolescent bulimia nervosa. *Archives of General Psychiatry, 64,* 1049–1056.

Le Grange, D., Crosby, R. D., & Lock, J. (2008). Predictors and moderators of outcome in family-based treatment for adolescent bulimia nervosa. *Journal of the American Academy of Child and Adolescent Psychiatry, 47,* 464–470.

Le Grange, D., Eisler, I., Dare, C., & Hodes, M. (1992a). Family criticism and self-starvation: A study of expressed emotion. *Journal of Family Therapy, 14,* 177–192.

Le Grange, D., Eisler, I., Dare, C., & Russell, G. F. M. (1992b). Evaluation of family treatments in adolescent anorexia nervosa: A pilot study. *International Journal of Eating Disorders, 12,* 347–357.

Le Grange, D., Hoste, R. R., Lock, J., & Bryson, S. W. (2011). Parental expressed emotion of adolescents with anorexia nervosa: Outcome in family-based treatment. *International Journal of Eating Disorders, 44,* 731–734.

Le Grange, D., Lock, J., Agras, W. S., Moye, A., Bryson, S. W., Jo, B., & Kraemer, H. C. (2012). Moderators and mediators of remission in family based treatment and adolescent focused therapy for anorexia nervosa. *Behaviour Research and Therapy, 50,* 85–92.

Lebow, J. (1997). The integrative revolution in couple and family therapy. *Family Process, 36,* 1–24.

Leff, J. P., & Vaughn, C. (1985). *Expressed emotion in families: Its significance for mental illness* (pp. 37–63). New York: Guilford Press.

Liddle, H. A. (1991). Empirical values and the culture of family therapy. *Journal of Marital and Family Therapy, 17,* 327–348.

Liddle, H. A., Dakof, G. A., & Diamond, G. (1991). Adolescent substance abuse: Multidimensional family therapy in action. In E. Kaufman, & P. Kaufman (Eds.), *Family therapy of drug and alcohol abuse* (pp. 120–171). Allyn and Bacon: Boston.

Lock, J. (2011). Evaluation of family treatment models for eating disorders. *Current Opinion in Psychiatry, 24,* 274–279.

Lock, J., Agras, W. S., Bryson, S., & Kraemer, S. (2005). A comparison of short- and long-term family therapy for adolescent anorexia nervosa. *Journal of the American Academy of Child and Adolescent Psychiatry, 44,* 632–639.

Lock, J., Couturier, J., & Agras, W. S. (2006). Comparison of long term outcomes in adolescents with anorexia nervosa treated with family therapy. *Journal of American Academy of Child and Adolescent Psychiatry, 45,* 666–672.

Lock, J., Couturier, J., Bryson, S., & Agras, W. S. (2006). Predictors of drop-out and remission in family therapy for adolescent anorexia nervosa in a randomised control trial. *International Journal of Eating Disorders, 39,* 639–647.

Lock, J., Garrett, A., Beenhakker, J., & Reiss, A. L. (2011). Aberrant brain activation during a response inhibition task in adolescent eating disorder subtypes. *American Journal of Psychiatry, 168*(1), 55–64.

Lock, J., & Le Grange, D. (2001a). Can family-based treatment of anorexia nervosa be manualized? *Journal of Psychotherapy Practice and Research, 10*(4), 253–261.

Lock, J., & Le Grange, D. (2013). *Treatment manual for anorexia nervosa: A family-based approach* (2nd ed.). New York: Guilford Press.

Lock, J., & Le Grange, D. (2014). Proposition: Family based treatment is overvalued. Position: Opposed. *Advances in Eating Disorders: Theory, Research and Practice*, 21–36.

Lock, J., Le Grange, D., Agras, W. S., & Dare, C. (2001a). *Treatment manual for anorexia nervosa: A family-based approach*. London: Guilford.

Lock, J., Le Grange, D., Agras, W. S., Moye, A., Bryson, S. W., & Jo, B. (2010). Randomised clinical trial comparing family-based treatment with adolescent-focused individual therapy for adolescents with anorexia nervosa. *Archives of General Psychiatry, 67*, 1025–1032.

Lock, J., Brandt, H., Woodside, B., Agras, W. S., Halmi, W. K., Johnson, C., ... & Wilfley, D.(2012). Challenges in conducting a multi-site randomized clinical trial comparing treatments for adolescent anorexia nervosa. *International Journal of Eating Disorders, 45*, 202–213.

Loeb, K. L., Walsh, T., Lock, J., Le Grange, D., Jones, J., Marcus, S., Weaver, J., & Dobrow, I. (2007). Open trial of family based treatment for full and partial anorexia nervosa in adolescence: Evidence of successful dissemination. *Journal of the American Academy of Child & Adolescent Psychiatry, 46*, 792–800.

Loeb, K. L., Wilson, G. T., Labouvie, E., Pratt, E. M., Hayaki, J., Walsh, B. T., ... & Fairburn, C. G. (2005). Therapeutic alliance and treatment adherence in two interventions for bulimia nervosa: A study of process and outcome. *Journal of Consulting and Clinical Psychology, 73*, 1097.

LoTempio, E., Forsberg, S., Bryson, S. W., Fitzpatrick, K. K., Le Grange, D., Lock, J. (2013). Patients' characteristics and the quality of the therapeutic alliance in family-based treatment and individual therapy for adolescents with anorexia nervosa. *Journal of Family Therapy, 35*, 29–52.

Luborsky, L., & DeRubeis, R. J. (1984). The use of psychotherapy treatment manuals: A small revolution in psychotherapy research style. *Clinical Psychology Review, 4*(1), 5–14.

Luepnitz, D. A. (1988). *The family interpreted: Feminist theory in clinical practice*. New York: Basic Books.

Madanes, C. (1981). *Strategic family therapy*. San Francisco, Jossey-Bass.

Madden, S., Miskovic, J., Wallis, A., Kohn, M., Lock, J., Le Grange, D., Jo, B., Clarke, S., Rhodes, P., Hay, P., & Touyz, S. (2014). A randomized controlled trial of inpatient treatment for anorexia nervosa in medically unstable adolescents. *Psychological Medicine*, available on CJO2014. doi:10.1017/S0033291714001573

Marcé, L. (1860). On a form of hypochondriacal delirium occurring consecutive to dyspepsia and characterized by refusal of food. *Journal of Psychological Medicine and Mental Pathology, 13*, 264–266.

Maturana, H. R., & Varela, F. J. (1987). *The tree of knowledge: The biological roots of human understanding*. Boston: Shambhala Publications.

McHugh, K. R., & Barlow, D. H. (2010). The dissemination and implementation of evidence-based psychological treatments: A review of current efforts. *American Psychologist*, 65, 73–84.

McHugh, K. R., Murray, H. W., & Barlow, D. H. (2009). Balancing fidelity and adaption in the dissemination of empirically-supported treatments: The promise of transdiagnostic interventions. *Behaviour Research and Therapy*, 47, 946–953.

Mehl, A., Tomanova, J., Kuběna, A., & Papežová, H. (2013). Adapting multi-family therapy to families who care for a loved one with an eating disorder in the Czech Republic combined with follow-up pilot study of efficacy. *Journal of Family Therapy*, 35, 82–101.

Messer, S. B., & Wampold, B. E. (2002), Let's face facts: Common factors are more potent than specific therapy ingredients. *Clinical Psychology: Science and Practice*, 9, 21–25.

Miller, S. D., & Duncan, B. L. (2000). Paradigm lost: From model driven to client directed, outcome informed clinical work. *Journal of Systemic Therapies*, 19, 20–34.

Miller, S. D., Hubble, M. A., Chow, D. L., & Seidel, J. A. (2013). The outcome of psychotherapy: Yesterday, today and tomorrow. *Psychotherapy in Australia*, 20(3), 64.

Minuchin, S. (1974). *Families and family therapy*. Cambridge, MA: Harvard University Press.

Minuchin, S., Baker, L., Rosman, B. L., Liebman, R., Milman, L., & Todd, T. C. (1975). A conceptual model of psychosomatic illness: Family organization and family therapy. *Archives of General Psychiatry*, 32, 1031–1038.

Minuchin, S., Rosman, B., & Baker, L. (1978). *Psychosomatic families: Anorexia nervosa in context*. Cambridge, MA: Harvard University Press.

Morgan, H. G., & Russell, G. F. M. (1975). Value of family background and clinical features as predictors of long-term outcome in anorexia nervosa: Four-year follow-up study of 41 patients. *Psychological Medicine*, 5, 355–371.

Murphy, S., Russell, L., & Waller, G. (2005). Integrated psychodynamic therapy for bulimia nervosa and binge eating disorder: Theory, practice and preliminary findings. *Eur. Eat. Disorders Rev.*, 13, 383–391.

Murray, S., Wallis, A., & Rhodes, P. (2012). The questioning process Maudsley Family Based Treatment Part 1: Deviation amplification. *Contemporary Family Therapy*, 34, 582–592.

Nathan, P. E., & Gorman, J. M. (1998). *A guide to treatments that work*. New York: Oxford University Press.

National Institute for Clinical Excellence (2004). *Eating disorders: Core interventions in the treatment and management of anorexia nervosa, bulimia nervosa and related eating disorders*. CG9. London: NICE.

Nielsen, S., & Bará-Carril, N. (2003). Family, burden of care and social consequences. In J. Treasure, U. Schmidt, & E. van Furth (Eds.), *Handbook of eating disorders*, 2 (pp. 191–206). London: Wiley & Sons.

Parsons, T., & Bales, R. F. (1955). *Family, socialization and interaction process*. Glencoe, IL: Free Press.

Patterson, G. (1971). Families: Applications of social learning to family life. Champaign, IL: Research Press.

Paulson-Karlsson, G., Engstrom, I., & Nevonen, L. (2009). A pilot study of a family-based treatment for adolescent anorexia nervosa: 18–36 month follow-ups. *Eating Disorders*, 17, 72–88.

Pereira, T., Lock, J., & Oggins, J. (2006). Role of therapeutic alliance in family therapy for adolescent anorexia nervosa. *International Journal of Eating Disorders, 39*, 677–84.

Pike, K. M. (1998). Long-term course of anorexia nervosa: Response, relapse, remission, and recovery. *Clinical Psychology Review, 18*, 447–475.

Pinsof, W. M., & Wynne, L. C. (1995). The efficacy of marital and family therapy: An empirical overview, conclusions, and recommendations. *Journal of Marital and Family Therapy, 21*, 585–613.

Pocock, D. (1995). Searching for a better story: Harnessing modern and postmodern positions in family therapy. *Journal of Family Therapy, 17*, 149–173.

Pote, H., Stratton, P., Cottrell, D., Shapiro, D., & Boston, P. (2003). Systemic family therapy can be manualized: Research process and findings. *Journal of Family Therapy, 25*, 236–262.

Rawlins, M. (2008). De testimonio: on the evidence for decisions about the use of therapeutic interventions. *Clinical Medicine, 8*, 579–588.

Rhodes, P., Baillee, A., Brown, J., & Madden, S. (2008). Can parent–parent consultation improve the effectiveness of the Maudsley model of family-based treatment for anorexia nervosa: A randomised control trial. *Journal of Family Therapy, 30*, 96–108.

Rhodes, P., Brown, J., & Madden, S. (2009). The Maudsley model of family-based treatment for anorexia nervosa: A qualitative evaluation of parent-to-parent consultation. *Journal of Marital and Family Therapy, 35*, 181–192.

Rhodes, P., & Madden, S. (2005). Scientist practitioner family therapists, postmodern medical practitioners, and expert parents: Second order change at the Eating Disorders Program, Children's Hospital at Westmead. *Journal of Family Therapy, 27*, 171–182.

Rhodes, P., & Wallis, A. (2009). The Maudsley model of family therapy for anorexia nervosa: History, practice and future directions. In S. Paxton, & P. Hay, (Eds.), *Interventions for body dissatisfaction and eating disorders: Evidence and practice* (pp. 58–74). Ip Communications: Melbourne.

Riskin, J., & Faunce, E. E. (1972). An evaluative review of family interaction research. *Family Process, 11*, 365–455.

Robin, A., & Foster, S. L. (1989). *Negotiating parent adolescent conflict*. Guilford Press: New York.

Robin, A. L., & Le Grange, D. (2010). Treating adolescents with anorexia nervosa using behavioural family systems therapy. In J. R. Weisz & A. E. Kazdin (Eds.), *Evidence-based psychotherapies for children and adolescents* (2nd ed.) (pp. 345–358). New York, NY: Guilford.

Robin, A. L., & Siegel, P. *Behavioral family systems therapy: An evidence-based approach for the treatment of eating disorders* (unpublished treatment manual).

Robin, A. L., Siegal, P. T., Koepke, T., Moye, A. W., & Tice, S. (1994). Family therapy versus individual therapy for adolescent females with anorexia nervosa. *Developmental and Behavioural Paediatrics, 15*, 111–116.

Robin, A. L., Siegel, P. T., & Moye, A. (1995). Family versus individual therapy for anorexia: Impact on family conflict. *International Journal of Eating Disorders, 17*, 313–322.

Robin, A. L., Siegel, P. T., Moye, A. W., Gilroy, M., Dennis, A. B., & Sikand, A. (1999). A controlled comparison of family versus individual therapy for adolescents with anorexia nervosa. *Journal of the American Academy of Child and Adolescent Psychiatry, 38,* 1482–1489.

Robinson, A. L., Strahan, E., Girz, L., Wilson, A., & Boachie, A. (2013). 'I know I can help you': Parental self-efficacy predicts adolescent outcomes in family-based therapy for eating disorders. *European Eating Disorder Review, 21,* 108–114.

Rockwell, R. E., Boutelle, K., Trunko, M. E., Jacobs, M. J., & Kaye, W. H. (2011). An Innovative Short-term, Intensive, Family-based Treatment for Adolescent Anorexia Nervosa: Case Series. *European Eating Disorders Review, 19,* 362–367.

Roemer, L., & Orsillo, S. M. (2002). Expanding our conceptualization of and treatment for generalized anxiety disorder: Integrating mindfulness/acceptance-based approaches with existing cognitive-behavioral models. *Clinical Psychology: Science and Practice, 9,* 54–68.

Rolland, J. S. (1994). *Families, illness, and disability: An integrative treatment model.* New York: Basic Books.

Rolland, J. S. (1994). In sickness and in health: The impact of illness on couples' relationships. *Journal of Marital and Family Therapy, 20,* 327–347.

Rolland, J. S. (1999). Parental illness and disability: A family systems framework. *Journal of Family Therapy, 21,* 242–266.

Rosman, B. L., Minuchin, S., & Liebman, R. (1975). Family lunch session. An Introduction to Family Therapy in Anorexia Nervosa. *American Journal of Orthopsychiatry, 45*(5), 846–853.

Russell, G. F. M. (1981). Comment: The current treatment of anorexia nervosa. *British Journal of Psychiatry, 138,* 164–166.

Russell, G. F. M., Szmukler, G. I., Dare, C., & Eisler, I. (1987). An evaluation of family therapy in anorexia nervosa and bulimia nervosa. *Archives of General Psychiatry, 44,* 1047–1056.

Sackett, D. L., Rosenberg, W., Gray, J. A., Haynes, R. B., & Richardson, W. S. (1996). Evidence based medicine: What it is and what it isn't. *British Medical Journal, 312,* 71–72.

Sackett, D. L., Straus, S. E., Richardson, W. S., Rosenberg, W., & Haynes, R. B. (2000). *Evidence based medicine: How to practice and teach EBM* (2nd ed.). New York: Churchill Livingstone.

Salaminiou, E., Campbell, M., Simic, M., Kuipers, E., & Eisler, I. (2014) Intensive multi family therapy for adolescent anorexia nervosa: An open study of 30 families. *Journal of Family Therapy* (in press).

Schmidt, U., Lee, S., Beecham, J., Perkins, S., Treasure, J., Yi, I., ... & Eisler, I. (2007). A randomized controlled trial of family therapy and cognitive behavior therapy guided self-care for adolescents with bulimia nervosa and related disorders. *American Journal of Psychiatry, 164,* 591–598.

Schoenwald, S. K., & Hoagwood, K. (2001). Effectiveness, transportability, and dissemination of interventions: What maters when? *Psychiatric Services, 52,* 1190–1197.

Scholz, M., & Asen, E. (2001). Multiple family therapy with eating disordered adolescents: Concepts and preliminary results. *European Eating Disorders Review, 9,* 33–42.

Scholz, M., Rix, M., Scholz, K., Gantchev, K., & Thömke, V. (2005). Multiple family therapy for anorexia nervosa: Concepts, experiences and results. *Journal of Family Therapy, 27,* 132–141.

Seligman, M. E. (1995). The effectiveness of psychotherapy: The Consumer Reports study. *American Psychologist, 50*(12), 965.

Selvini-Palazzoli, M. (1974). *Self-starvation: From the intrapsychic to the transpersonal approach to anorexia nervosa.* London: Chaucer.

Selvini-Palazzoli, M., Boscolo, L., Cecchin, G., & Prata, G. (1978). *Paradox and counterparadox.* New York: Aronson.

Selvini Palazzoli, M., Boscolo, L., Cecchin, G., & Prata, G. (1980). Hypothesizing-circularity-neutrality: Three guidelines for the conductor of the session. *Family Process, 19*, 3–12.

Sexton, T. L., & Alexander, J. F. (1999). Functional family therapy: Principles of clinical intervention, assessment, and implementation. *Henderson, NV: RCH Enterprises.*

Shafran, R., Clark, D. M., Fairburn, C. G., Arntz, A., Barlow, D. H., Ehlers, A., ... & Wilson, G. T. (2009). Mind the gap: Improving the dissemination of CBT. *Behaviour Research and Therapy, 47*, 902–909.

Sparks, J. (1997). Voices of experience: Inviting former clients to rejoin the therapy process as consultants. *Journal of Systemic Therapies, 16*, 367–375.

Speedy, J. (2004). Living a more peopled life: Definitional ceremony as inquiry into psychotherapy 'outcomes.' *The International Journal of Narrative Therapy and Community Work, 3*, 43–53.

Squire-Dehouck, B. (1993) *Evaluation of conjoint family therapy versus family counselling in adolescent anorexia nervosa patients. A two year follow-up study.* Institute of Psychiatry. unpublished M.Sc. dissertation. University of London.

Steinglass, P. (1998). Multiple family discussion groups for patients with chronic medical illness. *Families, Systems & Health, 16*, 55–70.

Steinglass, P., Bennett, L. A., Wolin, S. J., & Reiss, D. (1987). *The alcoholic family.* New York: Basic Books.

Strober, M. (2014). Proposition: Family based treatment is overvalued. Position: Proposer. *Advances in Eating Disorders: Theory, Research and Practice*, 1–36.

Strupp, H. H., & Anderson, T. (1997). On the limitations of therapy manuals. *Clinical Psychology: Science and Practice, 4*, 76–82.

Szmukler, G. I., & Tantam, D. (1984). Anorexia nervosa: Starvation dependence. *British Journal of Medical Psychology, 57*, 303–310.

Szmukler, G. I., Eisler, I., Russell, G. F. M., & Dare, C. (1985). Anorexia nervosa, parental expressed emotion and dropping out of treatment. *British Journal of Psychiatry, 147*, 265–271.

Tchanturia, K., & Lock, J. (2011). Cognitive remediation therapy for eating disorders: Development, refinement and future directions. *Current Topics in Behavioural Neuroscience, 6*, 269–87.

Tomm, K. (1987a). Interventive interviewing, Part I. Strategising as a fourth guideline for the therapist. *Family Process, 25*, 4–13.

Tomm, K. (1987b). Interventive interviewing, Part II. Reflexive questioning as a means to enable self healing. *Family Process, 26*, 167–183.

Tomm, K. (1988). Interventive interviewing, Part III. Intending to ask linear, circular, strategic or reflexive questions. *Family Process, 27*, 1–15.

Treasure, J., & Schmidt, U. (2005). Anorexia nervosa. *Clinical Evidence, 14*, 1140–1148.

von Bertalanffy, L. (1968). *General system theory.* New York: Braziller.

Voriadaki, T., Simic, M., Espie, J., & Eisler, I. (2015). Intensive multi-family therapy for adolescent anorexia nervosa: Adolescents' and parents' day to day experiences. *Journal of Family Therapy, 37*, 5–23.

Wallace, L. M., & von Ranson, K. M. (2012). Perceptions and use of empirically-supported psychotherapies among eating disorder professionals. *Behavior Research Therapy, 50,* 215–222.

Waller, J. V., Kaufman, R. M., & Deutsch, F. (1940). Anorexia nervosa: A psychosomatic entity. *Psychosomatic Medicine, 2,* 3–16.

Wallis, A., Alford, C., Baudinet, J., Cook, A., Robertson, A., Cubitt, A., Madden, S., & Kohn, M. *Enhancing Maudsley family based treatment: A specialist service response when the manual doesn't have the answers!—Two case studies.* submitted.

Wallis, A., Alford, C., Hanson, A., Titterton, J., Madden, S., & Kohn, M. (2013). Innovations in Maudsley family-based treatment for anorexia nervosa at the Children's Hospital at Westmead: A family admission Programme. *Journal of Family Therapy, 35,* S1, 68–81.

Wallis, A., Rhodes, P., Kohn, M., & Madden, S. (2007). Five-years of family based treatment for anorexia nervosa: The Maudsley model at the Children's Hospital at Westmead. *International Journal of Adolescent Medicine and Health, 19,* 277–283.

Watzlawick, P., Weakland, J., & Fisch, R. (1974). *Change: Principles of problem formation and problem resolution.* New York: W. W. Norton.

Webb, C. A., DeRubeis, R. J., & Barber, J. P. (2010). Therapist adherence/competence and treatment outcome: A meta-analytic review, *Journal of Consulting and Clinical Psychology, 78,* 200–211.

White, M. (1983). Anorexia nervosa: A transgenerational system perspective. *Family Process, 22,* 255–273.

White, M. (1986). Anorexia nervosa: A cybernetic perspective. *Dulwich Centre Review,* 56–65.

White, M. (1988/89). The externalizing of the problem and the re-authoring of lives and relationships. *Dulwich Centre Newsletter,* Summer, 3–21.

White, M. K. (1995). *Re-authoring lives: Interviews & essays.* Dulwich Centre Publications.

White, M. K. (2000). Reflecting teamwork as definitional ceremony revisited. In M. White (Ed.), *Reflections on narrative practice: Essays and interviews.* Adelaide: Dulwich.

White, M. K., & Epston, D. (1990). *Narrative means to therapeutic ends.* New York: Norton.

White, H. J., Haycraft, E., Madden, S., Rhodes, P., Miskovic-Wheatley, J., Wallis, A., Kohn, M., & Meyer, C. (2014). How do parents of adolescent patients with anorexia nervosa interact with their child at mealtimes? A study of parental strategies used in the family meal session of family-based treatment. *International Journal of Eating Disorders, 48,* 72–80.

Wilson, G. T. (1997). Treatment manuals in clinical practice. *Behaviour Research and Therapy, 35,* 205–211.

Wilson, G. T. (1998a). Manual-based treatment and clinical practice. *Clinical Psychology: Science and Practice, 5,* 363–375.

Woodside, D. B., Bulik, C. M., Halmi, K. A., Fichter, M. M., Kaplan, A., & Berrettini, W.H. (2002). Personality, perfectionism, and attitudes toward eating in parents of individuals with eating disorders. *International Journal of Eating Disorders, 31,* 290–9.

Part I

Innovative Adaptations of Family Therapy for Eating and Weight Disorders

Chapter 3

In Vivo Family Meal Training for Initial Nonresponders

Kathleen Kara Fitzpatrick, Alison M. Darcy,
Daniel Le Grange, and James Lock

Family-based therapy (FBT; Lock, Le Grange, Agras, & Dare, 2001) rests on the foundation that parents can be empowered to help their starving children meet their nutritional needs, thereby overcoming the far-reaching impact of malnourishment on the patient and restore both weight and health. Families have little experience with renourishment protocols for eating disorders and may question the veracity of this claim and perhaps the sanity of the clinician espousing it. The stance of FBT is that therapists and families must work together with their respective expertise in eating disorders or the patient, to develop a unique system that will respect the integrity of the parental authority and concern for the patient, hold sacrosanct the healthy part of the patient, and work to encourage a return to adolescent functioning, while also coaching the family in behaviors that might seem, at least on the surface, contrary to the two former goals. Although these tenets exist throughout the whole of treatment, nowhere are they more evident than in the family meal.

Why Do We Do a Family Meal?

The family meal, or session 2 of FBT, provides a unique learning experience for therapists and families. The injunction to bring a family meal is delivered at the close of session 1 and is both specific in its direction and vague enough to be open to interpretation. At the end of session 1, the therapist should state, "In the next session we are going to do something somewhat unique: I would like the two of you (indicating the caregiver/s) to bring a meal that you feel your starving child needs to eat in order to recover from anorexia." Additional guidance may be provided around the ability to heat or warm food or emphasizing that this should be a meal and not a snack, that the therapist will not eat the meal, but that the family will be eating in session; but further guidance on meal content should not be given. The interpretation of the content of the meal, when or how the family will plan the meal, and expectations for what will happen next remain open to interpretation.

The goal of this vague and yet compelling instruction is simple; the family meal helps the therapist to understand how the family perceives the injunction of renourishment, to provide the opportunity for the therapist to observe family dynamics and skills around engaging with the eating disorder, and to allow the family the opportunity to practice renourishment with direct coaching and intervention. Providing too much direction removes the therapist's ability to see existing family patterns and degree of symptom accommodation and fosters a dependence on prescriptive injunctions that limit the ability of the family to reason through the ways in which they will approach the daunting task of negotiating renourishment. Caregivers, understandably concerned about the health and welfare of their child, often long for the security of more directive guidance for intervening in the eating pathology. In contrast, therapists, knowing that each family will ultimately negotiate a unique path through renourishment, must be able to tolerate the family anxiety, knowing that this will ultimately play out in a manner that will support parental autonomy and provide information critical for furthering treatment.

It is hardly surprising, then, that the family meal session is somewhat controversial. Many therapists offer a "modified Maudsley" approach in which they do not offer family meals, and consistently, when trainees and therapists are asked about their experience of treatment, most express great concern about their ability to implement a family meal. This is not surprising as they are, almost by necessity, intense sessions. They may last long past the usually allotted 50-minute therapy time slot (although they need not do so). These sessions also require thoughtful scheduling at the end of the day to allow extra time for the adolescent to take "one bite more" than the adolescent had expected. And, of course, there may need to be extra time for the occasional cleaning of mashed potatoes off a wall or a ceiling.

Perhaps less acknowledged, many therapists fear that they will be unsuccessful in inducing the patient to eat that "one bite more" and they and the family will be disappointed at the outset of such a critical journey. While the treatment manual does not explicitly state the need to remain with the family until they experience success at attempting to get their anorexic adolescent to eat more than they had planned, in practice most therapists fear that failing to give parents this opportunity for empowerment to "win" against the anorexia risks making the rest of the treatment significantly more challenging. In this way, the more the adolescent resists the attempt, the greater the opportunity for magnifying the empowerment parents can experience from success. This is the perfect recipe for a hugely intense session, indeed, just after the first session, which was also *intentionally* intense. Thus it is understandable why therapists may be open to opportunities to avoid it. This fear, however prevalent, might reflect a misunderstanding of the goal and focus of this session: while helping parents take mastery over anorexia nervosa and working toward empowerment through successful nourishment is a stated goal, the skills training, coaching, and psychoeducation delivered throughout the session represent the most critical elements moving treatment forward. Even if no bites are taken, the family can be encouraged to continue to use the skills employed in the family session to forward their coaching efforts.

What Do We Know About Family Meals?

Perhaps most compelling about the conundrum of the family meal is the fact that we do not know for certain whether a family meal is necessary for successful outcome. Indeed, we have indirect evidence that it is not from earlier studies conducted by Eisler and colleagues (Eisler et al., 1997, 2000) comparing separated family therapy to conjoint family therapy. In the separated family treatment condition, the adolescent was seen separately from his or her parents and thus no family meal was conducted. In both of these studies, and *regardless* of treatment arm, about 70 percent of adolescents achieved weight restoration or had return of menses by the end of treatment, few necessitated hospitalization, and about 75 percent had favorable outcomes after a 5-year follow-up (Eisler, 2005).

However, we do know that we can predict outcome with considerable accuracy according to the family's response to treatment in the first four sessions of manualized FBT that *does* include a meal session (Doyle et al., 2010; Lock et al., 2006). Two studies using different data indicate that early weight gain predicts outcome in FBT. For example, using a signal-detection procedure, Doyle and colleagues identified a cut-off point of 2.88 percent Ideal Body Weight (IBW) (an absolute value of approximately 1.8 kg weight gain was identified) by session 4 as the best predictor of end-of-treatment remission with 90 percent accuracy (Doyle et al., 2010).

In an effort to examine what distinguishes those who achieve this predictor versus those who do not, our research group examined in vivo behavior in the first three sessions to see if any observable behaviors would be associated with early weight gain (Darcy et al., 2013). We coded therapy recordings from 21 patients for the first three sessions (1, 2, and 3) for the presence of predefined parental and child behaviors. The sample was divided between early responders and nonresponders and compared in the duration (time of observation divided by recording length) of behaviors to see if there was a relationship. The meal session (session 2) yielded the greatest number of between-group discrepancies, lending indirect support to the importance of including a family meal in maximizing treatment efficacy.

Behaviors that were indicative of parental control or pressure to eat in the face of refusal—for example, presenting food, serving food, and modeling eating appeared more often among nonresponding adolescents and in the context of food refusal. Nonresponding adolescents themselves also exhibited more negative verbal behaviors and were away from the table for longer than early responders. There was also a large difference between early responders and nonresponders on length of illness, suggesting that this may have a role as a mediator. In the absence of sufficient numbers required to conduct a formal mediator analysis, we concluded that the longer the illness was in place, the more entrenched were patterns of food coaxing and food refusal seen between parents and children, which, in concert with family-illness models, have evolved over time after caring for a loved one with a chronic illness (Eisler, 1995). This study thus suggests that we can observe entrenched behavior patterns that are related to poor prognosis as early as the second (meal) session. In addition, it suggests that the meal session may have specific therapeutic potency if the family system can be successfully intervened upon, amended, or restructured. An important path to improving treatment outcomes for nonresponders therefore might be to maximize the therapeutic benefit of the family meal.

Designing an In Vivo Meal Session Treatment Adaptation

One relatively obvious conclusion in pondering how to maximize the therapeutic benefit of the family meal was that an *additional* family meal might be a useful starting point for an adaptation for nonresponders. However, the timing, focus, and content of this meal session should not simply repeat a first meal experience but specifically target areas of challenge observed in family meals. This meant developing a specific goal-centered focus, so as to avoid repeating the same behaviors from the initial meal session and inadvertently reinforcing the unhelpful behavior patterns.

The importance of an early intervention is critical. This meant the meal needed to occur while family members remained activated around the illness and before sufficient time had passed to diminish hope and deplete the energy necessary to acquire and utilize new skills. However, only about half of patients will fail to make the required weight gain indicative of treatment response (Doyle et al., 2010) and would therefore be offered the intervention.

Given the intensity of the family meal, however, we also wanted families to have sufficient time between these sessions to secure additional skills and for the therapeutic relationship to uncover specific areas of challenge disrupting renourishment efforts. Said differently, families needed time to "digest" the family meal and the therapist benefitted from understanding which behaviors reflected more established patterns and "hard-wired" difficulties that would benefit from more directed intervention. As such, we built around the second family meal an additional two sessions aimed at maximizing the strategic potential of that session, in effect adding an additional three sessions to the treatment protocol for nonresponders. While a nonresponding family is identified at the start of session 4, ultimately, it was determined that session 6 would be ideal to introduce a second family meal, with session 4 used to "re-orchestrate the intense scene" and session 5 used to identify with the parents alone what the major barriers are to their renourishment efforts. Only then do we enter the second family meal. In this way, the family enters the second family meal with a specific target or goal in mind that aims to directly tackle whatever barrier was identified in the previous session, with their anxiety raised to within an optimal therapeutic window for action in the second meal session.

As noted earlier, a true repeat of the first meal is impossible, as the family would certainly know the expectation for the meal and the focus on identifying specific target strategies for renourishment. This was particularly important, as first family meals often involved a significant portion of time spent educating caregivers around appropriate nourishment, efforts toward aligning parents around these behavioral changes, and continuing psychoeducation. The second family meal was developed with an idea of "hitting the ground running" with a focus on efforts toward increasing nourishment, identifying themes and challenges from previous sessions to be directly elicited in this second family meal, and providing further opportunities for success. In this sense, the strategic potential of the second family meal is amplified by the preceding two sessions.

The goals of the initial meal session (Lock et al., 2001) are described next:

- To evaluate the efficacy of the strategies used by parents to assist with increasing nourishment
- To provide feedback to the family to assist with increasing nourishment
- To provide coaching to parents to assist them with facing challenging behaviors of anorexia nervosa
- To continue to empower parents to take over this role of renourishment
- To continue to empower siblings to assist their ill sibling in addressing challenges after eating

In the adaptation, knowledge from the separate parents-only session helps the therapist refine these goals and provide greater specificity of approach to target the individual needs of each family. In addition, the need for specific nutritional counseling is often attenuated in this second meal session as the family has had more time to understand the concept of "starvation nourishment." This lends more time in the session to be spent on other targeted behaviors.

Goals for the second family meal session are:

- *To evaluate the strategies used by parents to assist with increasing nourishment.* Has the family adopted new techniques or are they continuing to use the same techniques as in the first session? Helpful strategies to reinforce and practice in session include techniques such as the following: selectively ignoring nontarget behaviors; modeling a calm, patient approach to renourishment; capitalizing on successes at home; and identifying specific goals for each meal (e.g., shortened length of time for the meal, incorporating a feared food).

- *To disrupt the use of parental skills that may impede nourishment efforts.* This includes identifying "anorexic arguments," escalations of conflict, and reducing expressed emotion. Anorexia nervosa causes great distress, particularly during mealtimes, and certain strategies make renourishment more difficult. These include spending time on nontarget behaviors, engaging in verbal or physical arguments, or difficulties in sustaining a focus on anorexia nervosa during mealtimes. With respect to the last, families often have to learn to devote time to monitoring the patient and this may change other relationships or demands in the family (e.g., parents may need siblings to do dishes or start homework without prompting as mealtimes may be extended for the patient to complete a meal). In addition, families are often surprised by the level of scrutiny necessary to "catch" anorexic behaviors at mealtimes and a greater focus on these behaviors can be incorporated into the second meal session. No family comes to treatment with the intention of doing their child harm, and parents should be reminded that strategies that interfere with renourishment are not signs of "bad parenting" but rather habits and interactions brought about by the illness that need to be retrained.

- *To continue to assist the family with externalization of the illness.* This is targeted by using in vivo behaviors to enhance the difference between the healthy part of the patient and anorexia nervosa. Although some families can readily identify and separate their child from anorexia nervosa, others may find this difficult or may find the inverse challenging: to continue to see the healthy parts of their child under the burden of the illness.

- *To provide coaching to parents in developing emotional coping techniques to manage their own distress as well as the distress of their child.* Managing the emotional challenges of renourishment often means assisting parents in managing their grief over what the illness has taken from their child and their family; in managing their frustration with frequency/intensity of anorexia nervosa's presence, particularly with increased frequency of meals; and in tolerating anger or distress directed at them by the illness. Families expect to come to therapy to feel better and, if parents truly are pressuring anorexia nervosa and working toward renourishment, FBT often may feel a bit worse/uncertain/challenging than anticipated. Reminding parents of their own self-care and emotion regulation tools can be helpful in weathering the storms.

- *To continue to empower parents to take over the role of renourishment.* This is achieved by fostering alignment and communication between parents and identifying their skills and strengths. The therapist can use the meal to continue to assess and reinforce parents being "on the same page" both in terms of their overall goals and the goals of the meal session. If one parent feels confident and the other more uncertain, working together to empower both parents equally is key. When parents are "in the thick of it" with renourishment, it can also be challenging for them to see their successes. Furthermore, anorexia nervosa is not known to be constructive in its criticism of parents and thus parents are not likely receiving any positive feedback related to their efforts. The second family meal provides opportunity for the therapist to identify and praise specific techniques and strategies employed by the family that are supporting renourishment efforts.

- *To continue to empower siblings to assist their ill sibling in addressing challenges after eating.* By the time the second family meal arrives, the family as a whole is better known to the therapist. Efforts at aligning siblings can be more targeted, now that the therapist understands the impediments facing relationship-building. The healthy parts of the patient can be fostered through the sibling relationship, and siblings can also more directly describe the impact of renourishment efforts on their own lives. Another word about the healthy part of the patient: by the time of the second meal, the healthy part of the patient often has some relationship with the therapist and this stronger connection can also be used to help the sibling see the healthy parts of the sibling that parents may not see (e.g., the first author sometimes jokes with siblings in conflict that the only thing they agree on might be that they hate coming to treatment! The behavior is the same—reluctance to engage in treatment—but one is seen as pathological and the other as more typical adolescent behaviors).

- *To foster and maintain psychoeducation on nutrition and eating disorders.* As noted earlier, most families report fewer challenges with understanding what their child should be eating by the time of the second family meal. Rather, they struggle more with exactly how to go about doing exactly that. However, therapists should be aware of the need for ongoing education regarding the health risks of anorexia nervosa, the importance of calorie-dense, nutritious foods, and the risks of exercise while in a malnourished state.

There are several specific skills that can assist the therapist in knowing how to foster a more targeted and informative meal session. These relate to timing around meal delivery, parental engagement around nourishment efforts, and ways to further include siblings.

Family meal setup and serving

The novelty of the first family meal lends a nervous tension that is often not present in the second family meal. The goal here is to set straight about in delivering the meal to the table and coaching parents in the task of refeeding (Lock et al., 2001). The therapist should observe what the family has brought (ask questions if necessary to identify elements of the meal) and, as in the first meal session, inquire around the choice of the meal: Who decided on what to bring? How did they decide? What role did the patient play? However, in contrast to the initial family meal, the goal should be comparing these to the behaviors that family has engaged in previously or identifying new skills they are using and assess the efficacy of these. Knowing and anticipating the goals of this family meal, the family may be more aware of their questions, concerns, and process during meal preparation and these can be reviewed. In other words, now that the family knows what to expect, they are often more thoughtful about the choices regarding what they want to practice with you, where they have challenges and want guidance, and how they might utilize the session to overcome their challenges.

If the therapist has assigned a specific challenge to the family for this meal (e.g., work to introduce a higher fat food), how was this approached? How did the family manage the concerns that arose in the preparation of the meal? Encourage the family not to delay and to begin the meal in order to provide optimal time for coaching strategies. This time the therapist already knows family history around the meals, and the focus is less on understanding the impact of anorexia nervosa on family meals up to that point but the impact of anorexia nervosa on this particular meal. More time can be spent in directly addressing concerns, and the greater familiarity with each other allows for the therapist to modify his or her language or style in accordance with the family's particular needs. The risk of miscommunicating is decreased, and by this time the therapist and family should have a measure of comfort or greater ease in their interactions with one another, allowing for more candid and directive feedback from all parties. Having "joined the family," the therapist now has more knowledge on precisely where the family needs more information or improved skills in order to feel more empowered to challenge anorexia nervosa symptoms. Perhaps not surprisingly, the combination of decreased intensity with increased alliance between the parties often leads to a meal that is a bit lighter in spirit and less drama-filled than the first family meal.

Family meal strategies

During the family meal, it is critical to assist the parents in any efforts that keep renourishment front and center: plating appropriate amounts of food, assisting the parents in keeping the plate close, helping them remain unified in their emphasis that the patient must eat, using a language of statement rather than requests to help the patient eat (e.g., not "I *want* you to eat this" but "You need to eat this"), emphasizing continued urgency, keeping parents aligned, and keeping parents focused on renourishment efforts. In rare cases would all of these be targeted. Rather, the therapist should have in mind the skills or knowledge they would like the family to leave the session with and should state this somewhat directly (e.g., "We've been talking about how difficult it has been for you to help your daughter eat healthy fats, like butters and oils. I'm so glad to hear you brought butter and rolls tonight. I'd like to see how you set about trying to help her eat that this evening …"). If the patient "resists" by eating easily and one has utilized a paradoxical intervention, another potential strategy is to pay attention to elements that are difficult for anorexia nervosa and make provocative comments on that in the hope of activating it. For example, one might say, "I can see the cheese there and that is quite healthy as it has healthy fats and is calorically dense, so it adds quite a bit to this meal." These strategies are essential to help create resistance if none is present. While many parents would prefer to have a meal in peace and therefore dread therapist exhortations for the patient to resist eating unless they want to, it is important for the second family meal to be as similar to a typical meal at home as it can be. For coaching to be effective, the parents and therapist "need anorexia nervosa in the room" in order for parents to practice with the challenges they face at home. Familiarity also makes it more likely that no one will be on their "best behavior" any longer and more natural and dynamic interactions can be observed.

Sibling and patient strategies

Encouraging siblings to support the ill patient by providing support and identifying areas that siblings can provide a sense of normalcy to the family are roles of ongoing importance (Lock et al., 2001). The role of the sibling should absolutely move away from renourishment efforts and toward a sense of identifying aspects of the ill patient's true personality, goals, and aspirations. Additionally, assisting the siblings in identifying enjoyable activities that they can engage in with one another is an important focus. This not only has implications for family relationships, but also in helping everyone in the family nurture and support the healthy part of the patient who is working terribly hard at renourishment, too. Reminding parents and siblings that the patient's upset demonstrates just how hard the patient has had to fight against the illness. If parents are working this hard, can they imagine their child facing this terror alone? Fostering empathy for the patient is another important target in the second meal session.

Table 1 provides a description of problematic behaviors that tend to be identified in the adapted protocol for nonresponders with examples of strategies that can be applied in vivo.

Table 3.1 Behaviors observed in vivo and suggested coaching strategies

Problem/ Targeted Behavior	Coaching	Suggested Language
Parents not aligned	Probably the most commonly identified barrier to successful renourishment, this will be addressed in session 5 in a separate parents-only session. During the meal session, coaching will be provided on specific strategies to confer and agree on an amount of food to be eaten prior to instructing the patient. If alignment issues are more challenging (e.g., one parent does not think therapy is appropriate or does not want to continue), this is *not* an appropriate discussion at the family meal (and would suggest further consultation would be necessary before continuing treatment).	"In our first family meal, the two of you seemed to have very different ideas of how much your son needed to eat to gain weight. We've been discussing it and it sounds like this is still a bit challenging. Can you show me how you would work it out at home?" OR "You've said that you have really different styles in refeeding. I'd like to see your style, Dad/Mom." The therapist might also use circular questioning here. "So what would Dad do here? Where would he be sitting/eating?"
Patient passively avoids renourishment efforts (turns away from table, won't open mouth, attempts to leave)	The therapist will help parents identify escalating interfering behaviors in the earlier session and help them prevent, rather than intervene, with these. Therapist or parents might position a chair so that the door is harder to open and there is an obstacle between the patient and the exit. Parents may prepare for "fleeing" by having one standing, while the other parent sits with the patient. Parents will be coached on how to help the patient continue to eat, regardless of position at the table. Assist parents in helping to soothe their child until calm enough to begin the process again.	"I notice that [patient's name] has turned her back on the table. How do you think you might bring the food to anorexia nervosa instead of waiting for the illness to come to the food?"

Problem/ Targeted Behavior	Coaching	Suggested Language
Patient actively avoids renourishment (e.g., throwing food, spitting, verbally abusive behaviors)	Parents of more aggressive children often feel terribly disempowered. Help parents identify patterns to escalation. Help parents problem-solve ways to avoid target behaviors (e.g., providing a "splat mat" to catch food thrown on the ground, allowing the family to identify how much has been discarded in order to replace it. Coaching parents prioritize intake over normality at meals ("substance over style"). Help them problem-solve around those triggers; helping parents target a smaller number of total symptoms to prevent "overload"—focus parents on the skills that they can use repeatedly and with which they have had success. Parents might be reminded of how they solved these problems when the child was a much younger age (toddlerhood). Parents may encourage patient to eat in her own room to elicit the healthy part of the patient to be more active in preventing throwing and spitting behaviors.	"What have you noticed about when the illness gets most upset, are particular meals more challenging? Or on particular days?"
Patient or family bring up nonfood-related issues	Therapist models and/or coaches the parents on selective ignoring. Refocus parents on food and eating to the exclusion of all other behaviors not directly related this task. If necessary, continue to reorchestrate the intense scene to help raise parental anxiety sufficiently to view anorexia nervosa as the most significant challenge facing their family.	"It seems like the issue of school is one that comes up frequently, but I've noticed it seems to distract you from focusing on this meal. How can we come back to the meal right here to help your daughter eat?" "Of course, the biggest risk is not whether she misses the dance at school, but whether she misses out on the entire rest of her life. I know it can

(Continued)

Problem/ Targeted Behavior	Coaching	Suggested Language
		feel important to talk about these day-to-day activities, but we have to remember that while anorexia nervosa is in the picture, we need to keep it in our sights." "Sometimes families struggle to keep everything as it was before—to try to keep it "normal"—but once anorexia nervosa is at the table, life is anything but normal. I think focusing on what works, rather than what is "typical," is more helpful in overcoming this disease."

Clinical Case Material

We have piloted these adaptations in 20 families to date. Roughly half of those were enrolled in a small pilot randomized controlled trial evaluating the efficacy of these changes on weight trajectories in FBT. In those cases, half of the families were randomized to adaptations, the other half were randomized to "traditional" FBT. If the family was randomized to the adaptive arm and failed to achieve the required weight gain indicative of treatment response in the identified patient by session 4, they would receive all of the adaptations (session 4 reorchestrating the intense scene, session 5 with parents alone, and session 6 as a second family meal) before returning to standard of care FBT for sessions 7–10.

The other half of the cases who received these adaptations were cases that presented to our eating disorders outpatient clinic and had not achieved four pounds of weight gain by session 4. In these cases, families were told about adaptations to traditional FBT and agreed to participate in these adaptations. Anecdotally, the families randomized to adaptations were strongly similar to those who chose the adaptations. There were no particular distinguishing factors identified by clinicians to suggest that these families would be more challenged by weight gain, and the families did not differ in the range of challenges they faced. These were purely observational in nature, and assessment of moderators of outcomes will be assessed at the end of the pilot Randomized Clinical Trial (RCT) assessing Adaptive Family Therapy (FBT-A). Clinical cases have not been assessed for outcome, and the RCT has ended subject recruitment, but the study itself remains underway.

Therapist feedback on the second family meals has generally been positive. Therapists have described this session as "more instructive" and felt that parents were "more receptive" or "better able to understand the techniques and skills." Furthermore, therapists also noted that parents "came ready to problem-solve challenges" and often led with specific concerns or behaviors that they wanted to address. Feedback from therapists suggested parents felt more empowered to direct the session and this lent to the second family meal a sense of a "meeting of the minds" compared to the "deer in the headlights" feeling that often dominates the first family meal. Said more eloquently, by the second family meal the family has recovered somewhat from the shock of diagnosis and has become accustomed to the new normal of the renourishment routine and are better able to problem-solve and act on information.

No clinical families approached declined to participate in a second family meal, indicating that they found the suggestion to be helpful and saw it as having utility in improving the effectiveness of FBT. Anecdotally, many families expressed relief at the end of the second session and both therapists and parents reported greater success in both utilizing skills and in success in prompting "one bite more." Indeed, all of the clinical families using a second family meal were successful in getting their child to eat "one bite more." Although this group self-selected to this adaptation, this bodes well for the feasibility and acceptability of this intervention.

Outstanding Questions/Issues

The use of a second family meal to support renourishment efforts remains largely unstudied, but this continues to be a promising adaptation for families who may need further coaching. Therapists found the session helpful, and families were both open to trying and were successful in the target behavior of "one bite more." The family meal is a unique intervention, and capitalizing on the opportunity to specifically direct behavior change in an ecologically valid manner is a powerful tool.

Despite this, given therapist reluctance and fear around family meals, adding an additional family meal may be met with less enthusiasm by therapists already concerned about the feasibility and functionality of family meals in outpatient practice. Furthermore, both therapists and families may be reluctant to "try again" if they have previously faced a challenging meal session. Importantly, this should not be a session that incorporates any judgment or blame; nor should parents feel that this is because they have "failed" at their renourishment efforts. Rather, this meal should be approached with a spirit of collaboration and expectation of success.

References

Darcy, A. M., Bryson, S. W., Agras, W. S., Fitzpatrick, K. K., Le Grange, D., & Lock, J. (2013). Do in vivo behaviors predict early response in family-based treatment for anorexia nervosa? *Behavior Research and Therapy*, 51(11), 762–766.

Doyle, P., Le Grange, D., Loeb, K., Doyle, A. C., & Crosby, R. D. (2010). Early response to family-based treatment for adolescent anorexia nervosa. *International Journal of Eating Disorders, 43*, 659–662.

Eisler, I. (1995). Family models of eating disorders. In G. Szmuckler, C. Dare, J. Treasure (Eds.), *Handbook of eating disorders: Theory, treatment and research*. London: Wiley.

Eisler, I., Dare, C., Russell, G. F., Szmukler, G., le Grange, D., & Dodge, E. (1997). Family and individual therapy in anorexia nervosa. A 5-year follow-up. *Archives General Psychiatry*. 54(11),1025–1030.

Eisler, I., Dare, C., Hodes, M., Russell, G., Dodge, E., & Le Grange, D. (2000). Family therapy for adolescent anorexia nervosa: the results of a controlled comparison of two family interventions. *Journal Child Psychology and Psychiatry*. 41(6), 727–736.

Eisler, I. (2005). The empirical and theoretical base of family therapy and multiple family day therapy for adolescent anorexia nervosa. *Journal of Family Therapy*, 27, 104–131.

Le Grange, J., Lock, W. S., Agras, W. S., Moye, S. W., Bryson, B., Jo et al. (2012). Moderators and mediators of remission in family-based treatment and adolescent focused therapy for anorexia nervosa. *Behaviour Research and Therapy, 50*, 85–92.

Lock, J., Couturier, J., Bryson, S. W., & Agras, W. S. (2006). Predictors of dropout and remission in family therapy for adolescent anorexia nervosa in a randomized clinical trial. *International Journal of Eating Disorders, 36*, 639–647.

Lock, J., Le Grange, D., Agras, W. S., & Dare, C. (2001). *Treatment manual for anorexia nervosa: A family-based approach*. New York: Guilford Press.

Chapter 4

Parent-Focused Treatment

Elizabeth K. Hughes, Susan M. Sawyer,
Katharine L. Loeb, and Daniel Le Grange

One of the fundamental features of family-based treatment (FBT) for adolescent anorexia nervosa is that the whole family attends treatment sessions together, including the adolescent, his/her parents, and any siblings (Lock & Le Grange, 2013). Many therapists encounter difficulties in conducting whole family sessions, however, or choose to see parents and adolescents alone for at least part of therapy. Research suggests that a separated model of FBT, whereby the adolescent and parents attend separate individual sessions, may be just as effective as the traditional conjoint model of FBT (hereafter referred to as conjoint family therapy, CFT) and that separated FBT may be better suited to some families (Eisler et al., 2000; Eisler, Simic, Russell, & Dare, 2007; Le Grange, Eisler, Dare, & Russell, 1992).

In Australia, the Royal Children's Hospital specialist eating disorders program has developed a separated model of FBT called parent-focused treatment (PFT). This treatment has been delivered at the service since 2010 and is the subject of a current randomized controlled trial. In this chapter, we present the rationale for PFT, describe its features and process, and discuss the challenges and advantages of this model of treatment.

Background and Rationale

Benefits and Challenges of Conjoint Family Therapy

Having the whole family attend treatment sessions together can have benefits for the therapist, family, and, potentially, for treatment outcomes. With the family together, the therapist is able to directly observe family interactions, intervene as necessary, and model adaptive interaction styles to family members. Parents can observe how the therapist speaks to the adolescent about his/her illness and the ways by which the therapist manages eating disorder behaviors *in vivo*. This may include, for example, the ways by which the therapist contains the adolescent's distress, refuses to negotiate with the eating disorder, and sets limits for behavior in the office, all while remaining warm and compassionate. For adolescents in CFT, involvement in discussions between their parents and the therapist about the severity of the illness, the need for parental control of meals, and the ways the illness has affected their functioning, may help the adolescents come to terms with the need for treatment and to appreciate their parents' and therapist's strong advocacy for their "well self," even if it is difficult to express this in early stages of recovery. Finally, siblings who attend treatment may benefit from learning about the externalization of illness model, how their parents are trying to help their ill brother or sister, and how they can function in a supportive role without experiencing undue burden.

Despite the benefits of CFT, having the whole family in the therapy room can be difficult and may not have the desired effect. First, it may not be in the best interest of some family members to be exposed to the content of some sessions. The early stages of treatment are often very stressful and frustrating for parents, and some may voice their distress in a critical manner that is detrimental to the adolescent. Indeed, adolescents from highly critical families have been shown to have poorer outcomes in treatment for AN (Le Grange, Eisler, Dare, & Hodes, 1992). Even if phrased uncritically, hearing the distress the illness is causing his/her parents may provoke feelings of guilt and shame in the adolescent, which may likewise be detrimental. A second related difficulty with CFT is that it can suppress discussion of important topics that some family members do not feel comfortable talking about in the presence of other family members. For example, parents who are aware of how their feelings of frustration impact their child may avoid expressing these feelings and, in turn, struggle to engage fully in treatment while these feelings remain unaddressed. Other topics that may be avoided that could similarly interfere with treatment include parental psychiatric history, marital conflict, or other sensitive issues. For example, a parent who has residual or active eating disorder symptoms may refuse to disclose this to the family, making it difficult for the parents to provide their child with sufficient food to achieve weight restoration.

Another difficulty that may arise in CFT is when the adolescent is driven by his/her illness to disrupt therapy sessions, which can impede discussion of critical matters and halt progress towards recovery. Many adolescents with anorexia nervosa are unable to engage fully in the therapeutic process due to the cognitive impacts of starvation. Alternatively, they will refuse to engage in therapy due to the ego-syntonic nature of their illness and denial of the need for treatment. Others, however, will actively participate in treatment sessions, and while this participation can be helpful, in some cases the contributions are meant to thwart discussions focused on renourishment efforts. For example, some adolescents will display distress during much of the session, either verbally or through tears, or in severe cases, through self-harm or other aggressive threats and behaviors. At times, adolescents may undermine the therapeutic process by creating distractions from the goals of FBT. For instance, discussing unrelated school or friendship issues or presenting with unsubstantiated mood and physical complaints. It is important that the therapist does not view these behaviors as manipulative or willful but remembers that these are manifestations of the illness and attempts by the illness to derail progress.

Finally, there are the practical issues involved with having whole families attend treatment together. Some therapists do not have the physical space and facilities to accommodate whole families or to undertake the in-session family meal (Couturier et al., 2012). In addition, families can find it difficult to convene everyone for sessions, especially when there are multiple siblings with competing commitments such as school and recreational activities, or when there are other issues such as another family member's physical or mental health problems.

Research on Separated Family Therapy

In separated family therapy (SFT), the adolescent and parents are seen in separate individual sessions, thus overcoming many of the difficulties that can arise in CFT. In the earliest empirical study of SFT, Le Grange, Eisler, Dare, and Russell (1992) randomized eighteen adolescents with anorexia nervosa to CFT or 'family counseling.' Family counseling was a SFT model in which the therapist spent part of the session with the adolescent alone and part of the session with the parents alone. The families received an average of nine sessions over six months. Both groups had a significant increase in weight: the SFT group increased from a mean of 80.5 percent expected body weight (EBW) to 100.4 percent EBW, while the CFT group increased from 75.9 percent EBW to 89.1 percent EBW. Although the increase was greater for the SFT group (19.9% EBW) than the CFT group (13.2% EBW), the difference was not statistically significant. There was some evidence, however, that the outcome was poorer for CFT than SFT in families where there was high maternal criticism of the adolescent.

From these preliminary results, the researchers went on to conduct a larger study in which forty adolescents with anorexia nervosa were randomized to CFT or SFT (Eisler et al., 2000). In SFT, the therapist spent 45 minutes with the adolescent and 45 minutes with the parents. This compared to 1 hour spent with the whole family together in CFT. Families received around 16 sessions over 1 year (mean of 15.5 sessions for SFT and 16.4 for CFT). Using Morgan-Russell outcome criteria (Morgan & Russell, 1975), 76 percent of the SFT group had good or intermediated outcome at end of treatment compared to 47 percent of the CFT group, although the difference was just short of statistical significance ($p = 0.06$). At a 5-year follow-up, more adolescents in SFT had good/intermediate outcome (90%) compared to those in CFT (78%), although again the difference was not statistically significant (Eisler et al., 2007). Of importance: families with high levels of maternal expressed emotion (EE) had significantly better outcomes at the end of treatment in SFT (80% good/intermediate outcome) than in CFT (29% good/intermediate outcome). There was no significant difference between treatment groups for families with low maternal EE (Eisler et al., 2000). A similar pattern was found at a 5-year follow-up with adolescents from high EE families who received SFT having better outcome than those who received CFT (Eisler et al., 2007).

Although the sample size in these studies limited the power to detect potentially significant findings and, in turn, limits the conclusions that can be drawn, this research nevertheless provides preliminary indications that SFT and CFT produce similar outcomes. Further, the studies suggest that, at least for some families, SFT may be preferable.

It is perhaps not surprising that FBT can be effective when delivered in a separated model. A recent study of the components of FBT found that the strongest predictor of a positive treatment outcome (i.e., weight gain) was parental control of eating disorder behavior, followed by parental unity (Ellison et al., 2012). Therapists achieve these goals by working with the parents in-session to generate strategies for implementing and maintaining control at home and to assist parents in working together with shared goals and expectations (Lock & Le Grange, 2013). These processes can be untaken without the adolescent present in the therapy room. Many family therapists outside the eating disorder field do not include children in therapy sessions, arguing that the child does not need to be included in sessions to effect change in the family (Miller & McLeod, 2001). This stance aligns with family systems theory, which argues that changing one part of the system (i.e., the parent subsystem) will impact the larger family system and its members (Minuchin, 1985).

Parent-Focused Treatment

Based on the findings of earlier studies, our multidisciplinary team amplified the differences between CFT and SFT to develop a separated model of treatment in which the therapist sees only the parents in treatment sessions, while another team member (nurse and/or pediatrician) attends to the monitoring of the adolescent's weight, mental status, and medical status. The primary distinction between CFT, previous models of SFT, and this treatment model is that in this treatment model parents are not only enlisted as the active agents of change, but are, for the most part, the exclusive participants in therapy. Hence, this treatment was named parent-focused treatment (PFT). An unpublished version of this treatment manual is available from the authors, upon request (Le Grange, Loeb, Hughes, & Sawyer, 2010). In this respect, PFT represents family therapy in which the identified patient is absent from treatment sessions yet remains the target of the intervention. Consistent with the notion that in the active stages of anorexia nervosa and the early stages of treatment that the patient's self-concept is dominated by his/her illness, this model capitalizes on the parents as resources in the process of nutritional rehabilitation. This spares the patient the discomfort of attending sessions in which his/her identity, distorted by this ego-syntonic illness, is experienced as threatened. By extension, the time in sessions can be more effectively devoted to problem solving around renourishing efforts rather than managing the patient's active, *in vivo* resistance. In addition, the model provides a way to reduce the adolescent's exposure to counter productive expressions of criticism that might compromise treatment effectiveness.

PFT is fully based on the original FBT model and manual (Lock & Le Grange, 2013) and is an extension of the early models of SFT. PFT encompasses the same theoretical mechanisms of action and the majority of the specific therapeutic interventions, with the same duration and intensity of treatment as CFT. The three phases of treatment are followed with appropriate modifications as detailed in the sections below. The key differences and similarities between CFT and PFT are summarized in Table 4.1.

Table 4.1 Summary of Key Differences and Similarities between CFT and PFT

Differences	
Conjoint Family-Based Treatment	Parent-Focused Treatment
Therapist weighs adolescent (10 minutes)	Nurse/medical practitioner weighs adolescent (10–15 minutes)
Therapist sees parents and adolescent together (50 minutes)	Therapist sees parents alone (50 minutes)
Siblings included in sessions	Siblings not included in sessions
Family meal	No family meal
Adolescent's mental state monitored by therapist directly and via parent report	Adolescent's mental state monitored directly by nurse/medical practitioner and by therapist via parent report
Similarities	
Three phases of treatment	
Frequency and length of therapist's sessions and treatment duration	
Medical status monitored by medical practitioner*	
Psychiatric comorbidity managed by psychiatrist as indicated	

*In PFT, additional medical monitoring can be undertaken by the nurse at each session if needed.

PFT is family therapy despite only one or two parents being in the room during treatment; it is not couples therapy. Couple-related issues may be discussed, but they are limited to those which are identified to be interfering with effective implementation of key treatment strategies, and they are managed by the therapist at a practical level. For example, if a couple is not working together to renourish their child, the therapist would emphasize the importance of a unified front, explain the rationale for interparental consistency, explore concrete examples of the problem, and help the couple identify improved approaches. The therapist would not explore what this problem represents more broadly in the couple's relationship nor offer interpretations.

Implementation of PFT

The PFT protocol is an adaptation of the FBT manual for adolescent anorexia nervosa (Lock & Le Grange, 2013). The main goals and therapeutic interventions, as outlined in the FBT manual, are ostensibly preserved for PFT. The main difference between FBT and PFT lies in the mechanics; for PFT, the therapist works only with the parents in order to achieve the same goals that the FBT therapist would embark on. Therefore, PFT resembles or "looks like" SFT more so than FBT. Below is a brief summary of the three treatment phases. (The reader will clearly recognize the key mechanics of FBT here.)

Phase 1: Weight Restoration

Session 1

The adolescent first meets with the nurse for record of weight, review of eating disorder symptoms, assessment of mood and medical status (e.g., physical complaints, menstrual status), and provision of brief supportive counseling as needed (further described below). The nurse then conveys the weight and any other pertinent information to the therapist prior to the session with the family. In the first session, the therapist meets with the parents and adolescent to introduce himself/herself and the treatment before excusing the adolescent from the remainder of the session. Session 1 otherwise follows the core approach with the therapist greeting the parents in a sincere but grave manner, taking a history that engages each parent in the process, separating the illness from the patient, emphasizing the seriousness of the illness and difficulty in recovery, and charging the parents with the task of weight restoration.

Remainder of Phase 1

The remainder of this phase focuses on building the parents' understanding of the process of weight restoration and providing them with guidance and consultation to succeed in renourishing their child. Most of the remainder of this phase is characterized by the therapist's attempts to bring the patient's food intake under parental control by expanding, reinforcing, and repeating some of the tasks initiated at the beginning of therapy. The therapist reviews in detail with the parents, on a regular basis, their efforts to increase their adolescent's food intake, and the therapist systematically advises the parents how to proceed in curtailing the influence of the eating disorder over their offspring. Sessions remain focused on these themes throughout Phase 1 and, as such, are characterized by a considerable degree of therapeutically necessary repetition as the therapist may go over the same steps week after week to get the parents to become consistent and unified in their management of the patient's eating behavior and the eating disorder's attempt to defeat these efforts.

Session 2

Unlike CFT, there is no family meal in Session 2. In lieu of an in-session family meal, the parents describe their experience of family meals at home, and the therapist works through these experiences, coaching the parents about strategies to manage the patient's eating disorder as they would in CFT. This requires a detailed, step-by-step description of a meal, which allows the therapist to fully understand how family members interact at these times and prompt the parents about how the meal might be handled differently (Le Grange et al., 2010).

Phase 2: Helping the Adolescent Eat on His or Her Own

The mood displayed by the therapist in Phase 2 is different from the somber and sad tone characteristic of most of Phase 1. By the time the parents move into Phase 2, the patient will have demonstrated significant progress in terms of weight gain (information gathered from the nurse prior to each parent session). This advance should be reflected in the therapist's demeanor when he/she embarks on this next phase in treatment. The primary goal for this phase of treatment is for the therapist to guide the parents in their efforts to hand control over eating back to the adolescent. This should be done in a cautious manner so as to reassure the parents that when they start taking a step back, in terms of their vigilance, their child will continue to gain weight, albeit a little slower than before. In the transition to return of independent eating on the part of the adolescent, two trajectories must be simultaneously considered and navigated. First, the discrepancies between the adolescent's current symptom profile and ultimate health are identified and the necessary steps targeted. For example, if the adolescent is eating more, exhibiting reduced resistance, and meets criteria to transition to Phase 2 but is still engaging in eating rituals, the resolution of such behaviors would be a goal of Phase 2. Second, the distance between current levels of dependence on the parent for eating and symptom management and ultimate independence is tracked and steps are taken to gradually return agency to the adolescent. This is calibrated to the developmental stage of the child, in that healthy independence will look different for a 12 year old (who would serve himself/herself at a family meal) than for a late adolescent (who might prepare dinner on a night that parents work late). Unlike the more structured nature of treatment interventions concerning refeeding the adolescent up to this point, guidelines for the therapist's style/technique from this stage of treatment onward are less circumscribed. From a developmental perspective, the eating disorder can be seen as having "interfered" with the patient's normal adolescent development. Therefore, the therapist's task now is to help the parents get the patient "back into" adolescence. It should be noted that the parents also need to get "back into" adolescence; that is, they need to examine their own lives in relation to their son or daughter growing up. The specifics of this process are highly individualistic, and there is not a prescribed way to proceed (Le Grange et al., 2010).

Phase 3: Adolescent Issues

As is the case with standard FBT, the third phase in PFT is initiated when the patient achieves a stable weight, the self-starvation behaviors have abated, and control over eating has been returned to the adolescent. The central theme here is the establishment of a healthy adolescent–parent relationship in which the illness does not constitute the basis of interaction. Among other activities, this entails supporting the parents in their encouragement of increased personal autonomy for the adolescent and appropriate intergeneration family boundaries. In addition, there is the need for the parents to reorganize their life as a couple after their children's prospective departure from the family home. Attention to parental professional and leisure interests is a legitimate focus of this phase (Le Grange et al., 2010).

Role of Nurse/Medical Practitioner

The role of the nurse is to weigh the adolescent at the beginning of each session and monitor the adolescent's medical and mental status. The role is best untaken by a nurse with training and experience in mental illness, eating disorders, and adolescent health. The role could be filled by another medical practitioner with similar training and experience.

The nurse weighs the adolescent in light indoor clothing without shoes and records the weight for later communication to the therapist. Similar to CFT, weighing the adolescent in PFT is critical to the treatment process and will set the tone of the parents' session with the therapist. In weighing the adolescent and sharing that information with the patient, the nurse assists the adolescent through a potentially stressful time by communicating an understanding of the difficulty of this process and the dilemmas it raises for the patient. The nurse should be aware of the adolescent's reaction to the weight and should support the patient in managing the resulting emotions.

During this time, the nurse should inquire if there are any particular concerns or problems that the nurse should be aware of or any issues that the adolescent would like the therapist to raise with his/her parents. The nurse should ask the adolescent about the week, probing specifically about eating disorder symptoms and mood. Assessment of menstrual status, binge eating and purging behaviors, and physical complaints are also undertaken at this time. Concerns about the adolescent's mood should be conveyed to the therapist for follow-up, and any concern regarding the adolescent's safety should be acted upon immediately.

A medical assessment is not routine in these sessions. Instead, regular medical monitoring should be managed by the treating pediatrician as it would in CFT (Katzman, Peebles, Sawyer, Lock, & Le Grange, 2013). For some adolescents, however, it may be appropriate for the nurse to monitor heart rate and blood pressure for signs of medical instability. This includes adolescents who have been recently discharged from hospital, have border-line medical stability (e.g., low heart rate), complain of physical symptoms such as dizziness, or have lost considerable weight. Any acute problems should be referred to the treating pediatrician for immediate follow-up.

The therapeutic stance of the nurse should be one of general supportive counseling, for example, validating the adolescent's feelings, ensuring he/she feels heard, and encouraging the adolescent as progress is made. The nurse should encourage the adolescent to speak with family about how they are feeling and to lean on parents and siblings for support. It is impor-tant that the nurse is familiar with FBT and communicates frequently with the rest of the team to ensure their time with the adolescent is helpful, while not undermining the work that the therapist is undertaking with the par-ents. The nurse must refrain from giving directives and advising on meal plans. While questions related to treatment decisions are directed to the therapist and parents, the nurse can use these opportunities to demonstrate support of the adolescent and to seek further information. For example, if asked about returning to school, the nurse can inform the adolescent that this is a decision for his/her parents to make with the therapist but that the desire to return will be communicated to them. The nurse might inquire as to how the patient feels about eating meals at school.

The Remainder of the Team

The therapist and nurse should provide the team with regular treatment updates, including patient's weight progress, development of any new symptoms (e.g., purging, over-exercise), new diagnostic concerns (e.g., anxiety disorder, depression, suicidality, self-harm), and an overall sense of the parents' progress combating the illness. Regularly scheduled team meetings, if treatment is taking place in a hospital clinic or treatment center, are essential for ensuring sufficient support for the clinicians and adequate interdisciplinary communication about patient status.

Challenges of Parent-Focused Treatment

Although PFT has the potential to overcome many of the difficulties of CFT, as discussed earlier, it can also present its own challenges. Most often these challenges relate to not having the adolescent in the room. One of the earliest concerns raised at our service was that the therapist would be unable to monitor progress or deterioration in the adolescent and would have to rely on reports from the parents, nurse, or other team members. While this felt uncomfortable at first, especially for thera-pists accustomed to working directly with adolescents, concerns were allayed by frequent and clear communication between all team members, especially with the nurse. The need for such communication can actually serve to heighten the functioning of the team and ensure the treatment model is supported from all sides. In addition, the therapist's reliance on the parents to monitor their child's progress further reinforces the parents' centrality in treatment and their importance as the agents of change. It teaches the parents to be aware of changes in their child's health and wellbeing.

Parents engaged in PFT also raised concerns about not having the adolescent in room. Typically this included feelings that the therapist does not really know and understand the adolescent or beliefs that the adolescent needed to hear information directly from the therapist for the treatment to be effective. In these situations, the therapist must work carefully to ensure parents have confidence that the treatment can work despite the adolescent not being present. One way is to convey to the parents that, while the therapist is the expert on eating disorders, they are the expert on their child and that, even if the adolescent was physically in the sessions, the therapist would not have the same knowledge and understanding of their child as they do. In addition, the therapist can explain that having the adolescent in sessions would not change what the parents need to do at home. Although there is less opportunity to model behaviors and interactions with the adolescent, the therapist can overcome this by rephrasing or reframing parents' descriptions of their interactions with the adolescent or by working through specific scenarios in detail.

Research suggests that many FBT therapists do not conduct the in-session family meal as prescribed in the manual for Session 2 (Couturier et al., 2012). For some, this is due to facility constraints, but for many it is due to the fact that the family meal can be a very difficult and stressful session, for both the family and therapist, and a task which some therapists do not feel equipped to undertake. The absence of the family meal session in PFT can be a relief for some therapists; however, it is also appreciated that the family meal provides unique insights into the functioning of the family and an opportunity to assist the family *in vivo*. Indeed, some therapists will repeat the family meal in CFT in order to gain further insight into the family and help them through this process, especially when progress is slow. In the absence of the family meal session, therapists can use various strategies to gain this understanding and help the parents manage the meals at home. The simplest is to have the parents focus on a specific meal from the past week that was particularly difficult and describe the meal to the therapist in detail, beginning from preparation through to completion. The therapist should interrupt frequently to inquire about what each family member was doing at that point, what was being said, and the parents' interpretation. The therapist can then work with the parents to identify what was helpful and what wasn't and to generate ideas about what could be done differently next time. Similarly, a successful meal can be described and helpful strategies identified, reinforced, and applied to future meals.

In PFT, siblings are not included in sessions. When available, siblings can be a valuable source of support for the adolescent. Helping siblings to understanding the illness and how they can help their brother or sister and parents is a core feature of CFT (Lock & Le Grange, 2013). It is therefore important that the PFT therapist makes time to assist the parents in eliciting support from the sibling(s) and ensuring that the sibling(s) feel included in the process of their brother or sister's recovery. As in CFT, the therapist should explain to parents the expected role of the sibling as a friend and support to the ill child and discourage siblings from taking on a parental role in weight restoration. Parents can be encouraged to talk to the sibling(s) about the illness, explore concerns, and provide resources such as books or websites to further understanding.

Advantages of Parent-Focused Treatment

As described earlier in the chapter, PFT can be an effective way to overcome several of the problems arising in CFT. These problems include the practicalities of having a whole family attend treatment, exposure to parental criticism or distress, and disruption of therapy sessions by the adolescent. A separated model such as PFT simplifies treatment in many ways for the therapist, and it may be particularly attractive for therapists who struggle to adhere to some of the difficult aspects of CFT, such as the family meal and weighing the adolescent. Indeed, research suggests that therapists often avoid these aspects of the treatment (Couturier et al., 2012). PFT also encourages clinicians to share responsibility for the adolescent as, by design, it requires that a second clinician monitor and support the adolescent directly so that the therapist can focus efforts on assisting the parents. However, this may be practically difficult to implement, for example, in solo practices without a nurse or medical practitioner.

From the families' perspectives, some parents are initially confused that the adolescent will not be receiving the intensive one-on-one therapy that is often expected when they seek treatment. However, once the rationale for PFT, and FBT more generally, is explained and families are reassured that their child will be carefully monitored and supported throughout treatment, families' concerns can usually be overcome. Importantly, the idea that much of the therapy time will be focused on the parent reinforces the parents' role in recovery and arguably sends the strongest possible message that they are the most important players in their child's recovery. Some adolescents even express some relief or pleasure that their parents are "the ones in therapy," although this feeling may not last once parents start to implement changes at home. In general, however, many parents and adolescents in PFT appreciate having their own space to discuss their concerns and struggles.

In a qualitative study of satisfaction with CFT (Krautter & Lock, 2004), family members described the lack of individual support for patients and parents, the family meal, the involvement of siblings, and the arguments in sessions as unhelpful, and they expressed that they could not share (or did not feel comfortable sharing) issues with the whole family. PFT has the potential to successfully address these concerns. Moreover, previous research has found that separated models of FBT can be just as effective as conjoint models (Eisler et al., 2000; Eisler et al., 2007; Le Grange, Eisler, Dare, & Russell, 1992) and that families find these to be an acceptable form of treatment (Paulson-Karlsson, Nevonen, & Engström, 2006).

Conclusions

Conjoint models have been the most widely researched and disseminated form of family-based treatment for adolescent anorexia nervosa. However, separated models have many advantages, may be preferable for some families and therapists, and may be just as effective as conjoint models (Eisler et al., 2000; Eisler et al., 2007; Le Grange, Eisler, Dare, & Russell, 1992). PFT deviates from earlier separated models by intensifying the focus on parents and having shorter supportive sessions with the adolescent provided by a nurse or medical practitioner. PFT can overcome many of the difficulties of CFT but can present its own challenges of which the therapist should be cognizant. Our program has provided CFT for adolescents with anorexia nervosa since 2008 (Hughes, Le Grange, Court, Yeo, Campbell, Whitelaw, et al., 2014) and has subsequently developed and implemented PFT. We are now undertaking a randomized controlled trial to compare PFT to CFT (Hughes, Le Grange, Court, Yeo, Campbell, Allan, et al., 2014). The trial will not only test the overall effectiveness of the treatment but will provide an indication of its suitability in relation to highly critical families, illness severity and duration, and a range of other potential treatment moderators.

References

Couturier, J., Kimber, M., Jack, S., Niccols, A., Van Blyderveen, S., & McVey, G. (2012). Understanding the uptake of family-based treatment for adolescents with anorexia nervosa: Therapist perspectives. *International Journal of Eating Disorders, 46*(2), 177–188. doi: 10.1002/eat.22049

Eisler, I., Dare, C., Hodes, M., Russell, G. F. M., Dodge, E., & Le Grange, D. (2000). Family therapy for adolescent anorexia nervosa: The results of a controlled comparison of two family interventions. *Journal of Child Psychology & Psychiatry & Allied Disciplines, 41*(6), 727–736.

Eisler, I., Simic, M., Russell, G. F., & Dare, C. (2007). A randomised controlled treatment trial of two forms of family therapy in adolescent anorexia nervosa: A five-year follow-up. *Journal of Child Psychology & Psychiatry & Allied Disciplines, 48*(6), 552–560.

Ellison, R., Rhodes, P., Madden, S., Miskovic, J., Wallis, A., Baillie, A., ... Touyz, S. (2012). Do the components of manualized family-based treatment for anorexia nervosa predict weight gain? *International Journal of Eating Disorders, 45*(4), 609–614. doi: 10.1002/eat.22000

Hughes, E. K., Le Grange, D., Court, A., Yeo, M., Campbell, S., Allan, E., ... Sawyer, S. M. (2014). Parent-focused treatment for adolescent anorexia nervosa: A study protocol of a randomised controlled trial. *BMC Psychiatry, 14*, 105. doi: 10.1186/1471-244X-14-105

Hughes, E. K., Le Grange, D., Court, A., Yeo, M., Campbell, S., Whitelaw, M., ... Sawyer, S. M. (2014). Implementation of family-based treatment for adolescents with anorexia nervosa. *Journal of Pediatric Health Care, 28*(4), 322–330. doi: 10.1016/j.pedhc.2013.07.012

Katzman, D. K., Peebles, R., Sawyer, S. M., Lock, J., & Le Grange, D. (2013). The role of the pediatrician in family-based treatment for adolescent eating disorders: Opportunities and challenges. *Journal of Adolescent Health, 53*(4), 433–440.

Krautter, T., & Lock, J. (2004). Is manualized family-based treatment for adolescent anorexia nervosa acceptable to patients? Patient satisfaction at the end of treatment. *Journal of Family Therapy, 26*(1), 66–82.

Le Grange, D., Eisler, I., Dare, C., & Hodes, M. (1992). Family criticism and self-starvation: A study of expressed emotion. *Journal of Family Therapy, 14*(2), 177–192. doi: 10.1046/j..1992.00451.x

Le Grange, D., Eisler, I., Dare, C., & Russell, G. F. (1992). Evaluation of family treatments in adolescent anorexia nervosa: A pilot study. *International Journal of Eating Disorders, 12*(4), 347–358. doi: 10.1002/1098-108X(199212)12:4<347::AID-EAT2260120402>3.0.CO;2-W

Le Grange, D., Loeb, K., Hughes, E. K., & Sawyer, S. M. (2010). *Parent-focused treatment for adolescent anorexia nervosa: Treatment manual.* Royal Children's Hospital. Melbourne, Australia.

Lock, J., & Le Grange, D. (2013). *Treatment manual for anorexia nervosa: A family-based approach* (2nd ed.). New York: Guilford Press.

Miller, L. D., & McLeod, E. (2001). Children as participants in family therapy: Practice, research, and theoretical concerns. *The Family Journal, 9*(4), 375–383. doi: 10.1177/1066480701094004

Minuchin, P. (1985). Families and individual development: Provocations from the field of family therapy. *Child Development, 56*, 289–302.

Morgan, H. G., & Russell, G. F. M. (1975). Value of family background and clinical features as predictors of long-term outcome in anorexia nervosa: Four-year follow-up study of 41 patients. *Psychological Medicine, 5*, 355–371.

Paulson-Karlsson, G., Nevonen, L., & Engström, I. (2006). Anorexia nervosa: Treatment satisfaction. *Journal of Family Therapy, 28*(3), 293–306.

Chapter 5

A Brief, Intensive Application of Family-Based Treatment for Eating Disorders

Stephanie Knatz, Walter H. Kaye, Enrica Marzola, and Kerri N. Boutelle

The Intensive Family Treatment Program (IFT) is a brief, intensive, multi-family treatment program for children and adolescents with eating disorders based primarily on the underlying theoretical principles of family-based treatment (FBT) for eating disorders. The IFT model was developed by Walter Kaye, M.D, at the University of California, San Diego (UCSD) in response to the lack of FBT providers at the time of its inception. Since its creation in 2006, the program has undergone a series of evolutions that represent continued improvements based on experience, contemporary research findings, and expert consultation about effective ways to treat children suffering from eating disorders in a brief, intensive model. The contemporary model represents a comprehensive treatment program with a deeply rooted philosophy of parents as a necessary and critical resource for recovery, as was originally asserted by the founders of family-based methods for eating disorders (Dare, Eisler, Russell, & Szmukler, 1990; Lock & Le Grange, 2012; Russell, Szmukler, Dare, & Eisler, 1987). The comprehensive IFT model is composed of a combination of FBT techniques and other complementary methods appropriate for the brief, intensive format, all of which serve to mobilize parents to take action toward recovery, prepare families to manage recovery in the home, and facilitate change within the patient. In an effort to illustrate a method for applying family-based treatment over a brief, intensive course, this chapter describes the IFT program by reviewing its primary therapeutic components, associated strengths and innovations, and appropriate clinical applications.

Program Description

IFT is a brief treatment for families of children and adolescents with eating disorders delivered over the course of five days. Treatment is delivered in an intensive format, with families receiving approximately nine hours of treatment per day, for a total of 40+ hours of treatment delivered over the course of the week. The majority of treatment is conducted in a multi-family group format; however, other components include simultaneous parent-only and patient-only group sessions, and single-family psychiatric and medical evaluations. Treatment is conducted with between two and six families and occurs at monthly intervals. Groups are *not* intended to be matched on participant characteristics, and thus groups may consist of a wide range of illness and family demographics that vary from month to month. The program now fills a number of diverse family needs, including supporting transitions between phases of treatment or levels of care, augmenting traditional individual therapy, and as a booster for families failing to make gains in outpatient care.

History

IFT originally started as a single-family model to fill two needs: (1) to extend treatment to families in areas that lacked access to FBT services and (2) to offer ancillary services for treatment-resistant cases. The single-family model originally included approximately 40 hours of psychotherapy based on FBT principles, meal supervision, psychiatric and medication evaluations, and parent coaching. Outcomes for the first 19 single-family cases show significant improvements in post-treatment weight (Rockwell, Boutelle, Trunko, Jacobs, & Kaye, 2011). The model was later transitioned to a multi-family format (Dare & Eisler, 2000). To augment the FBT model, the program also evolved to incorporate other therapeutic components (discussed in a later section) that were found to support recovery and complement FBT principles.

Treatment Team

The IFT program includes two lead therapists, a clinical director, a child psychiatrist, a clinical nurse, and two senior faculty members. The two therapists are the primary treatment providers and are present and active throughout the entirety of treatment.

Lead therapists are responsible for conducting all interventions including family meals, group sessions, and any necessary single-family meetings or sessions. The clinical director oversees treatment and provides daily supervision to ensure targeted treatment planning and symptom-monitoring. The psychiatrist is responsible for medical monitoring of patients, including both review of medical status upon admission to the program, and the ongoing monitoring of medical status throughout their length of stay. Ongoing medical monitoring and medication issues are assisted by the clinical nurse, who is also responsible for taking patients' weights and vitals throughout their stay. Families receive a full psychiatric assessment and a follow-up session, for a total of two psychiatry visits throughout the week. Lastly, specific lectures are given by the UCSD Eating Disorder Treatment Program Director and UCSD faculty members with expertise in particular topics relevant to the treatment.

Training and Supervision

IFT is based on fundamental FBT principles delivered in a multi-family format and thus requires treatment providers that are trained extensively in both approaches. To ensure fidelity to key principles of family-based treatment, therapists leading the program receive ongoing training and supervision from a certified family-based therapy supervisor. Because IFT is conducted in the multi-family format, treatment providers also require specific expertise and training in conducting multi-family systemic therapy. Principal therapists leading the program have been trained and supervised directly by Dr. Ivan Eisler, one of the pioneers of multi-family therapy for adolescents with eating disorders.

Assessments

Prior to beginning treatment, families complete a diagnostic and family functioning assessment conducted by a trained intake coordinator, where both the patient and at least one parent are interviewed separately on the phone. Information from this assessment is used for insurance purposes, as well as to begin treatment planning and goal setting among the coordinated team. Because the majority of families attending come from outside the local area, a lead therapist is also typically in communication with families prior to their attendance to provide basic orientation to treatment and answer clinical questions in the interim period. Because the program is relatively small in size and consists of treatment components that have the capacity to be individually tailored, inclusion criteria are broad. Exclusion criteria include patients with active and imminent suicidality and those who lack significant family involvement.

Target Demographic

IFT participants vary in age, diagnoses, illness severity, treatment history, and other sample characteristics. Since its inception, the program has treated 120 patients between the ages of 8 and 26 at varying stages of recovery from anorexia nervosa (AN) (55 percent), bulimia nervosa (BN) (4 percent), and Eating Disorder, Not Otherwise Specified (ED-NOS) (41 percent). Demographic information on 40 past participants (both single-family and multi-family participants) has been collected as part of an ongoing research study examining patient and parent outcomes. Of the 40 participants, the mean age of participation was 14.57 years (SD = 2.88). Body mass index (BMI) at the time of admission was 17.62 (SD = 2.11), with 65 percent of patients exhibiting at least one diagnostic comorbidity. Ninety percent of participating families were Caucasian.

Treatment Format

Brevity and Intensity

Much of the novelty of the IFT program lies in the format in which the treatment is delivered. The brief, intensive format represents a paradigm shift from the weekly treatment model that is traditionally used in psychology. Whereas outpatient treatment models provide 24 hours of therapy over six months, IFT provides approximately 40 hours of treatment over the course of one week. Intensive models of treatment have been utilized extensively in the treatment of a range of anxiety disorders because of their ability to provide massed practice and training (e.g., Specific Phobia (Davis III, Ollendick, & Öst, 2009), Social Anxiety Disorder (Mörtberg, Karlsson, Fyring, & Sundin, 2006), and Obsessive-Compulsive Disorder (Mörtberg et al., 2006; Whiteside, Brown, & Abramowitz, 2008; Whiteside & Jacobsen, 2010). Many of these treatment programs are targeted at children and adolescents with a focus on training parents to continue necessary intervention in the home (Whiteside et al., 2008; Whiteside & Jacobsen, 2010). Research on such programs has shown that they lead to a reduction in targeted symptoms and, in some cases, at more accelerated rates than equivalent treatment occurring once a week (Abramowitz, Foa, & Franklin, 2003). To our knowledge, IFT is the first and only short-term, intensive program targeting families and their children with eating disorders. The benefits of massed practice and intensive parent training are made use of extensively in IFT and are particularly relevant for family-based models where the aim is for parents to be principal providers of treatment for their children. The intensive format offers the additional benefit of extensive in-vivo practice. Whereas in a traditional weekly outpatient setting, sessions revolve around the review of past events and a plan for how to proceed in the subsequent week, the treatment received in IFT is structured around in-vivo practice, as commonly occurring events that present as points of intervention such as meals, family interactions, emotional outbursts, and others take place in real time. Real-time therapist observation and intervention during surrounding these events allows for parents to receive applicative, hands-on training and management skills.

Multi-Family Format

IFT is modeled on multi-family-based treatment for eating disorders, where multiple families are treated simultaneously in a group format. The application of multi-family treatment approaches to eating disorders was originally pioneered by groups in Dresden, Germany (Scholz & Asen, 2001), and at the Maudsley Hospital in London, UK (Dare & Eisler, 2000; Eisler, 2005). Despite the relative novelty of multi-family treatment for eating disorders, the approach has an extensive history (Asen, 2002) and has been successfully applied to a number of child and adolescent issues, where parent involvement is critical (McKay, Harrison, Gonzales, Kim, & Quintana, 2002; Saayman, Saayman, & Wiens, 2006). Delivering family work in a group format appears to enhance the uptake of FBT principles, as well as accelerate necessary change and movement toward recovery. Indeed, a recent comparison of single-family and multi-family treatments for eating disorders showed that multi-family treatment was more effective at post-treatment, and at maintaining weight gain at the 6-month follow-up (Eisler, 2013). The synergistic effect of combining group and family modalities increases the opportunities for learning and change among family members by allowing for learning to take place from other attending families through direct observation, comparison, and consultation. Because IFT treatment occurs sequentially over the course of five full days, families have the opportunity to build intimate relationships, developing solidarity among the group. This level of group cohesion leads to more opportunities for parent-to-parent consultation among families—a process that has shown to have additive benefits—and enables parents and patients to learn from each other (Rhodes, Baillee, Brown, & Madden, 2008). Furthermore, the opportunity to observe and consult with other families stimulates a reflective process in families, through which they can consider their own behaviors, family patterns, ways of managing the eating disorder, and new and alternative perspectives (Rhodes, Brown, & Madden, 2009). Families also benefit from the supportive environment that is fostered through the group setting, where parents and patients alike have access to psychological support from other individuals undergoing a similar process. This supportive and safe environment also allows participants to take more risks in practicing new behaviors and strategies.

Therapeutic Stance

The IFT model is heavily informed by the theoretical philosophy underlying FBT, which demonstrates the impact of eating disorders on family functioning and the benefits of mobilizing families as the primary agents of change in achieving recovery (Eisler, 2005; Le Grange & Eisler, 2009; Lock, 2011). As such, the overarching goal of the program is to educate, train, and prepare parents to effectively manage the recovery of their child upon the transition home. The primary therapeutic components and treatment strategies included in IFT revolve around engaging the family in the recovery process, increasing parental competency, and providing a structure for promoting recovery-oriented behaviors in the home. Similar to FBT, therapists take the position of expert consultants, sharing knowledge and experience to support progression toward recovery, while focusing efforts on mobilizing parents. This is done while simultaneously empowering family members to make their own decisions about which strategies and approaches to adopt based on their own family values and culture.

The program follows a strength-based model, where the focus is on identifying and making use of family strengths, recognizing that disruptions in family functioning are likely primarily attributable to families' reorganization and accommodation around the illness (Eisler, 2005).

In addition to adopting a family systems approach, the therapeutic stance and associated treatment components utilized in the IFT model are guided by contemporary research and information about the neurobiology underlying eating disorders. We maintain a strong etiological position on the critical role of neurobiology as a primary cause of eating disorders. As such, tying symptoms, behaviors, and treatment approaches to neurobiology is something that is heavily interwoven into the treatment model. In addition to emphasizing education and orientation to neurobiology among attending families, complementary treatment strategies used in IFT to augment the FBT approach (described in a later section) represent ways of managing and coping with temperament and personality traits that typically characterizes individuals with eating disorders and that emerge within the context of the illness. Treatment strategies used have been constructed or adopted in response to the recognition that patients, and frequently their family members, exhibit high levels of anxiety, difficulty with tolerating uncertainty, interoceptive deficits, and altered responsivity to reward and punishment (Kaye, Fudge, & Paulus, 2009; Kaye, Wierenga, Bailer, Simmons, & Bischoff-Grethe, 2013). The perspective that eating disorders emerge as a function of a specific neurobiology is complementary to the FBT model because both emphasize the importance of dispelling blame and using existing family and individual characteristics as strengths to overcome the disease. Furthermore, the utility of many FBT strategies can be explained by effective management of neurobiological traits underlying eating disorders. For example, the insistence in FBT that patients consume appropriate calories, despite protest and resistance, acknowledges the motivational deficits and appetite dysfunction underlying restriction in anorexia. The externalization of the illness strategy borrowed from narrative therapy and used in FBT is another example of the complementary nature of FBT to a neurobiological perspective, where in both perspectives the emphasis is on dispelling blame. The neurobiological perspective and the FBT approach thus have mutual positive benefits and together make up the general philosophy underlying the IFT model.

Therapeutic Aims

The therapeutic aims in IFT can be divided into three broad phases: observation, intervention, and reinforcement/planning. The therapeutic stance shifts accordingly as treatment transitions through these phases. Because this therapy is brief and time-limited, it is important that therapists conducting treatment remain mindful of the therapeutic task at hand so that goals can be accomplished in a timely fashion. As such, planning for appropriate transition through each phase becomes critical for providers to ensure thorough and appropriate patient and family care.

Observation: Assessment

The first phase of treatment is devoted to observation of patient and family symptoms and behaviors that are pertinent to the eating disorder and treatment. During this stage, which roughly spans the course of the first complete day, therapists take an observational stance in order to gather information and assess the severity of the eating disorder, family functioning, and family patterns. Although the initial assessment is done through a structured interview before the family begins treatment, close observation throughout the day allows for treatment providers to assess family and patient strengths and weaknesses and establish treatment targets based on where patients and families appear to be struggling. One of the benefits of working with the families over massed sessions is the attainability of an assessment that is rich in information and that occurs more naturalistically. Although families are in a foreign, clinical setting, family patterns and individual attitudes inevitably emerge throughout the week due to the length of time that is spent in the therapeutic setting and the opportunities for observation during informal times, such as breaks and between groups. On finishing the first day, the clinical team conducts a review of each family that identifies strengths and weaknesses, points of stagnation, and potential points of intervention. The clinical team then uses this evaluation to create specific goals for each family.

Instruction: Intervention

Days two through four of the week are devoted to ensuring that families and individuals receive the appropriate instruction, education, and in-vivo experiences to begin to move them toward treatment goals identified in the observation phase. The therapeutic stance becomes much more active in this phase as therapists shift to providing family units and individuals with insight into the observed barriers for recovery, and direction for how to begin to change. To do this, therapists must think critically about how to make use of the multi-family setting by orchestrating group interactions that serve as family and individual interventions to raise awareness and develop the opportunity for change. With regard to direct therapist–family interactions, the primary roles assumed by the therapist are those of consultation and instruction, as well as one of support and guidance during in-vivo practice. The goal of treatment during this phase is for therapists to teach and facilitate the use of strategies that result in symptom reduction and promote recovery-oriented behaviors.

Table 5.1 Summary and Timeline of Treatment

Phases	Day 1	Day 2	Day 3	Day 4	Day 5
	Observation-Assessment	Instruction-Intervention		Reflection-Reinforcement	
Phased Treatment Goals	• Assessment of: Eating disorder symptoms and behaviors; • Family functioning; • Family/individual strengths and weaknesses; • Recovery-interfering behaviors and situations	• Facilitate insight of necessary change and barriers to recovery; • Provide instruction of necessary skills and management strategies; • Facilitate in-vivo practice and application of skills and management strategies; • Concretize guidelines for recovery and contingencies for target behaviors; • Assist families in practicing following recovery guidelines and implementing contingencies		Reinforce and crystallize positive changes in: • Parent management strategies; • ED symptoms and behaviors; • Family structure; • Individual roles. Facilitate reflection of transition home by: • Planning ways to maintain gains; • Brainstorming and problem-solving barriers to recovery	
Treatment Team Activities	• Establish treatment goals; • Plan interventions	• Assess progress; • Refine intervention techniques	• Formulate discharge plan; • Assess achievement of treatment goals	• Follow up with treatment providers; • Formulate formal discharge recommendations	
Implementation of Treatment Components	• Conduct multi-family group activities to build cohesion; • Introduce patient coping skills; • Facilitate parent discussion of barriers to recovery; • Conduct psychiatric evaluation	• Review treatment goals; • Provide didactic and in-vivo skills training (parent and patient); • Behavioral contract: identify target behaviors and contingencies	• Facilitate real-time practice of patient/ parent management and coping skills; • Formulate and implement recovery rules and guidelines; • Introduce discharge recommendations	• Finalize discharge recommendations; • Finalize written behavioral contract; • Conduct multi-family group activities to reflect on change and transition home	

Reinforcement: Planning

By the middle to end of the fourth day, families should be able to self-identify barriers and should have received significant therapist-assisted practice in using skills and strategies to promote recovery. It is expected that at this stage, families and individuals are making progress toward treatment goals. For the remainder of the treatment, therapists recede from their directive stance and a shift is made toward reinforcing any meaningful changes and positive shifts that are facilitating improvement. The team shifts the focus to assisting families in creating a positive memory of changes made to ensure continued movement toward recovery following IFT. Most importantly, facilitating a successful transition home or to the next phase of treatment is the primary aim of this phase of treatment. During the last day and a half, therapists work to solidify a structured treatment plan that includes follow-up care and a plan for how to navigate recovery in the home.

Primary Therapeutic Components

IFT consists of five primary treatment components with very specific aims. These components form the foundation of treatment, with all exercises and activities conducted throughout the program falling under the umbrella of one or more of these components. The five components include family therapy, supervised family meals, parent management training, patient skills training, and psychoeducation.

Family Therapy

Rationale. FBT strategies are used as a means of staying focused on symptom reduction by revolving the therapeutic content around appropriate management of food, eating, and weight behaviors. Elements borrowed from FBT are primarily Phase I FBT techniques due to the time-limited nature of the therapeutic encounter with families in the IFT model and the strong emphasis on symptom reduction. These strategies are utilized to assess the family structure as it relates to parent effectiveness in managing symptoms and to mobilize parents in assisting their child to overcome the eating disorder.

Although the primary focus throughout treatment is on symptom reduction because of the intensive nature, extended time, and multi-family context inherent in IFT, opportunities also arise for broader family therapy work to be conducted in conjunction with more acute interventions. Broader systemic work takes place through the use of multi-family therapy activities. Activities focus on systemic functioning and are utilized to facilitate both reflection and change. Activities designed to inspire reflection are intended to bring about awareness of current and past family functioning and structure and any changes that have occurred as a result of the eating disorder. Change-oriented exercises are intended to promote effective reorganization in family structure and open a family dialogue about the needs of all family members.

Description. Family therapy is conducted in both the multi-family group and in single-family sessions. Strategies borrowed from FBT include key interventions from Phase I such as assessing the family structure as it relates to the management of the illness, creating the crisis, illness externalization, prioritizing return to an appropriate weight, and framing therapeutic dialogue toward eating and weight behaviors. These strategies are applied in both the multi-family and single-family settings. Therapeutic techniques borrowed from FBT are applied throughout the entirety of treatment; however, there is an emphasis on applying these techniques in the initial phase of treatment because of their strong emphasis on symptom reduction. FBT strategies such as the prioritization on weight and physical health, creating the crisis, illness externalization and a pragmatic focus are introduced on the first day of treatment to facilitate immediate parent mobilization. These strategies are then continuously referred to and reinforced throughout the remainder of treatment.

The multi-family context is used to introduce and reinforce FBT techniques; however, multi-family group therapy activities surrounding broader family structure and functioning are generally weighted toward the latter parts of treatment (last day and a half), where the opportunity arises for exercises emphasizing broader change once skills for symptom reduction and management have been mastered. Multi-family activities used vary depending on the families involved and are chosen for each week program based on the needs of attending families. Many of the multi-family group activities used are modeled after exercises constructed by multi-family experts (Asen & Scholz, 2010). Typical multi-family group exercises include family sculpt, inter-family role plays, and cross-generational interviews among group members. Multi-family activities have also been devised to facilitate the delivery of other primary treatment components.

Patient Skills Training

Rationale. Eating disorders are driven by powerful biological mechanisms that explain the compulsion toward restriction, refusal to eat, and other eating disturbances. Recent research suggests that individuals with AN experience a degradation in mood and physical state following eating (Frank & Kaye, 2012), which explains the anxiety surrounding meals and eating that is commonly noted clinically and anecdotally. Furthermore, anxiety is overrepresented in individuals with eating disorders, with approximately two-thirds of individuals with eating disorders possessing one or more lifetime anxiety disorders (Kaye, Bulik, Thornton, Barbarich, & Masters, 2004). Thus, individuals with AN are prone to high levels of trait anxiety and further are confronted with the difficult task of eating, which more often than not elicits high levels of anxiety in conjunction with other negative emotions. A similar process has been shown to occur in bulimia, where altered negative emotional states appear to be intimately involved with binging and purging behaviors (Berg et al., 2013). This distress and negative emotionality is frequently a significant barrier to engaging in recovery-oriented behaviors, such as appropriate eating or abstinence from compensatory behaviors, and can lead to other negative coping behaviors that are detrimental to recovery. FBT has reliably demonstrated that parent intervention can facilitate recovery through normalized eating. In addition to adopting this philosophy, IFT teaches patients adaptive coping skills borrowed from Dialectical Behavior Therapy (DBT). Patients are taught DBT skills for tolerating distress and managing negative emotion to further facilitate parent intervention.

Description. Patients receive daily skills training sessions based on the DBT group modules and primarily the "Distress Tolerance" module. Sessions are conducted in traditional DBT group format, where patients are trained on the skills and then assigned practice. Patients are strongly encouraged to practice skills, particularly at mealtimes. The ability for therapists to be present at mealtimes and other times throughout the day where distress levels rise allows for therapist-directed skills practice on an as-needed basis, as patients acquire and master a "toolbox" of skills. Patients are taught a variety of skills and encouraged to use those that are the most effective. To facilitate skills usage, a number of objects and activities that promote distress tolerance are provided by the treatment staff and widely available for use by both patients and parents. While the majority of skills training occurs with patients only, one to two blocks throughout the week are devoted to "family skills training," in which skills are introduced to both patients and other family members in the group at large. The purpose of introducing caretakers and other family members to the skills is to encourage them to utilize skills for the purposes of both managing their own distress and modeling appropriate skills usage for patients. While the focus is weighted heavily toward distress tolerance skills, DBT skills from the interpersonal effectiveness and mindfulness modules have also been adapted for family therapy activities and are delivered through the week.

Family Meals

Rationale. The concept of the prescribed family meal used in FBT is made use of in the IFT model. The goal of a therapist-observed family meal includes assessment of family structure and functioning during eating and promoting an experience of mastery for parents in feeding their child (Lock & Le Grange, 2012). IFT is unique in that it includes multiple family meals over the course of treatment. On a daily basis, families eat breakfast, lunch, and two snacks under therapist observation/supervision as part of the program, resulting in approximately 15 to 20 therapist-supported family meals. The rationale for including multiple family meals is twofold. First, including therapeutic meals as part of treatment makes logical sense in a program designed as a brief partial hospitalization program, where families are receiving treatment throughout the day. Family meals also ensure simultaneously that the patients are eating throughout the week, as would be done under the care of any Partial Hospitalization Program (PHP). Additionally, therapeutic family meals throughout the program allow for in-vivo parent coaching to take place, where parents are learning appropriate feeding strategies and improving their self-efficacy around successful feeding and management of symptoms and behaviors. Providing continuous hands-on training around feeding by therapists allows for the caretakers of patients to receive meaningful training in a brief period of time that will translate into a reduction of primary symptoms, including restriction, binging, and purging. Lastly, family meals provide an opportunity for patients to practice skills to improve tolerance of eating, and become familiar with a meal schedule and routine to be translated to the home.

Description. Program meals comprise part of therapeutic treatment, with therapists remaining active in both observing families, intervening as necessary, and reinforcing behaviors and skills learned in the program. The therapeutic components of the meal extend beyond just the assistance offered during the meal but also to the preparation of the meal/snack beforehand and the management of patient symptoms and behaviors, when applicable. Thus, therapists are present and remain active as families prepare meals, as they eat, and once the meal is complete. Consistent with the overarching therapeutic posture of IFT, the therapeutic stance surrounding meals shifts as the week progresses from observation, to instruction, and finally to the reinforcement of effective practices. Prior to beginning program, families are instructed to provide their own meals and snacks based on what they feel their children's needs are, borrowing from FBT. In the observational stage, which typically spans the first two meals of program, the goal of the therapist is to observe and assess the appropriateness of meals being provided, the existing skill set of the caretakers in managing meals, and the extent of eating disorder symptomatology and resulting behaviors in the patient. Instruction given by therapists is intended to encourage caretakers to prepare an appropriate meal based on their children's needs. Once therapists have collected enough information about patient and parent functioning surrounding meals, a therapeutic shift is made toward providing any necessary coaching. Interventions with parents include direct feedback on the appropriateness of meal (caloric sufficiency, quantities, and type) and parent coaching on implementing behavioral strategies for both maximizing the likelihood of eating and managing negative affect or behavioral issues related to eating. Interventions directed at patients include positive reinforcement, redirecting and emphasizing the use of distress tolerance skills, and modeling appropriate behavioral management strategies for parents. The majority of therapist feedback is directed toward parents, with the ultimate goal of the therapist being to inform and assist parents in deciding on the appropriate ways to intervene but ultimately for parents, not therapists, to deliver the intervention. Like other portions of this intervention, this approach is informed by the need to facilitate a successful transition home, where parents will be fully skilled and capable of managing symptoms without the need for assistance from a health-care provider.

During the meals, therapists do not eat with families but instead actively monitor progress and problems through the meal, intervening with parents and patients when necessary. This is done by maintaining a distance to families that allows for the therapist to actively observe without disrupting family patterns that emerge around the meal. The therapist's presence ebbs and flows throughout the meal depending on the amount of coaching that is needed. As it becomes clearer that parents are mastering the skills and strategies needed to manage meals appropriately, the presence of the therapist again shifts to more observational and the primary therapeutic intervention becomes reinforcing effective parent and patient behaviors. Reflection is used to assist individuals with operationalizing effective strategies in a way that promotes crystallization and enhances the likelihood that these approaches will transfer to the home environment.

Parent Management Training

Rationale. While the IFT model recognizes that parents' existing skill sets can be used to facilitate recovery, the intensive format of IFT allows for the opportunity for parents to receive training on skills and strategies specifically designed to address the individual reactions and symptoms of the eating disorder. Parents are confronted with the difficult task of persuading their children to do something that, in most cases, they are resistant to doing. In addition to being in the difficult position of motivating their children to engage in something aversive (eating, avoiding compensatory behaviors), parents must also be equipped to manage any negative emotions that occur with eating. Both the lack of motivation and inherent anxiety associated with eating are powerful drives, in particular at the height of the illness. While it is true that parents must capitalize on their previous experiences in successfully directing children to healthy behaviors and managing negative emotions, many parents feel unequipped to deal with such powerful reactions like those associated with eating disorders. Furthermore, it is not uncommon to see parents who share the difficulties that their children are battling, such as managing anxiety, due to the strong genetic component underlying these diseases. Additionally, the intensity of reactions in patients with eating disorders may dissuade normally functioning parents from intervening. Accordingly, in an attempt to augment caretakers' skill set, IFT provides training in parent management skills. Skills taught are adapted from the Parent Management Training program (PMT) (Kazdin, 1997). PMT is a comprehensive set of parent-directed treatment techniques that were originally developed to enhance motivation and compliance in treatment-resistant youth. The program is based on basic behavioral principles and uses praise, reinforcement, and contingency management to assist parents with enabling their children to achieve specified target behaviors. PMT techniques are applicable to parent management of eating disorder symptoms and behaviors due to the tendency for patients to demonstrate resistance and lack motivation. The treatment is also consistent with principles of FBT because both treatments advocate for parents as the responsible party for managing symptoms and improving behavior.

Description. The majority of parent training is conducted within two broad components of treatment: parent-only skills training and behavioral contracting. This portion of treatment is devoted to teaching parents effective tools and skills to facilitate recovery-oriented behaviors within their children by enhancing motivation, managing negative affect, and promoting recovery-oriented behaviors. In addition to didactic training and discussion, IFT also emphasizes an experiential component, which includes the application and practice of these strategies. Therapist-guided practice occurs informally throughout the week and naturally surrounding meals (see Family Meals section).

Behavioral contracting. The behavioral contract, a written document specifying a plan for achieving recovery, is one of the primary therapeutic strategies in the IFT model. The behavioral contract specifies a plan for how recovery-oriented behaviors will be encouraged through the use of behavioral principles. A substantial portion of treatment provided during the week surrounds the goal of constructing a collaborative behavioral contract. The contract represents a set of guidelines for recovery to be followed by caretakers and patients alike, a critical necessity for a brief treatment model in which follow-up care may be limited. The behavioral contract encourages parents to stipulate a clear and concrete set of expectations for recovery and a protocol for how events will be managed. In addition to clarifying a recovery plan to be used at home, the contract is also used as a treatment tool for reducing uncertainty and imposing a clear structure, two things from which individuals with eating disorders may benefit (Frank et al., 2012). Importantly, a motivational system is a key part of the contract. The motivational system utilizes operant behavioral principles to both motivate positive, recovery-oriented behaviors, and discourage negative behaviors by posing individually tailored rewards and consequences attached to each target behavior. Behavioral contracts are highly individualized and are structured to take into account specific family circumstances, recovery needs, patient motivating factors, caretaker leverage, and patients' sensitivity to reward and punishment. Contracting sessions include the following: (1) separate parent and child brainstorming sessions for the purposes of drawing up rewards and consequences (children) and recovery guidelines and target behaviors (parents), and (2) "contract negotiations," during which parents and child present and come to an agreement about appropriate contract stipulations.

Skills training. Skills training sessions occur daily in a parent-only format in a group titled "parent coaching." Parent coaching sessions occur daily after lunch and are strategically scheduled in order to allow time to follow up on any occurrences at the meal. The purpose of the group is to assist parents in clarifying and operationalizing any recovery-interfering behaviors and to identify appropriate behavioral strategies for managing such behaviors. Parenting strategies are based on basic behavioral principles including positive and negative reinforcement, punishment, and extinction. Examples that are commonly taught include active ignoring of negative behaviors intended to provoke, praise of specific and concrete recovery-minded behavior, "if-then" statements based on contingencies set forth in the behavioral contract, statements to avoid intentional "derailing" away from target behaviors, and concise focus on primary target behaviors. Caretakers are also taught strategies to assist their children in managing distress and negative emotions. Such strategies include emotional validation versus problem-solving, managing perseveration by switching topics or refusing to engage in dysfunctional discussion, rerouting patients to distracting activities, or creating structured routine activities surrounding meals to reduce anxiety. As was previously stated, the application of such strategies is practiced informally throughout the week and surrounding mealtimes under the guidance of therapists (see Family Meals section).

Psychoeducation

Rationale. The presentation of important information pertinent to eating disorders is interwoven through the treatment program through psychoeducational sessions. Psychoeducation sessions are presented in an informal didactic style by university faculty associated with the program with expertise in specific eating disorder-related areas. The psychoeducational sessions that have been included in the treatment model have very specific aims that serve as complementary knowledge sources for specific components of our treatment. Educating attending families on important topics about the illness is valuable as many families lack access to experts in the field who possess specialized knowledge of medical, psychiatric, and psychological issues related to eating disorders. Additionally, the psychoeducation sessions serve the purpose of mobilizing caretakers by creating urgency and reducing familial blame. The framing of the illness as a crisis situation and the importance of reducing blame among families are two critical theoretical principles put forth by Phase I FBT that are seen as imperative for preparing caretakers to play the lead role in their children's recovery. Thus, psychoeducational sessions are structured around presenting medical information that increases urgency to act, as well as information and research related to the biologically driven etiology of eating disorders. Presentation of this information is done for the ultimate purpose of equipping families with the knowledge necessary to remain fully mobilized and ensure that they remain on a trajectory toward full health upon return home.

Description. The psychoeducation topics include physiological and psychological effects of starvation and other eating disturbances, medical consequences of eating disorders, temperament and personality contributors to eating disorders, neuroimaging research, and review of best medical practices for eating disorders. Topics are covered in two broad psychoeducation sessions. Topics related to medical information focus on pertinent medical information associated with eating disorders and physical starvation, as well as guidelines for appropriate medical treatment. In addition to educating families, the purpose of presenting this information is to provide evidence for the importance of prioritizing weight restoration and the necessity of full physical restoration to guarantee illness remission.

Topics related to the neurobiological underpinnings of eating disorders review temperament and personality traits that predispose individuals to developing an eating disorder. The neurobiological education received by families in the session serves to introduce families to the importance of biology in predetermining individuals stricken with eating disorders and allows families to deidentify with the notion that they are responsible for their children's illness, a popular belief held among attending families. This session introduces families to personality traits that are frequently found in those who develop eating disorders and an underlying theoretical neurobiological model that explains these mechanisms and their manifestation in eating disorders.

Table 5.2 Primary Treatment Components and Related Therapeutic Aims

Primary Treatment Components	Therapeutic Aims
Family Therapy	• Assess family structure as it relates to parental ability to manage symptoms and support recovery.[1]
	• Mobilize parents to take charge of eating and other recovery-related activities.[1]
	• Maintain family's focus on the eating disorder and recovery.[1]
	• Facilitate discussion on the impact of the illness of affected family members.[1,2]
	• Increase awareness of family structure and individual roles of members within the family.[2]
	• Clarify and revise individual roles within the family.[2]
	• Foster family cohesion and closeness.[2]

[1] Aims adopted from FBT and achieved through Phase I FBT techniques.
[2] Aims achieved through multi-family therapy activities.

(*Continued*)

Primary Treatment Components	Therapeutic Aims
Patient Skills Training	• Equip patients with skills for reducing negative emotion and tolerating distress to facilitate recovery. • Orient caretakers and other family members to skills for the purposes of modeling skills usage and tolerating own distress.

Family Meals	**I. Observation.**
	    • Assess family patterns and parenting strategies used around mealtimes.
	    • Assess caretaker ability to provide appropriate meals.
	
	II. Intervention.
	    • Provide feedback on meal appropriateness and necessary information to provide meals appropriate for respective stage of recovery.
	    • Provide in-vivo caretaker coaching on effective strategies for managing meal-interfering attitudes and behavior and negative affect.
	    • Provide in-vivo patient coaching on utilization of skills to manage mealtimes.
	
	III. Reinforcement.
	    • Reinforce the use of effective caretaker meal-management strategies.
	    • Observe, specify, and concretize effective meal-management strategies to be used at home.

Parent Management Training	• Provide parent training on the principles of positive reinforcement, punishment, and extinction, as they apply to parent management of eating disorder behaviors. • Provide therapist-guided, in-vivo training of appropriate parent management techniques. • Identify three target behaviors to be the focus of recovery, and specify a plan for how to achieve those behaviors. • Construct a clearly defined set of concrete rules for eating and other eating disorder-related behaviors. • Enhance motivation by creating consistent and predicable positive and negative contingencies for identified target behaviors.
Psychoeducation	• Provide education on the etiological factors associated with eating disorders. • Provide education on medical and psychological consequences of eating disorders. • Reduce blame in the family to mobilize energy toward recovery.

Ancillary Treatment Components

Medication Evaluation

Families receive individual consultative services from a resident psychiatrist with specialized knowledge of medication management specific to eating disorders and other common comorbidities. Although medication is not commonly prescribed throughout the stay in the program, a full psychiatric assessment is conducted with patients, and caretakers are advised on medication options that have the potential to facilitate recovery.

Case Management

Lead therapists also act as case managers in an effort to coordinate continuity of care and follow-up treatment services on transition home. The treatment team provides families with recommendations about appropriate follow-up care and makes their best efforts to provide appropriate community referrals to specialist treatment providers. Discharge recommendations and consultations with the follow-up treatment team are provided in the week following treatment.

Data

In 2011, a case series was published that summarized the outcomes of 19 families who attended single-family IFT between 2006 and 2010. Data collected from this study suggest that IFT is effective in restoring weight for patients across a wide range of age and diagnoses (Rockwell et al., 2011). Continued efforts to evaluate the program are ongoing. A retrospective follow-up study is currently underway to evaluate outcomes of those who attended our program between 2006 and 2013. Data (unpublished) collected on 40 past participants (including a follow-up assessment with initial 19 patients) indicate significant gains in BMI following participation in the program (mean = 3.06, SD = 3.21, CI (2.01 – 4.12), p <.001). All participating parents (100 percent) reported that the treatment was helpful and endorsed the following components as the most helpful: multi-family groups, behavioral contracting, and psychoeducation. Since July 2013, data collection efforts have begun to formally evaluate program data, and patient and caretaker outcomes including family functioning, eating disorder symptomatology, mood symptomatology, and weight at pre-, post- and 9-month follow-up.

Summary

The Intensive Family Treatment Program represents a brief, intensive model of treatment for children and adolescents with eating disorders, with the philosophical spirit of FBT at its root. Like FBT, the overarching purpose of the treatment is to position parents as the primary providers of treatment for their ill child. IFT accomplishes this by providing education, training, and practice for parents in an immersive setting, with the ultimate goal of positioning parents to assume responsibility and care over their children's recovery on transition home. To strengthen the chances of recovery, patients also receive training and practice on coping skills to improve their tolerance and willingness to engage in recovery-oriented behaviors. The end result is a comprehensive model that builds self-efficacy and improves families' chances of succeeding with recovery in the home.

Acknowledgements

The authors would like to acknowledge the following people who were involved in the creation, development, and administration of the IFT: Ivan Eisler, PhD, Roxanne Rockwell, MA, Joy Jacobs, PhD, Anne Clarkin, LCSW, Erin Parks, PhD, Erin Accurso, PhD, June Liang, PhD, and Mary Ellen Trunko, MD.

References

Abramowitz, J. S., Foa, E. B., & Franklin, M. E. (2003). Exposure and ritual prevention for obsessive-compulsive disorder: Effects of intensive versus twice-weekly sessions. *Journal of Consulting and Clinical Psychology, 71*(2), 394.

Asen, E. (2002). Multiple family therapy: an overview. *Journal of Family Therapy, 24*(1), 3–16. doi: 10.1111/1467–6427.00197

Asen, E., & Scholz, M. (2010). *Multi-family therapy: Concepts and techniques.* Routledge.

Berg, K. C., Crosby, R. D., Cao, L., Peterson, C. B., Engel, S. G., Mitchell, J. E., & Wonderlich, S. A. (2013). Facets of negative affect prior to and following binge-only, purge-only, and binge/purge events in women with bulimia nervosa. *Journal of Abnormal Psychology, 122*(1), 111.

Dare, C., & Eisler, I. (2000). A multi-family group day treatment programme for adolescent eating disorder. *European Eating Disorders Review, 8*(1), 4–18.

Dare, C., Eisler, I., Russell, G. F. M., & Szmukler, G. I. (1990). The clinical and theoretical impact of a controlled trial of family therapy in anorexia nervosa. *Journal of Marital and Family Therapy, 16*(1), 39–57.

Davis, III, T., E., Ollendick, T. H., & Öst, L. (2009). Intensive treatment of specific phobias in children and adolescents. *Cognitive and Behavioral Practice, 16*(3), 294–303.

Eisler, I. (2005). The empirical and theoretical base of family therapy and multiple family day therapy for adolescent anorexia nervosa. *Journal of Family Therapy, 27*(2), 104–131.

Frank, G. K. W., & Kaye, W. H. (2012). Current status of functional imaging in eating disorders. *International Journal of Eating Disorders, 45*(6), 723–736.

Frank, G. K. W., Roblek, T., Shott, M. E., Jappe, L. M., Rollin, M. D. H., Hagman, J. O., & Pryor, T. (2012). Heightened fear of uncertainty in anorexia and bulimia nervosa. *International Journal of Eating Disorders, 45*(2), 227–232.

Kaye, W. H., Bulik, C. M., Thornton, L., Barbarich, N., & Masters, K. (2004). Comorbidity of anxiety disorders with anorexia and bulimia nervosa. *American Journal of Psychiatry, 161*(12), 2215–2221.

Kaye, W. H., Fudge, J. L., & Paulus, M. (2009). New insights into symptoms and neurocircuit function of anorexia nervosa. *Nature Reviews Neuroscience, 10*(8), 573–584.

Kaye, W. H., Wierenga, C. E., Bailer, U. F., Simmons, A. N., & Bischoff-Grethe, A. (2013). Nothing tastes as good as skinny feels: The neurobiology of anorexia nervosa. *Trends in Neurosciences, 36*(2), 110–120.

Kazdin, A. E. (1997). Parent management training: Evidence, outcomes, and issues. *Journal of the American Academy of Child & Adolescent Psychiatry, 36*(10), 1349–1356.

Le Grange, D., & Eisler, I. (2009). Family interventions in adolescent anorexia nervosa. *Child and Adolescent Psychiatric Clinics of North America, 18*(1), 159–173.

Lock, J. (2011). Evaluation of family treatment models for eating disorders. *Current Opinion in Psychiatry, 24*(4), 274.

Lock, J., & Le Grange, D. (2012). *Treatment manual for anorexia nervosa: A family-based approach*: Guilford Press.

McKay, M. M., Harrison, M. E., Gonzales, J., Kim, L., & Quintana, E. (2002). Multiple-family groups for urban children with conduct difficulties and their families. *Psychiatric Services, 53*(11), 1467–1468.

Mörtberg, E., Karlsson, A., Fyring, C., & Sundin, Ö. (2006). Intensive cognitive-behavioral group treatment (CBGT) of social phobia: a randomized controlled study. *Journal of Anxiety Disorders, 20*(5), 646–660.

Rhodes, P., Baillee, A., Brown, J., & Madden, S. (2008). Can parent-to-parent consultation improve the effectiveness of the Maudsley model of family-based treatment for anorexia nervosa? A randomized control trial. *Journal of Family Therapy, 30*(1), 96–108. doi: 10.1111/j.1467-6427.2008.00418.x

Rhodes, P., Brown, J., & Madden, S. (2009). The Maudsley model of family-based treatment for anorexia nervosa: A Qualitative evaluation of parent-to-parent consultation. *Journal of Marital and Family Therapy, 35*(2), 181–192. doi: 10.1111/j.1752-0606.2009.00115.x

Rockwell, R. E., Boutelle, K., Trunko, M. E., Jacobs, M. J., & Kaye, W. H. (2011). An innovative short-term, intensive, family-based treatment for adolescent anorexia nervosa: Case series. *European Eating Disorders Review, 19*(4), 362–367.

Russell, G. F. M., Szmukler, G. I., Dare, C., & Eisler, I. (1987). An evaluation of family therapy in anorexia nervosa and bulimia nervosa. *Archives of General Psychiatry, 44*(12), 1047.

Saayman, R. V., Saayman, G. S., & Wiens, S. M. (2006). Training staff in multiple family therapy in a children's psychiatric hospital: from theory to practice. *Journal of Family Therapy, 28*(4), 404–419.

Scholz, M., & Asen, E. (2001). Multiple family therapy with eating disordered adolescents: Concepts and preliminary results. *European Eating Disorders Review, 9*(1), 33–42.

Whiteside, S. P., Brown, A. M., & Abramowitz, J. S. (2008). Five-day intensive treatment for adolescent OCD: A case series. *Journal of Anxiety Disorders, 22*(3), 495–504. doi: http://dx.doi.org/10.1016/j.janxdis.2007.05.001

Whiteside, S. P., & Jacobsen, A. B. (2010). An Uncontrolled examination of a 5-day intensive treatment for pediatric OCD. *Behavior Therapy, 41*(3), 414–422. doi: http://dx.doi.org/10.1016/j.beth.2009.11.003

Chapter 6

Exposure-Based Family Therapy

Tom Hildebrandt, Terri Bacow, and Rebecca Greif

Anxiety and Anorexia Nervosa

Anorexia nervosa (AN) is a chronic, severe condition that typically begins in adolescence and evidences poor treatment outcome among treatment seeking adults (Keel & Brown, 2010). Treatment for adolescents with AN has better prognoses, particularly if treatment occurs early during the course of the illness (Watson & Bulik, 2013). A relationship exists between AN and both trait anxiety (e.g., harm avoidance) and psychopathology. AN is comorbid with anxiety disorders (Godart et al., 2003), and these disorders overlap in clinical phenomenon such as perfectionism, rigidity, compulsivity, and harm avoidance (Collier & Treasure, 2004; Kaye, Bulik, Thornton, Barbarich, & Masters, 2004; Strober, 2004), which may reflect a shared genetic vulnerability among individuals with these pathologies (Bulik, Slof-Opt Landt, van Furth, & Sullivan, 2007; Halmi et al., 2005; Keel, Klump, Miller, McGue, & Lacono, 2005). Furthermore, anxiety (e.g., fear, worry, and disgust about food) and avoidance behaviors, such as severe dietary restriction, are core features of AN and indicative of a pattern of negative reinforcement common to behavioral symptoms found among anxiety disorders. The overlap between AN and anxiety has important implications for clinical models that have been relatively underdeveloped compared to other behavioral, nutritional, or pharmacological treatments for AN. For instance, dysregulation in fear conditioning is thought to contribute to both anxiety and AN (Strober, 2004). More recently, we have argued that AN treatment may be enhanced by targeting the broad range of anxiety experienced by these individuals (Hildebrandt, Bacow, Markella, & Loeb, 2012), and techniques that effectively target different types of anxiety (e.g., exposure) may be a component of effective treatments for AN. For example, traditional models of exposure with response prevention (EXRP) are now being used to reduce anxiety associated with eating (Steinglass et al., 2011).

Theoretical Models of Anxiety and Anorexia Nervosa

Several theoretical models of AN have been proposed based on the relationship between AN and anxiety, and each of these models has important, but unique, treatment implications. Strober's (2004) fear conditioning model of AN posits that the anxiety characteristic of these individuals is the result of vulnerability in the processing and storage of anxious/threat-based associations that constitute classic conditioning between stimulus and emotion. In theory, the relationship between fear and stimulus (e.g., food, body shape, etc.) is acquired much more quickly among individuals with AN and is more resistant to extinction. The consequences of this altered fear-conditioning trait is that feared associations with food, shape, and weight lead to rapid weight loss and subsequent difficulty extinguishing these associations. This model provides a clear rationale for the use of exposure techniques, which are commonly utilized in the treatment of anxiety disorders, for the treatment of AN (Steinglass et al., 2011). A pilot-test of EXRP for AN, however, resulted in a reduction in food anxiety but not a significant increase in food intake post-treatment (Steinglass et al., 2012). Thus, a fear conditioning model of food avoidance in AN may insufficiently explain this pathology, and therefore, techniques beyond traditional exposure therapy may be required to adequately treat this disorder.

Pallister and Waller's (2008) cognitive model of AN suggests overlapping cognitive biases between eating and anxiety disorders which center on maladaptive beliefs regarding the perceived dangerousness of the world and one's vulnerability, or inability to cope. As a result, environmental cues (e.g., food) are posited to elicit misperceptions regarding one's vulnerability (e.g., "this food is dangerous; this food will make me fat"). These misperceptions elicit anxiety and subsequent attempts to manage this affect via cognitive and behavioral strategies (e.g., food avoidance) to reduce the likelihood of a feared outcome (e.g., weight gain) or to avoid anxiety-provoking cognitions. These strategies reduce the individual's anxiety in the short term yet perpetuate the aforementioned maladaptive beliefs. These beliefs, in combination with increased attentional bias towards threatening stimuli, are believed to maintain anxiety among patients with eating disorders (Siep, Jansen, Havermans, & Roefs, 2011). This model suggests that treatment of AN should focus on restructuring the patient's cognitions regarding perceived vulnerability and propensity towards harm avoidance via strategies including behavioral experiments, cognitive restructuring, and reduction of safety behavior. Novel strategies to increase cognitive flexibility, such as cognitive remediation, have more recently been utilized as well (Abbate-Daga, Buzzichelli, Marzola, Amianto, & Fassino, 2012; Macleod, 2012). Cognitive behavioral therapy (CBT) commonly employs the aforementioned strategies; however, similar to exposure treatment, the effectiveness of CBT for AN has been mixed (Wilson, Grilo, & Vitousek, 2007), which further suggests that the current models of AN are incomplete.

A Broad Anxiety-Based Model for AN

Hildebrandt and colleagues (2012) proposed a broad anxiety-based model for AN that focuses on a distinct typology of anxious emotions that may act alone or in combination to support the complex range of compulsive and safety behaviors found in AN. Figure 6.1 summarizes the typology of anxiety encountered in the model. Fear is the most commonly referenced anxious emotion and operates under conditions of proximal threat (Misslin, 2003). The psychophysiology of fear involves activation of the autonomic nervous system in preparation for a fight-or-flight response. Fear manifests in AN when the threatening trigger poses an immediate threat to one's self, such as when an individual with AN believes that he/she is being judged or criticized by a peer or family member.

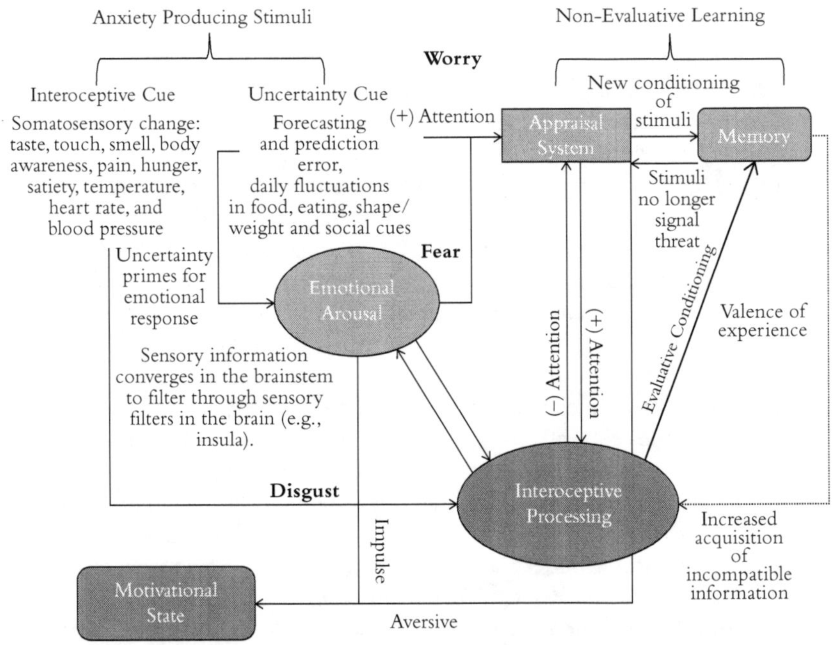

Figure 6.1 **A Model of Fear, Disgust, and Worry in Anorexia Nervosa.**
The broad model of anxiety summarized in Figure 6.1 describes how anxiety producing stimuli work through either interoceptively driven or cognitively driven pathways to support avoidance behavior. The interoceptive pathway favors sensory processing (taste, smell, etc.) in the formulation of a disgust-based association. This nonevaluative conditioning formulates an associative memory that is particularly difficult to extinguish and can influence motivational state and choice decisions about food independent of higher order processing. The cognitively driven pathway is heavily influenced by the degree of uncertainty indicated by the threat, leading to both higher levels of emotional arousal and attention dedicated to the threat cue. In extreme uncertainty, this can lead to worry-based associations or more immediately threatening fear-based associations. These emotions have direct influence over the motivational state (approach or avoid) but are more flexibly learned because of the role of cognition in modifying and updating threat levels to these stimuli.

Worry develops under conditions of distal threat and/or a high degree of uncertainty about the presence of the threat. Consequently, the autonomic responses to worry are attenuated (Hoehn-Saric, & McLeod, 2000; Starcevic & Berle, 2006) in order to focus attentional and sensory systems on gathering information that may prepare the individual to avoid the threat or reduce uncertainty about its presence. For example, a food trigger (e.g., a brownie) may elicit worries about future weight gain which may subsequently lead to food avoidance or other forms of safety behaviors (e.g., cutting the brownie into very small pieces) in an attempt to reduce the likelihood of this threatening outcome.

Disgust is unique among anxious emotions because the reflexive physiological and functional components support a highly evolved system designed to identify and avoid stimuli linked to disease and toxicity (Chapman & Anderson, 2012). The biological signatures of disgust include decreased heart rate (de Jong, van Overveld, & Peters, 2011), distinct facial expressions involving activation of the levator labii muscle (Cisler, Olatunji, & Lohr, 2009), and increased activation of the insula (Fusar-Poli et al., 2009). The last connection may help explain consistent findings from the neuroimaging literature implicating altered activation of the anterior insula in response to anticipation of food stimuli (Kaye, 2008; Nunn, Frampton, Fuglset, Torzsok-Sonnevend, & Lask, 2011). Functionally, the aversive response characteristic of disgust is associated with rapid acquisition and resistance to extinction. This mechanism was likely critical to our survival when food sources were often contaminated and infectious disease caused significant loss of life. In the context of AN, disgust is likely to manifest as the aversive somatic response to food/eating (e.g., fullness) or the discomfort associated with body checking (e.g., stomach folding over waistband).

The Hildebrandt et al. (2012) model also identifies reward processing as a key perpetuating factor of avoidance behaviors in AN. Five categories of triggers commonly perceived as threatening (food, eating, interoceptive cues, shape and weight, and social evaluation) can elicit either an aversive conditioned response, emotionally based impulsive response, or both due to several different factors, including the nature of the trigger, the environment in which the trigger is found, and previous learning associated with this trigger. Moreover, neuroscience suggests that these patients may experience heightened sensitivity to pain and pleasure (Keating, Tilbrook, Rossell, Enticott, & Fitzgerald, 2012) as well as heightened brain activation in the context of triggers associated with a high degree of uncertainty (Frank et al., 2012). Thus, from a neurobiological perspective, dysfunction in the motivation/reward system (Keating, 2010) may reinforce these avoidance behaviors and predispose these individuals to prefer short-term avoidance over long-term positive outcomes by facilitating a "relief reward" that occurs when avoidance functions as negative reinforcement.

Avoidance behaviors (e.g., prevention strategies, safety behaviors, and compulsions) function to manage the threat induced by the specific trigger and the context in which it occurs. These behaviors reduce anxiety short term (e.g., function via negative reinforcement) yet maintain anxiety long term because it denies the individual opportunities for experiential learning that could alter his/her maladaptive beliefs (e.g., eating a brownie leads to weight gain). Avoidance behaviors also perpetuate false beliefs regarding the function of safety behaviors; when the feared outcome (e.g., weight gain) does not occur, the individual attributes this to the safety behavior instead of the low probability of this event occurring. Social supports (e.g., family members, peers), particularly among adolescents with AN, may unintentionally further reinforce the individual's food avoidance. As the eating disorder progresses, pathology is further maintained by a dual process in which motivation to engage in healthy, age-appropriate activities (e.g., socializing with friends) declines while motivation to engage in eating disorder behaviors increases. Moreover, due to this population's propensity towards rapid fear conditioning, anxiety is transferred to additional triggers via associative learning (e.g., all carbohydrates elicit anxiety).

In summary, the Hildebrandt et al. (2012) model encompasses numerous different components of anxiety that characterize AN. When an individual encounters a trigger, the level of threat and degree of uncertainty are ascertained based on previous learning experiences with this trigger and the context in which the trigger occurs. Worry is experienced when the trigger is future–oriented or there is a high degree of uncertainty, and the individual typically manages this by utilizing avoidance behaviors intended to prevent the feared outcome. Fear is experienced when the trigger has immediate consequences or there is a low degree of uncertainty, and the individual often responds to this by utilizing avoidance behaviors intended to reduce emotional arousal. Disgust occurs when the threat involves a somatic exposure, and the somatic experience signals a high degree of uncertainty about the consequence. Associative learning, coupled with reduced opportunities for new learning, leads to generalization of anxiety over time and further maintenance of eating disorder pathology.

Treatment Implications for Broad Anxiety Model

Treatments based on the aforementioned fear conditioning and anxiety models of AN do not have strong empirical support. Family-based treatment (FBT) for adolescent AN, however, is an empirically supported stand-alone outpatient treatment (Eisler, et al., 2000; Le Grange, Eisler, Dare, & Russell, 1992; Lock, Agras, Bryson, & Kraemer, 2005) as well as an adjunctive treatment following hospitalization (Russell, Szmukler, Dare, & Eisler 1987), which evidences impressive long-term outcomes (Eisler et al., 1997; Eisler, Simic, Russell, & Dare, 1997; Lock, Couturier, & Agras, 2006).

FBT posits that modifications in familial functioning are the key impetus of change, and it does not directly identify anxiety as a treatment mechanism of change (Loeb, Lock, Le Grange, & Greif, 2012). We developed exposure-based FBT (FBT-E) to take advantage of the family's agency to execute a highly generalizable form of exposure therapy. By capitalizing on parental structure, FBT-E was designed to achieve intensive food and eating exposure in an individual's natural environment, while adapting the diverse strategies for exposure to specific types of anxiety. It is likely that some forms of exposure happen naturally (although not explicitly) in various treatment settings including inpatient units, intensive outpatient or partial hospital programs, and various outpatient settings. When food is presented in the context of anxiety (especially if safety/avoidance behaviors are eliminated), these interventions have the potential to achieve habituation and reduce anxiety. However, all of these methods are limited in their ability to bring exposure into the individual's natural environment with enough frequency to generalize the effect. We designed FBT-E to focus on "real world" exposure.

A second intended consequence of embedding a range of exposure approaches into family treatment is the ability to alter the associative mechanisms and incentive contingencies that reward eating. Having parents associate eating with health and linking health with engagement in other valued or pleasurable activities, the family may begin to decouple anxious associations with food/eating. Additionally, they have the ability to incentivize pro-health behavior as well as eating behavior while reducing collusion with safety/compulsive/avoidance behaviors.

The broad anxiety model further specifies that interventions should broadly target the individual's fear, worry, and disgust responses to symptom triggers. Fear may require classic exposure with response prevention. Targeting worry may require specific worry exposure techniques (e.g., to address catastrophic thinking about future shape and weight changes) (Hoyer et al., 2009), and disgust treatment may necessitate environmentally based exposures of greater frequency, duration, and intensity than traditional EXRP. Clinical research on specific phobias suggests that disgust habituates more slowly than fear (Olatunji, Smits, Connolly, Willems, & Lohr, 2007; Viar-Paxton & Olatunji, 2012), and conditioning of a neutral stimulus by disgust involves interoceptive-driven learning. This type of learning has distinct characteristics; its acquisition does not require higher order cognitive processing, and its extinction may require an explicit change in the interoceptive experience.

Hildebrandt and colleagues (in press) conducted a pilot open trial of FBT-E with a group of adolescents meeting DSM-IV diagnostic criteria for AN (n = 4) and eating disorder not otherwise specified-restricting type (SAN, n = 6). All participants gained weight over the course of treatment and 9/10 reached > 85 percent ideal body weight (IBW). Eating disorder and depressive symptom scales demonstrated improvement over treatment with moderate to large effects. These effects were statistically significant for global eating symptoms, eating concerns, and depressive symptoms. A total of 6/10 patients were below a clinical rating of "4" on both shape and weight subscales of the Eating Disorder Examination-Questionnaire (Fairburn & Beglin, 1994). Similar findings emerged for self and parent-rated adolescent anxiety. Patients reported significant improvements in global anxiety, panic and somatic symptoms, and school-related anxiety, whereas parents reported additional improvements in social anxiety. In sum, the results of this study provide preliminary evidence that FBT-E may effectively target disordered eating and anxiety symptoms.

Exposure-Based Family Behavioral Therapy (FBT-E)

FBT-E focuses on the use of exposure techniques and parental de/incentivization to (a) restore healthy weight status; (b) reduce anxiety associate with food, eating, and shape/weight; and (c) reduce compulsive, avoidance, and safety behaviors. All emotions, especially the anxious emotions, are discussed as temporary experiences that are quite difficult to control directly. This description helps reduce the expectation that exposure therapy will remove anxiety completely. Rather, the FBT-E therapists discuss the process of exposure as a method used to recalibrate emotions such as fear, worry, and disgust to be more functional for the individual. FBT-E retains some aspects of other family treatments including enlisting parents to take an authoritative role in refeeding, reducing blame on the patient, and focusing on initial weight restoration as the first goal in treatment. However, FBT-E targets anxiety-specific avoidance to achieve this weight gain and provides an explicit conceptual model for understanding the disorder that allows the clinician/family to target both eating disorder and body image symptoms.

FBT-E utilizes a three-phase, twenty-session format similar to the original approach (Lock, Le Grange, & Russell, 2013). The therapist uses the heuristic of the family as a "team" in which all members have an explicit role in defeating the eating disorder. The identified patient is typically engaged via (1) direct psychoeducation about anxiety and how it can interfere with the most basic of human needs from breathing to eating, (2) discussion of the range of methods used to target his/her experience of anxiety, and (3) the provision of different incentives associated with effort and progress towards defeating the eating disorder. Resistance is normal for the sick adolescent, and FBT-E explains this resistance as a function of the anxiety and reinforcement of the avoidance behaviors.

Table 6.1 A Comparison of FBT-E and FBT Treatment Components

Session	FBT-E Approach	FBT Approach
Session 1	Psychoeducation about anxiety and exposure Assign roles to family members Give parents Coach's Manual Introduce contingency management Plan for family meal (with challenge food)	Gathering history of the illness Separating the illness from the patient Emphasizing blame reduction Educating family about dangers of AN Planning for family meal

Session	FBT-E Approach	FBT Approach
Session 2	Family Meal: • Collect SUDS before and after meal • Gather therapist and family feedback • Assign task of meal monitoring (forms) • Ask parents to also monitor Firm Empathy	Family Meal: • Parents encouraged to get the adolescent to eat one more bite than he/she would typically eat • Monitoring not assigned/ collected
Session 3	Review and discuss monitoring forms Create Anxiety and Avoidance Hierarchy (AAH; of feared foods and beverages) Assign parent-facilitated exposure tasks Implement contingency management Review role of siblings (if present)	Discussing and supporting parent(s) efforts at refeeding including use of functional incentives for eating Continuing to separate the illness from the patient and reduce familial criticism Review progress
Sessions 4–8	Review monitoring forms weekly Approach each item on AAH with parent's direct assistance; tackle safety behaviors Teach adolescent skills for coping with anxiety Evaluate need for optional modules	Discussing and supporting parent(s) efforts at refeeding and reducing rituals Continuing to separate the illness from the patient and reduce familial criticism Evaluate readiness for Phase 2
Sessions 9–16	Criteria for Phase 2 are met Gradual return to independent eating Optional modules as needed for specific psychological symptoms using CBT: • Binge eating/purging • Body image concerns (mirror exposure) • AN specific worry (e.g., worry exposure)	Criteria for Phase 2 are met Gradual return to independent eating Family encouraged to examine link between adolescent issues and the development of his/her AN Continuing to separate the illness from the patient and reduce familial criticism
Sessions 17–20	Relapse prevention Planning for the future Celebration of progress/termination	Exploring adolescent issues with the family; planning for future issues Checking in how parents are doing as a couple (when two parents present) Terminating treatment

Over the course of treatment the therapist uses his/her extended exposure framework to match exposure technique with the appropriate aspect of anxiety (fear, worry, or disgust). The process for establishing the appropriate target involves the use of observation, feedback from family members, and, in cases of marked denial and/or alexithymia, the use of behavioral challenges designed to elicit emotions. Therapists focus observation/questions on cognitive and somatic experiences associated with use of a known aversive stimulus (e.g., weighing, specific food, etc.) in session. The goal initially is to develop a list of targets for exposure therapy that have specific functional significance for maintenance of the eating disorder. Initially, these exposures have the additional significance of facilitating weight restoration but may be used continually throughout treatment for goals associated with improving one's associations with food and eating.

Three primary types of exposure are used by the therapist in FBT-E. In EXRP exercises, exposure hierarchies are used and Subjective Units of Distress (SUDS) ratings are collected to document habituation and provide feedback to the patient about reductions in fear. Compulsive and/or safety behaviors are delayed or prohibited to facilitate habituation. Patients and/ or parents are asked to self-monitor these changes at meals between sessions, and they use a flexible hierarchy through the course of treatment to chart progress. Worry exposures typically involve developing a worry script that includes a detailed description of the specific worry domain that is repeatedly read aloud until the individual becomes bored by the content. Disgust exposures typically involve interoceptive focus with use of eliciting disgusting somatic experiences related to food, eating, or shape and weight. The interoceptive experience is captured by using triggers that elicit parallel somatic experiences and exposure executed by asking the patient to increase his/her tolerance of the specific sensory experience. One classic disgust exposure involves asking the family to facilitate a "fullness" exposure by having the patient eat a high-density food and then having the patient practice observing (rather than judging or avoiding) the somatic experience of fullness and how it changes with time and attention.

The complexity of the broad anxiety model is in its flexibility to include "stacked" or overlapping emotions associated with a specific symptom set. For example, fear and worry often co-occur in the context of scale avoidance/checking. Disgust and fear often co-occur when food avoidance persists in treatment. Worry and disgust often co-occur when avoidance of shape and weight exposure cause impairment. Fear, worry, and disgust may all operate in social situations where specific foods are present and the threat of social evaluation occurs. Clinically, these complex presentations are dealt with by adapting exposures to single components that contribute to the overall behavior. For example, the initial goal may be to reduce the disgust response to a specific food before tackling worry or fear associated with eating in a threatening social situation.

The broad anxiety model of FBT-E also links anxiety to a motivational system that is driven by "relief reward" which weights decision making towards short-term avoidance over long-term functioning. In FBT-E, parents receive psychoeducation about this motivational system and are asked to describe examples where they may have observed this system in operation. Using these examples, parents are charged with the goal of increasing positive drive by reducing familial and peer reinforcement of eating disorder behaviors (particularly avoidance) and incentivizing alternative noneating disorder behaviors. Ideally, pursuit of this goal leads to a broad range of positive experiences that interfere with positive associations connected to avoidance of anxiety. By positioning parents to decrease their child's access to avoidance and incentivize other (positive) life experiences (e.g., access to friends, meaningful leisure, etc.), parents can create positive associations between anxious triggers (eating, weight gain, etc.) and naturally rewarding experiences. This counter-conditioning may function not only to motivate adolescents to face their anxiety, but also facilitate extinction by changing the value of the trigger (rather than relying only on habituation to anxious emotions). Parents are coached in how to facilitate exposures in a variety of salient environments, generalizing the reduction of fear to a wide range of naturalistic contexts. Functionally, the home environment provides a learning context that contains the majority of relevant triggers. Moreover, parents either directly or indirectly facilitate healthy eating in other settings that are pertinent to sustained and generalized learning, such as school, restaurants, friends' homes, and vacation environments.

The 20-session standard FBT-E intervention involves three phases. Phase 1 involves a focus on weight gain and the initiation of exposure protocols. In Phase 2, FBT-E focuses on transfer of responsibility for feeding and weight management back to the adolescent through continuation of exposure exercises and use of five different modules designed to address persistent eating disorder symptoms. Phase 3 of FBT-E is designed to be a test of the patient and family's mastery over anxiety and their ability to use what they have learned to prevent relapse or reduce any residual symptoms. The three phases of FBT-E are as follows: Phase 1: Recovery from an Injury, Phase 2: Getting Back into the Game, and Phase 3: The Playoffs. The FBT-E treatment approach is described below.

Phase 1: Recovery from an Illness

The primary goals of Phase 1 of FBT-E are to present an anxiety-based model and anxiety-based treatment conceptualization of AN, explain the role of each family member in this treatment, and provide parents with clear instructions (in the form of a "Coach's Manual") regarding the re-feeding process. This includes descriptions of the three types of anxiety commonly encountered in AN (fear, worry, and disgust) and how they may be recognized in the context of the adolescent's eating disorder (e.g., refusal of food, aversion towards previously enjoyed foods accompanied by facial expressions signaling disgust, anticipatory worry about weight gain). These forms of anxiety are directly linked to the adolescent's avoidance of food and related triggers, while illustrating how anxiety in eating disorders can be overcome (i.e., by eating feared foods rather than avoiding them). This psychoeducation aims to help the adolescent and his/her family understand the patient's emotional and behavioral reactions to threatening stimuli and the process maintaining his/her eating disorder. Thus, the adolescent may feel more empowered to overcome this disorder knowing that he/she will be given specific tools to resolve the anxieties. Parents and family members are given the task in Session 1 of relating to the patient's anxiety through description of one of their own worst fears. After eliciting the worst fears from each family member, the therapist frames these fears in the context of the process of refeeding by asking individual family members to "imagine facing [feared situation] 3–5 times per day for the remainder of his/her life just to live." Family members are then assigned specific roles that are consistent with the emphasis on confronting different forms of anxiety. The parents are the "coaches" who help the patient face his/her fears of food and related stimuli. Siblings are "teammates" who play a supportive role. The patient with AN is an essential member of the team ("star player").

At the end of the first session, the parents are given a "Coach's Manual," which the therapist and parents review without the patient present. The Coach's Manual provides clear instructions for structuring the refeeding process (particularly when weight gain is indicated). Parents are, for example, instructed not to serve patients the most feared foods at the beginning of treatment and to gradually add more feared foods over time. Further, parents are provided with guidelines for supervised mealtimes derived from behavioral treatments (e.g., ignore negative behavior, attend to positive behavior, give labeled praise and model a calm, supportive stance when confronted with the adolescent's anxiety reaction).

The parent-coaches are instructed to bring a picnic meal to the next treatment session that is representative of a meal they may eat at home, including a "challenge" food (e.g., a food that the adolescent has been avoiding) that is not unreasonably difficult but that is currently avoided to some degree. This session directly targets fear and is the family's first concrete exposure practice, aided by the therapist.

During this initial phase of treatment, FBT-E focuses on reviewing the rationale behind conducting food/eating exposures and reducing safety/avoidance behaviors, creating an anxiety-and-avoidance hierarchy (AAH), and explaining how to properly use contingency management and associative learning to motivate/reinforce successful exposures. The "coaches" (i.e., parents) are assigned the task of serving the first item on the hierarchy to the "injured player" (i.e., patient) at home, and it is explained that they will be gradually tackling each item on the AAH throughout the course of Phase 1 in the context of eating enough to gain weight. Exposure, therefore, takes place primarily at home, allowing the adolescent (with the aid of his/her parent-coaches) to naturalistically confront feared and disgusted foods in a systematic way. The family is informed by the therapist that while both fear and disgust may be targeted effectively with exposure, it may take repeated trials of the exposure intervention to produce extinction of the disgust response that the patient finds particularly aversive (whether in terms of taste, texture, smell, macronutrient content, etc.). The patient is encouraged to place such items further along the hierarchy and to allow sufficient time for repeated exposure practice at home; in-office exposures may also occur in which the family brings a food that is primarily disgust-driven into session and coaching is provided by the therapist.

The therapist also explains to parent-coaches the importance of monitoring and curtailing any avoidance behaviors (e.g., cutting food into little pieces, weighing food, or chewing slowly) that the adolescent exhibits. Parents are encouraged to use contingency management to help enhance the adolescent's motivation for success. For example, privileges (such as exercise, spending time with friends) may be contingent upon the player's completion of meals with his/her family. During this phase, active coping on the part of the adolescent is also encouraged; skills for managing anxiety while confronting threatening stimuli (e.g., "riding the wave" of the anxiety during a meal, taking deep breaths, giving oneself a pep talk) (Kendall & Hedtke, 2006; March & Benson, 2006; Pincus, Ehrenreich, & Spiegel, 2008) are taught to the adolescent directly, with coaches and teammates present. The adolescent is encouraged to practice these skills during exposures outside of session.

Phase 2: Getting Back into the Game

In FBT-E, Phase 2 typically takes place from Sessions 9 through 16 (although more or less time is allotted to complete this phase as needed), and these sessions occur bimonthly (as opposed to weekly). There are specific criteria for progressing from Phase 1 to Phase 2. The adolescent (1) should be weight-restored or at a stable weight health-wise and (2) all foods on the hierarchy should be completed. The adolescent may need additional practice consuming his/her feared foods in different contexts (e.g., with friends) and is encouraged to continue incorporating these into all meals. However, he/she will have successfully exhibited a reduction in anxiety of all of the items on the hierarchy to proceed with Phase 2. The second phase of FBT-E involves a gradual increase in independence around eating. A first step may involve allowing the adolescent to serve him/herself portions of food, and a larger step may involve choosing his/her own meals and going out to eat with friends, unsupervised. The FBT-E manual allows for a return to Phase 1 if needed, if weight is lost or the adolescent exhibits a significant re-emergence of anxiety and avoidance (e.g., not being able to eat in social situations). There is no specific prescription for weight maintenance, and the ultimate goal of this phase is to fully normalize eating. Siblings also continue to be involved as teammates.

Phase 2 of FBT-E also addresses any residual eating disorder signs and symptoms, including (1) symptoms of rumination/worry that are interfering with exposure completion (i.e., worry that eating certain foods will lead to weight gain), (2) binge eating and purging, (3) compulsive exercise, (4) body image concerns, and (5) co-occurring internalizing symptoms. FBT-E includes five specific modules with suggested cognitive behavioral techniques for addressing each of these domains. (See Table 6.2.) These CBT interventions, which are employed on an as-needed basis, can be used with the adolescent alone and may also include his/her parents. For example, in the case of binge eating and/or purging, increased parental supervision may be indicated. At the same time, the adolescent may be independently educated about the benefit of regular meals in curtailing hunger and ways in which to manage binge eating triggers. With worry and rumination, the adolescent is coached on how to defuse his/her worries and engage in worry exposure. The parents may also be given psychoeducation about these symptoms. With body image concerns, a variety of exposure techniques may be used along with empirically supported CBT interventions for body image (Fairburn, 2008). The use of mirror-exposure for individuals with severe body image may also be indicated (Hildebrandt, Loeb, Troupe, & Delinsky, 2012). Both the adolescent and parents may be enlisted in monitoring and curtailing compulsive exercise. These modules have been extremely helpful in addressing residual symptomatology and fully addressing all aspects of the eating disorder. The modules are described more specifically in Table 6.2.

Table 6.2 FBT-E Phase 2 Optional Treatment Modules

Modules	Description
Optional Module 1	Psychoeducation
Binge Eating and NO Purging	Regular Eating
	Appetite awareness/triggers
Optional Module 2	Psychoeducation about ineffectiveness and/
Purging and/or Exercising	or impact of compensatory behavior
	Increased parental supervision
	Limit setting around behavior
Optional Module 3	Monitor body checking and avoidance
Body Image Concerns	Exposure to triggers (i.e., mirror exposure)
	Parent coaching
	CBT interventions (i.e., Fairburn, 1994)
Optional Module 4	Worry Exposure
Worry About Eating/Weight Gain	

Phase 3: The Playoffs

Phase 3 is the final phase of the treatment, and sessions now occur once per month (and may involve anywhere from one to four or more sessions). The "playoffs" occur when all treatment objectives are met, the adolescent is eating independently, and all disordered eating behaviors and additional eating disorder related issues are successfully addressed. Similar to many cognitive behavioral treatments, the final phase of treatment entails reviewing progress, discussing any remaining symptoms that need to be addressed, discussing relapse prevention, and planning for the future. The therapist explores what is needed for the adolescent to maintain gains and how to handle "bumps in the road" and potential lapses. Upon termination, the family is encouraged to do something to celebrate their progress, such as going out for pizza after a championship.

Clinical Application of FBT-E: A Case Example

Case Example: Phase 1

Elizabeth participated in 20 sessions of FBT-E that took place over approximately nine months. Phase 1 was comprised of six sessions. The first session involved an orientation to the treatment model and a discussion of how fear and anxiety manifest in eating disorders and how exposure is a beneficial way to overcome these emotions. Copies of the coach's manual were given to Elizabeth's parents. Session 2 of FBT-E, which consisted of the family meal, was held the following week. Elizabeth was encouraged to consume a portion of a challenging food or beverage in the form of one cup of chocolate milk. Her SUDs (subjective units of distress) rating went from a 30 to a 20 over the course of the meal. Positive feedback was given to Elizabeth and her parents, and they were encouraged to use monitoring forms to track Elizabeth's anxiety at meals over the course of the week and to generate a list of feared foods at home to bring to the next session. At the third session, Elizabeth admitted to "water loading" (inflating her weight by drinking large quantities of water) at the previous meeting. She was instructed to use the restroom before all sessions going forward. Elizabeth's parents reported that Elizabeth was struggling to eat larger portions of food but was able to get through it. At this session, a fear and avoidance hierarchy (AAH) was created that listed the foods that Elizabeth found fearful in increasing order of how difficult it was for her to consume them. During the remainder of Phase 1, Elizabeth's monitoring forms were reviewed each week, and she was assigned to eat a new item from the AAH. Elizabeth's parents were effective at assisting Elizabeth with these exposures, despite clear indications of Elizabeth's anxiety during meals (as measured by her monitoring forms and behavior). Elizabeth specifically expressed worry about weight gain and becoming "fat" from consuming calorically dense foods. As the family worked on the AAH, Elizabeth was given a "hypothesis testing" worksheet (see Appendix A, www.routledge .com/9780415714747) so that she could challenge some of her fears and worries and cope with her anxiety around eating. When Elizabeth was able to eat all items an the AAH and had increased her weight by six pounds, a discussion about transitioning to Phase 2 was held.

Case Example: Phase 2

Phase 2 began with a discussion of giving Elizabeth more control over what she was eating, for example, by allowing her to choose one of her snacks. At this point, Elizabeth's parents noted some difficulty. For example, they reported that Elizabeth was arguing about portion sizes, asking in advance what food would be served at meals, and making firm statements about what she was willing to eat. The therapist emphasized the need for Elizabeth to tolerate some uncertainty around meals and to tolerate not being able to control many aspects of her eating. Elizabeth was gradually given more independence with eating, for example, trying a few meals with friends without supervision. From Session 8 onward, sessions shifted to biweekly in frequency. Given Elizabeth's reported body image concerns, during this phase, interventions from the body image module were selected and implemented. Elizabeth self-monitored her feelings of fatness and learned the difference between these perceptions and her actual weight. As Elizabeth endorsed worry about weight gain, the therapist provided Elizabeth with psychoeducation regarding weight gain and normal weight fluctuation as well as a worry tracking form. During the middle of Phase 2, Elizabeth lost three pounds. A plan was generated for Elizabeth to increase her food intake on her own with some parental oversight. She returned to her healthy weight, and remaining aspects of the eating disorder were addressed, such as Elizabeth's attempt to control her snacks and only eat at certain times of day. Elizabeth's parents continued to take action to facilitate exposure and to help Elizabeth tolerate eating in a more flexible way with the aid of cognitive strategies. These strategies included cognitive defusion (detached mindfulness from negative thoughts) and placing positive coping statements on index cards to review during stressful meals. Elizabeth had completed all feared foods from her AAH; however, upon resumption of school after summer break, she expressed fear of eating certain foods in social situations. The next few sessions focused on Elizabeth completing food exposures based on a new AAH comprised specifically of foods she might eat at parties or related gatherings. Elizabeth was encouraged to approach these via systematic desensitization, and she worked her way up from eating lunches prepared at home to eating cafeteria food daily. She gained an additional pound and reported a noticeable decrease in her anxiety, commenting that she felt much more "free" to eat a variety of foods than she ever had in the past. Further, around this time, Elizabeth experienced a return of menses.

Case Example: Phase 3

This phase consisted of three sessions that entirely focused on managing anxiety issues unrelated to the eating disorder and relapse prevention. Elizabeth described more generalized anxiety around school, exams, and friendships. The therapist reviewed many of the anxiety management tools covered in Phase 2 (self-monitoring, cognitive therapy). The final session included a review of Elizabeth's progress and a discussion of what her parents could do should any symptoms of her eating disorder reoccur.

At the end of the intervention, Elizabeth was able to eat regularly with varied nourishment. She no longer met the DSM-IV criteria for an Eating Disorder Not Otherwise Specified (EDNOS) and weighed 106.2 lbs. (BMI = 20.1).

Summary and Future Directions

FBT-E draws on an evolving understanding of how specific types of anxiety maintain disturbances in eating, shape, and weight as well as an improved understanding of how deficits in reward processing may reduce motivation to change. This family-based treatment uses exposure techniques delivered by parents to catalyze change in eating disorder symptoms and instructs parents to utilize associative conditioning and contingency management to improve motivation and solidify changes in behavior. Initial evidence from our group suggests that patients and their families can tolerate this intervention and that it leads to increased weight and reduced anxiety (Hildebrandt, Bacow & Greif, in press). Future research will need to examine its efficacy in comparison to a credible control condition, as well as in comparison to traditional FBT. In addition, basic research into FBT-E treatment mechanisms will help to find creative ways to enhance the potency of this intervention.

References

Abbate-Daga, G., Buzzichelli, S., Marzola, E., Amianto, F., & Fassino, S. (2012). Effectiveness of cognitive remediation therapy (CRT) in anorexia nervosa: A case series. *Journal of Clinical and Experimental Neuropsychology, 34*(10), 1009–1015. doi: 10.1080/13803395.2012.704900

Bar, K. J., Berger, S., Schwier, C., Wutzler, U., & Beissner, F. (2013). Insular dysfunction and descending pain inhibition in anorexia nervosa. [Research Support, Non-U.S. Gov't]. *Acta Psychiatr Scand, 127*(4), 269–278. doi: 10.1111/j.1600-0447.2012.01896.x

Chapman, H. A., & Anderson, A. K. (2012). Understanding disgust. *Annals of the New York Academy of Sciences, 1251*, 62–76. doi: 10.1111/j.1749-6632.2011.06369.x

Cisler, J. M., Olatunji, B. O., & Lohr, J. M. (2009). Disgust, fear, and the anxiety disorders: A critical review. *Clinical Psychology Review, 29*(1), 34–46. doi: 10.1016/j.cpr.2008.09.007

de Jong, P. J., van Overveld, M., & Peters, M. L. (2011). Sympathetic and parasympathetic responses to a core disgust video clip as a function of disgust propensity and disgust sensitivity. *Biological Psychology, 88*(2–3), 174–179. doi: 10.1016/j.biopsycho.2011.07.009

Fairburn, C. G., & Beglin, S. J. (1994). Assessment of eating disorders: Interview or self-report questionnaire? *International Journal of Eating Disorders, 16*(4), 363–370. doi: 10.1002/1098-108X(199412)16:4<363::AID-EAT2260160405>3.0.CO;2-#

Frank, G. K., Roblek, T., Shott, M. E., Jappe, L. M., Rollin, M. D., Hagman, J. O., & Pryor, T. (2012). Heightened fear of uncertainty in anorexia and bulimia nervosa. [Research Support, N.I.H., Extramural Research Support, Non-U.S. Gov't]. *Int J Eat Disord, 45*(2), 227–232. doi: 10.1002/eat.20929

Fusar-Poli, P., Placentino, A., Carletti, F., Landi, P., Allen, P., Surguladze, S., ... Politi, P. (2009). Functional atlas of emotional faces processing: A voxel-based meta-analysis of 105 functional magnetic resonance imaging studies. *Journal of Psychiatry & Neuroscience, 34*(6), 418–432.

Hildebrandt, T., Bacow, T. L., Markella, M., & Loeb, K. L. (2012). Anxiety in anorexia nervosa and its management using family-based treatment. *European Eating Disorders Review, 20*(1), e1–16. doi: 10.1002/erv.1071

Hildebrandt, T., Bacow, T. L., & Greif, R. (in press). Exposure-based family behavioral therapy (FBT-E): An open case series of a new treatment for anorexia nervosa. *Cognitive and Behavioral Practice.*

Hoehn-Saric, R., & McLeod, D. R. (2000). Anxiety and arousal: Physiological changes and their perception. *Journal of Affective Disorders, 61*(3), 217–224.

Hoyer, J., Beesdo, K., Gloster, A. T., Runge, J., Hofler, M., & Becker, E. S. (2009). Worry exposure versus applied relaxation in the treatment of generalized anxiety disorder. *Psychotherapy and Psychosomatics, 78*(2), 106–115. doi: 10.1159/000201936

Kaye, W. (2008). Neurobiology of anorexia and bulimia nervosa. *Physiology & Behavior, 94*(1), 121–135. doi: S0031-9384(07)00463-5 [pii] 10.1016/j.physbeh.2007.11.037

Keating, C. (2010). Theoretical perspective on anorexia nervosa: The conflict of reward. *Neurosci Biobehav Rev, 34*(1), 73–79. doi: 10.1016/j.neubiorev.2009.07.004 S0149-7634(09)00101-8 [pii]

Keating, C., Tilbrook, A. J., Rossell, S. L., Enticott, P. G., & Fitzgerald, P. B. (2012). Reward processing in anorexia nervosa. [Research Support, Non-U.S. Gov't Review]. *Neuropsychologia, 50*(5), 567–575. doi: 10.1016/j.neuropsychologia.2012.01.036

Keel, P. K., & Brown, T. A. (2010). Update on course and outcome in eating disorders. *International Journal of Eating Disorders, 43*(3), 195–204. doi: 10.1002/eat.20810

Kendall, P. C., & Hedtke, K. A. (2006). *Coping cat workbook (Child therapy workbooks series)* (2nd ed.), Ardmore, PA: Workbook Publishing.

Le Grange, D., Lock, J., Agras, W. S., Moye, A., Bryson, S. W., Jo, B., & Kraemer, H. C. (2012). Moderators and mediators of remission in family-based treatment and adolescent focused therapy for anorexia nervosa. [Multicenter Study Randomized Controlled Trial Research Support, N.I.H., Extramural Research Support, Non-U.S. Gov't]. *Behav Res Ther, 50*(2), 85–92. doi: 10.1016/j.brat.2011.11.003

Lock, J., & Le Grange, D. (2013). *Treatment manual for anorexia nervosa: A family-based approach* (2nd ed.). New York, NY: Guilford Press.

Loeb, K. L., Lock, J., Le Grange, D. L., & Greif, R. (2012). Transdiagnostic theory and application of family-based treatment for youth with eating disorders. *Cognitive & Behavioral Practice, 19*(1), 17–30. doi: 10.1016/j.cbpra.2010.04.005

Macleod, C. (2012). Cognitive bias modification procedures in the management of mental disorders. *Current Opinion in Psychiatry, 25*(2), 114–120. doi: 10.1097/YCO.0b013e32834fda4a

March, J. S., & Benson, C. M. (2006). *Talking back to OCD: The program that helps kids and teens say "no way"—and parents say "way to go."* New York, NY: Guilford Press.

Misslin, R. (2003). The defense system of fear: Behavior and neurocircuitry. *Clinical Neurophysiology, 33*(2), 55–66.

Murphy, R., Straebler, S., Cooper, Z., & Fairburn, C. G. (2010). Cognitive behavioral therapy for eating disorders. [Research Support, Non-U.S. Gov't Review]. *Psychiatr Clin North Am, 33*(3), 611–627. doi: 10.1016/j.psc.2010.04.004

Nunn, K., Frampton, I., Fuglset, T. S., Torzsok-Sonnevend, M., & Lask, B. (2011). Anorexia nervosa and the insula. *Medical Hypotheses, 76*(3), 353–357. doi: 10.1016/j.mehy.2010.10.038

Olatunji, B. O., Smits, J. A., Connolly, K., Willems, J., & Lohr, J. M. (2007). Examination of the decline in fear and disgust during exposure to threat-relevant stimuli in blood-injection-injury phobia. *Journal of Anxiety Disorders, 21*(3), 445–455. doi: 10.1016/j.janxdis.2006.05.001

Pincus, D. B., Ehrenreich, J .T., & Spiegel, D. A. (2008). *Riding the wave workbook (treatments that work).* New York: Oxford University Press.

Shafran, R., Lee, M., Cooper, Z., Palmer, R. L., & Fairburn, C. G. (2008). Effect of psychological treatment on attentional bias in eating disorders. [Research Support, Non-U.S. Gov't]. *Int J Eat Disord, 41*(4), 348–354. doi: 10.1002/eat.20500

Siep, N., Jansen, A., Havermans, R., & Roefs, A. (2011). Cognitions and emotions in eating disorders. *Current Topics in Behavioral Neuroscience, 6*, 17–33. doi: 10.1007/7854_2010_82

Starcevic, V., & Berle, D. (2006). Cognitive specificity of anxiety disorders: A review of selected key constructs. *Depression and Anxiety, 23*(2), 51–61. doi: 10.1002/da.20145

Steinglass, J. E., Sysko, R., Glasofer, D., Albano, A. M., Simpson, H. B., & Walsh, B. T. (2011). Rationale for the application of exposure and response prevention to the treatment of anorexia nervosa. *International Journal of Eating Disorders, 44*(2), 134–141. doi: 10.1002/eat.20784

Strober, M. (2004). Pathologic fear conditioning and anorexia nervosa: On the search for novel paradigms. *International Journal of Eating Disorders, 35*(4), 504–508. doi: 10.1002/eat.20029

Viar-Paxton, M. A., & Olatunji, B. O. (2012). Context effects on bituation to disgust-relevant stimuli. *Behavior Modification, 36*(5), 705–722. doi: 10.1177/0145445512446189

Watson, H. J., & Bulik, C. M. (2013). Update on the treatment of anorexia nervosa: Review of clinical trials, practice guidelines and emerging interventions. *Psychological Medicine, 43*(12), 2477–2500. doi: 10.1017/S0033291712002620

Wilson, G. T., Grilo, C. M., & Vitousek, K. M. (2007). Psychological treatment of eating disorders. *American Psychologist, 62*(3), 199–216. doi: 10.1037/0003-066X.62.3.199

Chapter 7

Multi-Family Therapy

Mima Simic and Ivan Eisler

Therapeutic interventions delivered to a number of families at the same time in a multi-family setting have been used for the last six decades in the treatment of a variety of psychiatric and medical disorders as well as for families with high levels of social problems and risk of breakdown in adult, adolescent, and child populations (Asen & Scholz 2010; Laquer, La Burt, & Morong, 1964; McDonell & Dyck, 2004; O'Shea & Phelps, 1985; Steinglass, 1998). Despite the differences in theoretical models of interventions used in Multi-Family Therapy (MFT), as well as in participant populations and settings, benefits have been reported in improvement of the patient's symptoms, reduction of relapse and re-hospitalization rates, improvement in family communication and functioning, reduced family caregiver distress, increased social and vocational functioning, overcoming stigmatization and social isolation, and improving the collaboration among patient, family, and clinicians (Asen, 2002; McFarlane, 2002; Scholz et al., 2005; Steinglass, 1998). In addition, it has been suggested that MFT may be a more cost-effective alternative to other forms of treatment (Asen, 2002).

Involving families in treatment is particularly important for young people who often still live with, and have regular contact with, their family. Family treatments for Anorexia Nervosa (AN) have been recommended by international and national guidelines and endorsed by many reviewers (American Psychiatric Association, 2006; Bulik et al., 2007; Downs & Blow, 2013; National Institute of Clinical Excellence, 2004; Yager et al., 2012) and evidence suggests that AN-focused Family Therapy (FT-AN) (Eisler, Wallis, & Dodge, this volume) is a first-line treatment for the disorder. Multi-Family Therapy for Anorexia Nervosa (MFT-AN) draws on the principles and is an extension of FT-AN.

Development of Multi-Family Therapy for Anorexia Nervosa (MFT-AN)

For the last three decades, the Child and Adolescent Eating Disorders Service (CAEDS) at the Maudsley Hospital, London, has had extensive experience in treating severely ill patients with AN in an outpatient setting using FT-AN as the main therapeutic approach (Eisler, Simic, & team, 2012). Over time, concerns were raised that FT-AN was not intensive or safe enough to meet the needs of the subgroup of the most severely ill AN patients, but by the same token, the only other available alternative (inpatient treatment) was not deemed to always be the most effective and beneficial treatment because it disempowered patients' families, did not allow parents to learn ways of managing their child's anorexic behaviors, and there was evidence of high levels of relapse postdischarge from the hospital (Lay et al., 2002; Strober et al., 1997). MFT-AN was developed in 1999, concurrently in London and Dresden (Dare & Eisler, 2000; Scholz & Asen, 2001), as an alternative to inpatient admission for a subgroup of very ill anorexic children and adolescents.

The hope was that if FT-AN interventions were intensified and modified, delivered for at least six hours per day for four to five consecutive treatment days, within a therapeutic setting that includes five to seven families simultaneously, the level of change that could be potentially achieved would be enough to provide a realistic alternative to inpatient treatment. MFT-AN is conceptually an extension of FT-AN (Eisler, Simic, & team, 2012), which aims to strengthen the sense of self-efficacy in families and maximize their own resources to overcome their child's eating disorder. The overarching goal of MFT-AN is to enhance the speed of change, enable rapid improvement of anorexic symptomatology, and secure physical safety brought about with adequate and regular weight gain as a necessary prerequisite for recovery from AN. The collaborative environment of MFT is also an effective way of reducing the potential for the development of deleterious staff–patient relationships that can otherwise seriously hamper the progress of treatment (Scholz & Asen, 2001).

MFT-AN Theoretical Concepts

The MFT-AN integrates theoretical concepts of single FT-AN (Dare et al., 1990; Eisler, 2005; Eisler, Lock, & Le Grange, 2010; Eisler, Wallis, & Dodge, this volume) with more general concepts of MFT (Asen & Scholtz, 2010; Dare & Eisler, 2000; Simic & Eisler, 2012). FT-AN was developed and modified over the years by CAEDS clinicians at The Maudsley Hospital, London (Eisler, Simic, & team, 2012). The therapeutic model has four phases, the main goals of which are in Phase 1 to engage and develop the therapeutic alliance with the patient and his or her family; in Phase 2 to help the family to challenge the eating disorder; in Phase 3 to explore issues of individual and family development; and in Phase 4 to complete work around therapeutic endings and discussion of future plans for the patient and his or her family (Eisler, 2005).

The delivery of the intensified four phases of FT-AN interventions in a multi-family setting helps families to overcome a sense of isolation and stigmatization. Families that are brought together in MFT share their experiences, learn by example, and create new and multiple perspectives permitting them to learn from one another (Scholz & Asen, 2001;

Simic & Eisler, 2012). Asen and Scholz (2010) have described the MFT milieu as a creation of a "hothouse" learning environment in which it is safe to practice new behaviors, have new experiences, and express emotions. MFT is a highly integrative approach, which incorporates a broad range of systemic, cognitive, psychodynamic, and group therapy conceptualizations and intervention techniques.

MFT-AN Participants

The MFT-AN group consists of five to seven families, all with a young person suffering with AN, atypical AN, or Avoidant Restrictive Food Intake Disorder (ARFID), and a therapeutic team. In MFT-AN at the Maudsley Hospital, 10 MFT days are offered over the course of nine months to one year. Treatment starts with an introductory afternoon prior to four full consecutive days of therapy followed by six one-day follow-ups. The MFT group is a closed group, with the expectation that families attend both the intensive consecutive four days of treatment and subsequent one-day follow-up meetings. Follow-up days are initially more frequent, but then their frequency gets spread out, with typically a three-month gap between the last two follow-up meetings. Individual family sessions continue between follow-ups, and their frequency is dependent on the specific needs of each particular family.

Another conceptually very similar MFT model was developed around the same time at the University of Dresden, Germany (Scholz et al., 2005) using a somewhat different structure that offers 20 days of MFT; two-day follow-up meetings follow initial five consecutive days of treatment. Moreover, in Dresden no single-family therapy is offered in between MFT follow-up meetings. More recently, other centers have also started implementing MFT programs: Fleminger (2005) in the Netherlands; Hollesen, Clausen, and Rokkedal (2013) in Denmark; Marzola et al. (submitted) in San Diego; Mehl et al. (2013) in Prague; Rhodes et al. (2008); Wallis et al. (2013) in Sydney; Depestele and Vandereycken (2009); Depestele, Claes, and Lemmens (2014) in Belgium; Girz et al. (2013) in Toronto. The University of California, San Diego (UCSD) MFT program is of particular interest in that it provides just a brief intensive weeklong treatment with no further follow-up and has reported preliminary promising results at a three-year follow-up.

Young people and their families who join the MFT group are expected to be in different phases of treatment, in different stages of their illness with variable levels of motivation toward recovery. Variability has certain advantages and allows families and young people who are early in treatment or who have not made much progress to witness that change is possible. MFT interventions support mutual observation and reflections that promote insight into the eating disorder and its effects on people's lives and reduce the possibility of denial with many of the young people quickly finding ways of acknowledging that they have problems that they would like to overcome. For families and young people in later phases of treatment, observing consequences of anorexic symptoms in others can reinforce motivation not to go back into the life-suffocating grip of anorexia and build further on the changes they have already achieved.

MFT enables manifold perspectives by making use of various group constellations (whole multi-family group, parents/adolescents/sibling only groups or separate groups for mothers and fathers, run in parallel with the separate groups for young people and siblings) and multiple treatment contexts (formal treatment sessions using a variety of verbal and nonverbal interventions and informal breaks during the day). There are also tasks that each family works on individually or in which the young person discusses the issues with the parents from other families ("foster" family groups) before meeting together to discuss in the larger group. For a detailed structure of the first four days, see Table 1; description of the content of the groups in more detail will follow later. The authors of this chapter, in preparation for write-up, asked families who had completed treatment in different MFT groups to reflect on their experiences of the range of MFT exercises. The extracts from their feedback are included after descriptions of the various MFT exercises.

The MFT Team

Each MFT group is facilitated by two lead therapists who may be joined by other members of the multidisciplinary team including trainees in family therapy, psychology, and psychiatry. The MFT team meets regularly at the beginning and end of each therapy day but also 20 minutes during lunch break, or at any other break if review and reflection of the therapy process is deemed necessary. The team uses peer supervision as much as is required during the therapy days to ensure that safety and containment of the group is maintained, the group process understood, and that best-fit interventions/activities/role-plays for the current needs of the particular groups of families are used. Peer supervision is also used to share feedback from the interventions that team members have done during mealtimes with different families. While the team conversations take place away from the family, the process is very transparent and the team will often feedback their conversations to the families.

MFT therapists clearly convey the message to the group that they as a team own the expertise in eating disorders. However, they are equally clear about the limitations of their knowledge and always invite families to consider how relevant specific advice might be for them. Therapists also need to be self-reflective of the impact of being in the position of expert (e.g., reinforcing a sense of dependency on professionals) but they should not assume that these could be avoided by simply adopting a more neutral position. Use of humor, informality, and appropriate limited self-disclosures by therapists (c.f. a good discussion of the risks and potential benefits of therapist self-disclosure; Roberts, 2005) are an important ingredient in engaging families and promoting a more relaxed interactional flow in the group either during the formal group time or in breaks between the groups.

Table 7.1 Content of the First Four Multi-Family Therapy Days

Time	Day 1	Day 2	Day 3	Day 4
10–11am	• Introductions • Hopes and expectations of MFT	• Food plates-making symbolic Sunday lunch	• Family sculpts	• Family timeline with individual families
11–11:30am	Snack	Snack	Snack	Snack
11:30–1pm	• Portraits of AN (YP only) • Pros and cons for AN (YP only) • Lunch preparation (parents)	• Role reversal mealtime role-play	• Separate groups • Shield against AN (YP only) • Siblings' group • Parents' group	• Sharing timelines with other families
1–2pm	Lunch	Lunch-foster families	Lunch	Lunch
2–3pm	• Feedback from lunch • YP present portraits and pros and cons for AN to the whole group	• Feedback from the lunch with foster family • Internalizing other interview	• "Traps and Treasures" family game	• Toolbox to fight AN (separate groups: mothers, fathers, YP)
3–3:30pm	Snack	Snack	Snack	Snack
3:30–4pm	• Mindfulness or guided imagery relaxation exercise	• Mindfulness exercise	• Visualization of a relaxed place	• Feedback and planning of future follow-up

Abbreviations: Anorexia Nervosa: AN; Multi-Family Therapy: MFT; Young Person: YP

MFT Content

Introductory Afternoon

The MFT team meets all the families who will attend MFT for the first time at the introductory afternoon. This is a relatively formal session, held for 90 minutes on one afternoon in the week prior to the first four MFT days. The initial formality of the setting is achieved through setting up the seating like in a lecture theater with the therapy team sitting in one row facing the MFT participants. In the first part of the afternoon, the MFT team gives information about the structure of MFT days, the rationale for the treatment, an introduction to the therapy team, followed by a psychoeducational lecture on the effects of starvation, physical consequences of AN, and its prognosis. Alternatively, the team at the UCSD Eating Disorder Center starts their intensive one-week MFT program with a psychoeducational lecture on the temperament of the young people at risk of developing an eating disorder.

In the description of the therapy days, the MFT team emphasizes that joint meals are a key aspect of treatment. Prior to the MFT, the patient has been assessed with her or his family, and in most cases they have already engaged in the single FT-AN. For most families, but definitely for families where parents are unsure how much the young person should eat in order to gain weight or if the parents and anorexic child find themselves engaged in endless, destructive battles about how much and what kind of food the child should eat, a meal plan is developed in collaboration with dieticians. The meal plan is presented to the family often accompanied by a metaphor of it being like a medical prescription: "Food is medicine and the meal plan is a prescription how you take the medicine." Meal plans can play a useful purpose early on in treatment because they help provide structure and predictability that both parents and young people at this stage find reassuring. Therapists, however, need to be clear about the time-limited nature of this and that for young people who are in the later stages of treatment. It is crucial that meals have to become flexible usually at first by modifying and later abandoning the meal plan that is negotiated among patient, parents, and therapist and where relevant also involving the dietician (Eisler, Simic, & team, 2012).

During the MFT introductory afternoon, parents are instructed to bring food for snacks and lunches that they are expecting their child to have or according to the meal plan their child has been "prescribed." In order to promote engagement, it is important to acknowledge that it is likely that families will find multi-family meals quite challenging and at the same time the team conveys confidence that they have sufficient experience to support families to manage meals safely and to make it a useful learning context for families in how they can increase their effectiveness in helping their child in the process of recovery. The clear expectation is set from the start that young people eating what has been "prescribed" to them is an achievable goal in the MFT group.

In the second part of the afternoon the young people and their families are given an opportunity to talk to a "graduate family" who has previously completed the MFT and is either in the final phase of treatment or has recently completed it. In separated groups mothers, fathers, and young people meet with their contra parts from the "graduated" family who share with them their experiences of attending MFT, and the stepping stones of their journey through treatment toward recovery. It is not uncommon that listening to the experiences of the family who were once in their "shoes," but where the young person has much improved or even recovered from anorexia and has positive attitudes about the possibility that parents can help in the process of recovery, renews hope and enthusiasm for at least the parents who will be attending the new MFT group. The young people are often more skeptical but longer-term follow-ups suggest that many of them are at least sufficiently intrigued by hearing the account of MFT from the "graduate" young person to begin to consider that recovery might be possible although it generally takes some time before they can acknowledge this (Alexander & Eisler, in press).

A quote from a parent's feedback on how the introductory afternoon impacted their family follows:

> "Meeting with a "graduate family" in the week before we began gave us hope before it even started. That family said that they too hadn't known what to expect but that their daughter had benefitted. I think the term family therapy was a bit off-putting as you worry that a judgment will be made on you, but that turned out not to be the case. It is reassuring knowing how other families are dealing with the situation and definitely good to feel you have experts that can give advice and their thoughts."

First Four Days of MFT-AN

As stated previously, MFT-AN is based on FT-AN with the first four days of the group predominantly following and intensifying interventions and goals from the Phase 1 and 2 of FT-AN treatment. By the end of the fourth day, the aim is to introduce new time frames and a tentative vision of the future. Subsequent follow-up days combine Phases 2 and 3 of FT-AN with usually the last two follow-ups covering goals and interventions of the fourth phase focused on the ending of treatment. Though MFT therapists usually follow quite a similar structure of exercises in the first four days of MFT, the aim is for the structure to remain flexible and the therapists might decide to change the order, or the combination of exercises, in order to better address the specific dynamic of the particular MFT group.

Every MFT group is unique, and this is even more obvious in the follow-up days when exercises will vary greatly to reflect the specific stage of treatment or specific problems that differ from group to group. Through structured exercises families generate and share different ideas that can lead toward recovery from the eating disorder, while at the same time providing each other with mutual support.

Main Goals/Interventions in the First Four MFT Days

1   *Intensifying externalization/increasing insight into the illness*

A number of exercises in the first two days are specifically designed to intensify externalization, increase insight into the illness, and address motivation to change like the **Role Reversal Mealtime, Portraits of Anorexia,** and **Pros and Cons of AN.** All of these exercises tackle denial, promote realization and understanding of the seriousness of the illness, and serve as a reality check to families participating in the group.

The **Portraits of AN** exercise supports externalization of the illness, an intervention in which anorexic behaviors and cognitions are labeled as separate from the young person. Usually families respond positively to this separation of anorexic symptoms from the young person and may describe AN as having an intrusive "voice" that impacts/controls the young person's behavior. For some young people this exercise can be challenging, as they have either not yet accepted that they are unwell or find it difficult to acknowledge to others and can struggle with portraying AN as an entity separate from themselves. In this exercise young people, in a separate group from their parents, are instructed by group facilitators to think about how they would portray AN and to illustrate this in whatever way makes sense to them (draw write, use play dough or any other material).

This exercise gives an opportunity for the young people to get to know one another and to talk about their experiences of the illness, which in turn enables better understanding of the illness for the whole group. At the end of the exercise young people are encouraged to think about how they would like to present their "portraits of anorexia" to the whole MFT group. In nearly all instances even those who deny that they suffer from anorexia will complete the exercise and join in the discussion with the other young people.

Feedback from families:

Young person:

> "*I started believing I have a problem … just by what everyone else was saying here, because I could relate to it, and I thought that's what I feel … I could not see that before … I was surprised because I thought there was nothing wrong with me. I just thought I had an obsession with dieting.*"

Parent:

> *"It was good to see that the young people were aware of the very negative impact the illness was having on the family. Until that point the young person came across as selfish with no thought for the damage and hurt it was doing around them. However, this exercise does show that the young person, separated from their anorexic demon, does understand the damage being done to their family, but their anorexic demon/thoughts are so all consuming and focused that they are trapped within their own body/mind and are powerless to stop their negative behavior."*

Role reversal mealtime exercise is a role-play of a lunchtime, with the parent being instructed to take on the role of an anorexic young person who is finding mealtime very difficult and the young person taking the role of the parent instructed to do whatever they feel they should to get the "anorexic child" to eat. People from other families are invited into the role-play to support/consult the young person playing the "parent" and a member of MFT team plays a "voice of anorexia" amplifying from a whisper to a much louder volume, enacting externalization of the anorexic cognitions while being positioned on the side of the parent role-playing an anorexic youngster.

This exercise can be highly revealing for parents and young people as they face the extent of the struggle encountered, in being/feeding, an anorexic child. For parents, the role-play usually increases their understanding of the competing "voices" that their child is facing when eating. For young people, it can help them to appreciate the efforts that their parents are putting into feeding them. Parental mirroring of anorexic behavior is often met with laughter; however, it also opens a new perspective for young people to reflect on their illness behavior. Families find the role reversal very powerful, especially when the facilitators encourage gradual intensification of behavioral patterns in the role-play. The enactment of the voice of anorexia is usually immensely potent both for those in the role-play and those observing. The therapist facilitating the subsequent discussion will always check with all the young people to what extent they feel that the enactment represents what it is like for them. Most will generally acknowledge that it is an accurate representation of their experience, although it is always helpful to hear from young people about the nuances of their subjective experience of the anorexic cognitions.

Feedback from families on the mealtime role reversal exercise:

Young people:

> *"It was difficult—one of the hardest activities but most useful."*

> *"Helped me understand what it feels like to be my mum. How helpless and frustrated she must feel when pushing me to eat."*

"*Reinforced my motives for recovery, having observed the other patients and realizing, as an outsider, the effects of the illness.*"

Parents:

"*Very enlightening and useful. Did think there was a dawning on the young people and that they could see their actions in a different light, possibly because the parents acted all the worst scenarios in one go. Also useful to see how the young people thought they would feel as the parents, as they could appreciate the worry the parents felt rather than just feeling nagged. The parents acting as the young person again gives an awareness into how it must feel. It was good all round although quite a stressful one in a way.*"

"*This exercise was a real ice-breaker with the girls getting a real sense of how difficult and frustrating it was to be the parent. It caused quite a bit of laughter generally and many of the parents recognized the situations. I got great pleasure in being my daughter and giving her responses back to her ... it was very cathartic!*"

"*This was a very powerful exercise and the timing of it being done early in the four-day block was good. This was the first time a real insight into how awful this illness is and what the young people have to endure. The psychologist then playing anorexia (on shoulder of adult), was very emotional and again powerful, especially when they asked the young people in the room what anorexia was saying to them—'obese' was the word I know my daughter said at that point, but was also a word commonly used by my daughter before that during our many mealtime fights so I knew the scenario was an accurate reflection. This exercise was the dawning moment to my daughter that she had the illness as she recognized the scenario and was able to contribute.*"

2   *Exploring the impact of the illness on families*

In the initial phases of treatment, parents often have prevailing feelings of helplessness, hopelessness, and disempowerment. They often disbelieve that they can do something different or, even more so, to manage their child's disorder. At the same time, the young person often denies that they have a disorder. The therapeutic setting needs to provide the exhausted parents enough therapeutic sustenance for them to become reenergized and start believing that they can do something to help their child recover. The important part of treatment in this phase is to explore the role that anorexia has acquired in the management of emotions, feelings, and interpersonal relationships. This is particularly important if there has been no progress in weight gain. Such explorations should be focused on investigating how family interactions and relationships have changed around AN.

The MFT exercise that serves this purpose most visibly is the **Family sculpt** role-play in which the young person makes a 'sculpt' of the family relationships at particular points in time.

The MFT therapist invites the young person from the family the team has chosen, to become a "sculptor" and make a sculpture of their own family using other members of the group. The therapists ask the "sculptor" to place the family members however close or distant and in whatever pose that conveys how things were in their family before AN entered their life. Subsequently a new "sculpt" is instructed, moving family members into the positions they assumed with the arrival of AN, also introducing into the sculpt a member of MFT team as a personification of anorexia. The whole group participates in this strikingly visual exercise that brings powerful emotions followed by discussion and reflection on changes that all families have experienced due to the illness. The way in which the sculpt is developed may vary depending on the therapist's judgment of what is most relevant for the particular family. For instance, instead of comparing before, during, and after anorexia, a comparison may emerge between different perceptions of different family members.

The therapist may at some point invite the family members who are observing their own family being sculpted using other members of the group to "step in to the sculpture" to experience what it is like. When anorexia is introduced into the sculpture, the tension often increases considerably and the therapist might encourage the family members to respond if they wish (*"Sometimes sculptures come alive and begin to move"*). The therapist needs to be mindful of the very powerful emotions that are nearly always generated and if necessary, if the feelings become overwhelming, to shorten the exercise. Feedback from Families:

> *"Family sculpt is, I think, the most useful task. It was so visual and really made everyone think about what anorexia had done to the whole family, how it had isolated not only the girls but siblings and parents from each other too. It was there for all to see and the cure obvious. I liked the way in which the task was structured making the girls and parents work through gently. I don't think for a second that until then I had realized how divisive anorexia had and was being."*

> *"It was a powerful and emotional visual of what life was like before anorexia (i.e., happy and doing fun family things together), to how anorexia changes the family dynamic (i.e., angry and stressed parents and siblings keeping away from the unit/the stress)."*

> *"We were lucky enough to be one of only two families to do this. Ideally all the families should have had a go as each one revealed something unique."*

> *"The scene we sculpted that was then described back to us by staff and families was truly revelatory. Being a three-dimensional experience*

added a theatricality and sense of place that words couldn't match in their evocation of the emotions revealed—the physical separation of the parents and child when eating. I think this session also had a real effect on our daughter too—she also hadn't realized what we had been doing."

3   *Trying out new behaviors, eliciting new responses to AN symptoms*

The multi-family setting is a therapeutic laboratory where richness of multiple perspectives opens new horizons for families and generates new experiences. Therapists encourage MFT participants to experiment and try new things. The key component of MFT treatment are mealtimes, as at the beginning of treatment for most of MFT families, mealtimes are perceived as a battlefield usually controlled and dominated by anorexic symptoms that are the most disturbing part of the illness with a major impact on family life. In MFT, families have lunches and snacks together during which therapists intervene. While there is a clear expectation that the young people will eat during MFT mealtimes, the more important aim is for the families to try new ways of managing mealtimes. While initially the joint meals are difficult, for most families they quickly open up discussions about how the experience can be used to move forward interactional patterns and parental supervision into a more helpful and beneficial arena. The therapists take an active role, reinforcing positive parenting roles and being in charge of meal supervision, suggesting alternative strategies that can involve both parents but at the same time empathizing with the young person's predicament. After the meal, the interactive processes around food should be discussed in a matter-of-fact, non-judgmental way coupled with exploration of how patterns evolved over time and how they can move forward.

The aim of these discussions is to emphasize that all families get caught up in the processes around anorexia, which has the effect of preventing them from using their strengths to effectively support their ill child to eat. Therapists might also suggest some options (using distraction during meals) or rules around mealtimes (e.g., no negotiation around food during mealtime) and give examples of what other families have done. It is also important to avoid making the young person constantly mindful of eating and it is potentially useful to enquire about what kind of distraction techniques the young person finds helpful. Therapists might also explore how parents work together, how they deal with differences between themselves, emphasizing that all parents have different perspectives but when faced with something as serious as AN, they may need to develop a more united stance than usual in order to prevent anorexia from splitting them. Parental difference can also be explored as a potential resource for more effective meal supervision. As with all other MFT activities, it is crucial to ensure that the young people's voices are heard when processing the experience of MFT mealtimes once the meal is finished.

Feedback from parent:

> *"The lunches during the weeklong Multi-Family Workshop were instrumental in challenging and then shifting many of our daughter's ingrained anorexic eating fads. The simple act of bringing in food, storing it in the kitchen, and then eating our picnic lunches together every day was one of the most important and effective parts of the MFT."*

Usually, on the second MFT day in order to promote experimentation and break the fixed patterns around mealtimes, the therapists set up for the young people to have lunch with a "foster" family. In the lunchtime with the "foster" family the young person has lunch supervised by parents from two other MFT families allocated to the young person by the therapists. "Foster" parents are instructed by relevant parents what the child is expected to eat. Therapists emphasize that the aim of the exercise is to give an opportunity to all of them to try something different. It is explained that the focus of the exercise is on increasing flexibility in parental attempts to feed the child and tapping into their strengths and skills that may have become lost when faced with a long battle of supervising their own child's mealtime.

Parents will often report that feeding another child is an entirely different experience from feeding their own. They tend to take more risks and try things they no longer feel able to do with their own child. Also, young people appear to be more compliant with other adults than with their own parents, responding in a more cooperative way to the encouragement of "foster" parents. Parents feel encouraged when observing their child being able to respond differently during meal supervision by "foster" parents; by the same token, their confidence gets boosted realizing that they are able to feed somebody else's anorexic child.

The young people often have reservations about trying out the "foster meal," but the majority comment positively afterwards. Paradoxically, while most of them will acknowledge that they need their parents to encourage them to eat, the most common comments about the "foster meal" is that they appreciated not being nagged or watched all the time. Because the predictable routines that normally trap the whole family are unavailable, new interactions emerge and both young person and parents can learn what is helpful in managing the fear of eating. This is often a useful opportunity to discuss how and what type of distraction works best for each of them. The discussions of "foster meals" are often more light-hearted (*"I'm swapping my parents with yours ... they're much nicer!"*).

Feedback on Foster Family exercise

> *"This was a good way to get to know the other parents and young people in our MFT group. Although it might have been really scary for*

the young people, it was reassuring to see someone else's child doing the same thing as your own. It helped endorse this is a known illness/ pattern of behavior and that we were in the right place (the Maudsley) to work towards recovery."

"This was an extremely powerful tool, to challenge the strict and bizarre food choices that the girls were adhering to, such as a certain brand of crisp or a precisely measured amount of juice. The success was probably achieved by the staff, who lingered around asking useful questions, rather than the "foster" parents, but it was enabled by the girls not sitting with their parents, away from their comfort zone, or their enabling-parents zone. It also gave me a chance to get to know one of the other girls in an informal way, which was useful. Perhaps adding a certain level of trust both ways that helped once we were back in a session."

New experiences in the ability to successfully navigate the difficulties around mealtimes have a strong effect on the young person, showing them that the meals are not just about who is in control, and gives parents an increased sense of self-efficacy. Parents perceive that jointly the therapists, with the rest of group participants, are giving them permission to exercise positive parental authority resulting in strengthening parental roles.

The way in which families manage mealtimes during MFT varies from family to family and from group to group, but generally, most families will quickly establish a way of managing to help their child to eat and often by day three or four the need for the therapists to be very active during the MFT meals diminishes, at which point the therapists may join the families in a more social way and eat their lunch with them. A key factor in how quickly this happens appears to be the therapists' confidence in the parents being able to manage and the way in which they convey their expectation to the families.

4   *Increasing reciprocal empathy and trust*

For most families, participating in the MFT means talking openly with other people in the group in a way that the family may have not been able to do for some time. Often families report that attending MFT has helped them to reduce their sense of guilt and isolation and gave them the sense of belonging and being understood. Some MFT exercises such as the **Internalized Other Interview** and **Traps and Treasures** are developed to increase empathy between young people and parents and feelings of reciprocity between family members. The hope is that increased empathy and reciprocity will improve relationships and communication within the family.

In the **Internalized Other Interview,** either the parents are asked to take on the role of their children or the young people are interviewed as their parents by a therapist about life with anorexia while they are observed by the rest of the group (usually from behind a one-way screen or a video link). Those observing are invariably surprised how much the person role-playing them knows about how they feel. This exercise provides excellent opportunities to say things that are otherwise left unsaid (for instance, a young person who is still vehemently denying that she has an eating disorder may say [in role as her parent]: *"I think she knows she has anorexia but she finds it too difficult to admit"*). The ambiguity of whether what is being said is the person's perception of what the other would say, or in fact their own view, adds to the richness and multiplicity of perspectives that are central to MFT. Feedback from families:

"Another good one for empathizing with the other family members."

"I think one of the complaints the girls had about the parents was not being listened to. I think it gave the girls quite a surprise to hear actually how much the parents had heard and how well their parents knew and recognized how they were feeling. Even if the parents could, and should, not give into girls wanting more trust but actually being at a stage of anorexia where we could not give it."

Traps and Treasures is a game usually played on the third day of MFT, in which a young person is blindfolded and guided by parent to cross a 'minefield' and collect 'treasures.' Though the exercise is lighthearted and fun, it is aimed at building trust among family members and bringing awareness of how selective and sensitive people are to the voice of their close family member. It is critical for the optimum functioning on MFT group that therapists balance high-intensity role-plays with exercises that reintroduce laughter, humor, and sense of normality. This game is a good example of rebalancing strong emotions that emerged in the role-plays like the mealtime role reversal and family sculpt with enjoyment and fun. Feedback on **Traps and Treasures**

"Good fun! Lighthearted, good at bringing parents and young people together."

"Fun and a good diversion from the intense sessions."

"This was great and 'normalizing' more like a family team game—we played outside, which felt more like a summer picnic and I think the girls found it easy to join in. It also helped the families relate to each other in a more normal, less painful way. Obviously, it was great to get the underlying 'trust' message across too."

"This was good fun and helped to lighten the mood. It was also a visual that did show how hard it is to focus on the one good voice and screen out all the other voices."

Just as important as the structured sessions are the less formal breaks where members of the group, as well as the therapy team, interact in unplanned ways and adds enormously to the cohesion of the group and to each family's experience that they are in the same boat as other families. The sense of trust and positive regard for each other that quickly builds up is a key factor in enabling all group members to tackle some of the most difficult issues and to reflect on themselves in new ways. The therapists' relationships with the families is also strongly shaped in these informal moments, and both young people and parents will often use these times to talk in less guarded ways than they might normally do in formal therapy sessions.

5   *Rediscovering hope and increasing motivation for recovery*

Many, if not all, of the therapeutic interventions in MFT serve to increase the patient's motivation to recover and instill hope. From the start, events like meeting a graduate family or meeting families at different stages of the recovery journey or exploring at a group level advantages and disadvantages of maintaining the illness should enhance motivation for recovery. Witnessing small or big changes in young people and parents on a daily basis, especially in the first four days, and observing changes in behaviors during mealtimes or in young peoples' insight into the illness all contribute to this objective.

The **Timeline** exercise, usually completed on the fourth day of MFT, specifically tackles issues of hope, optimism, and determination, regarding a future without AN. In this exercise family members work together to draw their family's timeline for the next 12 months including the potential timeline of the process of recovery from anorexia. All the families are encouraged to think ahead and construct their timeline for all the upcoming family events they know about such as family birthdays, holidays, Christmas, exams, and so on. They are also asked to include in the timeline the incremental steps of supposed recovery; for example, if a young person has been out of school, they may want to think about when it would be possible for them to return to school and to put the steps toward this on the timeline. However, they are also asked to think and record on the timeline things that are not going to happen for the young person and their family if there is no improvement in their eating disorder. Later, on the same day, each family presents their timeline to other families in MFT. Feedback on **Timeline:**

> "*Very good as it focused on a time with anorexia more in the background. Our daughter had this up on her wall and when she was struggling we could focus her on things that she had said she wanted to do. It gives hope to the parents that the ED Service expects an improvement.*"

> "*This was a very positive way of looking forward as a family and hopefully beyond anorexia. It also helped us to focus on the other things going*

on in our lives and not just the black cloud of anorexia (e.g., holidays, sibling exams, etc.). Although in hindsight we were probably all too optimistic of recovery within a year, it didn't hurt to give us hope that our family lives would get back to normal, the stages we needed to go through beforehand and ideas on how we could work towards achieving these."

"This worked well for us as group—opening up our family lives, revealing interests, hobbies, family events, holidays, and a simple ambition of returning to a more predictable life. It also helped set some real goals for the girls too, as well as the parents. By this point in the MFT it was important that the parents also had something to look forward to, something as simple as attending a family wedding."

Young people:

"The timeline task made me and my mum feel happy and let me look into the future when I'm better. Everything seemed achievable."

"Good and used for looking ahead when times were tough."

6   *Enhancing skills in tolerating distress and expressing and regulating emotions*

In recent years, new exercises were developed for MFT drawing on a range of principles from other therapeutic approaches including cognitive behavior and dialectical behavior therapy (DBT) or attachment-based family therapy. Examples of those exercises are role-plays like wise/emotional/rational mind, assembling a toolbox to survive and manage anorexia, and constructing a family shield to protect oneself from anorexia. All of these exercises may be done with individual families, in "foster family" groups, or separate groups of mothers, fathers, young people with AN and siblings.

Feedback on **Assembling a survival toolbox:**

"By the time we did this activity at the end of the block four days, the different groups (men, women, and young people who worked in these groups) felt comfortable enough with each other, and knowledgeable enough from the last four days, to come up with the very practical tools which we could take home to help manage anorexia on our own. This was the point that the women suggested a 'group email' support system, which went on to be a great source of support in tough times between the various families, but also continues to be a great support even though most of us have now been discharged from the Maudsley. FYI, the women are better at opening up and keeping in touch. I understand the young people do keep in contact through Facebook, which must have been one of their tools in the toolbox."

7   *Mindfulness/relaxation techniques*

Over the years therapeutic approaches develop and change reflecting not only theoretical and conceptual developments but also changes happening in society and in the perception of mental health. As many more people are embracing the principles of mindfulness and accepting the necessity of being able to relax, new exercises were introduced at the end of each MFT day to help families to reestablish their emotional balance. These exercises incorporate body scan mindfulness, mindfulness exercises from DBT group skills protocols, and standard relaxation techniques using guided imagery.

Follow-Up Days—Toward Greater Autonomy and Independence

As treatment progresses there is a greater variety in the content of the follow-up days. While young people achieve greater flexibility with their meals, MFT exercises become more flexible, nonetheless, their critical component remains: attempting new behaviors and learning to take new risks. Flexibility fostered in new experiments should tackle the intolerance of uncertainty and rigidity that is so often present in young people with anorexia nervosa and that is reflected in their personal and family life.

Some young people who were following meal plans might have become rigid in their food choices as they consider them safe and certain. In those instances MFT exercises might focus on introduction of new foods, new timings, or new settings. Discussion with the "foster" parents, similarly to the previously described lunch with the "foster" parents, might be used to set up new challenges and tasks introducing more flexible behaviors around food and life in general.

As the young person moves along the path of recovery and takes over responsibility for their eating, the new task facing therapists is to begin to question aspects of externalization and introduce discussions in the group on the separation of illness behaviors from adolescent behaviors.

The relationship between the young people and mostly their mothers during the illness often becomes regressed and highly protective. The adolescent on the one hand complains about being told what to eat but at the same time finds it reassuring and often might insist on food being weighed and finds any changes to meal routines highly anxiety provoking. Parents are similarly reassured by the predictability as they are often scared that stepping back from meal supervision or becoming less available to their children will risk the return of anorexia. These patterns and the way they evolve of course vary from family to family, and observing other parents in the group taking risks and letting their children have more independence might reassure them to encourage their children toward more autonomy. Similarly the young people in the group will find encouragement observing others moving in new directions. Discussions in MFT also serve to encourage parents to regain back their own space both as individuals and as a couple, have some personal time separate from the young people, and support them in getting "their life back."

The achieved group cohesion and mutual support allow open expressions of feelings and the experience of being safe even when people are disclosing their individual vulnerabilities. Role-plays permit young people to see their parents and others vent their emotions and talk about their vulnerabilities, which reassures them and helps them accept who they are including the feelings of being vulnerable.

This is a time when a great deal has changed, with the young people mostly having moved beyond the danger zone and beginning to see recovery as a real and desirable option, while at the same time the uncertainty of what life would be like without the illness is anxiety provoking and can act as a block to progress. Anorexic cognitions will generally still be highly prevalent, at the same time scaring the parents from being too adventurous and prompting the adolescents to compare themselves with others. If a competitive undercurrent among young people is detected, this is discussed and openly acknowledged with the whole group and can be redirected from competition of "the best anorexic" to competition of being the best at recovery.

Anxieties around growing up and "safe uncertainty" (Mason, 1993) are explored, and skills that can help young people and their families in the management of anxiety are introduced and discussed. Young people are encouraged to discover fun and boost their social life while families are supported in having a good quality of life and close relationships without this having to be mediated by anorexia.

In the later stages, exercises like "**Antique Roadshow,**" "**Back From the Future Tea-Party,**" or "**Speed Consultations**" (Eisler, Simic, & team, 2012) are used to promote reflections of the treatment journey that families have gone through and future-oriented thinking. The meetings at this stage tend to be both lighthearted and reflective. The therapists increasingly take a less central role in the process, stepping back and letting the group find their own answers. For the final meeting of the MFT group the families are invited to come up with their own ending exercises (usually with parents and young people each preparing a task for the others in advance of the last meeting) to symbolize the ending of the group and time to move on. The group provides feedback to the therapists before saying their final good-byes.

Sibling Groups

Although siblings of young people with AN were invited to participate in MFT-AN from the very early beginnings of MFT-AN development, there was uncertainty around the nature of the impact that the illness has on patients' siblings and how sibling involvement should best be structured. In the early Maudsley studies, siblings were seen as a key support for the ill young person and were encouraged to attend all treatment sessions to encourage them to continue to provide support without being parental

(Dare et al., 1990; Lock & Le Grange 2013). Over time this practice has become more varied, recognizing that sibling relationships of course vary considerably and are impacted by the eating disorder in different ways in different families. In a recent study, Ellison et al. (2012) reported that sibling support during FT-AN did not predict weight gain in their anorexic sibling, raising questions about how best to include siblings in treatment. Siblings can be very helpful; they also have needs of their own and often their sense of loyalty makes it difficult for them to express their needs openly. Equally, some siblings will be openly angry with their sibling, feeling that anorexia has sidelined them, and direct request for them to help their sibling may simply exacerbate such feelings. All of this will depend on the specific family context and the siblings' age and relationship they had with their sister/brother before the illness started.

The current MFT-AN practice is to emphasize that siblings are seen as important, that the team welcomes their participation in MFT, recognizing that they too will have been affected by anorexia like everyone else in the family. Families are encouraged to bring siblings to the introductory afternoon where their future attendance is negotiated. The team acknowledges that not all siblings are likely to be able to attend every MFT session, and the aim therefore is to make sure that when they do attend, it is on days when other siblings can be there as well.

MFT provides a context for siblings that is not possible to create in single FT-AN. A recent study (Hutchison et al., submitted) in which siblings of AN patients were interviewed about their experiences of living with a sibling with AN and also their experience of the treatment they took part in, highlighted the impact on siblings and their sense of confusion and ambivalence about their relationship with their ill sibling with a mixture of feelings ranging from sadness, care, and frustration but also feeling sidelined and at times angry. Though they felt that their parents tried not to put the responsibility for their sibling's well-being on them, they nonetheless tried to help them and felt guilty if they did not succeed. They felt that their role was to keep their needs or feelings to themselves so as not to trouble or burden others, including their parents and friends. Most expressed more a sense of resignation than anger or frustration that their siblings' needs were above theirs. The most utilized coping mechanism was distancing themselves from the family home in order not to cause trouble or stay out of the way and "get on with things."

The siblings' experience of being involved in treatment mirrored their home experience, as they mostly did not feel that their needs were fully considered. They emphasized that what they would find most helpful would be to meet other siblings with similar experiences, which they thought would have a normalizing effect on them and to have a space to express how they feel without having to censor what they say for fear of burdening others.

Based on these findings, sibling groups were developed and are now offered as a standard part of MFT-AN. Separate sibling groups support expression of their needs and provide space for siblings to jointly explore and share their feelings and experiences about living with the ill sister or brother. The group allows them to process confusing feelings and enhances their well-being.

Evidence for MFT-AN

The evidence for the efficacy of MFT-AN is still relatively limited. A number of descriptive and open follow-up studies (Dare & Eisler, 2000; Hollesen, Clausen, & Rokkedal, 2013; Marzola et al., submitted, Salaminiou et al., in press; Scholz & Asen, 2001; Scholz et al., 2005) have reported promising improvements in ED symptoms, high levels of satisfaction with treatment, and very low drop-out rates.

Three studies have provided comparison with other treatments. In Toronto Gabel et al. (2014) compared a group of 25 adolescents with AN who received comprehensive treatment as usual (TAU) plus MFT with 25 case-matched controls who received only TAU, which include a range of treatments that were deemed clinically appropriate including single FT-AN. At one year, the MFT group had a significantly higher percentage of healthy weight than the controls (99.6% vs. 95.4%). The study was a retrospective case note study, so caution is needed in interpreting the findings. Also in Toronto, a small randomized controlled trial (RCT) compared eight sessions of single family therapy with eight sessions of family group psychoeducation in adolescent inpatients with anorexia nervosa (Geist et al., 2000). The study found comparable weight gain in both groups but the multi-family group was more cost-effective. The multi-family intervention used in the study was different from that described in this chapter focusing on psychoeducation and group discussion of the presented material in separate adolescent and parent groups. In London, Eisler et al. (submitted) conducted a multi-center RCT of 167 families with an adolescent with AN who were randomized to either FT-AN or a combination of FT-AN and MFT-AN. Those in the MFT group gained significantly more weight, and at the end of the one year outpatient treatment, a significantly greater number had achieved a good or intermediate outcome on the Morgan/Russell global outcome scales (Morgan & Russell, 1975).

Notable in all the descriptions of MFT-AN are reports of high levels of satisfaction by the families, particularly on the part of the parents. Scholz et al. (2005) reported results of an audit of a MFT intervention for teenagers with AN ($N = 30$) where MFT was rated satisfactory by 40% and very satisfactory by 60% of parents. While the adolescents were less satisfied than the parents, 40% of them found the treatment satisfactory and 39% very satisfactory.

Like most other psychotherapies, the mechanisms through which MFT-AN might bring about change are still poorly understood. A recent qualitative study of MFT participant perceptions of day-to-day changes during the four intensive group days (using daily journals and rating scales and adolescent and parent focus groups a week after the four-day treatment block) (Voriadaki et al., 2015) provides some indications as to factors that might be operating. The study suggests that the intensive MFT approach provides a rich learning experience that promotes profound insight into the illness within a setting that is perceived as safe, supportive, and cohesive to disclose feelings, discuss ideas, and try new behaviors. Young people reported a major increase in insight into the disorder gained from Day 1 to Day 3 of MFT that was assisted by the group's shared externalization of the illness. The sharing of experiences with other families was also felt to promote insight into the illness and a major shift in the adolescents' motivation toward recovery. It appeared that when young people in the group were faced with not being able to avoid observing other's anorexic behavior, seeing their own symptoms from an outsider perspective with all the similarities they mutually shared brought a greater awareness of their own illness behavior and of the "wall" that was separating them from their family and life.

The findings from the study echo many of the quotes reported earlier in the chapter about the way in which exercises facilitated adolescents' and parents' empathy for one another and promoted increased emotional expression. It appeared that these factors, as well as mutual learning, understanding, and support, contributed to the progress achieved in adolescents' motivation, parents' self-efficacy, and intra-family communication.

Confidence that recovery was possible usually increased gradually, first among parents who mostly, from the beginning of the group, appeared motivated to 'do something different' to help their children to recover, followed by most of their children showing the first glimpses of positive motivation for recovery while designing the family timeline on the fourth day of MFT.

New Applications of MFT in Eating Disorders

MFT Integrated into Day Programs

In the Intensive Treatment Program (ITP) day service at the Maudsley Hospital, in addition to standard 10 MFT-AN days, we dedicate one afternoon per week to parent skills for all the parents of the children that attend the program. In parent skills group, parents share their experiences of obstacles in managing their children's eating and the all-encompassing effects of the disorder. The parent skills group is followed by multi-family dinner during which staff model possible responses to challenges posed by young people with anorexia during the mealtime. ITP staff coach parents on how to respond with the clear expectation that children will comply with the boundaries of the day program that meals have to be fully completed within the allocated time.

Other day services have been incorporating MFT components into their programs (Girz et al., 2013; Marzola et al., submitted) as have some inpatient services (Depestele, Claes, & Lemmens, 2014; Fleminger, 2005; Honig 2005). An innovative whole family admission program for adolescents who have not responded to other treatments has been reported by Wallis et al. (2013), which also incorporates MFT elements.

MFT for Bulimia Nervosa (MFT-BN)

In contrast to treatment for adolescent anorexia nervosa, there is little empirical evidence for effective treatments for adolescent bulimia nervosa (BN). To date, there have been only two RCTs (Schmidt et al., 2007; Le Grange et al., 2007) evaluating treatment of BN in adolescents. Schmidt and colleagues compared family therapy (FT-BN) and a guided self-help version of CBT, and Le Grange and colleagues compared FT-BN and individual supportive therapy. In both studies, abstinent rates were relatively low and not exceeding 40% at the end of treatment or at the six-month follow-up. In Schmidt's study, 28% predominantly older adolescents refused to enter the study, as they did not want their family to be involved in treatment.

In order to bridge the gap in strongly effective treatments for adolescent BN, and with the clinical and research evidence-based experience of effectiveness of multi-family therapy in adolescent AN, the Maudsley CAEDS developed a new multi-family therapy program for adolescent bulimia nervosa (MFT-BN). The structure and content of the program were modified to meet the specific needs of adolescents with BN and their families and to promote family engagement in treatment.

The MFT-BN program is for six to eight adolescents with BN and their families. The program starts with an introductory afternoon followed by 16 sessions of 90 minutes' duration. The first 10 sessions are weekly, while the rest of the follow-ups are more spaced out. Individual sessions are added after the 10th session if requested by the patient and his or her family. In the initial phase of treatment, the focus is on a systemic cognitive behavioral therapy (CBT) formulation of the binge-purge cycle that is shared between adolescents and their families. Possible exit points from the binge-purge cycle are identified and solutions and strategies to exit/prevent the repetition of the binge-purge cycle are explored in separate young persons' group and then a joint group with their parents. Interventions used integrate the multi-family systemic perspective with validation, mindfulness, distress tolerance, and emotional regulation skills based on DBT skills groups. New acquired skills are aimed at a reduction of the binge-purge cycle and better emotional regulation. Adolescents are helped to prevent the repetition of the binge-purge cycle supported by their family. Both parties use skills and strategies explored in the MFT context. Additional

MFT interventions are aimed at opening the communication flow between adolescents and their family, sharing and reflecting on emotions and relationships using the richness of multiple perspectives and promoting better interpersonal effectiveness, and the reduction of parental anger triggered by bulimic symptoms.

Preliminary data (Simic et al., 2011; 2014) show high levels of satisfaction with the treatment reported both by parents and young people with low dropout rates. It was found that MFT-BN is a highly acceptable treatment effective in reducing bulimic symptoms, depressive symptoms, and increasing adaptive coping skills in adolescents. In parents, MFT-BN had a good effect on reducing the symptoms of anxiety and depression and negative experiences of parenting while increasing their positive parental experiences. In focus groups on the experiences of adolescents and their parents/caregivers with MFT-BN, the main themes identified were the group as a source of support that brought about improvements in adolescents and in family relationships, tackling BN as a secretive disorder and taboo, increasing parents' understanding and awareness of the disorder, and teaching parents and adolescents new coping mechanisms that are found to be helpful in the management of BN symptoms.

Quotes from focus groups:

> "... Because as a parent you're always going to blame yourself cause you think 'why didn't I see that coming? Why didn't I know this was going on?' and you blame yourself and then you see other people going through the same thing and somehow it makes you feel 'ok, you know, is not because I am a bad parent or is not because my daughter's gone completely off the rails, this stuff happens and you know, there's other people as well.'"

> "We actually started off with the introduction of BN—what it is, what it does, how it affects the body, then the young people did a really good presentation on the cycle of BN and the emotional effects, and then from there we built on the exit roots and how to distract and move them off on different tangents."

> "She uses all the techniques that were given to them you know to break the cycle (of bingeing and purging), so I think most of the time she manages well. There are days in which she just you know gives into temptation or whatever, but I think it's benefited her, she is managing to deal with it better than she did before."

Questions for the Future

Both the families and clinicians who have been involved in MFT programs are generally highly enthusiastic about its potential usefulness in treating eating disorders. We share this enthusiasm, and the research to date provides some encouragement that it is indeed an effective treatment. Nevertheless, a great deal more research is needed to evaluate the treatment both in the format developed at the Maudsley Hospital in London and the variations that teams in other contexts have used. The team in Dresden delivers a "pure" MFT-AN treatment (Scholz et al., 2005) consisting of only MFT days (20 days over one year) that has been attended by families travelling from across Germany. In San Diego, a stand-alone one-week intensive MFT-AN treatment has shown promise (Marzola et al., submitted) and again has been particularly valued by families who have been unable to access effective treatment locally. Similarly, the experience in London has been that families will travel for considerable distance for brief intensive blocks of treatment. Of course, acceptability and clinical utility of a treatment approach need to be accompanied by sound research to demonstrate efficacy as well. A number of groups in London, San Diego, Toronto, and Bodo have been developing MFT groups for adult AN patients, which have engendered similar enthusiasm, and again empirical evaluation is needed to support further developments.

An important aspect of MFT is that it readily lends itself to integrating ideas and therapeutic techniques from other therapy approaches. The previous account of the development of MFT-BN is a good example, but there are certainly many other possibilities (e.g., incorporating elements of CBT for anxiety in MFT-AN).

The MFT context encourages collaborative and very open communication with families and opens up discussions of areas that may not always be very readily accessible in other clinical settings. At the Maudsley CAEDS, a notable area of recent discussion in MFT has been the use of social media and technology, which have irrevocably changed the world in which we are living and have created, as any other significant change would do, unpredictable and unexpected risks and opportunities. In the context of MFT, one of the advantages that seems to be of undisputable benefit is the fact that many parents who attend MFT keep in regular e-mail communication that is perceived by them as being positive in maintaining the sense of feeling understood and belonging to the supportive community of people with the same goal of combating the eating disorder.

More unpredictable is the effect of social media on young people, as their communication on social media, even when it overtly appears to be supportive, can contain an undercurrent of competitiveness that in the world of anorexic sufferers might mean competitiveness about who is the one that is most severely ill. This needs serious consideration by the therapeutic team and further thinking about how social media could be used to better benefit young sufferers from eating disorders.

Conclusion

MFT for AN was initially developed with the idea that it would be an alternative for inpatient treatment for those who had not responded to

FT-AN. Though MFT-AN did not meet the expectation that it will resolve the need for inpatient, or day-patient treatment for AN, recent evidence confirms that it can lead to better outcomes for children and adolescents treated in outpatient settings. The model has been integrated into day programs where it has shown its strength in engaging families and skilling parents to help their child recover from their ED. Recently, MFT has found a new application in the treatment of adolescent BN. Further research is needed to confirm the effectiveness of these new applications of MFT. As all therapists gain invaluable knowledge from the feedback they receive from families they treat, we will finish this chapter with two last quotes from families:

> *"One of the most valuable elements was meeting the other families and understanding that we were all experiencing similar difficulties, no matter what the age or stage of the girl and the illness. For me it was brilliant to not be so alone with it all, as I was feeling very overpowered by responsibility for helping my daughter get better and it was great to know we all felt the same."*

> *"The caring environment certainly gave us confidence to follow the ideas and try the suggestions. Some exercises we felt to be less beneficial but then later on they would slot into place and seem more relevant. As a family, we were not having trouble bonding together as we were still close, but the activities were a good way to introduce more fun and give us more coping mechanisms. The sessions could be quite tough and draining after the whole day, but at that point any professional help was worth a try and looking back it played a worthwhile part."*

References

American Psychiatric Association. (2006). Treatment of patients with eating disorders (3rd ed.). *American Journal of Psychiatry, 163*(S7), 4–54.

Alexander, J., & Eisler, I. (in press). *Multi-Family Therapy for eating disorders: My family is back*. London: Routledge.

Asen, E. (2002). Multiple family therapy: An overview. *Journal of Family Therapy, 24*, 3–16.

Asen, E., & Scholz, M. (2010). *Multi-Family Therapy: Concepts and techniques*. London: Routledge.

Bulik, C., Berkman, N., Brownley, K., Sedway, J., & Lohr, K. (2007). Anorexia nervosa treatment: A systemic review of randomized controlled trials. *International Journal of Eating Disorders, 40*, 310–320.

Dare, C., & Eisler, I. (2000). A multi-family group day treatment programme for adolescent eating disorder. *European Eating Disorders Review, 8*, 4–18.

Dare, C., Eisler, I., Russell, G. F. M., & Szmukler, G. I. (1990). The clinical and theoretical impact of a controlled trial of family therapy in anorexia nervosa. *Journal of Marital and Family Therapy, 16*, 39–57.

Depestele, L., Claes, L., & Lemmens, G. M. D. (2014). Promotion of an autonomy-supportive parental style in a multi-family group for eating-disordered adolescents. *Journal of Family Therapy*. Early view doi: 10.1111/1467–6427.12047

Depestele, L., & Vandereycken, W. (2009). Families around the table: Experiences with a multi-family approach in the treatment of eating-disordered adolescents. *International Journal of Child Health and Adolescent Health*, 2, 255–261.

Downs, K. J., & Blow, A. J. (2013). A substantive and methodological review of family-based treatment for eating disorders: The last 25 years of research. *Journal of Family Therapy*, 35, 3–28.

Eisler, I., et al. (*submitted*). A multi-centre randomised trial of single and multi-family therapy for adolescent anorexia nervosa.

Eisler, I. (2005). The empirical and theoretical base of family therapy and multiple family day therapy for adolescent anorexia nervosa. *Journal of Family Therapy*, 27, 104–131.

Eisler, I., Lock, J., & Le Grange, D. (2010) Family-based treatments for adolescent anorexia nervosa. In Grilo C. and Mitchell J. (Eds) *The Treatment of Eating Disorders*. New York, Guilford Press.

Eisler, I., Simic, M., & team. (2012, unpublished manuscript. *Maudsley service model for the management of child and adolescent eating disorders*. Child and Adolescent Eating Disorders Service, South London & Maudsley NHS Foundation Trust. https://www.national.slam.nhs.uk/services/camhs/camhs-eatingdisorders/resources/

Eisler, I., Wallis, A., & Dodge, E. (2015) What's new is old and what's old is new: The origins and evolution of family therapy for eating disorders. Loeb, K., Le Grange, D., & Lock, J. (Eds). *Family Therapy for Adolescent Eating and Weight Disorders*. New York: Guilford Press.

Ellison, R., Rhodes, P., Madden, S., Miskovic, J., Wallis, A., Baillie, A., Kohn, M., & Touyz, S. (2012). Do the components of manualized family-based treatment for anorexia nervosa predict weight gain? *International Journal of Eating Disorders*, 45, 609–614.

Fleminger, S. (2005). A model for the treatment of eating disorders of adolescents in a specialized centre in The Netherlands. *Journal of Family Therapy*, 27, 147–157.

Gabel, K., Pinhas, L., Eisler, I., Katzman, D., & Heinmaa, M. (2014). The Effect of Multiple Family Therapy on Weight Gain in Adolescents with Anorexia Nervosa: Pilot Data. *Journal of the Canadian Academy of Child and Adolescent Psychiatry*, 23(3), 196–9.

Geist, R., Heinmaa, M., Stephens, D., Davis, R., & Katzman, D. K. (2000). Comparison of family therapy and family group psychoeducation in adolescents with anorexia nervosa. *Canadian Journal of Psychiatry*, 45, 173–178.

Girz, L., Lafrance Robinson, A., Foroughe, M., Jasper, K., & Boachie, A. (2013). Adapting family-based therapy to a day hospital programme for adolescents with eating disorders: preliminary outcomes and trajectories of change. *Journal of Family Therapy*, 35(S1), 102–120.

Hollesen, A., Clausen, L., & Rokkedal, K. (2013). Multiple family therapy for adolescents with anorexia nervosa: A pilot study of eating disorder symptoms and interpersonal functioning. *Journal of Family Therapy*, 35(S1), 53–67.

Honig, P. (2005). A multi-family group programme as part of an inpatient service for adolescents with a diagnosis of anorexia nervosa. *Clinical Child Psychology and Psychiatry*, 10, 465–475.

Hutchison, S., House, J., Coombs, B., Simic, M., & Eisler, I. Silent witnesses: experiences of siblings of adolescents with eating disorders (submitted).

Laquer, H. P., La Burt, H. A., & Morong, E. (1964). Multiple family therapy: Further developments. *Current Psychiatric Therapies, 4,* 150–154.

Lay, B., Jennen-Steinmetz, C., Reinhard, I., & Schmidt, M. H. (2002). Characteristics of inpatient weight gain in adolescent anorexia nervosa: Relation to speed of relapse and readmission. *European Eating Disorders Review, 10,* 22–40.

Le Grange, D., Crosby, R. D., Rathouz, P. J., & Leventhal, B. L. (2007). A randomized controlled comparison of family-based treatment and supportive psychotherapy for adolescent bulimia nervosa. *Archives of General Psychiatry, 64,* 1049–1056.

Lock, J., & Le Grange, D. (2013). *Treatment manual for anorexia nervosa: A family-based approach.* Guilford Press.

Marzola, E., Knatz, S., Murray, S. B., Rockwell, R., Boutelle, K., Eisler, I., & Kaye W. H. (submitted). Short-term intensive family therapy for adolescent eating disorders in individual and multi-family contexts: Thirty-month outcome.

Mason, B. (1993). Towards positions of safe uncertainty. *Human Systems, 4,* 189–200.

McDonell, M. G., & Dyck, D. G. (2004). Multiple-family group treatment as an effective intervention for children with psychological disorders. *Clinical Psychology Review, 24,* 685–706.

McFarlane, W. R. (2002). *Multifamily Groups in the Treatment of Severe Psychiatric Disorders.* New York, Guilford Press.

Mehl, A., Tomanova, J., Kuběna, A., & Papežová, H. (2013). Adapting multi-family therapy to families who care for a loved one with an eating disorder in the Czech Republic combined with follow-up pilot study of efficacy. *Journal of Family Therapy, 35*(S1), 82–101.

Morgan, H. G., & Russell, G. F. M. (1975). Value of family background and clinical features as predictors of long-term outcome in anorexia nervosa: Four-year follow-up study of 41 patients. *Psychological Medicine, 5,* 355–371.

National Institute for Clinical Excellence (2004). *Eating disorders: Core interventions in the treatment and management of anorexia nervosa, bulimia nervosa and related eating disorders.* CG9. London: NICE.

O'Shea, M., & Phelps, R. (1985). Multiple family therapy: Current status and critical appraisal. *Family Process, 24,* 555–582.

Rhodes, P., Baillee, A., Brown, J., & Madden, S. (2008). Can parent–parent consultation improve the effectiveness of the Maudsley model of family-based treatment for anorexia nervosa: A randomised control trial. *Journal of Family Therapy, 30,* 96–108.

Roberts, J. (2005). Transparency and self-disclosure in family therapy: Dangers and possibilities. *Family Process, 44,* 45–63.

Salaminiou, E., Campbell, M., Simic, M., Kuipers, E., & Eisler, I. (in press). Intensive Multi-Family Therapy for adolescent anorexia nervosa: An open study of 30 families. *Journal of Family Therapy.*

Scholz, M., & Asen, E. (2001). Multiple family therapy with eating disordered adolescents: Concepts and preliminary results. *European Eating Disorders Review, 9,* 33–42.

Scholz, M., Rix, M., Scholz, K., Gantchev, K., & Thomke, V. (2005). Multiple family therapy for anorexia nervosa: Concepts, experiences, and results. *Journal of Family Therapy, 27,* 132–141.

Schmidt, U., Lee, S., Beecham, J., Perkins, S., Treasure, J., Yi, I., Winn, S., Robinson, P., Murphy, R., Keville, S., Johnson-Sabine, E., Jenkins, M., Frost, S., Dodge, I., Berelowitz, M., & Eisler, I. (2007) A Randomized Controlled Trial of Family Therapy and Cognitive-Behavioral Guided Self-Care for Adolescents with Bulimia Nervosa or Related Disorders. *American Journal of Psychiatry, 164,* 591–598.

Simic, M., & Eisler, I. (2012). Family and multi-family therapy. In J. Fox & K. Goss (Eds.), *Eating and its disorders* (pp. 260–279). Chichester: John Wiley & Sons.

Simic, M., Pretorius, N., Bottrill, S., Voulgari, S., Coombes, B., Dimmer, M., & Eisler, I. (2011, September). *Multi-family therapy for adolescents with bulimia nervosa: Preliminary results from a new treatment programme.* Paper presented at the Eating Disorders Research Society 17th Annual Meeting, Edinburgh, Scotland.

Simic, M., Pretorius, N., & Eisler, I. (2014, March). *New treatment programme for adolescents with bulimia nervosa from the Maudsley: Multi-family therapy for bulimia nervosa (MFT-BN).* Paper presented at the Academy of Eating Disorders International Conference on Eating Disorders, New York, USA.

Steinglass, P. (1998). Multiple family discussion group for patients with chronic medical illness. *Families, Systems & Health, 16,* 55–70.

Strober, M., Freeman, R., & Morell, W. (1997). The long-term course of severe anorexia nervosa in adolescents: Survival analysis of recovery, relapse, and outcome predictors over 10–15 years in a prospective study. *International Journal of Eating Disorders, 22,* 339–360.

Voriadaki, T., Simic, M., Espie, J., & Eisler, I. (2015). Intensive multi-family therapy for adolescent anorexia nervosa: Adolescents' and parents' day-to-day experiences. *Journal of Family Therapy, 37,* 5–23.

Wallis, A., Alford, C., Hason, A., Titterton, J., Madden, S., & Kohn, M. (2013). Innovations in Maudsley family-based treatment for anorexia nervosa at the Children's Hospital at Westmead: A family admission programme. *Journal of Family Therapy, 35*(S1), 68–81.

Yager, J., Devlin, M., Halmi, K., Herzog, D., Mitchell III, J., Powers, P., & Zerbe, K. APA guideline watch (August 2012): Practice guideline for the treatment of patients with eating disorders, 3rd edition, *Psychiatry on Line,* 1–18.

Chapter 8

Parent Support as an Adjunct to Family Therapy

Roslyn Binford Hopf, Renee Rienecke Hoste, and Christian Pariseau[1]

"A challenging time was at dinner one night. Our daughter had been in the treatment program for about a month at this point. We were feeling like we had started to make a little progress, and were feeling a little hopeful with our small success so far. Meals still took a very long time, but it was getting a little better. On this particular night, I was feeling tired and burned out, not only from dealing with the eating issues, but also from work because I was working a lot of overtime. As soon as we sat down for dinner, our daughter just flat out refused to eat anything. Nothing was going to make her eat. It was very hard to motivate her because what could I do? Send her to her room without dinner? No, that was what she wanted. Tell her she couldn't hang out with her friends? She had already isolated herself from her friends, so that wouldn't motivate her. So we sat there, alternating between trying to distract her by talking about other things, to downright demanding that she eat, and giving her reasons why she had to. Well, as I'm sure you know, nothing was getting through to her. Finally I just snapped—I started yelling at her, telling her to 'JUST EAT! HOW HARD COULD IT BE? IF YOU DON'T EAT, YOU WILL DIE!' All kinds of things that did nothing to help, but at the time it was what I was feeling. The whole time she just looked at me defiantly, basically telling me 'Nope, I'm not going to eat, and there is nothing you can do to make me.' She at one point dropped her plate of food on the floor, an 'accident' of course. I wasn't going to let her get away with that, so I got her another plate, and in my frustration and anger, I flung the cupboard door open with such force, that to this day, it won't shut totally. I had just had enough, and I knew I had to get out of there. I went for a very long drive, leaving my husband to deal with everything. She did eventually eat dinner while I was gone. I remember that when I came back that evening, I found it very hard to be nice to her. I was so angry and hurt. I knew deep down it wasn't her fault, but it wasn't my fault either. Sometimes it was so hard to be the strong one, when all I really wanted to do was bury my head under the covers and cry."

— *Mother of AN patient*

After reading this description of one mother's experience implementing family-based treatment (FBT), it should come as no surprise that carers of people with eating disorders have been found to have high levels of psychological distress and caregiving burden (Zabala, Macdonald, & Treasure, 2009; Graap, Bleich, Herbst, Scherzinger et al., 2008; Perkins, Winn, Murray, Murphy, & Schmidt, 2004; Treasure et al., 2001; Winn, Perkins, Murray, Murphy, & Schmidt, 2004). In fact, carers of individuals with anorexia nervosa (AN) have reported comparable and even greater levels of distress and caregiving burden than carers of individuals with psychosis (Graap et al., 2008a; Treasure et al., 2001). Over half of carers of individuals with bulimia nervosa (BN) report feeling 'burned out,' depressed, or physically or mentally ill (Winn, Perkins, Murray, Murphy, & Schmidt, 2004). Feelings of helplessness, not knowing how they should best respond to their child, and fearing that their attempts to help were doing more harm than good were commonly reported (Perkins et al., 2004).

> *"Before we found the FBT program, we felt like we were watching our daughter slowly die, and there was nothing we could do to stop it."*
> —Mother of AN patient

> *"Our son was hospitalized twice. Each time after he was discharged, we were told not to interfere in his food intake. In other words, we should watch him starve to death. We did this because we trusted the therapists. After the second hospitalization, we were told the same thing, and our son rapidly lost even more weight than the first time. When we sought help once more, we were advised to put him in a group home as he was not able to eat at home ... Isn't it normal for parents to intervene when their child has a problem?"*
> —Mother of AN patient

> *"The powerlessness you feel when your child's body mass index (BMI) is so low that his brain is not functioning normally and prevents him from wanting to recover is challenging for a parent."*
> —Father of AN patient

Parents have described the refeeding process in FBT as "the hardest thing I've ever had to do" and "doubt whether we had enough strength to keep implementing this treatment long-term." The responsibility that parents have in FBT is a double-edged sword—empowering on the one side but time- and labor-intensive on the other. Parents are always "on duty" and often feel as if "all I'm doing is buying food, preparing food, feeding her, cleaning up afterward, and then moving on to the next meal or snack."

> *"The most challenging situation happened not long after we had started FBT, and our son only was supposed to eat a cookie for his*

evening snack. There he sat, motionless, stony-faced, not saying a word, and of course not eating one bite. My husband and I sat there with him for two hours and then we took turns until evening rolled into night and one of us knew that we were going to have to cover the night shift … to be completely honest, I was thankful that my husband volunteered to take over as I was completely wiped out. My husband, visibly exhausted, told me the next morning that he had sat with our son or rather 'Eddie, the eating disorder' (and the cookie!) until 2:00 a.m."

Despite these challenges, adjunctive support for FBT carers remains limited, at best (Collins, 2005). An assessment of carers of individuals with AN found high levels of unmet needs (Haigh, & Treasure, 2003). Carers expressed a desire for more information about eating disorders, more support from other people, including health care professionals, and the ability to share experiences with others in the same situation.

"As anyone with a child with an eating disorder knows, it is hard for others who aren't dealing with this to understand what you are going through. I mean most teenagers eat a lot and like hanging out with their friends. How can you describe sitting at the dinner table for 3 hours every night, or not being able to go anywhere because your child doesn't have the energy to even leave the couch, much less go shopping? I felt like I had failed as a parent. I mean, really, I can't get my teenage daughter to eat? I don't think I totally understood it, so how do I expect someone not dealing with this to understand it."

"The support that friends and family can offer is unfortunately limited because only parents who have a child with an eating disorder can truly imagine what you are going through. However, it does feel good to know that you have a place to vent your frustrations. It also is important to explain the illness and treatment approach to close family members or friends and inform them about how the treatment process is going in order for them to attempt to understand how the eating disorder affects the entire family—you included."

"No one can really understand what it's like unless they're directly confronted with it, however our friends and my brother do at least try to understand."

In light of the fact that FBT implementation often takes an emotional toll on parents, it would behoove FBT therapists to be cognizant of factors that could potentially influence outcome. Expressed emotion (EE) is a measure of a relative's attitudes and behaviors toward an ill family member. It is made up of five dimensions: criticism, hostility, emotional overinvolvement, warmth, and positive remarks, and has been found to be related to treatment outcome in families of patients with eating disorders. Specifically, parental criticism, hostility, and emotional overinvolvement have been associated with treatment drop-out and poor outcome (Le Grange, Eisler, Dare, & Hodes, 1992; Szmukler, Eisler, Russell, & Dare, 1985). Thus, therapists need to be aware of early signs of carer exhaustion and criticism and should encourage carers to express warmth toward their child, as parental warmth has been found to predict good treatment outcome (Le Grange, Rienecke Hoste, Lock, & Bryson, 2011).

Therapists also should be aware of personality traits or attributions made by parents that could impact their administration of FBT. For instance, a parent with perfectionistic tendencies might interpret slow weight gain as a treatment failure. Perfectionism or overly high expectations may promote a sense of hopelessness amongst parents who are already feeling overburdened, thus increasing the likelihood that they inadvertently will make critical comments toward their child. Parents or carers should be informed that thinking in all-or-none terms (i.e., "We are doing a 'good' or 'bad' job" with refeeding) or catastrophizing ("Our child is not gaining weight fast enough ... We will *never* be able to help her get well") regarding their implementation of FBT are counter-therapeutic and ultimately counter-productive.

Providing a platform for carers to hear "peer mentors" (Zucker, Loeb, Patel, & Shafer, 2011) recount their own ups and downs in using FBT would likely help carers challenge their perfectionistic thinking and expectations. Indeed, carers have reported that involvement in a support group with other carers who know firsthand the daily challenges in caring for an individual with an eating disorder would lessen social isolation and would allow them to reciprocally exchange experiences and provide advice and much-needed reassurance about how to cope with the person in their care (Cottee Lane, Pistrang, & Bryant-Waugh, 2004; Graap, Bleich, Herbst, Scherzinger et al., 2008; Graap, Bleich, Herbst, Trostmann et al., 2008; Winn et al., 2004).

It is worthy of mention that although there is a growing body of literature supporting the use of FBT for adolescent AN, it has been considered controversial in the very recent past. As chronicled by Collins (2005), implementers of FBT, like Collins, often are placed in the uncomfortable position of having to defend their rationale for choosing to use FBT—all of which is antithetical to feeling validated, empowered, and supported. Misperceptions of FBT continue to exist, particularly outside the United Kingdom, United States, Canada, and Australia where the approach remains relatively unknown. Indeed, one need only view the short list of FBT-certified therapists in continental Europe on the Training Institute for Child and Adolescent Eating Disorders website (www.train2treat4ed.com) to understand this issue more fully.

> "When we started with FBT, there was no one in our area, let alone Germany, who was in the same situation. It would have definitely

helped us if there would have been a group of parents where you could get advice and not have to try everything out on your own. When I now listen to other parents' stories, I understand their situation and think 'Yes, we went through that too' or 'That was the same for us.' Perhaps one wouldn't feel so lonely."

"It would be helpful to have more parents to exchange experiences with. Although participation in support groups with parents who are not involved in FBT also is helpful, it is not as helpful as talking to those who understand the unique challenges in using FBT."

Literature Review

An increasing recognition of the emotional strain that caregiving places on parents of patients with eating disorders, along with a movement away from blaming parents for causing disordered eating and instead viewing them as crucial to the recovery process (Le Grange, Lock, Loeb, & Nicholls, 2010; Whitney, & Eisler, 2005), has led to an increase in attempts to support them through this process. Several studies have investigated various interventions offered to parents while their child is concurrently in treatment for the eating disorder. These interventions often combine psychoeducation and skill development with support received from other group members.

Parent Groups

Holtkamp, Herpertz-Dahlmann, Vloet, and Hagenah (2005) evaluated a group offered to parents of adolescent patients with eating disorders. The group consists of five 90-minute sessions: the first two sessions are highly structured and didactic, while the latter three sessions allow more time for discussion. Topics covered include the physiological and psychological consequences of starvation; the etiology, course, and prognosis of eating disorders; basic principles of a healthy diet; and relapse prevention. One hundred fifteen parents completed a questionnaire evaluating the group sessions. The majority of parents found the group helpful in bettering their understanding of the treatment and enabling them to better cope with their child's illness, and 98 percent said they would recommend it to other parents.

Similarly, Uehara, Kawashima, Goto, Tasaki, and Someya (2001) offered five 2-hour group sessions to relatives of adolescents and young adults with disordered eating. During the first three sessions, one hour was spent on psychoeducation and one hour on group discussion, while the latter two sessions consisted of group discussion and group work. Topics covered included epidemiology, diagnosis, symptoms, etiology, course, complications, and treatment. In addition to increases in family cohesion and adaptability, the authors found decreases from pre- to post-treatment in the number of high EE relatives, particularly those showing high levels of emotional overinvolvement.

An ongoing parent support group consisting of general discussion as well as an educational component covering topics such as etiology, medical complications, and treatment modalities was found to be helpful in increasing parents' knowledge of and understanding of eating disorder behavior. It also provided a helpful setting in which to learn from other families' experiences (Pasold, Boateng, & Portilla, 2010).

Treasure and colleagues have investigated the utility of "the Maudsley eating disorder collaborative care skills workshops," a series of six workshops that offers education about eating disorders, helps carers to understand ways in which they can facilitate recovery by reducing high EE, and teaches carers skills such as motivational interviewing, communication, and problem solving (Sepulveda, Lopez, Todd, Whitaker, & Treasure, 2008). These workshops have been found to be acceptable to carers as reflected by high rates of attendance, and improvements were found in level of carer distress, level of general caregiving burden, and difficulties caused by the eating disorder symptoms. Qualitative feedback suggests that the workshop content is also useful for carers when delivered in DVD format combined with telephone coaching (Sepulveda, Lopez, Macdonald, & Treasure, 2008).

A group parent training program (GPT) has been developed by Zucker and colleagues (Zucker, Ferriter, Best, & Brantley, 2005; Zucker, Marcus, & Bulik, 2006) to develop caregivers as role models and to offer help in three domains: (1) disorder management (e.g., acute issues such as child resistance and caregiver frustration), (2) caregiver features (including maladaptive perfectionism, low self-efficacy, and high levels of EE), and (3) home environment (a supportive environment with caregivers modeling adaptive coping). The GPT occurred over sixteen 90-minute sessions with an open group format, where caregivers designed weekly homework assignments. Sixteen families who participated in the GPT completed a treatment satisfaction questionnaire (Zucker et al., 2006) and reported high levels of acceptability and perceptions of effectiveness. All group participants strongly agreed that GPT taught them how to manage their child's disorder and how to become better parents, and all said they would recommend the group to others. Ninety-one percent strongly agreed that GPT was essential for the improvement of their child.

Meal Support Training

Leichner, Hall, and Calderon (2005) describe a manual and 35-minute video offering meal support training (MST) that is focused on giving information, practical advice, and guidance on helpful interactions to families of young people with eating disorders. The approach of MST is one of collaborating with youth. It is recognized to be less helpful to youth in a precontemplative stage of change. MST includes reassuring statements during mealtimes; pre-, during, and post-meal planning; and examples of approaches to avoid (e.g., lecturing, bribing, and bargaining). The video reviews the manual content and provides additional vignettes and interviews with recovered patients and a mother and father who have used MST.

The approach was evaluated positively by caregivers of fifty-two consecutive patients with AN, BN, and eating disorder not otherwise specified (EDNOS) (Cairns, Styles, & Leichner, 2007). Carers found the information informative, with the section on the thoughts and feelings of youth who have struggled with eating disorders being the most highly rated part of MST.

Family Groups

Geist and colleagues (2000) compared two forms of family treatment: eight sessions of family therapy or eight sessions of family psychoeducation offered every two weeks for four months. The main goal of the family therapy sessions was to encourage parents to take an active role in managing the eating disorder. Topics covered in the psychoeducation groups included the physical and psychological sequelae of eating disorders, normal adolescent eating and development, body image and self-esteem, regulation of weight, and consequences of dieting. The authors found that patients in both groups gained weight, but improvements in family functioning were not found, and there was not sufficient power to determine whether there were differences between the two groups.

Parent Consultation

Rhodes, Baillee, Brown, and Madden (2008) compared ten families receiving FBT to ten families receiving an additional parent-to-parent consultation session. In this session the veteran, or more experienced, family shared their story, describing how they brought about their child's recovery and comparing their lives before and after treatment. This consultation served to help families feel less alone and more empowered to continue treatment (Rhodes, Brown, & Madden, 2009). Although there were no differences between the two groups in percentage ideal body weight (%IBW) at the end of treatment, the group receiving parent-to-parent consultation showed an immediate increase in the rate of weight restoration.

More controlled trials are needed to further investigate the utility of additional parent and family support, as there is currently no clear preferred intervention. Many studies did not include a control group, and several had small sample sizes or low participation or response rates. However, support for carers is requested by the carers themselves and reduces caregiver distress. There is also some evidence that it reduces high EE. Qualitative feedback from parents suggests that they appreciate the skills learned, the support provided, and the opportunity to interact with and learn from other families who are facing similar challenges.

> *"Listening to the other parents talk about their issues and struggles helped me realize that I was not alone. Just hearing someone else describe situations very similar to what we were going though, and to hear that they had all the same emotions that we did, was probably one of the most helpful things for us. When I would hear other parents talk about the struggles they were facing on a daily basis, it gave me a strength that I can't explain. There were times I would question myself and the things we had to do to get our daughter to eat, but when I heard the other parents explain the same situations, and how they handled it pretty much the same way we were, it made me feel like maybe I was doing the right things."*

Novel and Innovative Provision of Carer Support

Technology has been increasingly utilized for the provision of carer support. This development logically follows from the fact that Internet-delivered interventions are accessible, convenient, flexible, and time- and cost-efficient, as well as easy to use (see reviews by Bauer, Golkaramnay, & Kordy, 2005, and Cook Myers, Swan-Kremeier, Wonderlich, Lancaster, & Mitchell, 2004). Another important feature of online communication is that it allows parents to connect with others while maintaining their anonymity. For example, communicating under pseudonyms has been found to promote openness (Jaffe, Lee, Huang, & Oshagan, 1995) and online group members offer a "virtual shoulder," providing each other with high levels of support, acceptance, personal self-disclosure, and positive feelings regarding the approach that are commensurate with groups that meet in person (Kordy, Golkaramnay, Wolf, Haug, & Bauer, 2006).

Web-Based Skills Training

A series of studies have recently evaluated the technical feasibility, efficacy, and acceptability of the multimedia, web-based CBT program "Overcoming Anorexia Online" (OAO; Schmidt et al., 2007). This program is designed to reduce the emotional impact of carers of individuals with AN and to equip carers with skills to most effectively support their loved one with AN. OAO consists of the completion of nine interactive workbooks which include information on AN, CBT, how to successfully communicate with the individual with the eating disorder, meal support, understanding the functional aspects of maladaptive behaviors and how to support their abstinence of them, relapse prevention, and self-care/stress management (including a relaxation CD).

The first study was off-line and examined the workbook materials of OAO and found significant decreases in AN carer anxiety, depression, negative caregiving-related experiences, and EE at the end of the intervention and at a 10–12 week follow-up (Grover et al., 2011). In addition, positive caregiving experiences were significantly increased post-intervention. Parallel e-mail- or telephone-delivered clinician support also was offered. Qualitatively, participants liked the intervention and reported that involvement in such a program at an earlier point in the illness would have positively affected the course of the AN as they would have already possessed the knowledge and skills to provide the best possible support to their loved one.

The second study (Grover et al., 2011) compared online OAO with clinician guidance (via e-mail or telephone) to controls who received "ad hoc usual" support from BEAT (a U.K.-based organization for patients and carers). Results indicated significant reductions in carer anxiety and depression after participating in the web-based version of OAO that were maintained at a 3-month follow-up. A similar trend in carer EE also was found post-treatment.

In the third study (Hoyle, Slater, Williams, Schmidt, & Wade, 2013), carers were randomized to OAO with clinician guidance (OAO-G) or no guidance (OAO-NoG). The primary outcome measures were carers' ratings of their own EE and patients' ratings of their carers' EE. Although there were no changes in patients' perceptions of their carers' EE, significant improvements were found for carer intrusiveness (a component of EE), the negative experiences associated with caregiving, as well as the impact of starvation and guilt.

Moderated On-line Forum

Families Empowered and Supporting Treatment of Eating Disorders (F.E.A.S.T.) offers two platforms that make it possible for parents to connect to other parents from around the globe: "Around the Dinner Table" (ATDT) and "Coffee Breaks." ATDT is a moderated online adjunctive support forum in which carers post under usernames on various topics including implementing FBT when your child goes back to school, recipe exchange, eating out in restaurants, etc. It also is possible for users to e-mail one another via backchannel conversations. F.E.A.S.T.'s "Coffee Breaks" afford parents of persons with an eating disorder the opportunity to contact other parents in their geographic area via an online worldwide map.

> *"Just to hear from other parents that their child with an eating disorder recovered with FBT helped us tremendously and continues to give us strength and confidence. In Germany, where there are very few parents who are implementing FBT, Internet forums such as 'F.E.A.S.T.—Around the Dinner Table' allow us to profit from the experiences of other parents."*

Internet Relay Chat (IRC)

Carers have reported wanting to make use of modern technology such as synchronous Internet relay chat (IRC) or chat rooms to connect with fellow carers (Cottee-Lane et al., 2004). Accordingly, the purpose of one recently published study (Binford Hopf, Le Grange, Moessner, & Bauer, 2013) was to test the technical feasibility and acceptability of a therapist-guided, Internet-based chat support group for parents involved in FBT for adolescent AN. Thirteen parents who were involved in FBT for adolescent AN met at fixed times for fifteen 90-minute sessions in a virtual room. Communication was synchronous and in real time, and participants could join at any time. This heterogeneity of parents at various stages of FBT was thought to allow parents at earlier stages of FBT to profit from the experience of parents at later stages, as well as having the more veteran parents confirm the existence of the proverbial 'light at the end of the tunnel.'

The agenda was set at the beginning of each chat and dictated by member needs. Along with the therapist, parents helped each other problem-solve the challenges experienced in FBT, such as taking control of the refeeding process, discussing who to inform about AN, using proactive coping, and navigating through acute crises. Information regarding eating disorders, parental advocacy issues, media influences, and adolescent issues were further discussion points. An overarching goal was to provide parents with a space to vent the negative feelings related to the caregiving process as well as to glean pearls of wisdom from the more FBT-experienced parents regarding how they had coped. Role-play also was employed to help them choose more adaptive ways to respond to their child.

Participants reported a high degree of satisfaction (91.7%) with the chat program, looked forward to chat sessions, and would recommend the chat group to others. The accessibility and convenience that IRC afforded them helped them to better manage the logistics of attending the group.

> "I didn't have to leave the house."
> "No travel—doing it from home was very helpful. No babysitter to arrange, which can be especially difficult because of meal-times."

Participants also reported feeling less alone and more hopeful and confident about using FBT. Importantly, the chat group helped them to cope with their child's eating disorder and to implement FBT. The opportunity to "share concerns, experiences, and get advice from others who've 'been there'" and "have the same problem" as well as provide support to other parents were advantages of the chat group.

> "Just the actual knowing and 'talking' to someone who really knows what you are going through and to be able to share with another family—If they can do it ... we can do it."

"It's so nice to talk to others who 'get it.' My best friend just doesn't understand."

"I was able to compare notes with other parents."

These findings make a compelling (albeit preliminary) case for creating a supportive network for parents during FBT in order to lessen their psychological distress and caregiving burden and consequently help them to effectively implement FBT. The finite number of hours in parents' busy days may preclude them from committing to yet another appointment. IRC would therefore afford these parents the opportunity to reach out at a time (e.g., on a weeknight or weekend) and at a place (e.g., at home) convenient for them and thereby remove a substantial barrier to receiving support.

Conclusions and Implications

The ever-expanding research literature on adjunctive parental/carer support provides preliminary indication that carer support groups, either face-to-face or online versions, are valuable adjunctive supports to FBT. Involvement in carer support appears to help carers better manage their child's eating disorder, while it simultaneously boosts their self-confidence and improves their distress, caregiving burden, and eating disorder-related difficulties. Support offerings with psychoeducative components have effectively equipped carers with the knowledge and skills (e.g., improved communication and problem solving) to cope with their loved one's eating disorder. Moreover, the provision of psychoeducation can modify unhelpful carer attitudes, behaviors, and responses, as well as reduce the number of relatives with high EE. Additionally, modern technologies (e.g., web-based, online chat forums, IRC) have been effectively used to deliver adjunctive support. Results are indeed promising and this mode of delivery offers many additional conveniences for parents/carers, thus increasing the likelihood of them actively using such support programs.

Although FBT has been found to be effective in the treatment of adolescents with AN, full remission rates are 40–50 percent (Lock et al., 2010). It is possible that providing parallel support to parents or other carers who are in the process of implementing FBT would help improve outcome and increase remission rates. As demonstrated by Rhodes and colleagues (2008), participating in only one parent-to-parent consultation increased the rate of weight restoration and empowered parents to proceed with FBT. Enabling connections with other parents in FBT may be key to increasing the number of families who benefit from this form of treatment.

"One cannot go down this road alone. You need others who repeatedly confirm you are on the right track and encourage you to 'Keep at it!'"

> "*It was much easier once we talked to others that supported our efforts. I spent a lot of time doubting myself, and even my parenting skills when we first started going through this program. But once we had someone telling us that we were doing the right things, to just stick to it, and eventually it will get better, I got a sense of confidence that I had lost somewhere along the way. I'm not saying I didn't struggle everyday with it, but it helped to reinforce that we were doing what we had to do to help our daughter get her life back.*"

Findings also illuminate how pivotal therapists are in making connections for carers, especially those who are frustrated and display early signs of burnout, by referring them to forums such as F.E.A.S.T.'s "Around the Dinner Table" or "Coffee Breaks" and/or by encouraging and assisting them to form their own support network with their FBT carer peers.

> "*The contacts our FBT therapist provided us to other parents are extremely helpful; as the saying goes 'A problem shared is a problem halved.'*"

Future Research

Further investigation of the provision of support to carers of individuals with eating disorders in general, as well as those who are involved in FBT specifically, appears warranted. Efforts are currently underway to develop a skills group for parents who are in FBT for adolescent AN. Adapted from Treasure, Smith, and Crane's (2007) "New Maudsley Method" approach, the groups are designed to reduce the negative aspects of EE (hostility, criticism, and emotional overinvolvement) while increasing the positive aspects of EE (warmth, positive remarks) (Hoste, Treasure, & Le Grange, unpublished manuscript).

Future RCTs are required to further investigate the utility of additional parent and family support, as there is no clear front-runner to date. The paucity of controlled research designs, small sample sizes, and mediocre participation and response rates limit the extent to which these findings can be generalized. Nonetheless, qualitative data suggest that carers appreciate learning how to most effectively manage the eating disorder and how to respond to their loved one with the eating disorder. In addition, they feel supported and highly value the opportunity to connect with, as well as learn from, other carers who, to put it simply, "get it." The potential benefits of treating multiple families conjointly also are supported by work by Dare and Eisler (2000) (also see Chapter 7, this volume). Comparison of online and face-to-face modes of delivery as well as FBT with and without a parallel parental support group are further avenues of empirical investigation.

Note

1 The authors would like to generously thank Bernhard, Carmen, and Johannes Bambas, Walter, Paula, and Ashley Cummings, as well as parents from the ED Parent Support study for their contributions to this chapter.

References

American Psychiatric Association (2000). *Diagnostic and statistical manual of mental disorders* (4th ed., text rev.). Washington, DC: Author.

Bauer, S., Golkaramnay, V., & Kordy, H. (2005). E-mental-health—Neue medien in der medien in der psychosozialen versorgung [E-mental-health—New media in psychosocial provision]. *Psychotherapeut, 50*, 7–15.

Brown, H. (2011). A parent's perspective on family treatment. In D. Le Grange & J. Lock (Eds.), *Eating disorders in children and adolescents: A clinical handbook* (pp. 457–460). New York: Guilford Press.

Cairns, J. C, Styles, L. D., & Leichner, P. (2007). Evaluation of meal support training for parents and caregivers using a video and a manual. *Journal of the Canadian Academy of Child and Adolescent Psychiatry, 16*, 164–166.

Cook Myers, T., Swan-Kremeier, L., Wonderlich, S., Lancaster, K., & Mitchell, J. E. (2004). The use of alternative delivery systems and new technologies in the treatment of patients with eating disorders. *International Journal of Eating Disorders, 36*, 123–143.

Collins, L. (2005). *Eating with your anorexic: How my child recovered through family-based treatment and yours can too.* New York, NY: McGraw-Hill.

Cottee Lane, D., Pistrang, N., & Bryant Waugh, R. (2004). Childhood onset anorexia nervosa. The experience of parents. *European Eating Disorders Review, 12*, 169–177.

Dare, C., & Eisler, I. (2000). A multi-family group day treatment programme for adolescent eating disorder. *European Eating Disorders Review, 8*, 4–18.

Graap, H., Bleich, S., Wilhelm, J., Herbst, F., Trostmann, Y., Wancata, J., & de Zwaan, M. (2005). Needs and demands of the relatives of patients with anorexia or bulimia nervosa. *Neuropsychiatry, 19*, S155–161.

Geist, R., Heinmaa, M., Stephens, D., Davis, R., & Katzman, D. K. (2000). Comparison of family therapy and family group psychoeducation in adolescents with anorexia nervosa. *Canadian Journal of Psychiatry, 45*, 173–178.

Graap, H., Bleich, S., Herbst, F., Scherzinger, C., Trostmann, Y., Wancata, J., & de Zwaan, M. (2008a). The needs of carers: A comparison between eating disorders and schizophrenia. *Social Psychiatry and Psychiatric Epidemiology, 43*, 800–807.

Graap, H., Bleich, S., Herbst, F., Trostmann, Y., Wancata, J., & de Zwaan, M. (2008b). The needs of carers of patients with anorexia and bulimia nervosa. *European Eating Disorders Review, 16*, 21–29.

Grover, M., Naumann, U., Mohammad-Dar, L., Glennon, D., Ringwood, S., Eisler, I., Williams, C., Treasure, J., & Schmidt, U. (2011). A randomized controlled trial of an Internet-based cognitive-behavioural skills package for carers of people with anorexia nervosa. *Psychological Medicine, 41*, 2581–2591.

Grover, M., Williams, C., Eisler, I., Fairbairn, P., McCloskey, C., Smith, G., Treasure, J., & Schmidt U. (2011). An off-line pilot evaluation of a web-based systemic cognitive-behavioral intervention for carers of people with anorexia nervosa. *International Journal of Eating Disorders, 44*, 708–715.

Haigh, R., & Treasure J. (2003). Investigating the needs of carers in the area of eating disorders: Development of the Carers' Needs Assessment Measure (CaNAM). *European Eating Disorders Review, 11*, 125–141.

Holtkamp, K., Herpertz-Dahlmann, B., Vloet, T., & Hagenah, U. (2005). Group psychoeducation for parents of adolescents with eating disorders: The Aachen Program. *Eating Disorders: The Journal of Treatment and Prevention, 13*(4), 381–390.

Hoste, R., Treasure, J., & Le Grange, D. A skills group for parents in family-based treatment for adolescent anorexia nervosa. (unpublished manuscript).

Hoyle, D., Slater, J., Williams, C., Schmidt, U., & Wade, T. (2013). Evaluation of a web-based skills intervention for carers of people with anorexia nervosa: A randomized controlled trial. *International Journal of Eating Disorders, 46*, 634–638.

Jaffe, J. M., Lee, Y. E., Huang, L., & Oshagan, H. (July 1995). *Gender, pseudonyms, and computer-mediated communication: Masking identities and baring souls.* Paper presented at the Annual Conference of the International Communication Association, Albuquerque, New Mexico.

Kordy, H., Golkaramnay, V., Wolf, M., Haug, S., & Bauer, S. (2006). Internetchatgruppen in psychotherapie und psychosomatik: Akzeptanz und wirksamkeit einer Internet-brücke zwischen fachklinik und alltag. [Internet chat groups in psychotherapy and psychosomatics. Acceptance and effectiveness of an Internet-bridge between hospital and every day-life]. *Psychotherapeut, 51*, 144–153.

Le Grange, D., Eisler, I., Dare, C., & Hodes, M. (1992). Family criticism and self-starvation: A study of expressed emotion. *Journal of Family Therapy, 14*, 177–192.

Le Grange, D., Lock, J., Loeb, K., & Nicholls, D. (2010). Academy for Eating Disorders Position Paper: The role of the family in eating disorders. *International Journal of Eating Disorders, 43*, 1–5.

Le Grange, D., Rienecke Hoste, R., Lock, J., & Bryson, S. W. (2011). Parental expressed emotion of adolescents with anorexia nervosa: Outcome in family-based treatment. *International Journal of Eating Disorders, 44*, 731–734.

Leichner, P., Hall, D., & Calderon, R. (2005). Meal support training for friends and families of patients with eating disorders. *Eating Disorders: The Journal of Treatment and Prevention, 13*(4), 407–411.

Lock, J., & Le Grange, D. (2012). *Treatment manual for anorexia nervosa: A family-based approach* (2nd ed.) New York: Guilford Press.

Lock, J., Le Grange, D., Agras, W. S., Moye, A., Bryson, S. W., & Jo, B. (2010). Randomized clinical trial comparing family-based treatment with adolescent-focused individual therapy for adolescents with anorexia nervosa. *Archives of General Psychiatry, 67*, 1025–1032.

Pasold, T. L., Boateng, B. A., & Portilla, M. G. (2010). The use of an outpatient treatment group for children and adolescents with eating disorders. *Eating Disorders, 18*, 318–332.

Patel, S. J., Shafer, A., Zucker, N. L., & Bulik, C. M. (2011). Caring for yourself is caring for your child: Helping parents of children with eating disorders receive health care for themselves. In M. Brann (Ed.), *Contemporary case studies in health communication: Theoretical and applied approaches* (pp. 149–165). Dubuque, IA: Kendall Hunt.

Perkins, S., Winn, S., Murray, J., Murphy, R., & Schmidt, U. (2004). A qualitative study of the experience of caring for a person with bulimia nervosa, Part 1: The emotional impact of caring. *International Journal of Eating Disorders, 36,* 256–268.

Rhodes, P., Baillee, A., Brown, J., & Madden, S. (2008). Can parent-to-parent consultation improve the effectiveness of the Maudsley model of family-based treatment for anorexia nervosa? A randomized control trial. *Journal of Family Therapy, 30,* 96–108.

Rhodes, P., Brown, J., & Madden, S. (2009). The Maudsley model of family-based treatment for anorexia nervosa: A qualitative evaluation of parent-to-parent consultation. *Journal of Marital and Family Therapy, 35,* 181–192.

Salaminiou, E., Campbell, M., Simic, M., Kuipers, E., & Eisler, I. (2005). *Multi family therapy for adolescent anorexia nervosa: A pilot study.* Manuscript submitted for publication.

Salem, D. A., Bogar, G. A., & Reid, C. (1997). Mutual help goes on-line. *Journal of Community Psychology, 25,* 189–207.

Schmidt, U., Williams, C., Eisler, I., Fairbairn, P., McCloskey, C., Smith, G., & Treasure, J. (2007). *Overcoming anorexia online: Effective caring. A web-based programme for carers of people with AN.* Leeds, U.K.: Media Innovations Ltd.

Sepulveda, A. R., Lopez, C., Macdonald, P., & Treasure, J. (2008a). Feasibility and acceptability of DVD and telephone coaching-based skills training for carers of people with an eating disorder. *International Journal of Eating Disorders, 41,* 318–325.

Sepulveda, A. R., Lopez, C., Todd, G., Whitaker, W., & Treasure, J. (2008b). An examination of the impact of "the Maudsley eating disorder collaborative care skills workshops" on the well being of carers: A pilot study. *Social Psychiatry and Psychiatric Epidemiology, 43,* 584–591.

Szmukler, G. I., Eisler, I., Russell, G. F. M., & Dare, C. (1985). Anorexia nervosa, parental "expressed emotion" and dropping out of treatment. *British Journal of Psychiatry, 147,* 265–271.

Treasure, J., Murphy, T., Szmukler, G., Todd, G., Gavan, K., & Joyce, J. (2001). The experience of caregiving for severe mental illness: A comparison between anorexia nervosa and psychosis. *Social Psychiatry and Psychiatric Epidemiology, 36,* 343–347.

Treasure, J., Sepulveda, A. R., Whitaker, W., Todd, G., Lopez, C., & Whitney, J. (2007). Collaborative care between professionals and non professionals in the management of eating disorders: A description of workshops focused on interpersonal maintaining factors. *European Eating Disorders Review, 15,* 24–34.

Treasure, J., Smith, G., & Crane, A. (2007). Skills-based learning for caring for a loved one with an eating disorder: The new Maudsley method. New York: Routledge.

Uehara, T., Kawashima, Y., Goto, M., Tasaki, S., & Someya, T. (2001). Psychoeducation for the families of patients with eating disorders and changes in expressed emotion: A preliminary study. *Comprehensive Psychiatry, 42,* 132–138.

van Furth, E. F., Van Strien, D. C., Martina, L. M., van Son, M. J., Hendrickx, J. J., & van Engeland, H. (1996). Expressed emotion and the prediction of outcome in adolescent eating disorders. *International Journal of Eating Disorders, 20,* 19–31.

Whitney, J., & Eisler, I. (2005). Theoretical and empirical models around caring for someone with an eating disorder: The reorganization of family life and interpersonal maintenance factors. *Journal of Mental Health, 14,* 575–585.

Winn, S., Perkins, S., Murray, J., Murphy, R., & Schmidt, U. (2004). A qualitative study of the experience of caring for a person with bulimia nervosa, Part 2: Carers' needs and experiences of services and other support. *International Journal of Eating Disorders, 36,* 269–279.

Winzelberg, A. (1997). An analysis of an electronic support group for individuals with eating disorders. *Computers in Human Behavior, 13,* 393–407.

Zabala, M. J., Macdonald, P., & Treasure, J. (2009). Appraisal of caregiving burden, expressed emotion and psychological distress in families of people with eating disorders: A systematic review. *European Eating Disorders Review, 17,* 338–349.

Zucker, N. L., Ferriter, C., Best, S., & Brantley, A. (2005). Group parent training: A novel approach for the treatment of eating disorders. *Eating Disorders, 13,* 391–405.

Zucker, N. L., Loeb, K. L., Patel, S., & Shafer, A. (2011). Parent groups in the treatment of eating disorders. In D. Le Grange & J. Lock (Eds.), *Eating disorders in children and adolescents: A clinical handbook* (pp. 362–380). New York: Guilford Press.

Zucker, N. L., Marcus, M. D., & Bulik, C. (2006). A group parent training program: A novel approach for eating disorder management. *Eating and Weight Disorders, 11,* 78–82.

Part II

Specialty Populations

Chapter 9

Family-Based Treatment for Prodromal Anorexia Nervosa

Corinne Sweeney, Katharine L. Loeb, Amy Parter,
Lisa Hail, and Nancy Zucker

Subsyndromal or subthreshold Anorexia Nervosa (SAN) is a clinically significant eating disorder presentation meeting some but not all diagnostic criteria of Anorexia Nervosa (AN). SAN has been conceptualized as a transdiagnostic case of eating disorder psychopathology and traditionally labeled Eating Disorder–Not Otherwise Specified (EDNOS) in Diagnostic and Statistical Manual of Mental Disorders, Fourth Edition, Text Revision (DSM-IV-TR) (American Psychological Association [APA], 2000). To an extent, this category became a catchall for many child and adolescent cases that did not meet full criteria because of developmental factors such as an inability to articulate complex psychological symptoms. With *DSM-5*, we have moved toward a more developmentally sensitive paradigm that will presumably reduce the number of diagnostically ambiguous cases, thereby increasing meaningful case identification (APA, 2013). The diagnostic criteria for Anorexia Nervosa (AN) have been modified, including significant changes to make the criteria more applicable to youth. For instance, the criteria now allow for behavioral evidence or indicators of psychological symptoms. In addition to considerable alterations to specific eating disorder diagnoses, the terminology for transdiagnostic cases has changed in *DSM-5*, with EDNOS converting to Other Specified Feeding or Eating Disorder and Other Unspecified Feeding or Eating Disorder. Regardless of the label, though, given the dynamic quality of the case identification as a function of changes in the diagnostic system, disparate reports from multiple informants (Couturier, Lock, Forsberg, Vanderheyden, & Lee, 2007), and variations in clinical and research use of criteria, there will always be a group of children and adolescents who will not quite fit the full AN diagnosis despite their symptoms having compelling clinical significance. Some such cases will never have met criteria for AN while experiencing a progressive worsening of their eating disorder, raising the likelihood that SAN is signaling an AN prodrome. To understand how and when to intervene, a more thorough understanding of the nature and clinical significance of SAN is essential.

Conceptualizing Early Presentations

Based on the associated risks of SAN, researchers have proposed several differing conceptualizations of this constellation of symptoms to help determine where best to direct prevention and intervention efforts. Most notably, it has been suggested that for some cases, SAN may in fact represent a childhood presentation of full diagnosis when developmental factors are taken into consideration (i.e., early caseness); in others, as noted earlier, SAN may represent a prodromal phase of illness, which will eventually progress to a full presentation (Bravender et al., 2010; Le Grange & Loeb, 2007; Kreipe, Golden, Katzman, & Fisher, 1995). There are little data to guide predictions of which cases will worsen to full AN, which will stabilize and remain chronically subthreshold, or which are transient and will resolve with little or no intervention. However, there is an extensive literature evidencing the clinical risk of subsyndromal presentations and, by extension, the imperative for targeted, effective treatments (Crow et al., 2002; Eddy, Doyle, Hoste, Herzog, & Le Grange, 2008; Katzman, Christensen, Young, & Zipursky, 2001; Le Grange, Swanson, Crow & Merikangas, 2012; Neubauer et al., 2014; Peebles, Hardy, Wilson, & Lock, 2010; Swanson, Crow, Le Grange, Swendsen, & Merikangas, 2011).

Developmental Framework

It has been well-documented that *DSM-IV-TR* diagnostic criteria were not entirely applicable to youth, and as a result, this classification system may not have been sensitive enough to detect childhood presentations. In 2010, an international workgroup of experts in the field developed new recommendations for diagnosing eating disorders in youth that account for developmental stage (WCEDCA, 2007; Bravender et al., 2010). They asserted that lowering the overall symptom severity required for children and adolescents to meet diagnostic criteria for eating disorders will yield a more developmentally sensitive threshold. Specific recommendations included removing the amenorrhea criterion, as many children are prepubescent, consideration of significant deviations from the growth curve as opposed to a weight cut-off requirement, and decreasing the frequency and duration of binge episodes and compensatory behaviors required for a BN diagnosis. Regarding psychological criteria, the WCEDCA recommended removing the requirement that fear of weight gain be directly verbalized by patients and also suggested that behavioral observations or collateral report be adequate indicators for denial of seriousness of illness and body image disturbance. Furthermore, it was acknowledged that the very concept of denial, a construct whose relevance is debated even among adults with AN, may not be appropriate for children as their capacities to perceive current and future risk are just emerging. Moreover, the *DSM-IV-TR* criteria may miss actual caseness because of a child's inability to endorse certain symptoms, namely the more abstract cognitive features, despite these being truly present. As such, using behavioral indicators of symptoms, which are more reflective of how the disorder presents in youth may better promote case identification. For instance, while the concept of fear of weight gain may not be explicitly expressed in a child, behaviors such as affectively or behaviorally dysregulating when food is presented, rejecting food, or refusing to eat could serve as evidence for the presence of this symptom. This approach has been utilized in other child and adolescent realms, most notably anxiety disorders, where phobic symptoms may be expressed by "crying, tantrums, freezing, or clinging" (APA, 2000). These changes were ultimately incorporated in *DSM-5* for the purpose of greater developmental sensitivity as well as for the criteria to better align with important adult-based research findings (Call, Walsh, & Attia, 2013; Knoll, Bulik, & Hebebrand, 2011; Ornstein, et al., 2013).

Similarly, a position paper on adolescent eating disorders for the Society for Adolescent Health and Medicine asserts that the *DSM-IV* (APA, 1994) diagnostic criteria may have limited applicability to adolescents due to extensive variability in height and weight gains during puberty as well as variability in onset of menses (Kreipe et al., 1995). Furthermore, adolescents often lack the psychological insight to accurately report on cognitive symptoms, such as self-concept. The authors conclude that "the use of strict criteria may preclude the recognition of eating disorders in their early stages or subclinical form" (Kreipe et al., 1995). In a more recent position paper for the Society for Adolescent Health and Medicine, the authors recommend lowering the diagnostic threshold for adolescent eating disorders, particularly given the robust evidence suggesting that certain physiological consequences are irreversible and early intervention improves outcomes (Golden et al., 2003). Thus, according to this developmental framework, SAN and SBN are not exclusively partial syndromes but, rather, the developmental manifestation of the full syndrome that may have been failed to be detected or was inappropriately diagnosed due to the limitations of DSM-IV-TR for children and adolescents.

Stage-of-Illness Framework

Alternatively, as noted earlier, it may be that subsyndromal presentations represent prodromal stages that may eventually progress to a full eating disorder. This "subtype" of SAN (or stage of AN) and SBN would exist regardless of which version of the diagnostic system is applied, as AN and BN are not disorders that appear in full form suddenly in a healthy organism; rather, there is a natural progression of weight loss, binge eating/purging patterns and frequencies, and so on. Thus, the prodrome represents an important opportunity for preventive intervention to (a) avoid conversion to AN/BN, and (b) ameliorate extant clinically significant symptoms. An early study examining the course of EDNOS cases longitudinally showed that individuals with SAN may be at risk for developing the full-threshold diagnosis (Schleimer, 1983). Examined differently, all full AN cases in this study showed subsyndromal markers prior to reaching the AN threshold. Herzog, Hopkins, & Burns (1993) also found that 46% of their sample of participants with a subthreshold eating disorder converted to the full diagnosis over the course of a 41-month follow-up. More recent research has echoed these findings. In a prospective five-year study of both adolescents and adults with eating disorders, Ben-Tovim and colleagues (2001) found that 8% of EDNOS cases progressed to either AN or BN, and another prospective study (Milos, Spindler, Schnyder, & Fairburn, 2005) found that a large portion (41%) of EDNOS cases were assigned diagnoses of AN or BN at a one-year follow-up.

Adaptations Incorporated in the DSM-5

With the evolution to *DSM-5*, changes in the diagnostic criteria to AN and BN have improved their developmental sensitivity and applicability to youth. Most notably, the amenorrhea criterion was eliminated based on the extensive evidence that this criterion was more accurately conceptualized as an associated symptom rather than a requirement for AN. In fact, other physical symptoms, such as cardiac problems, are more universal and representative of sequelae of the disorder than amenorrhea (Katzman, 2005; Mehler & Krantz, 2003) and warrant serious medical attention (Rosen, 2010). The rationale for removing the amenorrhea criteria was particularly pertinent to children and adolescents, as menstruation in early puberty is often irregular or unpredictable and thus menses is not a reliable diagnostic indicator for this age group. Furthermore, this criterion cannot be applied to males, postmenopausal women, or women taking oral contraceptives. Research has also demonstrated that patients with all features of AN except amenorrhea do not differ from those with all criteria on most clinically relevant measures (Roberto, Steinglass, Mayer, Attia, & Walsh, 2008). These findings suggest that amenorrhea may be more indicative of weight or nutritional status rather than an independent characteristic (Attia & Roberto, 2009; Roberto et al., 2008). Furthermore, emerging evidence suggests that patients with and without amenorrhea do not significantly differ on treatment outcomes (Attia & Roberto, 2009).

The diagnostic criteria for eating disorders were also reshaped in *DSM-5* to capture behavioral indicators of the psychological features of illness. Specifically, *DSM-5* reframed the fear of weight gain criterion to further include "persistent behavior that interferes with weight gain." This increased focus on behaviors provides a more assessable measure and addresses the limitations in reporting of abstract concepts discussed previously. It also altered "refusal to maintain body weight" to the more behaviorally based "persistent restriction of energy intake" (APA, 2000; APA, 2013). These behaviors are more reflective of how the disorders present, particularly in children and adolescents, and consequently may better promote case identification. Another change to the diagnostic criteria for AN was the elimination of the example cutoff of 85% of expected weight for height (APA, 2000; APA, 2013). The 85% cutoff was frequently debated and often thought not to be established scientifically (Mitchell, Cook-Meyers, & Wonderlich, 2005) and was a moving target for youth, for whom the reference point for expected weight is dynamic, changing as a function of increasing age and height. The increased focus on behaviors, such as caloric restriction, serves as a more reliably measured construct, as well as eliminates the implication that low body weight is intentional on the part of the patient (Mitchell et al., 2005).

Challenges in Classification of SAN

While the shift to *DSM-5* represents progress in classifying subsyndromal presentations of AN, numerous barriers still make accurate identification a challenge. In addition to diagnostic issues related to irregular menstruation patterns early in puberty and variations in height and weight changes in adolescence, a further barrier remains typical assessment methods. Currently, assessment relies heavily on child or adolescent self-report of symptoms. Problems including cognitive and emotional factors, as well as denial and minimization, may greatly interfere with the accuracy of this approach. These factors, which must be taken into consideration when identifying children and adolescents with eating disorders, are described next.

Cognitive Factors

Cognitive factors in children and adolescents pose a unique challenge when attempting to assess symptoms that are largely cognitive in nature. The reliance on self-report of cognitive symptoms has been criticized in the adult eating disorders literature for a number of reasons. Namely, individuals may not endorse these symptoms due to lack of recognition (i.e., poor insight, minimization, denial) or in an attempt to conceal symptoms despite recognition for reasons related to stigma or desire to maintain symptoms (Becker, Eddy, & Perloe, 2009). While these same obstacles exist for child and adolescent self-report, the additional barrier of cognitive development also interferes. As noted earlier, because of their level of cognitive development, youth may not be capable of adequately expressing abstract concepts, such as body image dissatisfaction or fear of weight gain (Golden et al., 2003). Research shows that a variety of frontal lobe functions, such as abstract reasoning and attentional set shifting continue developing throughout adolescence and ability to complete tasks requiring these skills improves with progression through this age range (Rosso, Young, Femia, & Yurgelun-Todd, 2004; Yurgelun-Todd, 2007). Because of this immature development, youth may have limited insight regarding the motivation for restrictive eating patterns or attempts to control weight (Becker et al., 2009). Thus, child and adolescent reports of symptoms based on abstract concepts may be inaccurate due to their stage of cognitive development.

Research has also demonstrated that other neurobiological processes, such as inhibition and behavioral control, develop over the course of adolescence (Klenberg, Korkman, & Lahti-Nuuttila, 2001; Rosso et al., 2004). As a result of underdeveloped inhibitory abilities, children and adolescents may not be engaging in certain restrictive eating behaviors with premeditation as it is assumed adults do (Becker et al., 2009). Becker et al. (2009) provides the example of a youngster who restricts food intake without the intention of losing weight to illustrate this problem with the diagnostic criteria. Somatic discomfort may instead be primarily blamed. As a result of these limitations in reporting, many children and adolescents are not assigned diagnoses because they fail to fulfill full diagnostic criteria (Bunnell, Shenker, Nussbaum, Jacobson, & Cooper, 1990; WCEDCA, 2007). The 2007 Workgroup for the Classification of Child and Adolescent Eating Disorders (WCEDCA) clearly stated, "Diagnostic criteria that reference cognitive processes in AN are not sensitive to the timing of neurocognitive maturation in children and adolescents" (WCEDCA, 2007).

Affective Factors

In addition to cognitive processes that develop over the course of adolescence, several relevant emotional processes mature during this time period as well. Research shows that skills essential to emotion development, such as facial expression recognition and comprehension, progress through childhood and continue to mature during adolescence (Kolb, Wilson, & Taylor, 1992). Adolescents' ability to read social and emotional cues also continues to advance (Herba & Phillips, 2004). Youth utilize a wide variety of affective expressions during this stage, as their emotional responses have not yet consolidated (Yurgelun-Todd, 2007). Adolescence is also a marked period of growth for emotion regulation strategies, such as the capacity to identify, modulate, or suppress emotions (Luna & Sweeney, 2004). The immature nature of these emotion processes impacts adolescent reporting of their emotional state, as they may be incapable of doing so accurately given their developmental stage (WCEDCA, 2007). Numerous studies have shown that children and adolescents with pathological eating behaviors often fail to endorse a fear of gaining weight, a symptom that requires recognition and labeling of an affective state (Cooper, Watkins, Bryant-Waugh, & Lask, 2002; Fisher et al., 2001). Subsequently, self-report on these symptoms may not adequately capture the true severity of illness.

Denial and Minimization

As well as cognitive and emotional factors, denial and minimization of symptoms are further challenges to accurate self-report. Denial has long been thought to be an obstacle to accurate assessment of AN in adults (Vanderdeycken & Vanderlinded, 1983; Vitousek, Daly, & Heiser, 1991). More recently, denial of symptoms has been found to be even more common among adolescents as compared to their adult counterparts (Fisher et al., 2001). Couturier and Lock (2006) examined 86 adolescents with AN and divided the group into deniers, minimizers, and admitters based on congruence between the self-report Eating Disorder Examination (EDE) restraint subscale and clinical presentation. Results showed that deniers scored significantly lower than minimizers and admitters on all EDE subscales, despite showing no differences in weight, body mass index (BMI), and percent ideal body weight. Roughly half of the sample was categorized as a denier or minimizer, suggesting that denial and minimization are common processes among adolescents with AN, and ones that may interfere with accurate assessment and identification. It is important, however, to consider the role the aforementioned cognitive factors may play in denial and minimization. Adolescence is known as a time of increased risk-taking (Boyer, 2006), and immature frontal lobe processes such as inhibition may prevent youth from understanding the potential harm or negative consequences from their behavior (WCEDCA, 2007). Thus, denial and minimization may be less active or effortful processes among youth and more a result of their stage of brain development. Regardless, this combination of factors proves a true diagnostic challenge for accurately identifying those individuals in need of intervention.

Why Treat Subsyndromal AN?

Regardless of whether SAN truly represents a subthreshold version of AN or a full-threshold childhood presentation, treatment is imperative. Early identification and treatment of eating disorders in prodromal or early stages is considered by the field to be necessary for improved long-term prognosis (Deter & Herzog, 1994; Herzog, Nussbaum, & Marmor, 1996; Ratnasuriya, Eisler, & Szmukler, 1991; Russell, Szmukler, Dare, & Eisler, 1987; Steinhausen, 2002; Treasure & Russell, 2011; Von Holle et al., 2008). Proactively intervening on early symptom presentations may inhibit the disorder in early stages from progressing and is associated with more favorable treatment outcomes (Deter & Herzog, 1994). Additionally, detrimental physiological consequences can begin early in the course of illness. Delayed growth, decreased bone density, and alterations in brain structure and function have all been noted as early physical complications of eating disorders (Audi et al., 2002; Bachrach, Guido, Katzman, Litt, & Marcus, 1990; DiVasta, Feldman, Quach, Balestrino, & Gordon, 2009; Katzman, 2005; Katzman, Christensen, Young, & Zipursky, 2001; Modan-Moses et al., 2012; Root & Powers, 1983). Even more concerning, some research suggests these consequences may not be reversible with weight restoration or full recovery (Bachrach, Katzman, Litt, Guido, & Marcus, 1991; Kerem & Katzman, 2003, Miller et al., 2004; Misra & Klibanski, 2014). Younger age is also associated with more rapid weight loss, putting children at greater risk for growth problems (Peebles, Wilson, & Lock, 2006).

SAN is more prevalent than its full-threshold counterpart (Contrufo, Monteleone, Castaldo, & Maj, 2004; Crow et al., 2002). Prevalence estimates range from 0.8%–3.3% (Contrufo et al., 2004; Dancyger & Garfinkel, 1995; Patton, Johnson-Sabine, Wood, Mann, & Wakeling, 1990; Swanson et al., 2011; Walters & Kendler, 1995) as compared to 0.3%–0.5% for AN (Lucas, Beard, O'Fallon, & Kurland, 1991; Swanson et al., 2011; Walters & Kendler, 1995). EDNOS prevalence, which includes many SAN diagnoses as previously discussed, has been estimated at 2.3% (Machado, Machado, Goncalves, & Hoek, 2007). Furthermore, research has consistently demonstrated that the distress, impairment, and psychopathology associated with SAN is comparable to that of full AN. The physical health impairment in SAN is significant and, what is even more concerning, potentially irreversible. Walters and Kendler (1995) examined both anorexia nervosa and "anorexic-like syndromes" in adult females and found few distinct differences between groups. Likewise, Bunnell et al. (1990) compared adolescents with subclinical eating disorders to those meeting full criteria and found both groups demonstrated similar levels of eating disorder symptoms and related psychopathology. Similarly, Crow and colleagues (2002) examined full and partial syndrome AN and BN and found that while full syndrome BN can be distinguished from its subsyndromal counterpart, full and partial syndrome AN were essentially indistinguishable. More recent research has continued to find that partial and full-threshold diagnoses lack striking differences (Helverskov et al., 2011; Le Grange et al., 2013; McIntosh et al., 2004; Peebles, Hardy, Wilson, & Lock, 2010).

Not only are subthreshold presentations comparable to full blown diagnosis, but prepubertal onset has been shown to be an especially pernicious form of the disorder (Fosson, Knibbs, Bryant-Waugh, & Lask, 1987; Gowers, Crisp, Joughin, & Bhat, 1991; Hudson, Nicholls, Lynn, & Viner, 2012; Lantzouni, Frank, Golden, & Shenker, 2002; Peebles, Wilson, & Lock, 2006). In a study of physical sequelae in 20 patients with premenarchal anorexia nervosa, numerous devastating effects were identified, including marked delay in menstruation, reduced height growth, and disrupted breast development (Russell, 1985). Similarly, in a long-term follow-up study of 30 children with AN, age of onset prior to 11 years was associated with poor prognosis (Bryant-Waugh et al., 1988). Hudson and colleagues (2012) examined a sample of children with eating disorders under 13 years of age and found 35% of these cases were medically unstable, including bradycardic, hypotensive, dehydrated, and hypothermic. Notably, nearly half of the cases with medical instability (41%) were not underweight. Early onset has also been shown to be associated with irreversible growth delays and increased rates of weight loss (Lantzouni et al., 2002; Peebles et al., 2006). Especially worrisome is that adolescent girls with disordered eating patterns such as extreme dieting and attempts at weight control are at eight times greater risk for developing a full eating disorder than nondieters (Patton et al., 1990). Given the pernicious course of this disorder and evidence for early intervention, treating this subset of children and adolescents with SAN is imperative.

For all of the reasons outlined here, treatment research on FBT has often included cases whose clinical profiles do not align with strict DSM-IV definitions of AN (Le Grange, Binford, & Loeb, 2005; Lock, Le Grange, Forsberg, & Hewell, 2006; Loeb et al., 2007; Lock et al., 2010). One observational study of FBT specifically examined a subset of participants characterized as SAN. Loeb and colleagues (2007) conducted an open trial to test the feasibility and effectiveness of delivering FBT in the United States. In this study, 20 adolescents with AN or SAN were treated utilizing the published FBT manual (Lock et al., 2001). Of the 20 patients, seven had been categorized as SAN by a failure to meet full criteria for AN by virtue of weight or menstrual status. At the end of treatment, all of the participants with SAN met criteria for a good outcome.

If the diagnostic status of participants in these studies were revisited through the lens of DSM-5, it is likely that more cases would be identified as "true" AN. While there is little direct evidence at this point for the efficacy of FBT for subsyndromal and prodromal AN, there appear to be no contraindications, and early results suggest promise.

Overview of FBT for Prodromal AN

In light of the evidence that SAN is a clinically significant presentation with comparable consequences of the full disorder, and the importance of preventing full-syndrome AN, FBT has been adapted for clinically significant eating disorder patients who have never met the diagnosis of AN but are exhibiting a likely AN prodrome. These modifications have been detailed in Loeb, Craigen, Goldstein, Lock, and Le Grange (2011) but will be reviewed briefly here, with case examples to illustrate key SAN-specific considerations. The FBT-SAN model follows the foundation approach of FBT-AN (Lock, Le Grange, Agras, & Dare, 2001), as well as FBT-BN (Le Grange & Lock, 2007), with important modifications aimed at making the treatment more applicable and relevant to high-risk populations. The structure of FBT-SAN is largely comparable to the original models, with three separate phases. Phase 1 focuses on increased parent control of eating, externalization of the illness, blame-reduction, and sibling support. Phase 2 consists of gradual transfer of control back to the child as their symptoms improve. Phase 3 is focused on issues of broader adolescent development and return of the patient to typical functioning. The course of treatment is shorter than the original manual, consisting of 14 sessions over six months.

The FBT-SAN adaptation has been tested in youth with SAN. Loeb and colleagues (2012) presented the preliminary results of a controlled treatment trial comparing FBT-SAN to individual supportive psychotherapy (SPT) for the prevention of conversion to AN in high-risk youth (National Institute of Health grant K23 MH074506–01). Using a partially randomized preference design, participants were randomized to FBT-SAN or SPT; if they refused randomization they were presented with the opportunity to choose their study intervention. This design model retained families who were intent on receiving one treatment or the other (most cases of randomization refusers were loyal to FBT, having heard or read about the approach), thereby increasing generalizability of the sample. The sample consisted of 59 children and adolescents, ages 9–17, with prodromal or atypical AN. To be included in the study, participants must have never met criteria for full AN, having a clinically significant eating disorder that shares some but not all features of AN. Final analyses of the study are currently underway.

In Session 1, the SAN-FBT protocol diverges from the original approach in several notable ways. In contrast to the original manual, in which Session 1 underscores the dangerous consequences associated with AN, the crisis scene in Session 1 is focused on highlighting the risks inherent to SAN, as well as the importance of preventing the symptoms from progressing to full AN. Language consistent with these goals is used to convey the impending danger associated with conversion to AN. For example, "You must be so worried watching your daughter lose weight, and exhausted from working to keep the anorexia at bay." Considering the lesser degree of starvation and nutritional compromise in SAN as compared to AN, the FBT-SAN manual emphasizes the normalization of eating habits (quality/range of food types, quantity of food, and regularity of eating) more than a rigorous renourishment process, although weight gain is typically one treatment goal.

Challenges may arise around these components of treatment with SAN cases, as many families struggle to grasp the degree of nutritional rehabilitation required if their child does not appear as emaciated as a classic case of AN. Using a patient's historical growth curve is helpful to illustrate drops in percentiles, rather than abiding by standard ranges for acceptable BMI. Therapists must emphasize the urgency of the situation, using crisis-like language, to underscore the importance of increasing caloric intake. Citing multiple markers of health in addition to weight, such as menstrual status, cardiac indicators, and cognitive symptoms may assist families in understanding the full extent of expected recovery, and the discrepancy between the patient's current state and optimal health, despite falling short of an AN diagnosis. Providing education about the medical consequences of SAN is also imperative. It is also important to emphasize that the patient has a clinically significant eating disorder or he or she would not have been referred for treatment.

Maria is a 12-year-old female who presented for FBT with her biological parents and younger sister, at the recommendation of her pediatrician. Maria had lost 15 pounds over the course of six months in the context of an attempt to begin eating healthier foods, which rapidly progressed into restrictive eating. Though her BMI remained within the lower contingent of the normative range, her menstrual cycle had ceased for two months, she restricted overall caloric intake and avoided a long list of foods that elicited anxiety regarding weight gain, and experienced significant fear that she would become fat if compelled to eat "unhealthy" foods. While Maria's parents were extremely successful early in Phase 1, once Maria gained enough weight to place her further in the normative range, though still a significant drop from her historical growth trajectory, they became resistant to continued caloric increases. Maria's father asserted that foods containing large amounts of fats or sugars were detrimental for anyone to consume and that this was contraindicated to their family philosophy of health. The therapist worked with the parents to use indicators aside from weight as their gauge for the amount and types of food required. Emphasizing flexibility in eating as an independent treatment goal was essential in helping the parents understand the significance in Maria eating foods they may deem "unhealthy" and appreciating that a child with an eating disorder likely will require deviations from normative family practices, just as a child with diabetes requires special dietary considerations. In addition, the therapist continued to clarify that the continued rigidity in Maria's eating practices and thoughts about food was itself an indicator that she was not yet sufficiently restored to her individualized, pre-morbid place on the growth curve. While it was difficult for the parents to accept that further weight gain was necessary, and in fact medicinal, they were influenced by the therapist's stance of expertise in asserting that Maria's residual cognitive and behavioral symptoms represent a high risk for deterioration to baseline and a low probability of successful transition to Phases 2 and 3.

A change in Session 2, the family meal session, is the modified goal of helping parents convince their daughter to take one more bite of food than she is prepared to eat *or* to eat a mouthful of a forbidden food. This extends from the variability in SAN presentations and corresponding treatment goals, and derives from a combination of the original FBT BN and AN manuals (Le Grange & Lock, 2007; Lock et al., 2001). As such, therapists should encourage parents to bring a challenging food when packing the family meal. An obstacle may arise in that the patient eats all food provided to her, leaving seemingly no opportunity for the "one more bite" intervention. This is an optimal time for parents to help their daughter to confront the forbidden food. By convincing their daughter to eat food that she regularly avoids or restricts, this intervention encourages flexibility in eating and reinforces the message of nonrestrictive eating habits.

Lucy is a 14-year-old female who presented for FBT treatment with her parents and two older brothers. Lucy had failed to make weight gains for the past year and a half and had significantly dropped on the growth curve. She placed undue importance on shape and was particularly preoccupied with avoiding certain foods, such as those with high sugar content. During Session 2, Lucy's parents brought deli sandwiches, chips, and cookies for the family meal. They also brought peanut M&M's, a candy that Lucy had previously enjoyed but had stopped eating altogether. Lucy ate her sandwich, chips, and cookie with no persuasion or visible distress. The therapist used this opportunity to encourage Lucy's parents to convince her to eat the candy. At this point, Lucy became perceptibly anxious, tearful, and resistant. The therapist coached Lucy's parents to physically align them next to her, offer verbal encouragement, and facilitate her eating the candy by opening the package and placing a handful of pieces on her plate. Lucy slowly ate the M&M's on her plate as her parents offered continued support. The therapist underscored the parent's role in Lucy eating the forbidden food, and Lucy's parents commented that they felt empowered to follow their instincts when feeding Lucy foods she enjoyed prior to the eating disorder onset.

Additional variations in Phase 1 include the implementation of regular family meals at home (which research has shown to be associated with reductions in multiple child/adolescent psychopathologies, including eating disorders) and modeling of healthy eating habits by parents (Elan-Barak, Sztainer, Goldschmidt, & Le Grange, 2014; Fulkerson, Strauss, Neumark-Sztainer, & Boutelle, 2007; Neumark-Sztainer, Eisenberg, Fulkerson, Story, & Larson; 2008; Neumark-Sztainer, Wall, Story, & Fulkerson, 2004). Specifically, parents are encouraged to model flexible, nonrestrictive eating as a positive example for their child. This speaks to the potential for more overlapped eating habits profiles in SAN parents and offspring than in AN families, where the illness may be more visibly stark. With full AN, the case can be made that food is medicine for the starving child and that medicine is prescribed exclusively to the ill family member. With SAN, the topography of eating disorder symptoms might share more features of "normative" unhealthy dietary practices that may be exhibited by others in the family, prompting the need for a more systemic target of the intervention. This treatment strategy also speaks to the preventive aspect of this intervention in reversing the risk for progression from SAN to AN, and the importance of creating a protective family environment. A holistic, family-level approach will ideally buffer the child or adolescent against continued risk. An analogy to sleep hygiene may be presented: for a child with sleeping difficulties, precise regularity of bedtime and restriction of the use of the bed to sleeping only (as opposed to doing homework, playing on an iPad, etc.) is essential. However, for a child without vulnerability for poor sleep, such rules are not as important in ensuring ease of falling asleep.

This prescription sometimes elicits oppositional reactions from parents, who may have their own idiosyncrasies regarding food and eating. Modeling healthy eating may be especially challenging for parents who have their own difficulties with a past or current eating disorder, or who have self-imposed restrictive or avoidant eating behavior. Parents with their own eating struggles may be resistant to altering their habits as part of their child's treatment. Sensitivity around these issues is imperative, as parents may or may not have disclosed their problems with their families.

Natalia is a 16-year-old female who presented to FBT with her mother and stepfather. Natalia had begun dieting to lose weight for a school beach trip but continued losing weight following the trip as many peers told her how great she looked. Natalia counted calories every day and exercised excessively if she exceeded her goal caloric intake. Natalia's mother, Sue, had a history of AN as a teenager, for which she received treatment, but continued to exhibit symptoms into adulthood, and currently adheres to a vegan diet. During Phase 1, the therapist encouraged the family to eat meals together and for Natalia's parents to model healthy and nonrestrictive eating. In session, Natalia began complaining that although her stepfather ate healthy-sized servings at dinner, her mother refused to eat the majority of food prepared, usually ate only a small portion of the main dish, and declined dessert each night. Sue cited her veganism as the source of her eating habits, but descriptions of family meals revealed that she was even restricting vegan foods. The therapist navigated this sensitive situation by acknowledging that sometimes children with eating disorders are required to eat a larger quantity and greater range of foods than other family members require, while also highlighting the importance of parents exhibiting flexibility in the types of foods eaten. When this problem persisted and Sue's food avoidance became even more concerning by affecting what she was willing to feed her daughter, the therapist met with Natalia's parents alone to discuss the issue. The therapist noted that it appears difficult for Sue to eat a range of foods even within a vegan diet and asked whether she thinks some anxiety around food from her own history of an eating disorder may still be operative. Sue was much less defensive outside of the presence of her daughter and admitted to some residual eating disorder symptoms. The therapist responded empathically, suggesting that it must be difficult for the mother to be fully objective about Natalia's health needs in the context of her own related struggles. Sue expressed that she does not want her daughter to have these anxieties persist into adulthood as they had for her. The therapist indicated that some parents in this situation mutually agree that the parent who can be more objective about food requirements be disproportionately in charge of meal planning, while the affected parent assumes more of an active role in other aspects of caring for their ill child. In other words, the parents can function as a complementary team, capitalizing on relative strengths. The therapist also offered Sue a referral for her own treatment, which Sue said she would "think about."

The criteria for progression from Phase 1 to Phase 2 are modified in FBT-SAN to include weight gain or stabilization, as applicable, as well as a reduction in resistance toward eating and meals. Similar to the original protocol, parents must feel empowered by their own capabilities to exert control over the eating disorder and their child's eating habits. In Phase 2, the control of food and eating is gradually shifted back to the patient and family meals continue to be prioritized.

Consistent with the original manual, Phase 3 contains an emphasis on relapse prevention, but with an added accent on preventing progression to full AN. This stage also includes a focus on middle childhood issues, given the earlier development stage where SAN typically manifests, as compared to AN. Additionally, like in the core approach, problem-solving is modeled around childhood or adolescent issues that arise. Relapse prevention discussions center on caveats of unintentional weight loss (i.e., due to a stomach virus). Therapists should explain to parents that accidental weight loss may trigger the eating disorder if the child's weight drops significantly, and therefore, children must maintain a BMI-for-age percentile in the "safety zone" relative to their own personal growth curve, where unintentional weight loss will not leave them vulnerable to the eating disorder sneaking back in.

Jillian is a 15-year-old female who presented for treatment with her mother and grandmother. Jillian had successfully progressed through Phases 1 and 2 of FBT, and along with weight gain, cognitive symptoms had significantly remitted. During Phase 3, as the eating symptoms continually resolved and Jillian began engaging more socially, conflicts arose over curfew times and level of supervision required at various events. Jillian desired more independence and felt her mother and grandmother were being overly strict by not allowing her to attend social events in certain settings. The therapist modeled problem-solving by facilitating discussions of these conflicts calmly in session. During a moment of disagreement in session, the therapist interjected, highlighting the change in the nature of the session from the start of treatment until now. "I want to point out that instead of arguing over how many bites of dinner Jillian needs to take, we're disagreeing over how late she may stay out a party. Let's take a moment to celebrate that, even as we recognize the importance of these conflicts." This note served to underscore the progress Jillian made and highlight that this type of argument is a normative one for adolescence.

Conclusions

SAN is a clinically significant eating disorder presentation that, despite not fulfilling full diagnostic criteria, is comparable to full AN in distress, impairment, and psychopathology. These cases have typically been labeled EDNOS in the diagnostic system, although recent changes in *DSM-5* should improve case identification and reduce this group. However, given the dynamic quality of the diagnosis, as well as differing conceptualizations of subsyndromal as either prodromal or early caseness, a subset of children will likely never quite fit diagnostic criteria. In addition, given the nature of progression from well to ill in the case of eating disorders, there will always be an AN prodrome that represents a juncture for a hybrid prevention-treatment approach. The negative consequences of SAN, coupled with the improved prognosis associated with early identification, suggest that this presentation merits clinical intervention. FBT has been adapted for SAN to treat current symptoms, as well as prevent progression to the full disorder. The FBT-SAN protocol is a potentially effective method for addressing the unique needs of this transdiagnostic group of children and adolescents.

References

American Psychiatric Association (1994). *Diagnostic and statistical manual of mental disorders* (4th Ed.). Washington, DC: Author.

American Psychiatric Association (2000). *Diagnostic and Statistical Manual of Mental Disorders, Fourth Edition Text Revision.* Washington, DC: Author.

American Psychiatric Association (2013). *Diagnostic and statistical manual of mental disorders* (5th Ed.). Washington, DC: Author.

Attia, E., & Roberto, C. A. (2009). Should amenorrhea be a diagnostic criterion for anorexia nervosa? *International Journal of Eating Disorders, 42, 581–589.*

Audi, L., Vargas, D. M., Gussinye, M., Yeste, D., Marti, G., & Carrascosa, A. (2002). Clinical and biochemical determinants of bone metabolism and bone mass in adolescent female patients with anorexia nervosa. *Pediatric Research, 51, 497–504.*

Bachrach, L. K., Guido, D., Katzman, D., Litt, I., & Marcus, R. (1990). Decreased bone density in adolescent girls with anorexia nervosa. *Pediatrics, 86, 440–447.*

Bachrach, L. K., Katzman, D., Litt, I., Guido, D., & Marcus, R. (1991). Recovery from osteopenia in adolescent girls with anorexia nervosa. *Journal of Clinical Endocrinology & Metabolism, 72, 602–606.*

Becker, A. E., Eddy, K. T., & Perloe, A. (2009). Clarifying criteria for cognitive signs and symptoms for eating disorders in DSM-V. *International Journal of Eating Disorders, 42, 611–619.*

Ben-Tovim, D., Walker, K., Gilchrist, P., Freeman, R., Kalucy, R., & Esterman, A. (2001). Outcomes in patients with eating disorders: A 5-year study. *The Lancet, 357, 1254–1257.*

Boyer, T. (2006). The development of risk-taking: A multi-perspective review. *Developmental Review, 26, 291–345.*

Bravender, T., Bryant-Waugh, R., Herzog, D., Katzman, D., Kriepe, R. D., Lask, B., … Zucker, N. (2010). Classification of eating disturbance in children and adolescents: Proposed changes for the DSM-V. *European Eating Disorders Review, 18, 79–89.*

Bryant-Waugh, R., Knibbs, J., Fosson, A., Kaminski, Z., & Lask, B. (1988). Long term follow up of patients with early onset anorexia nervosa. *Archives of Disease in Childhood, 63, 5–9.*

Bunnell, D. W., Shenker, I. R., Nussbaum, M. P., Jacobson, M. S., & Cooper, P. (1990). Subclinical versus formal eating disorders: Differentiating psychological features. *International Journal of Eating Disorders, 9, 357–362.*

Call, C., Walsh, B. T., & Attia, E. (2013). From DSM-IV to DSM-5: Changes to eating disorder diagnoses. *Current Opinion in Psychiatry, 26*(6), 532–536. doi: 10.1097/YCO.0b013e328365a321

Contrufo, P., Monteleone, P., Castaldo, E., & Maj, M. (2004). A 4-year epidemiological study of typical and atypical eating disorders: Preliminary evidence for subgroups of atypical eating disorders with different natural outcomes. *European Eating Disorders Review, 12,* 234–239.

Cooper, P. J., Watkins, B., Bryant-Waugh, R., & Lask, B. (2002). The nosological status of early onset anorexia nervosa. *Psychological Medicine, 32,* 873–880.

Couturier, J., & Lock, J. (2006). Denial and minimization in anorexia nervosa. *International Journal of Eating Disorders, 39,* 212–216.

Couturier, J., Lock, J., Forsberg, S., Vanderheyden, D., & Lee, H. Y. (2007). The addition of a parent and clinician component to the Eating Disorder Examination for Children and Adolescents. *International Journal of Eating Disorders, 40,* 472–475.

Crow, S., Agras, W. S., Halmi, K., Mitchell, J. E., & Kraemer, H. C. (2002). Full syndromal versus subthreshold anorexia nervosa, bulimia nervosa, and binge eating disorder: A multicenter study. *International Journal of Eating Disorders, 32,* 309–318.

Dancyger, I. F., & Garfinkel, P. E. (1995). Relationship of partial syndrome eating disorder to anorexia nervosa and bulimia nervosa. *Psychological Medicine, 25,* 1019–1025.

Deter, H. C., & Herzog, W. (1994). Anorexia nervosa in a long-term perspective: Results of the Heidelberg-Mannheim study. *Psychosomatic Medicine, 56,* 20–27.

DiVasta, A. D., Feldman, H. A., Quach, A. E., Balestrino, M., & Gordon, C. M. (2009). The effect of bed rest on bone turnover in young women hospitalized for anorexia nervosa: A pilot study. *The Journal of Clinical Endocrinology & Metabolism, 94,* 1650–1655.

Eddy, K. T., Doyle, A. C., Hoste, R. R., Herzog, D. B., & Le Grange, D. (2008). Eating disorder not otherwise specified in adolescents. *Journal of the American Academy of Child & Adolescent Psychiatry, 47,* 156–164.

Elran-Barak, R., Sztainer, M., Goldschmidt, A. B., & Le Grange, D. (2014). Family meal frequency among children and adolescents with eating disorders. *Journal of Adolescent Health, 55,* 53–58.

Fisher, M., Schneider, M., Jennifer, B., Symons, H., & Mandel, F. S. (2001). Differences between adolescents and young adults at presentation to an eating disorders program. *Journal of Adolescent Health Care, 28,* 222–227.

Fosson, A., Knibbs, J., Bryant-Waugh, R., & Lask, B. (1987). Early onset anorexia nervosa. *Archives of Disease in Childhood, 62,* 114–118.

Fulkerson, J. A., Strauss, J., Neumark-Sztainer, D., Story, M., & Boutelle, K. (2007). Correlates of psychosocial well-being among overweight-adolescents: The role of the family. *Journal of Consulting and Clinical Psychology, 75,* 181–186.

Golden, N. H., Katzman, D. K., Kreipe, R. E., Stevens, S. L., Sawyer, S. M., Rees, J., Nicholls, D., & Rome, E. S. (2003). Eating disorders in adolescents: Position paper for the Society for Adolescent Medicine. *Journal of Adolescent Health, 33,* 496–503.

Gowers. S. G., Crisp, A. H., Joughin, N., & Bhat, A. (1991). Premenarchaeal anorexia nervosa. *Journal of Child Psychology and Psychiatry, 32,* 515–524.

Helverskov, J. L., Lyng, B., Clausen, L., Mors, O., Frydenberg, M., Thomsen, P. H., & Rokkedal, K. (2011). Empirical support for a reclassification of eating disorders NOS. *European Eating Disorders Review, 19*, 303–315.

Herba, C., & Phillips, M. (2004). Annotation: Development of facial expression recognition from childhood to adolescence: Behavioural and neurological perspectives. *Journal of Child Psychology and Psychiatry, 45*, 1185–1198.

Herzog, D. B., Hopkins, J. D., & Burns, C. D. (1993). A follow-up study of 33 subdiagnostic eating disordered women. *International Journal of Eating Disorders, 14,* 261–267.

Herzog, D. B., Nussbaum, K. M., & Marmor, A. K. (1996). Comorbidity and outcome in eating disorders. *Psychiatric Clinics of North America, 19*(4), 843–859.

Hudson, L. D., Nicholls, D. E., Lynn, R. M., & Viner, R. M. (2012). Medical instability and growth of children and adolescent with early onset eating disorders. *Archives of Disease in Children.* Advance online publication. doi: 10.1136/archdischild-2011–301055

Katzman, D. K. (2005). Medical complications in adolescents with anorexia nervosa: a review of the literature. *International Journal of Eating Disorders, 37,* S52–S59.

Katzman, D. K., Christensen, B., Young, A. R., & Zipursky, R. B. (2001). Starving the brain: Structural abnormalities and cognitive impairment in adolescents with anorexia nervosa. *Seminar of Clinical Neuropsychiatry, 6,* 146–152.

Kerem, N. C., & Katzman, D. K. (2003). Brain structure and function in adolescents with anorexia nervosa. *Adolescent Medicine, 14,* 109–118.

Klenberg, L., Korkman, M., & Lahti-Nuuttila, P. (2001). Differential development of attention and executive functions in 3- to 12-year-old Finnish children. *Developmental Neuropsychology, 20,* 407–428.

Knoll, S., Bulik, C. M., & Hebebrand, J. (2011). Do the currently proposed DSM-5 criteria for anorexia nervosa adequately consider developmental aspects in children and adolescents?. *European child & adolescent psychiatry, 20*(2), 95–101.

Kolb, B., Wilson, B., & Taylor, L. (1992). Development changes in the recognition and comprehension of facial expression: Implications for frontal lobe function. *Brain and Cognition, 20,* 74–84.

Kreipe, R., Golden, N. H., Katzman, D. K., & Fisher, M. (1995). Eating disorders in adolescents: A position paper of the Society for Adolescent Medicine. *Journal of Adolescent Health, 16,* 476–480.

Lantzouni, E., Frank, G. R., Golden, N. H., & Shenker, R. I. (2002). Reversibility of growth stunting in early onset anorexia nervosa: A prospective study. *Journal of Adolescent Health, 2,* 162–165.

Le Grange, D., & Loeb, K. (2007). Early identification and treatment of eating disorders: Prodrome to syndrome. *Early Intervention in Psychiatry, 1,* 27–39.

Le Grange, D., Binford, R., & Loeb, K. L. (2005). Manualized family-based treatment for anorexia nervosa: A case series. *Journal of the American Academy of Child and Adolescent Psychiatry, 44*(1), 41–46. doi: 10.1097/01.chi.0000145373.68863.85

Le Grange, D., Crosby, R. D., Engel, S. G., Cao, L., Ndungu, A., Crow, S. J., ... Wonderlich, S. A. (2013). DSM-IV-defined anorexia nervosa versus subthreshold anorexia nervosa (EDNOS-AN). *European Eating Disorders Review, 21,* 1–7.

Le Grange, D., Swanson, S. A., Crow, S. J., & Merikangas, K. R. (2012). Eating disorder not otherwise specified in the US population. *International Journal of Eating Disorders, 45,* 711–718.

Le Grange, D., & Lock, J. (2007). *Treating bulimia in adolescents: A family-based approach*. Guildford Press.

Lock, J., Le Grange, D., Agras, W. S., & Dare, C. (2001). *Treatment manual for anorexia nervosa: A family-based approach*. New York: Guildford Publications, Inc.

Lock, J., Le Grange, D., Agras, W. S., Moye, A., Bryson, S. W., & Jo, B. (2010). Randomized clinical trial comparing family-based treatment with adolescent-focused individual therapy for adolescents with anorexia nervosa. *Archives of General Psychiatry*, 67(10), 1025–1032.

Lock, J., Le Grange, D., Forsberg, S., & Hewell, K. (2006). Is family therapy useful for treating children with anorexia nervosa? Results of a case series. *Journal of the American Academy of Child and Adolescent Psychiatry*, 45(11), 1323–1328. doi: 10.1097/01.chi.0000233208.43427.4c

Loeb, K. L., Craigen, K. E., Goldstein, M. M., Lock, J., & Le Grange, D. (2011). Early Treatment for Eating Disorders. In D. Le Grange & J. Lock (Eds.), *Child and Adolescent Eating Disorders: A Clinical Handbook*. 337–361. Guilford Press.

Loeb, K. L., Walsh, B. T., Lock, J., Le Grange, D., Jones, J., Marcus, S., Weaver, J., & Dobrow, I. (2007). Open trial of family-based treatment for full and partial anorexia nervosa in adolescence: Evidence of successful dissemination. *Journal of the American Academy of Child and Adolescent Psychiatry*, 46, 792–800.

Loeb, K. L., Walsh, B. T., Newcorn, J., Striegel, R., Marcus, S., Taylor, C. B., Lock, J., & Le Grange, D. (2012, May). *Family-based treatment for prodromal anorexia nervosa: A hybrid efficacy-effectiveness trial*. International Conference on Eating Disorders, Austin, Texas.

Lucas, A. R., Beard, C. M., O'Fallon, W. M., & Kurland, L. T. (1991). 50-Year trends in the incidence of anorexia nervosa in Rochester, Minn.: A population-based study. *American Journal of Psychiatry*, 148, 917–922.

Luna, B., & Sweeney, J. A. (2004). The emergence of collaborative brain function: FMRI studies of the development of response inhibition. *Annals of the New York Academy of Sciences*, 1021, 296–309.

Machado, P. P., Machado, B. C., Gonçalves, S., & Hoek, H. W. (2007). The prevalence of eating disorders not otherwise specified. *International Journal of Eating Disorders*, 40, 212–217.

McIntosh, V. V., Jordan, J., Carter, F. A., McKenzie, J. M., Luty, S. E., Bulik, C. M., & Joyce, P. R. (2004). Strict versus lenient weight criterion in anorexia nervosa. *European Eating Disorders Review*, 12, 51–60.

Mehler, P. S., & Krantz, M. (2003). Anorexia nervosa medical issues. *Journal of Women's Health*, 12, 331–340.

Miller, K. K., Grieco, K. A., Mulder, J., Grinspoon, S., Mickley, D., Yehezkel, R., ... Klibanski, A. (2004). Effects of risedronate on bone density in anorexia nervosa. *The Journal of Clinical Endocrinology & Metabolism*, 89, 3903–3906.

Milos, G., Spindler, A., Schnyder, U., & Fairburn, C. G. (2005). Instability of eating disorder diagnoses: Prospective study. *The British Journal of Psychiatry*, 187, 573–578.

Misra, M., & Klibanski, A. (2014). Endocrine consequences of anorexia nervosa. *The Lancet Diabetes & Endocrinology*, 2, 581–592.

Mitchell, J. E., Cook-Myers, T., & Wonderlich, S. A. (2005). Diagnostic criteria for anorexia nervosa: Looking ahead to DSM-V. *International Journal of Eating Disorders*, 37, S95–S97.

Modan-Moses, D., Yarozlavsky, A., Kochavi, B., Toledano, A., Segev, S., Balawi, F., ... Stein, D. (2012). Linear growth and final height characteristics in adolescent females with anorexia nervosa. *PloS one, 7*, e44504.

Neubauer, K., Weigel, A., Daubmann, A., Wendt, H., Rossi, M., Lowe, B., & Gumz, A. (2014). Paths to first treatment and duration of untreated illness in anorexia nervosa: Are there differences according to age of onset? *European Eating Disorders Review, 22*, 292–298.

Neumark-Sztainer, D., Eisenberg, M. E., Fulkerson, J. A., Story, M., & Larson, N. I. (2008). Family meals and disordered eating in adolescents: Longitudinal findings from Project EAT. *Archives of Pediatric Adolescent Medicine, 162*, 17–22.

Neumark-Sztainer, D., Wall, M., Story, M., & Fulkerson, J. A. (2004). Are family meal patterns associated with disordered eating behaviors among adolescents? *Journal of Adolescent Health, 35*, 350–359.

Ornstein, R. M., Rosen, D. S., Mammel, K. A., Callahan, S. T., Forman, S., Jay, M. S., ... Walsh, B. T. (2013). Distribution of eating disorders in children and adolescents using the proposed DSM-5 criteria for feeding and eating disorders. *Journal of Adolescent Health, 53*(2), 303–305. doi: 10.1016/j.jadohealth.2013.03.025

Patton, G. C., Johnson-Sabine, E., Wood, K., Mann, A. H., & Wakeling, A. (1990). Abnormal eating attitudes in London schoolgirls—A prospective epidemiological study: Outcome at twelve month follow-up. *Psychological Medicine, 20*(2), 383–394.

Peebles, R., Hardy, K. K., Wilson, J. L., & Lock, J. D. (2010). Are diagnostic criteria for eating disorders markers of medical severity? *Pediatrics, 125*, e1193–e1201.

Peebles, R., Wilson, J. L., & Lock, J. D. (2006). How do children with eating disorders differ from adolescents with eating disorders at initial evaluation? *Journal of Adolescent Health, 39*, 800–805.

Ratnasuriya, R., Eisler, I., & Szmukler, G. (1991). Anorexia nervosa: Outcome and prognostic factors after 20 years. *British Journal of Psychiatry, 156*, 495–496.

Roberto, C. A., Steinglass, J., Mayer, L. E. S., Attia, E., & Walsh, B. T. (2008). The clinical significance of amenorrhea as a diagnostic criterion for anorexia nervosa. *International Journal of Eating Disorders, 41*, 559–563.

Root, A. W., & Powers, P. S. (1983). Anorexia nervosa presenting as growth retardation in adolescents. *Journal of Adolescent Health Care, 4*, 25–36.

Rosen, D. S. (2010). Identification and management of eating disorders in children and adolescents. *Pediatrics, 126*(6), 1240–1253.

Rosso, I. M., Young, A. D., Femia, L. A., & Yurgelun-Todd, D. A. (2004). Cognitive and emotional components of frontal lobe functioning in childhood and adolescence. *Annals of the New York Academy of Sciences, 1021*, 355–362.

Russell, G. F. M. (1985). Premenarchal anorexia nervosa and its sequelae. *Journal of Psychiatric Research, 19*, 363–369.

Russell, G. F., Szmukler, G. I., Dare, C., & Eisler, I. (1987). An evaluation of family therapy in anorexia nervosa and bulimia nervosa. *Archives of General Psychiatry, 44*, 1047–1056.

Schleimer, K. (1983). Dieting in teenage schoolgirls: A longitudinal prospective study. *Acta Paediatrica, 72*, 9–47.

Steinhausen, H. (2002). The outcome of anorexia nervosa in the 20th century. *American Journal of Psychiatry, 159*, 1284–1293.

Swanson, S., Crow, S. J., Le Grange, D., Swendsen, J., & Merikangas, K. R. (2011). Prevalence and correlates of eating disorders in adolescence: Results from the

National Comorbidity Survey Replication Adolescent Supplement. *Archives of General Psychiatry, 68,* 714–723.

Treasure, J., & Russell, G. (2011). The case for early intervention in anorexia nervosa: Theoretical exploration of maintaining factors. *The British Journal of Psychiatry, 199,* 5–7.

Vanderdeycken, W., & Vanderlinded, J. (1983). Denial of illness and the use of self-reporting measures in anorexia nervosa patients. *International Journal of Eating Disorders, 4,* 101–107.

Vitousek, K. B., Daly, J., & Heiser, C. (1991). Reconstructing the internal world of the eating disordered individual: Overcoming denial and distortion in self-report. *International Journal of Eating Disorders, 10,* 647–666.

Von Holle, A., Poyastro Pinheiro, A., Thornton, L. M., Klump, K. L., Berrettini, W. H., Brandt, H., ... Bulik, C. M. (2008). Temporal patterns of recovery across eating disorder subtypes. *Australasian Psychiatry, 42,* 108–117.

Walters, E. E., & Kendler, K. S. (1995). Anorexia nervosa and anorexic-like syndromes in a population-based female twin sample. *American Journal of Psychiatry, 152,* 64–71.

Workgroup for Classification of Eating Disorders in Children and Adolescents (WCEDCA) (2007). Classification of child and adolescent eating disturbances. *International Journal of Eating Disorders, 40,* 117–122.

Yurgelun-Todd, D. (2007). Emotional and cognitive changes during adolescence. *Current Opinion in Neurobiology, 17,* 251–257.

Chapter 10

Family-Based Treatment for Child and Adolescent Overweight and Obesity

A Transdevelopmental Approach

Katharine L. Loeb, Angela Celio Doyle, Kristen Anderson, Amy Parter, Corinne Sweeney, Lisa Hail, Katherine Craigen, Tom Hildebrandt, and Daniel Le Grange

Over the last quarter of a century, the prevalence of overweight and obesity has been increasing at an alarming rate and is now considered by many to be one of the leading public health problems facing our country. Pediatric obesity is defined as having a body mass index (BMI) meeting or exceeding the 95th percentile for age and sex; a BMI percentile between 85 and 95 is defined as pediatric overweight and represents an important juncture for prevention and intervention (Barlow, 2007). In the past 30 years, rates of childhood obesity have more than doubled in children and quadrupled in adolescents. The amount of obese children ages 6–11 has increased from 7 percent in 1980 to about 18 percent in 2012. Similarly, the rates of obese adolescents aged 12–19 has increased from 5 percent to about 21 percent over the same period of time (Center for Health Statistics, 2012; Ogden, Carroll, Kit, & Flegal, 2014). The rapidity of the increase suggests that genetic factors are not solely responsible (Dietz & Gortmaker, 2001; Marti, Moreno-Aliaga, Hebebrand, & Martinez, 2004; Mokdad et al., 1999).

Consequences and Correlates of Pediatric Overweight and Obesity

The consequences of this rapid increase in pediatric obesity are extensive. Obese youth are likely to be obese as adults (Dietz, 1998; Dietz & Gortmaker, 2001; Freedman et al., 2009; Guo & Chumela, 1999; Serdula et al., 1993; Singh, Mulder, Twisk, Van Mechelen, & Chinapaw, 2008), with one study showing that children who became obese as young as age 2 are greater than four times more likely to be obese as adults (Freedman et al., 2005). Independent of adult weight status, the long-term consequences of overweight in childhood and adolescence include increased morbidity and mortality in adulthood (Must, Jacques, Dallal, Bejema, & Dietz, 1992; Reilly & Kelly, 2011).

Medical

Overweight youth experience numerous physical health problems, such as elevated blood pressure, high cholesterol, greater risk for impaired glucose tolerance, insulin resistance, Type 2 diabetes, sleep apnea, asthma, and osteoarthritic difficulties (Freedman, Zuguo, Srinivasan, Berenson, & Dietz, 2007; Han, Lawlor, & Kimm, 2010; Kelsey, Zaeofel, Bjornstad, & Nadeau, 2014; Sutherland, 2008; Taylor et al., 2006; Whitlock, Williams, Gold, Smith, & Shipman, 2005). Many of these health problems are associated with higher risk for cardiovascular disease, with one study finding that 70 percent of obese youth had at least one cardiovascular risk factor and 39 percent had 2 or more (Freedman et al., 2007). The dramatic increase in Type 2 diabetes in children and adolescents has also been linked to obesity with the risk increasing as weight increases (Fleischman, & Rhodes, 2009; Mokdad et al., 2001; Pi-Sunyer, 2009). Furthermore, overweight and obesity are also associated with an increased risk of developing various types of cancer including those of breast, colon, kidney, and prostate among others (Kushi et al., 2006).

Economic

The economic consequences of pediatric obesity in the United States and in other countries are experienced both individually and nationally. Other countries have endured similar economic burden as a result of increasing rates of obesity (e.g., Comans et al., 2013; Wang & Zhai, 2013). The economic consequences are often characterized as either direct or indirect. Direct consequences include medical costs such as prescriptions, emergency room visits, outpatient costs, and inpatient costs. Indirect consequences refer to labor market costs to the obese individual and their employees such as absenteeism (Cawley, 2010). Obesity-related medical costs in the United States have recently estimated at $190 billion, or 20 percent of total annual U.S. healthcare expenditures in 2005 (Lehnert, Sonntag, Konnopka, Riedel-Heller, & Konig, 2013) and at $209.7 billion in 2008 (Apovian, 2013). However, the economic impact of obesity is not limited to healthcare costs, and therefore, it is likely that the overall economic burden resulting from obesity is even greater (Apovian, 2013).

Research indicates a strong positive relationship between excess weight and medical costs; however, this relationship is less evident for children and adolescents (Lehnert et al., 2013; Wright & Prosser, 2014). Wright and Prosser (2014) concluded that overweight and obese youth have greater healthcare visits and prescription costs than normal-weight youth; however, there was no significant difference in medical expenditures between the two groups. Nevertheless, the full impact of the obesity epidemic on U.S. health and economics is still largely unknown since such high rates of obesity have never previously been experienced.

Psychosocial

Research has indicated that overweight youth are targets of stigmatization, with obese youth being more likely to be bullied (Fox & Farrow, 2009; Griffiths, Wolke, Page, & Horwood, 2006; Haines & Neumark-Sztainer, 2009) and experiencing more difficulty making friends (Fonseca, Matos, Guerra, & Gomes Pedro, 2009) than their normal-weight peers. Furthermore, they are also more likely to experience suicidality (Eisenberg, Neumark-Sztainer, & Story, 2003; Haines, Neumark-Sztainer, Eisenberg, & Hannon, 2006; Menzel et al., 2010), parental criticism (Davison & Birch, 2002; Puhl & Latner, 2007), academic difficulties (Falkner et al., 2001), and behavioral problems (Lumeng, Gannon, Cabral, Frank, & Zuckerman, 2003). Overweight adolescents are less frequently named as friends by peers, which marks a vicious cycle, as such nominations are positively correlated with sports participation in school clubs, and decreased time watching television (Strauss & Pollack, 2003), all of which are variables protective against pediatric overweight (PO). Romantic peer relationships are negatively impacted by overweight status as well (Gortmaker, Must, Perrin, Sobol, & Dietz, 1993; Pearce, Boergers, & Prinstein, 2002; Sobal, Rauschenbach, & Frongillo, 1995).

Obese youth appear to have impaired psychological health compared to non-overweight children (Griffiths, Parsons, & Hill, 2010). Data on depression and obesity in youth are inconsistent across community and treatment seeking samples, with the latter indicating an association between the two (Erermis et al., 2004; Melnyk et al., 2006; Van Vlierberghe, Braet, Goosens, & Mels, 2009). Eating disordered behavior, especially binge eating disorder, has been observed in overweight and obese youth (Ackard, Neumark-Sztainer, Story, & Perry, 2003; Morgan et al, 2002; Puhl & Latner, 2007). Additionally, overweight and obese youth are more likely than their non-overweight peers to experience body dissatisfaction (Heinberg & Thompson, 2009; Wardle & Cook, 2005), with research indicating that this is especially salient in overweight and obese girls (Thompson et al., 2007). Health-related quality of life is significantly impaired among overweight youth (Griffiths et al., 2010; Schwimmer, Burwinkle, & Varni, 2003; Williams, Wake, Hesketh, Maher, & Waters, 2005), rivaling the compromised quality of life among children and adolescents diagnosed with chronic illnesses such as cancer (Schwimmer et al., 2003), Cystic Fibrosis, epilepsy, Type 1 diabetes, and inflammatory bowel disease (Ingerski et al., 2010).

Family-Level Factors

Family/Home Environment

In addition to less modifiable risk factors for PO, including genetic propensity (Demerath et al., 2007; Farooqi & O'Rahilly, 2000; Le Stunff, Fallin, & Bougnères, 2001) and socioeconomic and demographic factors (Zeller et al., 2007; Zeller et al., 2004), variables related to the persistence or increase of pediatric obesity include several parent-driven factors. Davison and Birch's (2001, 2002) longitudinal studies identified predominantly parental factors as the best predictors for change in girls' weight status over time. Specifically, the mothers' increase in BMI and the father's physical activity and caloric intake accounted for a significant proportion of their daughter's increase in BMI, when controlling for child-centric variables. Girls from families with "obesogenic environments" had significantly higher increases in BMI and skinfold thickness over two years compared to those in non-obesogenic families (Davison & Birch, 2002). As described in a follow-up study (Davison, Francis, & Birch, 2005), "These findings were noteworthy because they tested and confirmed the idea that parents create environments by way of their own behaviors that can promote, or protect their children from, accelerated weight gain" (p. 1981). Children's and adolescent's eating habits are strongly influenced by characteristics of the physical and social environment, which are heavily dictated by parents (Patrick & Nicklas, 2005; Van Strien, van Niekerk, & Ouwens, 2009). For example, children and adolescents are more likely to eat foods that are both accessible and frequently available in their households (Birch & Marlin, 1982; Story et al., 2002).

Additionally, the way in which families eat have changed from past generations who ate in a more regimented way by sharing mealtimes and preparing traditional (versus processed) meals to current families rarely eating together, and preparing quicker and more flexible meals (e.g., microwave meals, fast food; Kime, 2009). This is important because both quality and quantity of dietary intake appear to play a significant role in determining the weight status of a child or adolescent. Children who consume fast food, as compared to children who do not, have higher total energy and fat intake in addition to high saturated fat intake, lower fiber intake, and overall have diets consisting of high energy density (Powell & Nguyen, 2013; Sebastian, Wilkinson, Enns, & Goldman 2009). Fast food is also associated with greater consumption of sugar-sweetened beverages (Powell & Nguyen, 2013), which has also been correlated with increased obesity and overweight in youth (Hill, Wyatt, Reed, & Peters, 2003; Ludwig, Peterson, & Gortmaker, 2001; Malik, Schulze, & Hu, 2006; Martin-Calvo et al., 2014; Pan et al., 2013; Welsh, et al., 2005; Zheng et al., 2014). Notably, excess quantity and poor quality of food are not the only dietary-based variables that confer risk for pediatric obesity and overweight. Longitudinal research has also shown that dietary restraint and radical weight control behaviors place adolescent girls at increased risk for pediatric obesity and overweight (Stice, Cameron, Killen, Hayward, & Taylor, 1999; Stice, Presnell, Shaw, & Rhode, 2005).

Another factor relevant to the family environment is energy expenditure. Increased physical activity is associated with a lower risk of health issues in children and adolescents (Janssen & LeBlanc, 2010). However, daily participation in school physical education among adolescents has decreased over time (Eaton et al., 2012), placing greater responsibility on parents to compensate for this trend. However, outside of school, the data are equally discouraging (Powell, Slater, & Chaloupka, 2004), especially for children whose parents have lower incomes and education levels. Overweight youth are particularly disadvantaged in this regard (Boutelle, Neumark-Sztainer, Story, & Resnick, 2002; Patrick et al., 2004). Observational studies of activity patterns in youth suggest that a more natural integration of activity, through lifestyle activities or facilitation of spontaneous bouts of "play," may hold more promise for lasting behavior change (Goldfield & Epstein, 2002).

Conversely, sedentary activities in the home, such as watching television and playing video games, have been implicated in the rise in pediatric obesity due to the associated reduction in amount of physical activity and increased caloric consumption (Crespo et al., 2001; Pearson & Biddle, 2011; Thivel et al., 2013). Evidence from randomized controlled trials suggests that reduction in sedentary behaviors may result in reduced obesity (Epstein et al., 2008; Robinson, 1999; Tremblay et al., 2011). Research has shown that when youth are asked to reduce television time, they are more likely to engage in vigorous physical activity and their attitudes towards physical activity are more positive than when they are encouraged to directly increase activity (Epstein et al., 1997; Epstein et al., 1995).

Parent Feeding Styles

Overly restrictive and overly permissive parental feeding styles have both been implicated in pediatric obesity (Steele, Jensen, Gayes, & Leibold, 2014). Birch and Fisher (1995) developed a description of parent feeding styles that correspond with Baumrind's (1971) taxonomy of parenting styles: permissive, authoritarian, and authoritative. A permissive feeding style by parents, in which children are allowed to fully determine the quality and quantity of food eaten, is more common among families with overweight children (Berge, 2009; Johnson, Welk, Saint-Maurice, & Ihmels, 2012; Moens, Braet, & Vandewalle, 2013) and has been associated with unhealthy dietary intake and a more obesogenic environment (Johnson et al., 2012) and a positive relationship with child BMI (Humenikova & Gates, 2008; Johnson et al., 2012; Olvera & Power, 2010). An authoritarian feeding style, in which parents control children's eating without regard for their preferences, is negatively associated with healthy eating behaviors, such as consumption of vegetables (Patrick et al., 2004) and positively associated with child and adolescent BMI (Berge, Wall, Bauer & Neumark-Sztainer, 2010; Berge, 2009; Lane et al., 2013; Rhee, Lumeng, Appugliese, Kaciroti & Bradley, 2006). In fact, restricting children from "forbidden," high-calorie foods may have the effect of increasing these foods' desirability (Faith & Kerns, 2005) or prompting children to eat more sweet or savory snacks when away from direct parental supervision (Berge, 2009). Furthermore, restrictive food environments appear to affect children's health negatively when they are at high risk for overweight, and result in increases in BMI Z-score (Faith et al., 2004). An authoritative feeding style, in which parents encourage healthy choices while respecting child preferences, is associated with a less obesogenic environment and lower BMI (Arredondo et al., 2006; Johnson et al., 2012) as well as increased consumption of healhtier foods, such as fruits and vegetables (Park & Walton-Moss, 2012; Patrick, Nicklas, Hughes, & Morales, 2005; Patrick et al., 2004; Rodenburg, Oenema, Kremers, & van de Mheen, 2012), and is negatively associated with emotional eating (Topham et al., 2011). Furthermore, there is some evidence that an authoritative parenting style may lower the risk of a child becoming overweight or obese (Olvera & Power, 2010; Rhee et al., 2006; Wake, Nicholson, Hardy, & Smith, 2007).

The Use of Food as Reward or Punishment

Parental feeding styles that involve food as rewards or punishment are associated with an increase in intake of unhealthy foods and weight problems in children (Carnell, Cooke, Cheng, Robbins, & Wardle, 2011; Musher-Eizenman, de Lauson-Guillain, Holub, Leproc, & Charles, 2009; Ritchie, Welk, Styne, Gerstein, & Crawford, 2005). Birch (1999) found that children's preferences for specific foods increased after those foods were used as rewards for performing a task unrelated to eating. In addition, limiting the availability of the reward food increased liking of those foods.

Positive Parenting Factors

Parent-driven factors have also been associated with a reduced likelihood of childhood obesity or continued increases in overweight severity. Specifically, parental monitoring and modeling through frequent family meals has been linked to healthy eating and activity patterns and a decrease in overweight and obesity (Hammons & Fiese, 2011; Rollins, Belue, & Francis, 2010; Wansink & Kleef, 2014). Benefits of regular, frequent family mealtimes include increased consumption of fruits and vegetables; decreased consumptions of fried food, soda, and trans fats; increased likelihood of eating three meals a day; and decreased risk of disordered eating behaviors (Ackard & Neumark-Sztainer, 2001; Gillman et al., 2000; Neumark-Sztainer, Wall, Story, & Fulkerson, 2004). Meals eaten outside the home tend to contribute to increased portions sizes and caloric intake (e.g., Zoumas et al., 2001). Hammons and Fieses (2011) found that three or more family meals a week resulted in 12 percent reduction in odds for becoming overweight, 20 percent reduction in eating unhealthy foods, 35 percent reduction in disordered eating, and 24 percent increase in the odds of eating healthy foods for children and adolescents. Furthermore, frequent breakfast consumption was found to be associated with lower BMI scores in children aged 9–13 (Coppinger, Jeanes, Hardwick, & Reeves, 2012; Patro & Szajewska, 2010). Antonogeorgos and colleagues (2012) found that children who ate breakfast and more than three meals a day were two times less likely to be overweight or obese. Family mealtimes might exert a powerful effect on nutrition and behavior in children because they provide structure and organization in a child's life, allow a time for parents to monitor and model appropriate behavior, and foster a sense of connectedness (Feldman, Eisenberg, Neumark-Sztainer, & Story 2007; Story & Neumark-Sztainer, 2005). Higher frequency of family dinners is associated with meeting dietary guidelines for fruits and vegetables during the transition from childhood to adolescence (Burgess-Champoux, Larson, Neumark-Sztainer, Hannan, & Story, 2009) and improved diet quality in young adulthood (Larson, Neumark-Sztainer, Hannan, & Story, 2007). Moreover, when adolescents are served vegetables and milk at dinner, they are more likely to regularly consume these items five years later, highlighting the importance of parents choosing healthy items for their adolescents during family meals (Arcan et al., 2007).

Psychosocial and negative health risk factors associated with adolescent overweight are attenuated by the degree of family connectedness and parental monitoring (Mellin, Neumark-Sztainer, Story, Ireland, & Resnick, 2002). Overweight children and adolescents who perceived their family as more cohesive and supportive and reported more shared family meals were more likely, despite their overweight status, to engage in more physical activity, eat more nutritious diets, and report overall better psychological adjustment. Finally, adolescents who perceive that their mother is concerned with healthy eating are more likely to consume fruits and vegetables (Boutelle, Fulkerson, Neumark-Sztainer, Story, & French, 2007).

The Case for a Systems-Level Approach

Beyond the home, one of the greatest challenges to obese individuals in this country is what has been labeled the "toxic" environment (Wadden, Brownell, & Foster, 2002). This is an environment where high-fat, calorically dense foods are readily available and affordable for energy intake, while energy output is discouraged or inaccessible by virtue of passive forms of transportation, screen-based entertainment and recreation, and safety concerns in inner-city neighborhoods. Children and adolescents are particularly vulnerable to the toxic environment in that they have the least agency as consumers and must contend with multisystemic impediments to a healthy lifestyle. In addition to the difficulties faced by their adult counterparts, overweight and obese children are subject to their parents' and schools' food choices. Moreover, reductions in school-required physical activity are rarely compensated for in the home environment. Instead, sedentary home-based behaviors such as television viewing are compounded by incessant commercials advertising foods with poor nutritional value and increased weight liability (Lobstein & Dibb, 2005). Even on PBS, unhealthy food cues embedded in commercial-free television shows are given almost twice the airtime as healthy food cues (Radnitz et al., 2009).

Targeting children and adolescents exclusively in the weight loss process ignores these multisystemic challenges and is arguably a setup for failure. It is both relatively ineffective and developmentally inappropriate to apply a personal responsibility model to pediatric obesity. Instead, a socio-ecological model must be adopted that recognizes that environmental defaults are currently set to suboptimal levels, directing choice towards items with a negative health value (Brownell, Schwartz, Puhl, Henderson, & Harris, 2009; Radnitz, Loeb, DiMatteo, Keller, Zucker, & Schwartz et al., 2013). Parents must be enlisted in the process of shifting defaults in the home and school environments to prompt healthier choices for their children.

A Transdevelopmental Family-Based Intervention

The approach offered here does not merely suggest parents assume a role in providing healthy food and encouraging exercise for their children, but it proposes a developmentally sensitive continuum for parental involvement depending on the stage of the overweight child or adolescent. Parents have different roles depending on whether the patient is a child, preadolescent, or adolescent. These differences primarily encompass three general dimensions: quantity, quality, and intensity. For younger children, parents are charged with *fully* shouldering management of their child's eating and exercise behaviors until healthier patterns are established. For preadolescents, a somewhat more collaborative stance for parents is recommended. Older adolescents require the collaboration and support of their parents in implementing changes but must navigate their semi-independent lifestyle and prepare for the further independence afforded by the pending post high-school years when adolescents move outside of their parents' homes. For all ages, sustainable lifestyle changes are emphasized, not highly restrictive feeding practices or specific goal weights.

Noting the benefits of family-based treatment for child and adolescent eating disorders (Couturier, Kimber, & Szatmari, 2013; Stiles-Shields, Rienecke Hoste, Doyle, & Le Grange, 2012), an approach that sees parents as the most effective resource to remedy their child's disordered eating, we apply the underlying tenets of this method to childhood overweight and obesity. The consensus in the field is that children and young adolescents with obesity are most successfully treated through family-based interventions (American Dietetic Association, 2006; Epstein, Paluch, Roemmich, & Beecher, 2007; Janicke et al., 2014; Jelalian & Saelens, 1999; Shrewsbury, Steinbeck, Torvaldsen, & Baur, 2011). These intervention models have included parental involvement ranging from parents being the exclusive targets of treatment (e.g., Golan,

2006; Golan & Crow, 2004; Golan, Kaufman, & Shahar, 2006; Golan, Weizman, Apter, & Fainaru, 1998; Golley et al., 2007; Shelton et al., 2007; West, Sanders, Cleghorn, & Davies, 2010), to parents primarily being seen separately from their children (e.g., Jelalian, Mehlenbeck, Lloyd-Richardson, Birmaher, & Wing, 2005; Kalarchian et al., 2009), to families being seen conjointly at least for significant portions of the intervention (e.g., Epstein, 1993; Epstein, McCurley, Wing, & Valoski, 1990; Epstein, Valoski, Wing, & McCurley, 1990; Gunnarsdottir, Njardvik, Olafsdottir, Craighead, & Bjarnason, 2012; Epstein, McKenzie, Valoski, Klein, & Wing, 1994). While the literature clearly indicates that parental involvement is key for the long-term success of weight loss in children and adolescents, it does not provide clear guidance as to how the nature of that involvement should change depending on developmental level (Lo Presti, Lai, Hildebrandt, & Loeb, 2010; Shrewsbury et al., 2011). For instance, for young children, treatment can target the parents exclusively, and the child will lose weight by virtue of the changes and supervision that the parents impose in the home (Golan, 2006; Golan et al., 2006; Golan & Crow, 2004; Golley et al., 2007; Shelton et al., 2007; West et al., 2010); this would clearly not be appropriate for adolescents, whose developing autonomy requires them to navigate multiple external environments, each with its own foodscape. In fact, among overweight adolescent girls, a high level of parental monitoring is associated with extreme dieting behaviors, whereas moderate monitoring is correlated with healthy behaviors and psychosocial well-being (Mellin et al., 2002). Some studies with overweight or obese adolescents put parents in a support or parallel patient role, where they attend sessions separately from their teen (DeBar et al., 2012; Williamson et al., 2006) or are asked to merely provide food, transportation, and encouragement (Ebbeling, Leidig, Sinclair, Hangen, & Ludwig, 2003).

The core, foundation FBT approach targets adolescent anorexia nervosa (Lock & Le Grange, 2012) by initially putting parents fully in charge of the renourishment process and later working to return independence over eating back to the adolescent. This model works across developmental levels because the psychological nature of anorexia nervosa (i.e., the clear pathological distortions around food, eating, and body) arguably renders individuals of all ages in need of some degree of external control or support during weight restoration. In adults this is typically accomplished by an inpatient staff. With younger individuals, we can avoid hospitalization by facilitating parental agency for change. Meal plans and other rigid prescriptions of food intake are discouraged in favor of reliance on parental knowledge of basic nutrition in rectifying the health status of their child. The reason for this type of parental control (temporary, focused only on the eating disorder symptoms) is justifiable for adolescents is because this pernicious and deadly disorder interferes with self-care around food and exercise in a way that does not align with developmental stage. In the eating domain, individuals with anorexia nervosa can appear equally "regressed," regardless of chronological age. A primary goal of family-based treatment is to respect normal child and adolescent development by eliminating the obstacle of the illness and allowing the patient to progress in all developmental domains (e.g., physical, psychosocial).

In adapting this treatment model for pediatric overweight and obesity, the core approach must be modified to take into account that obesity is not a psychiatric disorder. In the absence of interfering cognitive distortions, sensitivity to the developmental stage becomes a primary goal, even at early stages of treatment. There are three stages of mastering weight control skills that loosely map onto child and adolescent development. Our adapted treatment model conceptualizes children as progressing from "novice," with parents exclusively in charge, to "student," whereby they begin to learn to make healthy choices even when their parents are not watching. Preadolescents may begin as "students," under their parents' guidance, but progress to "apprentice," with even more independence than their younger counterparts. Adolescents may begin as "apprentices" with their parents and move on to "partner" status as they demonstrate healthier choices and lose weight. This conceptualization, and its contrast with the anorexia nervosa model, are depicted in Figure 10.1.

Specific strengths of FBT as a foundation approach for pediatric overweight include its:

- Demonstrated efficacy in correcting maladaptive eating and related behaviors
- Mission to increase parental empowerment, competence, and efficacy around expecting and facilitating healthy behaviors and outcome in offspring
- Attention to parental engagement strategies
- Explicit agenda of blame reduction
- Framework in which overweight status is separated from the adolescent as a person
- Emphasis on promoting normal physical and psychosocial development for the child/adolescent
- Design to enhance parental capacities while ultimately fostering developmentally appropriate levels of independence in children and adolescents

This chapter will outline the transdiagnostic approach, which has been administered clinically in our treatment centers. We have also conducted a two-site randomized controlled trial comparing Family-Based Treatment for Pediatric Overweight (FBT-PO) to parent–child nutritional education counseling in a sample of adolescents at Mount Sinai School of Medicine and The University of Chicago Medicine (R21HD057394). Importantly, FBT-PO is a framework by which the practitioner can deliver, in a therapeutic

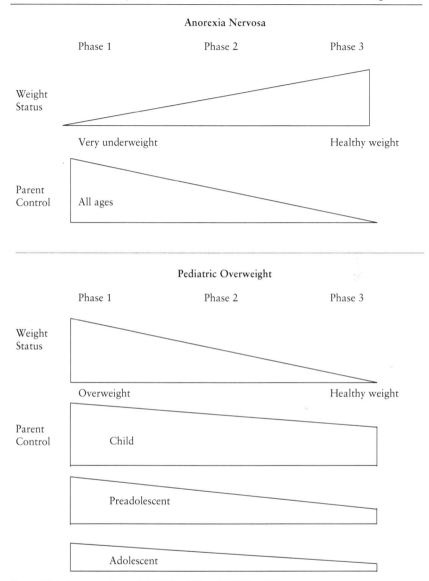

Figure 10.1 A comparison of FBT for AN and FBT for PO.

and effective manner, the nutrition and exercise information relevant to health promotion in children and adolescents. It is a treatment designed to increase uptake and use of such information by shifting responsibility for change to a systems level. As such, it is a family-level delivery mechanism, compatible with multiple nutrition programs, particularly as they evolve over time as new research data comes to bear on the optimal ways to achieve health.

Outline of Treatment

The intervention involves 16 family sessions, divided into 3 phases over 24 weeks. The locus of agency shifts from a parent-emphasis to more of a child-emphasis between Phase 1 and Phase 2, but the precise nature of parental involvement, and the degree to which responsibility is shifted toward the child in Phase 2, varies considerably by developmental stage. Phase 3 addresses broader issues of child and adolescent development and prepares the family for the conclusion of treatment. In Phase 1 (Sessions 1–8), sessions are weekly; in Phase 2 (Sessions 9–13) and Phase 3 (Sessions 14–16), sessions are biweekly. The therapist obtains the child/adolescent's height and weight at the start of each session. The treatment is applicable to families with traditional structures as well as single-parent families, grandparent-as-parent families, divorced families, and families where other caregivers have a prominent role. It is important that at least one parent or guardian commit to participating throughout the entire treatment. In two-caregiver households, parents/guardians need to be unified in their approach. Siblings attend the first two sessions at a minimum. Overweight siblings may participate in the entire treatment protocol.

As with the original FBT manuals for eating disorders (Le Grange & Lock, 2007; Lock & Le Grange, 2012), the therapist's style is directive to the extent necessary to provide critical information to the family, outline the mission and framework of treatment, and prescribe each family member's role in the process. At the same time, the therapist empowers parents to take charge and assert their authority as parents, not just over their child but over how the details of the treatment are implemented. In this respect, the therapist and parents provide complementary expertise: the therapist on pediatric overweight and obesity and the parents on their child and their home. Together, therapist and parents make a formidable collaborative team in the battle for health. FBT-PO sessions should be infused with a mission to change family structure to facilitate the health of each family member, with an emphasis on the overweight child(ren). While nutritional and exercise-related information is provided across the course of treatment, this knowledge is always imparted in the context of a discussion regarding family functioning. For example, education regarding the importance of breakfast is not complete without a detailed discussion of who will be responsible for planning breakfast (child, parents, or their collaboration depending on developmental stage and phase of treatment—see below) and how the change will apply to the entire family, not just the overweight child. If in the following session it is discovered that breakfast was not implemented as anticipated, the therapist should not simply reiterate the *facts* relevant to the importance of breakfast but highlight the necessary shifts in family authority and practice necessary to effect health-promoting change. As in any good family-based psychological treatment, this message should not be delivered in a lecture format but be explored with a curious stance via circular questioning. Like the foundation approach, FBT-PO goes well beyond psychoeducation to alter family coalitions, authority structures, and conflicts to improve parenting and family functioning in the service of improved health.

Tables 10.1 through 10.3 provide examples of how treatment techniques are modified as a function of developmental stage. Across stages, the entire family, including siblings (regardless of whether or not the siblings are overweight), attends Sessions 1 and 2. For these sessions, following the weight check, the format varies as a function of developmental stage of the patient. For the youngest and middle age ranges, the therapist meets with the parents alone for the first half of this first session and then meets with the entire family for the second half. For adolescents, the family convenes together for the remainder of the session following the weight check. (See a detailed description of Session 1 below for the rationale for this approach and additional information.) After the first two sessions, siblings are encouraged, but not required, to attend. Overweight siblings in particular may benefit from continued attendance. In phases of treatment where the session is divided (e.g., adolescent alone followed by adolescent plus parents), the siblings attend the portion that the parents attend. Sessions 1 and 2 are 90 minutes in length, while subsequent sessions are 60 minutes. Notably, in determining which module (child, preadolescent, or adolescent) to apply, it is important to consider not just chronological age but functional markers of developmental stage.

Table 10.1 Status of Overweight Child in Phases 1, 2, and 3

	Phase 1	Phases 2 and 3
Children	Novice	Student
Preadolescents	Student	Apprentice
Adolescents	Apprentice	Collaborator/Partner

Table 10.2 Who Is Responsible for Recording Daily Energy Intake and Expenditure?

	Phase 1	Phases 2 and 3
Children	Parents, with Child's Input	Parents, with Child's Active Involvement
Preadolescents	Parents, with Child's Active Involvement	Child, with Parents' Oversight and Contribution
Adolescents	Adolescent, with Parents' Input	Adolescent

Table 10.3 Structure of Sessions 3–16

	Phase 1 (Sessions 3–8)	Phases 2–3 (Sessions 9–16)
Children	Therapist meets with child alone for 5–10 minutes to obtain weight and check in, then with the parents alone for the remainder of the session.	Same as Phase 1.
Preadolescents	Therapist meets with child alone for 5–10 minutes to obtain weight and check in, then with the parents alone for the remainder of the session.	After weight check, therapist meets with the child and parents together for the remainder of the session.
Adolescents	Therapist meets with adolescent alone for 5–10 minutes to obtain weight and check in, then with the adolescent and parents together for the remainder of the session.	After weight check, adolescent alone for up to the first half of the session, then parents with adolescent for the remainder of the session.

Often, families may be motivated to attend the first session but find it difficult to prioritize treatment for their child's obesity over the long term. Sustained attendance is critical to success with FBT-PO, so the importance of weekly (and, later, biweekly) sessions should be emphasized. Some evidence-based engagement strategies from other populations include (McKay et al., 2004; Szapocznik et al., 1988):

- Reminder calls to parents about each upcoming appointment
- Identification of attitudes about and previous experience with weight loss treatment that might deter engagement with this treatment protocol
- Problem solving with the parents about any concrete obstacles to attendance, such as lack of time, transportation, child care, etc.

Phase 1 (Sessions 1–8)

In the first phase of treatment, parents are actively involved in making changes in their child's eating and exercise habits. Families should be oriented to the need for mobilization and the effort required to yield the maximum effect. This is especially true for this phase, which is characterized by a steep learning curve. Families will need to learn many new skills, adapt to the rhythm of treatment homework and lifestyle changes, and begin to adopt new attitudes. Recording of daily food intake and physical activity is introduced in the early sessions of Phase 1 in order to assist families in determining where changes in eating habits and activity might be warranted. However, a paramount goal is to enhance parenting capacities and knowledge about eating behavior, nutrition, and physical activity in an effort to "empower" parents. Therefore, rigid prescription of food choices through meal plans or strict exercise programs are discouraged. Instead, parents are guided in their efforts at making healthful choices. Monitoring of food intake and physical activity continues throughout treatment. For some families, changes in eating habits may be radical, and parents and offspring should be informed that children need to try a new or previously less familiar food many times before they develop a taste for it (Anzman-Frasca, Savage, Marini, Fisher, & Birch, 2012). Fruits and vegetables should not be quickly dismissed as unacceptable to the child or adolescent. Also, feelings of blame by the child and the parents for the child's overweight status must be addressed and reduced in order to improve the family's sense of efficacy and ultimately overcome this barrier to action. In two-parent/caregiver households, the adults must also be informed of the extreme importance of a unified stance. If one parent undermines the efforts of the other or is passively nonparticipatory, results may suffer. In single-parent/caregiver households, it is helpful to problem-solve around the challenges of being the only caregiver in the efforts to combat overweight on the family level.

Children: For children, this takes the form of parents assuming full responsibility for making decisions about the types of food the child eats, supervising directly or arranging supervision for all meals and snacks, and increasing physical activity by initiating exercise (formal/athletic, family-based, and/or lifestyle-based). The therapist meets with the parents alone for the majority of the session. The parents record their child's daily energy intake and expenditure, with the child's input, writing down precisely what has been eaten and the type and quantity of exercise that took place. The changes the parents make are implemented without elaborate explanation to the child, and changes are directed toward the entire family, including siblings. This is appropriate because, as discussed below, all changes that are made are health-oriented, not weight-loss oriented per se, and no food is eliminated entirely from the family diet. Patients may not lose weight with treatment, but they are expected to at least keep their weight stable while growth and age progress, thereby reducing BMI-for-age percentile. The parents begin to model more healthy behaviors for their children and, if questioned, may make general statements such as "we're doing things to be healthier as a family." For these younger patients, action—in the form of both modeling and supervision—is significantly more important than verbal instruction. Children this age have limited freedom of food selection, and if they are regularly consuming "junk food," parents must question and change their own grocery shopping habits, not blame the child or lecture the child about the merits of fruits and vegetables. In Phase 1, the child is regarded as a novice and the parents—with input from the therapist—as the experts.

Preadolescents: For preadolescents, Phase 1 is characterized by a teacher–student model, in which parents assume ultimate responsibility for food consumption and exercise, but they make their agenda more explicit with their overweight child. Parents balance direct behavior (modeling healthy behaviors and changing family eating and exercise habits) with a collaboratively instructional stance. At this age, children are spending more time eating independently, and while in Phase 1, extra supervision will be temporarily provided, children must begin to learn how to make better choices on their own. For this age range, the sessions in Phase 1 are primarily focused on the parents. Recording of daily energy intake and expenditure is done by the parents, with the child's active involvement. For instance, the parent might record the foods while asking their child to look up the calories/serving size and read them out loud. As with the younger patients, changes are implemented at a familial level and affect all family members including siblings. Weight may either remain stable and catch up to increasing height and age or decrease.

Adolescents: For adolescents, Phase 1 encompasses an apprenticeship model between parents and child where the triad/dyad learns about improving the family's health together and implements strategies in a cooperative way. The majority of the session is spent with the adolescent and parents together, with a focus on problem-solving ways to facilitate healthier eating and increase physical activity, keeping in mind that outside of sessions parents of adolescents will have less direct contact with their child than parents of younger children and preadolescents. In line with having greater autonomy than their younger counterparts, the adolescent self-monitors (records) energy intake and expenditure throughout this phase primarily on his/her own (and for the remainder of treatment). The parents will have some input into their adolescent's recording of daily energy intake and expenditure in Phase 1 of treatment (in a supportive and collaborative manner) but not in Phases 2 and 3. In Phase 1, the parents are still expected to change their own behavior and implement family-wide changes in all relevant habits. They commit to working with their adolescent to ensure success. For this age range, weight loss may be seen, especially for those adolescents who have achieved their adult height.

Checking in with the Child/Adolescent

Every session, regardless of modality or phase of treatment, will begin with the therapist and child/adolescent together for the first 5 to 10 minutes (this time alone will be longer for adolescents beginning in Phase 2). As with FBT for eating disorders (Le Grange & Lock, 2007; Lock & Le Grange, 2012), the therapist will check the child or adolescent's height and weight and plot the weight on a weight graph. The therapist will also ask how the child/adolescent's week went and ask if there are any issues that he/she would like to discuss before the session continues (e.g., without the parents or siblings present). Confidentiality parameters should be reviewed carefully during the informed consent for treatment process prior to the first session, specifying that most material presented by the patient during this alone time may be kept confidential (with typical exceptions related to safety concerns). However, matters related to eating and weight will be brought back to the family portion of the session so that parents can be helpful in these domains with full knowledge of any relevant behaviors or challenges.

Sessions 1 and 2

The first two sessions of treatment, the initiation of Phase 1, are unique in their structure and importance. It is within these early sessions that each family member is oriented to (a) the need for intervention, (b) the rationale for this particular treatment approach, (c) his or her specific role in facilitating change, and (d) ways of conceptualizing obesity that challenge the societal stereotypes and stigma. Across all developmental stages, the entire family, including siblings, attends the first two sessions of treatment. In Session 1, the session is divided into different parts, depending on developmental stage, with a different configuration of attendees in each segment (see below). In Session 2, which involves a family meal, all family members attend the entire session. As noted above, Sessions 1 and 2 are 90 minutes each in length, while all subsequent sessions are 60 minutes.

Session 1

Session 1 has multiple goals, and a large body of information must be introduced in this opening meeting. The therapist should keep in mind that there will be time throughout Phase 1, particularly in Sessions 3–8, to continue to clarify information, add details, and reinforce concepts introduced in Session 1. After the check-in described above, for the youngest and middle age ranges, the therapist meets with the parents alone for the first half of this first session and then meets with the entire family for the second half. The reason for this is that as the primary agents of change, the parents need to hear information that will appropriately raise their anxiety about the risks of obesity and become mobilized to take action. This is combined with an explicit message of blame reduction (self- and other-directed). Children and preadolescents may feel ashamed and be unduly frightened by this information and the necessarily dramatic delivery thereof. This shame and fear will not be productive and, in fact, may be counterproductive for their engagement in treatment. They, along with their siblings, will be informed of the essential messages in an age-appropriate manner in the second half of the first session. Therefore, not all the information will be repeated verbatim or delivered with the same intensity. The therapist must apply clinical judgment in determining how to convey the same messages to the identified patient and his/her siblings in a developmentally appropriate manner. For adolescents, after the check in, the entire family meets together. However, as described above, during the first 5–10 minutes alone with the adolescent, the therapist, in keeping with the increased agency that is afforded to the overweight adolescent in this treatment protocol, assesses whether there are any issues that the adolescent regards as private. This gives the adolescent a degree of decision power as to which personal information will be revealed to other family members. Issues that are explicitly and inextricably tied to eating and weight, such as sneak-eating or exercise avoidance, are openly discussed in the interest of giving parents the opportunity to provide family-level support for change.

Session 1 assumes that comprehensive medical and psychological evaluations have already taken place. Medical clearance should be based on the child or adolescent's ability to safely engage in at least moderate exercise. Any food restrictions related to medical conditions (e.g., food allergies) should be evaluated for compatibility with the protocol before proceeding. The information that should be obtained in advance of the first session by the physician and/or the therapist includes:

- Height and weight
- Growth curves (height, weight, BMI-for-age) over the course of development
- Medical history
- Family medical history, including obesity
- History of weight loss attempts
- Psychiatric diagnoses, history of psychiatric treatment, history of binge eating and other eating disorder behaviors
- Psychosocial history
- Genogram (abbreviated)

Similar to FBT for eating disorders (Le Grange & Lock, 2007; Lock & Le Grange, 2012), the goals of Session 1 are:

1   To orient the family to the treatment model, including the three phases of the intervention, and to engage each family member in the treatment process
2   To assign a specific role to each family member and to explain if and how this will change throughout the course of treatment
    a.   Parents (role varies as a function of developmental stage of child/adolescent)
    b.   Patient (role varies as a function of developmental stage)
    c.   Siblings: supportive role, regardless of patient's developmental stage
3   To assess family functioning, especially authority structure

4   To reduce blame toward the overweight child/adolescent while explaining potential contributory factors of overweight

5   To externalize the overweight and separate it from the child/adolescent as a person

6   To mobilize the parents and child/adolescent to make changes necessary to improve health (i.e., highlight the seriousness of overweight and obesity)

7   To provide initial information about behavior change necessary for improving health and reducing weight

8   To assign the tasks ahead, including the family meal to take place in Session 2

Goal #1: To orient the family to the treatment model, including the three phases of the intervention, and to engage each family member in the treatment process; Goal #2: To assign a specific role to each family member and to explain if and how this will change throughout the course of treatment. To accomplish these goals, the treatment is explained clearly and in lay terminology. The explanation is reiterated or elaborated at different points in the session as the attendee configuration shifts for younger patients (see above). For example, for a family in which the identified patient is 7 years old, the father is obese, and there is one sibling, age 9, who is within a normal weight range, the following might be said in the second half of the session (when all family members are present):

> *"I'm really pleased to see each and every one of you here today so that we can begin to work together to help you as a family become healthier. We're going to be making some changes at home to eat more foods that our bodies need and do things as a family to become more active. At first, your parents are going to do most of the thinking and planning around healthy behaviors, but later on, you're going to learn how to make more healthy choices on your own, such as during the school day. Some of these changes will be easy and fun, and some may be harder but good for you—like the way you might feel about going to the doctor. You each have an important job in helping your family become healthier. As I mentioned, you (turning to the parents) will have the job of planning changes, changes that make sense as a family and will apply to all of you. And you (turning to the two siblings) will have the job of being willing to try new things and of supporting each other when some changes seem harder than others."*

The therapist emphasizes that all changes will take place at a familial level. Even non-overweight parents and siblings will benefit from increased availability of healthy foods in the home and increased expectation of and engagement in physical activity, as well as from a decreased sedentary pursuits like television viewing. Moreover, no dietary changes should be overly restrictive in nature, and parents should not eliminate any food type completely nor leave the child hungry. Attitude and tone matter as well. A harshly critical parent who limits food intake has a completely different impact than a warmly supportive parent who provides an array of healthy food options for their child to eat until sated. The therapist also explains that the family is the best resource for managing health because the home is the child's immediate environment, and environment plays a critical role in the development and resolution of overweight.

It is important to review this treatment in contrast with other available options, with a focus on what has been tried historically. The pros and cons of any dieting strategies that have been attempted in the past should be discussed to create a backdrop and enthusiasm for the current strategy. The fact that studies support the positive impact of parents' active involvement in treatment (Epstein et al., 2007) should be noted. The therapist should explain why pediatric and adolescent overweight and obesity must be treated differently from adult obesity. Specifically, depending on the age, children have different nutritional requirements than adults. Parents should beware of trendy diets for this (and other) reasons. Parents must also keep cognitive and developmental levels in mind. While a "willpower" model of dieting does not work well in adults, it is even less effective in children and adolescents. Telling a child to exert willpower will have a cost on his/her self-concept when eating dysregulates.

Goal #3: To assess family functioning, especially authority structure. The therapist should pay close attention to coalitions in the family, the quality of the parents' relationship, and importantly, their parenting style (authoritarian, authoritative, or permissive). FBT-PO is designed to assign a clear authoritative role to parents during Phase 1 (correcting authoritarian or permissive styles with regard to eating/feeding and other health behaviors) with the degree of parental control and monitoring fading gradually as a function of developmental stage and phase of treatment. The parents must be able to function together in their efforts to either directly effect change (for the younger children and adolescents) or support change (for the older adolescents). Moreover, parents must be able to set limits with their children in a firm and kind manner. Some parents, notably of younger children, may need more general "parent training," which can be incorporated in those segments of the sessions in which the therapist meets with the parents alone. The therapist must also assess the role of siblings in the family. Siblings, even older ones, should not be expected to assume a supervisory or parental role and, in fact, should be discouraged from doing so. The therapist may ask questions that include:

- Who decides what you do when you get home from school?
- What sorts of household rules do you have?

- What is the authority structure around food and eating? Who makes the decisions around what is served, what is permitted, etc.?
- Who cooks?
- Do the parents make one meal for everyone or make multiple meals to address each family member's preference?

Goal #4: To reduce blame toward the overweight child/adolescent while explaining potential contributory factors of overweight status. Childhood obesity is not a matter of fault. It is an epidemic sweeping westernized countries and with a complex variety of contributory factors. Parents are not to blame for PO; rather, they are their child's greatest resource to combat it. Moreover, parents who have the foresight to recognize the seriousness of their child's overweight status and the willingness to address it should commend rather than blame themselves. Even in families where one or both parents are overweight, where parents may have not recognized the significance of their child's overweight status, or where they may have exhibited problematic parenting styles regarding food, active blame (by parents toward themselves, by the therapist toward the parents) will not be productive. Such families may need higher "doses" of basic nutritional and physical activity education, but a non-blaming stance is still therapeutically indicated as a clinical tactic. Similarly, a child should not be blamed. The child has fallen prey to a complicated set of biopsychosocial vulnerabilities and instead merits empathy and remedy. The therapist should encourage parents to see their role as a buffer against these influences.

The therapist explicitly labels the challenge of the "toxic environment." This terminology is powerful for families to hear, and it is important for the therapist to emphasize that children and adolescents are even more vulnerable to this toxicity than adults. In addition to providing psychoeducation on the toxic environment, the therapist should elicit examples from the family of how each member is affected by it. This is done interactively, in a manner that engages all family members simultaneously (e.g., with circular questioning) rather than just asking for a list from each person in sequence. The therapist will refer back to these examples throughout treatment.

The concept of "optimal defaults" can also be introduced to the parents, i.e., the notion that choices can be directed toward health-oriented options simply by making the defaults in the home healthier and less obesogenic. Specifically, by systematically manipulating the health value of the *default mode* (i.e., the usual and customary decisions that are made preemptively for the child), in combination with assuming an empowered stance with regard to the home environment, healthier choices can be elicited for all family members (Radnitz et al., 2013). The therapist can use accessible language such as "make health easier for your child" and "make the environment at home less challenging for him/her to be healthy." Examples of resetting defaults in the home include serving only water and skim milk at meals (reserving soda for a treat), serving fruits and vegetables for snacks (reserving other kinds of snack foods for dessert or for snacks after sufficient servings of fruits, vegetables, and proteins have been consumed throughout the day), and walking to destinations as a family whenever possible.

Across both of these concepts (toxic environment and optimal defaults), the therapist should emphasize that it is important to set the home environment to be extremely conducive to health and a robust buffer against the larger, obesogenic environment. Analogies to sleep disturbance can be used: for children who sleep well, bedtime can be somewhat flexible, homework can be done in bed, etc., without detriment to sleep. For a child with sleep disturbance, sleep hygiene is essential (e.g., a very regular bedtime, pure sleep associations with the bed). These analogies can help illustrate the point and also reduce blame when small changes do not seem to produce the expected yield. At each session, the therapist can ask, "What was particularly challenging about the environment this week? How can we create a stronger buffer to protect your child and make health easier for him/her?"

Goal #5: To externalize pediatric overweight—as a condition—and separate it from the child/adolescent. Overweight or obese status is not equivalent to the child but an outside factor that can jeopardize health. The benefits to this approach are twofold. First, it allows parents to target changes in health behaviors without the child feeling attacked. Second, it further reduces blame toward the overweight child/adolescent.

Goal #6: To mobilize the parents and child/adolescent to make changes necessary to improve health. For the younger two age groups, the primary target of mobilization efforts is the parents. Their anxiety must be raised to facilitate action. For adolescents, the therapist should direct this information not just to the parents but also to the adolescent, in a matter-of-fact, non-threatening manner. For example, the therapist can state, "I, as a doctor, have certain information about being overweight that likely pertains to you. You are old enough to hear this information directly, and I feel it's important to be working from the same knowledge base in order to move forward together." The adolescent will know you take him/her seriously and be less likely to dismiss the data. The therapist then proceeds to provide psychoeducation about the medical and psychosocial risks and correlates of obesity, after assessing what the family's baseline level of knowledge is in these areas. Many children/adolescents will deny emotional and social consequences of overweight, such as teasing and bias. In response to this, the therapist might say, "Maybe this is not a problem for you, which is good! A lot of other kids I work with tell me that this has been hard for them." That way, the therapist leaves the door open for them to talk about this later if it applies and as the therapeutic alliance is strengthened.

The therapist should also review the child/adolescent's personal weight status in terms of growth curves and BMI-for-age percentiles, as well as personal weight and growth history (assessed at the evaluation). Overweight is most conveniently assessed using body mass index (BMI, weight in kilograms divided by height in meters squared). Pediatric obesity, which parents should be made aware predicts obesity in adulthood (Dietz, 1998; Dietz & Gortmaker, 2001; Freedman et al., 2009; Guo & Chumela, 1999; Serdula et al., 1993; Singh et al., 2008), is defined as having a body mass index above the 95th percentile. Those above the 85th and below the 95th percentile are defined as overweight. As healthy BMI values vary by age, a BMI graph is required to evaluate a child's BMI percentile at a given age. The therapist should present the family with a BMI graph (this can be generated by following steps at http://apps.nccd.cdc.gov/dnpabmi/), specific to the patient's gender, and should point out where the child or adolescent's BMI is located on the curve, conveying the urgency to make changes in the home in light of related health risks, and mobilizing the parents to do so.

Goal #7: *To provide initial information about health behaviors necessary for improving health and reducing weight.* The emphasis here should not be simply on psychoeducation, compensating for knowledge deficits, and correcting maladaptive behaviors. Rather, the focus is on *how* changes will be implemented and by whom. For example, a discussion around developing and responding to satiety signals should include the idea that parents will initially need to provide a meal and snack structure, determine appropriate portion sizes, and decide what foods are appropriate for requested additional portions.

For adolescents, the apprentice model would take the form of parents discussing their decisions in Phase 1 with their adolescent and being transparent about the rationale for these decisions, with the aim to mentor their child and transition to more independence for the adolescent in Phase 2. In addition, the changes should be applicable to the entire family. The therapist could model such language in the session when a new concept is introduced, for example, "You as parents can organize your family's eating better so that your bodies can learn a pattern of eating that will help you eat when you are hungry and stop eating when you are full. I will provide you with the knowledge base to do this, and I will also keep reminding you that you have the authority to change your family's eating to improve health. You, in turn, can teach your adolescent how to ultimately eat well on his/her own by explaining the changes you are making and discussing obstacles in session. Most importantly, remember: you have the power as parents to change how your family eats."

Challenges to implementation of positive health behaviors on the part of parents should be discussed via circular questioning and be considered in the context of family coalitions, authority structures, and conflicts. In this sense, FBT goes well beyond nutritional counseling by providing family therapy to correct family functioning around health behaviors. Parents should be encouraged to provide a buffer for their adolescent from the toxic environment, and the therapist should encourage parents to come up with their own ideas for how to make changes at home.

Goal #8: *To assign the tasks ahead, including the family meal to take place in Session 2.* At the end of Session 1, the therapist briefly assigns the task of Phase 1 as well as the family meal for Session 2. For the youngest age range, the therapist would say to the parents: "Your child is young, and it is up to you to change the home environment to make it more conducive to decreased energy intake and increased energy expenditure. My primary caution to you may be counterintuitive, namely, that you should not become overly restrictive or let your child go hungry. You should provide hearty amounts of healthy foods and not eliminate any food entirely. For the next session, I'd like you to bring in a picnic dinner for your family that represents the changes you are making." For the pre-adolescent group, the message would be the same, with the first sentence changed to, "Your child is at an age where it is important to teach him/her how to eat more healthily and exercise more, and you must become his/her teacher by making changes in the home environment consistent with these goals, explaining as you go along." For adolescents, the therapist should tell the adolescent and his/her parents: "You need to work *together* to create a home environment conducive to decreased energy intake and increased energy expenditure. You (the adolescent) are responsible for your personal behaviors and you (the parents) are responsible for anything that happens at the broader familial level. For example, you (the adolescent) might tell your parents what foods you would like them to buy at the grocery store, and you (the parents) would provide these foods while limiting the availability of calorically dense, high-fat foods in the home. You will work out the details of this as you go along, with my help, but my main caution is to not become overly restrictive in what you eat or eliminate any particular food type entirely. This will backfire. For the next session, I'd like you to bring in a picnic dinner, for the whole family, that represents the changes you are making."

Session 2

There are two goals of Session 2:

1   To continue to evaluate the family in terms of structure and coalitions, as well as on their ability to facilitate healthier behaviors
2   To provide direct feedback on how the meal could be improved to be more consistent with familial goals

The therapist should keep in mind that the assignment for families was to bring in a meal that represents better health. Any "singling out" of the identified patient or overly restrictive feeding or eating practices should be actively corrected consistent with the model of treatment outlined above. It is also a direct opportunity to align siblings in support of one another, in vivo. The therapist asks the family to serve and eat the picnic meal, asking questions about who selected the foods, how selections were negotiated, if at all, how representative this experience is of eating at home, etc. The therapist continues to ask assessment questions and, at the end of the session, offers feedback. It is important that this is done collaboratively and sensitively, so that the parents and children feel empowered, not "graded" or criticized. If the family fails to bring a meal as planned, or brings inappropriate types or quantities of food, the therapist can direct the family to a cafeteria or local store to obtain a substitute meal.

Session 2, like all sessions, begins by obtaining height and weight with the child or adolescent alone and by inquiring whether there are any issues he/she would like to discuss individually. The therapist can also ask whether there are any concerns that the patient would like help raising in the family portion of the session. Following this segment, the entire family is invited in for the assigned picnic meal and instructed to wait before setting up the food. The therapist then explains the purposes of the in-session family meal:

- To observe a sample of the family's eating habits
- To find out more about how food choices are made in the family, especially with regard to the instruction to bring in a meal that represents the changes the family is about to implement
- To begin providing direction on the areas the therapist and family agree are useful to change initially

Following this introduction, the therapist prompts the family to begin laying out the meal and asks a few preliminary questions, such as:

- How did you decide what to bring today?
- Who made the ultimate decisions?
- Is this how meals are typically determined at home?

Once the meal is placed on the table, the therapist observes the following:

- The size of the portions being served and eaten
- The number of servings of food being served and consumed
- The speed of the participants' eating (e.g., do they eat extremely quickly, or do they eat at a more regular pace?)
- Parental or sibling criticism
- How active and directive (or passive and lax) the parents are during the meal
- Interactions between family members

The therapist can choose to intervene at various points. For example, if the child/adolescent begins eating quickly, the therapist may note this non-judgmentally and talk with the parents about why and how they might intervene. The therapist can also suggest that parents interrupt and slow down their child's pace of eating. The therapists can also initiate similar discussions and interventions around the child asking for or taking second or third helpings, filling up on less healthy options, etc.

As the meal progresses, the therapist will want to ask additional questions such as:

- Is this meal representative of what happens at home? How so or why not?
- What does the family typically do during mealtime at home?
- How do you know when you are full?
- How do you know when you are finished?

The therapist ends Session 2 by sharing his/her observations and providing constructive feedback (what was positive, what can be improved upon).

Session 3

Session 3 is the first session in which, after the individual time with the child or adolescent is complete, the therapist can spend time assessing the degree to which the parents are assuming an appropriate authoritative stance around eating and related health behaviors. This is accomplished via circular questioning and maintaining a focus on the principles of the approach established in Session 1, specifically the role assignment of parents versus offspring. Any efforts towards parents assuming more of a role in their child's health should be praised; any difficulties should be explicitly discussed. For example, the therapist can ask the parent, "What changes have you made in the home environment this week to make it easier for your child to be healthy?"

This session should encompass a basic introduction to the project of becoming healthier. To start, the therapist may engage the adolescent and parent in a discussion of "what is health" and discuss different types of health as well as general healthy/unhealthy eating and exercise habits. The connection between weight status and health is reviewed. For this segment of the session and subsequent sessions, the therapist can use any number of evidence-based nutrition and health-related published materials. It is important that therapists select the most current research-based information and guidelines, as recommendations in the field change over time.

The second task of Session 3 (after covering the basic introduction to health) is for the therapist to introduce recording of food intake and energy expenditure and assign roles. The therapist explains the benefits of self- (or parent-) monitoring. Specifically, this technique increases awareness of existing and changing eating and exercise habits; this awareness alone can be incredibly powerful. It also allows the therapist to make specific helpful suggestions about further changes that could be made and provide tailored feedback to the family. The therapist discusses potential barriers to self-monitoring and engages the family in problem-solving around such obstacles, while emphasizing that records will be reviewed at the beginning of every single session. Twenty-four hour recall methods can be used for assessment purposes in instances of low adherence to monitoring.

Session 4

The therapist starts the session with a review of food records, beginning with positive observations and specific, labeled praise (e.g., "I notice that you ate fruit three out of the seven days this week. Bravo!") Next, the therapist directs a constructive discussion around suggestions for potential areas of change in a constructive manner ("I noticed you ate fast food three days this week. Let's discuss the possibility of eating out less or making better choices at fast food restaurants.").

The next agenda item for this session is psychoeducation regarding how to read a food label, which will pave the way for improved monitoring going forward. Give the adolescent and parent a chance to practice reading a food label in session, to assess comprehension.

After this information is reviewed, if there is time remaining in the session, the therapist can begin addressing additional topics related to healthy eating and activity. Collectively, these topics should be covered throughout the remaining portion of Phase 1 and into Phase 2 as necessary. The order of topics is tailored to each family's unique needs and challenges, by level of relevance/importance. New topics may be added based on the specific needs of a particular family or, as research in the field of obesity progresses, changing guidelines for optimal health. These topics include:

- Social/familial support for healthy habits
- The importance of regular meals (three per day) and snacks (two per day)
- The importance of home-cooked meals, ideally eaten together as a family, while also knowing how to choose smartly among restaurants (i.e., avoiding fast food restaurants) and within a restaurant menu (e.g., if at a fast food establishment, determining which choices are best)
- Planning meals and snacks in advance to increase the likelihood of optimal choices and decrease the allure of in-the-moment options that may be convenient but lack nutritional value
- Context and behaviors associated with eating, such as stimulus control (e.g., eating at the table, without engaging in other activities such as watching television), eating slowly, and stopping when satiated but not overly full. Define the concept of hunger and distinguish this from psychological "cravings." Encourage family members to eat in relation to how hungry or full they feel (and how to accurately detect these sensations) rather than based on amounts they are accustomed

to eating. Review the ways in which marketing and presentation play a role in food choices and consumption.

- Dietary guidelines (e.g., www.choosemyplate.gov) and food groups. Explain that some prepared foods fall into multiple categories and highlight the importance of a variety diet.
- Portions sizes and servings. Introduce concept of portion sizes and the problem of portion "drift," where portions slowly grow over time without realization. Review factors that influence portion size, including size of plate/bowl and other environmental cues.
- Calories and caloric recommendations
- Consuming sufficient servings of fruits and vegetables per day
- Vitamins and minerals from foods
- Beverages. Discuss the topic of juice (not as good of a source of fiber as fruit itself), which is commonly misperceived as a health food. Encourage families to serve water and generally avoid sports drinks, soda, and other caloric drinks except skim or lowfat milk (note that guidelines differ for infants).
- Increasing physical activity and decreasing sedentary activities at a familial level. Provide education about the effects of physical exercise and low-cost exercise options in an urban environment. Address how to compensate for reduced physical activity provided by the school system. Explore obstacles to physical activity within home/built environment and any threats to safety. Consider a range of ways to obtain physical activity without compromising safety (e.g., joining a sports team at school or at a local youth center.) Have families review a recent day, identifying sedentary behaviors and setting goals for ways to substitute physical activities for screen-time. Decrease sedentary activity at a familial level; guidelines from the American Academy of Pediatrics is less than 1–2 hours per day (Strasburger et al., 2013), which may still be too much for families attempting to aggressively target PO.

Throughout Phase 1 and even into Phase 2, these topic areas should be covered in a didactic but collaborative manner. The therapist engages the family in discussion of how they might potentially use this information to make family-level changes. For example, if the topic of breakfast is being discussed, the therapist might actively engage the family in a conversation about their current breakfast-eating practices and collaboratively discuss whether these practices may be improved on a familial level (e.g., if breakfast is not eaten, educating the family about what breakfast options are healthy and realistic and discussing who could be in charge of purchasing and serving breakfast items, whether the meal should be supervised by the parent, etc.). A major goal of these sessions is to address knowledge deficits; importantly, this is not just done didactically but by guiding the family in the process of change using family therapy techniques.

From this session onward, once new material is introduced to families, the session should end with a collaborative goal-setting discussion between the family and the therapist in which the family is asked to articulate, with the therapist's help, up to three changes they are going to make in the coming week. These changes can be framed as goals and ideally incorporate new material learned. For example, if breakfast is discussed, one goal could be "eat breakfast at least four times this week." If exercise is discussed, another goal could be "go for a walk after school three times this week." Goals can be as simple as "complete all of my food records this week." The family is asked to bring the "Goals for the Coming Week or Two" handout (see Appendix B, www.routledge. com/9780415714747) back the following session so their success in meeting goals (as well as barriers to completion) can be discussed.

While covering all didactic topics, effort should be made by the therapist to repeatedly emphasize the role of the toxic environment and how this may (or may not) be impeding progress. The therapist should also be mindful to address the realities of the urban and/or socioeconomically disadvantaged environment throughout treatment. For example, when discussing fruit and vegetable consumption, the therapist may wish to evaluate the difficulties of finding fresh produce and cost of produce and to discuss the relative advantages of buying canned or frozen fruits and vegetables (less expensive than fresh and more available). The goal would be to compare costs with frequently purchased inexpensive foods (e.g., fast food dollar menus) to establish healthful decisions while minding expenses.

Additional topics that may be relevant to families participating in FBT-PO

Bing eating. While FBT-PO is not designed for or tested with patients with binge eating disorder (BED), the treatment can address the occasional loss-of-control eating episodes. Parents may not witness such episodes but may find clues of them, e.g., an excessive number of food wrappers in the garbage, or the child's money may disappear rapidly as he/she stops at the convenience store after school. Research on loss-of-control eating in children and adolescents (Goldschmidt et al., 2008; Tanofsky-Kraff et al., 2007) shows that it is preceded by the consumption of forbidden foods and associated with eating when not physically hungry, eating alone and/ or secretly, negative affect, and "numbing." Many of these triggers are modified in FBT-PO.

Addressing parental obesity. Parents of overweight children may be overweight themselves and may question their capacity to manage their child's challenges in the food and exercise domains. FBT-PO is designed to increase parental confidence around, as well as directly improve, parenting capacities related to health behaviors in offspring. Parents may also be pleased to know that their own weight status may improve as a "side effect" of their child's treatment, which is in fact a family-level intervention.

Creating and maintaining a positive home environment. Negative expressed emotion, particularly high levels of criticism in families, can interfere with FBT (Le Grange, Eisler, Dare, & Hodes, 1992). Therapists should directly correct and modify such criticism, especially around eating and weight issues, and help parents adopt nonevaluative language to discuss them. For example, instead of labeling foods as "diet" foods, parents can reference nutritious foods as ones that will make their child "healthy and strong." Parents should similarly take great care in discussing their own or their child's physical appearance. Effort and behaviors, not body size, should be the target of change-related comments. Parents should make direct efforts to mitigate any connection between appearance and self-esteem and develop their child's evolving self-concept as related to other domains, such as academics, work ethic, social and interpersonal functioning, talents and interests, etc.

Avoiding disciplinary choices related to food or exercise. Response cost is a common behavioral parenting practice. If punishment patterns have traditionally revolved around the denial of participation in activities that involve physical activity, the progress of the intervention could be greatly impacted by incidents that occur outside of treatment. The therapist should preemptively clarify that strategies to remove privileges related to food and exercise are counterproductive to the intervention. For example, parents should not take away recreational sports as a consequence for negative behavior in the context of this treatment but should consider other contingencies. Physical activity must be thought of as part of the prescription of this treatment, and the medical model conveys this message effectively.

The Remainder of Phase I

The remainder of Phase 1 focuses on continuing to make changes that will facilitate health. FBT-PO attempts to first capitalize on existing parenting capacities and parental knowledge base about eating behavior and nutrition in an effort to "empower" parents and then works to shape parents' decisions and behaviors from this foundation. In this respect, FBT-PO is initially less prescriptive than some other protocols for PO but does not rely exclusively on parents' common sense.

Phase 2 (Sessions 9–13)

In the second phase of treatment, parents become less directly or exclusively involved in making changes in their child's eating and exercise habits, and the child becomes more of an active agent of change. Education on nutrition and physical activity/sedentary behaviors continues during this phase, focusing on key stumbling blocks of the individual family. Any topics that were not adequately covered from Phase 1 can be addressed in Phase 2.

The clinical indicators for readiness to transition from Phase 1 to Phase 2, across all development stages, are threefold:

- The child or adolescent is no longer gaining weight; weight is at least stabilized, especially for those children who were gaining weight rapidly before presenting for treatment; and, ideally, BMI-for-age percentile is reduced.
- There is good compliance with food records.
- Parents feel confident in their ability to implement family-level, health-promoting changes in the home.

Children: For children, this phase is characterized by a teacher–student model, in which parents assume ultimate responsibility for food consumption and exercise but allow the child to begin to make food selections, choose portion sizes, and eat more independently. Parents may override a child's choices as necessary, while explaining the rationale for doing so. For example, if a child chooses a high-fat afternoon snack following a high-fat morning snack, the parent may say, "You haven't had a fruit or vegetable snack yet today, so let's save this for tomorrow. Would you like an apple or carrots for now?" Or, if a child takes too much food on his/her plate, the parent may say, "I think you might be full with less than that. Let's start with less and see how you feel when you're done." The parents still record energy intake and expenditure but do so with the child's active involvement, showing the child how it is done in greater detail than in Phase 1 and asking questions such as, "What did you eat for lunch today at school? Let's write it down. By writing things down, we can make sure that we're getting in all the healthy foods our bodies need." Supervision can be decreased. The session structure remains the same as Phase 1, meeting with the parents alone for the majority of the session. The parents continue to model more healthy behaviors for their children. Action—in the form of both modeling and supervision—remains more important than verbal instruction for this age range in Phase 2.

Preadolescents: In Phase 2, preadolescents shift from student to apprentice status. The child assumes more responsibility for food consumption and exercise, but the parents have ultimate veto or enforcement power. Supervision is decreased, and the child may take advantage of more and more opportunities for independent eating (e.g., sleepovers). Recording of energy intake and expenditure changes from parent-initiated with the child's active involvement to child-initiated with the parents' oversight and contribution. To reflect the child's increasing level of responsibility, the child now participates fully in the family sessions.

Adolescents: Adolescents become "collaborators" in Phase 2, and the partnership with the parents becomes more implied than explicit. This allowance for the increasing need for independence and autonomy on the part of adolescents is balanced against the reality that parents continue to influence the weight-relevant home environment of their adolescent offspring, for instance, by buying groceries, preparing meals, determining the mode of transportation for family outings. Parents should continue to bring their behavior and eating patterns in alignment with the goals of treatment and implement broad changes at the familial level (e.g., shopping for healthy foods, cooking healthy meals, expecting that the family eat at least one meal per day together, initiating family-based physical activity). Session structure shifts to meeting with the adolescent alone for up to half of each session, followed by meeting with the adolescent and parents together. At a minimum, the weight check and brief review is conducted with the adolescent alone for the first 5–10 minutes of each session, but adolescents who would like more time with the therapist one-on-one can have up to half an hour of individual contact. The adolescent continues to self-monitor energy intake and expenditure, but in Phase 2, this is completed without any assistance from parents. At this stage of treatment, the adolescent shoulders full responsibility for this task.

Phase 3 (Sessions 14–16)

The goals of Phase 3 are to:

1   Review principles of child and adolescent development with the patient and parents in an effort to track how aligned the patient is with expected physical and psychosocial functioning
2   Develop a maintenance plan with the family to ensure ongoing engagement with health-oriented behaviors
3   Review ways in which each family member has benefited or been affected by the changes made in treatment
4   Terminate treatment

These goals are consistent across all three developmental stages. Any Phase 2 topics that were not adequately covered can be continued to be addressed in Phase 3. As applicable, affect management without food and body image concerns can also be addressed in this phase.

All treatment goals are seldom accomplished in a fixed time period (such as that provided in this chapter), and the family should be encouraged to continue to implement the strategies they have acquired during the course of this treatment. To this end, the adolescent and his/her parent should also be prepared that the course forward may include some setbacks. However, such setbacks are quite typical, and most people have to learn to overcome such setbacks and continue to move forward. It will be important to prepare the family not only to expect such obstacles in their progress but to appreciate that the way in which they negotiate these obstacles (seeing it as a sign of failure and permanent setback, i.e., a relapse, versus a temporary bump in the road) will be crucial in their ultimate success.

Troubleshooting across Phases

What should the therapist do if the child or adolescent gains weight when the expectation is for the weight to remain stable while height increases (i.e., for younger children) or gains or maintains weight when the patient's expectation is to lose (i.e., for older adolescents who are near or have achieved adult height)?

Weight is only one indicator, and an imperfect one, of health-promoting behavioral change. Ideally, this treatment would achieve improvements in BMI-for-age percentile by targeting such behavioral domains and incorporating evidence-based dietary guidelines that represent current best practices in the fields of childhood obesity and nutrition. (Recall that FBT-PO is a transdevelopmental delivery mechanism for family-level uptake of scientifically developed and tested recommendations.) For some cases, modifications in quality and quantity of food consumption may be insufficient to yield a substantial shift in BMI percentile during the course of treatment, but the positive behavioral changes may be sufficient to confer health benefits and arrest a steep weight gain trajectory. In still other cases, change is insufficient to lead to health improvement and/or reductions in BMI Z-scores. While medical clearance and ongoing medical management are presumed adjunctive components to this intervention, the therapist will not always have immediate information about current health status to guide feedback to the family. Therefore, while weight is indeed only a single indicator of behavioral change, it is the most easily assessed and accessed piece of data for the therapist to use session to session, and as translated to BMI-for-age percentiles, it has powerful predictive value in terms of current and future health of the child. Therapists may be concerned that focusing on the number on the scale makes them complicit with the aspect of the toxic environment that promotes an unrealistic thin ideal and values weight loss more than a healthy lifestyle; however, the data cannot be disputed that obesity is a health risk. Therapists may also be sensitive to the misuse of weight readings by parents as an opportunity to blame or criticize the child/adolescent when the weight does not move in the expected direction or to blame themselves for insufficient effort. Children who worry that they will be "in trouble" for not losing weight will be more likely to lie on their self-monitoring forms. Parents who experience a detailed review of the week as critical scrutiny by the therapist will exhibit defensiveness. In both instances, the opportunity for positive mobilization and rational problem-solving is greatly reduced.

The therapist must therefore provide a great deal of psychoeducation about weight and conclude collaboratively with the parents that weight will be tracked throughout treatment. Weight should be noted on a graph at the start of each session (following the weight check with the child/adolescent) to provide a visual representation of progress over time. If the weight is as expected (stable or down, depending on the case), the therapist should inquire about and praise any efforts of the parents, child, or both (depending on developmental stage and phase of treatment) that may be contributory. If the weight is not as expected, the therapist would similarly conduct an analysis of potential contributory factors, with a matter-of-fact, non-blaming attitude, and with an emphasis on lifestyle changes as opposed to short-term extreme dieting "solutions." Statements such as "Let's look together at your monitoring forms to see which aspects of the toxic environment might have been particularly strong for your family this week" or "Let's figure out how, as a family, you can battle the toxic environment together" are appropriate. The therapist's tone is not confrontational or judgmental but rather serious, inquisitive, and collaborative. The therapist should not attach any affective valence to weight, positive or negative, as it relates to the child or adolescent's self-concept, and should actively discourage families from doing so. However, the therapist also unapologetically assumes a stance as an advocate for health, and obesity is a crisis that threatens health. The balance between these two positions lies in the externalized illness model, which positions obesity and the environment that supports it as what is "under attack," not the child.

How should the therapist handle families showing up to sessions without their self-monitoring forms?

The therapist reviews the self-monitoring forms at the start of each session, after the weight check and weight charting. If a family fails to bring these, the therapist instead conducts a 24-hour dietary intake and energy expenditure recall for the prior 24 hours and asks detailed questions about how representative the past day was of the prior week or interval since the prior session. This sends a message that the information is important enough to spend significant session time piecing together. All other agenda items (other than charting weight) should be put on hold until this is complete.

How should the therapist handle situations in which the parents discover evidence of sneak-eating, separate from binge eating?

Parents will sometimes report evidence of food being eaten in secret. For example, a family might notice the remainder of a pint of ice cream missing or a candy bar wrapper in the child's room. Parents may want to punish this behavior or resort to blame and criticism. Neither is appropriate. Instead, the therapist should conduct a functional analysis. Sneak-eating of normal to small amounts of food (i.e., not binge eating) can be a function of either overly restrictive feeding practices or poor stimulus control. The therapist should work with parents to make sure that they are providing a full range of food, including dessert and snack items, but that those foods with poor nutritional value represent the minority of their child's diet and are reserved for appropriate times and places. In addition, it is helpful to keep very limited amounts of these foods in the house, preferably in portions needed just for the upcoming day or so. These strategies will ensure that neither the patient nor his/her siblings feel deprived or overly tempted by the environment. If an adolescent denies secretive eating, the therapist may use the time alone with the adolescent to normalize this behavior via psychoeducation, provide support, and encourage the adolescent to be open about it in order to receive help from his/her parents in a noncritical or punitive way.

How should the therapist handle his/her own frustrations when the parents do not seem sufficiently mobilized or capable of handling their child's resistance to change?

Given the broader statistics on the difficulty combating the epidemic of obesity, the multi-faceted and poorly understood etiology of obesity, and the multitude of maintaining factors in a child's environments, therapists should expect to experience challenging and frustrating situations in working with families battling obesity. It is important for therapists not to take lack of progress personally or not to inadvertently model a blaming or critical stance toward the affected child. We strongly recommend supervision and/or peer consultation in administering this treatment protocol. This will help normalize a frustrated therapist's experiences and provide a forum for the therapist to seek ideas and feedback, in an effort to make sure his/her reactions are in check.

How should the therapist emphasize the need for family-level change?

Family-level change will both improve empathy for the affected child and create an environment conducive to health for all members of the household. Importantly, all changes should be appropriate to all family members, regardless of weight status. The therapist should encourage parents to not only monitor their child's eating but their own.

What is the role of incentives for weight loss in FBT-PO?

While weight loss can be celebrated in multiple ways, including the acquisition of desired material objects, certain things should not be exclusively contingent upon weight loss. For example, parents can certainly shop for new clothes with their child upon reducing size; however, they should be sure to provide sufficient and flattering clothing at any size. On a related topic, while most families will instinctively avoid food rewards to reinforce weight loss, food may still be used as a reward for other behaviors or accomplishments, or even for contingent eating that overrides satiety ("finish your plate and you can have dessert"). In general, it is best for families to limit the conditioned hedonic value of food, since the intrinsically pleasurable aspects of eating are already a sufficient challenge. The therapist should be clear that it is best for parents to reward specific behavioral changes (e.g., increases in physical activity, increased fruit and vegetable consumption) as opposed to weight loss per se.

What is the best way to track and chain goals and progress from one session to the next?

At the end of each session, the therapist should ask the family to verbalize and summarize several family-level changes that they agree to make before the next session (goal setting). For families who are overwhelmed, distracted by other stressors, disengaged, or exhibiting poor compliance, the therapist should reduce the task demand to one or two expected changes. Then, at the beginning of each session, in addition to weight charting and review of food records, the therapist will review the progress on specific goals that were set at the end of the prior session. The therapist praises the family for any and all changes, even approximations of their goals.

How should the therapist handle reports of behavioral change that are not plausible?

As noted earlier, weight is not a perfect indicator of behavioral change. However, when there are gross discrepancies in the direction of weight and the reports of behavioral change, it is reasonable for the therapist to be skeptical as to the veracity of the patient or family's report. It is important for the therapist not to "accuse" anyone directly or prematurely and not to risk rapport. It is equally important for the therapist not to respond with extreme enthusiasm and praise to positive reports that seem unlikely, as this can also compromise trust. Instead, the therapist can express being puzzled over the discrepancies. Therapists may also consider making general statements early on in treatment, especially to adolescents, such as, "Research shows that people tend to make things look better on self-monitoring forms than they are in reality. Sometimes, people might not even be aware that they are recording more what they wish had happened than what actually did occur! I would like you to be on the lookout for this and never to feel ashamed to tell me that things might not be as good as they look on paper." The therapist can then refer back to this in a manner that does not shame the patient.

Importantly, such report-versus-weight discrepancies can also be a sign that the patient is binge eating and is reluctant to admit it. If the therapist suspects this, he/she might say, "Sometimes out of control eating, or binge eating, can occur between sessions, and that can be very hard to write down or even to talk about. Has this been a problem for you recently?" Significant binge eating patterns (e.g., Binge Eating Disorder) may not respond to this intervention, and a referral to cognitive behavioral therapy or interpersonal psychotherapy may be more appropriate.

What should the therapist do if the parent explicitly asks for directives about what to do?

Assuming the therapist has already had the opportunity to provide thorough psychoeducation about the topic at hand, the therapist may wish to turn the question back to the parents and ask the parents what their ideas are about solving the particular problem. The therapist should convey that the parents are more competent than they might feel and instill confidence in the parents with regard to their parenting skills and abilities. If a parent maintains that he/she is at a loss for how to handle an aspect of the child's overweight status, the therapist may offer some options, framing the statement by beginning "Other families have tried. ..."

What if a parent starts becoming too restrictive in feeding their child or authoritarian (as opposed to authoritative) in their parenting style around food and eating?

In the case of families who are highly motivated to make changes to the home environment, some caution should be exercised by the therapist to make sure that the parent is not creating an environment that is overly restrictive. Creating a home environment that removes certain desired foods altogether may lead to an adolescent purchasing these desired foods outside the home where there is no parental support regarding healthier choices and portion size. The therapist should emphasize to the parents that the goal should be to decrease the child's access to less healthy options at home but not to restrict access altogether. Diets that involve categorically forbidden foods are harder to sustain and therefore not a good use of the parents' or child's energies. The goal of this intervention is to create durable changes at home that the child/adolescent carries to the external environment.

It is important that the therapist establish the power of the toxic environment and that parents need to help their child navigate it, starting with any toxic aspects of the home environment. Parents should take the stance with their child, "Your environment is challenging, and I'm going to help you manage it." Ideally, changes to food and meal options at home should be decided upon with an authoritative parental style, seeking input from the child while ultimately making decisions as parents. Parents can set the parameters for access to certain types of desired foods, such as cookies or juice, but involve the child or adolescent through an exploration of the challenges he/she faces.

An example of collaborative environmental planning at home with an adolescent follows:

> Parent: *We know you like juice. What are the chances that you will drink juice if it's in front of you?*
> Child: *Pretty good chance.*
> Parent: *Now what should we do with that information? Let's talk about ways that we can incorporate juice without cutting it out altogether. I'd be remiss if I served juice to you for dinner and breakfast given the challenge that it poses for you. What meal would you like to have it with? I can't serve it at every meal because that would be too challenging for your goals of becoming healthier.*

A collaborative approach should also be taken in session. The therapist might say to an adolescent, "Look, I'm the expert on health, and your mom is the expert on the home, but you are the expert on yourself, and if you have something to share about your experience, it is very important to us." The adolescent should be made to feel like an active participant in the environment restructuring process because their participation is essential to success. One way that parents and adolescents can collaborate, for example, is by completing food records together. However, collaboration should not be prioritized at the expense of identifying parents as the ultimate decision makers, particularly in Phase 1, and especially for younger children. Parents shouldn't be compelled to *convince* their child of the wisdom of a health-oriented decision; rather, they should *implement* changes, albeit ideally with a teaching style so that their child can ultimately transition to greater independence in the health behaviors domain.

Case Example

We end this chapter with a case example of FBT-PO.

Background Information

"Jennifer" is a 16-year-old African-American female who presented to treatment with her biological mother, "Carol," and younger brother, "David." Jennifer reported gaining 25 lbs. over the past six months. At the time of assessment, Jennifer was 180 lbs. and 64 inches tall, placing her at the 96th percentile of BMI-for-age. Per her growth charts, she had met the threshold for overweight for a majority of her life. Jennifer became interested in treatment when a school counselor told her about a research study that was being conducted at a local medical center. She stated upon presenting for the study that her motivation to lose weight is to "feel better about herself." Jennifer lives at home with her mother and brother, but due to her mother's work schedule, she often stays with her maternal grandmother. Jennifer does not have contact with her biological father. Jennifer reported that many members of her extended family are overweight. Mother, Carol, is overweight, and brother, David, is obese.

Jennifer reported limited activity due to safety concerns in her neighborhood. Additionally, due to budget constraints, the public high school she attended eliminated gym class as part of the curriculum in her grade. Jennifer currently eats breakfast on her way to school, a government subsidized lunch in the cafeteria, and dinner at home with her family. Due to Carol's work schedule, Jennifer and David are home alone after school for a period of three hours. Jennifer denied a history of binge eating, but Carol reported that she often finds candy and chip wrappers in Jennifer's bedroom. Jennifer denied any history of mood concerns but reported that "sometimes she feels sad about the way her body looks."

Session 1

The therapist arranged to meet with the family for the first session in the evening. Carol expressed that it was necessary for her family to meet with the therapist in the evening to accommodate her work schedule. During the session, Jennifer's family initially had a difficult time understanding what factors might be associated with Jennifer's recent weight gain. The therapist led a collaborative review of the family's environment and experiences through questions posed to each family member. This review included discussing reduced physical activity, difficulty with preparing meals at home, and unsupervised time after school. Carol also raised concern that Jennifer's grandmother often fed the children high-fat, high-sugar foods and liked to "spoil them with food."

Excerpt from Session 1

Therapist: *"Carol, how are meal times handled in your house?"*
Carol: *"We typically have breakfast when we are running out of the house, you know ... a doughnut or breakfast pastry."*
Therapist: *"What about the other meals, David?"*
David: *"Well, I get lunch at school, I get to pick pizza or a sandwich."*
Therapist: *"Jennifer, is your lunch structured the same as David? How do you decide what to have at lunch?"*
Jennifer: *"I get whatever my friends are having, and then sometimes they give me their leftovers too."*

Session 2—The Family Meal

Jennifer and her family arrived on time for their family meal. After the therapist weighed Jennifer, they joined Carol, David, and Jennifer's grandmother, "Betty." The family had purchased a meal at a local rotisserie chicken restaurant. The meal was placed in the center of the table, and everyone in the family served themselves. The meal consisted of cornbread, rotisserie chicken, corn, mashed potatoes and gravy, macaroni and cheese, brownies, and milk. Jennifer served herself a large portion of chicken and macaroni and cheese but did not take any other items. Carol intervened and said, "You can't eat that much, you are trying to lose weight" and took the plate away. When this occurred, Jennifer looked distressed, while the rest of the family members plated their dishes.

The therapist used this as an opportunity to intervene to better understand Carol's reaction. Carol explained that she often reacts in this way because she feels responsible for her daughter's weight gain. The therapist asked Carol to plate Jennifer's dish in a manner that may help her "achieve her health goals." Carol plated her dish to include chicken and a small portion of macaroni and cheese and mashed potatoes, a glass of milk and half of a brownie. The therapist praised mother for including the brownie and explained that throughout treatment that small, planned treats should be included in order to reduce "sneak-eating" and/or Jennifer perceiving foods as "forbidden."

Remainder of Phase I

During Sessions 3 and 4, the therapist introduced food logs to Jennifer. Jennifer developed a plan to complete food logs on her smart phone using a food log application. After approximately 15 minutes of individual time with the therapist, Jennifer's mother joined the session, and Jennifer presented her plan to her mother. The therapist explained that, during Phase 1, it was very important for Carol to ensure that she take the lead on making changes in the home. Carol suggested that she create a binder of food logs that they would leave in the kitchen island of their home. She suggested that she would check in with Jennifer every evening to ensure that food logs were completed. At Session 5, the family did not bring complete food logs. Jennifer raised concern with her therapist that she is being criticized at home. Jennifer stated, "My mom doesn't think I am doing a good job, and she tells me I should be trying harder." Carol reported feeling upset because "Jennifer is not holding up her end of the bargain." The therapist used this as an opportunity to talk about the effects of blame and criticism on behavioral changes. Jennifer and Carol decided that, moving forward, Carol will work towards providing support by reminding Jennifer to complete food logs and praising her when she remembers to do so. The therapist also used this opportunity to illustrate the separation of Jennifer from her weight status. The therapist engaged the family in a discussion of how obesogenic habits as well as developmental stage may be contributing to her ability to complete all tasks independently. During Session 6, Jennifer and Carol developed a new strategy. Carol created a notebook for Jennifer to take to school. Jennifer logged her breakfast at home, lunch at school, and afternoon snack and dinner at home. At the end of each evening, Jennifer and Carol reviewed the day. They found this very helpful to use the logs to make new changes for the week. During this same time, Carol began making a grocery list for the week that supported the family-created meal plans. Between Sessions 6 and 8, Jennifer experienced significant weight loss. Carol attributed this to planning for the week and changing the content of breakfast from a pop-tart or doughnut to oatmeal and fruit. Overall, the family felt that they were making significant changes around meals where there was parent/grandparent oversight. However, during the end of Session 8, David disclosed that when they are home alone, they sometimes "sneak food." Jennifer was very upset following this disclosure. The therapist worked to normalize this experience and learn more about what was happening. Carol remained very calm and did not say anything critical. The therapist noted Carol's alternative response compared to previous sessions. The therapist assessed the nature of these episodes. Jennifer tearfully explained that she often will eat a small bag of candy or slice of fruit pie and sometimes, when they are home for long periods of time, she eats more food because she is bored. Jennifer admitted to this occurring many times over the past three months, since the family began cutting out sweets. The therapist assessed the behaviors and determined that these episodes did not meet criteria for binge eating. The therapist also reminded the family that the presence of small, controlled treats was an important component of healthy eating and could aid in Jennifer not feeling that these foods were forbidden. The family supported Jennifer by giving her a hug and telling her it is "okay." The therapist asked Carol how she felt it might be best to address this issue. Carol was unsure at first but then discussed reintroducing some sweets in small portions, as well as finding an alternative activity for Jennifer and her brother after school. After much discussion, Carol proposed that Jennifer begin volunteering at the library after school. She suggested that Jennifer and her brother could go to the library after school and that Carol would pick them up after her work was complete. Although Jennifer initially protested, Carol remained firm that this will be a helpful strategy to curb eating in the absence of hunger. Throughout the remainder of Phase 1, Jennifer and her family focused on how to make healthy choices at lunch. They did so by requesting the menu from school, and making a meal plan for the week.

Jennifer and her family struggled with how to incorporate healthy exercise in their unsafe neighborhood. Due to the lack of sports and gym class at school, Jennifer and her family were faced with determining how they would add exercise into their daily lives. The family began by waking up earlier in the morning and mother walking with Jennifer and her brother to the train instead of taking the bus to the train station. This small change added 15 minutes of walking each day. The family also began going to the local YMCA on the weekends to participate in a family swim program. The family's therapist was able to help the family by providing a letter of support outlining their financial limitations, which enabled them to obtain a reduced-price pass.

Phase 2

Phase 2 began with Jennifer starting to choose lunch at school. At Session 9 it was noted that Jennifer's weight increased. Through discussion with the family, Carol attributed Jennifer's weight gain to the change in schedule at home. This change included the beginning of a 12-week summer break for Jennifer and David. Although some attention had been paid to this in the previous session, Jennifer and her mother reported that the transition had been more difficult than expected, as plans for Jennifer to be employed at the library, following her volunteer position, had not materialized. A majority of Session 9 was focused on how the family could continue to brainstorm around these changes, including finding additional time for activities and other events to structure the family's schedule. At this time, eating in the absence of hunger had ceased, and the family continued to exercise together on the weekends at the YMCA. Jennifer's goals for the week were to find another part-time job and to ask her friend to begin taking walks together around the track at a local high school. Jennifer's mother felt that this activity would be safe as a summer school program was taking place at the high school, which ensured security staff would be on-site. Jennifer and her mother decided to no longer meet every evening to discuss food logs, and Jennifer decided to go back to tracking on her smart phone. Throughout the remainder of Phase 2, Jennifer was able to engage in regular exercise with her friend and secured a job at the local mall. After several weeks of not packing her lunch and buying food in the food court, Jennifer decided that she should start packing a lunch to bring to work. She struggled with this because she found it difficult to eat with her co-workers when she was not eating similar food as they were. Jennifer and her therapist discussed ways to respond to co-workers' comments. During the end of Phase 2, Jennifer also struggled with the belief that she had not "lost enough weight." The therapist used this as an opportunity to review expectations related to goals of treatment and redefine success in terms of health promoting behavioral changes rather than a specific "goal weight." The family expressed commitment to continuing to engage in health-oriented behaviors at a family systems level.

Phase 3

At this point, Jennifer was interested in talking about ways to "feel better about her body," and Carol described her hope to better understand how to prevent "relapse." Jennifer and Carol decided not to include David in Sessions 14 and 15. The therapist led them in a conversation to explore Carol's experiences as a teenager with body image and dissatisfaction. After describing her teenage years, Carol emphasized the importance of other factors in Jennifer's life (e.g., school, family, church) and how these factors will, over time, elaborate her self-concept, beyond weight. During the final session, the family and therapist discussed how the family could work together to maintain the healthy habits they had developed, as well as to continue integrating new habits into their lifestyle. The family decided they will continue to go to the YMCA every weekend. They made a family goal to complete a 5k walk during the year. Jennifer expressed interest in trying out for the cheer squad during the fall of her junior year. The family believes they should eat a majority of meals at home for both health and budget reasons and decided that they will track weight once per week at the YMCA as one outcome of Jennifer and her family's efforts to sustain health-oriented behaviors and choices.

References

Ackard, D. M., Neumark-Sztainer, D., Story, M., & Perry, C. (2003). Overeating among adolescents: Prevalence and associations with weight-related characteristics and psychological health. *Pediatrics, 111*(1), 67–74.

Ackard, D. M., Neumark-Sztainer, D. (2001). Family mealtime while growing up: Associations with symptoms of bulimia nervosa. *Eating Disorders, 9*(3), 239–249.

American Dietetic Association (2006). Position of the American Dietetic Association: Individual-, family-, school-, and community-based interventions for pediatric overweight. *Journal of the American Dietetic Association, 106*(6), 925.

Antonogeorgos, G., Panagiotakos, D. B., Papadimitriou, A., Priftis, K. N., Anthracopoulos, M., & Nicolaidou, P. (2012). Breakfast consumption and meal frequency interaction with childhood obesity. *Pediatric Obesity, 7*(1), 65–72.

Anzman-Frasca, S., Savage, J. S., Marini, M. E., Fisher, J. O., & Birch, L. L. (2012). Repeated exposure and associative conditioning promote preschool children's liking of vegetables. *Appetite, 58*(2), 543–553.

Apovian, C. M. (2013). The clinical and economic consequences of obesity. *The American Journal of Managed Care, 19*(10 Suppl), s219–228.

Arcan, C., Neumark-Sztainer, D., Hannan, P., van den Berg, P., Story, M., & Larson, N. (2007). Parental eating behaviours, home food environment and adolescent intakes of fruits, vegetables and dairy foods: Longitudinal findings from Project EAT. *Public Health Nutrition, 10*(11), 1257–1265.

Arredondo, E. M., Elder, J. P., Ayala, G. X., Campbell, N., Baquero, B., & Duerksen, S. (2006). Is parenting style related to children's healthy eating and physical activity in Latino families? *Health Education Research, 21*(6), 862–871.

Barlow, S. (2007). Expert committee recommendations regarding the prevention, assessment, and treatment of child and adolescent overweight and obesity: Summary report. *Pediatrics, 120* (suppl 4), s164–s192.

Baumrind, D. (1971). Current patterns of parental authority. *Developmental Psychology, 4*(1p2), 1.

Berge, J. M., Wall, M., Bauer, K. W., & Neumark-Sztainer, D. (2010). Parenting characteristics in the home environment and adolescent overweight: A latent class analysis. *Obesity, 18*(4), 818–825.

Berge, J. M. (2009). A review of familial correlates of child and adolescent obesity: What has the 21st century taught us so far? *International Journal of Adolescent Medicine and Health, 21*(4), 457–484.

Birch, L. L. (1999). Development of food preferences. *Annual Review of Nutrition, 19*(1), 41–62.

Birch, L. L., & Fisher, J. A. (1995). Appetite and eating behavior in children. *Pediatric Clinics of North America, 42*(4), 931–953.

Birch, L. L., & Marlin, D. W. (1982). I don't like it; I never tried it: Effects of exposure on two-year-old children's food preferences. *Appetite, 3*(4), 353–360.

Boutelle, K. N., Fulkerson, J. A., Neumark-Sztainer, D., Story, M., & French, S. A. (2007). Fast food for family meals: Relationships with parent and adolescent food intake, home food availability and weight status. *Public Health Nutrition, 10*(01), 16–23.

Boutelle, K., Neumark-Sztainer, D., Story, M., & Resnick, M. (2002). Weight control behaviors among obese, overweight, and nonoverweight adolescents. *Journal of Pediatric Psychology, 27*(6), 531–540.

Brownell, K. D., Schwartz, M. B., Puhl, R. M., Henderson, K. E., & Harris, J. L. (2009). The need for bold action to prevent adolescent obesity. *Journal of Adolescent Health, 45*(3), S8–S17.

Burgess-Champoux, T. L., Larson, N., Neumark-Sztainer, D., Hannan, P. J., & Story, M. (2009). Are family meal patterns associated with overall diet quality during the transition from early to middle adolescence? *Journal of Nutrition Education and Behavior, 41*(2), 79–86.

Carnell, S., Cooke, L., Cheng, R., Robbins, A., & Wardle, J. (2011). Parental feeding behaviours and motivations: A qualitative study in mothers of UK preschoolers. *Appetite, 57*(3), 665–673.

Cawley, J. (2010). The economics of childhood obesity. *Health Affairs, 29*(3), 364–371.

Comans, T. A., Whitty, J. A., Hills, A. P., Kendall, E., Turkstra, E., Gordon, L. G., ... & Scuffham, P. A. (2013). The cost-effectiveness and consumer acceptability of taxation strategies to reduce rates of overweight and obesity among children in Australia: Study protocol. *BMC public health, 13*(1), 1182.

Coppinger, T., Jeanes, Y. M., Hardwick, J., & Reeves, S. (2012). Body mass, frequency of eating and breakfast consumption in 9–13-year-olds. *Journal of Human Nutrition and Dietetics, 25*(1), 43–49.

Couturier, J., Kimber, M., & Szatmari, P. (2013). Efficacy of family-based treatment for adolescents with eating disorders: A systematic review and meta-analysis. *International Journal of Eating Disorders, 46*(1), 3–11.

Crespo, C. J., Smit, E., Troiano, R. P., Bartlett, S. J., Macera, C. A., & Andersen, R. E. (2001). Television watching, energy intake, and obesity in US children: Results from the third National Health and Nutrition Examination Survey, 1988–1994. *Archives of Pediatrics & Adolescent Medicine, 155*(3), 360–365.

Davison, K. K., & Birch, L. L. (2001). Child and parent characteristics as predictors of change in girls' body mass index. *International Journal of Obesity and Related Metabolic Disorders: Journal of the International Association for the Study of Obesity, 25*(12), 1834.

Davison, K. K., & Birch, L. L. (2002). Obesigenic families: Parents' physical activity and dietary intake patterns predict girls' risk of overweight. *International Journal of Obesity and Related Metabolic Disorders: Journal of the International Association for the Study of Obesity, 26*(9), 1186.

Davison, K. K., Francis, L. A., & Birch, L. L. (2005). Reexamining obesigenic families: Parents' obesity-related behaviors predict girls' change in BMI. *Obesity Research, 13*(11), 1980–1990.

DeBar, L. L., Stevens, V. J., Perrin, N., Wu, P., Pearson, J., Yarborough, B. J., ... & Lynch, F. (2012). A primary care-based, multicomponent lifestyle intervention for overweight adolescent females. *Pediatrics, 129*(3), e611–e620.

Demerath, E. W., Choh, A. C., Czerwinski, S. A., Lee, M., Sun, S. S., Chumlea, W. M., ... & Siervogel, R. M. (2007). Genetic and environmental influences on infant weight and weight change: The Fels Longitudinal Study. *American Journal of Human Biology, 19*(5), 692–702.

Dietz, W. H. (1998). Health consequences of obesity in youth: Childhood predictors of adult disease. *Pediatrics, 101*(Supplement 2), 518–525.

Dietz, W. H., & Gortmaker, S. L. (2001). Preventing obesity in children and adolescents. *Annual Review of Public Health, 22*(1), 337–353.

Eaton, D. K., Kann, L., Kinchen, S., Shanklin, S., Flint, K. H., Hawkins, J., ... & Wechsler, H. (2012). Youth risk behavior surveillance-United States, 2011. *Morbidity and Mortality Weekly Report. Surveillance Summaries (Washington, DC: 2002), 61*(4), 1–162.

Ebbeling, C. B., Leidig, M. M., Sinclair, K. B., Hangen, J. P., & Ludwig, D. S. (2003). A reduced-glycemic load diet in the treatment of adolescent obesity. *Archives of Pediatrics & Adolescent Medicine, 157*(8), 773–779.

Eisenberg, M. E., Neumark-Sztainer, D., & Story, M. (2003). Associations of weight-based teasing and emotional well-being among adolescents. *Archives of Pediatrics & Adolescent Medicine, 157*(8), 733–738.

Epstein, L. H. (1993). Methodological issues and ten-year outcomes for obese children. *Annals of the New York Academy of Sciences, 699*(1), 237–249.

Epstein, L. H., McCurley, J., Wing, R. R., & Valoski, A. (1990). Five-year follow-up of family-based behavioral treatments for childhood obesity. *Journal of Consulting and Clinical Psychology, 58*(5), 661.

Epstein, L. H., Paluch, R. A., Roemmich, J. N., & Beecher, M. D. (2007). Family-based obesity treatment, then and now: Twenty-five years of pediatric obesity treatment. *Health Psychology, 26*(4), 381–391.

Epstein, L. H., Roemmich, J. N., Robinson, J. L., Paluch, R. A., Winiewicz, D. D., Fuerch, J. H., & Robinson, T. N. (2008). A randomized trial of the effects of reducing television viewing and computer use on body mass index in young children. *Archives of Pediatrics & Adolescent Medicine, 162*(3), 239–245.

Epstein, L. H., Saelens, B. E., Myers, M. D., & Vito, D. (1997). Effects of decreasing sedentary behaviors on activity choice in obese children. *Health Psychology, 16*(2), 107.

Epstein, L. H., Valoski, A. M., Vara, L. S., McCurley, J., Wisniewski, L., Kalarchian, M. A., ... & Shrager, L. R. (1995). Effects of decreasing sedentary behavior and increasing activity on weight change in obese children. *Health Psychology, 14*(2), 109.

Epstein, L. H., Valoski, A., Wing, R. R., & McCurley, J. (1990). Ten-year follow-up of behavioral, family-based treatment for obese children. *JAMA, 264*(19), 2519–2523.

Epstein, L. H., Valoski, A., Wing, R. R., & McCurley, J. (1994). Ten-year outcomes of behavioral family-based treatment for childhood obesity. *Health Psychology, 13*(5), 373–383.

Erermis, S., Cetin, N., Tamar, M., Bukusoglu, N., Akdeniz, F., & Goksen, D. (2004). Is obesity a risk factor for psychopathology among adolescents? *Pediatrics International, 46*(3), 296–301.

Faith, M. S., & Kerns, J. (2005). Infant and child feeding practices and childhood overweight: The role of restriction. *Maternal & Child Nutrition, 1*(3), 164–168.

Faith, M. S., Berkowitz, R. I., Stallings, V. A., Kerns, J., Storey, M., & Stunkard, A. J. (2004). Parental feeding attitudes and styles and child body mass index: Prospective analysis of a gene-environment interaction. *Pediatrics, 114*(4), e429–e436.

Falkner, N. H., Neumark-Sztainer, D., Story, M., Jeffery, R. W., Beuhring, T., & Resnick, M. D. (2001). Social, educational, and psychological correlates of weight status in adolescents. *Obesity Research, 9*(1), 32–42.

Farooqi, I. S., & O'Rahilly, S. (2000). Recent advances in the genetics of severe childhood obesity. *Archives of Disease in Childhood, 83*(1), 31–34.

Feldman, S., Eisenberg, M. E., Neumark-Sztainer, D., & Story, M. (2007). Associations between watching TV during family meals and dietary intake among adolescents. *Journal of Nutrition Education and Behavior, 39*(5), 257–263.

Fleischman, A., & Rhodes, E. T. (2009). Management of obesity, insulin resistance and type 2 diabetes in children: Consensus and controversy. *Diabetes, Metabolic Syndrome and Obesity: Targets and Therapy, 2,* 185.

Fonseca, H., Matos, M. G., Guerra, A., & Gomes Pedro, J. (2009). Are overweight and obese adolescents different from their peers? *International Journal of Pediatric Obesity, 4*(3), 166–174.

Fox, C. L., & Farrow, C. V. (2009). Global and physical self-esteem and body dissatisfaction as mediators of the relationship between weight status and being a victim of bullying. *Journal of Adolescence, 32*(5), 1287–1301.

Freedman, D. S., Khan, L. K., Serdula, M. K., Dietz, W. H., Srinivasan, S. R., & Berenson, G. S. (2005). The relation of childhood BMI to adult adiposity: The Bogalusa Heart Study. *Pediatrics, 115*(1), 22–27.

Freedman, D. S., Mei, Z., Srinivasan, S. R., Berenson, G. S., & Dietz, W. H. (2007). Cardiovascular risk factors and excess adiposity among overweight children and adolescents: The Bogalusa Heart Study. *The Journal of Pediatrics, 150*(1), 12–17.

Freedman, D. S., Wang, J., Thornton, J. C., Mei, Z., Sopher, A. B., Pierson, R. N., ... & Horlick, M. (2009). Classification of body fatness by body mass index-for-age categories among children. *Archives of Pediatrics & Adolescent Medicine, 163*(9), 805–811.

Gillman, M. W., Rifas-Shiman, S. L., Frazier, A. L., Rockett, H. R., Camargo Jr, C. A., Field, A. E., ... & Colditz, G. A. (2000). Family dinner and diet quality among older children and adolescents. *Archives of Family Medicine, 9*(3), 235.

Golan, M. (2006). Parents as agents of change in childhood obesity-from research to practice. *International Journal of Pediatric Obesity, 1*(2), 66–76.

Golan M. & Crow S. (2004). Targeting parents exclusively in the treatment of childhood obesity: Long-term results. *Obesity Research, 12,* 357–361.

Golan, M., Kaufman, V., & Shahar, D. R. (2006). Childhood obesity treatment: Targeting parents exclusively v. parents and children. *British Journal of Nutrition, 95*(05), 1008–1015.

Golan, M., Weizman, A., Apter, A., & Fainaru, M. (1998). Parents as the exclusive agents of change in the treatment of childhood obesity. *The American Journal of Clinical Nutrition, 67*(6), 1130–1135.

Goldfield, G. S., & Epstein, L. H. (2002). Can fruits and vegetables and activities substitute for snack foods? *Health Psychology, 21*(3), 299.

Goldschmidt, A. B., Jones, M., Manwaring, J. L., Luce, K. H., Osborne, M. I., Cunning, D., & Taylor, C. B. (2008). The clinical significance of loss of control over eating in overweight adolescents. *International Journal of Eating Disorders, 41*(2), 153–158.

Golley, R. K., Magarey, A. M., Baur, L. A. et al. (2007). Twelve month effectiveness of a parent-led, family focused weight-management program for prepubertal children: A randomized, controlled trial. *Pediatrics, 119,* 517–525.

Gortmaker, S. L., Must, A., Perrin, J. M., Sobol, A. M., & Dietz, W. H. (1993). Social and economic consequences of overweight in adolescence and young adulthood. *New England Journal of Medicine*, *329*(14), 1008–1012.

Griffiths, L. J., Parsons, T. J., & Hill, A. J. (2010). Self-esteem and quality of life in obese children and adolescents: A systematic review. *International Journal of Pediatric Obesity*, *5*(4), 282–304.

Griffiths, L. J., Wolke, D., Page, A. S., & Horwood, J. P. (2006). Obesity and bullying: Different effects for boys and girls. *Archives of Disease in Childhood*, *91*(2), 121–125.

Gunnarsdottir, T., Njardvik, U., Olafsdottir, A. S., Craighead, L., & Bjarnason, R. (2012). Childhood obesity and co-morbid problems: Effects of Epstein's family-based behavioural treatment in an Icelandic sample. *Journal of Evaluation in Clinical Practice*, *18*(2), 465–472.

Guo, S. S., & Chumlea, W. C. (1999). Tracking of body mass index in children in relation to overweight in adulthood. *The American Journal of Clinical Nutrition*, *70*(1), 145s–148s.

Haines, J., & Neumark-Sztainer, D. (2009). Psychosocial consequences of obesity and weight bias: Implications for interventions. In Leslie J. Heinberg, J. Kevin Thompson (Eds.), *Obesity in youth: Causes, consequences, and cures* (pp. 79–98). Washington, DC: American Psychological Association.

Haines, J., Neumark-Sztainer, D., Eisenberg, M. E., & Hannan, P. J. (2006). Weight teasing and disordered eating behaviors in adolescents: Longitudinal findings from Project EAT (Eating Among Teens). *Pediatrics*, *117*(2), e209–e215.

Hammons, A. J., & Fiese, B. H. (2011). Is frequency of shared family meals related to the nutritional health of children and adolescents? *Pediatrics*, *127*(6), e1565–e1574.

Han, J. C., Lawlor, D. A., & Kimm, S. (2010). Childhood obesity. *The Lancet*, *375*(9727), 1737–1748.

Heinberg, L. J., & Thompson, J. (2009). *Obesity in youth: Causes, consequences, and cures*. American Psychological Association.

Hill, J. O., Wyatt, H. R., Reed, G. W., & Peters, J. C. (2003). Obesity and the environment: Where do we go from here? *Science*, *299*(5608), 853–855.

Humenikova, L., & Gates, G. E. (2008). Social and physical environmental factors and child overweight in a sample of American and Czech school-aged children: A pilot study. *Journal of Nutrition Education and Behavior*, *40*(4), 251–257.

Ingerski, L. M., Modi, A. C., Hood, K. K., Pai, A. L., Zeller, M., Piazza-Waggoner, C., ... & Hommel, K. A. (2010). Health-related quality of life across pediatric chronic conditions. *The Journal of Pediatrics*, *156*(4), 639–644.

Janicke, D. M., Steele, R. G., Gayes, L. A., Lim, C. S., Clifford, L. M., Schneider, E. M., ... & Westen, S. (2014). Systematic review and meta-analysis of comprehensive behavioral family lifestyle interventions addressing pediatric obesity. *Journal of Pediatric Psychology*, jsu023.

Janssen, I., & LeBlanc, A. G. (2010). Systematic review of the health benefits of physical activity and fitness in school-aged children and youth. *International Journal of Behavioral Nutrition and Physical Activity*, *7*(40), 1–16.

Jelalian, E., Mehlenbeck, R., Lloyd-Richardson, E. E., Birmaher, V., & Wing, R. R. (2005). 'Adventure therapy' combined with cognitive-behavioral treatment for overweight adolescents. *International Journal of Obesity*, *30*(1), 31–39.

Jelalian, E., & Saelens, B. E. (1999). Empirically supported treatments in pediatric psychology: Pediatric obesity. *Journal of Pediatric Psychology, 24*(3), 223–248.

Johnson, R., Welk, G., Saint-Maurice, P. F., & Ihmels, M. (2012). Parenting styles and home obesogenic environments. *International Journal of Environmental Research and Public Health, 9*(4), 1411–1426.

Kalarchian, M. A., Levine, M. D., Arslanian, S. A. et al. (2009). Family-based treatment of severe pediatric obesity: Randomized, controlled trial. *Pediatrics, 124*(4), 1060–1068.

Kelsey, M. M., Zaepfel, A., Bjornstad, P., & Nadeau, K. J. (2014). Age-related consequences of childhood obesity. *Gerontology, 60*(3), 222–228.

Kime, N. (2009). How children eat may contribute to rising levels of obesity Children's eating behaviours: An intergenerational study of family influences. *International Journal of Health Promotion and Education, 47*(1), 4–11.

Kushi, L. H., Byers, T., Doyle, C., Bandera, E. V., McCullough, M., Gansler, T., ... & Thun, M. J. (2006). American Cancer Society guidelines on nutrition and physical activity for cancer prevention: Reducing the risk of cancer with healthy food choices and physical activity. *CA: A Cancer Journal for Clinicians, 56*(5), 254–281.

Lane, S. P., Bluestone, C., & Burke, C. T. (2013). Trajectories of BMI from early childhood through early adolescence: SES and psychosocial predictors. *British Journal of Health Psychology, 18*(1), 66–82.

Larson, N. I., Neumark-Sztainer, D., Hannan, P. J., & Story, M. (2007). Family meals during adolescence are associated with higher diet quality and healthful meal patterns during young adulthood. *Journal of the American Dietetic Association, 107*(9), 1502–1510.

Le Grange, D., Eisler, I., Dare, C., & Hodes, M. (1992). Family criticism and self-starvation: A study of expressed emotion. *Journal of Family Therapy, 14*(2), 177–192.

Le Grange, D., & Lock, J. (2007). *Treatment manual for bulimia nervosa: A family-based approach*. New York: Guilford.

Le Stunff, C., Fallin, D., & Bougnères, P. (2001). Paternal transmission of the very common class I INS VNTR alleles predisposes to childhood obesity. *Nature Genetics, 29*(1), 96–99.

Lehnert, T., Sonntag, D., Konnopka, A., Riedel-Heller, S., & König, H. H. (2013). Economic costs of overweight and obesity. *Best Practice & Research Clinical Endocrinology & Metabolism, 27*(2), 105–115.

Lobstein, T., & Dibb, S. (2005). Evidence of a possible link between obesogenic food advertising and child overweight. *Obesity Reviews, 6*(3), 203–208.

Lock, J., & Le Grange, D. (2012). *Treatment manual for anorexia nervosa: A family-based approach*. New York: Guilford Press.

Lock, J., Le Grange, D., Agras, W. S., & Dare, C. (2000). *Treatment manual for anorexia nervosa: A family based approach*. London, UK.

Lo Presti, R., Lai, J., Hildebrandt, T., & Loeb, K. L. (2010). Psychological treatments for obesity in youth and adults. *Mount Sinai Journal of Medicine, 77*, 472–487.

Ludwig, D. S., Peterson, K. E., & Gortmaker, S. L. (2001). Relation between consumption of sugar-sweetened drinks and childhood obesity: A prospective, observational analysis. *The Lancet, 357*(9255), 505–508.

Lumeng, J. C., Gannon, K., Cabral, H. J., Frank, D. A., & Zuckerman, B. (2003). Association between clinically meaningful behavior problems and overweight in children. *Pediatrics, 112*(5), 1138–1145.

Malik, V. S., Schulze, M. B., & Hu, F. B. (2006). Intake of sugar-sweetened beverages and weight gain: A systematic review. *The American Journal of Clinical Nutrition, 84*(2), 274–288.

Marti, A., Moreno-Aliaga, M. J., Hebebrand, J., & Martinez, J. A. (2004). Genes, lifestyles and obesity. *International Journal of Obesity, 28*, S29–S36.

Martin-Calvo, N., Martínez-González, M. A., Bes-Rastrollo, M., Gea, A., Ochoa, M. C., & Marti, A. (2014). Sugar-sweetened carbonated beverage consumption and childhood/adolescent obesity: A case–control study. *Public Health Nutrition*, 1–9.

McKay, M. M., Hibbert, R., Hoagwood, K., Rodriguez, J., Murray, L., Legerski, J., & Fernandez, D. (2004). Integrating evidence-based engagement interventions into "real world" child mental health settings. *Brief Treatment and Crisis Intervention, 4*(2), 177.

Mellin, A. E., Neumark-Sztainer, D., Story, M., Ireland, M., & Resnick, M. D. (2002). Unhealthy behaviors and psychosocial difficulties among overweight adolescents: the potential impact of familial factors. *Journal of Adolescent Health, 31*(2), 145–153.

Melnyk, B. M., Small, L., Morrison-Beedy, D., Strasser, A., Spath, L., Kreipe, R., ... & Van Blankenstein, S. (2006). Mental health correlates of healthy lifestyle attitudes, beliefs, choices, and behaviors in overweight adolescents. *Journal of Pediatric Health Care, 20*(6), 401–406.

Menzel, J. E., Schaefer, L. M., Burke, N. L., Mayhew, L. L., Brannick, M. T., & Thompson, J. K. (2010). Appearance-related teasing, body dissatisfaction, and disordered eating: A meta-analysis. *Body Image, 7*(4), 261–270.

Moens, E., Braet, C., & Vandewalle, J. (2013). Observation of parental functioning at mealtime using a sibling design. *Appetite, 68*, 132–138.

Mokdad, A. H., Ford, E. S., Bowman, B. A., Dietz, W. H., Vinicor, F., Bales, V. S., & Marks, J. S. (2003). Prevalence of obesity, diabetes, and obesity-related health risk factors, 2001. *JAMA, 289*(1), 76–79.

Morgan, C. M., Yanovski, S. Z., Nguyen, T. T., McDuffie, J., Sebring, N. G., Jorge, M. R., & ... Yanovski, J. A. (2002). Loss of control over eating, adiposity, and psychopathology in overweight children. *International Journal of Eating Disorders, 31*(4), 430–441.

Musher-Eizenman, D. R., de Lauzon-Guillain, B., Holub, S. C., Leporc, E., & Charles, M. A. (2009). Child and parent characteristics related to parental feeding practices. A cross-cultural examination in the US and France. *Appetite, 52*(1), 89–95.

Must, A., Jacques, P. F., Dallal, G. E., Bajema, C. J., & Dietz, W. H. (1992). Long-term morbidity and mortality of overweight adolescents: A follow-up of the Harvard Growth Study of 1922 to 1935. *New England Journal of Medicine, 327*(19), 1350–1355.

National Center for Health Statistics (US, 2012). Health, United States, 2011: With special feature on socioeconomic status and health.

Neumark-Sztainer, D., Wall, M., Story, M., & Fulkerson, J. A. (2004). Are family meal patterns associated with disordered eating behaviors among adolescents? *Journal of Adolescent Health, 35*(5), 350–359.

Ogden, C. L., Carroll, M. D., Kit, B. K., & Flegal, K. M. (2014). Prevalence of childhood and adult obesity in the United States, 2011–2012. *JAMA, 311*(8), 806–814.

Olvera, N., & Power, T. G. (2010). Brief report: Parenting styles and obesity in Mexican American children: A longitudinal study. *Journal of Pediatric Psychology, 35*(3), 243–249.

Pan, A., Malik, V. S., Hao, T., Willett, W. C., Mozaffarian, D., & Hu, F. B. (2013). Changes in water and beverage intake and long-term weight changes: Results from three prospective cohort studies. *International Journal of Obesity, 37*(10), 1378–1385.

Park, H., & Walton-Moss, B. (2012). Parenting style, parenting stress, and children's health-related behaviors. *Journal of Developmental & Behavioral Pediatrics, 33*(6), 495–503.

Patrick, H., & Nicklas, T. A. (2005). A review of family and social determinants of children's eating patterns and diet quality. *Journal of the American College of Nutrition, 24*(2), 83–92.

Patrick, H., Nicklas, T. A., Hughes, S. O., & Morales, M. (2005). The benefits of authoritative feeding style: Caregiver feeding styles and children's food consumption patterns. *Appetite, 44*(2), 243–249.

Patrick, K., Norman, G. J., Calfas, K. J., Sallis, J. F., Zabinski, M. F., Rupp, J., & Cella, J. (2004). Diet, physical activity, and sedentary behaviors as risk factors for overweight in adolescence. *Archives of Pediatrics & Adolescent Medicine, 158*(4), 385–390.

Patro, B., & Szajewska, H. (2010). Meal patterns and childhood obesity. *Current Opinion in Clinical Nutrition & Metabolic Care, 13*(3), 300–304.

Pearce, M. J., Boergers, J., & Prinstein, M. J. (2002). Adolescent obesity, overt and relational peer victimization, and romantic relationships. *Obesity Research, 10*(5), 386–393.

Pearson, N., & Biddle, S. J. (2011). Sedentary behavior and dietary intake in children, adolescents, and adults: A systematic review. *American Journal of Preventive Medicine, 41*(2), 178–188.

Pi-Sunyer, X. (2009). The medical risks of obesity. *Postgraduate Medicine, 121*(6), 21.

Powell, L. M., & Nguyen, B. T. (2013). Fast-food and full-service restaurant consumption among children and adolescents: Effect on energy, beverage, and nutrient intake. *JAMA pediatrics, 167*(1), 14–20.

Powell, L. M., Slater, S., & Chaloupka, F. J. (2004). The relationship between community physical activity settings and race, ethnicity and socioeconomic status. *Evidence-Based Preventive Medicine, 1*(2), 135–144.

Puhl, R. M., & Latner, J. D. (2007). Stigma, obesity, and the health of the nation's children. *Psychological Bulletin, 133*(4), 557.

Radnitz, C., Byrne, S., Goldman, R., Sparks, M., Gantshar, M., & Tung, K. (2009). Food cues in children's television programs. *Appetite, 52*(1), 230–233.

Radnitz, C., Loeb, K. L., DiMatteo, J., Keller, K. L., Zucker, N., & Schwartz, M. (2013). Optimal defaults in the prevention of pediatric obesity: From platform to practice. *Journal of Food & Nutritional Disorders, 2*(5), 1–8.

Reilly, J. J., & Kelly, J. (2010). Long-term impact of overweight and obesity in childhood and adolescence on morbidity and premature mortality in adulthood: Systematic review. *International Journal of Obesity, 35*(7), 891–898.

Rhee, K. E., Lumeng, J. C., Appugliese, D. P., Kaciroti, N., & Bradley, R. H. (2006). Parenting styles and overweight status in first grade. *Pediatrics, 117*(6), 2047–2054.

Ritchie, L. D., Welk, G., Styne, D., Gerstein, D. E., & Crawford, P. B. (2005). Family environment and pediatric overweight: What is a parent to do? *Journal of the American Dietetic Association*, *105*(5), 70–79.

Robinson, T. N. (1999). Reducing children's television viewing to prevent obesity: A randomized controlled trial. *JAMA*, *282*(16), 1561–1567.

Rodenburg, G., Oenema, A., Kremers, S. P., & van de Mheen, D. (2012). Parental and child fruit consumption in the context of general parenting, parental education and ethnic background. *Appetite*, *58*(1), 364–372.

Rollins, B. Y., Belue, R. Z., & Francis, L. A. (2010). The beneficial effect of family meals on obesity differs by race, sex, and household education: The national survey of children's health, 2003–2004. *Journal of the American Dietetic Association*, *110*(9), 1335–1339.

Schwimmer, J. B., Burwinkle, T. M., & Varni, J. W. (2003). Health-related quality of life of severely obese children and adolescents. *JAMA*, *289*(14), 1813–1819.

Sebastian, R. S., Wilkinson Enns, C., & Goldman, J. D. (2009). US adolescents and MyPyramid: Associations between fast-food consumption and lower likelihood of meeting recommendations. *Journal of the American Dietetic Association*, *109*(2), 226–235.

Sepulveda, A. R., Todd, G., Whitaker, W., Grover, M., Stahl, D., & Treasure, J. (2010). Expressed emotion in relatives of patients with eating disorders following skills training program. *International Journal of Eating Disorders*, *43*(7), 603–610.

Serdula, M. K., Ivery, D., Coates, R. J., Freedman, D. S., Williamson, D. F., & Byers, T. (1993). Do obese children become obese adults? A review of the literature. *Preventive Medicine*, *22*(2), 167–177.

Shelton, D., Le Gros, K., Norton, L., Stanton-Cook, S., Morgan, J., & Masterman, P. (2007). Randomised controlled trial: A parent-based group education programme for overweight children. *Journal of Pediatrics and Child Health*, *43*(12), 799–805.

Shrewsbury, V. A., Steinbeck, K. S., Torvaldsen, S., & Baur, L. A. (2011). The role of parents in pre-adolescent and adolescent overweight and obesity treatment: A systematic review of clinical recommendations. *Obesity Reviews*, *12*(10), 759–769.

Singh, A. S., Mulder, C., Twisk, J. W., Van Mechelen, W., & Chinapaw, M. J. (2008). Tracking of childhood overweight into adulthood: A systematic review of the literature. *Obesity reviews*, *9*(5), 474–488.

Sobal, J., Rauschenbach, B. S., & Frongillo, E. A. (1995). Obesity and marital quality analysis of weight, marital unhappiness, and marital problems in a US national sample. *Journal of Family Issues*, *16*(6), 746–764.

Steele, R. G., Jensen, C. D., Gayes, L. A., & Leibold, H. C. (2014). Medium is the message: Moderate parental control of feeding correlates with improved weight outcome in a pediatric obesity intervention. *Journal of Pediatric Psychology*, jsu035.

Stice, E., Cameron, R. P., Killen, J. D., Hayward, C., & Taylor, C. B. (1999). Naturalistic weight-reduction efforts prospectively predict growth in relative weight and onset of obesity among female adolescents. *Journal of Consulting and Clinical Psychology*, *67*(6), 967.

Stice, E., Presnell, K., Shaw, H., & Rohde, P. (2005). Psychological and behavioral risk factors for obesity onset in adolescent girls: A prospective study. *Journal of Consulting and Clinical Psychology*, *73*(2), 195.

Stiles-Shields, C., Rienecke Hoste, R., M Doyle, P., & Le Grange, D. (2012). A review of family-based treatment for adolescents with eating disorders. *Reviews on Recent Clinical Trials, 7*(2), 133–140.

Story, M. T., Neumark-Stzainer, D. R., Sherwood, N. E., Holt, K., Sofka, D., Trowbridge, F. L., & Barlow, S. E. (2002). Management of child and adolescent obesity: Attitudes, barriers, skills, and training needs among health care professionals. *Pediatrics, 110*(Supplement 1), 210–214.

Story, M., & Neumark-Sztainer, D. (2005). A perspective on family meals: Do they matter? *Nutrition Today, 40*(6), 261–266.

Strasburger, V. C., Hogan, M. J., Mulligan, D. A., Ameenuddin, N., Christakis, D. A., Cross, C., ... & Swanson, W. S. L. (2013). Children, adolescents, and the media. *Pediatrics, 132*(5), 958–961.

Strauss, R. S., & Pollack, H. A. (2003). Social marginalization of overweight children. *Archives of Pediatrics & Adolescent Medicine, 157*(8), 746–752.

Sutherland, E. (2008). Obesity and asthma. *Immunology and Allergy Clinics of North America, 28*(3), 589–602.

Szapocznik, J., Perez-Vidal, A., Brickman, A. L., Foote, F. H., Santisteban, D., Hervis, O., & Kurtines, W. M. (1988). Engaging adolescent drug abusers and their families in treatment: A strategic structural systems approach. *Journal of Consulting and Clinical Psychology, 56*(4), 552.

Tanofsky-Kraff, M., Goossens, L., Eddy, K. T., Ringham, R., Goldschmidt, A., Yanovski, S. Z., ... & Yanovski, J. A. (2007). A multisite investigation of binge eating behaviors in children and adolescents. *Journal of Consulting and Clinical Psychology, 75*(6), 901.

Taylor, E. D., Theim, K. R., Mirch, M. C., Ghorbani, S., Tanofsky-Kraff, M., Adler-Wailes, D. C., ... & Yanovski, J. A. (2006). Orthopedic complications of overweight in children and adolescents. *Pediatrics, 117*(6), 2167–2174.

Thivel, D., Aucouturier, J., Doucet, É., Saunders, T. J., & Chaput, J. P. (2013). Daily energy balance in children and adolescents. Does energy expenditure predict subsequent energy intake? *Appetite, 60*, 58–64.

Thompson, J. K., Shroff, H., Herbozo, S., Cafri, G., Rodriguez, J., & Rodriguez, M. (2007). Relations among multiple peer influences, body dissatisfaction, eating disturbance, and self-esteem: A comparison of average weight, at risk of overweight, and overweight adolescent girls. *Journal of Pediatric Psychology, 32*(1), 24–29.

Topham, G. L., Hubbs-Tait, L., Rutledge, J. M., Page, M. C., Kennedy, T. S., Shriver, L. H., & Harrist, A. W. (2011). Parenting styles, parental response to child emotion, and family emotional responsiveness are related to child emotional eating. *Appetite, 56*(2), 261–264.

Tremblay, M. S., LeBlanc, A. G., Kho, M. E., Saunders, T. J., Larouche, R., Colley, R. C., ... & Gorber, S. C. (2011). Systematic review of sedentary behaviour and health indicators in school-aged children and youth. *International Journal of Behavioral Nutrition and Physical Activity, 8*(1), 98.

van Furth, E. F., van Strien, D. C., Martina, L. M., van Son, M. J., Hendrickx, J. J., & van Engeland, H. (1996). Expressed emotion and the prediction of outcome in adolescent eating disorders. *International Journal of Eating Disorders, 20*(1), 19–31.

Van Strien, T., Van Niekerk, R., & Ouwens, M. A. (2009). Perceived parental food controlling practices are related to obesogenic or leptogenic child life style behaviors. *Appetite, 53*(1), 151–154.

Van Vlierberghe, L., Braet, C., Goossens, L., & Mels, S. (2009). Psychiatric disorders and symptom severity in referred versus non-referred overweight children and adolescents. *European Child & Adolescent Psychiatry*, 18(3), 164–173.

Wadden, T. A., Brownell, K. D., & Foster, G. D. (2002). Obesity: Responding to the global epidemic. *Journal of Consulting and Clinical Psychology*, 70(3), 510.

Wake, M., Nicholson, J. M., Hardy, P., & Smith, K. (2007). Preschooler obesity and parenting styles of mothers and fathers: Australian national population study. *Pediatrics*, 120(6), e1520–e1527.

Wang, H., & Zhai, F. (2013). Programme and policy options for preventing obesity in China. *Obesity Reviews*, 14(S2), 134–140.

Wansink, B., & Kleef, E. (2014). Dinner rituals that correlate with child and adult BMI. *Obesity*, 22(5), E91–E95.

Wardle, J., & Cooke, L. (2005). The impact of obesity on psychological well-being. *Best Practice & Research Clinical Endocrinology & Metabolism*, 19(3), 421–440.

Welsh, J. A., Cogswell, M. E., Rogers, S., Rockett, H., Mei, Z., & Grummer-Strawn, L. M. (2005). Overweight among low-income preschool children associated with the consumption of sweet drinks: Missouri, 1999–2002. *Pediatrics*, 115(2), e223–e229.

West, F., Sanders, M. R., Cleghorn, G. J., & Davies, P. S. (2010). Randomised clinical trial of a family-based lifestyle intervention for childhood obesity involving parents as the exclusive agents of change. *Behaviour Research and Therapy*, 48(12), 1170–1179.

Whitlock, E. P., Williams, S. B., Gold, R., Smith, P. R., & Shipman, S. A. (2005). Screening and interventions for childhood overweight: A summary of evidence for the US Preventive Services Task Force. *Pediatrics*, 116(1), e125–e144.

Williams, J., Wake, M., Hesketh, K., Maher, E., & Waters, E. (2005). Health-related quality of life of overweight and obese children. *JAMA*, 293(1), 70–76.

Williamson, D. A., Walden, H. M., White, M. A., York-Crowe, E., Newton, R. L., Alfonso, A., … & Ryan, D. (2006). Two-year Internet-based randomized controlled trial for weight loss in African-American girls. *Obesity*, 14(7), 1231–1243.

Wright, D. R., & Prosser, L. A. (2014). The Impact of Overweight and Obesity on Pediatric Medical Expenditures. *Applied Health Economics and Health Policy*, 12(2), 139–150.

Zeller, M. H., Reiter-Purtill, J., Modi, A. C., Gutzwiller, J., Vannatta, K., & Davies, W. (2007). Controlled study of critical parent and family factors in the obesigenic environment. *Obesity*, 15(1), 126–126.

Zeller, M., Kirk, S., Claytor, R., Khoury, P., Grieme, J., Santangelo, M., & Daniels, S. (2004). Predictors of attrition from a pediatric weight management program. *The Journal of Pediatrics*, 144(4), 466–470.

Zheng, M., Rangan, A., Olsen, N. J., Andersen, L. B., Wedderkopp, N., Kristensen, P., … & Heitmann, B. L. (in press). Substituting sugar-sweetened beverages with water or milk is inversely associated with body fatness development from childhood to adolescence. *Nutrition*. http://www.nutritionjrnl.com/article/S0899-9007(14)00209-3/abstract

Zoumas-Morse, C., Rock, C. L., Sobo, E. J., & Neuhouser, M. L. (2001). Children's patterns of macronutrient intake and associations with restaurant and home eating. *Journal of the American Dietetic Association*, 101(8), 923–925.

Chapter 11

Family Therapy for Transition Youth

Gina Dimitropoulos, James Lock, Daniel Le Grange, and Kristen Anderson

This chapter presents an innovative model for working with transition age youth (TAY, ages 17–25) with anorexia nervosa (AN) and their families. This model builds on the empirically supported Family-Based Treatment (FBT) for Adolescents with AN and BN (Lock & Le Grange, 2012; Le Grange & Lock, 2007). This chapter begins with a review of empirical evidence regarding FBT for adolescents and young adults with eating disorders. The next part of the chapter highlights evidence that demonstrates the rationale for using a family-based intervention to support TAY or emerging adults with AN. An overview of how FBT can be adapted and potential challenges that must be addressed when working with young adults with AN is discussed. An application of the model to a clinical example will be used throughout the chapter.

Literature Review: The Importance of Using Family-Based Treatment for Young Adults with AN

AN is associated with severe medical consequences, psychosocial impairment, and psychiatric co-morbidity (Klump et al., 2009; Steinhausen, 2002, 2009) and the typical age of AN diagnosis occurs during mid to late adolescence (average 14–18 years of age) (Nicholls et al., 2008). AN is associated with high rates of mortality (Rosling et al., 2011; Arcelus et al., 2011), which peaks in the 20–30 year old age group with a Standardized Mortality Ratio (SMR) of 18.0 (Arcelus et al., 2011). Older adolescents and young adults with eating disorders (EDs) have a high frequency of co-morbidities (Fischer & Le Grange, 2007; Le Grange et al., 2012) such as mood (McElroy et al., 2011; Nunes Campos et al., 2013; Wade, Bulik, Neale & Kendler, 2000; Touchette et al., 2011), anxiety disorders (Kaye et al., 2004; Swinbourne et al., 2012) or substance use disorders (Baker et al., 2010; Harrop & Marlatt, 2010; Gregorowski, Seedat, & Jordaan, 2013). Overall, the risk for mortality and for the development of co-morbid conditions peaks during a period of time when adolescents are becoming emerging adults (ages 17–21) (Doyle, Smyth, & Le Grange, 2011; Fischer & Le Grange, 2007; Jones, 2013; Kessler et al., 2008; Merikangas et al., 2010).

Approximately 50% of adolescents with EDs develop a chronic illness course (Lock et al., 2010; Treasure & Russell, 2011) necessitating a transfer of care from pediatric to adult health care services (Baldock, 2010). A number of barriers to a successful transition from pediatric to adult Eating Disorder Programs (EDPs) were identified through qualitative interviews with expert clinicians (Dimitropoulos et al., 2012a; Dimitropoulos et al., 2012b). The transfer of care to adult intensive EDPs is often abrupt and uncoordinated, leaving older adolescents and young adults with inadequate care for their illness. Clinicians also reported that *transition age youth* often lack necessary skills to engage autonomously in adult treatment because prolonged starvation, malnourishment, and sustained weight loss disrupt neuro-cognitive development and psychosocial maturation of young people afflicted with EDs. Such developmental disruptions leave the young adult dependent on their parents to manage the illness even when it is no longer developmentally appropriate, hindering young adults from taking the opportunity to direct their treatment and recovery (Dimitropoulos et al., 2012a). Finally, illness-related factors, such as ambivalence about weight gain, prevent or delay young adults from accepting a transfer from pediatric providers to adult health-care services and from independently pursuing eating disorder treatment. These findings suggest that clinicians recognize the strivings for greater independence in older adolescents and young adults with AN but that illness-related factors interfere with their autonomous engagement in treatment without the supportive assistance of family members and clinicians.

The importance of parental support in assisting with weight restoration and eating rehabilitation in young adults with AN is demonstrated by the ego-syntonic nature of the illness, which leads to minimization of the severity of eating disorder symptoms (Bulik & Kendler, 2000; Roncero, Belloch, Perpina, & Treasure, 2013). In a systematic review of qualitative studies (Westwood & Kendel, 2011) individuals with AN described internal tensions stemming from a profound desire to exert control over their lives through starvation and weight loss while simultaneously experiencing relief when others such as their parents support them to recover from the illness. Although individuals with AN have difficulties acknowledging the consequences of their illness, their attitudes about engaging in behavioral changes shift as they progress through treatment (Westwood & Kendel, 2011; Watson, Fursland, & Byrne, 2013; Schmidt, Tiller, & Treasure, 1993). This shift in attitudes can be further aided by supportive others who can assist with behavioral changes. Although it is important to develop a therapeutic alliance with the young adult, research demonstrates that this in and of itself is not a sufficient ingredient for the achievement of weight restoration and normalized eating, regardless of whether patients participate in individual or family-based treatment (Forsberg et al., 2013). Alliance-building facilitates the engagement of young people in treatment but it is the alliance of the parents and their active efforts to assist with eating and weight gain, especially early in treatment, that contributes to positive outcomes in individuals with AN (Forsberg et al., 2013).

Family-Based Treatment for Adolescents with Eating Disorders

FBT is an adolescent-focused intervention that emphasizes parent involvement in addressing starvation and eating disorder symptoms and parental responsibility for ensuring that the youth adheres and complies with treatment (Lock & Le Grange, 2012; Lock et al., 2010). Ever since it was first developed, there has been evidence that conventional FBT contributes to good outcomes for young adolescents with a short duration of illness but is less effective with older adolescents with a more chronic illness course (Russell et al., 1987; Eisler et al., 1997). One seminal research study suggested that there are other subgroups that do not respond well to FBT (Eisler et al., 1997). Specifically, older adolescents with AN with a late illness onset showed improvement from individual counseling in some outcomes (psychosexual adjustment and mental state) at a five-year follow-up, but older adolescents with late onset AN did not improve with FBT. Adolescents with a young age of onset and a longer duration of illness and adults with BN were poor responders to both FBT and individual counseling (Russell et al., 1987; Eisler et al., 1997). This study had several limitations including a small sample size and interventions that were not manualized. In a recent randomized controlled trial comparing manualized FBT to manualized individual therapy, adolescents did not significantly improve with individual treatment regardless of age (Le Grange et al., 2011). Older adolescents experienced a greater decline in remission rates over time compared with younger adolescents, regardless of the treatment modality used (Le Grange et al., 2012). Taken together, these findings raise important questions about whether FBT may require some adaptations to increase its utility with older adolescents and young adults.

More recently, a small case series was conducted on four young adult outpatients (ages 18–21) with AN with duration of illness ranging from 1 to 3.5 years (Chen et al., 2010). This model consisted of FBT that was slightly modified for young adults. It can be differentiated from FBT for adolescents in that a more collaborative relationship is emphasized between parents and the young adult. Young adult patients are encouraged to take a more active role in discussions regarding treatment, but in circumstances where discussions are not progressing, decision-making reverts to the parents for promoting weight restoration. The treatment was associated with weight restoration and a return of menses in three out of four participants.

Although FBT appears effective for some adolescents, particularly when they are younger and have a shorter illness duration, the original format and structure requires modifications to increase effectiveness in older teenagers and young adults with a chronic illness, or for individuals with a late onset of AN in mid to late adolescence. In this chapter, an adapted version of FBT for adolescents with AN and BN that aims to address some of the limitations of applying the original family intervention to older adolescents and young adults is presented. We recently received funding from the Ontario Mental Health Foundation to conduct a feasibility study on an adapted FBT model for young adults. This study consists of two stages: (1) The first phase integrates research based on patient, parent, and expert clinicians using family-based treatment with adolescents and adults to establish an adapted and standardized FBT model for working with transition age youth with AN; and (2) The second stage consists of conducting a multi-site study to assess the feasibility, acceptability, and tolerability of this intervention to clinicians, young adults, and their parents. This study is currently underway at four major pediatric and adult eating disorder programs in Ontario, Canada. While data are not yet available on the outcomes of the study, the adapted version of FBT for transition age youth including the goals and interventions required to deliver this model has been constructed and is described later in the chapter. The differences and similarities between the foundational models and the adapted version are illustrated. However, prior to discussing FBT-TAY, the unique challenges of working with transition age youth are described to illustrate the rationale underlying the adaptations to FBT for AN and BN.

Challenges of Working with Transition Age Youth

Heterogeneity of Young Adults with AN

Like adolescents with eating disorders, young adults with these disorders are a heterogeneous group. By early adulthood, many individuals may have a complicated history including repeat hospitalizations for their eating disorder throughout adolescence. Some young adults who have been ill throughout their adolescence may have been unable to achieve important milestones associated with this developmental time period and may appear more regressed or dependent on their parents. On the other hand, a late onset AN in adolescence and young adulthood may mean that individuals have already achieved greater independence in various domains of their lives. An independent older adolescent or young adult may be more resistant and opposed to parental control, even if temporary, over eating and weight gain compared with individuals who are emotionally, psychologically, and financially dependent on their parents.

Disempowered Parents Experiencing Burden, Guilt, and Shame

Due to the chronicity of the illness and frequent treatment episodes in pediatric care, parents of young adults may express significant demoralization, hopelessness, and despair (Coomber & King, 2013; Sepulveda et al., 2012). Parents may experience greater burnout if they have been supporting their offspring with AN for a longer period of time, compared to a recent onset of illness. As demonstrated in empirical research on caregivers of people with eating disorders (Nielsen & Bara-Carril, 2003), higher rates of burden are associated with anxiety, depression, and poor quality of life in caregivers (Martin et al., 2013; Padierna et al., 2013; Raenker et al., 2012; Treasure et al., 2001; Whitney et al., 2005; Whitney et al., 2007). Consequently, parents may express significant blame and guilt especially if they perceive themselves as ineffectual due to the illness becoming chronic in their daughter or son.

Co-Morbidity in Young Adults with AN

Older adolescents and young adults may present with more co-morbid mental illnesses including substance abuse and anxiety disorders compared with young teenagers (Swanson et al., 2011). As with other forms of FBT, FBT for young adults is a behaviorally focused treatment that engages parents in addressing eating disorder symptoms. Similar to FBT-BN, co-morbid psychiatric illnesses may need to be addressed simultaneously especially if other illnesses are exacerbating eating disorder symptoms and interfering with the efforts of the young adult and parents to address starvation and purging symptoms. FBT therapists working with young adults will need to work closely with psychiatrists or physicians who can treat co-morbidities and prescribe effective medications when required.

Given that psychiatric co-morbidities are more likely to increase in older adolescents and young adults (Fischer & Le Grange, 2007; Le Grange et al., 2012), FBT therapists must also network with other clinicians with extensive expertise in various treatment modalities or training to ameliorate other mental illnesses. For instance, FBT-TAY clinicians should work collaboratively with clinicians in their community who have training in empirically based interventions such as cognitive behavior therapy (CBT) and dialectical behavior therapy (DBT) to assist young adults with AN who are struggling with emotion dysregulation, self-injurious behaviors, and chronic suicidality (Chugani, Ghali, & Brunner, 2013; Gonzales & Bergstrom, 2013; Pistorello et al., 2012; Tarrier, Taylor, & Gooding, 2008). The utilization of individual counseling for the patient is especially warranted when treatment interfering behaviors such as self-harm and suicidality prevent the FBT therapist and the parents from focusing on problematic eating behaviors in the young adult. FBT-TAY clinicians should similarly request for consultations from clinicians with expertise in other mental illnesses such as depression, anxiety, and obsessive compulsive disorder especially if these other illnesses are impeding the young adult responding to FBT treatment. Young adults with substance abuse problems may similarly require assistance to reduce their use of alcohol and illicit drugs (Gregorowski, Seedat, & Jordaan, 2013).

Family-Based Treatment for Young Adults: A Developmentally Tailored Approach to Work with Older Adolescents and Young Adults with AN

FBT-TAY is grounded in the original FBT-AN and FBT-BN manuals (Lock & Le Grange, 2012; Le Grange & Lock, 2007). FBT-TAY is different from FBT for adolescents as it:

1   Is tailored to address the unique developmental needs of older adolescents and young adults with AN.
2   Promotes greater collaboration with the young person and their parents.
3   Assists with behavioral changes and the psychological tasks associated with emerging adulthood in the final phase of this treatment.

FBT-TAY is also designed to be longer and more intensive than FBT for adolescents with AN and BN. FBT-TAY offers more individual time prior to family meetings for the purpose of preparing and engaging the young adult in every phase of the treatment. Borrowing more heavily from the FBT-BN approach (Lock & Le Grange, 2007), FBT-TAY places greater primacy on building a collaborative relationship between the young adult and the parents. This goal is paramount in FBT-TAY and must be continuously assessed and reevaluated at every step of the treatment process.

As FBT-TAY will typically be delivered in adult outpatient eating disorder programs, community-based organizations, and health and counseling services on university and college campuses, there are important legal, philosophical, and developmental issues that must be taken into consideration and respected. In many Western societies, individuals over the age of 18 have the legal right to autonomously decide if they require medical and psychiatric treatment for AN (Byrick & Walker-Renshaw, 2012). The right to self-determination and autonomous decision-making, free of coercion in capable individuals with mental illnesses (including AN), is highly valued in Western societies over a more paternalistic approach (Clayman & Makoul, 2009; Makoul & Clayman, 2006). In North America, clinicians abide by various acts and legislations that protect the legal rights of competent young adults to decline treatment even when it is in their best interest and even when their wishes contrast with the wishes of their family members (United Nations Human Rights Office, 1989). Given these legal and philosophical realities, FBT-TAY should not be employed with young adults who emphatically refuse eating disorder treatment. This intervention is designed for young adults who are willing, even if with considerable reluctance and ambivalence, to agree to their parents supporting them with eating until they are better equipped to make such behavioral changes themselves. In the FBT-TAY model, parental control of eating rehabilitation and weight restoration in a young adult is viewed as temporary and necessary and must occur in a supportive and nurturing family environment. On the other hand, parental support with eating for a prolonged period of time in a young adult who appears willing to experiment with eating independently and engaging in behavioral changes is also developmentally inappropriate. In FBT-TAY, young adults must be provided with the opportunity to experiment with preparing meals and eating without excessive supervision and parental control in order to develop the necessary skills for recovery.

Family Is Defined Broadly

An important consideration in the initiation of family-based treatments with young adults is that they have greater input in how family is conceptualized. Although parental involvement is highly valued in FBT-TAY, we acknowledge that young adults may elect to involve their family of choice, partner, or peers in their recovery process. Young adults may decline to engage their family of origin due to a range of reasons, for example:

1   Significant physical distance between the affected individual and their family members making it difficult for the latter to be consistently available to help with eating and meals
2   Impairing mental illnesses and physical ailments such as cancer in parents preventing them from providing instrumental support with meals
3   History of parental sexual, physical, emotional abuse that creates a lack of safety for the affected individual within the context of their family

In contrast to younger adolescents, young adults need to be engaged much more in the decision-making process about who attends therapy and supports their recovery. For instance, some young adults may be unable to involve their parents in all aspects of their treatment (particularly Phases 2 and 3) if they are attending university or living away from home. In such instances, a young adult may elect to involve close friends who are willing to work together to assist with meal support. In such circumstances, it may be useful to utilize communication technology (e.g., Skype) to continue to involve parents with meal support even if there is considerable physical distance between the young adult and his or her family members.

Sibling Involvement Is Not Mandatory but Strongly Encouraged

Like FBT for adolescent AN and BN, sibling involvement is highly recommended. Along the same lines as the family-based treatments for adolescents, siblings attend the family meetings because they have the potential to be an important source of support. From the outset of treatment, clinicians should inquire about the involvement of siblings from the perspective of the young adult and his or her parents. Young adults may choose not to include a sibling in treatment who has disordered eating or a full-blown eating disorder. Conversely, young adults may prefer to have their siblings assist with some meals especially if their parents cannot help with addressing eating disorder symptoms. Some young adults may choose to involve a supportive sibling who can help with eating, while others may elect not to include siblings whose support would be deemed problematic. To protect their confidentiality, young adults may also request to have only their parents (or other supportive individuals) and not their siblings in FBT-Transition Age Youth (FBT-TAY). Clinicians should support the right to privacy in young adults who may express discomfort with the disclosure of personal information to their siblings.

Theoretical Tenants of FBT-TAY

The philosophy of FBT with young adults is the same as what has been described previously in the FBT manual for adolescents (Lock & Le Grange, 2012; Le Grange & Lock, 2007). We continue to take an agnostic view of the causes of AN and focus exclusively on behavioral changes rather than the identification of underlying and familial reasons for the cause of the illness and do not assign meaning to starvation and weight loss. Despite this agnosticism about causes of AN, we argue that certain individual factors may maintain AN, including an overvaluation of control over eating, a strong drive for thinness, dietary restrictions, compensatory behaviors, and excessive exercise (Fairburn, 2008). Similar to FBT for AN and BN, the chief objectives of FBT-TAY continue to be focused initially on behavioral change through symptom reduction and weight restoration. A secondary objective, which is particularly emphasized in the third phase of treatment for FBT-TAY, is to work with young adults and their parents to identify and address factors that may contribute to illness behaviors and might lead to relapse.

From the outset of FBT-TAY, clinicians work diligently to communicate to the family that a *collaborative approach* between the parents and the healthy side of the young adult is needed to effectively address AN. Given the egosyntonic nature of the illness, individuals with AN are often unwilling to gain weight and increase their food consumption without external assistance from supportive family members. Depending on the degree of ambivalence on the part of the young adult, clinicians may be required to work with the young adult to recognize that they need the support of their family to initially begin the process of eating rehabilitation and the weight gain process. In the brief individual meetings with the young adult, clinicians build an alliance with the young person by briefly addressing core features of the illness that may interfere with parental involvement in treatment. To align with the healthy side of the young adult, clinicians should continuously recognize the strengths and resiliency of the young adult for seeking support despite ambivalence about involving their parents and the treatment process.

The therapist acts as a *consultant* and resource to the young person and his or her family throughout this family-based treatment. The therapist strikes a balance of supporting the young adult as an individual while challenging their eating behaviors and valuing the role of parental control in supporting behavioral changes. Therapists foster collaboration with the young adult and his or her parent by avoiding messages that convey that the patient independently direct their own recovery or that the parents must solely be responsible for ensuring that their daughter or son eat. In order to support the autonomy of the young adult, it is vital that patients have input into the treatment process, albeit on different aspects of the treatment and during different phases of FBT. Throughout FBT-TAY, young adults are empowered to have influence over their own lives by engaging in discussions that are age-appropriate and respectful of their desire for independence and autonomy, but in nonfood-related areas especially in Phase 1. The role of the parents is to effectively use their parental control to assist the young adult with eating disorder behaviors and to act as a support and a resource to them as they struggle to eat and gain weight with greater independence.

Target Weights and Individual Meetings with Young Adults

Although the best method for determining expected body weight (EBW) for adolescents is to use the body mass index (BMI) percentile method, when working with young adults BMI is preferred (Fairburn, 2008). As in FBT for adolescents, while FBT clinicians weigh patients at the beginning of each session for clinical purposes, it is not the role of the FBT clinician to determine BMI. These calculations should be made by the pediatrician or family doctor. Although we strive for young adults to achieve the targeted BMI—typically 19.5 to 20 (Fairburn, 2008)—recovery and progress in FBT treatment is about more than a specific targeted number. As described in Lock and Le Grange (2012), criteria for determining progress are based on a combination of factors:

- Eating a variety of foods
- Evidence of increased ability to eat independently and with less anxiety and preoccupation as well as eliminate excessive exercise
- The cessation of binge/purge symptoms
- Resumption of menses in females

Family-Based Treatment for Transition Age Youth

The following clinical example will be referenced throughout the discussion of the three phases of FBT-TAY.

Elizabeth is a 19-year-old, first-year college student with a four-year history of AN. Elizabeth had been treated for AN in high school but, during her transition to university, began restricting her eating and engaging in excessive exercise. While attending university, Elizabeth lost 17 pounds in five months. When Elizabeth returned home for winter break, her parents were very concerned with the significant weight loss and worried about her health. Elizabeth's family consists of her parents, both who are in their 50s. Elizabeth's mother works part-time as a home health aide, and Elizabeth's father works as a bank manager. Elizabeth has an older brother who is living out of state at university and a younger sister who is a sophomore in high school. Elizabeth's boyfriend is away at school but comes to Elizabeth's hometown often to visit family and friends.

Elizabeth's mother called the clinic to express concern about her daughter's relapse and wanted more information about FBT-TAY. On medical evaluation, no major abnormalities were discovered. Currently Elizabeth is not taking any psychiatric medications and expresses loss of interest in some activities (choir, dorm council) and trouble concentrating on schoolwork. On clinical assessment by the specialized eating disorders service, Elizabeth was diagnosed with Anorexia Nervosa. Elizabeth agreed to remain at home for the following semester to engage in treatment and voiced concern over her parents becoming "too involved" in her treatment and that they were treating her as if she were a teenager again.

Phase I

Sessions 1–10 over 4–8 weeks

As noted earlier, FBT-TAY is based on the foundational models of FBT for AN and BN. In contrast to the number of sessions described in FBT for AN and BN, a greater number of sessions within a shorter period of time are recommended in Phase 1 for young adults. Phase 1 consists of 10 sessions offered over 4–8 weeks. The clinician may meet twice a week with the young adult and their family for the first few weeks of FBT and then weekly for the rest of Phase 1. The goals of the first session are similar to the ones delineated in the FBT manual for AN and BN. However, the aims are tailored to address the unique developmental issues pertaining to young adults, which are as follows:

1   To engage the young adult and their family in the therapeutic process.
2   To obtain information about how AN has interrupted the growth and physiological and psychological development of the young adult.
3   To gain specific information about how AN has restricted freedom and autonomy of the young adult and opportunity to become independent from their parents.
4   To obtain preliminary information about how the family functions (i.e., degree of autonomy and independence in the TAY, parenting style(s), conflicts, and warmth) and how this may promote or impede weight restoration.

Borrowing from the original FBT for AN and BN, at the beginning of each session the patient is weighed and a symptom log is used to document subjective and objective over eating and purging behaviors. In contrast to FBT for adolescents, to facilitate alliance building, the young adult is engaged in a discussion about what approach to employ to share the information about their weight and symptoms to their family. The TAY may have the following types of options discussed with them to consider:

- At the request of the patient, the therapist presents the weight and symptom chart.
- The patient presents this information to their family.
- The patient and therapist share this information together by identifying in advance what information will be shared and by whom.

Along the same lines as FBT for AN and BN, clinicians take a history of what young adults and parents have done to address the ED symptoms (what has worked and has not worked). The clinician also begins to gather information about how the family functions (i.e., degree of autonomy and independence in the TAY, parenting style(s), conflicts, and warmth) and how this may promote or impede weight restoration. As in the first session of FBT in the adolescent models, clinicians need to *externalize* the illness (separate the illness from the healthy side of the young adult) by utilizing the information provided by young adults and their parents during the history. It may be helpful to use metaphors or examples from popular novels and movies with content that will have persuasive relevance to young adults as well as their parents. Externalization of the illness provides the young person and their family with an opportunity to think about how they can work as a team to undermine the illness when it is powerful.

For both the young adult and their parents, clinicians use their expertise about this life-threatening illness by communicating that the young adult will prematurely die or become chronically ill from AN unless considerable parental control is exerted over eating and the weight gain process and the parents support the young adult. The urgent message is directed at increasing the anxiety of both the individual and his or her parents as is the case in FBT for adolescents. In contrast to a shorter duration of illness in adolescents, clinicians may need to pay careful attention and take greater time orchestrating the intense scene if parents have been living with a young adult affected by the illness since childhood or adolescence. It may be more challenging to create an intense scene if parents are demoralized by the chronicity of the illness and exhausted by ongoing efforts to convince the affected individual to eat and gain weight over a prolonged time and often many years. In these circumstances, clinicians may consider conveying the following information:

- The high mortality and morbidity rates associated with AN.
- The increased medical, psychological, academic, and social consequences associated with this illness.
- The lack of other empirically based treatments for adults with AN.

- The short- and long-term effects of AN (illustrated by clinical case examples of these effects on the lives of clients with whom the clinician has previously worked).

In the context of persistent AN, clinicians must emphasize that parental control of the eating disorder is imperative to help mitigate against further chronicity, increase medical and psychiatric morbidity, and a decrease in social and academic achievements. Clinicians must acknowledge parental burnout and apathy while also emphasizing that parents have the skills, resources, and knowledge to help the young adult with AN recover. To elicit hope, clinicians may further describe that they will utilize their expertise and skills to support the parents in working together to help their daughter or son overcome AN.

The parents are charged with the task of actively controlling the illness in the young adult because regardless of age, the young adult has a life-threatening illness with significant repercussions that have a ripple effect throughout his or her life. The content of the urgent call to action is similar to the message that clinicians would communicate if they were working with children and adolescents. However, the emphasis of the message needs to take into account the developmental stage of the patient. For this to work, the young adult will need to "allow" their parents to support them with eating and meals. In contrast to working with children and young adolescents in FBT, young adults must accept or acquiesce to the support of their parents in their treatment. It would be inappropriate to ask a 12 year old if his or her parents can help her recover from a serious illness such as AN. However, young adults have the legal right to pursue treatment (or not) without any parental involvement. When working with individuals over the age of 18, FBT therapists must acknowledge that the young adult is in a difficult predicament and it will not be easy to have her or him involve parents in meal support. It is important to emphasize to the young adult that this level of parental involvement is temporary and necessary for recovery. The parents are the best people to address restrictive eating and other ED symptoms because they know the young person and they are the most invested in his or her health and future.

Once the therapist has described the seriousness of the illness, the need for urgent action, and the work that must be undertaken to support recovery and has charged parents with the task of supporting weight gain and normalized eating, the therapist must directly ask the parents to make a commitment. The FBT therapist may ask:

> "What are your thoughts about taking control of the illness? Is this something that you are willing to do? What would you like to communicate to your child about the illness? What do you think he or she needs to know about the lengths that you will take to control the illness and support her in recovery?"

FBT therapists cannot assume that parents have accepted the charge to engage in this intensive behavioral treatment if they have not explicitly made a commitment to themselves and the young adult with AN. It is at this point in the session that the parents will share their thoughts about whether they think AN is a serious enough illness to warrant their involvement. FBT therapists must directly address parental ambivalence about taking control over the illness and support with eating and weight gain in their adult offspring.

Preparation for the Family Meal

The statements that clinicians make in this session to ask the parents to prepare for the second session (the family meal) are the same as they would be with children and adolescents. The clinician emphasizes that for the next session, the family will be asked to bring a meal for them to eat during the session. The clinician looks directly at the parents and asks that they bring a meal that they think is needed to overcome the AN. It will be imperative that the clinician convey that the parents must work collaboratively with each other to ensure that the AN is not dictating what foods the family can prepare and bring to the session. The clinician will want to reiterate the importance of both parents attending and the siblings (if any and the young adult has agreed). Although the clinicians may respond to logistical questions (i.e., where the meal will be held), clinicians may want to steer away from responding to any specific questions about what food the family should bring to the session.

Session 2: The Family Meal

Duration: 60 to 90 minutes

The goals of and interventions employed in Session 2 are similar to the ones delineated by Lock and Le Grange (2012) and Le Grange and Lock (2007). A slight variation in the family meal with TAY is that clinicians must assess how much a family has accommodated the illness, especially if the young adult has been ill for a prolonged period of time. When AN has become chronic, clinicians may also observe the degree to which the parents and the young adult have become entrenched in patterns of interacting and relating surrounding the eating disorder and in other aspects of their relationship. FBT therapists must similarly pay special attention to the degree to which the young adult has become independent with respect to eating and meal preparation. Although not necessarily the case for all young adolescents, it can be assumed that most parents are preparing the majority of the meals, grocery shopping for their young children and adolescents, and therefore have greater decision-making power over eating. However, young adults may have taken up the task of preparing some of the meals or eating outside of the home while working at a part-time job or with peers for many years.

As in the FBT manual for AN and BN, the family is asked to begin laying out the meal and the clinician again reiterates that they will not be eating with them. The following questions may be used to assess the structure of meals in a family of a young adult:

- How often is the family eating meals together? Does the young adult prepare any of the meals? What meals are "sacred" requiring attendance by all?
- What activities/work schedules interfere with family meals?
- How much independence does the young adult have with grocery shopping, preparing meals, and eating on his or her own?
- How much has the family organized itself around the emerging independence of the young adult (or the illness) with eating and meal times?
- If the young adult is living outside of home, how often is he or she eating alone or with other friends, partner, and other supportive people in their lives?

Another salient goal of the therapeutic meal is to help the parents to assist the young person to eat more than they previously would have during a meal. The clinician should encourage the parents to think about how they can work together against the power of the illness by assisting their daughter or son to eat either one mouthful more or a piece of food previously avoided. To do this, and to maintain trust and alliance with the young adult (and their parents), the clinician must describe that the illness can be particularly "loud" during these moments and may be critical of the efforts of the young adult for eating more food (or eating food that has been avoided). It is important to be as transparent as possible with the young adult about why this intervention is being used in Session 2. Parents are coached to use directive, encouraging, and emotionally supportive statements to help the young person eat and to decrease the power of the illness. If left up to the young adult alone, it would be difficult for the young adult to eat enough to gain weight and to increase their intake as needed because AN thinking interferes with these processes.

During Elizabeth's family meal, the therapist observed that her parents brought a meal for themselves consisting of sandwiches, soup, soda, and chips. Elizabeth purchased her own meal, which was a small side salad and a bottle of water. The therapist also learned that Elizabeth was doing her own grocery shopping and eating a majority of her meals alone. Typically, Elizabeth's mother, father, and sister ate breakfast and dinner together during weekdays and lunch together on weekends. During the family meal, the therapist questioned the parents about whether Elizabeth brought sufficient food to eat to help her overcome AN. The parents agreed that they thought Elizabeth's meal was insufficient and that she needed to eat more than what she brought to the session. The therapist further questioned Elizabeth on whether the food that she had brought with her was adequate to beat her illness, and reluctantly Elizabeth stated she "may need more." The therapist engaged Elizabeth in a discussion about how she thought her parents can help her to eat more and challenge the AN from preventing her from eating. With her parents' support, she was able to take several bites of her mother's sandwich. During the discussion, the parents also asked Elizabeth if it might be helpful for them to take over grocery shopping and prepare meals with her. Elizabeth agreed to this change.

Remainder of Phase 1

The goals of the remainder of Phase 1 are similar to the ones described in the manual for AN and BN (Lock & Le Grange, 2012; Le Grange & Lock, 2007). In contrast to original FBT, it is imperative that clinicians continuously assess the degree of engagement of the young adult and work to support and build the collaboration between the patient and his or her parents. As noted earlier in this manual, throughout the course of FBT clinicians work carefully to keep both the young adult and their parents engaged in the process of achieving the goals of weight restoration and eating rehabilitation. In young adults with a chronic illness course (developed AN in early to mid-adolescence), it may take parents longer to disrupt interaction patterns surrounding eating disorder symptoms. It is common for parents to require substantial assistance during Phase 1 to find ways to work together in order to effectively challenge AN. There are some unique challenges in the young adult age group that may interfere with parents working together. When working with young adults, parents may be locked in disagreements and tensions for a longer period of time especially if the illness has become chronic. In such cases, parents may have greater difficulties finding new ways of working together when patterns of relating and communicating with each other have become habitual.

An important caveat when working with adults with AN is that they are likely to present with persistent or emerging co-morbid mental health issues. In contrast to young adolescents with a short duration of illness, a narrow focus on eating in Phase 1 (and 2) may not be appropriate if the young adult and the parents raise concerns about serious co-morbid diagnosis such as depression, mood disorders, OCD, and anxiety disorders. If the family (including the young adult) is concerned about co-morbid diagnoses, the clinician should respond to this concern by referring the young adult to an appropriate clinician who can further assess and treat as needed. It is not the responsibility of the clinician conducting FBT for young adults to investigate the presence of other mental health issues. An appropriate referral and assistance with mental health issues may also help validate the feelings and experiences of a young adult who has perceived others as overlooking other sources of pain and stress in their lives.

In contrast to FBT-AN for adolescents, special attention should be given to developing and strengthening collaborations between young adults and their parents. A salient goal of FBT-TAY is to assist parents and young adults to perceive themselves as working on the same team. Due to profound ambivalence about eating and weight gain (Fairburn, 2008), the willingness of young adults to collaborate with their parents will wax and wane throughout the treatment process. In fact, clinicians should provide educational information that helps normalize the ambivalence associated with engaging in behavioral changes by emphasizing that a majority of young adults with AN seem to want support but resist it as well. Throughout FBT-TAY, clinicians should raise questions about how young adults and parents are preventing the ambivalence from adversely affecting their collaborative relationship in the treatment process. Every effort should be made to ensure that parents are working to align themselves with the healthy side of the young adult. As parents know their child better than anyone else, clinicians should elevate their knowledge and understanding of how to intervene when their daughter or son becomes discouraged, hopeless, ambivalent, and distressed by the work required to overcome this life-threatening illness.

Criteria for Determining When to Enter Phase 2

- Steady and persistent weight gain in Phase 1 (achievement of a BMI of 17.5–18.5)
- Normal eating patterns (three meals and two snacks) and no excessive exercise, binge eating, purging, or other unhealthy strategies to maintain low weight
- Parental agreement that the young adult can take on increasing responsibility to eat
- Dissipation of the level of tension and anxiety in the family and consistent expressed empathy by the parents for the young adult

During Phase 1, Elizabeth slowly but steadily began to gain weight. With her parents' assistance she began eating breakfast with her mother and sister and dinner with her family. Elizabeth's father continued to do the grocery shopping, but each week the family would sit down together to generate and discuss the shopping list. Due to her absence from school, Elizabeth decided early on in treatment to secure a volunteer position at the local animal shelter. Two days per week Elizabeth ate lunch there, and to offer meal support, her mother would often call patients during lunch to chat and provide distraction. Elizabeth's sister would also text support to her throughout the day. As Elizabeth had begun engaging in excessive exercise at school, the family determined that they would not renew Elizabeth's gym membership until she was in a healthier state. At the end of Phase 1, Elizabeth would meet her mother for lunch at a local restaurant once per week. At times during Phase 1, Elizabeth would tell her parents that she no longer wanted their support and wanted to "do this on her own." When this occurred, parents would warmly, but firmly, tell Elizabeth that they wanted her to be well and they would help her continue in treatment. Although these periods slowed weight progress, Elizabeth and her parents were able to continue to create other ways to collaborate with each other.

Phase 2

Sessions 11 to 20, biweekly meetings

Phase 2 consists of three main components:

1   Transitioning the full control over eating back to the young person
2   Identifying behaviors that may be associated with binge eating, purging, and compensatory behaviors including excessive physical activity
3   Addressing general adolescent issues (and issues of emerging adulthood toward the latter part of this phase)

Lock and Le Grange (2012) state that "*much of the focus in the early part of Phase 2 is on experiments with transitioning control over eating and exercise back to the adolescent child safely*" (p. 179). Even more than in younger adolescence, transition of control should be a major focus of Phase 2, encouraging the young adult to increasingly gain independence over eating with progressively less parental management and support during meals. The interventions of Phase 2 have been modified to address the unique developmental needs of the young adult. For instance, the active role of the clinician in relaying information about weight and symptoms discussed in the individual meeting with the young adult diminishes in this phase. Young adults should become increasingly responsible for communicating to their parents when they are progressing well with their treatment and when they are struggling with ED symptoms. During the individual time with the patient, discussions about how to transfer the role of communicating weight progress and the binge/purge log from the clinician to the young adult should be discussed. The clinician and the young adult also identify any potential challenges that arise (AN hampers the abilities of the patient to accurately relay information about weight and ED behaviors) in the family sessions.

Another difference between the original FBT models and FBT-TAY is that young adults are asked to document and track what they eat daily. The goals of self-monitoring are twofold:

1   To assist young adults to become responsible for monitoring their eating every day and communicating what meals may be more challenging for them in and outside of the sessions
2   To learn how to self-monitor their eating in order to develop and practice skills that will assist them in the short and long run to maintain their recovery from AN

As a consultant, clinicians leave it entirely up to the young adult to decide the best way to monitor their eating. Clinicians may provide a range of examples of how to self-monitor including the following:

1   Initially focus on the exact time and frequency of when they eat their meals and snacks.
2   Identify with whom they are eating and how much instrumental and emotional support is needed.
3   Assess what helps and interferes with them asking for assistance during eating/meals from their parents (and others) when the illness is stronger.
4   Describe in detail the quality and quantity of food eaten for some or all meals.

Collaboratively with clinicians, young adults work to identify which monitoring approach or combination of approaches are beneficial for building skills and promoting recovery. It is important to note that self-monitoring is not employed in the same way as a cognitive behavioral therapy approach (Fairburn, 2008). The chief objective is to empower the young adult to become simultaneously more self-aware of their eating patterns and to seek assistance from supportive others when they are struggling. A subtle but important shift occurs when a young adult, rather than his or her parents, gains the skill of self-monitoring and can describe their struggles with AN and assert that they need assistance.

At the beginning of the family meeting, young adults demonstrate the direction of their weight using the weight chart and the binge/purge log to note any changes in symptoms. This may initially occur with considerable support from the clinician especially in the early stages of phase 2. Next, young adults are to report on how they think their eating/meals may explain the direction of their weight. At this point, the clinician should intervene to solicit the thoughts of parents regarding weight, the symptom log, and meals in the previous weeks. Clinicians carefully work to promote discussions between the parents and the young adult by highlighting similarities and differences in what has been discussed. Increased discrepancies between the reporting of the young adult and the parents communicates that the illness continues to be stronger/louder for the former. Rather than take sides, clinicians merely repeat that the illness manifests itself behaviorally and is evidenced by weight loss, weight stagnation, and the presence of symptoms/compensatory behaviors. Clinicians then summarize the objective data gleaned from the weight/binge-purge log, to help reinforce the idea that the parents and young adult must work more carefully to ensure that eating occurs at every meal without restrictions. Similar to phase 1, clinicians ask detailed questions about how parents worked together (either with or without the healthy side of the young adult) during each meal over the previous week. Young adults are similarly called on to identify where they may require support from the family in the upcoming week.

Lock and Le Grange (2012) advocate that the clinician work collaboratively with patients and their parents to develop a plan for how to transition greater independence and control from the latter to the former. In the adapted version of FBT for TAY, the focus is on helping the young adult transition to eating independently in a variety of contexts and with various people. The manner in which young adults take on more responsibility for eating will be decided upon by them collaboratively with their family, not by the clinician. The clinician does not advocate the manner in which this transfer of parental control over eating is given back to the young adult. However, clinicians may use their ED expertise to ensure that the young person and the family make informed decisions about any proposed plans for independent eating.

Elizabeth and her family worked together to modify their plan from Phase 1 with the primary goal of giving Elizabeth more independence. This began by Elizabeth accompanying her father to the grocery store and utilizing a list to guide her shopping. Following these grocery store visits, Elizabeth began grocery shopping alone, but she felt that utilizing a predetermined list helped reduce feelings of being "overwhelmed and anxious." Elizabeth also began to work part-time, which meant that she had several dinners per week at work. Initially parents helped her pack "sack dinners," and over time Elizabeth began to experiment with getting takeout and packing her own dinner. In order to keep track of food intake, Elizabeth photographed her meals using her smart phone. Elizabeth reviewed these photographs in session and sometimes with her mother. When meal sizes were not adequate, Elizabeth and her family would discuss and implement additional snacks, or Elizabeth's mother or father would prepare dinner for several days. Elizabeth's boyfriend also started having more meals with her on the weekend when he visited. He attended several of the sessions in person or by Skype to hear about the struggles and challenges associated with learning to eat again with greater parental support. During these sessions, Elizabeth was able to relay that she found it helpful when she could call her boyfriend after meals and identified content that was helpful and unhelpful to keep her safe. As Phase 2 progressed, Elizabeth resumed going to the gym. This started by going with her father and limiting time spent at the gym. Over time, this progressed to attending the gym three times a week for 45 minutes at a time. Elizabeth and her family also began discussing the resumption of school. Elizabeth researched local options and determined that she would begin classes at a local college and continue living at home, with the goal of returning to her university the following semester.

Criteria for Determining When to Enter Phase 3

- A BMI of 19–20 is achieved.
- The young adult is maintaining a normal weight.
- The young adult is able to eat a variety of food, and there is cessation of ED symptoms.

- The young adult is able to eat independently without any parental supervision/monitoring.
- The young adult and his or her parents are exploring issues pertaining to adolescence and emerging adulthood.

Phase 3

Sessions 21–25, biweekly

Phase 3 consists of biweekly sessions with the TAY and his or her parents. Parallel to the description of the goals and interventions in Phase 3 FBT for adolescents, in this adapted model, clinicians similarly review tasks and challenges associated with launching from adolescence to adulthood and the inevitable changes in the family as interactions between the parents and the young adult are no longer defined by the illness and the management of symptoms. It may be helpful to review information about adolescent development (see Lock & Le Grange, 2012; Le Grange & Lock, 2007) and emerging adulthood (see following brief description) in the family meetings. Compared with FBT with adolescents, clinicians should expend more time in Phase 3 exploring with young adults and their parents what has been lost due to the illness and what areas of growth may still be required to progress into adulthood. In contrast to FBT for BN and more similar to FBT for AN, this treatment focuses on issues regarding autonomy because AN has stifled age-appropriate independence with eating in young adults. The FBT therapist encourages the family to think about how the parents may support their adult offspring to become autonomous, independent, and to become involved in activities and build relationships that will help create a sense of identity separate from AN. As older adolescents, young adults are likely to be experiencing multiple life transitions including a transfer from pediatric to adult health care providers. Clinicians may also consider working with parents and the young adult to identify strategies that can be used to access appropriate health and mental health services as required.

Elizabeth began taking classes at a local college and continued to volunteer and work part-time. She continued to eat some meals with her parents but spent an increased amount of time with coworkers and friends. Elizabeth worked toward transitioning back to university. Due to her concerns about living in the dormitory, she pursued other group housing arrangements. With her parents' support, she has reached out to the university health system and initiated treatment with the university counseling and medical services for periodic follow-up.

Primer on Emerging Adulthood

There is growing recognition that older adolescents and young adults are in a unique phase of life. Older adolescents (age 16 onwards) and young adults (ages 18–25) are newly recognized as a unique developmental group called "emerging adulthood" (Arnett, 2000; 2004; 2007), during which time many important psychosocial and neurobiological changes occur. Significant brain and cognitive development occurs in adolescence and continues throughout early adulthood as well (Blakemore, Burnett, & Dahl, 2010). Historically, developmental tasks such as residence, school, career, marriage, or the birth of children were used to define the transition from adolescence (ages 13–17) to adulthood (age 18+), but in today's context, many of these markers are reversible and less enduring than how they were experienced by previous generations, making the progression from adolescence to adulthood a much more variable process. During the period of emerging adulthood, young people experience many life changes including the formation of intimate relationships, building meaningful links with a social network, moving from secondary to postsecondary school, and transitioning from education to employment opportunities and then a career (Arnett, 2000; Salmela-Aro, Aunola, & Nurmi, 2014). For emerging adults suffering from AN, co-residence with families is common and literature has shown that extended co-residence with family during the period of EA for typically developing emerging adults is associated with diminished success in achieving adult goals and decreases subjective well-being unless it is freely chosen by both the family and the emerging adult (Kins et al., 2009). It is important to encourage adolescents during this therapy to regain their place on a path to continued success in achieving adult goals throughout this critical period. Examples of topics that may be of importance to emerging adults can be anticipated from literature focused on other serious illnesses that interrupt development. In instances of physical illness such as cancer in the late teens or early 20s, emerging adults express the need for help in four critical areas: navigating adult personal responsibilities, developing personal beliefs/values, renegotiating relationships with parents, and obtaining financial independence (Patterson et al., 2012).

Relapse Prevention

Along the same lines as FBT-BN, discussions about the future are encouraged but for young adults the focus is more extensive. Due to the high rate of relapse in adults with eating disorders (Carter et al., 2012; Lewinsohn, Striegel-Moore, & Seeley, 2000; Steinhausen, 2009), it is important that clinicians work with young adults and their families to prevent relapse from occurring and increase the possibility for recovery. Additional relapse prevention work is needed for a number of reasons. First, young adults are more likely to have the illness for a longer period of time and therefore require more planning and assistance with recovery. Second, young adults are more likely to return to greater independence than adolescents with ED and therefore need to conduct extensive preparatory work to ensure that they (and their parents) have the strategies and knowledge to rapidly intervene if restrictive eating, binge/purging, and other disordered eating occurs. Third, young adults will naturally have less parental involvement as they progress into adulthood and transition to postsecondary school or residing on their own. Consequently, clinicians should work closely to support the young adult to think about how they can stay well and potential situations that may put them at risk (stress associated with school, changes to their bodies, difficulties meeting new people).

During Phase 3, FBT therapists meet individually with the young adult to identify and prepare plans to avoid slips and relapses. Depending on the duration of the illness and treatment process, clinicians may need to meet for two to three sessions with the young adult to discuss relapse-prevention issues. In these sessions, the young adult delineates risk factors and plans for how parents and other supportive people can be called upon if eating becomes challenging and weight loss occurs. Young adults discuss their relapse-prevention plan with their parents and elicit their thoughts about how they may be helpful. Parents are encouraged to ask questions and provide suggestions to help solidify the plan for how to stay recovered. The final session is used to say good-bye to the young adult and the family and to celebrate their accomplishments.

Conclusion

This chapter has presented an adapted version of FBT for young adults and highlights how this model approximates and deviates from the foundational models for adolescents with AN and BN. Although a relentless focus on eating and weight restoration is paramount throughout Phases 1 and 2 in FBT-TAY, clinicians should not delay involving other experts who may assist with the amelioration of other impairing mental health problems. Due to the entrenchment of eating disorder behaviors over time, greater effort should be put into assisting parents to develop new strategies for working together in an effective way to support the young adult.

Although there are fewer differences between FBT for TAY and FBT for adolescents in Phase 2, some important modifications have been made. Control and responsibility with eating may be relinquished over to the young adult from the parents somewhat more quickly than to an adolescent. The rationale for this is that the young adult likely has greater freedom and independence (outside of the illness) requiring him or her to practice eating in a variety of contexts (e.g., work and school environment) and with different people (e.g., friends, partner, colleagues). In contrast to adolescents, young adults should also take on the responsibility of sharing their progress weight (and binge/purge symptoms). Another important modification is that young adults are encouraged to learn how to monitor their eating and to communicate any potential challenges with food to their parents.

The greatest adaptations to original FBT can be found in Phase 3. A major deviation from adolescent FBT is that clinicians meet individually with young adults to assist them in identifying potential risk factors for relapse. The young adult also works collaboratively with their parents to solidify their relapse-prevention plans. Finally, the family work in Phase 3 focuses on assisting with issues related to emerging adulthood rather than adolescence.

References

Arcelus, J., Mitchell, A. J., Wales, J., & Nielsen, S. (2011). Mortality rates in patients with anorexia nervosa and other eating disorders: A meta-analysis of 36 studies. *Archives of General Psychiatry, 68*(7), 724.

Arnett, J. J. (2007). Emerging adulthood: What is it, and what is it good for? *Society for Research in Child Development, 1*(2), 68–73.

Arnett, J. J. (2004). Emerging adulthood: The winding road from the late teens throughout the twenties. New York, NY: Oxford University Press.

Arnett, J. J. (2000). Emerging adulthood: A theory of the development from the late teens through the twenties. *The American Psychologist, 55*(5), 469–480.

Baldock, E. (2010). An ethico-legal account of working with careers in eating disorders. In J. Treasure, Ulrike, Schmidt, & P. MacDonald (Eds.). *The clinician's guide to collaborative caring in eating disorders: The new Maudsley Method* (pp. 30–42). New York, NY: Routledge.

Baker, J. H., Mitchell, K. S., Neale, M. C., & Kendler, K. S. (2010). Eating disorder symptomatology and substance use disorders: Prevalence and shared risk in a population based twin sample. *International Journal of Eating Disorders, 43*, 648–658.

Blakemore, S. J., Burnett, S., & Dahl, R. E. (2010). The role of puberty in the developing adolescent brain. *Human Brain Map, 31*(6), 926–933.

Bulik, C. M., & Kendler, K. S. (2000). "I am what I (don't) eat": Establishing an identity independent of an eating disorder. *American Journal of Psychiatry, 157*(11), 1755–1760.

Byrick, K., & Walker-Renshaw, B. (2012). A practical guide to mental health and the law in Ontario. Ontario Hospital Association.

Carter, J. C., Mercer-Lynn, K. B., Norwood, S. J., Bewell-Weiss, C. V., Crosby, R. D., Woodside, D. B., & Olmsted, M. P. (2012). A prospective study of predictors of relapse in anorexia nervosa: Implications for relapse prevention. *Psychiatry research, 200*(2), 518–523.

Chen, E. Y., Le Grange, D., Doyle, A. C., Zaitsoff, S., Doyle, P., Roehrig, J. P., & Washington, B. (2010). A case series of family-based therapy for weight restoration in young adults with anorexia nervosa. *Journal of Contemporary Psychotherapy, 40*(4), 219–224.

Chugani, C. D., Ghali, M. N., & Brunner, J. (2013). Effectiveness of short-term dialectical behavior therapy skills training in college students with cluster B personality disorders. *Journal of College Student Psychotherapy, 27*(4), 323–336.

Clayman, M. L., & Makoul, G. (2009). Conceptual variation and iteration in shared decision-making: the needs for clarity. In A. Edwards & G. Elwyn (Eds.), *Shared Decision-Making in Health Care*. Oxford University Press, 109–116.

Coomber, K., & King, R. M. (2013). A longitudinal examination of burden and psychological distress in carers of people with an eating disorder. *Social Psychiatry and Psychiatric Epidemiology, 48*(1), 163–171.

Dimitropoulos, G., Tran, A. F., Agarwal, P., Sheffield, B., & Woodside, B. (2012a). Navigating the transition from pediatric to adult eating disorder programs: Perspectives of service providers. *International Journal of Eating Disorders, 45*(6), 759–767. doi: 10.1002/eat.22017

Doyle, P. M., Smyth, A., & Le Grange, D. (2011). Childhood and adulthood: when do eating disorders start and do treatments differ. In J. Alexander & J. A. Treasure, *Collaborative Approach to Eating Disorders*, ED. New York, NY: Routledge.

Eisler, I., Dare, C., Russell, G. F. M., et al. (1997). Family and individual therapy in anorexia nervosa. A 5-year follow-up. *Archives of General Psychiatry, 54*, 1025–1030.

Fairburn, C. G. (2008). *Cognitive Behaviour Therapy and Eating Disorders*. Guilford Press.

Fischer, S., & Le Grange, D. L. (2007). Comorbidity and high-risk behaviors in treatment-seeking adolescents with bulimia nervosa. *International Journal of Eating Disorders, 40*(8), 751–753.

Forsberg, S., LoTempio, E., Bryson, S., Fitzpatrick, K. K., Le Grange, D., & Lock, J. (2013). Parent-therapist alliance in family-based treatment for adolescents with anorexia nervosa. *European Eating Disorders Review, 22*(1), 53–58.

Gonzales, A. H., & Bergstrom, L. (2013). Adolescent Non-Suicidal Self-Injury (NSSI) Interventions. *Journal of Child and Adolescent Psychiatric Nursing, 26*(2), 124–130. doi: 10.1111/jcap.12035

Gregorowski, C., Seedat, S., & Jordaan, G. P. (2013). A clinical approach to the assessment and management of co-morbid eating disorders and substance use disorders. *BMC Psychiatry, 13*(1), 289.

Harrop, E. N., & Marlatt, G. A. (2010). The comorbidity of substance use disorders and eating disorders in women: Prevalence, etiology, and treatment. *Addictive Behaviors, 35*, 392–398.

Jones, P. B. (2013). Adult mental health disorders and their age at onset. *The British Journal of Psychiatry, 202*, S5–S10.

Kaye, W. H., Bulik, C., Thornton, L. et al. (2004). Comorbidity of anxiety disorders with anorexia and bulimia nervosa. *American Journal of Psychiatry, 161*, 2215–2221.

Kessler, R. C., Amminger, G. P., Aguilar-Gaxiola, S., Alonso, J., & Ustun, T. B. (2008). Age of onset of mental disorders: a review of recent literature. *Current Opinions in Psychiatry, 20*(4), 359–364.

Kins, E., Beyers, W., Soenens, B., & Vansteenkiste, M. (2009). Patterns of home leaving and subjective well-being in emerging adulthood: The role of motivational processes and parental autonomy support. *Developmental Psychology, 45*(5), 1416.

Klump, K. L., Bulik, C. M., Kaye, W. H., Treasure, J., & Tyson, E. (2009). Academy for eating disorders position paper: eating disorders are serious mental illnesses. *International Journal of Eating Disorders, 42*(2), 97–103.

Lewinsohn, P. M., Striegel-Moore, R. H., & Seeley, J. R. (2000). Epidemiology and natural course of eating disorders in young women from adolescence to young adulthood. *Journal of the American Academy of Child & Adolescent Psychiatry, 39*(10), 1284–1292.

Le Grange, D., Lock, J., Agras, W. S., Moye, A., Bryson, S. W., Jo, B., & Kraemer, H. C. (2012). Moderators and mediators of remission in family-based treatment and adolescent focused therapy for anorexia nervosa. *Behaviour Research and Therapy, 50*(2), 85–92.

Lock, J. D., & Le Grange, D. (2007). Family treatment of eating disorders. *Clinical Manual of Eating Disorders*, 149–170.

Lock, J., Le Grange, D., Agras, W. S., Moye, A., Bryson, S. W., & Jo, B. (2010). Randomized clinical trial comparing family-based treatment with adolescent-focused individual therapy for adolescents with anorexia nervosa. *Archives of General Psychiatry, 67*(10), 1025.

Lock, J., & Le Grange, D. (2012). *Treatment Manual for Anorexia Nervosa: A Family-Based Approach.* Guilford Press.

Makoul, G., & Clayman, M. L. (2006). An integrative model of shared decision making in medical encounters. *Patient Education and Counseling, 60,* 301–312.

Martín, J., Padierna, A., Aguirre, U., González, N., Muñoz, P., & Quintana, J. M. (2013). Predictors of quality of life and caregiver burden among maternal and paternal caregivers of patients with eating disorders. *Psychiatry Research, 210*(3), 1107–1115.

Merikangas, K. R., He, J. P., Brody, D., Fisher, P. W., Bourdon, K., & Koretz, D. S. (2010). Prevalence and treatment of mental disorders among US children in the 2001–2004 NHANES. *Pediatrics, 125*(1), 75–81.

McElroy, S., L., Frye, M. A., Hellemann, G., Altshuler, L., Leverich, G. S., ... & Post, R. M. (2011). Prevalence and correlates of eating disorders in 875 patients with bipolar disorder. *Journal of Affective Disorders, 128*(3), 191–198.

Nielsen, S. & Bara-Carril, N. (2003). Chapter 11: Family, burden of care and social consequences. In Treasure, J., Schmidt, U., & Furth, E. V. (2nd ed). *Handbook of Eating Disorders.*

Nunes Campos, R., Rodrigues dos Santor, D. J., Cordas, T. A., Angst, J., & Moreno, R. A. (2013). Occurrence of bipolar spectrum disorder and comorbidities in women with eating disorders. *International Journal of Bipolar Disorders, 1,* 25.

Padierna, A., Martín, J., Aguirre, U., González, N., Muñoz, P., & Quintana, J. M. (2013). Burden of caregiving amongst family caregivers of patients with eating disorders. *Social Psychiatry and Psychiatric Epidemiology, 48*(1), 151–161.

Patterson, P., Millar, B., Desille, N., & McDonald, F. (2012). The unmet needs of emerging adults with a cancer diagnosis: A qualitative study. *Cancer Nursing, 35*(3), E32–E40.

Pistorello, J., Fruzzetti, A. E., MacLane, C., Gallop, R., & Iverson, K. M. (2012). Dialectical behavior therapy (DBT) applied to college students: A randomized clinical trial. *Journal of Consulting and Clinical Psychology, 80*(6), 982.

Raenker, S., Hibbs, R., Goddard, E., Naumann, U., Arcelus, J., Ayton, A., ...& Treasure, J. (2013). Caregiving and coping in carers of people with anorexia nervosa admitted for intensive hospital care. International Journal of Eating Disorders, 46(4), 346–354. doi: 10.1002/eat.22068

Roncero, M., Belloch, A., Perpiñá, C., & Treasure, J. (2013). Ego-syntonicity and ego-dystonicity of eating-related intrusive thoughts in patients with eating disorders. *Psychiatry research, 208*(1), 67–73. doi: 10.1016/j.psychres.2013.01.006

Rosling, A. M., Sparén, P., Norring, C., & von Knorring, A. L. (2011). Mortality of eating disorders: A follow-up study of treatment in a specialist unit 1974–2000. *International Journal of Eating Disorders, 44*(4), 304–310.

Russell, G. F., Szmukler, G. I., Dare, C., & Eisler, I. (1987). An evaluation of family therapy in anorexia nervosa and bulimia nervosa. *Archives of General Psychiatry, 44*(12), 1047–1056.

Salmela-Aro, K., Kiuru, N., Nurmi, J.-E., & Eerola, M. (2014). Antecedents and consequences of transitional pathways to adulthood among university students: 18-year longitudinal study. *Journal of Adult Development, 21*(1), 48–58. doi:10.1007/s10804-013-9178-2

Schmidt, U., Tiller, J., & Treasure, J., (1993). Setting the scene for eating disorders: childhood care, classification and course of illness. *Journal of Psychological Medicine*, 23(3), 663–672.

Steinhausen, H. C. (2002). The outcome of anorexia nervosa in the 20th century. *American Journal of Psychiatry*, 159(8), 1284–1293.

Steinhausen, H. C. (2009). Outcome of eating disorders. *Child and Adolescent Psychiatric Clinics of North America*, 18(1), 225–242.

Sepúlveda, A. R., Graell, M., Berbel, E., Anastasiadou, D., Botella, J., Carrobles, J. A., & Morandé, G. (2012). Factors associated with emotional well-being in primary and secondary caregivers of patients with eating disorders. *European Eating Disorders Review*, 20(1), e78–e84.

Swanson, S. A., Crow, S. J., Le Grange, D., Swendsen, J., & Merikangas, K. R. (2011). Prevalence and correlates of eating disorders in adolescents: Results from the national comorbidity survey replication adolescent supplement. *Archives of General Psychiatry*, 67(7), 714–723.

Swinbourne, J., Hunt, C., Abbott, M., Russell, J., St. Clare, T., & Touyz, S. (2012). The comorbidity between eating disorders and anxiety disorders: prevalence in an eating disorder sample and anxiety disorder sample. *Australian & New Zealand Journal of Psychiatry*, 46(2), 118–131.

Touchette, E., Henegar, A., Godart, N. T., Pryor, L., Falissard, B., Tremblay, R. E., & Cote, S. M. (2011). Subclinical eating disorders and their comorbidity with mood and anxiety disorders in adolescent girls. *Psychiatry Research*, 185(1–2), 185–192.

Tarrier, N., Taylor, K., & Gooding, P. (2008). Cognitive-behavioral interventions to reduce suicide behavior a systematic review and meta-analysis. *Behavior Modification*, 32(1), 77–108.

Treasure, J., & Russell, G. (2011). The case for early intervention in anorexia nervosa: theoretical exploration of maintaining factors. *The British Journal of Psychiatry*, 199(1), 5–7.

Treasure, J., Murphy, T., Szmukler, T., Todd, G., Gavan, K., & Joyce, J. (2001). The experience of caregiving for severe mental illness: a comparison between anorexia nervosa and psychosis. *Social Psychiatry and Psychiatric Epidemiology*, 36(7), 343–347.

United Nations Human Rights Office of the High Commissioner for Human Rights (1989). Convention on the Rights of the Child.

Wade, T. D., Bulik, C. M., Neale, M., & Kendler, K. S. (2000). Anorexia nervosa and major depression: shared genetic and environmental risk factors. *American Journal of Psychiatry*, 157, 469–471.

Watson H. J., Fursland A., & Byrne S. (2013). Treatment engagement in eating disorders: whoexits before treatment? *International Journal of Eating Disorders*, 46(6), 553–559.

Westwood, L. M., & Kendal, S. E. (2012). Adolescent client views towards the treatment of anorexia nervosa: A review of the literature. *Journal of Psychiatric and Mental Health Nursing*, 19(6), 500–508.

Whitney, J., Murray, J., Gavan, K., Todd, G., Whitaker, W., & Treasure, J. (2005). Experience of caring for someone with anorexia nervosa: Qualitative study. *The British Journal of Psychiatry*, 187(5), 444–449.

Whitney, J., Haigh, R., Weinman, J., & Treasure, J. (2007). Caring for people with eating disorders: Factors associated with psychological distress and negative caregiving appraisals in carers of people with eating disorders. *British Journal of Clinical Psychology*, 46(4), 413–428.

Chapter 12

Family-Based Therapy for Avoidant Restrictive Food Intake Disorder

Families Facing Food Neophobias

*Kathleen Kara Fitzpatrick, Sarah E. Forsberg,
and Danielle Colborn*

"Alex has always been a picky eater. Even as a baby he didn't nurse right, sometimes nursing for hours and, at other times, refusing to nurse at all. I was a first-time mother and really nervous, but the lactation consultant assured me he was fine. When we switched to solid foods, he refused certain foods but loved others. He would cry, turning his head away from foods he didn't like. He never seemed to choke or have difficulty taking food; in fact, when he liked something he ate as much of it as he could get! This pattern just continued. By age 4 he was healthy but so picky the preschool asked us to pack snacks for him, as he would refuse to eat many things they served, and they were worried about him going an entire day without eating. He has never refused fruits or most vegetables, except squash. He won't eat anything crunchy or 'dry,' and he refuses all meats. We were able to get him to eat fish sticks once, when he was very hungry, but he has refused them since. I know it sounds like we are just giving in to his demands, but he really does refuse! When he was little, he would become so upset that he literally could not breathe or eat. Now that he is older, he doesn't temper so much as refuse, delay, become upset, or 'accidentally' drop food; or he avoids us and situations that require him to eat what he does not want to eat. Even if he is starving, unless he can eat a favored food, he'd rather not eat at all. Now that he will be in middle school next year, it is getting harder and harder to find foods he can eat! The school has a blanket 'no nuts' policy, and peanuts are pretty much his only protein source. Despite all this, he's pretty normal in every other way, developing well, social at school. He is anxious, always takes a little while to warm up to new situations and activities, but he almost always adjusts well. He has had separation anxiety from mom when younger, but we've been able to work through that, too. Even with his limited diet he is healthy, but has not been gaining weight the way we would like as he is growing. We love food, and it is hard on us to always eat at the same restaurants, always try to make sure they have something he wants. And we have had to restrict foods that are unhealthy because he fills up on them—he would live on French fries if we let him! We've tried rewards and punishments, waiting him out and giving in. Everyone says he will 'grow out of it,' but at this point we just want to be able to feed him enough to keep him growing!"

"Penelope is ten and has high-functioning autism. We've been doing a parent training program for two years, supplemented with ABA [applied behavior analysis] therapy. Things have gone really well in most areas, and she has made great improvement in her language, is integrated into regular education, and generally is doing well. Her pediatrician and psychologist both feel like she is healthy and growing well, but we are so concerned. Her eating is so unusual! She has always had textural sensitivities: tags on clothes, 'scratchy' fabrics, being too hot or too cold. But it seems to us that she has these same problems with food! She likes to eat bread and will sneak bread and will fill herself up on that, then not have room for other healthy foods. And she hates vegetables! We call them hell-getables behind her back because she acts like we are poisoning her. We have tried different plans to help her eat more, but it seems like she always goes back to the same, plain, 'white foods' that she favors: bread, peanut butter, sweets, chips, and other 'junk' foods. She is incredibly sensitive to any changes; she will only eat the same brands and will gag and spit out foods she does not like. We ate out at a restaurant, and they served ketchup in a cup—she wouldn't touch it even though she usually slathers her food in the stuff. It was even the same brand she likes, but because it looked different, she couldn't be coaxed to try it. She's normal weight, but she cannot possibly be healthy eating the same four foods over and over again at each meal!"

Avoidant restrictive food intake disorder (ARFID), sometimes called food neophobia, is a new eating disorder classification for Diagnostic and Statistical Manual, 5th Edition (DSM-5) (American Psychiatric Association, 2013). To many families it is a relief to finally have a category to describe the significant dietary attenuation they have been fighting against, often since their child was an incredibly young age. To the uninitiated, it may seem that picky eaters have finally earned designation as mentally ill; something that pediatrician and parents alike eschew. In fact, a designation of ARFID represents a significant departure from a more typical developmental eating trajectory and is characterized by such limited intake as to require medical intervention or supplementation. Beyond just "picky eating," the group comprising those with ARFID represent those with truly limited intake, in both type and range of foods, and an intense fear of novel foods and eating behaviors that impair development. The DSM-5 outlines the criteria for diagnosis, which emphasize the restricted intake without associated concerns around body image, shape, and weight. The severity and significance of the dietary restriction and the associated nutritional deficiencies are the primary symptoms of this disorder and, as such, must exist in a severe enough degree to result in one of the following:

1 Failure to attain growth milestones in either height or weight or loss of weight.
2 Nutritional deficiencies as evident through exclusion of entire food groups (e.g., vegetables or proteins).
3 Dependence on enteral feeding or nutritional supplementation such as vitamin/mineral supplementation and use of liquid nutrition supplements.
4 Marked interference in psychosocial functioning, such as challenges in eating outside the home or when favored foods are not available.

Importantly, patients presenting with ARFID report a lifetime of attenuated eating, with parents often reporting restricted intake at the earliest ages of food introduction. Thus, unlike anorexia nervosa (AN), bulimia nervosa (BN), and binge eating disorder (BED), which often appear after a history of more normative eating, ARFID typical represents an early and trenchant pattern of deviant eating patterns. Table 12.1 highlights important consideration points in making a differential diagnosis.

Table 12.1 Differential Diagnosis

ARFID versus	Symptom Differences	Symptom Overlap
Anorexia Nervosa	• AN onsets after a period of normal or typical eating development, while ARFID is typically a long standing developmental pattern (much younger age of onset of symptoms). • AN is characterized by intense body image disturbance, which is lacking in ARFID. • Focus on AN is weight/shape concerns, while in ARFID anxiety centers around novelty/change.	• Weight loss and/or failure to meet expected weight gains • Attenuated eating or food "rules" • Possible strong preference for routine in food and eating behaviors; significant upset if food behaviors are altered

Bulimia Nervosa	• BN onsets after a period of normal or typical eating development, while ARFID is typically a long standing developmental pattern (much younger age of onset of symptoms). • BN is characterized by intense body image disturbance, which is lacking in ARFID. • Focus on BN is weight/shape concerns, while in ARFID anxiety centers around novelty/change. • BN has compensatory behaviors that are not present in ARFID.	• Attenuated eating or food "rules" • Possible strong preference for routine in food and eating behaviors • Significant upset if food behaviors are altered • Both groups may show a high drive/preference for sweet or carbohydrate rich foods (during a binge episode for BN and during everyday eating for ARFID).
Binge Eating Disorder	• BED is characterized by normative eating punctuated with periods of binge eating behavior. • ARFID is characterized by consistently attenuated food intake (although some report binge-like episodes when presented with favored foods that have been restricted).	• Both groups may show a high drive/preference for sweet or carbohydrate rich foods (during a binge episode for BED and during everyday eating for ARFID).
Rumination Disorder	• Regurgitation of foods is the primary symptom, while food is typically consumed in ARFID, even if spitting out or gagging occurs.	• Both may occur for long periods of time. • Both impact nourishment. • Neither are associated with body image disturbance or weight/shape concerns. • Both may lead to weight loss or failure to thrive if sufficient amounts are regurgitated.
Pica	• Characterized by eating of nonfood items, while ARFID is a preference for specific or limited range of foods/eating behaviors.	• Often have a younger age at development, although both can be present at older ages.

In the context of diagnosis, it is important to consider culturally normative developmental eating patterns. Of note, these have changed considerably in the West over the past century (see Beal, 1957). Babies are born with reflexes that support intake, in particular, the turn and suck reflex, and, for the first 6 to 9 months (the latter in some cultures), babies are sustained on largely liquid supplementation through breast milk or baby formula. Given that feeding patterns vary widely among infants, it is difficult to describe more normative eating patterns, but by and large, infants nurse frequently and with increasing amounts as they age.

True independent interest in eating develops by 5 to 9 months of age, as parents begin introducing pureed and soft foods for their children. While there are wide cultural differences here, for the most part parents introduce single foods for toddlers, focusing largely on fruits and vegetables. Most toddlers will readily eat single foods, pureed to appropriate consistency. By one year of age, children can express desire for food in a rudimentary way (typically grabbing it and squeezing it while mashing it in their faces) and have sufficient eye–hand coordination to eat smaller finger foods. By one year of age, parents are typically mixing foods, serving mixed fruits, vegetables, and strained meats. It is at this age that many parents of children with ARFID report noticing challenges in their child's range of intake. Specifically, these children may show a strong preference for certain foods, may refuse to eat foods that are not favored, and may demonstrate more extreme disgust reactions to nonpreferred foods. Many parents report difficulties transitioning to mixed foods or specific sensitivities, such as to "mushy" or "crunchy" textures. Around age 2, children should largely be eating the food their parents eat, albeit in smaller portions and adjusted in bite size to fit the chewing ability of the child and to avoid choking. Just as communication skills are increasing, so is appetite and willingness to try new foods. Indeed, toddlers are often quite a bit more interested in what is on someone else's plate than their own and will often readily sample foods given to them by parents or trusted others. The expansion of types, textures, and amount of food eaten generally progresses until age 6 or 7. Most children of early school age experience an attenuation of tastes and many become more "picky" in their eating, often strongly favoring the carbohydrates that fuel growth and development. This may explain why the children's menu at almost every restaurant looks similar. By late childhood or early adolescence, both appetite and flexibility around food increase again, with a return to a wider range of intake and greater balance within and across meals.

The importance of this progression is that many parents and pediatricians expect a certain level of "pickiness" in eating, and this often is brushed aside as developmentally typical unless symptoms are unusually severe or significantly impact psychosocial functioning. Another reason these difficulties may be highlighted at an earlier age is if the symptoms occur in the context of other developmental difficulties, such as autism spectrum disorders. Many parents report concern around their child's eating at a young age but are repeatedly told by others that this is "normal" and their child will grow out of it. While many children do express food preferences and many will have strong aversions to certain foods, ARFID is distinguished by the global and pervasive nature of food refusal. This is, in part, why some have described this as "food neophobia" (Bryant-Waugh, Markham, Kriepe, & Walsh, 2010), where rather than displeasure with food, the reticence, even outright refusal, to try new foods leads to a limited diet. This would suggest that one of the primary mechanisms leading to the disorder is novelty aversion rather than taste aversion, although both of these may exist in concert.

Little is known of the features that distinguish children with ARFID from their more typically eating peers. Given the recent establishment of this diagnosis and the lack of any population studies on these behaviors, we are left to speculate on the risk factors, prevalence, and cross-cultural validity of these symptoms. However, it seems reasonable to assume that these behaviors exist on a continuum, as most parents of more than one child will readily tell you. There are some children who will adventurously eat most things, are quick to try new foods and flavors, and are saddled with a sibling who wants nothing more than blandness and routine in his diet. But ARFID is distinguished by a refusal to try something new and, therefore, is a much more extreme and clinically concerning version of a "boring" eater. In our clinical evaluations and observations, we took note of similar features among those presenting with these features, as well as the source of these referrals. Interestingly, it was clear that a disproportionate number of these referrals came from Gastroenterology when compared to concerns related to AN, BN, or BED. The latter referrals were more often from pediatricians and community therapists than specialty medical services. In addition, parents reported having sought help from a wider array of service providers before going to an eating disorders clinic. Many families had already seen occupational therapists, school therapists, nutritionists, and pediatricians seeking advice on ways to increase dietary flexibility. ARFID referrals were also skewed toward a younger age, with referrals as young as 4 and as old as 22. In addition, clinical cases present with significant anxiety, although with a different "flavor" than that found in AN, BN, and BED. Children presenting with ARFID often expressed a very high number of worries, around which food was only one. This tended to give the flavor of obsessive-compulsive disorder (OCD) or generalized anxiety disorder (GAD). These worries were often tied to intake as well as more general somatization fears. This latter set of concerns often distinguished ARFID cases, as they expressed more concern around stomach upset, fear of not liking foods and fear of negative outcomes associated with eating. Although these sound similar to what we see in AN, the content and focus were slightly different, with an increased somatic vigilance and response to experts encouraging intake that is not seen in AN.

Specifically, when encouraging patients with ARFID, the response is typically interest or fear of trying things they do not like. In contrast, with AN the response to urges to change eating are typically met with agitation and fears regarding weight gain (see Table 12.1 for additional differentiation).

Despite increasing evidence that ARFID, left untreated, will not resolve itself (Wildes, Zucker, & Marcus, 2012) and can lead to chronic, long-term health difficulties, there are no treatments that have been evaluated for ARFID. There are suggestions around treatment, often drawn from occupational therapy approaches. In general, these focus on hierarchical food exposure exercises, decreasing novelty, and improving taste/sensation pairings (Fraker, Fishbein, Cox, & Walbert, 2007). Ellyn Satter's work on helping parents provide adequate intake and encouraging a neutral, compassion-based feeding stance has also influenced work with more "picky" eaters (www.ellynsatterinstitute.org). This program generally focuses on the presentation of a variety of foods, allowing the child to choose with some parental direction. Rather than utilizing an "authoritarian" approach with a "finish your plate" policy, this method focuses more on parental responsibility to provide nutrition and to encourage consistent intake. This practice also focuses on limiting conflict in the parental feeding dynamic. There is an emphasis on development, developmental nutrition, and parental education.

Given that there is an established history of using families in the treatment of eating disorders (Murray & Le Grange, 2014; Lock & Le Grange, 2012, as examples) and the importance of early feeding behaviors in ARFID, it seemed a natural extension to apply standards of Family Based Therapy (FBT) to clinical levels of food neophobia. The aspects of standard FBT that remain in place include the principles of parental empowerment, psychoeducation on nutrition, and eating behaviors. Additionally, therapists also are able to demonstrate therapeutic skill in managing behaviors and relationships. However, there are also significant differences between an ARFID population and children with AN/BN that make application of "pure FBT" principles more challenging. Unlike AN/BN symptoms, which represent a change in functioning, ARFID symptoms are generally life-long challenges in food novelty and are often coupled with novelty aversiveness in several domains. Thus the separation of patient and illness that is an essential component of traditional FBT becomes more complicated when applied to an ARFID population. Further, specific skills, such as orchestrating an intense scene, proved both challenging and problematic. Given that parents had expressed concerns for a long time and had often seen a number of professionals, raising parental anxiety regarding the challenge of renourishment felt more like "preaching to the choir" than a deliberate therapeutic intervention designed to focus parental efforts. Orchestration of intensity efforts were similarly hampered by the sheer duration of the symptoms, making it more challenging for parents to identify the parts of their child that were not occupied by ARFID symptoms. This is a corollary to FBT with young adults, whereby the length of time and previously unsuccessful efforts to address AN have led to frustration, feelings of defeat and disempowerment, and a sense that these symptoms, however damaging, have an element of willfulness about them. As a result of these and other symptomatic differences, modifications to FBT were made, with efforts to retain the fundamental theories behind the approach and modifying skills for the current application. Below is an introduction to ARFID-FBT. By no means sufficient to capture all of the clinical variability present in these cases, we hope to invite the reader to consider these adaptations for the use with children and adolescents presenting with ARFID symptoms.

ARFID-FBT Phase I

Just as in Phase 1 of standard FBT, the goal in Phase 1 of ARFID FBT is to unite the family in a focus on eating behaviors that are supportive of the increase of both types and variety in food consumption. The overall goals in this phase are an understanding of feeding/eating behaviors in the family, assessment of the range of foods eaten, and identifying successful efforts at renourishment.

Session I

The first session is similar to standard FBT in several ways. The main skills of greeting the family, taking a history specific to ARFID symptoms (see Appendix C, www.routledge.com/9780415714747), providing education and information to the family regarding the risks associated with ARFID and food neophobia behaviors, externalizing the illness, and charging parents with the task of renourishment remain in place, although the focus is shifted to better address the unique features of ARFID. The session opens with greeting the family and gathering a focused history. The therapist should present with a serious demeanor while making every effort to remain warm and welcoming, particularly for the novelty-averse child. The skill of taking a focused history also remains primary. In the first session the goal is an understanding of the current impact of restricted eating behaviors on functioning at home, relationally, academically, and socially. Rather than orchestrating an intense scene, this treatment emphasizes education on the challenges of ARFID.

ARFID Adaptations to the Intense Scene

There are several points to amplify for families. The first point is that novelty-averse eaters tend to engage in several behaviors that keep their diets restricted. First, the tendency to eat the same foods again and again, within a day or at each meal, serves to amplify differences in other tastes or presentations. In other words, if one eats the same bread and peanut butter daily for several weeks, switching peanut butter will lead to an amplified sensation of differences between the traditional and novel peanut butters. While this is true for all people (habituation leads the brain to "tune out" nuances of a stimuli but heighten differences between that stimuli and novel ones), it appears that these mechanisms may be amplified for children with ARFID, just as they are in children with ASD and OCD. Breaking these patterns means that completely novel introductions will be perceived with more disgust and aversive experience of difference than subtle changes in foods.

One important principle we cover in the first session is the need to rotate presentations of preferred foods. For example, if a child is eating the same breakfast every day (e.g., waffles) but has, in the recent past, also eaten another suitable food (e.g., French toast sticks), the goal would be to rotate this presentation. Although these foods have similar nutritional value and do not represent a change in baseline eating, encouraging greater novelty within a known or comfortable range sets the stage for practice with greater flexibility with novel foods at a later time. We often refer to the tendency to have a high demand for specific foods as "glut" eating, as patients will often eat the same food repeatedly until they tire of it and refuse to eat it again.

Another important area for education is the frequency with which novel foods need to be presented to lose their inherent novelty. The average person typically requires several presentations before stimuli are no longer experienced as novel, often as many as eight. For "picky" children this number skyrockets to thirty. For truly novelty-averse children the number is often upwards of fifty presentations before a food is no longer experienced as novel. Children with ARFID are often reacting more toward the novelty of a presentation than the taste itself. As parents of picky eaters can attest, their child will express disgust about a food that parents are certain their child will like, based on a difference in appearance, presentation, or simply because they have never tried it before. We encourage families to replace "I don't like it" with "I haven't tried it enough to know if I like it." On occasion, all of us will have experienced trying a food for a first time and truly enjoying it and this is also true for children with ARFID.

The tendency to focus on—even amplify—characteristics of foods they do not like often leads to frustration for children and keeps parents from repeating their presentations of novel foods. "It has seeds!" was the cry of one patient we treated when presented with fresh strawberries, though he loved strawberry jam, filled with the same seeds. Similarly, another child refused to eat an ice cream bar of his favorite ice cream covered with chocolate as he was used to having these same items in a dish. Such idiosyncrasies often frustrate parents and make it challenging for them to understand the patterns of their child's limited eating. Children with food neophobias also endorse only wanting to eat highly favored foods. Most healthy adults eat a range of foods, rarely drawing on foods we really despise, but also eating foods that may not be strongly preferred, or we attempt to shape those tastes toward more palatable presentations. For example, if we do not prefer spinach but know that we "should" eat it, we might dress it with a flavored dressing. We are open to eating foods in a percent-preferred taste range, while ARFID patients routinely limit their intake to only their most preferred foods (90–100 percent on the "yummy" scale). We help families recognize that, while we expect that some of the foods will not become ready favorites, no one eats only foods they do not like. The goal of the treatment is not to force the child to live on a diet of nonpreferred foods. The end goal of treatment, then, is the ability to respond flexibly when presented with nonpreferred foods and provide a sufficient variety and range in intake of foods to address the growing child/adolescent's nutritional needs.

In the first session, we introduce the concept of parental empowerment over eating, with a focus on having parents monitor and observe eating behaviors and provide an "accounting" of foods that their child eats. We call this is the "Always, Sometimes, Never list," and this can be started collaboratively in session, but it almost always ends up as "homework" between the first two sessions. An example of this appears in Appendix D (see www.routledge.com/9780415714747), but it is deserving of additional discussion. The goal of this list is to explore the foods that are eaten regularly, as this will become a base for increasing the frequency of food presentations. As noted above, increasing the presentation of non-novel foods is a critical part of treatment and sets the stage for introduction of increasingly novel foods. Helping children habituate to comfortable change is a key Phase 1 goal. Foods that are sometimes eaten are also targets for increasing the frequency of presentation and providing a window into exploring areas of taste, texture, and presentation that signal novelty for our patients. Sometimes foods may also be foods that were highly favored but have now been "dropped" due to fatigue after repeated presentations. The "Never" list is not, as the name suggests, a list of foods the child never eats, but instead captures the foods that are traditional or frequently eaten by the family members and that would represent important in-roads in food flexibility and normalcy for the family. The ultimate goal is to increase the number of foods on the Never list to the child's eating repertoire and reduce parental burden.

Lastly, we challenge parents with the task of assisting their child with expanding the range of nourishment. We instruct parents to bring a meal to the next session that includes items from the Always, Sometimes, and Never lists. The goal is to observe families in their approach to meal-time coaching behaviors and to assist them in developing renourishment skills.

Despite differences in some aspects of eating behaviors, it is important to note that families facing ARFID report many of the same challenges as those facing AN and BN. Namely, temper outbursts with food presentations, food refusal, negotiation behaviors/food "swapping" (though swaps are generally for preferred foods rather than for lower-calorie foods that are the focus of more traditional eating disorder [ED] treatments), and an ability to tolerate or ignore hunger cues that might direct eating behaviors. Therapists who can predict and explain these behaviors to families can help smooth the course of treatment. Assisting parents with understanding basic behaviorism, and avoidance behaviors in particular, therapists will find that parents often feel tremendous benefit from someone explaining the patterns of avoidance to them, rather than simply coaching them to push through these behaviors. Parents have been trying, unsuccessfully, often for years to coax their child to eat, and these families benefit from understanding the importance of patient, consistent, small steps toward a goal to avoid burnout.

Session 2

This session carries the same overtones and utilizes the same skills as Session 2 in standard FBT. The focus is on understanding the family history of eating skills utilized to assist their child in eating a bite of nonfavored food, providing continued education on developing a feared-food hierarchy, and encouraging intake. The family begins by demonstrating how they serve meals and providing information to the therapist on the items chosen and the progression of the meal. Parents are then coached in helping the identified patient eat a bite of a feared or novel food. Some differences in this session that highlight the distinctions in diagnostic criteria between AN and ARFID include structuring meals such that novel foods are eaten before preferred foods. Reinforcement strategies may also need to be identified for the family, specifically introducing patterns of rewarding target behaviors. These include strategies such as negative reinforcement, such as removing an unwanted task in response to appropriate eating (e.g., you do not have to help with the dishes if you finish this bite), setting up visual reward systems, such as reward charts, and finding novel rewards to keep motivation high. These techniques may dovetail with AN strategies but are often adjusted for the typically younger developmental age of ARFID patients. The use of more visual strategies is also appropriate for younger patients. Older patients may establish their own reward system, which can include eating favored foods after trying a novel food, but in general we try to avoid using eating as a reward for food exposures.

General principles that are important to follow include helping parents keep the amount of novel food small but significant (approximately 2 tablespoons of a novel food) and explaining the importance of tasting the food while eating, rather than choking down the food and swallowing it or "washing it down" with water. It is also important to remind parents of the frequency of exposures, such that they are choosing the same food for repeated exposures. Many parents begin to become lax in presentations after a week or so, particularly when presentations are challenging. Or, parents feel the need to change the presentation by presenting a different form of the food or adding spices (e.g., broccoli is served raw or roasted). When the preparation is changed, this would be considered a new food presentation, although in our experience, changing the presentation is far less difficult once the taste has been secured. Similarly, adding salt, garlic, etc., to foods may help with initial presentations (if these are favored tastes) but should be removed to consider a taste exposure completed. As a result, unless a food is immediately enjoyed, the same presentation should be utilized until the food is no longer considered novel.

Sessions 3–15

As in standard FBT, the remainder of Phase 1 focuses on helping parents implement hierarchies of food and practicing food-based exposures. There are two foci: (1) rotating already secured foods such that the timing and frequency of secured foods is more varied and the identified patient has more practice in eating different meals with favored foods and (2) introduction of simple, related new foods. The general principles are to find a food that is similar to (or almost identical, if possible) to foods that are already eaten. These foods are then slowly expanded until there is a multiple array of presentations. Most families would prefer to start with mixed foods, but this is an area that many identified patients struggle with the most—the contrast of tastes and flavors is entirely too novel for the more sensitive palates. Instead, we encourage presentations of single foods at a time.

For example, one patient was eating Nutrigrain bars in a strawberry flavor, and the family focused on introducing raspberry flavored bars to reduce the overall novelty. These were first introduced as a "two bite" rule, where the patient took two bites and then could finish the remainder of his snack with a strawberry bar. After only five presentations, the patient noted that the tastes were similar enough as to be indistinguishable from one another, and he began to freely eat either bar. As a result, parents provided a different bar each day and moved on to a blueberry bar. When this was tolerated sufficiently (again requiring approximately five presentations), the family moved this into an overall rotation where each day a different bar was presented with little concern. The family identified a desire to switch to other foods for exposures, as they saw little benefit to this type of dietary expansion. They moved on to serving toast (a secured food) with small bites of strawberry jam, which was tolerated well, as was seedless raspberry jam. However, they were also open to trying the remaining flavor of Nutrigrain bars, apple. This was significantly harder than they expected and required multiple presentations. After more than twenty presentations, this flavor was still being experienced as novel, but parents were able to keep this up continuously. As a result, efforts moved to focus on other ways to support the flavor of apple in other presentations.

Parents purchased apple cinnamon waffles to introduce small bites, supporting the already secured food of waffles. This led to two simultaneous presentations of apples baked into grains that were tolerated, but not enjoyed. The waffles were preferred and were more quickly adapted than the apple bar. Parents then began to serve applesauce in small portions. After only three months of presentations, the family was able to serve toast with several flavors of jam, bars of multiple types, and a first serving of fruit—applesauce. Parents were then able to practice with berry waffles, waffles with jam (introducing the use of condiments in a child who was previously averse), and applesauce with cinnamon. In this way, one can see that "chaining" flavors often allows for faster adaptations of flavors and accepting can occasionally occur simultaneously. In addition, there is rarely a large leap into difficult food groups or even "healthier" foods, although that is always the ultimate goal. The building upon already established flavors helps build trust that "disgusting" foods will not be the focus of treatment. Further, as more foods or food pairings are conquered, the accepted rotations within the diet also expand. As such, at the end of this phase of treatment, the family was able to serve a unique breakfast each day of the week. The expanded range and frequent sampling of these items prevents them from being "dropped out" of the diet and also prevents boredom, for both parents and child.

One specific change in ARFID treatment is the longer period of time spent in Phase 1. While standard FBT tends to focus on ten sessions for the first phase, FBT-ARFID typically requires fifteen sessions and, in cases of extremely limited range of intake, may require an even longer course of treatment. This is due to several factors: teaching parents to structure behavioral experiments and secure new behaviors takes longer than returning to previously established skills. In addition, as one can tell from the example above, this type of food-based exposure takes a tremendous amount of time and patience. In addition to teaching hierarchies, several other skills are typically beneficial to families in this first phase of treatment. These include teaching relaxation skills and identifying strategies to help parents and patients cope with upset and manage fears around exposure exercises. One area that we often teach parents and children is a "visualization for mastery" exercise. In this relaxation skill, the goal is to help patients identify a time when they felt very strong, powerful, relaxed, or confident (the specific emotion may depend upon the challenges presented before/during/after meals). Once the patients can "fill their body" with the strong positive feelings, we have them engage in imaginal exposures in which they feel this way after eating a challenge food. The goal is to improve paired-associations with food. We might start these exercises at a time other than food presentation, such as bedtime or at a restful transition point in the day. They then continue to practice the technique. The goal is to help break the cycle of negative, avoidant thinking and replace this with strong feelings of competence and mastery.

For more anxious children, the introduction of standard relaxation skills, such as diaphragmatic breathing, progressive muscle relaxation, or visualization for relaxation can be taught to the family. Parents would be in charge of assisting their child in the practice of these skills—ideally as an entire family—and this is one additional area where we encourage parental empowerment in addressing their child's fears and concerns. This represents a significant departure from traditional FBT, in which we might encourage use of problem-solving skills, coping strategies, and communication skills but rarely specifically teach these strategies. Again, the introduction and mastery of skills in ARFID requires more focus on "teaching" rather than redirecting parents to existing skills and mastery behaviors. "Re-feeding" assumes that "feeding" behaviors have been secured and can be strengthened, while in the case of ARFID there is a bit more focus on introduction of new skills than shoring up existing ones.

Phase 2

The second phase of this treatment begins when parents understand the basics of food exposures and can set about determining the next appropriate exposures and/or are able to independently introduce and carry forward a food exposure. Additionally, such exposures are experienced with relatively little distress by the identified patient, who may also be able to direct to these challenges. For example, the child may be able to identify a food that would be useful for them to eat or a food that sounds interesting to them. This shift in motivation is not present in all children and should also be tied to the developmental level of the patient. Our patients with developmental disabilities often struggle to identify or be motivated toward foods, and these children may need to be directed by parents even throughout this phase. Regardless, the increasing competencies of the patient and family are reflected in a spacing of sessions to every other week, as in Phase 2 of standard FBT.

The largest gains in Phase 2 are introducing mixed or complex presentations of foods, for example, sandwiches that contain both favored and nonfavored items. For children who have not been eating any mixed presentations, introducing mixing of flavors or tastes is a critical next step. As such, if one has presented strawberries and blueberries separately, presenting those as mixed berries would be a next step. They can still be eaten separately (all the blueberries, then all the strawberries) but the presentation itself can begin to be varied. If there are particularly favored foods, such as a brand of peanut butter or a specific type of bread, there may also be an effort to move away from just that type, to allow for greater flexibility in eating with others (e.g., eating a peanut butter and jelly sandwich at a restaurant or a friend's house).

Social eating is also a target in this phase of treatment, reinforcing eating at school, restaurants, or family gatherings. This phase also allows for greater integration into more typical family meals, reducing the burden on families who have often been preparing multiple meals. This reduction in burden on family resources allows greater time for the family to focus on more enjoyable activities and communication. The patient may be of the age where independent eating behaviors should be reinforced, and this is also an area where families may focus their efforts by encouraging self-directed snacks and ensuring that variety continues to be part of dietary efforts. This can be further reinforced by encouraging independent eating with peers in social/playtime situations. Moving from food as the focus of meals to a focus on others is an important step in normalizing eating.

As concerns around food abate, other issues in the family or the patient may arise and should be managed clinically as necessary, without losing focus on feeding and eating behaviors. Some families need assistance in addressing challenges in communication or comorbidities that may arise or eclipse the challenges presented by ARFID. Just as in standard FBT, if significant comorbidities make management of independent eating more challenging, this may be a time where a referral for additional services or a medication evaluation may be clinically indicated. For some, a referral for exposure therapy or cognitive behavioral therapy (CBT) for anxiety may be necessary. For others, there may be a need for support around developmental issues; this can be managed differently depending upon the case and clinical expertise. In our case series, for some patients the treating clinician continues to address anxiety symptoms in sessions, maintaining a weekly schedule and working on more specific anxiety during "off weeks," while in other cases a referral to a new clinician is in order. The same also stands for referrals for additional family or marital therapy.

Phase 3

The question of when to terminate treatment for ARFID remains a question. No treatment studies exist and certainly no information on long-term outcomes is available. Additionally, for food neophobes, it is unlikely that treatment will end when all eating concerns and rigidities are resolved. Rather, treatment may be terminated when sufficient progress has been made such that eating issues no longer present nutritional and social impairments and the family is capable of managing eating concerns with little intervention from the treatment team. Another treatment target is the ability for families to serve only one meal that satisfies most members of the family with few modifications. As with standard FBT, sessions in this late phase are spread to once per month, and the focus is largely on developmental adjustments, identifying areas for future concern and general communication and familial adjustment. It should be noted that, for ARFID patients, significant changes in eating represent areas of risk for returning to a limited diet. Switching to a school lunch, being responsible for their own after-school snacks or meals, and a departure to college all should be viewed with an eye toward continued expansion, rather than limiting, of the diet. Dating and social adjustment are also appropriate targets in this stage of treatment, if developmentally relevant.

The use of a family-based protocol for ARFID presents many opportunities to address a unique variant of restrictive eating disorders. While there remain fundamental differences between AN and ARFID, the use of the family as a context for renourishment and an emphasis on parent-led exposure exercises combines to teach behaviors in the context in which we expect them to be expressed. Additionally, the use of parent direction of eating behaviors that can be supported in the family creates a "virtuous cycle" in which all parties are rewarded for their efforts by reduced stress and increased feelings of mastery.

Below is a case report outlining the implementation of these tenets in a clinical context.

Presenting Issue

Oliver, an 11-year-old biracial male, first came to an outpatient eating disorders clinic in a university medical center following referral to evaluate the nature of ongoing food refusal and picky eating. Oliver's refusal to eat outside of a limited repertoire of foods had resulted in failure to make expected weight gain milestones, and by age 5 his weight had dropped from the 30th BMI percentile to the 5th, raising parental concern. Further, he required supplements to treat vitamin and mineral deficiencies, and his food refusal began to limit his social engagements outside of the home and resulted in strain between family members.

According his parents, Oliver had seemed disinterested in food from a very young age. He was born several weeks early and never initiated breast-feeding. He began eating pureed baby foods without difficulty around 6 months of age, and by the time he went to day care at age 2, he was eating a limited repertoire of solid foods including cream of wheat, mashed potatoes, graham crackers, and cereal. His preschool providers often reported home to the parents that he did not seem interested in food or seek food out like other children. Like many parents, Oliver's mother and father raised their concern about his limited intake and failure to expand his intake with his pediatrician. However, the parents continued to receive the message that Oliver would eventually grow out of his picky eating habits. By the time Oliver was around 4 or 5 years old, he stopped trying new foods entirely. When encouraged to try something new, Oliver often clamped his mouth and burst into tears. This resulted in initial encouragement, followed by pleading, and ultimately resignation by his parents. Often, Oliver's mother would burst into tears and leave the table, and his father would concede to Oliver's wishes, not wanting to upset him further.

His parents expressed exasperation at Oliver's difficulties and confusion over what seemed like nonsensical and unpredictable food refusal.

For example, his parents often would buy bulk quantities of foods they thought Oliver preferred, and then he would suddenly refuse these foods. Alternatively, they might buy a new brand of a preferred food, and Oliver would refuse to eat it. They rearranged their lives in many ways to accommodate Oliver's eating challenges: going to multiple supermarkets to find preferred brands, bringing special foods to restaurants or family gatherings, and picking Oliver up early from social engagements involving meals.

Upon interview, Oliver shared that he experienced a significant amount of anticipatory anxiety around trying new foods. He was acutely aware of and sensitive to his parents' perceptions. He asked for his parents' approval and expressed embarrassment and guilt about his eating difficulty. Oliver described physiological arousal in the form of stomachaches, muscle tension, and feelings of being on edge or restless. Over time, his anxiety around mealtimes resulted in increasingly defiant behaviors. For example, in the past year, he had begun refusing to come to the table for dinner and on occasion would "drop" food on the floor or hide it in his napkin. Oliver's parents gave in to his requests to eat the same meal every night because it alleviated arguments at the dinner table. When they did encourage Oliver to try something new, Oliver would engage in bargaining and ultimately remind them of their "promise" that he could eat what he preferred.

Oliver denied any worries about gaining weight, his physical appearance, or body shape. Although, he did note embarrassment about being smaller than other boys his age, and he experienced bullying about his size on a number of occasions. There remained transient fear of vomiting following a bout of food poisoning around the time Oliver stopped trying new foods at age 4. Oliver did not complain of any ongoing gastrointestinal symptoms or medical illness upon interview or historically.

Treatment History

Given the parents' ongoing concerns, they eventually took Oliver to see a nutritionist who recommended brief treatment for what they diagnosed as a feeding disorder secondary to food aversion. Sessions involved exposure to food with practice smelling, touching, and holding food in the mouth to decrease sensitivity to such sensory elements. Oliver did expand his food repertoire slightly during treatment; however, once the family terminated treatment, they found it difficult to maintain the gains they had made.

Current Symptoms

Oliver presented with a number of perceptual sensitivities, including sensitivity to texture, smell, sight, and temperature. He was bothered by food smells like cabbage, cauliflower, and fish and plugged his nose when in the presence of these foods. He reported not liking foods that were "wet" or "slimy" and avoided sauces and spreads. On the other hand, he preferred "crunchy" foods, and the majority of his preferred foods were texturally crispy, including food items like crackers, cereal, chips, peanuts, and granola bars. Combined foods like sandwiches, hamburgers, and soup were a particular challenge, and these were items that the family wanted Oliver to try given their own meal preferences. Oliver tended to eat the same exact foods for each meal, with little variation. Oliver's parents noted that on occasion he would switch to a new kind of cereal, for example, but then would eat the same cereal for months on end. He often skipped lunch at school despite his parents' efforts to pack a range of preferred foods.

Oliver reported significant anxiety in a number of domains. Oliver often worried about his family members, resulting in some separation fears with a history of school avoidance. He expressed significant anxiety and sadness related to the loss of an aunt two years prior to initiating treatment. He also described worry about losing his own parents and his younger sister. He frequently sought reassurance from his parents in the form of checking to see what their response would be—looking to them, asking them their opinion, and seeking positive reinforcement in the context of self-critical thoughts. Oliver's self-criticism existed around whether he was "good enough" or an "embarrassment" to his family and with peers. He frequently worried about others' perceptions of him, and he became embarrassed easily in front of peers leading to occasional social withdrawal. He had increasingly stopped attending play dates over the past year. He also expressed uncertainty around his abilities—for example, he enjoyed competitive swimming but despite evident talent, he lacked self-confidence.

The impact of his anxiety and food refusal resulted in social impairment—often Oliver would not go to friends' homes, especially during a mealtime due to worry about whether he would be able to eat with his friends. Further, at family gatherings Oliver often refused to sit at the table with his family while they ate, again due to embarrassment.

Response to Psychoeducation around Eating Challenges

At outset of treatment, the therapist provided psychoeducation about ARFID, linking specific diagnostic symptoms to Oliver's current presentation. For example, the family expressed confusion about why Oliver would eat a particular food on one occasion but then subsequently refuse the food. The therapist explained different perceptual sensitivities associated with ARFID, including those to texture, temperature, smell, and sight, that may lead a child to refuse a food that was otherwise consumed due to differences that would be imperceptible to individuals without ARFID. The therapist encouraged the family to consider how these sensitivities applied to Oliver. Treatment emphasized the need for consistent and repeated trials of foods that were not in the "preferred" category, in order to decrease sensitivity and encourage habituation. The family would often quickly react to successful intake of a novel food by buying large quantities of that food. Oliver would then refuse to eat it, leading to frustration and confusion. The family expressed relief as they found this new information provided useful structure and guidance, where previously they had tried a number of strategies, many of them only briefly.

Shaping and Chaining

Phase 1 of FBT-ARFID was focused on providing psychoeducation to the family to enhance their understanding of Oliver's food difficulties, decrease parental blame and Oliver's shame, and increase hopefulness for change given longstanding difficulties. The therapist used externalization strategies to support separation of food difficulties from Oliver as a person with the goal of decreasing subtle criticism towards Oliver (e.g., parents might roll their eyes at each other, withdraw, or act disinterested in the context of Oliver discussing food difficulties). The parents expressed a great deal of self-criticism for not having been successful in managing Oliver's food difficulties up until this point and for not acting on their concerns earlier despite physician recommendations. The therapist normalized their concerns by providing psychoeducation about the range of picky eating behaviors seen in childhood, which can often lead to confusion about behaviors that fall outside of a developmentally typical range.

Early treatment targets involved teaching the parents about shaping, or slowly changing, Oliver's eating to increase the frequency of new presentations of food. In the assessment phase, Oliver and his parents each created a separate list of the foods that they felt were "preferred" foods, or foods that he always ate, foods that he sometimes ate or were inconsistently eaten, and those foods that the family would like for him to eat but he consistently refused (see Appendix D, www.routledge.com/9780415714747). From that point, the therapist asked Oliver and his parents to compare their lists, observing differences and resolving these to create a final master list to work from. The family was informed that an initial treatment goal would be to improve flexibility and to increase habituation to change in routine. Oliver's parents started with the easiest meal of the day (dinner), which was often when Oliver was hungriest. They collaborated with Oliver to choose foods on his "Always" list to rotate daily so that he would not have the same meal twice in one week. The aim of this intervention was to decrease "glut" eating and increase novelty of foods presented and flexibility. Within the range of preferred foods, the therapist supported the family in identifying ways they could creatively introduce flexibility, which included buying different flavors of preferred food, different brands of preferred food, and different ratios or combination of food items.

Within the first month of treatment, as Oliver gained mastery over eating his favorite foods with increased variability, therapy began to target introduction of foods from his "Sometimes" list. In doing this, treatment first emphasized the importance of increasing the number of presentations, encouraging a focus on frequency rather than quantity. Each week, Oliver and his parents collaborated to identify the food item they wanted to practice multiple exposures of for the subsequent session. The therapist supported the family in identifying antecedents to successful food intake and to food refusal. She encouraged them to modify environmental factors (e.g., where family members were positioned at the table, how they presented a visual reminder of established rewards, and a reward chart) and situational factors (e.g., the order in which food is presented, quantities placed on the plate, and the presence of reward foods following successful completion of a novel food). The therapist also encouraged the family to modify behavioral patterns that appeared to reinforce the cycle of food refusal. For example, Oliver's parents were helped to understand the impact of subtle criticism, or the ways in which their own anxiety that Oliver would not be successful were apparent in their behaviors. The therapist redirected criticism as it occurred in a session as a model for out-of-session behavior. Oliver found it helpful to have a visual reminder of a reward for which he and his family had agreed he could work. He also felt increasingly confident when he was more actively involved in the structuring of food exposures. These food presentations continued, often over a period of 2–3 weeks, with upwards of ten presentations per week until Oliver reported habituation to the food and a desire to place the food on his "Always" list. In addition, the therapist began to teach the process of "chaining," referring to the linking together of experiences to create new, more complex behaviors. First, the family and therapist identified foods that are similar to one another (e.g., toast and English muffins) and then switched back and forth between the two. Once these new foods were secure, the family expanded to other, similar foods, including French toast and waffles.

In Oliver's case, a focus on Phase 2 treatment goals was slow and included developmentally and situationally appropriate independence. For example, Oliver practiced eating out with friends, first bringing preferred foods and then practicing in advance with foods he was aware would be served. The majority of treatment in Oliver's case, however, focused on Phase 1, with significant generalization of skills used to manage food-related anxiety also being used to manage anxiety in a number of other domains. Many of the strategies employed are consistent with cognitive behavioral models of anxiety management in children. For example, given the significant anxiety associated with food exposures, as well as broad anxiety in a number of domains (e.g., illness, separation, going new places), relaxation skills were introduced at the very outset of treatment. The structure of these didactics involved teaching Oliver these skills in a separate individual session, rehearsing, and then bringing his parents in so he could subsequently teach them newly learned skills. Relaxation strategies were delivered in succession, as is the case in anxiety treatment more generally, beginning with breathing retraining (diaphragmatic breathing), progressive muscle relaxation, guided imagery, and guided imagery for mastery. The therapist supported Oliver and his family in identifying physiological cues associated with anxiety. In Oliver's case, he often experienced anxiety in the form of feelings of restlessness, muscle tension, and stomach upset. Developmentally appropriate scripts, audio recordings, and books were utilized to enhance family learning of these skills. Oliver and his parents were encouraged to practice these skills on a regular basis and to choose a time of day they could introduce the routine of practicing relaxation. They used these skills at the end of the school day, and from there, the therapist encouraged generalization of these skills to food trials. In-session exposures to food allowed Oliver to practice using progressive muscle relaxation followed by guided imagery for mastery. These exposures were presented as an opportunity to practice calming the body in the presence of challenge food, rather than an opportunity to practice eating the food itself. Further, the therapist adopted a playful attitude, supporting the family in creatively adopting strategies to make these experiences fun rather than aversive. The aim of this approach was to model decreased seriousness, encourage family connection, and decrease pressure that often led to defiant behaviors in Oliver's case. While not the aim of many of these activities, oftentimes following practice of these new skills, Oliver successfully ingested the presented food—an unexpected benefit. These in-session experiences were used as a model for discussing effective and ineffective strategies for encouraging successful food intake. The family was able to adopt a playful attitude, enjoying brainstorming methods to involve Oliver in the experience of planning, preparing, and structuring meals to increase his self-confidence and decrease feelings of guilt and embarrassment around eating challenges.

Ultimately, these structural changes allowed for a change in family perspective around Oliver's eating difficulties. The family was able to increase the frequency of successful food exposures, and their overall anxiety was greatly decreased and no longer serving as a barrier to applying skills learned in treatment in the home.

References

American Psychiatric Association (2013). *Diagnostic and statistical manual of mental disorders* (5th Ed.). Washington, DC.

Beal, V. A. (1957). On the acceptance of solid foods, and other patterns, of infants and children. *Pediatrics, 1957*(20), 448.

Bryant-Waugh, R., Markham, L., Kreipe, R., & Walsh, B. T. (2010) Feeding and eating disorders in childhood. *International Journal of Eating Disorders, 43*, 98–111.

Fraker, C., Fishbein, M., Cox, S., & Walbert, L. (2007). *Food chaining: The proven 6-step plan to stop picky eating, solve feeding problems, and expand your child's diet*. Boston, MA: De Capo Press.

Lock, J. D., & Le Grange, D. (2012). *Treatment manual for anorexia nervosa*, 2nd Ed. New York: Guilford Press.

Murray, S. B., & Le Grange, D. (2014). Family therapy for adolescent eating disorders: An update. *Current Psychiatry Reports, 16*(5), 447.

Wildes, J. E., Zucker, N. L., & Marcus, M. D. (2012). Picky eating in adults: Results of a web-based survey. *International Journal of Eating Disorders, 45*, 575–582.

Chapter 13

Family-Based Therapy for Adolescent Weight Loss Surgery

Danielle Colborn and Kathleen Kara Fitzpatrick

The rate of adolescent obesity has increased rapidly in recent years (Michalsky, Reichard, Inge, Pratt, & Lenders, 2012; Black, White, Viner, & Simmons, 2013; Treadwell, Sun, & Schoelles, 2008). In addition, obesity in adolescents is associated with a number of serious health outcomes. Given these factors, weight-loss surgery (WLS) is increasingly being turned to as one solution to promote weight loss, prevent the development of adult obesity, and change the course of many of the comorbidities associated with adolescent obesity. Evidence increasingly supports WLS as a viable option for weight-loss and health improvement in severely obese adolescents who have been carefully screened and selected, and thus it is not surprising that the rates of WLS within this population are also very much on the rise (Michalsky et al., 2012; Treadwell et al., 2008). However, WLS in adolescents is not without its risks and does not always lead to desired outcomes. Identifying factors and interventions that promote the likelihood of long-term success for adolescents undergoing this procedure is of high importance. It is critical to note that WLS is not for teens who have had an uncomplicated history of obesity but is reserved for only those adolescents who have multiple, significant medical comorbidities that threaten longevity and hamper other weight loss efforts. Based on our review of relevant research, our clinical experiences with this population, and our success in using this intervention with other populations, we propose that increasing the involvement of the adolescent's family, through the implementation of family-based therapy for weight loss surgery (FBT-WLS), is likely to promote successful outcomes and minimize the risks associated with WLS in adolescents. In this chapter, we present background on the use of bariatric surgery to treat adolescent obesity, background on family involvement in treatment of pediatric obesity, background on family involvement in preparing teens for weight loss surgery, and present a proposed plan for implementing FBT-WLS. We finish with a presentation of clinical examples to support and illuminate our recommendations.

Background on WLS for Adolescents

Rates of Obesity and WLS in Adolescents

The rate of obesity among adolescents in the United States has increased swiftly in recent years. The percentage of adolescents with a BMI greater than the 95th percentile almost tripled from 1970–99, going from 5 percent to 14 percent, and it is estimated to have increased to 16 percent from 1999–2002 (Treadwell et al., 2008). Although recent analysis of prevalence rates of obesity for children, adolescents, and adults in the United States suggests that obesity rates seem to have plateaued, with no increase from 2003–04 to 2011–12 estimates (Ogden, Carroll, Kit, & Flegal, 2013), obesity remains a major health concern given the high number of medical comorbidities with which it is associated, not to mention psychological and quality of life concerns.

Severe and morbid obesity have been associated with a number of serious health comorbidities in both adults and adolescents. What is particularly concerning is that adolescents with obesity appear to experience medical comorbidities that are equivalent to those observed in adults. That is, many of the major health concerns associated with obesity appear to develop rather rapidly after the onset of obesity, rather than several decades later, and are not protected against by younger age. Given these concerns and the rising rates of obesity in adolescents, it is not surprising that rates of bariatric surgery as an intervention with this population have risen significantly as well in recent years. One research article found WLS in adolescents more than tripled from 2000 to 2003 (Treadwell et al., 2008).

Comorbidities

Obesity in adolescents is associated with a number of comorbidities, including type 2 diabetes mellitus; obstructive sleep apnea; nonalcoholic fatty liver disease (NAFLD) and nonalcoholic steatohepatitis (NASH); pseudotumor cerebri; cardiovascular disease risk factors including hypertension and dyslipidemia; and predictors of metabolic syndrome such as hyperinsulinemia, insulin resistance, and abnormal lipid metabolism. Obesity in adolescents has also been associated with negative quality of life and depression (Michalsky et al., 2012; Black et al., 2013). In addition to immediate comorbidity concerns, obesity in adolescence has been clearly linked to health concerns in adulthood including all-cause mortality, coronary heart disease, atherosclerosis, colorectal cancer, gout, and arthritis (Treadwell et al., 2008).

Many of the above mentioned comorbidities appear to resolve or significantly improve following WLS. Type 2 diabetes appears to go into complete remission following Roux-en-Y Gastric Bypass (RYGB) in both adolescents and adults. Obstructive sleep apnea appears to significantly improve or resolve in adolescents who undergo bariatric surgery, similar to adult outcomes (Michalsky et al., 2012). Pseudotumor cerebri improves several months after bariatric surgery in adolescents, again consistent with adult data (Chandra et al., 2007). Hypertension and dyslipidemia improve within one year in adolescents who have RYGB (Black et al., 2013). Finally, recent research suggests significant improvement in quality of life for adolescents undergoing both RYGB and gastric sleeve (Loux et al., 2008), as well as an improvement in depressive symptoms (Zeller, Modi, Noll, Long, & Inge, 2009).

In addition to resolution of a number of comorbidities, WLS in adolescents has been shown to have a positive impact on weight loss, similar to outcomes found in adults. This is hardly surprising, given that the point of surgery is weight loss, but in actuality the resolution of comorbidities is more important, as this is the sole reason a surgical weight loss option would be proffered. A recent literature review suggested a mean BMI change of -13.5 kg m^{-2} at one year post surgery (Black et al., 2013). In this review, BMI at baseline ranged from 38.5 to 60.2 kg m^{-2} (mean 47.9 kg m^{-2}) and decreased to 25.2 to 41.5 kg m^{-2} (mean 34.7 kg m^{-2}) at one year post-operatively. These findings are similar to rates of weight loss observed in adults following WLS (Colquitt, Picot, Loveman, & Clegg, 2009). It is noteworthy that these findings indicate that the vast majority of WLS patients, both adult and adolescent, remain in the overweight to obese category. This suggests that management of patient expectations following surgery is an important part of any pre-surgery protocol and will be a significant component of FBT-WLS.

Given the negative health consequences of medical comorbidities associated with pediatric obesity, and the resolution of many following WLS, comorbidities have been taken into account when selecting patients for bariatric surgery. The current criteria for considering adolescents for bariatric surgery can be found in Table 1.

Table 13.1 Criteria for selection of adolescent patients for bariatric surgery

Adolescent candidates must meet one of the below criteria	
1.	BMI ≥ 35 kg/m^2 with major comorbidities: type 2 diabetes mellitus, moderate sleep apnea (apnea-hyponea index > 15), pseudomotor cerebri, severe NASH
OR:	
2.	BMI ≥ 40 kg/m^2 with other comorbidities (i.e., hypertension, insulin resistance, glucose intolerance, significantly impaired quality of life or activities of daily living, dyslipidemia, sleep apnea (apnea-hyponea index > 5)
Plus:	Consideration of the potential for the individual patient to incur long-term health risks due to untreated or inadequately treated obesity.

From: Michalsky, M., et al. (2012). ASMBS pediatric committee best practice guidelines. *Surgery for Obesity and Related Diseases, 8,* 1–7.

Risks of WLS in Adolescents

Although WLS for adolescents appears to have many potential benefits, it is not without its risks. Some of these risks are related to the surgical procedures themselves, whereas others are unique to this developing adolescent population. In addition, the risks of WLS are not well defined in the relevant research, partially due to the developing nature of WLS as a viable option for treating adolescent obesity. As with any major medical procedure, particularly those that are newly in use and done with a developing population, adolescent WLS should be conducted with caution, careful patient screening, and full discussion of the risks and benefits with patients and their families. Given the potential impact for long-term development and health behaviors, adolescents, in particular, present challenges for selection and follow-up for those eligible for weight loss surgery. These are further reasons we believe FBT-WLS is an appropriate and worthwhile intervention.

Surgical Risks. A recent meta-review of peri-operative complications following adolescent WLS found more complications following RYGB compared to gastric banding, with nutrient deficiencies, hernias, wound infections, small bowel obstructions, cholelithias, and ulcers being the most frequent (Black et al., 2013). However, lap band surgery is not an option for adolescents moving forward. Therefore, evaluation of only RYGB complications is relevant. A number of common nutritional deficiencies following WLS include low levels of iron, vitamin B12, vitamin D, and calcium, particularly after RYGB, making nutritional supplementation essential (Xanthakos & Inge, 2006). Given that adolescents are particularly known to be non-compliant with medical regimens, the risk of nutritional deficiencies following WLS is even greater with this population compared to adults (Rapoff, 2010).

Pregnancy. A recent study found a twofold increase in pregnancy in adolescents who had undergone WLS (Roehrig et al., 2007). This suggests increased risk of pregnancy is a concern for adolescents undergoing WLS. This may be due to resolution of polycystic ovarian syndrome (PCOS) as well as increased sexual activity associated with greater confidence and sociability following WLS. Female patients should be informed about the increase in fertility following weight loss within the first 18 months after WLS. Pregnancy is a dangerous outcome, both for the patient as well as the fetus, and efforts should be taken to provide education and protection to patients.

Psychosocial. Although little data exist on the psychosocial risk factors of adolescent WLS, we know that having a surgical procedure such as this is a life-changing operation. Adolescents and their families should be educated on the distressing impact even positive changes can have in our lives. Many adolescents, who are undergoing a critical developmental period, may not be prepared for either the increased attention they receive after weight loss or the changed way in which people are likely to relate to them. Some respond to increased attention with upset, "You want to be my friend now, but not when I was heavier?" while others are terribly eager to engage in what they perceive themselves as having missed while obesity kept them facing medical challenges and limited mobility. For this latter group, drinking, drug use, and risk-taking behaviors can present significant challenges. Discussing these changes with the adolescent and their family prior to surgery provides opportunity to plan for the impact of these changes and develop necessary coping skills. Families are uniquely placed to assist in these efforts as they know their child and can contain and address these risk factors.

Bariatric Surgical Options for Adolescents

Although a variety of types of bariatric surgical procedures are being practiced, only two are currently approved for use with pediatric patients: Roux-en-Y gastric bypass (RYGB) and gastric sleeve (GS). Gastric banding has been suspended as a choice for adolescents (AGB), due to post-surgical complications but has been used as a comparison against other weight loss methods and therefore may be discussed. As we will see, the choice of surgery has important implications for adolescents and their families, and supporting them in making this decision is an important component of FBT-WLS. RYGB has been conducted on adults in the United States since the 1960s and on adolescents since 1980. It has been shown to be associated with sustained weight loss in adults with comparable outcomes for adolescents (Treadwell et al., 2008; Black et al., 2013). Although RYGB is associated with more significant weight loss and has been more heavily studied than AGB, due to its having been longer in use, it is also associated with more post-surgical complications, including anastomotic leak, sepsis, bleeding, complications, and thromboembolic events. Gastric sleeve avoids resection of the intestine and uses only the restrictive method of reducing stomach size, in this case to roughly that of a banana. Characteristics of GS make it an appealing option for adolescents: it requires less stringent dietary adherence following surgery, it is relatively safe, and if additional weight loss is required, a post-surgical modified RYGB can be performed. This last factor is of particular importance given the developing nature of adolescents for whom, after years of growth and maturity, may find that their earlier choices and preferences have changed. It is also noteworthy that in our evaluations of youth who have undergone WLS at our clinic, there have been no differences in weight loss outcomes when comparing RYGB and GS. Although these are unpublished data, the findings are important. It may be that for adolescents who are still growing, GS will produce weight loss outcomes similar to adults who have undergone the more stringent RYGB, without concerns for malnourishment.

Family Involvement in Pediatric Weight Loss Efforts

In the frustrating, overwhelming, and often futile arena of pediatric obesity treatment, family involvement in weight loss efforts appears to offer some hope of effectiveness. In their ten-year review of outcomes for pediatric obesity treatment, Epstein and colleagues demonstrated that family-based behavioral treatment for obese children promoted the likelihood of maintaining weight loss through adolescence and into adulthood (Epstein, Valoski, Wing, & McCurley, 1994). Another more recent literature review found that the majority of articles supported the use of family-based treatment in the management of pediatric obesity (Nowicka & Flodmark, 2008). In another review, this one of Clinical Practice Guidelines (CPG) for pre-adolescent and adolescent overweight and obesity treatment, it was found that all documents reviewed recommended that a parent or family should be involved in the treatment of pediatric obesity (Shrewsbury, Steinbeck, Torvaldsen, & Baur, 2011). When discussing children, the level of parental involvement recommended was clear and direct, with increasing age associated with decreased parental involvement. The recommendations for family involvement with adolescents were more ambivalent. However, one document clearly indicated that when interventions are directed at the teen and parent outcomes were better (AACE/ACE Obesity Task Force, Position Statement, 1998). Finally, a randomized controlled trial (RCT) comparing a family-based behavioral intervention with usual care (i.e., two nutrition consultation sessions) found that the family-based intervention had a significantly larger decrease in child percentage overweight compared to usual care and that these changes were sustained over time (i.e., 18 months) in families who had good session attendance (≥75 percent) (Kalarchian et al., 2009). Interestingly, one of the most effective weight loss strategies in a family is to have a family member undergo RYGB; not only does the surgical candidate lose weight, family members who are overweight or obese also lose up to 30 percent of their excess weight. Having the entire family implement changes provides support and lessens the risk that poor food choices will be available.

Given the profound impact family involvement appears to have on pediatric weight loss efforts on overweight and obese youth, it stands to reason that family involvement in adolescent WLS would promote more long-term, sustainable change, compared to protocols that focus primarily on the teen. We challenge the tendency for professionals to recommend little to no family involvement for weight loss and health promotion interventions targeted at adolescents as compared to children. Although we want to respect developing adolescent autonomy and individuation, we believe that adolescence is a time of turbulence and change in which teens need their parents' support more than ever, albeit in a different manner from when they were younger. Empowering parents to be involved in their teen's lives in a way that allows them to effectively support their teen will promote healthy development, and therefore healthy autonomy, that will benefit the teen and the family as a whole.

One final note: Although family involvement seems to promote weight-loss in pediatric populations, all interventions in this area have demonstrated minimal effectiveness. Many families, even after multiple attempts to support their child's weight loss efforts are faced with the ongoing challenge of managing obesity and the associated health problems in their children. Bariatric surgery has been found to be more effective for improving the risk factors associated with juvenile obesity compared to family-therapy and behavior modification. Thus it appears that for many families, having been carefully screened and selected, bariatric surgery may offer the best option for sustained weight loss and comorbidity resolution. It also suggests that combining family-therapy with bariatric surgery may be more efficacious in treating juvenile obesity, and its associated health risks, than either alone.

Family Involvement in Adolescent Weight-Loss Surgery

Adequate and appropriate family involvement is considered a prerequisite for adolescent participation in WLS. Familial support both before, during, and after surgery is essential for success. In fact, some authors have argued that when evaluating potential surgery candidates it is important to remember that the "patient" is both the adolescent and their family (Austin, Smith, & Ward, 2013). Further, maintaining supportive family relationships throughout the year following surgery can help maintain focus and maximize weight loss.

It has also been noted by practitioners in this field that adolescents and parents often differ in their views on obesity, its consequences, and the implications of surgery. Often obesity and its related health risks are more of a concern for the parents than they are for the teen. Adolescents may fail to grasp the gravity of certain medical issues, and all adolescents have challenges in understanding future thinking and planning, as these aspects of cognition are still under development. Parceling out parental concern from adolescent focus is an important component of the assessment process when screening patients for bariatric surgery. The adolescent must both want and commit to surgery and be able to implement the numerous self-care skills to thrive post-surgically.

Family-Based Therapy for Weight Loss Surgery (FBT-WLS)

Given that bariatric surgery is increasingly being turned to as an option for treating adolescent obesity and associated health risks, coupled with evidence of the effectiveness of family involvement in juvenile weight loss efforts, we propose that family-based therapy for adolescent weight loss surgery is a practicable intervention and one that is likely to promote successful outcome of this endeavor. However, the targets of this treatment are obviously different from those in standard FBT. Specific differences include greater collaboration in the selection of treatment targets, an emphasis on shared family efforts in adopting the practices discussed in treatment, and an emphasis on progression toward a specific goal of surgery. Although the therapist retains a stance of parental empowerment, a greater degree of education and behavioral shaping is present in FBT-WLS. Particular attention is given in our recommendations on the following issues:

- Adherence: working with families to promote attendance at medical appointments, compliance with dietary recommendations both before and after surgery, compliance with medical recommendations, and adherence to vitamin and supplement recommendations, which are critical components of post-surgery follow-up and need to be practiced prior to surgical intervention.
- Education: knowledge regarding surgical types and their necessary pre-surgical evaluations (e.g., endoscopy), as well as post-surgical follow-ups (e.g., vitamin supplementation differs between types of surgery).
- Developmental issues: given that adolescents are still well embedded in the family structure, involving families in their treatment makes sense particularly for this population where most of their meals are still being had with family members. Adolescents are notorious for pushing the limits, and this means closer observation to prevent breakthrough eating that may result in plugging, dumping, or other challenges. Further, adolescents are more drawn to rewards and tend to minimize risks (Casey, Jones, & Hare, 2008), and therefore they may over-estimate the benefits of WLS while minimizing the impact on their daily living.
- Empowerment: meeting families where they are and working to develop a plan that works for them while also reducing guilt and blame, similar to what has been done in traditional FBT. Families have often been working along with their youth to engage in weight loss efforts, and while may feel they have been ineffective in doing so, families have a lot of information about shape, weight, dietary, and lifestyle issues.

FBT-WLS as compared to traditional FBT for AN is much more collaborative and involves the teen in decision making. Transition between Phase 1 efforts targeting parental empowerment occur simultaneously with adolescent efforts at autonomy. Phase 2 focuses on the balance between these skills and continued practice or expansion of techniques targeting weight loss and adherence. We are working with the families to address how to shape family structure rather than parents taking over. The behaviors and activities practiced have to be things that teens will ultimately do themselves. Thus, parental empowerment is largely around "surveillance" rather than parental authority.

Initial Evaluation

Every bariatric patient seen at our clinic starts out with a thorough psychological evaluation and history taking that includes the family (see Appendix E, www.routledge.com/9780415714747). The information gathered in this assessment lays the groundwork for working with the family as they seek to support their child in promoting his or her health. This evaluation covers a variety of areas including diet and weight history, previous weight loss attempts, medical comorbidities and adherence history, family history of overweight and obesity, psychosocial functioning, quality of life, developmental history, insight into their current situation, academic and social functioning, knowledge and expectations of surgery, eating and activity habits, and motivation to change.

Assuming is it determined through the initial evaluation that the patient does not have significant psychiatric comorbidities that would impede their ability to be successful candidates for bariatric surgery, we would proceed with the following treatment protocol. If patients do have psychological, physical, or familial factors that are likely to make them ill-suited as candidates for surgery, we recommend referring them to appropriate providers who can address issues such as depression, binge eating disorder, anxiety or panic attacks, social phobia, agoraphobia, and school refusal. Addressing these issues first, through the appropriate treatment intervention, will give them the opportunity to return as candidates for surgery with the likelihood of success being greatly increased.

Three Phases of FBT-WLS

Phase I

Just as in standard FBT (Le Grange & Lock, 2007; Lock & Le Grange, 2013), the focus of the initial phase of treatment is designed to establish the importance of family in the weight loss efforts, to empower parents to engage and assist with those efforts. The therapist assumes the same sincere but grave manner as outlined in the initial session, gathers history on eating patterns and the impact on the patient and family, as well as orchestrates an intense scene around weight issues during the first session. The fundamental difference is in the provision of WLS specific didactics, and the focus of the intense scene is on medical comorbidities specific to this patient's illness.

An important distinction between traditional FBT for AN and FBT-WLS is that with the former, the main "push" for change occurs early on in the beginning of treatment when there is grave concern about the patients' malnourished state. In FBT-WLS this emphasis is shifted, with a slower build-up at the start of treatment, in which initial sessions are spent preparing for a significant change in the future. As a result the tenor and pacing of FBT-WLS is different than FBT for AN. There is a significant focus on providing families with knowledge that will allow them to make decisions to promote sustainable long-term change over time. An important early target therefore is to provide families with information about the surgical procedural options and the associated dietary and lifestyle changes. In our program, we also utilize a group training format to provide education around the surgical options, a service provided by a nurse practitioner specializing in WLS. This allows for a programmatic discussion of the path to surgery and provides information in a broad context, while the supporting therapy targets specific family/patient concerns regarding this process.

Where we follow weight in AN, we will follow weight, medical follow-up, and lab reports in our bariatric patients. Regular labs should include heart rate, blood pressure, cholesterol levels, hormone levels, and hemoglobin A1C's; while these are ordered by the physician team overseeing the weight loss, therapists should be prepared to discuss these findings with the family, using these as additional measures of success in treatment, much the same way vital sign stability can be celebrated with families facing AN. We do recommend weighing bariatric patients in sessions just as we do for AN and encourage them not to weigh outside of sessions as these frequent check-ins can provide information that is not meaningful yet can be distressing and misleading. Weight is an important variable for these patients just as it is in AN.

As discussed previously, adolescents seeking WLS have two options: RYGB or GS. While in some ways having these limited options may make the process of education easier, it may also leave the family with some difficulty in decision making that may lead them to seek knowledge and expertise from the therapist. It will be the therapist's job to educate the family on the implications of both RYGB and GS and to work with them to identify which option is most appropriate for them. However, it will be important for the therapist to explain that ultimately the choice about surgery is a family decision, with pros and cons to both surgical options.

Just as Venn diagrams are used in FBT-AN, they can also serve an important function in FBT-WLS. In FBT-WLS the different spheres represent the patient and the life he or she wants and can be used to illustrate how weight is impacting his or her ability to engage in this life. We want to encourage patients to think about the activities that they can begin to practice now, that are not tied to weight and shape issues, and therefore should be started to be practiced right away. Said a different way, it will be necessary to begin to develop coping skills early on in treatment, i.e., psychological coping skills. For example, how does the family negotiate what should be eaten early on in treatment, when should independence be increased, and what skills should patients have at their disposal? In contrast to FBT-AN, where all of the skills are fostered in the parents early on in treatment, and then later taught to the adolescent, in FBT-WLS we want the family deciding what skills to teach the adolescent, and where to have them take on more independence, early on in treatment.

We want families to select a procedure that they are likely to be successful with. If families remain on the fence, we recommend proceeding with preparing them for RYGB. Because RYGB has more significant limitations post-surgery and requires more radical lifestyle adjustment, preparing families for this procedure will promote their success should they choose to go this route and will only enhance their readiness for the less invasive GS.

Addressing Medical Comorbidities

Because adolescents who seek bariatric surgery have at least three major medical comorbidities, surgery should not begin until these are being managed by the adolescent and their family. Managed does not mean resolved, but it should be stressed during therapy that adherence to medical regimens, including regular attendance at medical appointments, is an essential part of the bariatric surgery process. For example, use of a C-PAP, follow-up with sleep study, endoscopy to check for H-pylori, pulmonary function, GI appointments. We are looking for greater consistency in these patients and families than may be typical for adolescents because that is exactly what is necessary for their health and successful outcome following surgery. Just as we would not see a patient with AN who was not medically stable for outpatient treatment, we would not continue to see patients for bariatric surgery who were not medically stable in the sense of being compliant and pro-active at addressing their medical comorbidities through regular medical monitoring and visits with physicians who are monitoring the ramifications of obesity. Thus our initial focus early on it treatment is on adherence, with the goal of managing the individual's comorbidities. Some families may need assistance with adherence—for example, they may need assistance with ensuring that their child uses their C-PAP and understanding the types of behavioral reward protocols that are well documented in the pediatric literature as promoting adherence to medical regimens. This can include interventions such as having structure around drinking appropriate amounts of fluids, taking medications and supplements, and understanding interactions between various medications and supplements. It is not the therapist's job to provide the education on the specific medical protocols and procedures; it is the therapist's job to help families with the adherence to these pre-existing regimens that are recommended by medical professionals. That is, parents are taught, in this therapy, behavioral principles about how to support their son or daughter in adhering to the necessary medical regimens, not taught what those specific regimens should be. The latter is the job of other medical professionals involved in the patient's care. This makes the therapist an important point person on the patients' team and highlights the necessity of working as members of a multi-disciplinary medical team. The therapist will necessarily be required to integrate recommendations from other team members, such as dieticians, primary care physicians, GI specialists, pulmonologists, endocrinologists, surgeons, sleep specialists, and pain specialists, to name a few. This is a potential challenge in FBT-WLS as the patient's team may be wider and more spread out compared to other multi-disciplinary teams, making coordination and integration of care more challenging. It is important that the therapist stay in contact with other team members to update them about psychosocial issues that have the potential to impact other aspects of the patient's care.

In working to encourage and highlight for families the reasons why early adherence and management of behaviors early on is important, we want to stress that adherence to medical regimens is likely to speed weight loss, improve healing, and promote resolution of comorbidities post-surgically. An excellent example of this is the area of sleep apnea. Many families we work with may not know how essential sleep is to promoting health and healing. The use of a C-PAP or Bi-PAP if indicated, or tonsillectomy adenoidectomy if necessary, will actually speed up weight loss and enhance healing post-surgically. Symptoms of obstructive sleep apnea can appear similar to ADHD and therefore can be particularly challenging because they can interfere with attention and learning as well as overall adherence.

Thus adherence to medical protocols is likely to enhance and improve desired outcomes from surgery. Adolescents' inherent tendency to have difficulty comprehending the impact of their current behaviors on future outcomes points to the reasoning behind involving parents in this process. When parents work collaboratively with teens, it increases the likelihood of medical compliance and, therefore, successful outcome post-surgically.

Adherence to Diet, Exercise, and Supplementation

The focus on adherence at this point in treatment may take up to 10 sessions. This will of course vary based on the needs of the individual patient and family, and therapists will need to be flexible at this stage in order to orchestrate treatment to each individual's and family's unique needs. It may also not be necessary to focus on adherence for the entire session, and this focus may actually change forms. For example, the same types of behaviors and strategies that are necessary for compliance with sleep apnea treatment may also apply to adherence with exercise requirements.

Following medical comorbidities, the second set of behaviors that we focus on are nourishment behaviors. Changing and shaping family expectations around food is key—in particular, reducing portion sizes, reducing caloric density, and adjusting frequency of eating, such that there are punctuated periods of re-nourishment, as much as five to six times per day, but of much smaller size. Our job is to educate families on the need for these changes and find out where they may be willing and able to make these changes. Typically for the families we work with this involves reducing sugars as initial treatment target goals. However, rather than reducing use of, it may be more effective to think about replacements. Helping families identify and find foods that are already preferred by the family, but in lower caloric density options, may be important and useful. Oftentimes this starts with eliminating sodas, then reducing fast foods, then reducing juices, and then reducing eating out behaviors. Sodas and other carbonated beverages are a first target, as these are a restriction following surgery and meet a secondary target of increasing the intake of other hydrating beverages. Other behaviors that can be targets, depending on a family's eating behaviors, include reducing fats and starches in the family's diets, switching from white starchy foods to whole grains, and limiting other types of sweets; eating more regular meals and eating more meals together as a family; and increasing vegetables and proteins.

The important task for the therapist is helping families think through *how* they are going to make these changes, in a manner that is suitable for each particular family. This can involve helping them identify recipes and consider what foods it makes the most sense to cut back on first, gauging how to best cut back on those foods and what to replace them with. They learn to identify what types of fruits and vegetables are most easily enjoyed, including raw, roasted, steamed, or sautéed vegetables; frozen vegetables are an excellent option. In some cases, we can encourage families to "think ahead" to the reintroduction of foods and find lower calorie mashed foods that can be tolerated in the weeks after surgery. We suggest families engage in practice with these changes as well as experimentation. In this way it is unlike standard FBT; we encourage the acquisition of new eating behaviors rather than a return to a more typical baseline set of behaviors.

Phase 2

Phase 2 is begun when the family is certain of the type of surgery they want and have made sufficient gains with medical adherence to begin to introduce more complex behaviors. The family will have been given sufficient dietary information and initiated change in eating habits. As we get closer to surgery, there is a need to focus on exercise, including increasing activities of daily living and reducing sedentary behaviors. These are often ideal places for families to focus energy because it increases family time and monitoring in ways that can be considered pleasurable. Finding ways to increase activities of daily living are often mutually beneficial to family members. Activities such as walking the dog, cleaning, vacuuming, gardening, and car-washing not only increase one's level of physical movement, they also have secondary benefits of accomplishing needed tasks and teaching youth important responsibility behaviors that can decrease the load on parents.

Another important area of consideration is identifying activities that are both adaptive for individuals of a larger size and do not cause pain. For many of our bariatric patients, walking, sitting, or engaging in other activities excessively can cause pain. We need to educate families around strategies that involve starting with small amounts of activity and building up as increasing levels are tolerated. For example, walking for 10 minutes, twice a day and then increasing to 15, 20, and so forth. This activity can also be incorporated into activities of daily living, such as having parents drop kids off within 10 minutes' walking distance from school, and then picking them up a mile away. Reducing sedentary behaviors can include things such stretching or practicing particular yoga exercises during commercials, sitting on a physio-ball while watching TV, and gradually increasing the length of time during which this is done: Start with sitting on the ball up to the first commercial, then switch to the couch, and work up to watching a full hour while sitting on the ball. They can also engage in strength training during usual sedentary activities—lifting weights or even soup cans while watching TV.

Three areas of exercise should be considered: aerobic, balance, and muscle building. We want our patients engaging in all three of these. Muscle building will help increase basal metabolic rate, keep the body strong, and prevent excessive muscle wasting post-surgery when the body is essentially starved of calories; we want the body to access fat stores, not just muscle sources. Thus strength training has multiple benefits for these patients. It will allow them to burn more calories at rest and will promote recovery post-surgery. Many muscle building tasks can be done while sedentary; for example, lifting small weights with legs while sitting, doing arm raises with soup cans while watching TV or engaging in other sedentary activities and using resistance bands and following videos that are appropriate for these patients, many of which can be found online, is another option.

Another important consideration regarding exercise is increasing aerobic capacity to strengthen the heart, speed gastric motility, and to address issues such as fatty liver, issues that are not as responsive to dietary changes as they are to exercise. Examples may include walking during therapy sessions to support methods for combining activities for families. Typically exercising in 10-minute bursts and participating in physical education activities at school are key targets. Also helping families understand the benefits of stretching, which can help reduce pain, increase flexibility, and help maintain a certain level of physicality while also promoting balance. With significant weight loss, balance often becomes impaired; the body shifts its center of gravity, and muscle is lost, so patients may become less stable. We know from the adult literature that falls and other balance accidents are common concerns post-surgically. Basic stretching and balance exercises can assist with reducing the likelihood of these events and promoting increased stability. They can also help alleviate pain for these patients.

In addition, many of our bariatric surgery patients have significant limitations on typical developmental activities that are not present in our AN and BN patients. For example, many of our bariatric patients are not performing up to par academically and may be on home hospital due to their high level of medical comorbidities. In addition, poverty may limit the available resources and ability to access services, including even access to healthy, viable food options to support their dietary changes. The therapist needs to evaluate the extent to which the family resources can support more typical and more adequate adolescent functioning. Engaging teens in regular academic functioning and involvement in school will actually boost their caloric needs. We need to be sensitive to the fact that academic environments are often not set up to accommodate larger patients, and they may need our support to intervene and ensure appropriate seating environments and allow for adequate time to transition in between classes. Therapists can help support adjustment by providing necessary documentation to help ease this transition and keep teens nested in appropriate services. Attempts to return the adolescent to more typically developmental functioning are a critical focus in Phase 2. Keeping our patients nested in the environments in which they will find themselves post-surgically can enhance their success with weight loss and allows them to "practice it like you will live it" in terms of lifestyle adaptations for weight loss.

The final area of adherence focuses on vitamin and mineral supplementation. The regular consumption of these post-surgically is essential, and research has shown that adolescents struggle with adherence to these requirements in particular (Modi, Zeller, Xanthakos, Jenkins, & Inge, 2013). Helping families set up a regular schedule and practicing these behaviors prior to surgery, for example by taking daily multi-vitamins, is an important component of FBT-WLS. Following dietician guidelines for other vitamins and minerals, including ones that may need to be taken in larger doses, can be incorporated as well. Most adolescents' lives do not have the consistency and predictability of adult lives, and so helping them design and adhere to vitamin and supplement regimens that can be incorporated into their often shifting, transitioning and unstructured routines can be a challenging task. Considering challenges, such as blocked schedules at school, school year versus summer vacation, and changing after school activities, will be important for families as they work to set up viable schedules for health behaviors.

Inconsistency with structure can also impact physical activity. During summer, adolescents may be more physically active or the opposite may occur—without motivation or reason to walk to and from school, they may become more sedentary. Concerns with teasing from others, excessive sweating, or other impediments are important to address in treatment. Helping *parents* find ways to address this and promote physical activity year round is an important component of FBT-WLS. This falls squarely in Phase 2, as such discussions include ways in which the adolescent will take greater control over directing these choices as a means of supporting their efforts at lifestyle change. This is also the time in treatment when initial motivations have worn off, but weight loss may not have occurred (although weight stabilization is common and evidence of consistent behavioral change). As such, it may become harder for the patient and family to engage in or reward the changes mastered in Phase 1.

Exercise can be supported in several ways. The first is to encourage "workout buddies" and partners in these efforts, most commonly from family members. Friends may also be a useful support. While walking is free, relatively easy, and can be part of directed efforts at activities of daily living, we also encourage other forms of exercise in order to maximize weight loss and minimize boredom, such as sitting on a balance ball while watching television, using a standing desk, using resistance bands to engage in strength training, or doing seated stretches while on the laptop; these are all ways of adding in small doses of physical activity.

Additional areas of dietary concerns. While the strategies taught in Phase 1 focus on changing diet and exercise, these are refined in Phase 2 to address the specific needs of the adolescents facing surgical intervention. These may vary based on the differences in post-surgical requirements of the different interventions. The main interventions include cutting out carbonated beverages and juices, chewing and swallowing foods, monitoring satiety and feelings of fullness, and managing social events and activities. Cutting out carbonated beverages is a positive, as most are filled with empty calories, but is a must following surgery where carbonated beverages are prohibited. Another important factor influencing both satiety and post-surgical care involves mindful eating practices such as slow and methodical chewing of food. Adolescents are encouraged to practice chewing food 30–50 times and getting support with this from family members. Ironically, paying attention to chewing and swallowing can often result in biting of the tongue or cheeks, as formerly smooth motor movements are re-modeled and slowed. A side benefit of excessive chewing is that it slows the consumption of the meal, allowing for physiological regulating processes to "catch up" with intake, trending toward decreased overall intake.

The challenges facing our patients are also those that face families as a whole. Families may need help recognizing that meal times may take longer, thus the need to adjust family and homework schedules to accommodate mealtime adjustments. Prior to and early post-surgery, a liquid diet prevails. Practice being on a liquid diet and tolerating the hunger that comes with this are key goals for Phase 2. Adolescents can practice by learning to tolerate meal replacement with liquid supplements at one meal, then increasing this to two meals per day. Rarely do we encourage complete supplementation, as we prefer that patients practice eating sufficiently to support nutrition post-surgically. Going too quickly can lead to great hunger and compensatory eating behaviors, even binges, which should be avoided where possible. Given that small, frequent eating behaviors are key, particularly following RYGB, the challenge of finding healthy snacks that can be easily transported presents real difficulties. The introduction of high protein, low fiber, easily reduced foods, such as eggs (scrambled, mashed) or small portions of ground meats can assist with dietary efforts. Practicing with making these meals sufficiently different as to satisfy the palate while also addressing eating challenges are worth good practice. Protein supplementation is also important, given the different metabolic needs post-surgically, particularly following RYGB. Liquid supplements or protein "shakes" come in many types and flavors and should be sampled by patients and their families; whey-, soy-, and nut-based products all exist, and many are flavored (e.g., vanilla, strawberry), but care should be taken to avoid supplements that also have unknown ingredients and attention should be paid to sugars. In addition, consuming too much soy through supplementation has been linked to endocrine disruption in women, although no data exists on such difficulties arising post-bariatric surgery. Also, it is important to be careful of the sugar content and herbal supplementation that is often present in these foods; many of these products have stimulants in them, presenting significant concern and strongly discouraged for these patients at any point but particularly post-surgically.

Phase 3: Adjustment and Coping

The final phase of FBT-WLS focuses on adjustment issues. Although we anticipate that WLS will have a positive impact on the adolescent's life, it is important for the therapist to prepare the patient and the family for the impact of these changes. Positive changes can still be stressful, and it is important to provide an opportunity for the patient and family to explore and plan for potential issues that may arise. Just as in Phase 3 of traditional FBT for AN, the focus is on returning the teen to typical adolescent development that the eating disorder interrupted. Phase 3 in FBT-WLS focuses on socialization changes that are due to both surgery as well as issues that may have been interrupted in the teen's life due to limitations on health prior to weight loss.

The first area we want to address in the section of adjustment and coping is that of self- and other-perception. When change happens rapidly, even when it is change that is desired, the impact can be stressful. Adolescent patients in particular are unlikely to be prepared for the shift in how they view themselves, how they perceive others viewing them, and the changing way others will relate to them. Although research has suggested that overall, adolescents show improved psychosocial functioning following WLS, evidence shows a portion of teens may deteriorate, and it is difficult to determine who may be affected this way (Järvholm et al., 2012). We want to help our patients and their families think about how they are going to cope with these often unexpected changes. Many overweight patients report feeling that others "look through" them. When patients change to having a more normal-sized body, they experience a marked shift in the degree of attention they receive, and while this can be exciting, it can also be disconcerting. Helping our patients and their families think through how they might respond to and cope with this is an important task of FBT-WLS.

Some adolescent WLS patients have limited social experience due to ostracism because of their size, or worse, may have experienced direct teasing and bullying. Others develop coping strategies, such as the use of humor or an "edgy" style that may successfully mask challenging feelings but also leave them without close relationships. These experiences can severely and negatively impact the development of social skills and may result in difficulties in this area. The therapist must sensitively and empathically address these issues with the family. Families should be encouraged to think about age-appropriate social activities that they believe their child should participate in and work to develop strategies to assist them in these endeavors. In-vivo opportunities to shape social skills and dialogue are also important, and the therapist can serve as a model for more appropriate relationships, development of intimacy, and appropriate emotional self-disclosure. Indeed, this is an excellent use of the therapeutic relationship itself, as the "unfolding" of the therapeutic relationship is akin to the subtle levels of intimacy that sustain friendships.

In this discussion, it is important to consider that while bariatric surgery may have a positive impact on an adolescent's socialization, it can also pose real limitations. For example, eating out is a common social activity for teens. Especially immediately following surgery, adolescent patients will have dietary restrictions that may limit their ability to eat in restaurants. Planning how to engage in social activities while still adhering to necessary nutritional behaviors and guidelines is an important part of Phase 3 in FBT-WLS. Suggestions include scheduling time with peers focusing on an activity other than eating.

After adult bariatric surgery, the risk of death is higher compared to the general population, due to both accidents and suicide (Peterhänsel et al., 2014). Although some of these may be related to increased opportunities for risk-taking behaviors, an increased risk for death by suicide remains a potent risk factor with very few useful determinants of this most tragic of outcomes. Evaluating and improving upon existing coping strategies and self-management techniques bears significant attention. Distress may be caused by many factors, including significant changes in activities, relationships, and future planning. Among the more challenging aspects is helping imprint a realistic expectation of post-surgical life. Patients often think that having surgery is going to change everything in their lives, and while often it changes many things, it may not always do so in the manner expected. Bariatric surgery changes how you eat, how you interact with food, and what you can do socially in terms of mobility and accessibility. However, it does not fix all social and interpersonal problems. People often enter bariatric surgery with beliefs about what the outcome and their life afterwards will be like. Frequently these expectations do not fit the actual experience. We want to explore with our patients and families what their individual beliefs are, how realistic they are, and how they might cope if things turn out differently.

Preparations for the physiological outcomes of surgery are also important areas to review at the end of treatment. Following surgery, particularly with RYGB, the body does not metabolize alcohol the same way: higher levels of intoxication are reached on lower quantities of alcohol, and these effects take significantly longer to wear off. This is not just a function of losing weight, and patients should be well-aware of the unexpected outcome of intoxication and associated risks (e.g., DUIs, accidents). Certain medications may also be metabolized differently, and all prescription and over-the-counter medications and supplements should be regularly reviewed by a pharmacist and the treatment team to guard against interactions and ensure that the doses are appropriate for each patient. This is particularly true with psychiatric medications as this period of rapid personal transition is a risk factor for relapse.

Post-Surgical Follow-Up

Post-surgery is a time of significant psychosocial as well as physical risk. The adult literature is most informative here, as there is no extant literature on adolescents. It is relatively well documented in the literature that post-surgical complications include heightened risk for accidents, death, and psychiatric complications such as anxiety (often related to changes in the body) as well as depression (Peterhänsel et al., 2008). Accidents and heightened risk for death are correlated with substance use, in particular alcohol use, in adults. However, other unknown factors likely contribute to these risks and may be exacerbated for adolescents. For example, their younger age suggests fewer experiences with alcohol or drugs—and certainly active substance use would be a rule-out against surgical interventions—and they are likely to be less familiar with symptoms of intoxication than adults.

Another area related to physical concerns is that of excessive skin following surgery. With rapid weight-loss, skin loses elasticity, and patients are often left with large amounts of excess skin. Skin folds can be substantial and can, in some cases, mask some of the effects of weight-loss. The treatment for this is a body-shaping surgery, an intervention that is rarely covered by insurance as it is considered a cosmetic procedure. When told about the potential for excessive skin following WLS, patients often say they don't mind and don't think they will want or need body-shaping surgery. In fact, when asked pre-surgery about body-shaping surgery, only a minority of bariatric patients say they would like this and are planning for it; post-surgery, as much as three years later, a strong majority of patients express a desire for body shaping treatments, and this is especially true for women (Staalesen, Fagevik Olsén, & Elander, 2013). The more weight people lose (i.e., the more successful they are), the more likely they are to want body-shaping surgery. This is likely to be particularly true for our adolescent patients, for whom self-image and appearance-related concerns are often highly salient. We want our patients to at least consider these issues, so they and their families can begin to think through how these concerns might be approached.

We conclude our chapter with a case study.

Case Study

Sebastian is a sixteen-year-old male presenting with a life-long history of being overweight, becoming morbidly obese by age eight. He presented to the weight loss clinic for bariatric surgery consideration after one year of being followed by clinicians to assist him with weight loss. During this time period, he and his family met with medical specialists, dieticians, and a pain clinic for pain that limited his mobility, in addition to joining a gym and working with a personal trainer. Despite efforts by the family, weight loss was minimal, although the family was able to halt Sebastian's weight gain. The family and medical team decided upon a bariatric surgery consultation to determine if he was an appropriate candidate for surgical interventions to address his weight and medical comorbidities.

Assessment for Surgical Readiness

Sebastian and his family were seen by the team psychologist for two sessions over approximately three hours. The information gathered can be found in Appendix E (see www.routledge.com/9780415714747; Bariatric Surgery Evaluation form), developed by Rebecca S. Bernard and modified by the child and adult bariatric teams at Stanford. The family reported that Sebastian had a lifetime history of being overweight. He was a healthy eater in infancy, fed primarily by bottle. His family reported no early health concerns, and all milestones were met within normal limits.

Weight History. By the time Sebastian completed fifth grade, however, he was morbidly obese, weighing in at 150 pounds at a height of 59 inches. His parents reported that their entire family was overweight, on both sides, but that this was particularly prominent on the maternal side. Even with this positive history, Sebastian was clearly the largest among his nuclear family and his weight trajectory was a steep upward line on his growth charts, falling above the 99.9th percentile and with a BMI of 49.6. His family had then spent time looking at diets. They participated in Weight Watchers as a family, following the diet for roughly six months. They also tried to increase his participation in athletic activities and physical education at school. Sebastian began playing American football for his high school team. However, he was prone to injury and felt significant pain in his knees and back. His coaches provided nutritional advice and encouraged the use of weight loss supplements, of which his parents were unaware. These were largely appetite suppressants and herbal formulas. They also recommended a high-protein diet and weight lifting. Sebastian found working out with the team was useful for weight maintenance but again felt pain with weight lifting. At the end of his first year of high school, Sebastian was tall, at close to six feet in height weighing 405 pounds.

Medical History. Although he had few medical concerns in early childhood, Sebastian had a host of health concerns at the time of his presentation for weight loss surgery consideration. His medical comorbidities included obstructive sleep apnea (OSA) for which he had a prescription CPAP. He had also been diagnosed with hyperinsulinemia, hypercholesterolemia, dyslipidemia, and acanthosis nigricans. At the time of referral, he was being evaluated by cardiology due to some concerns regarding episodes of tachycardia and both orthopedics and pain clinic regarding his knee and back pain. His pain was significant enough that he had been placed on exercise restriction; though he still attended all practices, he did not participate athletically. He was also scheduled to complete several follow-up tests, including an endoscopy and a follow-up sleep study.

Eating Behaviors. Sebastian and his family denied most symptoms of eating disorder. Sebastian denied any purging episodes, use of diet pills, herbal supplements, diuretics, laxatives for weight loss, or caffeine for appetite attenuation. However, his coach had given him an unknown "appetite suppressant," which was likely an over-the-counter diet pill. The family also denied extended periods of fasting, though he had tried a "cleanse" on the advice of his coaches where he consumed only liquids: cranberry juice with lemon, orange, and cinnamon. On the fifth day of this diet, Sebastian reported being very dizzy at football camp, and when he came home, he and his mother described an episode of frank binge eating: the family was at a family party with a buffet style of food; Sebastian ate until he felt sick, then continued to eat until he "couldn't move." Although it was difficult to ascertain the degree to which there was a true "loss of control" from Sebastian's report, it was evident from the family report that Sebastian was unable to cease eating, that he ate well past the point of fullness, and other family members attempted to intervene and were unsuccessful. Sebastian reported great shame around this event but also was able to note that his diet over the days preceding the binge-eating episode contributed to feelings of deprivation and hunger that resulted in significant rebound eating. In general, however, the family described Sebastian's eating as being a strong drive toward food, frequent feelings of hunger, eating while bored, eating larger portions, and "enjoying food[s] that are more fattening." He reported a strong preference for sweets, carbohydrates, and fats. He felt he "couldn't resist" when being offered foods by friends or others and was particularly prone to over-eating cookies and tortilla chips. The family had been working with a dietician and had eliminated all sodas from the home, although these were still available at parties and sporting events, and Sebastian considered these "treats" that he could have when not at home, approximately two times per week on average. He had juice most days and sports drinks during practice. Although the family had been working to reduce eating out and fast food in particular, the busy family schedule and frequent team events meant that Sebastian often ate fast food and take-out with his family. The family had breakfast and dinner together most days, but Sebastian was engaging in eating behaviors outside the home on most occasions.

The family's 24-hour recall of Sebastian's intake was as follows: His 24-hour recall of intake was extremely limited as he "can't remember" even when prompted by the examiner. He stated that he wakes early to help in the family business, but he typically does not eat until around 7:30. The day prior to the intake he had two pears for breakfast, then later stated that he "may have had some chips" but could not say what kind or how much. He skips lunch and often sleeps during the day or goes out with his "uncles" (who are relatively close in age to Sebastian). He reported that he ate dinner at a taqueria with his uncle and friends where they ate nachos with chips, cheese, beans, meat, salsa, guacamole, and sour cream. He reported only eating half but indicated a very large serving size. He felt this was somewhat typical of his eating, describing a light breakfast typically of fruits (pears and apples, predominantly) or cereal at times. He frequently eats fruits and frequently skips meals, in particular lunch.

Sebastian's exercise is limited and sporadic. His uncle has weights and has been "trying to get more fit," and he has included Sebastian in weight lifting and healthy exercises although this sounds inconsistent. He reported that he plays (American) football and rides bikes, but then stated he does not have his own bike and "borrows" one—just to "ride around," and he was unable to elaborate as to where he goes or with whom. Sebastian could state that he cannot do the things he would like to do, such as more football, but this is also due to his failure to attend school at this time (see below), and his grades were too poor to participate in school athletics. He noted some interest in boxing but then stated that he does not think he would do this.

He continues to engage in significant screen time, watching television or spending time playing video games, but most often movies and television. The family has attempted to reduce this, but with the recent birth of Sebastian's brother and ongoing difficulties in managing Sebastian's behavior, he has continued to have a minimum of four to five hours of screen time per day as well as some daytime napping. Suggestions for increasing activities associated with daily living were provided to Sebastian and his mother, although Sebastian was resistant to these as they "meant doing more chores in addition to work!"

Sebastian denied being dissatisfied with his body shape and weight. In contrast, his mother reported that Sebastian is sensitive to discussions and teasing around his weight. He has been teased at school by peers, and this has been very challenging—and a reason why Sebastian is no longer in school. Sebastian expressed a desire to lose 75 to 100 pounds for "health reasons." He does not want to return to school and desires to return to home-schooling, as he has been from kindergarten to ninth grade and denied that weight loss was a factor in this. He would like to lose weight

Bariatric Surgery Knowledge. Sebastian expressed a strong interest in bariatric surgery although he noted he has some reluctance in seeking assistance in meeting health or weight loss goals. He has attended a bariatric surgery information session, though he admitted he had difficulty retaining this information and was not certain about the different surgery types. These were reviewed with him, and he noted that he had been leaning toward gastric sleeve, although he admitted he would prefer gastric bypass if it meant more weight loss. When we reviewed the need for greater dietary restrictions associated with gastric bypass, Sebastian quickly stated that he would not pursue the more invasive surgery due to his concerns about the dietary restrictions.

Surgical Determination

Sebastian did not present with any specific rule-outs for surgery, despite numerous concerns regarding his ability to be successful with surgery at the time of the initial assessment. It was determined that the examiner concerns could be addressed with FBT for weight-loss surgery with a highlight on the following features: continued education on surgical preparations, surgical interventions, and post-surgical expectations. Following education, treatment goals should emphasize family changes to intake and exercise with a goal of reducing Sebastian's screen time and increasing adherence with eating smaller, more frequent meals. Establishing coping strategies that support post-surgical behaviors, including spending time with friends, developing work or educational skills, and strategies for managing changing emotions (e.g., frustration, pride, sadness).

Course of FBT

The sessions begin with an explanation of the process of therapy, all relevant disclosures and gathering informed consent. In family therapy, we note that we are the therapist for the entire family and that any family member's behaviors may be a target of interventions, focusing particularly on letting parents and siblings know that we may be asking them to modify their behaviors. Sebastian's family was very open with this and consented to videotaping of sessions as well.

The therapist then laid out the process of pursuing weight loss surgery as a map to identify targets for treatment. This included mapping out goals for weight loss, as Sebastian's surgeon expressed concerns around fatty liver disease and requested that Sebastian aim for weight loss to reduce risks associated with having to retract his liver during surgery. In addition, Sebastian had several other areas for follow-up as he progressed to surgery, and these were added as targets for therapeutic intervention. Most importantly, the family was encouraged to describe the behaviors that they felt were limiting weight loss and health-related behaviors. Sebastian noted that feelings of pain were limiting his healthy behaviors, while his mother felt that it was lack of structure that led to fast food and hectic, pressured eating. This led to two focal points for the initial part of therapy: Sebastian's regular attendance at appointments, including therapy appointments, and a reduction in fast-food intake.

With regard to the first aspect, Sebastian and his mother compiled a list of appointments, and together in treatment, we made efforts to determine which would be most important. Because pain impacted Sebastian's ability to engage in continuous exercise, the first set of appointments were to the pain clinic. Sebastian's mother helped him make appointments and set these on the schedule, with plans to take notes and determine additional appointments. This took relatively little of the session time, as making the initial appointment took a sum total of 10 minutes. The remainder of the time was focused on noting all the times that Sebastian ate fast food with and without the family. Sebastian's mother reported that all family members would benefit from a reduction in fast food and this would be an area that she could also assess for compliance. Needless to say, Sebastian's family was not thrilled with this idea, as all reported enjoying fast food. They determined that breakfast was the least enjoyable fast-food meal and therefore the one to be least contested. Of course, determining what to eliminate is only half the battle, as it also requires that the meal be replaced with something homemade, of superior quality, and with fewer calories than what could be eaten outside the home. As such, a good portion of the first few sessions was in problem solving what to serve for breakfast. The focus was on serving a higher protein, high fiber meal to lend feelings of fullness to prevent early snacking and, hopefully, reduce snacking and the potential for further eating outside of the home. The family tried several options: cereals, waffles, pancakes, muffins, and finally settled on a meal of scrambled eggs in a corn tortilla with salsa, which could be carried out the door and eaten "on the go" as well as prepared prior to breakfast time. Most importantly, all family members enjoyed these and found ways to vary them up (changing salsa, adding some cheese or avocado) to provide differences in flavors so as to avoid boredom. Weekends were often a bit different, with a focus on later, larger family breakfasts.

During the time that breakfasts were being worked out and problems identified and overcome, Sebastian also had his consultation with the pain clinic and was referred to ongoing physical therapy. This led to an increasing number of appointments for the family, which was challenging, but also beneficial, as Sebastian reported feeling stronger and decreased pain. As part of his physical therapy, he was instructed to engage in physical activity on a daily basis. He practiced walking as well as engaging in core exercises. He was given a therapy ball for strengthening his back and core, and he worked on sitting on the ball during screen time. This meant he was both more aware of how long he was engaging in screen time (as it was challenging to sit on the ball and balance for more than 15 minutes). In this way, one can see that the goal of weight loss was targeted through multiple interventions. By session six, Sebastian was eating breakfast at home, had reduced his fast-food consumption by three meals per week, and had increased his exercise from almost completely sedentary behavior to 15 to 20 minutes of exercise five days per week. He was also attending physical therapy twice per week.

In the second part of Phase 1, the family reported wanting to target increasing exercise and eliminating sweetened beverage intake entirely. The former was met with several ready suggestions for activities, including boxing, hip hop dancing, and walking. The latter, however, was met with groans and displeasure by most members of the family. They noted enjoying soda, feeling deprived by the lack of soda, and also expressed great surprise at the impact of juice on both calorie and sugar intake. The children of the family, in particular, endorsed feeling that eliminating these beverages would also impact social activities. As such, the family adopted a "scale back" model. First, they replaced all sweetened beverages with diet versions and aimed to cut back on the consumption of these by 50 percent. The family reported this was generally quite successful and met with relatively little resistance, which was surprising to parents. The family was encouraged to find other options, such as fruit-infused waters and unsweetened teas, in addition to increasing water intake. Sebastian struggled with this, reporting he did not want to give up sodas, but discovered that he liked sparkling water with lemon. In addition, at a follow-up visit with the endocrinologist, his doctor immediately noted an improvement in urine specific gravity and complimented Sebastian. Sebastian volunteered at football practice, despite being ineligible due to grades and non-attendance, and he received kudos from his peers and coaches regarding his changes. His peers were willing to walk with him and engage in "cool downs," and he was given permission to use the weight room and engage in training. This led to many more opportunities for physical activity as well as peer engagement.

This led to the family making several additional changes during Phase 2. Despite all of the activity and several steps toward change, Sebastian's weight changed relatively little, though he was more physically active and quite a bit more fit. He reported fewer days of pain and agreed to enroll in school for the fall semester. However, he began experiencing periods of "rebelliousness" with his parents and his diet. At school he would eat school lunches, binge on cookies, and avoided coming home to allow himself the opportunity to eat with his peers, again returning to fast food and other less health-based choices. His team staged a family meeting, noting that he was unlikely to be eligible for surgery without concerted effort to change several areas: continuing to reduce his intake of sweets and "junk" foods, eating regular meals, and continuing to exercise regularly. This spurred the family to increased resolution and efforts were made to target lunch, particularly when the family was reminded about their success with breakfasts, which had continued with some changes. The family reported a desire to try Weight Watchers and this was encouraged, provided Sebastian did this with his family, rather than alone.

The emphasis on this portion of treatment was on continued emphasis on health-related behaviors and identifying triggers for maladaptive eating. Sebastian's family noted that they associated eating out with family time and began to work toward more healthy family activities. They attended folk dances and school activities and also began going to football and other sporting activities together. Replacing sedentary with physical behaviors became a significant focus, and the family worked out ways to try different activities. In this case, Sebastian's mother tied rewards to activities (going to a sporting event) and rewards were also linked to physical activity. The family continued to work on changing their diet with a focus on continuing to reduce eating out. Sebastian's struggles with school intensified, and he was referred for psychological testing. Testing revealed some learning difficulties, and school accommodations were put in place. This helped alleviate family stress, and the parents reported decreased conflict at home, and Sebastian's own mood improved. Given his academic improvements, he had the ability to become eligible for sports, which further increased his motivation.

Phase 3, unlike being considered a period of remission from illness, instead focuses upon surgical preparation. For Sebastian, this meant practicing with liquid diets and continuing to practice reducing portion sizes and eating more frequent meals. Sebastian's family was encouraged by tests indicating that his medical difficulties were improving. He was more physically active and, although he still had periods of eating more than would be considered appropriate post-surgically, his family supported him in pursuing foods that would be suitable post-surgically. Daily supplements were introduced, giving Sebastian time to practice with his medication regimen post-surgically. Continued adjustment at school assisted with these efforts.

Sebastian had a sleeve-gastrectomy nine months after initiating a surgical evaluation. He was capable of eating several small meals, was engaged in school, and has a social life and peers that supported his change in lifestyle. Although he did not tell many people, his weight loss, which had started pre-surgically, was maximized post-surgically. At his three-month follow-up he had lost 30 pounds and was noticeably more active and quick in his movements. His family reported continued adherence with post-surgical protocols.

References

AACE/ACE Obesity Task Force (1998). Position statement on the prevention, diagnosis and treatment of obesity. *Endocrine Practice, 4,* 297–330.

Austin, H., Smith, K., & Ward, W. L. (2013) Psychological assessment of the adolescent bariatric surgery candidate. *Surgery for Obesity and Related Diseases, 9,* 474–481. doi: 10.1016/j.soard.2012.12.004

Black, J. A., White, B., Viner, R. M., & Simmons, R. K. (2013). Bariatric surgery for obese children and adolescents: A systematic review and meta-analysis. *Obesity Reviews, 14,* 634–644. doi: 10.1111/obr.12037

Casey, B. J., Jones, R. M., & Hare, T. A. (2008). The adolescent brain. *Annals of the New York Academy of Sciences, 1124,* 111–126. doi: 10.1196/annals.1440.010

Chandra, V., Dutta, S., Albanese, C. T., Shepard, E., Farrales-Nguyen, S., & Morton, J. (2007). Clinical resolution of severely symptomatic pseudotumor cerebri after gastric bypass in an adolescent. *Surgery for Obesity and Related Diseases, 3,* 198–200. doi: 10.1016/j.soard.2006.11.015

Colquitt, J. L., Picot, J., Loveman, E., & Clegg, A. J. (2009). Surgery for obesity. *Cochrane Database of Systematic Reviews, 2,* CD003641.

Epstein, L. H., Valoski, A., Wing, R. R., McCurley, J. (1994). Ten-year outcomes of behavioral family-based treatment for childhood obesity. *Health Psychology, 13,* 373–383.

Hofmann, B. (2013). Bariatric surgery for obese children and adolescents: a review of moral challenges. *BMC Medical Ethics, 14:18,* 1–13. http://www.biomedcentral.com/1472-6939/14/18.

Järvholm, K., Olbers, T., Marcus, C., Marild, S., Gronowitz, E., Friberg, P., & Johnsson, P. (2012). Short-term psychological outcomes in severely obese adolescents after bariatric surgery. *Obesity (Silver Spring), 20,* 318–323.

Kalarchian, M. A., Levine, M. D., Arslanian, S. A., Ewing, L. J., Houck, P. R., Cheng, Y., Marcus, M. D. (2009). Family-based treatment of severe pediatric obesity: Randomized, controlled trial. *Pediatrics, 124,* 1060–1068; originally published online September 28, 2009; doi: 10.1542/peds.2008-3727

Le Grange, D., & Lock, J. (2007). *Treating bulimia in adolescents: A family-based approach.* New York, NY: The Guilford Press.

Lock, J., & Le Grange, D. (2013). *Treatment manual for anorexia-nervosa: A family-based approach* (2nd ed.). New York, NY: The Guilford Press.

Loux, T. J., Haricharan, R. N., Clements, R. H., Kolotkin, R. L., Bledsoe, S. E., Haynes, B., Harmon, C.M. (2008). Health-related quality of life before and after bariatric surgery in adolescents. *Journal of Pediatric Surgery, 43,* 1275–1279. doi: 10.1016/j.jpedsurg.2008.02.078

Michalsky, M., Reichard, K., Inge, T., Pratt, J., & Lenders, C. (2012). ASMBS pediatric committee best practice guidelines. *Surgery for Obesity and Related Diseases, 8,* 1–7. doi: 10.1016/j.soard.2011.09.009

Modi, A. C., Zeller, M. H., Xanthankos, S. A., Jenkins, T. M., & Inge, T. H. (2013). Adherence to vitamin supplementation following adolescent bariatric surgery. *Obesity, 21,* 190–195. doi: 10.1002/oby.20031

Nowicka, P. & Flodmark, C. E. (2008). Family in pediatric obesity management: a literature review. *International Journal of Pediatric Obesity, 3*, 44–50. doi:10.1080/17477160801896994

Ogden, C. L., Carroll, M. D., Kit, B. K., & Flegal, K. M. (2014). Prevalence of childhood and adult obesity in the United States, 2011–2012. *The Journal of the American Medical Association, 311*, 806–814. doi:10.1001/jama.2014.732

Peterhänsel, C., Petroff, D., Klinitzke, G., Kersting, A., & Wagner, B. (2014). Risk of completed suicide after bariatric surgery: A systematic review. *Obesity Reviews, 14*, 369–382. doi: 10.1111/obr.12014

Rapoff, M. (2010). *Adherence to pediatric medical regimens* (2nd ed.) New York, NY: Springer Science+Business Media.

Roehrig, H. R., Stavra, A., Xanthakos, M. D., Jenny Sweeney, R. N., Zeller, M. H., & Inge, T. H. (2007). Pregnancy after gastric by-pass surgery in adolescents. *Obesity Surgery, 17*, 873–877. doi: 10.1007/s11695-007-9162-7

Shrewsbury, V. A., Steinbeck, K. S., Torvaldsen, S., & Baur, L. A. (2011). The role of parents in pre-adolescent and adolescent overweight and obesity treatment: A systematic review of clinical recommendations. *Obesity Reviews, 12*, 759–769. doi: 10.1111/j.1467-789X.2011.00882.x

Staalesen, T., Fagevik Olsén, M., & Elander, A. (2013). Experience of excess skin and desire for body contouring surgery in post-bariatric patients. *Obesity Surgery, 23*, 1632–1644. doi: 10.1007/s11695-013-0978-z

Treadwell, J. R., Sun, F., & Schoelles, K. (2008). Systematic review and meta-analysis of bariatric surgery for pediatric obesity. *Annals of Surgery, 248*, 763–776. doi: 10.1097/SLA.0b013e31818702f4.

Xanthakos, S. A., & Inge, T. H. (2006). Nutritional consequences of bariatric surgery. *Current Opinion in Clinical Nutrition & Metabolic Care, 9*, 489–496. doi: 10.1097/01.mco.0000232913.07355.cf

Zeller, M. H., Modi, A. C., Noll, J. G., Long, J. D., & Inge, T. H. (2009). Psychosocial functioning improves following adolescent bariatric surgery. *Obesity, 17*, 985–990. doi: 10.1038/oby.2008.644

Integrating Dialectical Behavior Therapy with Family Therapy for Adolescents with Affect Dysregulation

Kelly Bhatnagar and Lucene Wisniewski

A comprehensive review was recently published highlighting the efficacy of family-based interventions for the treatment of adolescent eating disorders (EDs) (Downs & Blow, 2013). Of these interventions, Family-Based Treatment (FBT), or the "Maudsley Model" (Lock, Le Grange, Agras, & Dare, 2001; Lock & Le Grange, 2012), is considered particularly efficacious in treating a large number of adolescents suffering from Anorexia Nervosa (AN) and Bulimia Nervosa (BN) (Eisler et al., 2000).

Despite these promising findings, not all adolescent patients respond satisfactorily to existing family-based treatment models. In fact, as many as 50 percent of adolescent patients may not achieve full ED remission using FBT alone, thus requiring alternative or supplementary treatment (Le Grange, Binford, & Loeb, 2005; Lock et al., 2010). If research can identify predictors of treatment response, then novel approaches can be developed in the hope of ameliorating outcome. Although still early in the scientific study process, certain variables have been found to be related to successful or poorer outcomes in FBT. In terms of successful outcomes, the FBT model is considered most viable and effective for individuals with early onset (before age 19) and short duration (less than three years) illnesses (Eisler et al., 1997; Russell, Szmukler, Dare, & Eisler, 1987). Early response to treatment (i.e., gaining a minimum of four pounds in four weeks) has also been found to predict success in FBT (Doyle, Le Grange, Loeb, Doyle, & Crosby, 2010; Lock, Couturier, Bryson, & Agras, 2006). Poor treatment response in FBT has been linked to several variables. Data suggest that young patients with moderate to severe ED symptoms, presenting with comorbid psychiatric disorders, parent history of psychiatric illness, greater emotion dysregulation (e.g., suicidal/self-injurious behaviors, problems with anger), and/or personality disorder features (e.g., emerging borderline personality disorder traits) may not do as well with the standard FBT model and are considered "difficult to treat" using FBT alone (Le Grange, Crosby, & Lock, 2008; Lock et al., 2006). Families considered high in expressed criticism and expressed emotion may also make FBT in its standard form more of a challenge and less effective (Eisler et al., 2000; Eisler, Simic, Russell, & Dare, 2007; Treasure et al., 2008).

While many adolescent patients will respond positively to standard FBT, it is imperative that the ED field explore other models that might help those who are not fully helped by standard FBT. Given FBT's success rate, however, the authors speculate that it may make more sense to *add* to FBT rather than to replace it. Ideally, an adjunctive treatment would support the basic tenets of FBT while still directly addressing factors that can lead to poorer treatment response in the standard model and/or interfere with FBT delivery by requiring a clinical algorithm to concurrently manage emergent comorbidity. Dialectical Behavior Therapy (DBT) may offer such a model. DBT provides a theoretical framework and intervention toolbox for addressing complex ED presentations due to comorbidities, emotion dysregulation, and problematic family (i.e., expressed criticism) or patient (e.g., self-harm, having multiple problems) behaviors.

The goals of this chapter are to (1) provide an overview of DBT, (2) offer rationale for how DBT may be used to augment standard FBT when treatment response is insufficient, particularly when affect dysregulation is part of the clinical picture, and (3) present a model for how an integrated FBT-DBT approach is used in the authors' clinical practice.

DBT & DBT-A: An Overview

DBT is a comprehensive outpatient treatment that was originally designed to target recurrent suicidal and self-injurious behaviors in adult women suffering from borderline personality disorder (BPD) (Linehan, 1993a). It is considered a "third wave" cognitive-behavioral therapy (Kahl, Winter, & Schweiger, 2012) because it blends the change-based strategies of CBT with mindfulness and acceptance-based approaches. DBT focuses specifically on teaching patients skills to effectively manage emotions, while directly addressing problematic behaviors that interfere with treatment. According to DBT theory, difficulties in emotion regulation are believed to develop when an individual with an inherent biological vulnerability to intense and enduring emotions is paired with an environment that dismisses or punishes emotional experiences (i.e., an environment that is invalidating). For a review, see Crowell, Beauchaine, & Linehan, 2009. It is important to note that this invalidating environment can take many forms. As in FBT, the DBT model is agnostic as to the source of the invalidation. Some examples of an invalidating environment include, but are not limited to, families who do not have the skills to manage intense emotions, siblings or peers who engage in weight and shape teasing, and a culture that values a certain body type or style of emotional expression. Such an individual may never learn to effectively manage his/her emotions and may come to believe that the emotions themselves are "the problem." Maladaptive behaviors (e.g., self harm, purging) are conceptualized, therefore, as the individual's "solution" to the problem of ineffective emotion regulation. Since the original publication of Linehan's treatment manual, randomized trials evaluating the treatment have shown DBT to be associated with fewer hospital admissions, lower rates of substance abuse and angry outbursts, increased patient commitment to therapy, fewer dropouts, and decreased therapist burnout. Please see reviews by Lynch, Trost, Salsman, & Linehan, 2007; Robins & Chapman, 2004. In its standard form, DBT involves a one-year commitment to weekly individual therapy, group skills training, telephone skills coaching, and a therapist consultation team (Linehan, 1993a, 1993b).

In 2007, Miller, Rathus, and Linehan adapted DBT for use with adolescents (DBT-A) who engage in non-suicidal self-injury (NSSI). Several studies have demonstrated this model's effectiveness in decreasing self-harm, suicidality, aggression, general psychiatric symptoms, and symptoms of borderline personality disorder (Fleischhaker et al., 2011; James, Taylor, Winmill, & Alfoadari, 2008; Katz, Cox, Gunasekara, & Miller, 2004; Miller, Rathus, & Linehan, 2007; Rathus & Miller, 2002). In standard DBT-A, treatment is typically provided over a 12–16 week period and involves weekly individual psychotherapy and multi-family group skills training. During this period, patients are offered telephone skills coaching outside of sessions and the therapist is required to participate in a consultation team. DBT-A includes adaptations from the original DBT model that incorporate developmental and family factors in the treatment. For example, parents attend skills training sessions and are included in the adolescent's individual therapy sessions when there is concern that parental behavior or interactions are a prompting event for the child's maladaptive behaviors. Additionally, parents are required to learn the same DBT skills that their adolescents learn so that they can model the use of emotion regulation skills in the home environment. Families are trained in the four standard DBT skill modules (mindfulness, emotion regulation, distress tolerance, and interpersonal effectiveness) as well as an additional fifth module (walking the middle path) that was designed specifically for adolescents and families (Miller et al., 2007).

DBT for Eating Disorders

DBT has also been adapted for eating disorders, conceptualizing maladaptive eating and weight regulatory behaviors as extending from ineffective affect regulation. Modified DBT interventions (e.g., group or individual DBT skills training, adding appetite awareness training) have been successful in reducing binge eating and purging behaviors in adult women suffering from BN and BED (Safer, Telch, & Agras, 2001; Telch, 1997; Telch, Agras, & Linehan, 2000, 2001). Preliminary work describing a model of DBT further adapted for adolescents with BED is also promising (Safer, Lock, & Couturier, 2007). While these studies using modified DBT are encouraging, they were designed to treat a less severe (e.g., mild-moderate symptoms, few comorbid conditions) patient population so they do not include the full DBT treatment (i.e., individual therapy, skills group, phone coaching, and consultation team). This adapted DBT model may therefore be insufficient for the population of adolescents who are not helped by FBT alone.

There is increasing interest in the application of standard DBT for individuals with complex and comorbid ED presentations (Wisniewski, Safer, & Chen, 2007). Preliminary evidence from the authors' and others' clinics suggest that the standard DBT model, which includes all components of the treatment, may be an effective intervention for multidiagnostic adult ED patients when blended with standard ED interventions (Ben-Porath, Wisniewski, & Warren, 2009, 2010; Federici & Wisniewski, 2013; Kröger et al., 2010; Palmer et al., 2003). The authors are aware of only one study to date that has evaluated the use of the full DBT model in adolescent patients with eating issues. Salbach-Andrae and colleagues (2008) reported on a case series of adolescent AN & BN patients who received full DBT-A. This study demonstrated significant reductions in ED behaviors and pathology at the end of treatment (Salbach-Andrae, Bohnekamp, Pfeiffer, Lehmkuhl, & Miller, 2008). Further research is needed, however, to validate these findings.

Rationale for the Integration of DBT into FBT for Adolescents with Affect Dysregulation

One may speculate as to the compatibility of a model focused on parental leadership and control (FBT) with a model based on collaboration with the patient (DBT). The authors strongly feel that the theoretical underpinnings of the two treatments can be combined into a working model, albeit with the use of creative thinking, flexibility, and systems in place for ongoing review of fidelity. Thoughts on how the two philosophies might be combined are presented in Table 1.

Table 14.1 The Marriage of DBT and FBT Philosophies

DBT Philosophy (Linehan, 1993a)	How It Works with FBT
Balancing Acceptance and Change	Assists with *effective problem-solving** and promotes empathy for a more collaborative approach to renourishment and restoring the adolescent to his/her healthy developmental trajectory.
"Consultation-to-the-Client" Approach	FBT therapist also takes an active yet noncontrolling stance. FBT therapist serves as the "expert consultant" to the family while family members are encouraged to become observers and leaders of their own process. FBT strives to maintain respect for the adolescent developmental status, and this approach supports autonomy and individuation needs.

(continued)

DBT Philosophy (Linehan, 1993a)	How It Works with FBT
People are doing the best they can.	Assists with *blame reduction** for both patient and parents and frees parents to engage in trial-and-error necessary for finding a plan for weight restoration that works for them.
People want to improve.	If this notion is adopted, it may be easier for the family to engage in *externalization** or *separating the child from the illness** when behaviors indicate otherwise.
People need to do better, work harder, and be motivated to change.	Provides rationale for understanding why past interventions may have been ineffective and encourages stamina and creative thinking regarding how to best restore health to the ill child.
The lives of suicidal and ED individuals are unbearable as they are currently being lived.	Language that helps to *establish that there is a crisis** in the family.
People must learn new behaviors in all areas of their lives.	Supports *pragmatic, solution-focused work*.*
You may not have caused your problems, but you need to take responsibility to solve them anyway.	Fits with FBT's *agnostic view of etiology*,* blame reduction*,* and provides language to support the FBT intervention "*Charging parents with the task of refeeding."**
People cannot fail in DBT.	Supports *blame reduction** and provides *hope** needed to mobilize families to take charge of the illness.

Both models are considered frameworks guided by fundamental assumptions and philosophies—there are no specific or "right or wrong" pathways to promoting change. Both models emphasize a "team approach" that includes the adolescent and family as integral members of the team.

Note: Starred items (*) indicate fundamental FBT assumptions and techniques.

In addition to the proposed theoretical compatibility, the authors believe DBT to be a useful adjunct to FBT for several reasons:

1. Treatment Hierarchies Help Focus Treatment

Standard DBT provides a structure for managing and prioritizing multiple behavioral targets to be addressed in treatment simultaneously. This framework will be particularly helpful for the subset of adolescent ED patients who are diagnosed with comorbid conditions (e.g., depression, anxiety, substance use disorders) and will be especially relevant when the patient is suicidal and/or engages in NSSI. When considering depression and anxiety, thorough history taking will be necessary to determine the appropriate time to address the comorbid conditions. For example, if the comorbid condition emerged *after* weight loss or restrictive eating, then weight gain using the techniques described in the standard FBT model (e.g., laser focus on food) will likely resolve the problematic symptoms. Conversely, if there is a long and well-documented history of the comorbids and/or they appear to be primary to the ED illness, then the immediate use of an adjunct treatment model (such as DBT) may be indicated.

DBT's notion of a treatment hierarchy helps the therapist to identify which behavior to address first in session, thus providing a clear path to prioritizing the goals of treatment (Linehan, 1993a). The need for a well-organized treatment hierarchy is illustrated by the following example of a fictitious patient:

> *Lauren, a dangerously low-weight 15-year-old adolescent patient with a history of multiple suicide attempts, presents for FBT treatment with her parents. In session, Lauren and her parents report that Lauren became dysregulated at dinner the previous evening after being offered a new food. Lauren left the home in the midst of her dysregulation and engaged in self-harm by cutting herself with a pair of scissors. When searching Lauren's room to look for clues as to where Lauren may have gone, her parents found bags of vomit in her room, which greatly upset Lauren's parents. Lauren's father further discovered that Lauren has been visiting "thinspiration" / "proANA" chatrooms on her computer. Upon Lauren's return late at night, the family engaged in a shouting match over the events of the day, which resulted in Lauren's father smashing Lauren's computer and Lauren threatening suicide if her parents continued to invade her privacy and "force her" to eat. When the parents shared their concern about Lauren's suicidality with their FBT therapist, another argument was triggered, which ultimately ended up with Lauren refusing to talk for the rest of the session and dozing off in her chair.*

In standard FBT, getting a child to eat is top priority, particularly if he/she is dangerously low weight. The case scenario above, however, prompts the following question: How do we manage the other issues that have the potential to be life-threatening as well? Without a targeting framework, deciding how to focus a session for patients such as these could be a challenge. Following a target hierarchy is core to DBT treatment and provides a theoretical justification for how to manage multiple maladaptive behaviors. The standard DBT target hierarchy has been adapted for use with ED patients (Wisniewski & Kelly, 2003; Wisniewski, Safer, & Chen, 2007) and is structured as follows:

Target I: Life-Threatening Behaviors

(e.g., suicide, NSSI). As in standard DBT, suicidal ideation and self-injury are the first targets to be addressed in treatment. ED behaviors may be moved to Target I, however, when they present an imminent threat to the patient's life as in a medical emergency (e.g., evidence of bradycardia, electrolyte imbalances, EKG abnormalities, syrup of ipecac use). When Target I non-ED issues are present, they are addressed without ever losing focus on ED issues and with awareness that some non-ED Target I behaviors may inadvertently function as escape or avoidance of the ED.

Target II: Therapy-Interfering Behaviors (TIBs)

The active attention to behaviors that interfere with treatment compliance and progress is one of several reasons why DBT has the potential to augment standard FBT treatment. Therapy-interfering behaviors that may occur within the context of adolescent ED treatment include family members not regularly attending sessions, the adolescent becoming withdrawn or refusing to talk in session after parents express criticism about the adolescent's eating behaviors, inability to focus in session due to malnourished state, parents not being on the same page about how weight restoration should happen, participants not attending medical appointments, and absence from treatment due to the need for medical intervention, etc. Therapist behavior can be therapy-interfering as well and, as such, is directly addressed in DBT. Therapist's TIBs include being late for appointments, a judgmental stance toward the patient or family, and failure to provide adherent treatment.

Target III: Quality of Life Interfering Behaviors

ED and/or problematic behaviors stemming from comorbidities that are not associated with imminent medical risk nor interfering with treatment are considered Target III behaviors. These behaviors include, but are not limited to, restrictive eating, binge-eating, vomiting, laxative use, diuretic use, diet pill use, excessive exercise, excessive need for sleep due to depressed mood, anger outbursts, substance use, running away from home, etc.

In her book, Linehan considers *how* an issue is discussed to be just as important as *what* issue is discussed in session (Linehan, 1993a). The bulk of treatment for ED patients who are not suicidal or at imminent medical risk will occur within Targets II and III. In cases such as Lauren's, however, the DBT therapist would focus first on the Target I behaviors (suicidality, self-harm) before addressing Target II (Lauren's withdrawal in session and dozing off) or Target III (food refusal, running away, purging, pro-ANA chatroom visits) behaviors. It is important to note that the same behavior may be considered a different target depending on the context. For example, Lauren's purging behavior typically would be considered Target III. It would shift to Target I if she were also diagnosed with hypokalemia, as further purging could result in imminent death. The purging may be moved to Target II if it begins interfering with effectiveness of her antidepressant medication (i.e., she took the medicine at breakfast and purged soon after). Focus on purging behavior in session, therefore, would change with the status of the target.

2. Validation and Acceptance Principles Can Increase Collaboration in Treatment

DBT's specific focus on teaching validation and acceptance has the potential to be especially useful in working with families in which high expressed emotion (EE) is part of the clinical picture. In DBT-A, parents and offspring are taught how to validate each other. Validation is the recognition and acceptance that one's thoughts, feelings, or actions make sense and are understandable given the current situation. This does not necessarily mean that the individual providing validation has to concur with the other's thoughts or feelings, as validation is not the same as agreement. Validation instead requires one to actively accept the patient and not discount or trivialize his/her responses to events. Validation is useful in that it helps regulate emotions, is good for relationships, and can decrease the intensity of conflicts (Linehan, 1993a). This may be incredibly helpful and powerful for parents working to restore their child's weight. In the case example, Lauren's family's communication style was plagued by shouting matches, which would oftentimes lead to aggression and ineffective ways of managing problematic behaviors. Alternatively, a validating statement such as "Lauren, it makes sense, given your ED, that you do not want to eat this new food. I am sorry that eating upsets you, and I want you to recover, so you will need to eat it nonetheless" still accomplishes the parents' objectives of needing to feed their daughter while still attending to and finding truth in Lauren's experience. Validation in this sense could be a mechanism through which effective communication can be taught to families exhibiting high expressed emotion in order to promote more successful outcomes in FBT.

3. Skills-Training Helps with Symptom Management and Promotes Effective Coping Behaviors

Skills training is necessary when a solution to a problem requires skills not readily available in an individual's behavioral repertoire. The integration of skills is emphasized in DBT because individuals exhibiting affect regulation difficulties and/or personality disorder features may require assistance in generating or producing actions required to respond to situations adaptively or effectively (Linehan, 1993a). DBT skills have been shown to mediate the effects of DBT and are helpful in decreasing suicidal behavior and depressive symptoms as well as in promoting better anger control (Neacsiu, Rizvi, & Linehan, 2010), all of which can be of great help to an FBT therapist treating a patient with an eating disorder who is concurrently struggling with such issues. Parents can also benefit from learning skills.

Parents who have their own biological tendency towards intense emotions may need skills to better tolerate the distress they see in their child. Take, for example, Lauren's father in the case illustration. In response to Lauren's dysregulation and problematic behaviors (e.g., visiting inappropriate websites), Lauren's father's solution was to shout and engage in aggressive acts (e.g., break her computer). Lauren's father may also have a deficit in his ability to produce more effective behaviors to handle the situation, which skills training could ameliorate. Research has shown, in fact, significant improvement in psychosocial adjustment, increased problem-focused coping, and enhanced emotional well-being when skills are taught to caregivers (Drossel, Fisher, & Mercer, 2011).

In order to teach patients and their families how to better manage their symptoms and engage in more effective coping behaviors, the following five skills modules are taught in DBT-A:

Mindfulness

Mindfulness skills are designed to teach people how to focus their attention on the present moment without judgment. Mindfulness teaches patients how to step away from distracting and painful thoughts that often trigger symptoms. The "what" skills (i.e., observing, describing, participating) and the "how" skills (taking a nonjudgmental stance, focusing on one thing in the moment, being effective) can augment FBT sessions by promoting family participation with awareness, as opposed to participation without awareness, which is a key characteristic of impulsive and mood-dependent behaviors (Linehan, 1993a).

Interpersonal Effectiveness

Interpersonal effectiveness skills teach people how to effectively communicate with others and how to increase the likelihood of getting what we want and need. An interpersonally effective style of communicating can be generalized to the FBT session, allowing for increased collaboration among family members who are trying to figure out the best way to restore health in a sick child (Linehan, 1993a).

Distress Tolerance

Distress tolerance skills teach individuals new ways of getting through a crisis without making matters worse (Linehan, 1993a). When emotions feel overwhelming and situations get difficult, people who lack distress tolerance skills will turn to their symptoms as a way of coping and regulating themselves. Distress tolerance training instead teaches people how to bear pain skillfully (e.g., not engaging in symptoms that make the situation worse) and how to radically accept reality for what it is (without judgment) in order to move forward. Adolescents with EDs undergoing FBT may feel that they are in crisis each time a meal is presented by parents, and distress tolerance skills can help the adolescent identify alternative means of coping and to radically accept that *not* eating is *not* an option.

Emotion Regulation

Emotion regulation skills teach people how to observe and describe their emotions and how to understand their emotional world without fear, judgment, or self-hatred. Instead of rejecting or suppressing emotions, these skills emphasize the adaptive nature of emotions and teach people how to reduce their vulnerability to negative emotions and how to generate more positive emotions (Linehan, 1993a).

Walking the Middle Path

Walking the middle path is a new skills module developed specifically for adolescents and families. This module emphasizes the balance between change-oriented skills and acceptance-oriented skills in order to manage dialectical dilemmas commonly occurring in families. The module encourages families to think in dialectics, practice validation (i.e., acceptance), practice problem-solving (i.e., change), and offset extreme behavior patterns (Miller et al., 2007).

As a whole, the DBT skills provide a tool kit to support fundamental assumptions of FBT. For example, in Phase I of FBT treatment, the DBT-A skills can be used to better tolerate the refeeding process. In Phases II and III, the skills can be used to resolve pending adolescent developmental issues, thus leading to an increased quality of life, or "life worth living."

4. DBT offers in-vivo coaching outside of session

In standard DBT treatment, between-session telephone contact with a primary therapist is standard practice and is used to assist patients in generalizing the skills they are learning in treatment to everyday situations (Linehan, 1993a). This is referred to as "telephone skills-coaching" (TSC). The goal of TSC is to provide therapeutic contact and problem-solving support to patients during crises while at the same time extinguishing passive, dependent behaviors. TSC sessions can improve patients' ability to manage their environment. It may also increase patients' effectiveness in a given context and lead to improved generalization of skills to a variety of circumstances.

In order of importance, the targets addressed in standard DBT telephone coaching are (1) decreasing suicidal crisis behaviors, (2) increasing generalization of behavioral skills, and (3) decreasing the sense of conflict, alienation, and/or distance from the therapist (Linehan, 1993a).

TSC for patients with EDs follows the same principles outlined by Linehan (1993a) with some modifications (Wisniewski & Ben-Porath, 2005). Similar to standard DBT, ED patients are expected to call for coaching *before* engaging in self-harm or ED behavior. Telephone contact with the therapist *after* the behavior has occurred may inadvertently reinforce the behavior if the therapist's attention happens to be reinforcing. In standard (non-ED) DBT, there is a *24-Hour Rule* that states that a patient cannot call for coaching until 24 hours after they have engaged in Target I, suicidal, or self-harming behaviors. This 24-Hour Rule is used with ED patients who engage in self-harm; however, it has been adapted to manage ED-specific behaviors. The 24-Hour Rule was deemed ineffective when addressing ED behaviors, as patients with EDs are likely exposed to a potentially triggering stimulus (i.e., meal/snack) every 4 to 6 hours of the day. Each meal/snack presents an opportunity for the patient to engage or not engage in targeted behaviors. For patients with numerous daily scheduled exposures with potentially triggering stimuli, the 24-hour rule may never allow them to call for coaching, thus rendering it useless in assisting patients in shaping their ED behaviors (Wisniewski, Safer, & Chen, 2007). Instead, the 24-Hour Rule was modified to be the *Next Meal/Snack Rule* (see Wisniewski & Ben-Porath, 2005, for detailed protocol). The Next Meal/Snack Rule allows the patient to call for coaching at the next scheduled meal or snack whether or not they had a behavior at the previous one. So as not to inadvertently reinforce ED behavior, the Next Meal/Snack Rule does stipulate that the focus of the call be related to the current situation only.

Aside from skill-coaching to manage triggering situations, TSC may also be used to help repair the therapeutic relationship when necessary. Due to their emotional reactivity, patients with BPD are particularly sensitive to emotional slights and may elicit strong negative reactions from others. Some suggest that the same may be true for patients diagnosed with an eating disorder (McCabe, LaVia, & Marcus, 2004). The use of TSC to manage and ameliorate the therapeutic relationship in DBT sets it apart from standard ED treatments. Eating disorder patients are encouraged to call their therapist if they are feeling alienated or angry in order to repair the relationship rather than waiting for the next session to do so.

As related to FBT, TSC may allow families the opportunity for immediate practice of more skillful behavior as opposed to having to wait until the next session to problem-solve alternative means of handling less-than-ideal situations. Had Lauren phoned her DBT individual therapist immediately upon experiencing the urge to refuse the new food parents offered, she may have been able to use distress tolerance skills reviewed in session to make it through the meal. Similarly, had parents contacted their DBT skills coach (the skills group leader), they may have been able to generate more validating and effective ways of managing Lauren's (and dad's) dysregulation, not to mention save themselves the cost of a new computer!

5. DBT Offers Therapy for the Therapists

The consultation team, a multidisciplinary group of professionals dedicated to treating DBT patients, supports the therapist in being committed and effective in his/her treatment with the DBT patient. The consultation team meets weekly and is considered to be "therapy for the therapists." During this meeting, the consultation team is expected to apply DBT to the therapists, just as the therapist is expected to apply DBT to the patient. The goals of the consultation team are to keep each therapist treating his/her patient, to keep the therapist's interactions with the patient balanced, and to maintain DBT treatment integrity. This may be especially helpful when treating individuals or families high in EE, which could be a contributing factor to eventual therapist burnout.

The Cleveland Center for Eating Disorders FBT-DBT Treatment Model

In response to the need for alternative or adjunctive clinical interventions for adolescents with complex ED presentations, the Cleveland Center for Eating Disorders (CCED) is exploring the effectiveness and feasibility of an integrated FBT-DBT model. The approach calls for an innovative combination of strategies well-established in the successful use of FBT for the management of eating pathology as well as DBT in the treatment for emotion dysregulation. Although the compatibility of the two models has at times been called into question, the authors firmly believe in the usefulness of the integrated approach, particularly for youth with EDs and a history of suicidal or self-injurious behaviors. This belief is supported by extensive clinical observation as well as pilot research data collected onsite.

Guiding Treatment Philosophy

The DBT model strives to honor the balance between acceptance and change and work towards helping patients act as their own agents. This philosophy blends nicely with the "phase approach" of FBT that increasingly encourages autonomy as the adolescent becomes behaviorally and psychologically less involved with the ED. Families are coached to find balance and move away from extreme ways of thinking and behaving. Similar to what the adolescent is learning in DBT sessions, the FBT therapist can support parents in adopting an approach towards weight restoration that is grounded in a *Dialectical Philosophy*, which states that two seemingly opposite entities can co-exist. For example, an adolescent in Phase I may require the highest level of supervision for all meals and parents may not be able to personally provide around-the-clock supervision due to the need to work full-time. The Dialectical Philosophy would recognize that there is truth to both sides of the dilemma and aim to find a "middle path," or a *synthesis* between these two opposites, rather than proving that one option is better than the other, leading to more effective problem-solving and a concrete plan to continue the weight restoration process. In all discussions and situations, the family is encouraged to find a balance between acceptance (i.e., accepting the current state of their lives and their emotions as they are in any given moment) and change (in order to develop a life worth living). The dialectical philosophy is apparent in the following clinical example of "Sarah," who is being treated using the combined model. Since Sarah is suffering from AN, Sarah's parents are following the treatment guidelines for Phase I of FBT. Sarah has a significant history of emotion dysregulation, self-harm, and suicidality and is therefore also receiving DBT treatment. When Sarah's parents attempt to feed her desserts, Sarah threatens to harm herself and has at times become physically aggressive toward her mom. Parents historically (and perhaps understandably) back off from feeding Sarah desserts when these events occur. A dialectical philosophy will embrace the notion that both issues are valid and need to be addressed: It is both true that feeding Sarah desserts (something the family regularly does) is necessary for recovery AND when she is fed desserts, she becomes dysregulated and may hurt herself. The dialectical synthesis in this situation is that parents will continue to feed Sarah desserts AND will sit with her calmly until the urges to self-harm decrease.

To uphold these guiding treatment philosophies and promote the highest level of fidelity to each model as is possible, all members of the treatment team are required to participate in a weekly patient staffing meeting and DBT therapists participate in a traditional weekly consultation team meeting, where the DBT "therapy for the therapists" discussed earlier takes place.

Admission Criteria

Initially, the CCED FBT-DBT model required all adolescent patients to start out receiving standard FBT, as that is the treatment with the most empirical support. This remains true for most patients at our clinic; however, our team became increasingly challenged by a subgroup of patients and families whose complex clinical presentations (usually due to a well-established history of psychiatric comorbidities and emotion dysregulation) required that the admissions criteria be adjusted so that a select group of adolescents may qualify for integrated FBT-DBT treatment immediately after assessment. This decision was necessary for many reasons. First, it has been suggested that there is a three-year "window of opportunity" to intervene on adolescent EDs before chances of full recovery diminish (Eisler et al., 1997). For youth with the most complex of clinical presentations, we thought it important to respond immediately and aggressively with a model that adequately addresses all presenting symptoms so as not to miss out on the recovery window. Also with respect to these cases, our FBT team struggled to apply standard FBT in the context of recurrent suicidal/self-injurious behaviors, explosive and often uncontrollable angry outbursts and/or substantial opposition to treatment goals. Maintaining the focus of therapeutic discussion on food and eating behaviors, although important, was quite difficult to do with a family whose child was regularly engaging in self-injurious behaviors and threatening suicide. It is speculated by our team that parents were left feeling disempowered and helpless (which had direct negative effects on the FBT) because the standard model alone did not provide a means to address these risky behaviors. The difficulty in engaging these families in standard FBT often resulted in our clinicians (and the families they treat) feeling ineffective and burned out. By the time the families were deemed unresponsive to standard FBT and identified as being candidates for FBT-DBT treatment, the families were tired, disheartened, and had exhausted insurance benefits, all of which made it more difficult to make the required DBT commitment. Therefore, the FBT-DBT admissions criteria presently used was designed to assist in the early identification of these complex cases in the hopes of facilitating recovery sooner. See Table 14.2 for a complete listing of the specific criteria required for admission into FBT-DBT treatment.

Table 14.2 FBT-DBT Admissions Criteria

	Admissions Criteria
(A)	Meets diagnostic criteria for eating disorders and is medically stable for outpatient treatment.
(B)	Presents with an established and documented history of emotion regulation difficulties, supported by a clinically significant Difficulties in Emotion Regulation Scale (DERS) (Gratz & Roemer, 2004).
(C)	Exhibits two or more symptoms that DBT has evidence in managing (e.g., recurrent self-harm, suicidality, impulsivity with the potential for danger, substance abuse/dependence, pattern of affective instability, disturbance in interpersonal relationships).
For Youth Already Participating in Standard FBT:	
(D)	Presents with a comorbid Axis I diagnosis that is complicating standard ED treatment.
(E)	There is evidence that the adolescent is not being fully helped by standard FBT alone, as evidenced by slow treatment response or inability to meet treatment goals.
(F)	There is evidence of Therapy Interfering Behaviors (e.g., high degree of criticism by parents, invalidating environment) that make it difficult to follow the manualized FBT agenda and contribute to ineffectiveness of the standard model.

Structure of the FBT-DBT Model

Once an adolescent has been identified as a potential candidate for FBT-DBT treatment based on the admissions criteria listed above, the case is presented to the FBT-DBT treatment team for review and case acceptance.

In DBT, every provider on the DBT consultation team is considered a member of each patient's treatment team, regardless if they have direct contact with the patient or not. This is true to the extent that if one DBT patient commits suicide, then all the providers on that team are meant to answer "yes" when asked if he/she has had a patient who committed suicide. The DBT consultation team provides support and consultation to the primary provider in order to facilitate the highest level of adherence to DBT and protect against clinician burnout. Our clinic modified the notion of a traditional DBT consultation team to include not just DBT providers who participate in the traditional DBT consult team, but also the FBT providers so that both theories would have input and be equally represented when reviewing a case. The DBT providers alone still participate in a traditional DBT consultation team; however, case acceptance and review is discussed in the weekly staffing meeting and includes all members of the treatment team.

Once the FBT-DBT treatment team has reviewed the case and provided agreement with the recommendation for FBT-DBT, the family is assigned a specially trained FBT therapist (i.e., one well-versed in DBT principles) and the adolescent is assigned a specially trained DBT therapist (i.e., one well-versed in FBT principles). Manualized FBT commences (beginning with session 1) in addition to the motivation and commitment phase of DBT. Once the family has signed the DBT commitment contract agreeing to the following non-negotiable criteria for participation—(1) a commitment to staying alive, (2) a willingness to work on eating disorder symptoms, and (3) a willingness to attend the DBT component of treatment for a minimum of six months—the family is considered formally enrolled in FBT-DBT treatment.

In our clinic, treatment is structured to maximize exposure to emotion regulation concepts and skills to both facilitate compliance with FBT and to reduce maladaptive or ineffective behaviors. In this model, our FBT-DBT adolescent patients meet with their DBT individual therapist weekly in addition to attending regular (phase-dependent) FBT family sessions. The FBT therapist is primarily responsible for supporting parents to become leaders in the weight restoration and ED behavior elimination process. As indicated for FBT, all weight, meal-planning, and food management discussions take place in the family session. The DBT therapist focuses on helping patients and families tolerate and skillfully manage the painful and distressing emotions that arise as a response to food exposure and weight gain. The DBT is conducted in adherence to the DBT target hierarchy model, with issues related to life-threatening behaviors being targeted first, therapy-interfering behaviors being targeted second, and quality of life issues being targeted last. Adolescents are required to complete weekly goal sheets, diary cards (see Figure 14.1), and behavior chain analyses (see Figure 14.2), which are thoroughly reviewed in session with their DBT therapist. The adolescent is encouraged (not required) to share these documents in the FBT sessions, which works to increase

Chain Analysis

Date Filled Out: _____ Date of Problem Behavior: _____

WHAT EXACTLY IS THE MAJOR *PROBLEM BEHAVIOR* THAT I AM ANALYZING?

WHAT THINGS IN MYSELF AND MY ENVIRONMENT MADE ME *VULNERABLE?*
Start day:_____

WHAT *PROMPTING EVENT* IN THE ENVIRONMENT STARTED ME ON THE
CHAIN TO MY PROBLEM BEHAVIOR? Start day:_____

WHAT ARE THE *LINKS* IN THE CHAIN BETWEEN THE PROMPTING EVENT
AND THE PROBLEM BEHAVIOR?

Action	Thought	Emotion	Urge

WHAT EXACTLY WERE THE *CONSEQUENCES* IN THE ENVIRONMENT?
Immediate:

Delayed:

AND IN MYSELF?
Immediate:

Delayed:

Solution Analysis

WAYS TO REDUCE MY *VULNERABILITY* IN THE FUTURE:
WAYS TO PREVENT *PROMPTING EVENT* FROM HAPPENING AGAIN:
WAYS TO WORK ON CHANGING THE *LINKS*:
WHAT *HARM* DID MY *PROBLEM BEHAVIOR* CAUSE?
PLANS TO *REPAIR, CORRECT,* AND *OVER-CORRECT* THE HARM:

Figure 14.1 Example of a Diary Card Used in FBT-DBT Treatment

communication and collaboration among family members. Diary cards can be particularly useful, as they can assist a family to recall and reflect upon problematic meals throughout the week so that ineffective behaviors are not repeated the following week. Sporadically throughout treatment, it is requested that parents join the DBT session. This request is most often related to the need for safety-planning, discussions surrounding ways to create a more validating environment for the adolescent (e.g., addressing expressed criticism and/or blame that also may be interfering with the FBT), and family coaching surrounding overall skills generalization. It is understood that the DBT "Consultation-to-the-Client" approach (i.e., the DBT therapist will not talk on behalf of the adolescent; instead, the DBT therapist will act as a consultant to the adolescent helping him/her to negotiate needs) will be used when parents are in session in order to allow the adolescent to practice the vital life skill of effective communication. The same approach is used when the adolescent wishes to convey information to the FBT therapist or in a family session. The DBT therapist does not serve as the "go-between," talking on behalf of the adolescent. Instead, the DBT therapist works with the adolescent so that he/she gains comfort talking in session about his/her needs.

DIARY CARD Treatment Plan A

CLEVELAND CENTER for Eating Disorders
Living with Food™

Name:
Day/Date:

Mark (*) if you engaged in a behavior.
Rate (0-5) if you had an urge but did not engage in the behavior.

Time of Day	MEALS	Location	Supplement	Emotions	Binge	Purge	Restrict	Pills	Exercise	SI	SH	Body Diss.	Skills (0-6)
	BREAKFAST												
	SNACK												
	LUNCH												
	SNACK												
	DINNER												
	SNACK												

Emotions Today	Rating (0-5)
Pain/Misery	___
Anxiety/Fear	___
Sadness	___
Shame	___
Anger	___
Joy	___
Urge to quit tx/recovery	___
Lying/withholding	___

Skills
0= Not thought about or used
1= Thought about, didn't use
2= Wanted to use, but didn't
3= Tried to use, but couldn't
4= Tried, didn't help
5= Tried, helped
6= Used without trying, helped

VITAMINS	Yes	No	Orthostasis Protocol!	Yes	No	Bradycardia Protocol!	Yes	No

Skills Diary Card	(Circle the days you practiced the skills)							
	How did you practice the skill?							
Core Mindfulness Skills								
Wise Mind		Mon	Tues	Wed	Thurs	Fri	Sat	Sun
Observe: just notice		Mon	Tues	Wed	Thurs	Fri	Sat	Sun
Describe: put words on		Mon	Tues	Wed	Thurs	Fri	Sat	Sun
Nonjudgemental stance		Mon	Tues	Wed	Thurs	Fri	Sat	Sun
One-mindfully: in the moment		Mon	Tues	Wed	Thurs	Fri	Sat	Sun
Effectiveness: focus on what works		Mon	Tues	Wed	Thurs	Fri	Sat	Sun
Interpersonal Effective Skills								
Objective Effectiveness: DEAR MAN		Mon	Tues	Wed	Thurs	Fri	Sat	Sun
Relationship Effectiveness: GIVE		Mon	Tues	Wed	Thurs	Fri	Sat	Sun
Self-Respect Effectiveness: FAST		Mon	Tues	Wed	Thurs	Fri	Sat	Sun
Emotion Regulation Skills								
Reduce Vulnerability: PLEASE		Mon	Tues	Wed	Thurs	Fri	Sat	Sun
Build Mastery		Mon	Tues	Wed	Thurs	Fri	Sat	Sun
Build Positive Experiences		Mon	Tues	Wed	Thurs	Fri	Sat	Sun
Opposite to emotion action		Mon	Tues	Wed	Thurs	Fri	Sat	Sun
Distress Tolerance Skills								
Distract		Mon	Tues	Wed	Thurs	Fri	Sat	Sun
Self-Soothe		Mon	Tues	Wed	Thurs	Fri	Sat	Sun
IMPROVE the moment		Mon	Tues	Wed	Thurs	Fri	Sat	Sun
Pros and Cons		Mon	Tues	Wed	Thurs	Fri	Sat	Sun
Radical Acceptance		Mon	Tues	Wed	Thurs	Fri	Sat	Sun
Willingness		Mon	Tues	Wed	Thurs	Fri	Sat	Sun
Turning the mind								
Walking the Middle Path								
Thinking dialectically		Mon	Tues	Wed	Thurs	Fri	Sat	Sun
Validation/self-validation		Mon	Tues	Wed	Thurs	Fri	Sat	Sun
Positive reinforcement		Mon	Tues	Wed	Thurs	Fri	Sat	Sun

Figure 14.2 Example of a Behavior Chain Analysis Form Used in FBT-DBT Treatment

In addition to the DBT and FBT sessions, the family participates in a 90-minute DBT multi-family skills group that is designed to help patients and their families develop a range of adaptive coping skills with an emphasis on emotion regulation, distress tolerance, interpersonal effectiveness, mindfulness, and "walking the middle path." The multi-family skills group is based on the Miller, Rathus, and Linehan model (Miller et al., 2007) and involves weekly participation over the course of the six-month DBT treatment. Per the adolescent DBT model, telephone skills-coaching is offered to both the adolescent and the parents while participating in treatment. The purpose of between-session phone contact is to assist family members in their attempts to generalize skills learned in sessions and group to their real-world environments. Phone coaching involves a brief (e.g., ten-minute) phone conversation between the adolescent and his/her therapist and/or a parent and the multi-family skills group leader. The family is oriented to the purpose and appropriate use of telephone skills coaching at the onset of DBT treatment, resulting in a brief, highly structured brainstorming conversation surrounding which skills may be effective in managing difficult situations as they arise. In accordance with the FBT model, parents are not told what to do or given a "prescription" for how to manage a difficult situation. Instead, parents are empowered to come up with a skills plan that they think will best work for that given situation, with input from the therapist as the expert on eating disorders. The adolescent is also encouraged to be an active participant in the skills coaching conversation in order to enhance self-efficacy (Limbrunner, Ben-Porath, & Wisniewski, 2011; Wisniewski & Ben-Porath, 2005).

Conclusions and Future Directions

This chapter describes a novel approach to treating adolescents with affect regulation difficulties who suffer from eating disorders. The authors propose that a blended FBT-DBT model can be a useful alternative to standard treatment approaches when an adolescent patient presents with significant emotion dysregulation that predates the onset of the eating disorder, suicidal, or self-injurious behaviors, and/or has not responded sufficiently to standard FBT on its own. It is important to note that at present, the ideas put forth in this chapter are just theory grounded in scientific evidence. The authors are in the process of systematically evaluating the feasibility and efficacy of this integrated model and plan to present the scientific data collected at our site in the near future. Future research focusing on this blended model and other innovative approaches for managing affective regulation difficulties in adolescents presenting with an eating disorder is necessary and encouraged.

References

Ben-Porath, D. D., Wisniewski, L., & Warren, M. (2009). Differential treatment response for eating disordered patients with and without a comorbid borderline personality diagnosis using a dialectical behavior therapy (DBT)-informed approach. *Eating Disorders: The Journal of Treatment & Prevention, 17*(3), 225–241. doi: 10.1080/10640260902848576

Ben-Porath, D. D., Wisniewski, L., & Warren, M. (2010). Outcomes of a day treatment program for eating disorders using clinical and statistical significance. *Journal of Contemporary Psychotherapy, 40*(2), 115–123. doi: 10.1007/s10879-009-9125-5

Crowell, S. E., Beauchaine, T. P., & Linehan, M. M. (2009). A biosocial developmental model of borderline personality: Elaborating and extending linehan's theory. *Psychological Bulletin, 135*(3), 495–510. doi: 10.1037/a0015616

Downs, K. J., & Blow, A. J. (2013). A substantive and methodological review of family-based treatment for eating disorders: the last 25 years of research. *Journal of Family Therapy, 35*(S1), 3–28. doi: 10.1111/j.1467-6427.2011.00566.x

Doyle, P. M., Le Grange, D., Loeb, K., Doyle, A. C., & Crosby, R. D. (2010). Early response to family-based treatment for adolescent anorexia nervosa. *Int J Eat Disord, 43*(7), 659–662. doi: 10.1002/eat.20764

Drossel, C., Fisher, J. E., & Mercer, V. (2011). A DBT skills training group for family caregivers of persons with dementia. *Behavior Therapy, 42*(1), 109–119. doi: 10.1016/j.beth.2010.06.001

Eisler, I., Dare, C., Hodes, M., Russell, G., Dodge, E., & Le Grange, D. (2000). Family therapy for adolescent anorexia nervosa: The results of a controlled comparison of two family interventions. *Journal of Child Psychology and Psychiatry, 41*(6), 727–736. doi: 10.1111/1469-7610.00660

Eisler, I., Dare, C., Russell, G. F. M., Szmukler, G., Le Grange, D., & Dodge, E. (1997). Family and individual therapy in anorexia nervosa: A 5-year followup. *Archives of General Psychiatry, 54*(11), 1025–1030. doi: 10.1001/archpsyc.1997.01830230063008

Eisler, I., Simic, M., Russell, G. F. M., & Dare, C. (2007). A randomised controlled treatment trial of two forms of family therapy in adolescent anorexia nervosa: A five-year follow-up. *Journal of Child Psychology and Psychiatry, 48*(6), 552–560. doi: 10.1111/j.1469-7610.2007.01726.x

Federici, A., & Wisniewski, L. (2013). An intensive DBT program for patients with multidiagnostic eating disorder presentations: A case series analysis. *International Journal of Eating Disorders, 46*(4), 322–331. doi: 10.1002/eat.22112

Fleischhaker, C., Böhme, R., Sixt, B., Brück, C., Schneider, C., & Schulz, E. (2011). Dialectical Behavioral Therapy for Adolescents (DBT-A): A clinical trial for patients with suicidal and self-injurious behavior and borderline symptoms with a one-year follow-up. *Child and Adolescent Psychiatry and Mental Health, 5*. doi: 10.1186/1753-2000-5-3

Gratz, K. L., & Roemer, L. (2004). Multidimensional assessment of emotion regulation and dysregulation: Development, factor structure, and initial validation of the difficulties in emotion regulation scale. *Journal of Psychopathology and Behavioral Assessment, 26*(1), 41–54. doi: 10.1023/B:JOBA.0000007455.08539.94

James, A. C., Taylor, A., Winmill, L., & Alfoadari, K. (2008). A preliminary community study of dialectical behaviour therapy (DBT) with adolescent females demonstrating persistent, deliberate self-harm (DSH). *Child and Adolescent Mental Health, 13*(3), 148–152. doi: 10.1111/j.1475-3588.2007.00470.x

Kahl, K. G., Winter, L., & Schweiger, U. (2012). The third wave of cognitive behavioural therapies: What is new and what is effective? *Current Opinion in Psychiatry, 25*(6), 522–528.

Katz, L. Y., Cox, B. J., Gunasekara, S., & Miller, A. L. (2004). Feasibility of dialectical behavior therapy for suicidal adolescent inpatients. *Journal of the American Academy of Child & Adolescent Psychiatry, 43*(3), 276–282. doi: 10.1097/00004583-200403000-00008

Kröger, C., Schweiger, U., Sipos, V., Kliem, S., Arnold, R., Schunert, T., & Reinecker, H. (2010). Dialectical behaviour therapy and an added cognitive behavioural treatment module for eating disorders in women with borderline personality disorder and anorexia nervosa or bulimia nervosa who failed to respond to previous treatments. An open trial with a 15-month follow-up. *Journal of Behavior Therapy and Experimental Psychiatry, 41*(4), 381–388.

Le Grange, D., Binford, R., & Loeb, K. L. (2005). Manualized Family-Based Treatment for Anorexia Nervosa: A Case Series. *Journal of the American Academy of Child & Adolescent Psychiatry, 44*(1), 41–46. doi: 10.1097/01.chi.0000145373.68863.85

Le Grange, D., Crosby, R. D., & Lock, J. (2008). Predictors and moderators of outcome in family-based treatment for adolescent bulimia nervosa. *Journal of the American Academy of Child & Adolescent Psychiatry, 47*(4), 464–470. doi: 10.1097/CHI.0b013e3181640816

Limbrunner, H. M., Ben-Porath, D. D., & Wisniewski, L. (2011). DBT telephone skills coaching with eating disordered clients: Who calls, for what reasons, and for how long? *Cognitive and Behavioral Practice, 18*(2), 186–195. doi: 10.1016/j.cbpra.2010.01.010

Linehan, M. M. (1993a). *Cognitive-behavioral treatment of borderline personality disorder*. New York, NY US: Guilford Press.

Linehan, M. M. (1993b). *Skills training manual for treating borderline personality disorder*. New York, NY US: Guilford Press.

Lock, J., Couturier, J., Bryson, S., & Agras, W. S. (2006). Predictors of Dropout and Remission in Family Therapy for Adolescent Anorexia Nervosa in a Randomized Clinical Trial. *International Journal of Eating Disorders, 39*(8), 639–647. doi: 10.1002/eat.20328

Lock, J., Le Grange, D., Agras, W. S., & Dare, C. (2001). *Treatment manual for anorexia nervosa: A family-based approach*. New York, NY US: Guilford Press.

Lock, J., & Le Grange, D. (2012). *Treatment manual for anorexia nervosa: A family-based approach (2nd ed.)*. New York, NY US: Guilford Press.

Lock, J., Le Grange, D., Agras, W. S., Moye, A., Bryson, S. W., & Jo, B. (2010). Randomized clinical trial comparing family-based treatment with adolescent-focused individual therapy for adolescents with anorexia nervosa. *Archives of General Psychiatry, 67*(10), 1025–1032. doi: 10.1001/archgenpsychiatry.2010.128

Lynch, T. R., Trost, W. T., Salsman, N., & Linehan, M. M. (2007). Dialectical behavior therapy for borderline personality disorder. *Annual Review of Clinical Psychology, 3*, 181–205. doi: 10.1146/annurev.clinpsy.2.022305.095229

McCabe, E. B., LaVia, M. C., & Marcus, M. D. (2004). Dialectical Behavior Therapy for Eating Disorders. In J. K. Thompson (Ed.), *Handbook of eating disorders and obesity*. (pp. 232–244). Hoboken, NJ US: John Wiley & Sons Inc.

Miller, A. L., Rathus, J. H., & Linehan, M. M. (2007). *Dialectical behavior therapy with suicidal adolescents*. New York, NY US: Guilford Press.

Neacsiu, A. D., Rizvi, S. L., & Linehan, M. M. (2010). Dialectical behavior therapy skills use as a mediator and outcome of treatment for borderline personality disorder. *Behaviour Research and Therapy, 48*(9), 832–839. doi: 10.1016/j. brat.2010.05.017

Palmer, R. L., Birchall, H., Damani, S., Gatward, N., McGrain, L., & Parker, L. (2003). A dialectical behavior therapy program for people with an eating disorder and borderline personality disorder-description and outcome. *International Journal of Eating Disorders, 33*(3), 281–286. doi: 10.1002/eat.10141

Rathus, J. H., & Miller, A. L. (2002). Dialectical Behavior Therapy adapted for suicidal adolescents. *Suicide and Life-Threatening Behavior, 32*(2), 146–157. doi: 10.1521/suli.32.2.146.24399

Robins, C. J., & Chapman, A. L. (2004). Dialectical Behavior Therapy: Current Status, Recent Developments, and Future Directions. *Journal of Personality Disorders, 18*(1), 73–89. doi: 10.1521/pedi.18.1.73.32771

Russell, G. F., Szmukler, G. I., Dare, C. & Eisler, I. (1987). An evaluation of family therapy in anorexia nervosa and bulimia nervosa. *Archives of General Psychiatry, 44*(12), 1047–1056. doi: 10.1001/archpsyc.1987.01800240021004

Safer, D. L., Lock, J., & Couturier, J. L. (2007). Dialectical behavior therapy modified for adolescent binge eating disorder: A case report. *Cognitive and Behavioral Practice, 14*(2), 157–167. doi: 10.1016/j.cbpra.2006.06.001

Safer, D. L., Telch, C. F., & Agras, W. S. (2001). Dialectical behavior therapy for bulimia nervosa. *The American Journal of Psychiatry, 158*(4), 632–634. doi: 10.1176/appi.ajp.158.4.632

Salbach-Andrae, H., Bohnekamp, I., Pfeiffer, E., Lehmkuhl, U., & Miller, A. L. (2008). Dialectical behavior therapy of anorexia and bulimia nervosa among adolescents: A case series. *Cognitive and Behavioral Practice, 15*(4), 415–425. doi: 10.1016/j.cbpra.2008.04.001

Telch, C. F. (1997). Skills training treatment for adaptive affect regulation in a woman with binge-eating disorder. *International Journal of Eating Disorders, 22*(1), 77–81. doi: 10.1002/(SICI)1098-108X(199707)22:1<77::AID-EAT10>3.0.CO;2-F

Telch, C. F., Agras, W. S., & Linehan, M. M. (2000). Group dialectical behavior therapy for binge-eating disorder: A preliminary, uncontrolled trial. *Behavior Therapy, 31*(3), 569–582. doi: 10.1016/S0005-7894(00)80031-3

Telch, C. F., Agras, W. S., & Linehan, M. M. (2001). Dialectical behavior therapy for binge eating disorder. *Journal of Consulting and Clinical Psychology, 69*(6), 1061–1065. doi: 10.1037/0022-006X.69.6.1061

Treasure, J., Sepulveda, A. R., MacDonald, P., Whitaker, W., Lopez, C., Zabala, M., … Todd, G. (2008). The assessment of the family of people with eating disorders. *European Eating Disorders Review, 16*(4), 247–255. doi: 10.1002/erv.859

Wisniewski, L., & Kelly, E. (2003). Can DBT be used to effectively treat eating disorders? *Cognitive and Behavioral Practice, 10*, 131–138.

Wisniewski, L., & Ben-Porath, D. D. (2005). Telephone skill-coaching with eating-disordered clients: Clinical guidelines using a DBT framework. *European Eating Disorders Review, 13*(5), 344–350. doi: 10.1002/erv.657

Wisniewski, L., Safer, D., & Chen, E. (2007). Dialectical behavior therapy and eating disorders. In L. A. Dimeff & K. Koerner (Eds.), *Dialectical behavior therapy in clinical practice: Applications across disorders and settings.* (pp. 174–221). New York, NY US: Guilford Press.

Chapter 15

Emotional Experience and Regulation in Eating Disorders

Theory, Evidence, and Translational Application to Family Treatment

Nancy Zucker

One increasingly accepted framework for understanding the function or purpose of eating disorder symptoms is that the symptoms serve to dampen or help to avoid emotional experience (Haynos & Fruzzetti, 2011; Zucker & Harshaw, 2012; Merwin, Moskovich et al., 2013). Rather than experience the full onslaught of an intense emotional episode, symptoms may lessen emotional intensity. For example, rather than thinking about the rejection of a friend, an adolescent with an eating disorder may divert his or her attention by focusing on counting calories. Alternatively, eating disorder symptoms may alter emotional experience by changing the way in which the body feels. Emotions are embodied: individuals physically feel their emotions. The gut churns when an individual is anxious; the heart pounds in excitement. Eating disorder symptoms can have direct physiological effects on somatic experience: starvation is associated with bradycardia, or a slowed heart rate; excessive exercise is associated with decreased pain sensitivity, while the somatic consequences of purging have yet to be explored. There is increasing evidence that those with eating disorders may be deficient in possessing alternative emotion regulation strategies, though this research is limited to date (Merwin, 2011). Combined, this knowledge suggests several important implications for treatment, in general, and family-based treatment, in particular. First, treatments that directly and exclusively targets or challenges the performance of eating disorder symptoms are essentially depriving the individual of an emotion regulatory strategy. Thus, such treatments would be accompanied by a surge in intensity in emotional experience, particularly if the individual with an eating disorder lacks an alternative strategy. Second, given this proposed skill deficit, treatments must give adolescents tools to better understand, integrate, and regulate their emotional experience. Third, such a surge in emotional intensity with treatment necessitates that therapists and caregivers be prepared for the turmoil that is to ensue and capitalize on this period as a pivotal opportunity for teaching emotional awareness and empathic responding. This chapter is designed to guide therapists and caregivers through this tumultuous period and to provide a framework for researchers to better guide the study of emotion regulation in those with eating disorders.

To begin, the nature of emotional experience and the relationship of emotional experience to goal pursuit is discussed. Next, there is discussion of emotion regulatory capacities in those with eating disorders and how family-based treatment can help augment emotion regulatory skills.

The Nature and Function of Emotional Experience

Despite debate, there is relative agreement among researchers that the term *emotion* is a useful verbal shortcut that encapsulates the complex coordinated responses (from multiple systems) that occur in response to motivationally salient stimuli (Scherer, 2005; Bradley & Lang, 2007; LeDoux, 2007). In general, common components of emotional experience include the somatic "feeling" of emotion (e.g., an individual's conscious awareness of changes in visceral organs, such as increased frequency and intensity of a heart beating), alterations in central and peripheral physiology, automatic (e.g., tightening of particular facial muscles) and instrumental behavioral changes (e.g., response preparation, such as urges to fight in anger or flee in fear), and cognitive appraisals and related subjective experience ("I feel nervous") (Fontaine, Scherer et al., 2007). These complex, full-body reactions are in response to internal or external stimuli that capture attention because of their salience. Yet, the organization of these response systems (Scherer, 2005; LeDoux, 2007) and even the utility of conscious emotional experience continues to be debated (Bargh & Williams, 2007). As will be discussed, such beliefs have important implications for adaptive norms about the experience and display of emotions within a family system.

Emotions are useful. Emotional states are full-bodied response tendencies that facilitate goal pursuit and otherwise guide behavior to satisfy the motivational state of the individual. Put differently, an emotion signals to oneself and others, "This is important. Pay attention and do something." This functionalist conceptualization descends from the writings of Darwin, who stressed the social utility of emotions as vehicles of rapid communication for social organisms (Darwin, 2002). Of importance, Darwin's conceptualization of affective utility deviated sharply from earlier philosophers who emphasized the frivolity of emotional experiences—considering emotions as barriers to goal pursuit or indications of weakness of character (as noted in Bargh & Williams, 2007), or as inevitably interfering with rational decision making (e.g., James, 1884, p. 199). Yet, although extensive research supports the value of emotion as a vehicle of communication and facilitator of goal pursuit, this perennial debate continues to shape lay thought about both the norms of emotional display ("Men don't cry") and what those displays indicate about character ("She's too emotional") (Zucker & Harshaw, 2012). At its essence, such debate indicates that, despite advances in affective neuroscience supporting the necessity of emotional experience, individuals are socialized to feel guilty about unavoidable biological reactions.

This deep-seated ambivalence regarding the value of emotion is of great importance for understanding the development of emotional experience and rules for emotional expression in those with eating disorders and their families. First, consider the interpersonal nature of emotion as depicted in Figure 15.1. Given that emotions communicate needs to others, if an individual fosters a belief that one should *not* display emotions, then others have difficulty perceiving the needs of the individual who is suppressing emotional experience. Critically, as time progresses, what may have begun as a deliberate attempt to suppress emotion may have become so automatic that the individual does not appreciate the disjunction between what one is feeling and what one is expressing and thus may feel confused or abandoned when individuals do not respond to their emotional needs (Figure 15.2). This example illustrates how the function of emotion is thwarted when emotions are not expressed.

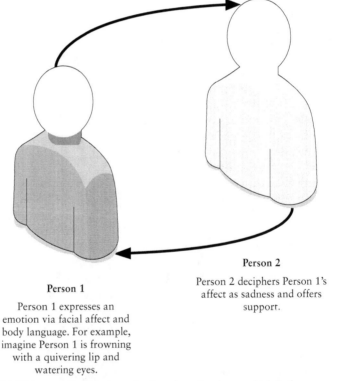

Person 2

Person 2 deciphers Person 1's affect as sadness and offers support.

Person 1

Person 1 expresses an emotion via facial affect and body language. For example, imagine Person 1 is frowning with a quivering lip and watering eyes.

Figure 15.1 This example illustrates the function of sadness, which is the communication of support.

Second, there are intrapersonal costs to emotional suppression. If emotions signal needs, and an individual is either unwilling to acknowledge or to respond to one's own internal state, such denial or neglect could

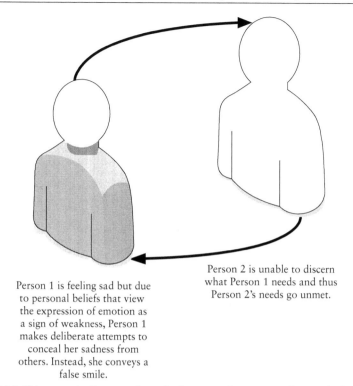

Person 1 is feeling sad but due to personal beliefs that view the expression of emotion as a sign of weakness, Person 1 makes deliberate attempts to conceal her sadness from others. Instead, she conveys a false smile.

Person 2 is unable to discern what Person 1 needs and thus Person 2's needs go unmet.

Figure 15.2 This example illustrates how the function of emotion is thwarted when emotions are not expressed.

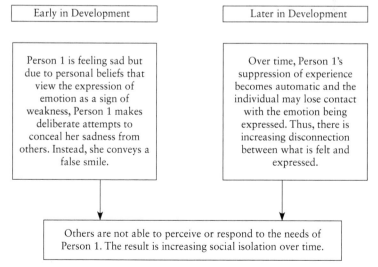

Early in Development

Person 1 is feeling sad but due to personal beliefs that view the expression of emotion as a sign of weakness, Person 1 makes deliberate attempts to conceal her sadness from others. Instead, she conveys a false smile.

Later in Development

Over time, Person 1's suppression of experience becomes automatic and the individual may lose contact with the emotion being expressed. Thus, there is increasing disconnection between what is felt and expressed.

Others are not able to perceive or respond to the needs of Person 1. The result is increasing social isolation over time.

Figure 15.3

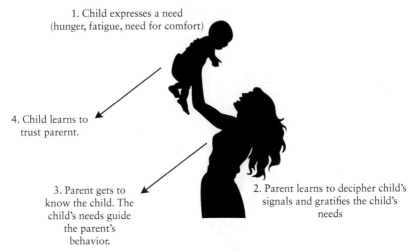

1. Child expresses a need
(hunger, fatigue, need for comfort)

4. Child learns to
trust parernt.

3. Parent gets to
know the child. The
child's needs guide
the parent's
behavior.

2. Parent learns to decipher child's
signals and gratifies the child's
needs

Figure 15.4 **The infant-parent transactions that serve as the foundation of a secure attachment.**

have profound implications for the development of self-awareness, self-knowledge, and self-trust (Figure 15.3). Such dire consequences may be better understood from the framework of healthy development, particularly the parent–infant transactions that establish the foundation for the development of a secure attachment (Figure 15.4). Consider a healthy infant who appropriately signals wants and needs (e.g., hunger, comfort, fatigue). Using the infant's cries of distress, the parent learns to decipher the nuances of these signals and responds with food to a hunger cry, with nurturance to a distressed cry, and so on. In part as a result of the reliable response to such infant cries, the parent comes to know his or her infant. The infant's needs help guide the parent's behavior. In turn, the infant comes to trust the parent, accepting him or her as the reliable source of needs gratification. Furthermore, the repeated back and forth between infant and parents, particularly the growing realization of the infant that he or she is something that facilitates a response from others helps the infant to develop self-awareness—the infant is someone who exists and elicits responses from others. Thus, the results of this responsive parent–infant transaction are trust, knowledge, and self-awareness.

By corollary, one of the goals of development is co-opting caregiver caretaking and becoming one's own "self-parent" (Figure 15.5). Just like a responsive parent responds to his or her child's need, a responsive self-parent would reliably and adaptively respond to his or her own needs (e.g., of hunger, thirst, fatigue, distress) and, consequently, would develop self-knowledge, self-trust, and self-awareness. Unfortunately, the nature of eating disorders is that of denial of neglect of these internal needs, and consequently, the cost is not only physical but also broad deficits in self-awareness, self-trust, and self-knowledge. If a secure attachment creates the safety necessary for

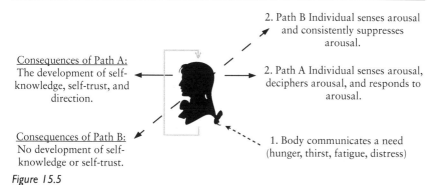

Figure 15.5

exploration, this self-neglect creates a context of insecurity. As in any state of insecurity, an individual in a state of threat sticks to what is predictable and known rather than daring to engage in novel activities. Consequently, the self-denial that characterizes individuals with eating disorders has additional negative consequences: narrowing an individual's behavioral repertoire with implications for the availability of a range of emotion regulatory strategies.

Individuals with eating disorders need to acknowledge and identify emotional experience; however, there are also contexts in which emotional experience needs to be channeled (Zucker & Harshaw, 2012). In fact, the regulation of emotion is a crucial adaptive skill. Despite the utility and importance of emotional experience described earlier, emotions are sometimes undesirable, sometimes an annoyance, and sometimes inconvenient. As eloquently described by Goldsmith, Pollack, and Davidson, "Among the most consequential behavioral and neural changes that have occurred over the course of phylogeny is the capacity to regulate emotion" (2008, p. 132). Thus, although emotions can usefully facilitate goal pursuit and signal motivational needs, contemporary rules of civilization demand that individuals sometimes inhibit emotional impulses. Indeed, complex social situations contain multiple competing demands, and this conflict in goal pursuit (e.g., hating your boss but wanting to keep your job) often necessitates that we suppress one emotional urge in order to potentiate and satisfy another. Thus, proficient emotion regulation requires that a hierarchy be established whereby the competing demands are prioritized based on complex stopping rules (Williams, Bargh et al., 2009). In other words, based on an individual's priorities and values, the presence of competing goals and associated emotional experiences will dictate which emotions are suppressed and which emotions are selectively expressed to facilitate one goal while postponing the acquisition of a second goal. Combined, this requires negotiation of inner response conflict. In contrast, if there were no conflict, there would presumably be no need to regulate. We will return to this issue as we discuss the role of attention and emotion regulation as deficits in executive function in individuals with eating disorders, which may complicate the flexible response conflict demanded by emotion regulation.

Emotion regulation has been variably defined. Most definitions none-theless cluster around the theme of cognitive and behavioral facilitation of goal pursuit. Specifically, emotion regulation is considered to be those behaviors and strategies that inhibit or integrate emotional experience to facilitate goal acquisition (Gross & Thompson, 2007; Eisenberg, Spinrad et al., 2010). As mentioned earlier, given that emotional experience itself facilitates goal pursuit, emotion regulation only becomes necessary when a conflict exists in goal pursuit. Furthermore, emotion regulatory strate-gies can be either conscious or nonconscious. For example, infants display capacities to regulate arousal via shifts in attention, certainly performed without conscious intention (Posner & Rothbart, 2009). And, in fact, there is evidence that infants begin to use emotion regulation strategies (such as attention disengagement) as early as three months of age (Posner & Rothbart, 1998; Calkins, Dedmon et al., 2002). Given the early age at which emotion regulatory capacities begin to emerge, numerous regula-tory strategies likely occur outside of conscious awareness and thus may be automatically executed (Williams, Bargh et al., 2009). As pointed out by Bargh and Williams (2007), automaticity of emotion regulation may, in theory, become increasingly likely the more a given strategy is performed in a given context, as distributed neural circuits become increasingly potentiated by repeated coactivation in particular contexts (Hebb, 2002). This is consistent with current emphases in emotion regulation research, in that a given strategy or even the broad construct of regulating emotions is relatively adaptive or maladaptive, given the goal in question and the given context. Theoretically, if a person engages in a particular regulatory strategy within a particular context and encounters that context with great frequency, over time, he may become increasingly better at inhibiting emo-tional experience to facilitate goal pursuit in that context. Furthermore, he may be unaware that he is regulating his emotions, and even further, these processes may become so automatic that the initial emotional experience and trigger(s) may not enter awareness. Additionally, Bargh and Williams (2009) examined how goal pursuit itself can even become nonconscious with repetition. If these assumptions are tenable, the end result of highly proficient emotion regulation could, over time, be a general lack of emo-tional awareness (Zucker & Harshaw, 2012).

Synthesis

Let's consider this knowledge of conscious and nonconscious emotion regulation when considering the developmental trajectories of those who develop eating disorders. Figure 15.6 shows two divergent developmental paths. In Path A, the child, prior to developing an eating disorder, was emotionally volatile and impulsive. There were no deficits in the display of emotional experience as emotions were expressed freely, but there may have been putative deficits in capacities to regulate emotions. Enter the

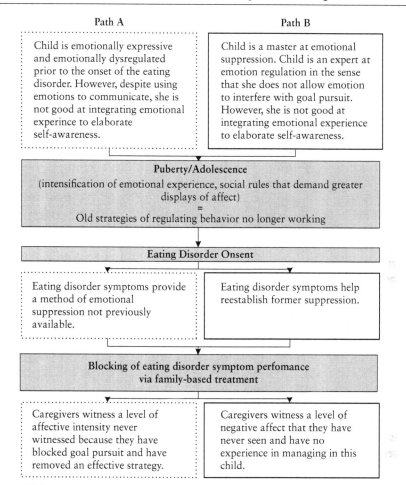

Figure 15.6

eating disorder. For these individuals, eating disorder symptoms may be one of the few successful strategies to suppress affect. This situation raises several consequences for treatment. First, eating disorder symptoms may be both a means to an end (facilitate the goal of weight loss) and may have the secondary "benefit" of suppressing emotional experience. Predictably then, the interruption of eating disorder symptoms, as occurs via family-based treatment, would pose a "double whammy" in terms of emotional expression. First, emotions would be expressed intensely because there is a barrier to goal pursuit. Second, emotions would be expressed intently because the individual has just been deprived of an emotion regulation strategy. Knowing this can help therapists and caregivers put the display of affect of Path A in context. Consider Path B. Prior to illness onset, individuals that corresponded to Path B were expert emotion regulators to the extent that they were masters at not allowing emotional experience to interfere with goal pursuit (e.g., as would occur in those with elevated achievement striving). With adolescence and the intensification of emotional experience that may accompany puberty, it could be the case that old strategies are proving increasingly ineffective or that new goals have surfaced that demand increasing or different capacities to regulate affect. The eating disorder symptoms could be viewed as emergency strategies that are more necessary to return the individual back to a prepubertal state physiologically (where former strategies may once again be effective), or as additions to the emotional suppression armamentarium (e.g., along with intense studying, overzealous pursuit of extracurricular activities, etc.). With Path B, the prevention of eating disorder symptoms as with family-based treatment results in something potentially unexpected: a display of emotions that have never yet been witnessed by the family system or experienced by the individual with the eating disorder. Thus, it would be easy to conclude that treatment is somehow not working as it is making the family system more upset. In fact, this novel and intense display of emotional experience is actually a unique opportunity: individuals along Path B can be taught to be aware of and interpret the meaning of emotional experience so that the deficits in self-awareness alluded to earlier can be addressed.

The sections that follow delve into invention. Using emotion regulatory frameworks of Thompson and Gross (2007), we discuss how current eating disorder symptoms may function to suppress emotional experience and how strategies integrated into family-based treatment may be used to capitalize on this symptomatic period not only to improve eating disorder symptoms but also to enhance self-awareness of both the individual with the eating disorder and his or her caregiver.

Types of Emotion Regulatory Strategies

Several classification schemes have been developed to organize emotion regulation strategies. Research into specific regulatory strategies has indicated that some strategies may be more adaptive than others in facilitating downregulation of physiological arousal and permitting subsequent goal pursuit (Ochsner, Bunge et al., 2002). Notwithstanding, delineation of an emotion regulatory strategy as adaptive or maladaptive is ultimately contextually specific. In the section that follows, we first consider the strategies that have received the most empirical support; namely, emotional suppression (e.g., distraction) and reappraisal. We then examine how cognitive capacities may influence choice of emotion regulatory strategy (for a more detailed discussion, see Zucker & Harshaw, 2012). Finally, we consider whether these strategies are adaptive or maladaptive with implications for treatment.

The emotion regulation classification scheme of Gross and Thompson (2007) employs the temporal dynamics of a situation to frame both the timing and functioning of certain regulatory strategies. Antecedent strategies refer to those techniques undertaken prior to or *in anticipation of* the occurrence of an emotional response elicited by some evocative situation. Response-focused strategies, on the other hand, are analogous to "damage control," representing attempts to modify emotional experience *after* a response has been generated. Gross and Thompson (2007) delineated five families of emotion regulatory processes: situation selection, situation modification, attention deployment, cognitive change, and response modulation. In the sections that follow, we consider the use of these strategies with due consideration to the phenomenology of eating disorders, since research evidence is lacking to support the preferential use of these strategies. Where possible, we bring in evidence that may indirectly support the use of these strategies.

Situation Selection

Situation selection refers to the intentional avoidance of situations likely to be emotionally evocative. Many individuals with eating disorders endorse elevations in the trait feature of harm avoidance, with the implication that individuals high in this trait feature do indeed avoid situations with the potential for emotional volatility (Zucker & Harshaw, 2012). What would these situations be? Any situation involving uncertainty would have the potential to be emotionally evocative, so one hypothesis is that those with eating disorders gravitate toward those situations and activities with very clearly defined rules. For example, the high achievement striving reported in those with anorexia nervosa may be manifested by excessive participation in extracurricular activities with clearly defined rules rather than those that lack structure (e.g., participating in ballet versus modern dance, joining a club after school rather than inviting a friend over) (Zucker, Losh et al., 2007). The ill state of anorexia nervosa may further influence situation selection. Seminal studies of human starvation by Dr. Ancel Keys and colleagues (Keys, 1950) revealed increased social isolation among adult males who were calorically deprived over a prolonged period. Similarly, the starvation pathognomonic of anorexia nervosa may potentiate the avoidance of ambiguous situations specifically, or more rule-governed and predictable social venues, more generally. Whether such situation selection is a way of *avoiding* more nuanced and ambiguous social contexts, a way of *seeking* activities that bring a sense of pleasure and accomplishment, or likely a weighting of both, necessitates that researchers understand the function and relative adaptiveness of situation selection in those with anorexia nervosa, in particular, or eating disorders, more generally.

Notwithstanding, for an adolescent, particularly a young adolescent, situation selection is not always the sole choice of the child. Rather, sensitive parents intending to protect their children from harm may also preselect those environments less likely to be threatening. The closest body of evidence to support this possibility is research related to anxious parents. Studies of anxious parenting indicate that parents may sometimes underestimate their child's capacity to deal with threat and subsequently may only expose their children to low-threat situations. Although well-intended and certainly empathic to the child's emotional needs, over time, such protection may have the unintended effect of giving the children less practice in dealing with complicated social situations (Gruner, Muris et al., 1999; Shortt, Barrett et al., 2001). Indeed, finding the balance of when to protect and when to gently nudge is one of the many complex tasks of parenting. Whether the same dynamic extends to parents of those with eating disorders remains to be investigated. However, it is also conceivable that the extreme perfectionism and related achievement striving of those with eating disorders and their parents is protective of such avoidance—given the potential ramifications of avoidance of feared situations with a loss of status (e.g., missing a competition, fear of friends talking about you if you are not there) (Zucker & Harshaw, 2012). If so, then other emotion regulatory strategies, such as situation modification and cognitive change, may be more useful for those with eating disorders, as explained in the following sections.

Situation Selection: Implications for Symptom Expression

In the ill state, those with eating disorders may abuse the strategy of situation selection to the extent that it interferes with the development of mastery over novel situations. As will be discussed, while certain aspects of this avoidance may be appropriate and even adaptive in the beginning stages of treatment, the continuance of avoidance, as in the stage of treatment when the adolescent has regained control over eating and is reestablishing healthy adolescent trajectories, would be maladaptive. Because of this difference, we discuss maladaptive avoidance and subsequent treatment strategies in the beginning (e.g., Stage 1 in family-based treatment) and end of treatment (e.g., Stage 3 in family-based treatment).

Beginning of Treatment

It is worthwhile to spend a moment inside the head of an individual with an eating disorder. When adolescents with eating disorders are developing strategies to reduce their eating disorder symptoms, a great deal of mental effort is required. Those with eating disorders have described their internal experience as having the presence of intrusive, cruel thoughts.

"Don't eat that, you fat pig. You disgust me. If you eat that, you will never be able to accomplish anything. You will lose all self-discipline and become nothing."

While eating foods that were previously restricted or while resisting the urge to vomit, the intensity (e.g., of content, of volume) of these thoughts/

voices will increase. Thus, situations that are pleasantly distracting may reduce distress; situations with excessive stimulation may make it more difficult to eat. For example, adolescents may report that they have an easier time eating with the television on, while reading a book, or in the company of friends but may struggle a great deal with all the commotion of a big family meal with extended relatives or in a restaurant. In fact, some adolescents may struggle to eat within the nuclear family and may make requests to eat at a separate time without other family members, but in the company of a parent. Whether this is adaptive or maladaptive coping depends on how this is framed and on what behaviors are reinforced. For example, to ensure that all children in the family receive one-on-one time with their parents, a parent who is engaging in one-on-one meal support may allot other one-on-one time with the other children (presumably doing things other than meal support). As the adolescent gets well and no longer needs the one-on-one meal support, this special one-on-one time can be maintained so that the adolescent learns that he or she does not have to be ill to get parental attention. Indeed, the quality of the time will improve. Alternatively, the parents may choose to make sure that the adolescent gets the support of the entire family and so continues to eat with everyone. However, in this circumstance, the family may have to employ exercises so that the adolescent's internal struggle is made a family struggle. For example, the adolescent may write down the cruel messages passing through her mind on slips of paper so the entire family can unite in disempowering the power of the words. The overall strategy then is that antecedent emotion regulation strategies such as situation avoidance may be adaptive in the early phases of treatment but become maladaptive as treatment progresses.

Treatment Progress

The question then becomes, what is the appropriate degree of avoidance of situations? As stated, it would be appropriate to avoid certain situations in the beginning of treatment and to "work up to them" as families get more comfortable with strategies to manage eating. Thus, it is not "giving into the eating disorder" or "letting the eating disorder control the family" to deliberately avoid family events or restaurants in the beginning of treatment. However, as treatment progresses and strategies around symptom improvement are more firmly established, the continued avoidance of more complicated eating environments would be more maladaptive. This is the case because such avoidance would prevent the establishment of new skills of mastery around these complex environments.

Eating contexts represent only one type of environment that may be avoided. Those who are high in the temperament trait of harm avoidance value certainty and predictability. Thus, organized social activities, such as extracurricular activities, may be sought, while relatively unstructured and unpredictable activities, such as inviting a friend over after school, may be avoided. We discuss other strategies that may be employed to avoid potentially distressing circumstances *within* a situation in the following sections.

Situation Modification

Situation modification refers to alterations in chosen environments to reduce emotion arousal (Lewinsohn, Sullivan et al., 1980). Because there are a multitude of strategies that can be employed, this section highlights two that are well-documented and that have the potential for abuse. These include knowledge acquisition and conflict avoidance. One pattern of behavior that may reduce arousal in the short term, but exacerbate symptoms in the long term, is the need for information. Mealtimes are a salient example. Caregivers may have successfully established the child's regular attendance at mealtimes and so Situation Avoidance is no longer occurring. The adolescent may then move to the next antecedent emotion regulation strategy: trying to alter the nature of the situation so that it causes less distress. One way the adolescent may try to do this is to find out all the information she can about the situation so that she is minimizing her distress by decreasing her uncertainty. This scenario may be very familiar to caregivers.

"Did you use butter on those vegetables? Are you sure you just gave me one serving? What kind of turkey is this? ...

As an aside, this constant pressing for information and seeking of reassurance is one of the most exhausting aspects of the disorder for caregivers. It is also seductive for both caregivers and the individuals with eating disorders in that responding may seem to provide the adolescent with short-term comfort and the caregiver with a short-term break from the relentlessness of eating disorder symptoms. However, this behavior and response pattern is a never-ending and all-encompassing black hole. This is the case because there is always more information that can be obtained, and thus the "need to know" can become an avoidance strategy that further narrows options in that within a situation, only options with complete information will be sought.

However, seeking information is also an adaptive strategy in that it helps an individual to be prepared. This process thus illustrates a key feature of the behavioral and subsequent emotional dysregulation of those with eating disorders: the belief that more (more information, more effort, more dieting, more exercise) is always better. Unfortunately, this interpersonal and intrapersonal process does not promote the development of self-regulatory skills as the individual is not learning to cope with anxiety—just to suppress the experience of anxiety and to necessitate further information seeking to facilitate avoidance.

Clinical Strategies for Seeking Information

In fact, this pattern is an opportunity to practice limit setting on both the part of the caregiver and the individual with an eating disorder. Aristotle's

Golden Mean, Confucius' Doctrine of the Mean, or the Middle Path of Buddhist philosophy all emphasize that that there is a state of optimal synthesis that lies between two extremes. This point is empirically illustrated by the Yerke-Dodson Law, an upside-down u-shaped curve that illustrates the trade-off between anxiety and performance. While increasing arousal can facilitate performance, once arousal surpasses a certain threshold, performance declines. This same framework can be applied to any context in which the child with an eating disorder is pushing past optimal limits to gather information/achieve outcomes. For example, the parent can set a limit on the number of questions the child can ask per day (about eating disorder related issues, of course). This would be an example of helping the child move an antecedent emotion regulation strategy, that of seeking information, from dysfunctional to adaptive (the child gets some information to help prepare, but not so much that the object becomes to eliminate all uncertainty).

Applying a strategy that deprives an individual of a coping strategy, no matter how maladaptive, will initially greatly exacerbate distress. The classic phenomenon of extinction burst provides a learning framework of why this would be the case. Let's stick with this same example, that of seeking information (Figure 15.7). In Step 1, the child with an eating disorder asks for information. If the parent chooses Option 1, giving him or

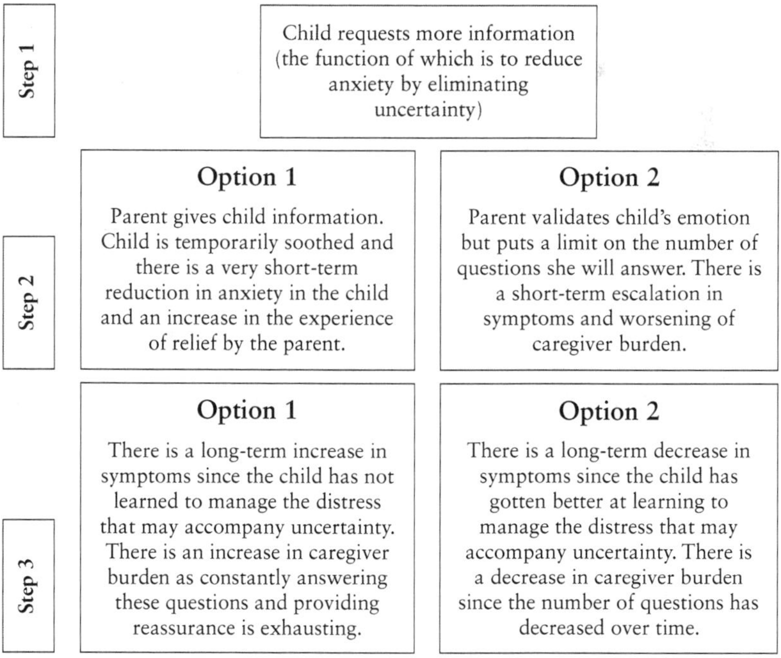

Step 1

Child requests more information (the function of which is to reduce anxiety by eliminating uncertainty)

Step 2

Option 1

Parent gives child information. Child is temporarily soothed and there is a very short-term reduction in anxiety in the child and an increase in the experience of relief by the parent.

Option 2

Parent validates child's emotion but puts a limit on the number of questions she will answer. There is a short-term escalation in symptoms and worsening of caregiver burden.

Step 3

Option 1

There is a long-term increase in symptoms since the child has not learned to manage the distress that may accompany uncertainty. There is an increase in caregiver burden as constantly answering these questions and providing reassurance is exhausting.

Option 2

There is a long-term decrease in symptoms since the child has gotten better at learning to manage the distress that may accompany uncertainty. There is a decrease in caregiver burden since the number of questions has decreased over time.

Figure 15.7

her information, the child is temporarily soothed. However, this behavior on the part of the parent reinforces the behavior of asking for information in the child. In Step 2 along this path, the behavior of asking has increased in frequency. The parent continues to supply the answers, and the child is soothed—but now such asking is exacting a greater toll on both caregiver and child. Step 3 shows the longer term result of this strategy: an overall increase in eating disorder symptoms and worsening of caregiver burden. Option 2 illustrates the short-term aftermath of a change in strategy. The parent decides that the strategy of giving information is backfiring and explains to the child that he or she will not be answering this continual stream of questions because it is not helping the child learn to cope with not knowing. Instead, the child can ask one question before each meal. The short-term aftermath of this change in strategy is a sharp escalation in symptoms: there are more questions asked, there may be an increase in verbal abuse on the part of the child, there may even be an escalation in self-harm behaviors. Step 2 describes how the parent manages the escalation of an extinction burst. Basically, the parent validates the child's feelings while not reinforcing maladaptive behaviors. This may include ignoring the escalation of behaviors while sticking to the strategy of not providing information.

A second example of situation modification is that of conflict avoidance. In individuals with eating disorders, conflict avoidance represents one consistently reported interactional style that may help to minimize the need for emotion regulation due to the avoidance of emotional displays that may result from interpersonal disagreement (Lattimore, Gowers et al., 2000; Lattimore, Wagner et al., 2000). For example, Lattimore, Gowers, and Wagner (2000) report that individuals with anorexia nervosa exhibited greater autonomic reactivity in a laboratory conflict task with their mothers. While not supporting conflict avoidance, these findings support the intensity with which conflictual reactions are experienced. Those individuals who displayed such reactivity also endorsed greater impairment in the ability to problem-solve interpersonal conflict. If we assume that those with anorexia nervosa, specifically, and eating disorders, more generally, typically avoid such conflicts, increased reactivity and decrements in problem-solving may be the interpersonal costs of such avoidance (Zucker & Harshaw, 2012). In other words, although the avoidance of future conflicts would potentially circumvent such autonomic reactivity acutely, the long-term consequence is reduced proficiency in dealing with interpersonal conflict, particularly if such avoidance is a stable interpersonal pattern.

There are long-term interpersonal and intrapersonal consequences when strategies of situation modification are overused. For instance, conflict avoidance may interfere with the development of *theory of mind*. Theory of mind is a complex construct whereby we understand that others have minds different from our own, minds with distinct thoughts, opinions, and experiences, originating from others' unique perspectives (Baron-Cohen,

Leslie et al., 1985). Theory of mind has been found to be enhanced in families with siblings and decreased in families in which parents are elevated in harm avoidance, the hypothesis being that sibling conflict is a potent teacher about different states of mind (Cole & Mitchell, 2000). Conflict arises when people differ in their opinions, and thus, conflict among siblings and family members may facilitate the development of theory of mind. As a corollary, the avoidance of conflict may impair development of theory of mind.

Alternatively, the avoidance of conflict may prevent elaboration of the individual's own beliefs and opinions (Zucker & Harshaw, 2012). A poorly operationalized lay term used among many parents of children with eating disorders is that they are "people pleasers"—presumably going out of their way to attend to the emotional needs of others. Conflict avoidance would be but one example of such interactional tendencies. Although such interactional styles would presumably facilitate the development of theory of mind (i.e., awareness that others have a mind with related preferences, opinions, etc.), what may fail to develop is the opposite: that the individual with an eating disorder has a mind of his or her own, with the potential for differing beliefs or opinions. Although a discussion of self-deficits in individuals with eating disorders is beyond the scope of this chapter (instead, see Goodsitt, 1997), what is germane is the developmental consequences of particular emotion regulatory strategies if applied rigidly and systematically across contexts. For those with eating disorders, the tendency to rigidly engage in situation modification strategies such as avoiding conflict may also have implications for the development of interpersonal relationships. Asher, Parker, and Walker (1996) reviewed studies of friendship formation in adolescence to derive a list of those features that are necessary for the creation of affective relationships. The ability to resolve conflict and the ability to express differing opinions were among the ten features listed. This is not surprising, given the prior discussion that conflict facilitates the development of theory of mind, whereas the expression of differing opinions helps individuals get to know each other. Unfortunately, the nature of friendships in those with eating disorders, let alone the barriers and assets in the formation of these relationships, is vastly understudied.

Treatment implications of conflict avoidance

To be sure, the nature of family-based treatment, with its emphasis on renourishment and symptom reduction, will inevitably create situations in which interpersonal conflict is unavoidable. However, the availability of such situations is necessary but not sufficient to facilitate improved authentic interpersonal communication. Another piece is the capacity to facilitate emotional arousal to permit the exchange of differing opinions in a manner that facilitates communication but not personal attacks. To help achieve this goal, a metaphor that both caregivers and their children have found to be helpful is that of an emotional wave (Figure 15.8). While

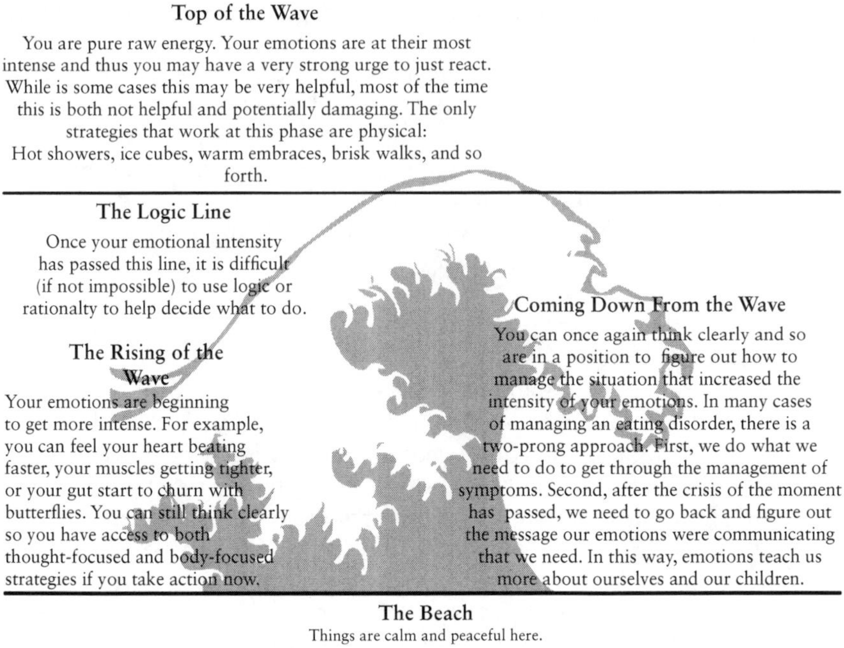

Top of the Wave
You are pure raw energy. Your emotions are at their most intense and thus you may have a very strong urge to just react. While is some cases this may be very helpful, most of the time this is both not helpful and potentially damaging. The only strategies that work at this phase are physical: Hot showers, ice cubes, warm embraces, brisk walks, and so forth.

The Logic Line
Once your emotional intensity has passed this line, it is difficult (if not impossible) to use logic or rationalty to help decide what to do.

The Rising of the Wave
Your emotions are beginning to get more intense. For example, you can feel your heart beating faster, your muscles getting tighter, or your gut start to churn with butterflies. You can still think clearly so you have access to both thought-focused and body-focused strategies if you take action now.

Coming Down From the Wave
You can once again think clearly and so are in a position to figure out how to manage the situation that increased the intensity of your emotions. In many cases of managing an eating disorder, there is a two-prong approach. First, we do what we need to do to get through the management of symptoms. Second, after the crisis of the moment has passed, we need to go back and figure out the message our emotions were communicating that we need. In this way, emotions teach us more about ourselves and our children.

The Beach
Things are calm and peaceful here.

Figure 15.8

the concept of the emotional wave is fully described in the later section on response modulation, this construct is raised here to demonstrate the identification of intensity of emotional arousal. Simply, the height of the wave corresponds to the intensity of emotional experience. The rising of the wave corresponds to rising intensity of emotional experience and the falling of the wave represents the decrease in intensity that follows the peak experience. As will be discussed in the section on response modulation, the choice of strategy is most optimally matched to the level of intensity of emotional experience.

Attention Deployment

The ability to manipulate attention is an emotion regulation strategy that emerges early in development (Gaertner, Spinrad et al., 2008; Eisenberg, Spinrad et al., 2010). Shifting eye gaze toward something pleasing to amplify positive affect or away from something distressing remains a powerful way to alter emotional experience (Gaertner, Spinrad et al., 2008). Consequently, capacities to shift attention, whether consciously or nonconsciously, have implications for abilities to regulate emotional experiences (Simonds, Kieras et al., 2007). This has profound implications for those with eating disorders, for whom deficits in executive attention have been the most consistently neurocognitive feature. In the specific case of anorexia nervosa, deficits in shifting attention between cognitive sets, or set-shifting, have been demonstrated to persist with weight restoration in adult samples (Roberts, Tchanturia et al., 2007). Such deficits in shifting attention may impact the ability of those with eating disorders to use this as an emotion regulatory strategy (Zucker & Harshaw, 2012). Research supports attention biases to illness-related stimuli and the association of such biases on symptom severity (Jansen, Nederkoorn et al., 2005; Smith & Rieger, 2006), although the etiological significance of such illness-related biases remains unclear (Side Box 1).

Side Box 1. Clinical Significance of Deficits in Executive Attention

Earlier in this chapter, we mentioned how individuals with eating disorders may excessively engage in situation avoidance as a way to regulate affect. Considering that the capacity to shift attention is a crucial emotion regulatory strategy, and given that indiviudals with eating disorders have documented deficits in this capacity, it may be that this avoidance is quite adaptive as once in a high risk situation, they have trouble modulating affect.

Eating disorder symptoms may function as a way to redirect attention. Distraction is the direction of attention toward events other than the emotionally provocative event. Numerous formulations of the function of eating disorder symptoms have posited that symptoms such as binge eating and cognitive dietary restraint may be negatively reinforced, in part, because these symptoms distract attention from other threatening (but arguably less "controllable") concerns (Heatherton & Baumeister, 1991; Pokrajac-Bulian, Tkalcic et al., 2009; Zucker, Herzog et al., 2011). Consider the symptom of binge eating. During the actual binge eating event, the individual is distracted from other events (both external and internal) as attention is narrowed to the hedonic qualities of the food. Binge eating has even been described as an altered level of conscious awareness, although the relationship between binge eating and memory has been a limited focus of study. Binge eating may facilitate attention shifting even after the binge eating event is over, as attention that was previously perseveratively focused on a stressful life event is now shifted to a perseverative focus on the binge eating episode that just occurred. Given prior evidence of set-shifting, it could be argued that it would take another emotionally evocative event of equivalent or greater magnitude to facilitate such a shift of attention. Dietary rumination may also serve as a distraction, such as counting calories and planning meals. These very cognitive activities have been found to downregulate visceral arousal (see Cognitive Change). In fact, work by Merwin, Moskowich, and Zucker (2010) reported that dietary restraint was uniquely related to emotion regulatory deficits in adults with AN, even those with a prior history, relative to healthy controls. Eating disorder symptoms have long been posited to serve as regulators of emotional experience. Emotion regulatory classification schemes provide a useful framework to organize these strategies and thereby derive specific hypotheses about the compensatory function of specific symptom profiles.

Treatment Implications of Attention Deployment

Should caregivers be instructed to make their home "safe" by eliminating stimuli that may be provocative and distracting and thus may elicit eating disorder cognitions and behaviors? Should caregivers make meals safer by providing sources of distraction during a meal? Given the challenges that those with eating disorders have in shifting cognitive sets, and the resulting perseveration and acute exacerbation of symptoms that may ensue following a cue-triggering event, it is very tempting for caregivers to do both of those things. Given the acute medical severity posed by an eating disorder, it is also tempting for therapists to encourage strategies that lead to attention allocation to less threatening stimuli. None of these strategies are maladaptive in of themselves, and at times, such strategies may be very adaptive. However, the use of distraction or the determined avoidance of distracting cues may become maladaptive if they are used inflexibly (e.g., if caregivers always promote avoidance). Thus, the effective use of attention deployment comes down to sequencing and timing.

Distraction may be appropriate and helpful in the initial stages of treatment. For example, in the initial phases of renourishment, a child may be in a starved state and his or her capacities to shift attention may be severely impaired. Alternatively, an adolescent may be prevented from using dangerous weight loss behaviors for emotion regulation, but it is too early in the treatment of the adolescent to have acquired more adaptive emotion regulatory strategies. In such initially fragile circumstances, there is so much flooding already occurring in terms of consuming adequate nutrition, that watching a television show of emaciated runway models may be too much to ask. Thus, caregivers may legitimately try to make the home environment safer by eliminating provocative cues and may wish to limit plans with other friends who are engaged in unhealthy weight loss behaviors. However, as treatment progresses, there will be a need to increasingly approach and integrate objects, people, and situations that are preoccupying.

A parallel context occurs in the use of exposure-based treatments for those with anxiety disorders. Traditionally, an individual may make a list of the objects, people, and situations that are feared; may rank them according to how fearful they are, and then may work to gradually approach them one by one. More recently, it has been reported that approaching items and situations randomly from across this distribution promotes greater reductions in fear and greater generalization (Lang & Craske, 2000; Kircanski, Mortazavi et al., 2012). Thus, rather than systematically going one by one through the list of avoided circumstances from least to most fearful, parent and child would be constantly "shaking things up"—approaching situations unpredictably in random orders. This strategy also helps to prevent the overuse of antecedent emotion regulation strategies as there is less opportunity to plan.

An additional strategy involves improving capacities to shift attention. One example is the use of mindfulness. Mindfulness is proposed to be comprised of two facets: present moment awareness and nonjudgmental acceptance of thoughts, sensations, and emotions (Cardaciotto, Herbert et al., 2008; Teper, Segal et al., 2013). The practice of mindfulness actively engages the three facets of the attention network: alerting, orienting, and shifting. First, the practice of mindfulness involves honing one's ability to be "awake." This sense of being awake is not just the opposite of sleeping; rather, it is a state of intense sensibility where one is ready to receive the sensory information that unfolds. However, mindfulness is distinctly characterized by present-focused awareness. As our mind is constantly flooded with thoughts of past and future, the capacity to maintain this present focus involves a gentle guiding of attention from distracting thoughts and redirecting attention to ongoing experience as it unfolds. These actions mimic the processes of alerting, orienting, and shifting that form the basis of executive attention.

Mindfulness can be a family practice. Mindfulness can be a deliberate meditative exercise that is incorporated into a family's daily routine or the practice of mindfulness can be interspersed throughout the day in short snippets. For example, we have families insert a pause before the start of a meal. A pause cues individuals to slow down and to guide attention to observe all aspects of the meal (not just the food): one's family, one's surroundings, the smells, the sounds. Technological advances offer some rather unique opportunities for mindfulness. For example, there are Smartphone® applications that contain programmable "mindfulness bells." The sound of the mindfulness chime is a cue to focus on one's breathing. The breath is used as an entry point to gently guide attention to focus on ongoing experience. The framework of a mindful stance is one of nonjudgmental detachment. An individual notices broadly but describes objectively without bias. Thus, the use of strategies that capitalize on attention deployment can focus broadly on changing the environment, on enhancing the ability to flexibly shift attention, or on altering the framework from which one views ongoing experience.

Cognitive Change

Cognitive change refers to those strategies that impact our appraisal of a situation, including the meaning or significance of the event itself, our physiological response(s) to an event, or our capacity to handle that event. Reappraisal, the process of changing our appraisal of the emotional significance of an event, is an example of a cognitive change strategy that has been the focus of systematic empirical research (Gross, 1998). Reappraisal demands that the meaning of a situation be reframed (but could be applied to any aspect of emotional experience, such as somatic arousal or mood-congruent cognitions). For example, a person about to give a speech in front of class could evaluate the situation as being crucial to receiving the desired grade (an appraisal that would putatively increase anxiety) or as excellent practice for future job interviews (an appraisal that may increase enthusiasm) (Zucker & Harshaw, 2012). Similarly, those suffering from performance anxiety are often instructed to reframe intense feelings of arousal prior to a performance as being indicative of the necessary pump in adrenalin that enhances performance (see Roland, 1998). Thus, reappraisal may be utilized anywhere along the time sequence of an unfolding emotional event and the associated choice in behaviors that are motivated by emotional events.

There is accumulating evidence that reappraisal facilitates goal pursuit. To evaluate whether reappraisal is a relatively adaptive strategy in regulating emotion, the utility of reappraisal in facilitating goal pursuit in a given context can be examined. In this regard, the process of reappraisal appears to function as an adaptive regulatory strategy in that it increases neural activity associated with goal pursuit (Ochsner, Bunge et al., 2002). For instance, a study using oxygen-dependent functional neuroimaging examined the importance of individual differences in the use of reappraisal as a regulatory strategy. When individuals were asked to employ reappraisal during a functional neuroimaging task, those individuals who endorsed habitual use of reappraisal evidenced less activation in the distributed neural circuitry that accompanies perception of motivational salience and the accompanying visceral arousal that accompanies that experience of emotion (Drabant, McRae et al., 2009). There was also greater activation in distributed neural circuits implicated in planning and visceral—motor integration—that is, those cognitive functions necessary for the achievement of complex goal-directed actions. Simply, the pattern of results indicates that those individuals who habitually engage in reappraisal are doing more motivated planning in the context of emotionally evocative situations. This finding has been replicated in several investigations. However, what is particularly interesting in the study by Drabant et al. (2009) is that the habitual use of reappraisal was a stronger predictor of patterns of neural activation than were individual difference measures of neuroticism and trait anxiety, suggesting that it is the manner in which one integrates emotional experience rather than the intensity of the experience that is critical for adaptive self-regulation.

While previously discussed in the context of attention deployment, mindful observation may serve as another form of cognitive change that helps to regulate arousal. Prior work examining the somatic component of motivated states of emotional experience (i.e., studies of physiological changes that accompany emotion) have consistently reported that the act of perception (e.g., observation) decelerates heart rate (Bradley & Lang, 2007). In contrast, "thinking" that involves action selection involves heart rate acceleration. This makes logical sense. Reserving energetic resources while one takes stock of a situation would be advantageous, as would a rapid deployment of energy to facilitate the chosen action plan. Accordingly, mindful observation of situations without judgment or bias, the foundation of mindfulness, may function in part because these strategies facilitate perception and associated parasympathetic activation. Likewise, reappraisal may be a form of perception as individuals observe a situation to arrive at a different, less motivationally salient, global meaning.

How does this relate to those with eating disorders? Intriguingly, individuals with eating disorders may co-opt reappraisal to maintain the ill state (Zucker & Harshaw, 2012). In principle, those with eating disorders ought to be concerned about their life-threatening weight loss behaviors on several levels; this includes threats to health, potential morbidity, and extreme duress and worry caused to family members by such behaviors. Yet, those with eating disorders seem surprisingly impervious to these realities. A number of hypotheses have been put forward to explain this, including level of cognitive development, "denial," and deficits in social cognition (Bravender, Bryant-Waugh et al., 2007; Zucker, Losh et al., 2007). An additional hypothesis (or elaboration) would be that the poorly operationalized construct of denial is actually superior reappraisal: the ability to construe behaviors from a more optimal viewpoint that helps to resolve cognitive dissonance and helps facilitate the maintenance of behavior patterns.

Consider a typical scene in the life of someone with anorexia nervosa. Her mother gives her a hug and then breaks into sobs because the feel of her child's emaciated frame is emotionally overwhelming to the mother. She fears her child's death and verbalizes these concerns. How is it that someone with AN can be so immune to these emotional displays from a critical attachment figure? One possibility is reappraisal. Rather than attuning to the message and emotion of her mother, a far more effective solution from an emotion regulatory standpoint (when goal pursuit is further weight loss) is to reframe the situation via reappraisal: "My mother is too melodramatic," "My mother is jealous of my size," or "My mother is too overweight to know what healthy really is." Indeed, reappraisal in this context, in addition to decreasing emotional arousal and facilitating illness behaviors, may be further negatively reinforced due to the added incentive of reducing cognitive dissonance (Festinger, 1999). Dissonance is an increased experience of discomfort that results when our behavior does not match our values. To resolve this experience of discomfort, an individual has two choices. She can either change her values or change her behavior. Thanks to reappraisal, those with anorexia nervosa do not have to change either. They can resolve dissonance by changing their appraisal of the situation. For example, the thought process of those with anorexia nervosa would be, "Mom is worried without cause because she is the real problem. She is far too emotional." The result, according to the literature on reappraisal, is suppression of emotional experience to facilitate goal acquisition. It would then appear that those with anorexia nervosa are indeed masters of emotion regulation (Zucker & Harshaw, 2012).

Treatment Implications of Cognitive Change

Education about the processes of reappraisal is essential to help circumvent self-denial in those with eating disorders. This education is most helpfully delivered to the entire family, and the adolescent is encouraged to share how this process operates from his or her own experience. For example, we may have an adolescent provide a verbal description of walking through her day and to slowly describe the points in her day when she is faced with a critical choice: to act in the direction of her eating disorder or act in the direction of the valued life she is building. The adolescent can articulate the reappraisal strategies she uses to justify the choice, and then the therapist and family can observe with her the direction in which this choice will take her. The point is not to try to get the adolescent to think differently (which will just be met with resistance), but rather to help the adolescent understand how she is deceiving herself.

Innocuous somatic sensations may be conditioned to be experienced as aversive by those with eating disorders. Consequently, the meaning of those aversive sensations can be reappraised. For example, the state of fullness has been conditioned by many individuals with eating disorders to signal fatness, laziness, or loss of control. In this context, the meaning of fullness would be reappraised as a necessary experience to achieve one's academic aspirations. There is an important difference between this type of reappraisal versus more classic restructuring. In reappraisal, we are altering the relationship between objects or situations; we are not trying to alter the state itself or dispute the meaning of that state in isolation. We are altering the context in which the state occurs.

Response Modulation

Response modulation refers to the ways in which individuals directly intervene to impact the experience of an emotion, once the emotional response has already begun to occur. This strategy has been the most frequent focus of functional models of eating disorder symptomatology. These models consider how eating disorder symptoms may be maintained by the individual's attempts at increasing positive feelings (e.g., euphoria, with excessive exercise) or decreasing negative feelings (e.g., guilt, by adhering to a strict dietary regimen). Many of these models examine the distal relationships of emotion and eating disorder symptoms by employing self-report measures and examining longitudinal relationships among sizable groups of participants. For example, the dual-pathway model of Stice, Nemeroff, and Shaw (1996) highlights the role of elevated negative affect as a predictor of subsequent bulimic pathology independent of appearance-related concerns. Such distal relationships suggest that bulimic behaviors, such as binge eating and purgative behavior, may impact the experience of emotions.

Eating disorder symptoms, in general, have also received some preliminary support as emotion regulatory strategies. Wildes, Ringham, and Marcus (2010) examine the relationship of emotional avoidance as a mediator of depressive and anxiety symptoms and eating pathology. Findings reveal both enhanced endorsement of emotional avoidance relative to control samples and confirmation of emotional avoidance as a mediator between affective and eating disorder symptoms. Merwin et al. (2010) examined relationships between dietary restraint and emotion regulation in a sample of adults with a history of AN who were weight-restored, currently diagnosed with AN, or healthy control adult females. They reported that dietary restraint was associated with emotion regulatory strategies in both clinical groups but not in the healthy control group (Zucker & Harshaw, 2012).

Laboratory manipulations provide more proximal support for these relationships and have largely been examined in the context of stress manipulations, in which the degree of stress experienced by the participant is manipulated and effects on subsequent eating behavior are observed (Levine & Marcus, 1997; Oliver, Wardle et al., 2000). For example, when an eating disordered individual is in a stressful situation and experiences an increase in negative affect, he or she changes his or her eating behavior, presumably to mitigate negative emotional experience. Eating disorder symptoms can—by their very nature and subsequent influence on physiological parameters, changes in metabolism, and other effects—directly impact somatic experience with putative effects on emotional experience. To the degree that eating disorders influence cognitive parameters such as attention, they may additionally influence emotional experience via this mechanism.

Treatment Implications of Response Selection

If eating disorder symptoms function, in part, to regulate emotion, then preventing the performance of eating disorder symptoms will result in a surge of negative emotional experience and behaviors. This is a critical fact of which families must be made aware. Given the life-threatening nature of eating disorder symptoms, caregivers must intervene to reduce the frequency of eating disorder symptoms, a maladaptive coping strategy, before more adaptive coping strategies have been acquired or mastered. In essence, we are taking away the children's crutches before their bones have healed.

Often, the intense expression of negative emotion is the first time that the caregivers have ever seen such emotional intensity from their child. It would be natural to conclude that the treatment they are undertaking is not helpful and may even be harmful to their child. It is imperative that therapists explain how eating disorder symptoms may function to suppress or divert emotional experience and that this surge of negative affect is actually progress: the family can now face and figure out the needs the child was not communicating.

This does not imply that parents are instructed to tolerate rude or disrespectful behavior. It does mean that they are helped to validate the child's feelings while setting gentle limits on the forms of expression that are acceptable. Consider the following dialogue:

"I hate you. You are a fat ugly bitch and you are the worst mother in the world. All my friends hate you. I wish you weren't my mother."

"I hear that you are really angry, but I cannot listen to what you need when you speak to me like that."

To help parents and children navigate this challenging landscape, we employ the metaphor of the emotional wave mentioned earlier. Parents are instructed to locate themselves and their child along the wave as a way of determining their child's current level of emotional intensity. They are then instructed to match their chosen emotion regulatory strategy to their child's level of emotional intensity (and to their own). For example, if their child is "on the top of the wave," a location on the emotional wave that has crossed the Logic Line (Figure 15.8), then using logic and reasoning with the child will not be effective. Rather, the parent should join the child in using a sensory-based strategy to lower arousal before reengaging in the situation that first provoked the arousal. For example, imagine that the previous verbal diatribe occurred during a meal. The parent may decide to gently guide the child outside so that mother and child can sit quietly on the porch for a bit before going back inside to start dinner over again. What is most important about this strategy is the parent did not use words, she used touch. If instead, she had said:

"Let's go outside and get some fresh air."

She would have been met with a furious "NO!" The top of wave is no place for rationality; rather, parents should think of the strategies they used to help their children calm down when they were toddlers. Hugs and back rubs are still needed by adolescents (as much as they will not admit that they need them).

However, regulating arousal so it does not interfere with the goal of the moment (e.g., completing a meal or completing a meal without counterregulatory behaviors) is just the first part of building adaptive self-regulation in the child. If emotions communicate needs, then there is an additional step required if parents and child are to truly gain the self-knowledge that comes with adaptive emotion regulation. That additional step is that parents and children must explore the need that their emotion was communicating and work to validate that need and devise strategies to meet that need. Table 15.1 provides a quick shorthand of some putative needs that emotions may be expressing. Via this exploration of emotional awareness, parents and children can learn that emotions are vital communicative signals that can guide the development of adaptive solutions—rather than viewing emotions as something to be feared and avoided.

Example of eating disorder thought content

"Don't eat that, you fat pig. You disgust me. If you eat that, you will never be able to accomplish anything. You will lose all self-discipline and become nothing."

Table 15.1

Emotion	Potential Function of Emotions	Actions that May Address the Need
Guilt	In appropriate guilt, the feeling of guilt arises because one's actions have violated the rights of others. In inappropriate guilt, no one's rights were violated, but the feeling of guilt may ensue following a failure to achieve one's designated standards.	For appropriate guilt, an adaptive action is to repair the wrong that was committed. Apologize. Take actions to repair or fix the rights violation. For inappropriate guilt, an adaptive action is to engage in an act of self-compassion (e.g., allowing oneself to go to sleep when tired).
Shame	Shame is a complex emotion with usually an unclear but long history. Shame involves feelings of revulsion or disgust towards oneself.	An adaptive approach to shame may involve the open-minded exploration of the history of an individual so that there can be forgiveness and understanding for past events. An additional necessary approach to shame is the active engagement in behaviors towards the self that are loving and nurturing. Given the difficulty that those with eating disorders may have in doing this, I have found it helpful to have individuals take out baby pictures and direct actions of compassion to the young child that they once were.
Sadness	Sadness often communicates a loss and need for support.	Reach out to others. There is a need for nurturance and restoration. Thus, one might need to withdraw from activities and rest. The crucial thing here is that withdrawal is done from a context of nurturance and is not accompanied by guilt and blame for a loss of productivity. Demand a hug.

(Continued)

Emotion	Potential Function of Emotions	Actions that May Address the Need
Anger	Anger communicates that one's rights have been violated and that there is a need to protect oneself.	One option is to assertively request one's need. The important aspect to remember here is that assertiveness is about maintaining self-respect and self-dignity—not about changing the other person's behavior. The latter is out of an individual's control, and thus one can't rely on the change in the other person's actions to meet the need of anger. Voicing one's concern firmly may be the necessary first step.
Contentment	Contentment signals that all is well. One's needs are met and the current situation is worth maintaining.	Mindfulness awareness to the ongoing moment is essential. Individuals with eating disorders often have an aversive reaction to pleasant emotions—perhaps because they become too focused on the potential loss of when the emotion will end. Mindfulness can help to allow an individual to fully experience an emotion as it unfolds—not focus on the future termination of the experience.

Conclusion

This chapter has attempted to provide a framework for understanding emotion regulatory strategies in individuals with eating disorders so that family-based interventions can integrate this information into ongoing family-based treatment. In addition to discussing the temporal sequence of emotion regulatory strategies (antecedent/during/consequent), this chapter attempted to delineate the boundary between when a particular strategy is adaptive or maladaptive. For instance, strategies may be maladaptive if they promote such extensive avoidance (e.g., of situations or individuals) such that the acquisition of new skills is prevented. Furthermore, strategies can be maladaptive if they prevent the attainment of valued life directions (e.g., if they reduce arousal in the moment but create further distance between what the individual ultimately wishes to achieve). Ultimately, the goal of emotion regulation as incorporated into family-based treatment is to help families to regard and utilize emotional experience as the path to guide the emergence of self-knowledge, self-trust, and mutual trust. For it is by tuning into one's own emotions that an individual learns what he or she wants or needs. It is by acknowledging and responding to one's emotional needs that one comes to trust oneself, a process of self "secure attachment" that mimics the process of secure attachment between parent and child. Thus, by corollary, the consistent acknowledgment and responsiveness between parent and child of each other's emotional experience can promote mutual trust and understanding. From this framework, the emotional outbursts of an adolescent can be understand as hitherto unexpressed or ineffectively expressed and unmet needs. Ultimately, we want families to embrace and integrate emotional experience, not suppress and run from these crucial communicative signals.

References

Asher, S. R., Parker, J. G., & Walker, D. (1996). Distinguishing friendship from acceptance: Implications for intervention and assessment. In W. M. Bukowski, A. F. Newcomb, & W. W. Hartup (Eds.), *The Company They Keep: Friendship in Childhood and Adolescence* (pp. 366–406). Cambridge, UK: Cambridge University Press.

Bargh, J. A., & Williams, L. E. (2007). On the automatic or nonconscious regulation of emotion. In J. J. Gross (Ed.), *Handbook of emotion regulation* (429–445). New York, Guilford Press.

Baron-Cohen, S., Leslie, A. M., & Frith, U. (1985). Does the autistic child have a "theory of mind"? *Cognition, 21*(1), 37–46.

Bradley, M. M., & Lang, P. J. (2007). Emotion and motivation. In J. T. Cacioppo, L. G. Tassinary, & G. G. Berntson (Eds.), *Handbook of psychophysiology* (581–607). New York: Cambridge University Press.

Bravender, T., Bryant-Waugh, R., Herzog, D., Katzman, D., Kreipe, R. D., Lask, B., ... Adolescents. (2007). Classification of child and adolescent eating disturbances. Workgroup for Classification of Eating Disorders in Children and Adolescents (WCEDCA). *International Journal of Eating Disorders, 40 Suppl*, S117–122.

Calkins, S. D., Dedmon, S. E., Gill, K. L., Lomax, L. E., & Johnson, L. M. (2002). Frustration in Infancy: Implications for Emotion Regulation, Physiological Processes, and Temperament. *Infancy, 3*(2), 175–197. doi: 10.1207/s15327078in0302_4

Cardaciotto, L., Herbert, J. D., Forman, E. M., Moitra, E., & Farrow, V. (2008). The assessment of present-moment awareness and acceptance—The Philadelphia Mindfulness Scale. [Article]. *Assessment, 15*(2), 204–223. doi: 10.1177/1073191107311467

Cole, K., & Mitchell, P. (2000). Siblings in the development of executive control and a theory of mind. *British Journal of Developmental Psychology, 18*, 279–295.

Darwin, C. (2002). *The expression of emotion in man and animals.* Oxford, UK: Oxford University Press.

Drabant, E. M., McRae, K., Manuck, S. B., Hariri, A. R., & Gross, J. J. (2009). Individual Differences in Typical Reappraisal Use Predict Amygdala and Prefrontal Responses. *Biological Psychiatry, 65*(5), 367–373. doi: 10.1016/j.biopsych.2008.09.007

Eisenberg, N., Spinrad, T. L., & Eggum, N. D. (2010). Emotion-Related Self-Regulation and Its Relation to Children's Maladjustment. *Annual Review of Clinical Psychology, 6*, 495–525.

Festinger, L. (1999). Reflections on cognitive dissonance: 30 years later. In E. Harmon Jones & J. Mills (Eds.), *Cognitive Dissonance: Progress on a Pivotal Theory in Social Psychology* (381–385).

Fontaine, J. R. J., Scherer, K. R., Roesch, E. B., & Ellsworth, P. C. (2007). The world of emotions is not two-dimensional. *Psychological Science, 18*(12), 1050–1057.

Gaertner, B. M., Spinrad, T. L., & Eisenberg, N. (2008). Focused attention in toddlers: Measurement, stability, and relations to negative emotion and parenting. *Infant and Child Development, 17*(4), 339–363. doi: 10.1002/icd.580

Goldsmith, H. H., Pollak, S. D., & Davidson, R. J. (2008). Developmental Neuroscience Perspectives on Emotion Regulation. *Child Development Perspectives, 2*(3), 132–140.

Goodsitt, A. (1997). Eating disorders: A self-psychological perspective. In D. M. Garner & P. Garfinkel (Eds.), *Handbook of treatment for eating disorders* (205–228). New York, Gilford Press.

Gross, J. J. (1998). Antecedent- and response-focused emotion regulation: Divergent consequences for experience, expression, and physiology. *Journal of Personality and Social Psychology, 74*(1), 224–237.

Gross, J. J., & Thompson, R. A. (2007). *Emotion regulation: Conceptual foundations. Handbook of emotion regulation.* New York, Guilford Press.

Gruner, K., Muris, P., & Merckelbach, H. (1999). The relationship between anxious rearing behaviours and anxiety disorders symptomatology in normal children. *J Behav Ther Exp Psychiatry, 30*(1), 27–35.

Haynos, A. F., & Fruzzetti, A. E. (2011). Anorexia nervosa as a disorder of emotion dysregulation: Evidence and treatment implications. *Clinical Psychology-Science and Practice, 18*(3), 183–202.

Heatherton, T. F., & Baumeister, R. F. (1991). Binge eating as escape from self-awareness. *Psychological Bulletin, 110*(1), 86–108.

Hebb, D. O. (2002). *The organization of behavior: A neuropsychological theory.* Lawrence Erlbaum.

James, W. (1884). What is an emotion? *Mind, 9,* 188–205.

Jansen, A., Nederkoorn, C., & Mulkens, S. (2005). Selective visual attention for ugly and beautiful body parts in eating disorders. *Behaviour Research and Therapy, 43*(2), 183–196.

Keys, A. (1950). *The biology of human starvation.* Minneapolis, MN: University of Minnesota Press.

Kircanski, K., Mortazavi, A., Castriotta, N., Baker, A. S., Mystkowski, J. L., Yi, R., & Craske, M. G. (2012). Challenges to the traditional exposure paradigm: Variability in exposure therapy for contamination fears. *Journal of Behavior Therapy and Experimental Psychiatry, 43*(2), 745–751. doi: 10.1016/j.jbtep.2011.10.010

Lang, A. J., & Craske, M. G. (2000). Manipulations of exposure-based therapy to reduce return of fear: a replication. *Behaviour Research and Therapy, 38*(1), 1–12.

Lattimore, P. J., Gowers, S., & Wagner, H. L. (2000). Autonomic arousal and conflict avoidance in anorexia nervosa: A pilot study. *European Eating Disorders Review, 8*(1), 31–39.

Lattimore, P. J., Wagner, H. L., & Gowers, S. (2000). Conflict avoidance in anorexia nervosa: An observational study of mothers and daughters. *European Eating Disorders Review, 8*(5), 355–368. doi: doi: 10.1002/1099-0968(200010)8:5<355::aid-erv368>3.0.co;2-b

LeDoux, J. (2007). Unconscious and conscious contributions to the emotional and cognitive aspects of emotions: a comment of Scherer's view of what an emotion is. *Social Science Information, 46,* 395–405.

Levine, M. D., & Marcus, M. D. (1997). Eating behavior following stress in women with and without bulimic symptoms. *Annals of Behavioral Medicine, 19*(2), 132–138.

Lewinsohn, P. M., Sullivan, J. M., & Grosscup, S. J. (1980). Changing reinforcing events: An approach to the treatment of depression. *Psychotherapy: Theory, Research & Practice, 17*(3), 322–334.

Merwin, R. M. (2011). Anorexia nervosa as a disorder of emotion regulation: Theory, evidence, and treatment implications. *Clinical Psychology-Science and Practice, 18*(3), 208–214.

Merwin, R. M., Moskovich, A. A., Wagner, H. R., Ritschel, L. A., Craighead, L. W., & Zucker, N. L. (2013). Emotion regulation difficulties in anorexia nervosa: Relationship to self-perceived sensory sensitivity. *Cognition & Emotion, 27*(3), 441–452. doi: 10.1080/02699931.2012.719003

Merwin, R. M., Moskovich, A. A., & Zucker, N. L. (2010). *Dietary restraint as a maladaptive emotion regulation strategy among individuals with anorexia nervosa.* Paper presented at the Accepted for presentation at the annual meeting of the Association for Behavioral and Cognitive Therapies.

Ochsner, K. N., Bunge, S. A., Gross, J. J., & Gabrieli, J. D. E. (2002). Rethinking feelings: An fMRI study of the cognitive regulation of emotion. *Journal of Cognitive Neuroscience, 14*(8), 1215–1229.

Oliver, G., Wardle, J., & Gibson, E. L. (2000). Stress and food choice: A laboratory study. *Psychosomatic Medicine, 62*(6), 853–865.

Pokrajac-Bulian, A., Tkalcic, M., Kardum, I., Sajina, S., & Kukic, M. (2009). Perfectionism, Private Self-Consciousness, Negative Affect and Avoidance as Determinants of Binge Eating. *Drustvena Istrazivanja, 18*(1–2), 111–128.

Posner, M. I., & Rothbart, M. K. (1998). Attention, self-regulation and consciousness. *Philosophical Transactions of the Royal Society B-Biological Sciences, 353*(1377), 1915–1927.

Posner, M. I., & Rothbart, M. K. (2009). Toward a physical basis of attention and self-regulation. *Physics of Life Reviews, 6*(2): 103–120.

Roberts, M. E., Tchanturia, K., Stahl, D., Southgate, L., & Treasure, J. (2007). A systematic review and meta-analysis of set-shifting ability in eating disorders. *Psychological Medicine, 37*(8), 1075–1084.

Roland, D. (1998). *The confident performer.* London: Heinemann.

Scherer, K. R. (2005). What are emotions? And how can they be measured? *Social Science Information, 44*(4), 695–729.

Shortt, A. L., Barrett, P. M., Dadds, M. R., & Fox, T. L. (2001). The influence of family and experimental context on cognition in anxious children. *Journal of Abnormal Child Psychology, 29*(6), 585–596.

Simonds, J., Kieras, J. E., Rueda, M. R., & Rothbart, M. K. (2007). Effortful control, executive attention, and emotional regulation in 7–10-year-old children. *Cognitive Development, 22*(4), 474–488. doi: 10.1016/j.cogdev.2007.08.009

Smith, E., & Rieger, E. (2006). The effect of attentional bias toward shape- and weight-related information on body dissatisfaction. *International Journal of Eating Disorders, 39*(6), 509–515.

Stice, E., Nemeroff, C., & Shaw, H. E. (1996). Test of the dual pathway model of bulimia nervosa: Evidence for dietary restraint and affect regulation mechanisms. *Journal of Social and Clinical Psychology, 15*(3), 340–363.

Teper, R., Segal, Z. V., & Inzlicht, M. (2013). Inside the Mindful Mind: How Mindfulness Enhances Emotion Regulation Through Improvements in Executive Control. [Article]. *Current Directions in Psychological Science, 22*(6), 449–454. doi: 10.1177/0963721413495869

Wildes, J. E., Ringham, R. M., & Marcus, M. D. (2010). Emotion Avoidance in Patients with Anorexia Nervosa: Initial Test of a Functional Model. *International Journal of Eating Disorders, 43*(5), 398–404. doi: 10.1002/eat.20730

Williams, L. E., Bargh, J. A., Nocera, C. C., & Gray, J. R. (2009). The Unconscious Regulation of Emotion: Nonconscious Reappraisal Goals Modulate Emotional Reactivity. *Emotion, 9*(6), 847–854. doi: 10.1037/a0017745

Zucker, N. L., & Harshaw, C. (2012). Emotion, attention, and relationships: A developmental model of self-regulation in anorexia nervosa and related disordered eating behaviors. In J. Lock (Ed.), *The Oxford Handbook of Developmental Perspectives on Child and Adolescent Eating Disorders* (67–87). London: Oxford Press.

Zucker, N. L., Herzog, D., Moskovich, A., Merwin, R., & Linn, T. (2011). Incorporating dispositional traits into the treatment of anorexia nervosa. In R. A. H. Adan & W. H. Kaye (Eds.), *Behavioral Neurobiology of Eating Disorders* (pp. 289–314). Berlin: Springer-Verlag.

Zucker, N. L., Losh, M., Bulik, C. M., LaBar, K. S., Piven, J., & Pelphrey, K. A. (2007). Anorexia nervosa and autism spectrum disorders: guided investigation of social cognitive endophenotypes. *Psychological Bulletin, 133*(6), 976–1006.

Part III

Dissemination and Implementation

Chapter 16

Implementing Behavioral Family Therapy in Complex Settings

Blake Woodside, Brooke Halpert, and Gina Dimitropoulos

The development of novel forms of family therapy in the treatment of adolescent eating disorders has represented an important advance in the field. Behavioural Family Therapy (FBT), developed first for the treatment of Anorexia Nervosa (AN) (Lock & Le Grange, 2012) and later for the treatment of Bulimia Nervosa (BN) (Le Grange & Lock, 2007), is an evidence-based, manualized treatment that has been demonstrated to have good efficacy (Lock, Agras, Bryson, & Kraemer, 2005; Lock, Couturier, & Agras, 2006) and disseminability (Lock et al., 2006).

One of the fundamental elements of FBT is the empowerment of the parents in driving and shaping the treatment. The FBT therapist, while knowledgeable about AN or BN, does not presume to be an expert about the specific family she/he is treating. This change in locus of control is at the very core of the treatment modality, and the treatment cannot be implemented without very active support of this principle. Complex settings, such as hospitals, day hospitals, and other institutional locations, typically have a different approach to the treatment of illness and disease.

While respecting parents and wishing to keep them informed about the nature and progress of treatment, it is more usual for complex settings to work from the perspective of the health-care professionals directing almost all elements of treatment. In such settings, the locus of control is firmly within the grasp of the professionals involved, and the parental role is to provide consent for the recommended treatment and to be supportive while it is being implemented.

Here rests the fundamental problem when attempting to implement an FBT-like approach in a complex setting: Who is in charge of the treatment? Who is fundamentally making decisions? How can conflicts in these areas be reconciled with an FBT-centered approach?

This chapter will review these issues and present some strategies to enable such implementation in these types of settings. There is no significant literature on this topic, aside from one paper examining the role of the pediatrician in FBT (Katzman et al., 2013), so the chapter is exploratory in nature and based on the experience of the authors. For the purposes of this chapter, the authors assume that the typical complex setting is a hospital or other residential-based treatment program with an ambulatory and an inpatient setting and has experience in the treatment of AN and BN.

Nature of Decision Making in Complex Settings

Complex settings include formal hospitals, day hospitals, and other institutional entities. Such settings are typically hierarchical, with some professions granted more decision-making power than others. In settings that treat AN or BN, pediatricians or child psychiatrists typically have the greatest authority. Very often the overall treatment program will be structured around an outpatient assessment and treatment service, and more intensive settings where emergency or more intensive care are provided.

Because of the significant increase in cost of treatment provided within these more intensive treatment settings, they are usually reserved either for emergency care or the care of the most complex and challenging cases of the illness in question. This further promotes a hierarchical system, where in an emergency there needs to be an "expert" who is prepared to make rapid decisions about potentially life-saving treatment and, in the case of complex or treatment-resistant illness, an individual or team regarded as having special knowledge and experience to be able to manage the complexity.

Parents in such settings may be routinely involved in decision making about their children, depending on local laws about consent and capacity to make treatment decisions. However, most often this limits parents to being informed about the diagnosis and proposed treatment and being asked for permission to proceed. While a range of options may be presented to a parent, there is usually a recommendation—that is, after all, what the expert professional is paid to do—and the parent is left in the position of whether to agree or disagree with the recommendation.

Even in the best of circumstances, with understanding and compassionate institutional staff, who are careful to be respectful, there are many situations where conflict can arise between parents and staff. Sometimes this is related to the emergency nature of such treatment, where the attending staff are of the opinion that one intervention or another is urgently required and that there is no time to delay. Parents in such situations can be panic-stricken and deathly afraid, which can result in paralysis about making decisions, or they can be significant confused, which can be interpreted as resistance or interference. Alternatively, in complex cases, parents may struggle to understand complicated rationales and explanations for what is happening and again either become paralyzed or appear to be resisting agreeing to one course of action over another.

In such cases conflict can at times escalate significantly, sometimes to the point where local Child Protection Services may become involved. Regardless of the care with which such involvement is organized, it often results in a significant rupture of communication between the parent and the institutional staff. Both parties have the same goal—improved health for the child—but the nature of the circumstances can at times present opportunities for significant conflict.

Obviously, care needs to be delivered, and there are many situations where decisions simply must be made, in short order, to preserve the life of an ill child. It should also be said that often institutional-based interventions are marked by concordance between parents and staff and that there is no conflict at all. However, the hierarchical nature of such settings is always present, and it is this hierarchical decision-making process that can lead to difficulties when FBT is the primary mode of treatment.

Managing this difficulty—the apparent opposed modes of decision making and locus of control—is the key issue when considering attempting to implement a FBT approach in a complex setting.

Issues and Strategies to Manage Implementation

Consensus Building

The first question is why a decision is to be made to implement, or switch to, a primarily FBT-driven model. Has this been a gradual process, or was it an abrupt decision? In either case, such a decision is likely to be seen as a criticism of the existing model. Given that staff in the setting may have practiced the existing model for many years, it would not be too surprising if some staff were heavily invested in the existing model.

It is worth taking the time, in a nonthreatening way, to engage all members of the treatment team in a discussion about what they think is and is not working about the current model. This needs to be a genuine and thoughtful discussion focused not so much on perceived failures but seen as an opportunity to improve outcomes. Even staff who are heavily invested in a given model will often be able to identify gaps in service or problematic outcomes.

This process should eventually generate common themes around the efficacies and deficiencies of the current model. At this point options can be introduced that attempt to address the areas of consensus. FBT may well be a part of a solution, one that can be endorsed by the staff group.

Another helpful strategy is to involve the parents of current and recent patients and perform some focus group/qualitative study on their opinions about what is and is not working well with the current system. Again, a genuine engagement across a spectrum of families, some of whose ill children had good, and others less good, outcomes is very helpful. Care is designing such activities and in the presentation of results can avoid this turning into a staff or program-bashing activity.

It is not likely that an "imposition" of an FBT model in a complex setting will be successful. Because of the alterations in roles and locus of decision making, there needs to be a clear process where the advantages and disadvantages of the model are reviewed and discussed. Many changes in roles and behaviors are required in a FBT-driven system, and an adoption will go best when there has been sufficient buy-in from all concerned. This is a problem common to the implementation of many evidence-based treatments (McHugh & Barlow, 2010).

Careful Training of Staff

Staff who have not been directly involved in FBT should have a thorough training experience about the rationale for the use of the model and become familiar with the fundamental principles of the model. It is not necessary to train all staff to be proficient in FBT as therapists. This training should include specific examples of behaviors that are compatible, or not compatible, with a FBT approach. This is especially important because of the locus of control in FBT, which shifts much of the responsibility for the treatment to the parents. In this model, the notion of working with parents as a collaborative team will arise over and over again. It can happen that old-fashioned ideas about parents being to blame for their child's illness will surface at regular intervals, usually as a response to a bad clinical outcome. Providing training that continuously emphasizes the strengths and abilities that parents can bring to the treatment process is most helpful. It may be a relief to staff who have experienced much conflict with parents that the model, once implemented, should reduce the overall conflict level.

It is key that every member of the clinical team carefully consider how their actions and words are affecting the FBT treatment. For example, physicians must consciously avoid labeling emergency admissions as failures in treatment and instead frame as collaborative experiments in learning about what can help an ill child eat more and gain weight and then how this learning can be transferred to the home setting. Excessive advice giving, which tends to disempower the family, needs to be avoided as well. It is most helpful for physicians in this situation to adopt a stance that recognizes the core treatment approach as family therapy, positively endorses this, and views the admission as an interruption in the course of the treatment.

The role of medical clinic visits occurring outside of a family therapy session need to be carefully considered: Are these meant to support the FBT or do they have a therapeutic component (Katzman et al., 2013)? If so, how will this be implemented in a way that facilitates the FBT? It may help parents to understand that such visits may become less frequent while family therapy sessions continue, if matters are going smoothly.

A number of other considerations are important for such visits. Will medical staff weigh patients? What will be said to the patient and family about the weight? How can this support the FBT treatment? How will medical staff respond to questions about sports and exercise in a way that supports the underlying goal of facilitating the FBT?

Nursing staff need to learn how to assist parents in specific tasks, ranging from meal supervision to calming agitated patients, in a collaborative way that does not disempower the family. A collaborative problem-solving approach may work best, where a nurse might say, "Here's something that other families have told me is helpful, is this something you are willing to try? I'm happy to support you while you do so." It is very important that nursing staff—who always spend the most time with the patients—are very thoroughly trained in FBT principles and have input into how they can design patterns of practice that allow both for the core nursing work to be done while at the same time reinforce the importance of supporting the parents in their ongoing efforts.

The role of the registered dietitian in an inpatient admission is critical. While FBT has sometimes been described as an anti-dietitian treatment, this is not the case. The dietitian has enormous influence on the parents, many of whom will be desperate about their ill child. This calls for a thorough FBT training experience for the dietitian, who can have an enormous positive influence on the course of treatment. The dietitian, through well-meaning advice giving, can inadvertently totally disempower the parents by being proscriptive about what the child should or should not eat. A FBT-informed dietitian approach will again be collaborative, where the enquiries about the child's eating are respectful, positive efforts are praised, and difficulties are identified and seen as a collaborative opportunity to discover ways to make more progress. To be compatible with FBT, it is particularly important that the dietitian avoid indicating to the ill child that his or her parents are incompetent to feed them and that staff "know better." A typical example of this type of problem is the proscriptive, structured meal plan, which can either be imposed on the child while in the hospital or as an outpatient. This very common practice disempowers the parents and sets up a dynamic where the child, at every turn, will challenge the parents as to their food choices, referring back to the "real" expert, the dietitian. This is totally contrary to the fundamental premise of FBT, where the professionals, while authoritative about AN generally, are not authoritarian- and respect the family's expertise about the family itself.

Communication

A clear pattern of communication between ambulatory and inpatient staff is an essential requirement for successful implementation of a FBT-focused approach. While there will be unavoidable difficulties with children being assessed in the emergency department, or admitted by staff on call with limited knowledge either about the child, the family, or the nature of the treatment provided, once the child is under the care of the inpatient care providers there needs to be close integration between the ambulatory care plan and the inpatient care plan. It is important to avoid sending a message such as "we're in charge of the treatment now," as such messages will disempower the entire course of treatment.

Role Clarification and Goals for Interruption of Outpatient FBT

It is most important to carefully consider the role not only of each staff member but of the elements of the treatment program as a whole. This first should be done as a systemic exercise by the treatment service. So, for example, if a major modality of treatment is going to be FBT, then by definition the outpatient elements of the overall treatment program will be the primary driver of treatment in the program, and other elements of the program need to be identified as secondary and supportive of the main treatment modality.

The role and purpose of other elements needs to be reconsidered in the context of the FBT model. What is the revised purpose of an inpatient service? Of a Day Hospital service? If FBT is a major modality of treatment, what should those working in an inpatient service think about the nature of the treatment that they are providing?

In settings where an inpatient service, for example, has been seen to be the important or critical element of care, implementing a FBT approach will most likely seem like standing everything on its head, as suddenly the outpatient, "ancillary" treatment becomes the central focus of the overall treatment effort, and as the responsibility for decision making is partially shifted away from predominantly medical staff to allied health care professionals and family members. This can be a particularly difficult transition if it happens that an inpatient setting had inadvertently developed a culture consistent with a family-blaming attitude or if such a unit has had a rigid professional hierarchy.

In FBT the authority of the parents is a critical part of the treatment. While parents require assistance and support, they are to be the critical decision makers for their child. In a clinical setting where FBT is a major modality of treatment, this principle needs to be respected at every level. This is fairly straightforward in an outpatient or ambulatory setting, where the situation is not an emergency and the child is medically stable.

However, in a more intensive setting all the issues reviewed above come into play. One way to approach this is to define the role of a more intensive element of treatment as temporary and supportive but with the express goal supporting the child for the minimum length of time necessary in this setting. The goals of having an admission as short as possible would include avoiding the risk of disempowering the parents, interrupting the child's normal activities and development, and reducing both the overall cost of treatment and possible stigmatizing labeling of the child or the parents as "failures."

Having very clear criteria for both admission and discharge helps this process immensely. Such clear criteria, provided in advance, will reduce parental distress around admissions and allow for care to be provided in a more consistent fashion at times when patients are receiving care from multiple medical providers. It is also very important to avoid identifying such episodes of care as failures on the part of either the family or other professional staff. Clarity around the need for admission in the context of FBT needs to be explained. The overall goal of an admission in this sense would be to strengthen the family's ability to be successful with the FBT treatment.

How best to incorporate parental involvement in the intensive treatment setting should be resolved by the treatment team and ultimately clearly communicated to the parents, the ill child, and staff. To accomplish this, decisions about what is a medical or professional decision, where the health-care professionals will be the primary drivers of decision making, and what is not will be needed. So for example, determining the need for intravenous fluids is a fairly obvious medical decision, as would be identifying an appropriate level of calories for the ill child to consume. However, perhaps there is a role for the parents to meet with the dietitian and discuss what they would like to choose for their child to make up those calories. In this example, the professional—the dietitian—might offer professional advice about food choices, but at least some element of the parental responsibility for feeding the child can be preserved.

Admissions should include a careful analysis of how the admission will assist the family in being more effective with their FBT. For example, if the sense of the treating family therapist is that the family is not very effective in coaching the ill child to eat, it would make sense for inpatient staff to work directly with the family to enhance their coaching skills. If the family is having difficulty with the intense anorexic panic that often occurs during meal times, perhaps staff can work with parents during actual meals to coach them on techniques that staff have learned to be helpful. If the problem is that the family is having difficulty in locating additional resources to organize supervision, then this should be addressed during the admission. The overall goal of the admission should be to strengthen a family's ability to do the work that they need to do with their ill child, and all inpatient staff members should be viewed as important resources to the family.

Involving the family is an important focus even in the face of a medical emergency such as bradycardia or low potassium. While it is natural that the immediate focus will be on correcting the acute medical problem, such interventions should be framed as temporary interruptions of the key therapeutic approach, which is the ongoing family therapy. Clinicians involved in such interventions need to be trained in the principles of FBT so as to avoid undue disempowerment of the family. There are rich opportunities to use such an admission to advance the work of the BFT. For example, as detailed below, additional educational materials about BFT can be provided, along with the opportunity to meet with other families engaged in the process, to receive and offer peer support.

Special Problems

Child Being Admitted to a Nonexpert Hospital Setting

It is not uncommon for ill children with AN or BN to be admitted to pediatric services that have limited expertise in treating either illness. It would be unrealistic to assume that such a setting had any meaningful expertise in

FBT, and it is very likely that the family will receive mixed messages about how the treatment is going or how to proceed in the future.

Any efforts by the family therapist's team to assist attending staff in a nonexpert setting may help prevent such mixed messages. In addition, it is likely most useful for the family therapist to stay in contact with the family during the period of such a hospitalization and also to try to assist the family in understanding the purpose and the nature of such an admission. This may include helping the family to understand the differences between an admission to an expert and a nonexpert setting. Such differences might include a lower awareness on the part of nonexpert staff about the nature of FBT, which could result in the family receiving advice or information that varied from what they might have received in the expert setting and which seemed contradictory to the nature of the FBT treatment.

Deciding to End FBT

Not every course of FBT will be successful, and many families will have great difficulty in mobilizing the resources, practical and emotional, to continue to grapple with the illness. It is important to have a clear, agreed-upon process for a team to use when deciding to end a course of FBT. Failure to respond will usually involve an inability on the part of the family to generate adequate weight gain, of course as a consequence of the family being unable to effectively re-feed their child at home. There is limited literature on correlations of poor outcome from FBT. Criteria used by a specific program should be made explicit to the family at the initiation of treatment, and if it appears that the family is unable to use the treatment effectively, the family therapist and responsible other staff should meet with the family and review the progress of the treatment. Sometimes such a meeting will reinvigorate a family; in any event, it is best if the family understands the decision and at least assents to it, even if they do not agree with it.

Decisions to end the family therapy made on the fly, often in the course of an emergency situation, are to be avoided. It can be especially hard for staff working only in inpatient settings, who tend to see only very sick individuals, often over and over again. Maintaining a hopeful stance in such a setting can be difficult.

Clinical Example

Here is an example of some of the principles described above.

> *June, aged 15, has been losing weight and not eating well for several months. Her parents, John and Miranda, were concerned enough to take her to see her family doctor, who suspected she was suffering from Anorexia Nervosa and referred her for an assessment at a local hospital that had a program for adolescent AN.*

The assessment occurred in the ambulatory part of the facility. While everyone was nervous, it went well. Despite having been warned, it was a shock to actually hear the diagnosis. The assessor said that the multidisciplinary team would discuss June's case later in the week and make recommendations for treatment.

At the team meeting, her psychiatric and medical situation was reviewed. She was deemed to be medically stable, and given the lack of any contraindication, it was suggested that the family be offered FBT and have a first session to see if they would accept the charge.

The next week the family attended their initial FBT session, where, with some distress, the parents accepted the charge to re-feed their daughter. June was adamant that she did not need their help and that the whole thing was an over-reaction.

At the end of the session, after giving June's parents their instructions for session two, the family therapist offered to show the family around the rest of the facility, including the inpatient unit. The family agreed, and they toured first the ambulatory part of the clinic and then went upstairs to the inpatient unit. June was very frightened and initially refused to enter the unit, stating that she thought the family had agreed to outpatient treatment. Their family therapist located the unit manager, who was able to spend some time with the family, reassuring them that the inpatient unit was there only for emergencies, or for complications, and that the core modality of treatment was the family therapy. She explained that if June needed an admission, then her parents would continue to be very involved in her care and any admission would be as short as possible to ensure her safety.

The FBT sessions initially went well, with June being able to eat a bit more with her parents' assistance. By about the fifth session, however, when she had gained about 5 lbs, her distress at meals began to escalate from unhappiness to crying to panicky outbursts. Her parents, who had been very active, found this to be very personally distressing and, despite the efforts of the family therapist, began to back off at meals.

Over the course of a month, her weight declined and her heart rate began to slow significantly. At a team meeting, where the family therapist was describing the difficulty that the parents were having in confronting the AN, the attending pediatrician reported that June had shown signs of abnormal heart function on her EKG that week and that he felt she should come into the hospital for a period of medical stabilization.

The team discussed goals for an admission beyond simple medical stabilization. They agreed that having nursing staff help teach June's parents skills to tolerate the anorexic panic that she was experiencing would be a key goal of an admission. Because of the difficulty that June's parents had been experiencing, they were finding it hard to make appropriate food choices for June and the dietitian offered to meet with them, primarily to reassure them that they had been making good choices before this setback and to encourage them not to doubt themselves. The child psychiatrist offered to assess June for a possible depression, and it was agreed that the family would continue to meet with the family therapist during the admission. It was finally agreed that the end-point of the admission would be when June was medically stable, which was estimated to be after about two weeks, given that while her cardiac function was impaired, her weight was not yet critical.

Both June and her parents were very distressed about the admission. The inpatient pediatrician made a point when meeting with them to reassure them that June would be fine medically and that the staff could help her parents learn skills to assist them with her re-feeding while she was in the hospital.

A caloric level was prescribed by staff, and the dietitian met with June's mother to discuss what to feed her to achieve the necessary caloric level. June's parents agreed to come to the hospital every morning to participate in supervising breakfast and every evening after work to help supervise dinner and evening snack.

The initial part of June's admission was marked by extreme distress around meals and difficulty in tolerating any change in her weight. Experienced staff coached her parents on methods to help de-escalate June's distress while ensuring that the calories were consumed. Staff worked hard to normalize the distress and reassure June's parents that they were doing the right thing ... and that if they were not present that staff would be ensuring that the food was consumed.

June's parents were able to meet with other parents of hospitalized patients, in the setting of an informal peer-support setting. Hospital staff provided June's parents with additional written material about BFT to increase their knowledge base about and confidence in the treatment.

Gradually over the course of the two weeks June became somewhat less distressed by the process of eating, and her parents became less concerned that in helping her to eat, they were somehow harming her. June's parents met with the dietitian again, who helped them make up a "book" of sample meals that the parents thought would be suitable for June. The assessment by the child psychiatrist suggested that June was not depressed, which reassured her parents further. At her family meeting in the second week June was able to admit that she was reassured that others were able to help her eat and that at least a part of her knew it was the right thing to do and that she was happy that her parents had been able to help her while she was in the hospital.

The family was able to utilize the hospitalization to be much more effective at home in June's treatment, and she again started to gain weight. The remainder of her treatment was uneventful.

Summary

Given the evidence supporting FBT and despite the challenges, it is likely that it will be adapted to other clinical settings beyond outpatient care. Implementing FBT in intensive treatment settings is challenging because it requires that an entire treatment team accept the approach, learn it, and support its use. Further, implementing FBT in an intensive setting also requires a thorough ongoing revisiting of all aspects of the program to make sure it is consistent with the principle tenets of FBT, including parental empowerment, nonblaming, externalization of the eating disorder, and consultation with parents, as opposed to prescribing expert driven treatment. Careful approach to process, a building of consensus, and thorough training in new skills and modified roles will help ensure a successful implementation of FBT.

References

Lock, J., & Le Grange D. (2012). *Treatment manual for anorexia nervosa, second edition: A family-based approach.* New York: The Guilford Press.

Le Grange, D., & Lock J. (2007). *Treating bulimia nervosa in adolescents: A family-based approach.* New York: The Guildford Press.

Lock, J., Agras, W. S., Bryson, S., & Kraemer, H. (2005). A comparison of short- and long-term family therapy for adolescent anorexia nervosa. *Journal of the American Academy of Child and Adolescent Psychiatry, 44,* 632–9.

Lock, J., Couturier, J., & Agras, W. S. (2006). Comparison of long-term outcomes in adolescents with anorexia nervosa treated with family therapy. *American Journal of Child and Adolescent Psychiatry, 45*(6), 666–72.

Lock, J., Brandt, H., Woodside, B., Agras, W. S., Halmi, W. K., Johnson, C., Kaye, W., & Wilfley, D. (2012). Challenges in conducting a multi-site randomized clinical trial comparing treatments for adolescent anorexia nervosa. *Int J Eat Disord., 45*(2), 202–13. Epub 2011/04/16.

Katzman, D. K., Peebles, R., Sawyer, S. M., Lock, J., & Le Grange, D. (2013). The role of the pediatrician in family-based treatment for adolescent eating disorders: opportunities and challenges. *Journal of Adolescent Health, 53*(4), 433–40.

McHugh, R. K., & Barlow, D. H. (2010). The dissemination and implementation of evidence-based psychological treatments. *American Psychologist, 65*(2), 73–84.

Chapter 17

Delivering Family-Based Treatment in a Specialty Practice Setting

Peter M. Doyle and Angela Celio Doyle

The use of evidence-based treatments (EBT) for psychological disorders is an aspiration held by many clinicians in an endeavor to engage in evidence-based practice. However, despite the shared commitment of researchers and clinicians to provide the most efficacious treatments to patients, the uptake of EBTs by clinicians has been challenging due to concerns about generalizability of research findings to practice, discomfort with using treatment manuals, and practicalities of obtaining adequate training and consultation (Kazdin, 2008). In the treatment of eating disorders, many clinicians do not "take up" EBTs. In one study, 23 percent of community clinicians used a cognitive behavioral approach to treat eating disorders and many of these practitioners did not use specific cognitive behavioral interventions regularly (von Ranson, Wallace, & Stevenson, 2013), in spite of CBT being the most researched EBT for bulimia nervosa and binge eating disorder (Wilson, Grilo, & Vitousek, 2007). However, in a study of clinicians who are members of eating disorder professional organizations, more than 80 percent used EBTs either alone or in combination with non-empirically supported treatments (Wallace & von Ranson, 2012). These findings are more encouraging, although it was unclear from these findings how closely EBTs were followed and how other treatment approaches were integrated.

More specifically, therapists' use of family based treatment (FBT) for anorexia nervosa (AN) in adolescents was explored and 50 percent of the sample of therapists, who were part of a national eating disorder treatment provider organization, used FBT alone or in combination with another approach in their practice (Couturier, Kimber, Jack, Niccols, Van Blyderveen, & McVey, 2013). Barriers to the uptake of FBT in therapists' practice included organizational factors (e.g., if the director of the clinical service supported training and use of FBT); interpersonal factors (e.g., experience and comfort working with adolescents with their families); patient/family factors (e.g., treatment preference of family); and illness factors (e.g., belief that comorbidities and complexities of treating AN suggest need for inpatient or day treatment). Finally, of those who were using FBT, fidelity to the model was lacking. Specifically, practitioners were reluctant to weigh patients, provide nutritional advice, and implement a family meal during treatment; no therapists interviewed reported using all three of these elements, indicating a lack of fidelity with the model by all respondents. The time commitment in the early part of treatment and inclusion of siblings were also viewed as barriers to uptake by therapists. A second study assessing therapist fidelity to FBT showed that "considerable" fidelity was observed in ratings of taped therapy sessions 72 percent of the time in Phase I, 47 percent of the time in Phase II, and 54 percent of the time in Phase III (Couturier, Isserlin, & Lock, 2010). Overall, participants demonstrated improvements in weight and psychological measures, but a lack of fidelity to the FBT model engenders serious questions about whether practicing FBT in this way will be effective in the community given its dissimilarity to the way FBT was delivered in randomized controlled trials.

EBTs could be provided within any mental health practice, yet specialty practices with a focus narrowed to a particular disorder or set of disorders (e.g., eating disorders, anxiety disorders) may be superior to generalist practices as a forum for the dissemination of EBTs such as FBT. Specialty practices can more aptly provide support for FBT training and consultation and prioritize environmental needs (e.g., room to conduct family meals, scales for weighing, and offices large enough to see an entire family). Different levels of care, such as intensive outpatient, partial hospitalization, and outpatient services may be offered within a specialty practice or there may be a more singular focus on outpatient treatment.

Given the existing evidence supporting FBT as an efficacious treatment for adolescents with anorexia nervosa, bulimia nervosa, and eating disorders not otherwise specified (Stiles-Shields, Hoste, Doyle, & Le Grange, 2012), an eating disorder specialty practice should provide FBT as a treatment option to patients as part of evidence-based practice. FBT is manualized (Lock, Le Grange, Agras, & Dare, 2001) and training and consultation opportunities are available through a training institute, both of which increase the possibility of specialty practices offering FBT. Furthermore, an eating disorder specialty practice embracing evidence-based practices should be able to provide high fidelity FBT (i.e., FBT that closely follows the treatment manual and tenets of FBT) to patients. Providing FBT in a specialty practice demands attention to the following elements to optimize its delivery in a manner consistent with evidence-based practices.

Clinical Competence and Support

Implementing FBT in specialty clinical practice calls for a high level of competence in this treatment approach. First, it is important to have received formal training in FBT through the Training Institute for Child and Adolescent Eating Disorders and, ideally, certification. Certification includes attendance at the 1.5-day training as well as 25 hours of consultation by an Institute faculty member for at least three patients who complete all three phases of FBT. This is considered the minimal experience necessary in order to offer FBT in a specialty clinical practice. Additionally, it is preferred if clinicians are engaged in ongoing peer consultation with colleagues who have also been fully trained and certified in FBT. Colleagues can be connected locally or distantly through Internet teleconferencing, telephone, or e-mail communications. Additional training is also available through the Institute in the form of an advanced workshop, which is currently offered annually.

Broad-based training in eating disorder treatments is also essential in achieving competence in FBT. Strober and Johnson (2012) argued in a recent paper that an overfocus on training and provision of FBT at the expense of other treatment approaches will not adequately prepare clinicians for the complexity of an eating disorder. While there is no evidence to date of other approaches being more effective or of an overfocus on FBT (see Le Grange & Lock, 2014 and Lock & Le Grange, 2014), experience in the treatment of eating disorders assists in efforts to be a competent FBT provider. FBT does not initially target etiological factors in the development of the eating disorder (e.g., low self-esteem, weight concerns, fears of sexual development), nor does it actively address comorbidities, yet an FBT therapist must be aware of different theories, approaches, and the individual's personal experience when using FBT. Furthermore, similar to any treatment approach, not all patients will benefit from FBT and it is crucial to have a full range of clinical tools to assist patients.

Quality Assurance

Data collection, while an integral part of every research setting, can be a difficult task for a private practice clinician. Obtaining measures; tracking administration of measures; entering, coding, and analyzing data are all potentially time consuming and costly prospects. However, for a variety of reasons, measurement of change in therapy and therapy outcomes is a crucial part of delivering EBTs like FBT in a clinical setting. Assessing our own therapy outcomes regularly can help keep us mindful of what we are targeting in our interventions. In the case of FBT for AN, early in treatment there is an unrelenting focus on weight restoration and symptom reduction is prioritized. Evaluating eating disorder symptoms on an ongoing basis can help us maintain that focus and ensure a higher quality intervention that does not drift too far astray in the face of all the competing issues that present themselves in sessions. Furthermore, data collection in these "real-world" settings can provide an important contribution to our understanding on the effectiveness and applicability of treatments.

There are a number of public domain instruments clinicians can use free of charge to gather objective data on the treatments they deliver. Clearly, anthropomorphic measures can be collected easily at each session. Patients are weighed without shoes and heavy outerwear in the therapist's office at the beginning of each session, and height is measured periodically. The most obvious data point of patient weight is instrumental in guiding treatment when using FBT. The majority of adolescent patients who will respond to FBT show a marked gain in weight during the first four sessions (Doyle et al., 2010), so consistently tracking and recording patient weight is a simple step that can help clinicians assess whether they are seeing expected treatment progress or need to reevaluate something about their approach. The addition of other standardized paper-and-pencil measures helps to keep clinicians focused (among other things) on measurable outcomes and to continue asking themselves, "Is what I'm doing working for this patient?" Therapy can "feel" like it is working well and we are making strides, but if weight is dropping and measures of ED symptomatology are climbing, we must confront the fact that we are not achieving the desired results.

Clinics' outcome data are also becoming increasingly used as a screening tool for educated consumers of therapy to determine whether to seek treatment there. Patients in every field of health care are taking a more proactive role in their own care and making inquiries such as "What do your outcomes look like? How many patients recover under your care? How do you know if patients are getting better?" Providing more than an anecdotal answer to empirical questions about the clinic's practice is valuable. It is additionally valuable to be able to compare a clinic's outcomes to larger samples' outcomes studied in the literature. These types of comparisons, however, have no real meaning unless we are utilizing EBTs.

Establishing a Highly Coordinated Treatment Team

A multidisciplinary team is a central element in the provision of FBT due to the complex interplay of medical and psychiatric problems in an eating disorder. The leader of the team is the therapist, who has the responsibility to coordinate the different providers. The second essential team member is the physician or nurse practitioner, who may specialize in pediatrics, adolescent medicine, or family medicine. Ideally, this medical specialist will have an interest in eating disorders and will be familiar with their role in FBT (see Katzman et al., 2013). A medical specialist will expertly reinforce the tenets of FBT (e.g., having the parents in charge of refeeding), will be confident in the ability of families to help an ill adolescent, and will be knowledgeable about the medical tests recommended for individuals struggling with an eating disorder. A third team member may be a psychiatrist, in case psychiatric medication is deemed useful for comorbid disorders such as depression or anxiety. A fourth team member may be a registered dietitian, who may provide consultation in case of nutritional issues that are more complicated during the process of weight restoration, such as food allergies, irritable bowel syndrome, celiac disease, or diabetes. A psychiatrist (unless they are also the primary therapist) and a dietitian are not always required members on the team, and their inclusion is typically not determined until the therapist has evaluated the patient for the appropriateness of the inclusion of these team members.

The use of a team provides support and expertise that are needed but also introduces several challenges for a specialty clinic that does not employ a full complement of medical providers, psychiatrists, and dietitians. First, finding providers who have experience, expertise, or interest in treating eating disorders can be difficult, particularly within smaller cities or rural areas. Second, the therapist has the task of educating the providers about FBT if they are unfamiliar with it and inviting them to take part in this team approach. Third, some patients initiate therapy with providers already involved with whom the therapist has never worked before. At times, it might be appropriate to provide referrals to providers with whom the therapist frequently works. For instance, an adolescent's pediatrician may not have experience in eating disorders or may feel more comfortable with a specialist working temporarily with their patient on this issue. In other situations, it might be more appropriate to have the patient continue with their already-established physician, psychiatrist, or dietitian. In this situation, it is vital that a common commitment to the FBT approach is verified with the team members and, if there is disagreement about the approach, that the therapist help facilitate with the parents the construction of a unified team. Educating providers and establishing a commitment to FBT can be accomplished through meetings, preferably face-to-face. A brief visit by the therapist to a provider's office can allow for collegial conversation about FBT and experiences using this treatment. Also, it is ideal to provide opportunities for other providers to learn more about FBT through invitations to informal journal clubs, presentations, or webinars being offered by professional organizations.

In the context of a patient already in treatment, phone conversations on a regular basis with the other providers can help to shape involvement by each provider such that everyone is practicing in a manner consistent with FBT tenets. How this might look in day-to-day practice: The therapist meets weekly with the patient for Phase 1. Following sessions, the therapist often contacts the physician through whatever means the physician tends to communicate in order to briefly update them with any progress and current challenges. It is the role of the physician to communicate information on the patient's medical status, offer observations of the patient and family interactions during medical visits, and support the FBT therapist's efforts to lead the treatment team in empowering the adolescent's parents in the treatment of the eating disorder (Katzman et al., 2013). The therapist might also highlight any issues that the medical provider would likely want to address. For instance, if the patient is pressing the therapist or his or her parents in session to return to sports practice soon, the therapist can alert the medical provider that this request may arise in the next visit. If the therapist has concerns about reintroducing sports at the current time due to psychological concerns (e.g., difficulty on the patient's part with feeling compelled to exercise) or concerns about interference of sports in weight restoration progress, these are important to share and to consider with the medical provider when and how a return to sports should occur. Having all treatment team members on the same page is essential in reducing confusion for families regarding whose advice they should follow.

Starting Well: Logistical Issues of Starting FBT

When does therapy begin? It may seem like a straightforward question that the clock could easily answer, but clinicians know that often intervention begins with that very first contact, whether in person or over the phone. In the case of an EBT like FBT, which clearly spells out the therapeutic tasks and considerations of Session 1, the initiation of treatment can be anxiety provoking for a clinician who wants to adhere to the letter of the manual but has clinic protocols and procedures to also consider. An initial consideration for practitioners in a specialty practice that only provides outpatient care is the importance of obtaining medical clearance for the initiation of outpatient treatment. This clearance should include an evaluation of electrolytes (including potassium, phosphorus, and magnesium), electrocardiogram, full vital signs (including orthostatics and temperature), and any other tests suggested by the physician (see Katzman et al., 2013). The physician is asked to provide his or her signature to either deem the patient medically stable for outpatient treatment or to indicate that the patient needs inpatient care where more extensive medical monitoring will be possible. Patients should be asked to provide this clearance prior to an intake appointment in order to most quickly provide direction to the patient, should inpatient care be more appropriate on a medical basis.

Ideally, clinicians seeing an adolescent for the first time will schedule a 90- to 120-minute intake to complete a full psychiatric evaluation with the patient and at least one caregiver for collateral information. However, if a clinician is on insurance panels and depending on insurance coverage, clinicians (or their patient) may not be reimbursed for an intake session (CPT 90791[1]). As a result, clinicians might schedule their intake sessions as a 45-minute session (CPT 90834) due to these insurance constraints and out of consideration for the patient. A third option is to schedule an intake session as a 60-minute crisis session (CPT 90839) with an add-on code of 90840 for each additional 30 minutes of treatment beyond the initial 60-minute 90839 code. "Crisis" per the CPT manual, is defined as a presenting problem requiring urgent assessment that is either "life threatening" or "complex and requires immediate attention to a patient in high distress." Repeated use of this code may invite an audit by insurance companies but could arguably be an appropriate code for families seeking help for a child acutely ill with AN. When in doubt, it is advisable to contact the client's insurance companies to discuss the most appropriate use of codes. At the conclusion of this intake session, options for treatment are discussed and, if FBT is determined to be the appropriate treatment, Session 1 is scheduled.

We are often asked whether or how to combine an intake session with FBT Session 1, which is not typically a concern for clinical settings in which the assessment and treatment plan is developed by a separate assessor (e.g., in academic medical setting specialty clinics). To avoid the potential redundancy of information gathered in these sessions, it is helpful if the therapist focuses the intake on facts (such as symptom profile, treatment history, and assessment of comorbid conditions) and leaves Session 1 for discussion of the more subjective experiences of the family members, how the eating disorder has disrupted the adolescent's life, and daily rhythms and dynamics of the family in order to orchestrate the intense scene on which recommendations for refeeding are based.

Optimally, Session 1 and Session 2 are scheduled as soon as possible after the intake and within a few days of each other. This is done both to quickly and effectively build the parent empowerment that is a foundation of FBT and to address the seriousness of the eating disorder. AN frequently demands rapid initiation of treatment as a result of the medical sequelae of starvation. Session 2, the family meal, is best scheduled as a 90-minute session (CPT 90837) to allow for the extra time it may take for the meal to be eaten and the "one more bite" to be consumed. All subsequent sessions are scheduled for 50 minutes, unless some crisis emerges that would require additional time to address.

It is not uncommon for families to request some out-of-session contact, especially in the beginning of treatment as parents are assuming the role of refeeding their child and coping with their own uncertainties and anxieties about this process. Arrangements regarding type of contact (e.g., phone, e-mail, text), frequency of contact, and fees associated with out-of-session contact should be established at the outset of treatment. This can help families know what resources are available to them between sessions. An additional benefit is minimizing burnout for a therapist who may be fielding many requests for out-of-session contact that will be easier to manage if the terms for frequency and payment are already established. Also, it is usually helpful for a therapist to anticipate between-session requests for support in order to plan for phone calls, etc., rather than allow persistent, intermittent contacts.

Educating the Community about FBT

Although many individuals and families seeking treatment find the idea of evidence-based practice compelling, and some may seek out information on best practice for the treatment of eating disorders, others may not be aware that FBT exist for anorexia nervosa. Providing this information in many different formats is helpful. For instance, describing FBT and the evidence supporting it on a practice website (or linking to other sites that have this information) can provide information otherwise hard to find for families and patients. When a patient's family calls to find out more information about treatment options, information on FBT can also be provided, as well as other options for treatment. Handouts with brief descriptions of FBT can be provided to families and possible referral sources, as well as recommendations for the book *Help Your Teenager Beat an Eating Disorder* (Lock & Le Grange, 2015), which is written for parents and describes the main tenets of FBT. Meeting with other providers to talk about FBT aids not only in possibly constructing a strong treatment team for certain types of practitioners, but also may assist in creating a large, well-informed referral network.

One aspect of EBTs that may interfere with individuals or their families seeking EBT is the fear that "one size does not fit all" and that practitioners will not take into account their unique story and needs while providing the treatment. Providing an EBT and being responsive to unique aspects of a patient are not mutually exclusive, and therapists might need to assuage any fears that these are not compatible. Clinicians providing FBT should exercise appropriate clinical flexibility within the framework of the manual and strike the balance between treatment fidelity and adjusting elements for unique individuals. A helpful rule of thumb is to default to maintaining high fidelity to the tested intervention and any deviations from this need to be well-defended. For instance, if one decides to schedule time alone with the parents in the early part of Phase 1, one might need to defend the rationale. This modification may make sense if parents are having a particularly difficult time talking openly about their observations regarding the eating disorder in front of their ill child. Taking a brief part of a session to discuss their concerns about being open in front of their child or other family members could help to increase effective communication in treatment that would, in turn, optimize their ability to feel empowered in working to fight the eating disorder. On the other hand, this deviation in Phase 1 would not be recommended in most situations because excluding the adolescent would reduce their ability to hear discussions about treatment and communicate with their parents and the therapist around the issues being brought up.

An added consideration in a specialty practice is maintaining patient satisfaction; a family may not like aspects of FBT, and balancing the integrity of the treatment with keeping an adolescent in treatment becomes a delicate process.

Addressing Comorbidities

As with the research studies, comorbidities such as depression, bipolar disorder, obsessive compulsive disorder, social anxiety, and other forms of anxiety may coexist with the eating disorder. Suicidality is the only condition that trumps the focus on low weight within anorexia nervosa in FBT, and as such, other comorbidities may not be addressed immediately. Clarifying expectations for parents on this front will be important, and involving a psychiatrist, if medication is deemed helpful, can help reduce psychiatric symptoms during FBT. Once the eating disorder is well-addressed, other psychiatric issues are more able to be treated and additional treatment may need to be sought outside of the specialty practice setting.

Beyond FBT

FBT is the most efficacious treatment for adolescent AN known at present, and although it was originally developed as an outpatient weight restoration treatment, studies have observed improved psychological symptoms beyond mere weight restoration. While FBT may be effective as a stand-alone treatment where no additional psychotherapy is required, we might estimate that in as many as half of the adolescents treated, there are those who benefit initially from FBT but fail to regain momentum in healthy adolescent development for a variety of reasons or are not able to sustain their improvements in weight status over longer periods of time. These situations suggest a sequenced approach to FBT with an emphasis on making a deliberate decision in collaboration with the adolescent and their family to transition into other evidence-based treatments for additional psychiatric difficulties. Other evidence-based treatments can be provided by the FBT therapist, if they have expertise in these areas, or by another therapist in the community with that expertise. If there is a reoccurrence of eating disorder symptoms, booster sessions of FBT can be provided (whether integrated into individual work with the therapist who had done FBT or in synchrony with treatment by another therapist) and can be utilized as needed. In the case of involving a second therapist to take over the treatment of a comorbidity, clarity on how the treatment plan would work in the case of a reoccurrence of the eating disorder is important. For instance, it might be decided that treatment of a comorbidity is temporarily suspended if the ED symptoms return and a revisit of FBT strategies is needed or the two therapies might go on concurrently. Parents are told that through FBT, "they cannot unlearn what they have learned in the process of becoming empowered against the eating disorder" and that they will always have these tools on hand as their adolescent progresses through the recovery process.

One example of a patient that might benefit from a sequenced approach to FBT is an adolescent with anorexia nervosa and comorbid social anxiety. Once the patient completes FBT, the patient and their family would likely want treatment for social anxiety as well. As Phase 3 of FBT concludes, individual CBT for social anxiety can commence. It is important to have conversations with the patient and his or her parents to clarify the distinct change in treatment that will occur; in the case of social anxiety, the adolescent will be meeting alone with the therapist more often with less involvement from the parents, although the parents may be involved with treatment according to the adolescent's wishes. If the therapist is not trained in treatment of anxiety disorders, then a referral to an anxiety specialist is warranted.

In other situations, cognitive aspects of the eating disorder (e.g., weight/ shape concerns) may still be distressing to the patient. In these cases, the role of parents as part of their "team" to combat the eating disorder behaviors can be retained, but additional therapy could be useful in ensuring a full and sustained recovery. As such, a sequenced approach could benefit the patient; following FBT, a change might be made to cognitive behavioral therapy for body image, which would be done on an individual basis with parents "on retainer" for FBT-style support in case of a reoccurrence of eating disorder symptoms. For instance, if during the course of CBT for body image an adolescent is starting to skip breakfast due to urges to restrict, parents would be invited to a session to discuss how they can help their adolescent stay on track with a regular pattern of eating, while CBT strategies are used to help adolescents learn the importance of regular eating. Clinical judgment can also be used to determine when adolescents may be asked to try out individual skills learned in CBT to reduce urges to restrict, for instance, without reinvigorating FBT interventions utilizing parent involvement.

A final example is in the case of an adolescent being treated for an eating disorder with FBT but who also exhibits emotional dysregulation that results in self-harm behaviors or suicidal ideation. In these situations, completion of FBT may be achievable before sequencing in a referral to a dialectical behavior therapy program/therapist. However, in this and other situations where there exist comorbidities that cannot be easily sequenced (e.g., severe OCD), treatment via psychiatric medication during FBT may be warranted. In some rare cases, individual treatment for the severe comorbidity might be recommended concurrent with FBT, although this is a situation to generally avoid due to possible conflicting therapeutic messages and competing therapeutic goals that could distract from parents' intense efforts to treat the eating disorder.

Conclusion

The use of FBT in clinical practice with attention to the manualized protocol can be the realization of many individuals' aspirations to make EBTs more widely available to people suffering from eating disorders. However, steps must be taken to remain faithful to the treatment as it was developed and tested if we are to truly deliver evidence-based treatment. These steps include: an emphasis on clinical competence and support; quality assurance over the course of treatment; constructing a unified, multidisciplinary team; starting FBT well by thoughtfully approaching the logistical translations of implementing the manual in private practice; educating the community and other providers about FBT in order to develop a strong network/interest; finding the balance of appropriate clinical flexibility within the manual and fidelity; and considering "what's next" following FBT in some situations, especially in the case of psychiatric comorbidities. With these elements in place, the delivery of evidence-based psychotherapy can thrive and benefit individuals suffering from eating disorders.

Note

1 Current Procedural Terminology (CPT) codes are set by the American Medical Association and used to communicate what medical services have been rendered during an appointment with a provider. Clinicians must report CPT codes to insurance companies when seeking reimbursement for services provided.

References

Becker, E. M., Smith, A. M., & Jensen-Doss, A. (2013). Who's using treatment manuals? A national survey of practicing therapists. *Behaviour Research and Therapy, 51*(10), 706–710.

Couturier, J., Isserlin, L., & Lock, J. (2010). Family-based treatment for adolescents with anorexia nervosa: A dissemination study. *Eating Disorders, 18*, 199–209.

Couturier, J., Kimber, M., Jack, S., Niccols, A., Van Blyderveen, S., & McVey, G. (2013). Understanding the uptake of family-based treatment for adolescents with anorexia nervosa: Therapist perspectives. *International Journal of Eating Disorders, 46*(2), 177–188.

Doyle, P. M., Le Grange, D., Loeb, K., Doyle, A. C., & Crosby, R. D. (2010). Early response to family-based treatment for adolescent anorexia nervosa. *International Journal of Eating Disorders, 43*, 659–662.

Katzman, D. K., Peebles, R., Sawyer, S. M., Lock, J., & Le Grange, D. (2013). The role of the pediatrician in family-based treatment for adolescent eating disorders: Opportunities and challenges. *Journal of Adolescent Health, 53*, 433–440.

Kazdin, A. (2008). Evidence-based treatment and practice: New opportunities to bridge clinical research and practice, enhance the knowledge base, and improve patient care. *American Psychologist, 63*(3), 146–159.

Le Grange, D., & Lock, J. Family-based treatment is overvalued: reply to Strober, *Advances in Eating Disorders: Theory, Research and Practice*, May 2014. doi: 10.1080/21662630.2014.898397

Lock, J., & Le Grange, D. Debate Proposal: Family-based treatment is undervalued. *Advances in Eating Disorders: Theory, Research and Practice*, March 2014. doi: 10.1080/21662630.2014.898393

Lock, J., & Le Grange, D. (2015). *Help Your Teenager Beat an Eating Disorder*, Second Edition. New York: Guilford Press.

Lock, J., Le Grange, D., Agras, W. S., & Dare, C. (2001). *Treatment manual for anorexia nervosa: A family-based approach*. New York: Guilford Press.

Stiles-Shields, C., Hoste, R. R., Doyle, P. M., & Le Grange, D. (2012). A review of family-based treatment for adolescents with eating disorders. *Reviews on Recent Clinical Trials, 7*, 133–140.

Strober, M., & Johnson, C. (2012). The need for complex ideas in anorexia nervosa: Why biology, environment, and psyche all matter, why therapists make mistakes, and why clinical benchmarks are needed for managing weight correction. *International Journal of Eating Disorders, 45*, 155–178.

von Ranson, K. M., Wallace, L. M., & Stevenson, A. (2013). Psychotherapies provided for eating disorders by community clinicians: Infrequent use of evidence-based treatment. *Psychotherapy Research, 23*(3), 333–343.

Wallace, L. M., & von Ranson, K. M. (2012). Perceptions and use of empirically-supported psychotherapies among eating disorder professionals. *Behaviour Research and Therapy, 50*, 215–222.

Wilson, G. T., Grilo, C. M., & Vitousek, K. M. (2007). Psychological treatment of eating disorders. *American Psychologist, 62*, 199–216.

Chapter 18

Internet Assisted Family Therapy and Prevention for Anorexia Nervosa

Megan Jones, Corinna Jacobi, and C. Barr Taylor

The prevalence of anorexia nervosa (AN) is estimated at 0.3–0.7 percent among adolescent females between 15–19 years of age; yet the age of onset is even younger (Hoek and Hoeken, 2003; Hoek et al., 2005; van Son et al., 2006; Swanson et al., 2011b). AN can be medically serious in developing adolescents with malnutrition, leading to growth retardation, pubertal delay or interruption, and peak bone mass reduction. Follow-up studies of varying lengths suggest that the aggregate mortality rate is approximately 5.6 percent per decade. While about half of the deaths were due to suicide, the remainder were due to the physical complications of AN. Comorbid psychological conditions are also common in AN (Golden et al., 2003, Rome et al., 2003, Swanson et al., 2011b), and some 60 percent of all eating disorder patients have a lifetime affective disorder (Herzog et al., 1996).

Treatment Outcome

Existing clinical trials for AN treatments demonstrate that approximately half have good outcome, a quarter have intermediate outcomes, and about a quarter do poorly. Distressingly, even when AN symptoms have remitted, some studies indicate that associated psychiatric and social impairments persist (Herzog et al., 1993; Fichter et al., 2006; Vandereycken and Pieters, 1992; Zipfel et al., 2000). Prognosis depends in part on age of onset and duration of illness. Associated with a poor outcome in follow-up studies are longer duration of illness and older age of onset; the presence of symptoms of vomiting, bulimia, and purging; obsessive-compulsive personality disorder and compulsivity; and the extent and severity of dietary and eating patterns and other factors (Fichter et al., 2006; Steinhausen, 2002; Steinhausen, 2009).

Family-Based Interventions

Several recent reviews have examined the evidence supporting Family-Based Treatment (FBT) for individuals of all ages with eating disorders

(Couturier et al., 2013b; Fisher et al., 2010; Lock, 2011; Smith and Cook-Cottone, 2011; Stiles-Shields et al., 2012). FBT is the current recommended first-line treatment for adolescents with AN (American Psychiatric, 2006). FBT demonstrates recovery rates of approximately 50 and 90 percent maintenance of recovery one year post-treatment (Lock et al., 2010). Couturier et al. (2013b) conducted a systematic review and meta-analysis of family-based treatment studies for eating disorders and found 12 randomized controlled trials. Of these, three met the inclusion criteria for the meta-analysis. Results indicated that there was no difference between FBT and individual treatment at end of treatment, yet there was a clear advantage to FBT at the 6- to 12-month follow-up (Couturier et al., 2013b). A Cochrane review and meta-analysis concluded that FBT may be advantageous for remission compared to treatment as usual (RR 5 3.83, 95% CI 1.60–9.13; Fisher et al., 2010) and have specific utility with adolescents.

Despite demonstrated efficacy, few families have access to FBT because it is a difficult treatment to implement well in conventional settings (Fairburn and Wilson, 2013). There is good evidence to suggest that FBT is not widely practiced nor practiced with fidelity (Couturier et al., 2013a). Only one quarter of adolescents with AN report receiving specialized treatment (Swanson et al., 2011a). That the majority of individuals with AN go without specialized treatment is especially concerning, as early intervention is imperative in preventing a chronic course of the disorder, for which there are currently no known effective treatments (Doyle et al., 2010; Bulik et al., 2007).

Prevention of AN

Summary of Risk Factors for AN

Given the limited results of treatment studies for AN and the severity, course, and prognosis of the disorder, interventions targeting risk factors early before the onset of the fully developed disorder are of great importance and may reduce both the severity and consequences of AN. Effective preventive interventions should target specific risk factors, as well as those that can be changed and have some "potency" (= effect size of clinical significance; Kraemer et al., 2001; Kraemer et al., 1997). In an update of a large meta-analysis examining risk factors for eating disorders (ED), Jacobi & Fittig (2010) reviewed data from 23 longitudinal studies. Due to the low incidence of AN, the majority of cases identified in these studies were subclinical or "eating disorders not otherwise specified (EDNOS)" cases. Most of the EDNOS cases comprised subclinical BN and BED cases, while only a minority of cases were AN. Despite these limitations, the following risk factors for AN could be confirmed: *During childhood*, risk factors for AN include genetic factors, gender, ethnicity, season of birth, preterm birth or birth trauma, early childhood health problems, early childhood digestive problems, picky eating, AN symptoms, eating conflicts and struggles around meals, and being adopted or in foster care. Risk factors and markers confirmed *during adolescence* are adolescent age, pubertal status, weight concerns/dieting, and neuroticism.

In addition to these longitudinally assessed, probable risk factors (i.e., retrospectively assessed correlates of AN) include pregnancy complications or gestational age; high-concern parenting and infant sleep pattern difficulties; childhood anxiety disorders; obsessive-compulsive personality traits; feelings of loneliness, shyness, and inferiority; a high level of exercise; body dysmorphic disorder; sexual abuse; adverse life events; negative self-evaluation; perfectionism; obsessive-compulsive disorder; and acculturation.

Since the publication of the last update of the risk factor meta-analysis, only two new studies with prospective risk factor assessment including a sufficient number of AN cases as outcome have been published. The first prospective study used data from the 1970 British Cohort Study (Viner et al., 2000) and found that the risk of lifetime self-reported AN was independently predicted by female sex, infant feeding problems, maternal depressive symptoms in early childhood, and a history of undereating in late childhood. The second study, a large Swedish birth cohort study including over 14,000 participants born in 1953, found higher maternal education to be associated with a higher risk for hospitalization for AN. In addition, the risk for AN was increased among females who stated that they "often compare their future prospects with others" (Ahrén et al., 2012).

Evidently, not all of these factors are equally suited or practical to be targeted by preventive interventions. Some factors are "fixed" and not alterable. Some have been examined in just one study and are in need or replication. The age of the occurrence of the factors ranges from birth to young adulthood. There is a large variation in the potency of some risk factors. Evidence of risk factors specific for AN versus other more prevalent EDs is limited (Jacobi & Fittig, 2010). Accordingly, most of the risk factors targeted in preventive trials are common risk factors for anorectic and bulimic syndromes (e.g., weight and shape concerns). Moreover, little is known about the prevalence of risk factors for AN (Jacobi & Fittig, 2010; Jacobi et al., 2004; Völker et al., 2013). However, in the context of preventive interventions, targeting factors that can be manipulated and are also specific, highly prevalent, and potent is essential to reduce the onset of the disorder.

Summary of Prevention Effects for AN

In the past decade, an impressive number of prevention programs for eating disorders (EDs) in general have been developed and evaluated in randomized controlled trials (RCTs) and have allowed meta-analyses to be conducted (Beintner et al., 2011; Sinton and Taylor, 2010; Stice et al.,

2007; Jacobi et al., 2012). In the largest meta-analysis, effects of preventive interventions of almost 70 studies were examined. Overall, effect sizes of these interventions are usually small and in many studies restricted to changes in knowledge. Some studies observe changes in eating disorder-related attitudes (e.g., weight and shape concerns, body dissatisfaction), whereas to date only very few studies demonstrate effects of preventive interventions on behavioral outcomes (Stice, 2008; Taylor et al., 2006). Effect sizes (ES) are mostly small, and for selected outcomes they are in the small to medium range. Moderator analyses showed that highest effect sizes (ESs) are achieved for targeted (selective and indicated) and interactive (i.e., Internet-based) interventions with more than one session and for programs designed for female participants of 15 years and older (Beintner et al., 2011; Sinton and Taylor, 2010; Stice et al., 2007; Jacobi et al. 2012).

While many programs are generally directed at individuals with eating disorders (thus including AN), both the selection criteria of these studies and the outcomes considered do not reflect a focus on the more specific behavioral symptoms and/or risk factors for AN. Due to the low incidence of AN, targeting high-risk populations with initial symptoms of AN, such as low body mass index (BMI) or restrained eating, may be more promising. Unfortunately, previous selective prevention programs for EDs usually based their selection of high-risk groups on high weight and shape concerns/dysfunctional body shape preoccupations, only without consideration of BMI or other (potentially) early symptoms as an entry criterion. In addition, the mean BMI in these samples is in the normal range (M = 23.3, SD = 2.8), and restrained eating has never been used as inclusion criterion in any of the trials (Stice et al., 2007). Accordingly, it is very likely that participants with a lower BMI (i.e., <21) are not reached by these programs and that existing programs would need to be more specifically tailored for participants at risk for AN.

Given the above mentioned limitations regarding both the results and focus of previous prevention trials (inclusion criteria, targeted risk factors, observed effects on outcomes) and the positive results of family-based treatment trials for AN (see above), we decided to design a preventive intervention that acknowledges both the strengths of therapeutic interventions and the strengths and limitations of previous preventive studies. Accordingly, the intervention was based on Family-Based Treatment for Anorexia, as described above, and was delivered through the Internet to parents of children at risk for AN. The definition of risk was based on a combination of confirmed and putative risk factors for AN onset and on early symptoms of AN selected from three broad symptom categories common to EDs: (1) weight and shape concerns, (2) physical health indicators (weight status and amenorrhea), and (3) correlates (perfectionism, excessive exercise, and family history of an ED) of AN (Völker et al., 2013). The prevalence of these factors was 10.8 percent in the whole sample.

Why Use the Internet?

In 2013, in the United States, 85 percent of all adults and 95 percent of those ages 14–25 used the Internet (http://pewinternet.org/Trend-Data-%28Adults%29/Whos-Online.aspx). The Internet is a key source of health information (Kazdin and Blase, 2011; Carlbring et al., 2009; Christensen and Griffiths, 2002; Carroll and Rounsaville, 2010; Marks et al., 2007; Portnoy et al., 2008; Kohl et al., 2013). Interventions offered through the Internet and mobile applications such as "eHealth" (Eng, 2001) and "m-Health" (Free et al., 2010) comprise pure psychoeducational interventions, guided or nonguided self-help interventions, universal to indicated preventive interventions, counseling, and therapeutic interventions (Munoz, 2010; Riper et al., 2010). In addition, a mix of face-to-face interventions combined with online interventions ("blended interventions") is becoming more frequent (Munoz, 2010), and programs range from changing behaviors on an individual level to community-wide approaches in a variety of settings (Marks et al., 2007; Munoz, 2010).

Internet-based (preventive) interventions offer several potential advantages compared to face-to-face interventions (Christensen and Hickie, 2010). They are accessible at (almost) all times and therefore especially useful for people with limited access to health care or prevention providers, improving the reach of these interventions. They can be easily modified and updated to keep information accurate and can be tailored to the individual's specific needs and/or motivation. Greater anonymity may encourage individuals to seek out and/or reveal more sensitive health information, especially when the target behaviors are associated with shame or guilt. Finally, depending on the amount and efficiency of guidance provided by the intervention, online programs may be more cost-effective compared to face-to-face interventions (Portnoy et al., 2008; Atkinson and Gold, 2002).

Overall Effects of Internet-Based Parental Studies

The Internet is widely used by parents to obtain health information and for other activities, such as participating in support groups. Recently, programs have been developed for teaching skills to parents with children with various difficulties and problems (e.g., conduct problems, disruptive behavior disorder, and eating/weight). For example, in their latest evaluation, Sanders et al. (2012) evaluated the use of the online version of the Triple P program, a widely used and effective parenting program (Sanders, 2012) to help parents of children with early-onset conduct problems. At post-intervention assessment, parents receiving the Internet intervention had significantly better outcomes on measures of problem child behavior, dysfunctional parenting styles, parents' confidence in their parenting role, and parental anger. At a 6-month follow-up, assessment intervention gains were generally maintained and in some cases enhanced. Parents liked the programs. As another example, McGrath et al. (2013) evaluated the effects of an Internet-assisted parent training program for disruptive behavior.

In both of these examples, and in most published studies, online parenting courses have focused either on teaching general parenting skills or on helping parents cope with a problem. To our knowledge, only one study has focused on the use of Internet-based programs directed at helping parents of students participating in an Internet-based eating disorder prevention program. In this study Bruning Brown et al. (2004) provided a 4-week program to complement the students' in-classroom activities related to Student Bodies, an eating disorders prevention program. Parents had four weeks to complete the program. Parents could log on to the website at any time. Similar to the student group, the parent program included an online discussion group, providing a forum for participants to ask questions, discuss and react to the content of the program, or simply to interact with other parents. To protect confidentiality, parent participants logged on using an alias. The program encouraged parents to accept variations in weight and shape and to discourage negative attitudes and behaviors that might affect their daughters. Specific exercises and educational materials were provided to help parents determine whether or not they might be contributing to unhealthy attitudes about weight and shape and how they can recognize the signs and symptoms of unhealthy eating behaviors. In addition, the program assisted parents in identifying how miscommunication may occur between themselves and their children. Parents could view hypothetical scenarios demonstrating common behaviors and their potential implications.

Parents were also given guidelines to help them determine whether their daughters might need to diet and were educated about using supportive communication skills to begin a dialogue with their daughters about weight- and shape-related issues. Sixty-nine parents completed the baseline assessments. Of these, 49 had daughters who were in the Student Bodies intervention and the remainder (n = 20) had daughters who were in the student comparison group. Parents of the daughters in the Student Bodies intervention were assigned on the basis of their daughter's class period to either the Student Bodies parent intervention (intervention group, n = 22) or the wait-list control group (n = 27). The percentage of parents who agreed to participate was similar for those whose daughters were in the intervention (40 percent) and for those whose daughters were not in the intervention (39 percent). From baseline to post-intervention, significant differences were found between the intervention and control groups on the subscale assessing critical attitudes and behaviors toward others (p = .008). Between group effect sizes for the parent intervention were 0.48 for Critical to Self, 0.59 for Critical to Daughter, 0.57 for Critical to Others, and 0.61 for Healthy Outlook. Eleven of twenty-two intervention group parents logged on to the Student Bodies parent program. Most (8 of 11) parents reported reading over 80 percent of the content; two parents indicated that they read between 50 and 80 percent. Of the parents who read the material on the website, 10 of 11 responded that they found the site helpful and interesting and reported that they talked to others about the content. Overall, parents posted a total of nine messages over the 1-month period. Parents also had the opportunity to e-mail the consulting psychiatrist, though only one did. To examine if students in the intervention whose parents were randomized to the parental intervention did better than students in the intervention whose parents were not, changes in students' primary and secondary outcomes were compared at baseline to post- and baseline to follow-up. No significant differences were found. This study demonstrated that parent programs can be added in parallel to online programs. Although effective, the relative low participation (only 50 percent logged on) by parents was surprising.

An Internet-Assisted Family Intervention: Parents Act Now

For parents who are interested in preventing the onset or progression of a child's AN symptoms—or who otherwise are not able to access FBT—mobile and online interventions present the opportunity to increase access, reduce costs, and establish sustainable systems for providing care. When linked to in-person medical services, such as medical monitoring by a pediatrician, Internet-delivered programs may help reduce mental health care disparities for adolescent AN. Internet-delivered guided self-help interventions have been successfully implemented among individuals with BN and BED and at a minimum appear to promote symptom reduction beyond a wait-list control condition (Ljotsson et al., 2007; Carrard et al., 2011; Sanchez-Ortiz et al., 2011). There are no comparable treatments developed at this time for AN. A fundamental principle of FBT is parental empowerment, making it ideal for dissemination as an approach for parents.

Parents Act Now Intervention

Parents Act Now (P@N; German version: "Eltern als Therapeuten (E@T)") was originally designed in collaboration by the Stanford and Dresden group as an early intervention for girls who were screened as being at risk or high risk for the development of AN based on established risk factors and early symptoms of AN (Jones et al., 2012). In two small pilot studies (one in the United States, one in Germany), it was also offered to parents of adolescents with AN as an ancillary support and educational program. The program is based on FBT principles and was evaluated in Germany and the United States.

Parents Act Now includes six weekly online sessions for parents, an online parent discussion board, and two phone-delivered coaching calls with a moderator (psychology graduate and postdoctoral students). The online sessions were comprised of psychoeducational readings and videos, monitoring journals, and case examples. Parents Act Now was derived directly from the first phase of FBT (Lock et al., 2001; Lock and Le Grange, 2005b; Lock and Le Grange, 2005a) and an Internet-based intervention for adolescent eating disorder prevention (Jacobi et al., 2007). Parents are educated about AN, the devastating consequences of this illness, and the vital importance of early intervention. Parents Act Now encourages definitive steps to prevent the continuation and/or exacerbation of weight loss efforts. Sessions activate parental concern, facilitate parent empowerment, encourage parental action, and provide concrete and practical approaches for intervention. Parents receive support in problem-solving skills and guidance about ongoing monitoring of their daughters' behaviors.

Intervention Content and Structure

Session 1: The principle aim of Session 1 is to activate parental concern about the possibility of AN developing in their child in order to encourage them to take action to modify their child's behaviors before they become entrenched. To achieve this aim, parents are educated about the seriousness and dangers of the illness: bone loss, cardiac arrhythmias, infertility, depression, and suicide. This is illustrated through clinical vignettes, bone scans, brain scans, photographs, interviews, as well as graphics illustrating data. Additional aims are to help parents to recognize early symptoms of AN (e.g., problematic hidden behaviors, denial of problematic behaviors) and to educate them about healthy eating and exercising versus the dangers of restrictive eating, weight loss, and over-exercising. This session is followed by a phone call from moderators to discuss parents' questions about the contents provided in Session 1 and to encourage them to take action.

Session 2: The principle aim of Session 2 is to empower parents to take action to challenge the worrying behaviors that their child is demonstrating. In order to do so, this session also aims to increase the parents' sense of efficacy (confidence) that they can and should do something. These aims are accomplished by providing a variety of information about how parents have been successful challenging AN behaviors in their children. The most effective way to communicate this information is through videotaped illustrations and case vignettes of parents and former patients discussing their experience and success. Other strategies include more educational materials on the systematic studies demonstrating effectiveness of parental weight restoration in adolescent AN.

Session 3: The principle aim of Session 3 is to provide parents with some practical approaches that have been used successfully by other parents. Parents and clinicians describe what they did and how it worked.

For example, they might approach it just like any other serious medical problem: keeping the students home if the student is not gaining weight or is over-exercising; monitoring their intake; restricting physical, academic, and social activity that would lead to weight loss. Session 3 is followed by a phone call from moderators with the aim of supporting parental decisions about how to challenge the AN-related behaviors in their child.

Session 4: The aim of Session 4 is to practice and think through possible strategies parents are considering using to challenge AN behaviors. The strategy involves several practice scenarios common to parents trying to challenge these behaviors (e.g., grocery shopping, meal planning, covert exercise, tantrums, withdrawal).

Session 5: The aim of Session 5 is to help parents identify problems in their own behaviors that might limit the effectiveness of their interventions with their child. The strategy also involves practice scenarios of common dilemmas parents face (e.g., disagreement with co-parent on approach, criticism, overreaction, over-negotiating with child, not sticking with plan long enough to test its effectiveness, poor role modeling about weight concerns, own weight and shape issues).

Session 6: The aim of Session 6 is to deal with potential ongoing lapses into problematic behaviors and relapse monitoring.

Pilot Study Results

The results of the two pilot studies with P@N and E@T (n = 21 and n = 25) demonstrated that we are able to identify between 11 and 22 percent of girls with some clear indications of risk for anorexia nervosa (high weight and shape concerns, low weight/weight loss, family history of ED/low self-esteem/high perfectionism/driven exercise). The P@N/E@T program addresses these issues well, supported by a reduction in risk status in the majority of participants and an increase in mean percent of ideal body weight (%IBW), with medium-large effect sizes for all participants except those in the German sample whose %IBW remained the same (M = 102.1%) (Jones et al., 2012). In addition, the overall evaluation of parents who participated in the program was very good. Evidently, sample sizes were small in both pilot studies and participation of parents was rather low as was the rate of parents willing to take up the intervention. While parents of children with ED-NOS (included in the Stanford pilot study) used the program more frequently, they also rated the program less favorably, likely reflecting the fact that program content was originally designed for the purposes of prevention of development of full-syndrome EDs. While the results generally showed promise for the acceptance and potential effectiveness of the parent-based preventive intervention, they also suggest that parents are more likely to be effectively mobilized when their child is visibly ill rather than when they are exhibiting warning signs. Further, parents of children with ED-NOS in the

Stanford sample expressed an interest in accessing in-person FBT but were unable to find specialized services in their area.

Conclusions from Pilot Studies and Revisions for the Main Study

While our exploratory results demonstrated some remarkable changes in attitudes and behaviors of disordered eating given the (short) parent-based intervention, they also demonstrated necessary revisions to be addressed in the main study to improve both the screening and recruitment of high-risk participants and increase the rate of participating parents. Apart from many smaller changes, we shortened the time span between screening and parental feedback as well as better screening and start of the intervention. To deal with parental motivation and compliance problems, we added a motivational assessment and enhancement module (adapted from motivational interviewing) to the first assessment when parents receive feedback on the risk status of their daughters. Prior to starting the program, we encouraged parents to write down the reasons why they are interested in participating in the program, elicited concerns/worries about their daughter, elicited knowledge of medical/psychological/social consequences of AN, and then provided motivational enhancement based on this by building upon it, providing information, and providing reminders to parents in their own words throughout the program. We acknowledged the problem of denial and downplaying of eating problems in the first session, addressed parents' fear of triggering more problematic behaviors by talking about the eating problem and/or acting, and emphasized the danger of not acting by explaining negative somatic and cognitive consequences more upfront in the program. We also provided feedback about program use in conjunction with a message about the importance of taking action now.

Main Study

Following the two pilot studies, we initiated a larger randomized controlled trial in Dresden in 2009. For this trial, we applied a multi-stage procedure: (1) adolescents (aged 11 to 17 years) were screened and high-risk adolescents identified based on the above mentioned selected risk factors and early symptoms of AN, and (2) eligible participants and their parents were then randomized to the E@T program and compared with an assessment-only control group. Assessments took place at baseline, six weeks later at post-intervention, and at 6- and 12-month follow-ups. Between 2010 and 2013, a total of 12,377 screens were handed out in 86 schools in Saxony. Overall, 3,939 girls (and parents) took part in the screening, 473 (12 percent) of these were identified as at-risk for AN and informed about their daughter's risk status. Of those, however, only 96 families agreed to participate in baseline interviews;

of these, finally 66 families could be randomly assigned to the intervention or the control condition. Due to the relatively low participation rate of parents in relation to the number of handed out and returned screens, resulting in a rather long recruitment process, recruitment for the study was terminated in spring 2013. Complete follow-up results regarding parents' adherence and (daughters') primary outcomes are available by July 2014. However, it is already evident that, despite a variety of means implemented in the study to raise parental awareness and increase parental participation, parental willingness to participate and adherence to the intervention was low.

Discussion

We report on two pilot studies and a larger, controlled trial now underway designed to evaluate the effectiveness of an online family-based intervention to prevent anorexia. The two pilot studies were promising and suggested that an online intervention could be effective. In order to have a sample large enough to adequately evaluate the effects of the intervention, we then decided to develop a screen that might capture most at-risk for anorexia students and apply it to a large population with the notion that parents of these students would then be notified and agree to participate in a prevention intervention. We were also hoping that the sample would be large enough to permit moderation analysis so that the intervention might be directed at those at highest risk. Unfortunately, relatively few students (32 percent) agreed to complete the screen and even fewer of their parents agreed to participate in the randomized study. We are left with a number of unresolved issues.

Is it worthwhile to screen for anorexia using the risk factors we identified? The answer is probably not. As Offord et al. (1998) notes, screen sensitivity and specificity rates need to be very high when screening for low prevalent conditions. Otherwise, a large number of individuals need to be treated to prevent a case. For instance, in our data, assuming that 12 to 20 percent of students are at risk and the risk factor data captures all individuals at risk, incidence data suggest that only one or two of them would become cases. For instance, if 1,000 students in a defined population filled out the survey, 120–200 would be at risk, of whom only 1 or 2 might become cases. Preventive interventions can be delivered to large populations at relatively low cost (Beintner et al., 2011) so that lack of specificity is not necessarily a problem as long as the intervention is intrinsically beneficial to those who turn out not to be at risk and can be delivered at low cost. However, P@N is relatively expensive to deliver in terms of requiring moderators and participant time. The small numbers of students and parents who enrolled will preclude us from the types of analysis that might reveal who is most at risk and would benefit from the preventive intervention.

The most disappointing part of this work thus far is that only about 14 percent of the parents with at-risk students agreed to be part of the research study. We can only speculate as to why so few parents agreed to part of the study. One strong possibility is that parents may be reluctant to see their child as being at risk based on what would appear to be severe restricted eating, excessive exercise, and/or a very low weight. It is possible that some parents may view their child's thinness and weight loss as positive and may even have encouraged it. The rapid onset of AN, and associated rapid decline in health status, seen in many children and adolescents affected by this disorder often comes as a shock to parents. Hence, what may be initially seen as an interest in healthful eating and/or exercise or a socially and developmentally "normative" experiment with dieting may not be sufficient to raise parents' alarm—even in spite of feedback to the contrary. As experts know, for children vulnerable to AN, these behaviors can quickly spiral out of control, making the window for "prevention" quite narrow.

If there is a tendency for some parents not to fully appreciate feedback about their child's risk for AN, it is not clear what strategy, if any, would be ethical to try to reduce the minimizing/denial for students at risk but without clinical symptoms. Some public health campaigns (e.g., those directed at smoking cessation) have used "scare" techniques to try to break through a smoker's denial, and those techniques seem to have been every effective (McAfee et al., 2013). Such an approach might increase the number of parents who would be willing to use the program but at what cost? For instance, a public health intervention delivered to a defined population (e.g., high school students) would target a large number of parents/students who might be very unlikely to go on to develop anorexia. Thus, the harm/benefit of the intervention needs to be considered. An intervention might be considered if it provides general, useful skills (e.g., Metzler et al., 2012) or recommends positive behaviors (e.g., avoiding criticisms, encouraging family meals) but does not unduly frighten the target audience. Further, any effort focused on AN prevention should seek to both *activate concern* and *empower* parents, as these are a core tenet of effective parental involvement (i.e., FBT; Lock et al., 2006). It is critical to reduce parental blame (Le Grange et al., 2009) and yet find a way to help parents make early intervention a priority in spite of many competing demands.

Another strategy would be to provide universal/targeted prevention programs to defined populations (e.g., all students in a school) and to monitor students' progress (including weight). In this model the parents of students who are not doing well would then be contacted. Models that combine universal messages (general healthy weight regulation behaviors, positive body image) while addressing a targeted audience (students at risk for eating disorders) have proven effective for reducing eating disorder behaviors (Jones et al., 2014a; Jones et al., 2014b). They more recently have been expanded to include indicated preventive interventions (Wilfley et al., 2013). These programs can combine screens with interventions and have had high acceptance rates in school populations (45–95 percent, from Jones et al., 2014b).

More practically, the online program might be offered to parents who already are worried about their daughter (or son) and see a need for an intervention. The low enrollment observed in the German school-based screening compared to recruitment through other methods as reported above may relate to the large discrepancy observed between the baseline %IBW at the two sites (Dresden = 102.1, Stanford = 88.3–90.1). It may be difficult for parents to take action when their daughter is at a normal body weight, as was the case in the Dresden sample. This suggests that parents whose daughters already have noticeable signs of AN may be more interested and willing to participate in an early intervention program. Parents could learn about the program through websites and eating disorders organizations, sites where they might go anyway to find resources to help their children. However, before being disseminated, the efficacy of the program needs to be proven. Parents appear to want and need additional support in intervening with children who are at-risk for or already suffering from AN. Internet-based parental or "carer" support may also be provided as a treatment adjunct (Binford Hopf et al., 2013; Grover et al., 2011). Binford Hopf et al. (2013) found high acceptability of a therapist-led, online discussion group for parents ancillary to participation in FBT. Authors noted that parents reported feeling supported and better able to cope with their child's eating disorder.

The results of these studies suggest that the use of an online family-based therapy for students presumably at risk is not an effective prevention strategy, at least as provided to a universal population, although it may have some benefit for parents who are already concerned about their child's behavior and could be part of a stepped care program. Prevention of anorexia should also focus on symptomatic students. Efforts need to be made to determine the best way to identify such students and engage them and their parents in prevention programs.

References

Ahrén, J. C., Chiesa, F., af Klinteberg, B., & Koupil, I. (2012). Psychosocial determinants and family background in anorexia nervosa—results from the Stockholm birth cohort study. *International Journal of Eating Disorders, 45*(3), 362–369.

American Psychiatric Association (2006). Treatment of patients with eating disorders, third edition. *American Journal of Psychiatry, 163*(7 Suppl), 4–54.

Atkinson, N. L., & Gold, R. S. (2002). The promise and challenge of eHealth interventions. *American Journal of Health Behavior, 26*(6), 494–503.

Beintner, I., Jacobi, C., & Taylor, C. B. (2011). Effects of an Internet-based prevention program for eating disorders in the U.S. and Germany—A Meta-analytic Review. *European Review of Eating Disorders, 20*, 1–9.

Binford Hopf, R. B., Le Grange, D., Moessner, M., & Bauer, S. (2013). Internet-based chat support groups for parents in family-based treatment for adolescent eating disorders: A pilot study. *European Eating Disorders Review, 21*(3), 215–223. doi: 10.1002/erv.2196

Bruning Brown, J., Winzelberg, A. J., Abascal, L. B., & Taylor, C. B. (2004). An evaluation of an Internet-delivered eating disorder prevention program for adolescents and their parents. *Journal of Adolescent Health, 35*(4), 290–296.

Bulik, C. M., Berkman, N. D., Brownley, K. A., Sedway, J. A., & Lohr, K. N. (2007). Anorexia nervosa treatment: A systematic review of randomized controlled trials. *International Journal of Eating Disorders, 40*(4), 310–320. doi: 10.1002/eat.20367

Carlbring, P., Nordgren, L. B., Furmark, T., & Andersson, G. (2009). Long-term outcome of Internet-delivered cognitive-behavioural therapy for social phobia: A 30-month follow-up. *Behavior Research and Therapy, 47*(10), 848–850. doi: 10.1016/j.brat.2009.06.012

Carrard, I., Crepin, C., Rouget, P., Lam, T., Golay, A., & Van der Linden, M. (2011). Randomised controlled trial of a guided self-help treatment on the Internet for binge eating disorder. *Behavior Research and Therapy, 49*, 482–491.

Carroll, K. M., & Rounsaville, B. J. (2010). Computer-assisted therapy in psychiatry: Be brave—It's a new world. *Current Psychiatry Reports, 12*(5), 426–432. doi: 10.1007/s11920-010-0146-2

Christensen, H., & Griffiths, K. M. (2002). The prevention of depression using the Internet. *Medical Journal of Australia, 177*, S122–S125.

Christensen, H., & Hickie, I. B. (2010). E-mental health: a new era in delivery of mental health services. *Medical Journal of Australia, 192*(11), S2–S3.

Couturier, J., Kimber, M., Jack, S., Niccols, A., Van Blyderveen, S., & McVey, G. (2013). Understanding the uptake of family-based treatment for adolescents with anorexia nervosa: Therapist perspectives. *International Journal of Eating Disorders, 46*, 177–188.

Couturier, J., Kimber, M., & Szatmari, P. (2013). Efficacy of family-based treatment for adolescents with eating disorders: A systematic review and meta-analysis. *International Journal of Eating Disorders, 46*(1), 3–11. doi: 10.1002/eat.22042

Doyle, P., Le Grange, D., Loeb, K., Doyle, A., & Crosby, R. (2010). Early response to family-based treatment for adolescent anorexia nervosa. *International Journal of Eating Disorders, 43*, 659–662.

Eng, T. R. (2001). *The eHealth Landscape: A Terrain Map of Emerging Information and Communication Technologies in Health and Health Care.* Princeton, NJ: The Robert Wood Johnson Foundation.

Fairburn, C. G., & Wilson, G. T. (2013). The dissemination and implementation of psychological treatments: problems and solutions. *International Journal of Eating Disorders, 46*(5), 516–521. doi: 10.1002/eat.22110

Fichter, M. M., Quadflieg, N., & Hedlund, S. (2006). Twelve-year course and outcome predictors of anorexia nervosa. *International Journal of Eating Disorders, 39*(2), 87–100. doi: 10.1002/eat.20215

Fisher, C. A., Hetrick, S. E., & Rushford, N. (2010). Family therapy for anorexia nervosa. *Cochrane Database Syst Rev* (4), CD004780. doi: 10.1002/14651858.CD004780.pub2

Free, C., Phillips, G., Felix, L., Galli, L., Patel, V., & Edwards, P. (2010). The effectiveness of M-health technologies for improving health and health services: A systematic review protocol. *BMC research notes, 3*, 250. doi: 10.1186/1756-0500-3-250

Golden, N., DK, K., RE, K., SL, S., SM, S., J, R., ... ES, R. (2003). Eating disorders in adolescents: position paper of the Society for Adolescent Medicine: Medical Indications for Hospitalization in an Adolescent with an Eating Disorder. *Journal of Adolescent Health, 33*, 496–503.

Grover, M., Naumann, U., Mohammad-Dar, L., Glennon, D., Ringwood, S., Eisler, I., ... Schmidt, U. (2011). A randomized controlled trial of an Internet-based cognitive-behavioural skills package for carers of people with anorexia nervosa. *Psychological Medicine, 41*(12), 2581–2591. doi: 10.1017/S0033291711000766

Herzog, D. B., Hopkins, J. D., & Burns, C. D. (1993). A follow-up study of 33 sub-diagnostic eating disordered women. *International Journal of Eating Disorders, 14*(3), 261–267.

Herzog, D. B., Nussbaum, K. M., & Marmor, A. K. (1996). Comorbidity and outcome in eating disorders. *Psychiatry Clinics North America, 19*(4), 843–859.

Hoek, H. W., & van Hoeken, D. (2003). Review of prevalence and incidence of eating disorders. *International Journal of Eating Disorders, 34*, 383–396.

Hoek, H., van Harten, P. N., Hermans, K. M., Katzman, M. A., Matroos, G. E., & Susser, E. S. (2005). The incidence of anorexia nervosa on Curacao. *American Journal of Psychiatry, 162*, 748–752.

Jacobi & Fittig, 2010. Who is really at risk? Identifying risk factors for subthreshold and full syndrome eating disorders in a high-risk sample. *Psychological Medicine, 41*(9), 1939–1949. doi: S0033291710002631 [pii]

Jacobi, C., Hayward, C., de Zwaan, M., Kraemer, H. C., & Agras, W. S. (2004). Coming to terms with risk factors for eating disorders: application of risk terminology and suggestions for a general taxonomy. *Psychological Bulletin, 130*(1), 19–65. doi: 10.1037/0033-2909.130.1.192003-11000-002 [pii]

Jacobi, C., Morris, L., Beckers, C., Bronisch-Holtze, J., Winter, J., Winzelberg, A. J., & Taylor, C. B. (2007). Maintenance of internet-based prevention: a randomized controlled trial. *International Journal of Eating Disorders, 40*(2), 114–119. doi: 10.1002/eat.20344

Jacobi, C., Jones, M., & Beintner, I. (2012). Prevention of Eating Disorders in Children and Adolescents. In J. Lock (Ed.), *The Oxford Handbook of Child and Adolescent Eating Disorders: Developmental Perspectives.*

Jones, M., Kass, A. E., Trockel, M., Glass, A.; Wilfley, D. E., & Taylor, C. B. (2014). A universal screening and intervention platform for eating disorders on college campuses: The Healthy Body Image Program. *Journal of American College Health*, DOI: 10.1080/07448481.2014.901330

Jones, M., Taylor Lynch, K., Kass, A., Burrows, A., Williams, J., Wilfley, D. E., & Taylor, C. B. (2014). Universal and targeted intervention for healthy weight regulation and eating disorder prevention in high school students. *Journal of Medical Internet Research, 16*, e57.

Jones, M., Volker, U., Lock, J., Taylor, C. B., & Jacobi, C. (2012). Family-based early intervention for anorexia nervosa. *European Eating Disorders Review, 20*(3), e137-143. doi: 10.1002/erv.2167

Kazdin, A. E., & Blase, S. L. (2011). Rebooting Psychotherapy Research and Practice to Reduce the Burden of Mental Illness. *Perspectives on Psychological Science, 6*(1), 21–37. doi: 10.1177/1745691610393527

Kohl, L. F. M., Crutzen, R., & de Vries, N. K. (2013). Online prevention aimed at lifestyle behaviors: a systematic review of reviews. *Journal of Medical Internet Research, 15*(7), e146. doi: 10.2196/jmir.2665

Kraemer, H. C., Kazdin, A. E., Offord, D. R., Kessler, R. C., Jensen, P. S., & Kupfer, D. J. (1997). Coming to terms with the terms of risk. *Archives of General Psychiatry, 54*(4), 337.

Kraemer, H. C., Stice, E., Kazdin, A., Offord, D., Kupfer, D. (2001). How Do Risk Factors Work Together? Mediators, Moderators, and Independent, Overlapping, and Proxy Risk Factors. *American Journal of Psychiatry, 158*(6), 848–856.

Le Grange, D., Lock, J., Loeb, K., & Nicholls, D. (2009). Academy for Eating Disorders position paper: The role of the family in eating disorders. *International Journal of Eating Disorders, 43*(1), 1–5. doi: 10.1002/eat.20751

Ljotsson, B., Lundin, C., Mitsell, K., Carlbring, P., Ramklint, M., & Ghaderi, A. (2007). Remote treatment of bulimia nervosa and binge eating disorder: A randomized trial of Internet-assisted cognitive behavioral therapy. *Behavior Research and Therapy, 45*(4), 649–661.

Lock, J. (2011). Evaluation of family treatment models for eating disorders. *Current Opinions in Psychiatry, 24*(4), 274–279. doi: 10.1097/YCO.0b013e328346f71e

Lock, J., Le Grange, D., Agras, W. S., & Dare, C. (2001). *Treatment Manual for Anorexia Nervosa: A Family-Based Approach*. New York, NY, US: The Guilford Press.

Lock, J., & Le Grange, D. (2005a). Family-based treatment of eating disorders. *International Journal of Eating Disorders, 37*(S1), S64–S67. doi: 10.1002/eat.20122

Lock, J., & Le Grange, D. (2005b). *Help Your Teenager Beat an Eating Disorder*. New York, NY: The Guilford Press.

Lock, J., Le Grange, D., Agras, W. S., Moye, A., Bryson, S. W., & Jo, B. (2010). Randomized clinical trial comparing family-based treatment with adolescent-focused individual therapy for adolescents with anorexia nervosa. *Archives of General Psychiatry, 67*(10), 1025–1032. doi: 10.1001/archgenpsychiatry.2010.128

Lock, J., le Grange, D., Forsberg, S., & Hewell, K. (2006). Is family therapy useful for treating children with anorexia nervosa? Results of a case series. *Journal of the American Academy of Child and Adolescent Psychiatry, 45*(11), 1323–1328. doi: 10.1097/01.chi.0000233208.43427.4cS0890-8567(09)61914-6 [pii]

Marks, I. M., Cavanagh, K., & Gega, L. (2007). *Hands-on Help: Computer-Aided Psychotherapy* (1 ed.): Psychology Press.

McAfee, T., Davis, K. C., Alexander Jr., R. L., Pechacek, T. F., & Bunnell, R. (2013). Effect of the first federally funded US antismoking national media campaign. *The Lancet, 382*(9909), 2003–2011. doi: http://dx.doi.org/10.1016/S0140-6736(13)61686-4

McGrath, P. J., Sourander, A., Lingley-Pottie, P., Ristkari, T., Cunningham, C., Huttunen, J., ... Watters, C. (2013). Remote population-based intervention for disruptive behavior at age four: study protocol for a randomized trial of Internet-assisted parent training (Strongest Families Finland-Canada). *BMC Public Health, 13*(1), 985. doi: 10.1186/1471-2458-13-985

Metzler, C. W., Sanders, M. R., Rusby, J. C., & Crowley, R. N. (2012). Using consumer preference information to increase the reach and impact of media-based parenting interventions in a public health approach to parenting support. *Behavior Therapy, 43*(2), 257–270. doi: 10.1016/j.beth.2011.05.004

Munoz, R. F. (2010). Using Evidence-Based Internet Interventions to Reduce Health Disparities Worldwide. *Journal of Medical Internet Research, 12*(5). doi: 10.2196/jmir.1463

Offord, D. R., Kraemer, H. C., Kazdin, A. E., Jensen, P. S., & Harrington, R. (1998). Lowering the burden of suffering from child psychiatric disorder: Trade-offs among clinical, targeted, and universal interventions. *J Am Acad Child Adolesc Psychiatry, 37*(7), 686–694. doi: 10.1097/00004583-199807000-00007

Portnoy, D. B., Scott-Sheldon, L. A. J., Johnson, B. T., & Carey, M. P. (2008). Computer-delivered interventions for health promotion and behavioral risk reduction: A meta-analysis of 75 randomized controlled trials, 1988–2007. *Preventive Medicine, 47*(1), 3–16. doi: 10.1016/j.ypmed.2008.02.014

Riper, H., Andersson, G., Christensen, H., Cuijpers, P., Lange, A., & Eysenbach, G. (2010). Theme issue on e-mental health: A growing field in Internet research. *Journal of Medical Internet Research, 12*(5). doi: 10.2196/jmir.1713

Rome, E., Ammerman, S., Rosen, D., Keller, R., Lock, J., Mammal, K., ... Silber, T. (2003). Children and adolescents with eating disorders: The state of the art. *Pediatrics, 111*, e98-e108.

Sanchez-Ortiz, V., Munro, C., Stahl, D., House, J., Startup, H., Treasure, J., ... Schmidt, U. (2011). A randomized controlled trial of internet-based cognitive-behavioural therapy for bulimia nervosa or related disorders in a student population. *Psychological Medicine, 41*, 407–417.

Sanders, M. R. (2012). Development, evaluation, and multinational dissemination of the triple P-Positive Parenting Program. *Annu Rev Clin Psychol, 8*, 345–379. doi: 10.1146/annurev-clinpsy-032511-143104

Sanders, M. R., Baker, S., & Turner, K. M. (2012). A randomized controlled trial evaluating the efficacy of Triple P Online with parents of children with early-onset conduct problems. *Behav Res Ther, 50*(11), 675–684. doi: 10.1016/j.brat.2012.07.004

Sinton, M., & Taylor, C. (2010). Prevention: Current status and underlying theory. *The Oxford Handbook of Eating Disorders*, 307-330.

Smith, A., & Cook-Cottone, C. (2011). A review of family therapy as an effective intervention for anorexia nervosa in adolescents. *J Clin Psychol Med Settings, 18*(4), 323–334. doi: 10.1007/s10880-011-9262-3

Steinhausen, H.-C. (2002). The outcome of anorexia nervosa in the 20th century. *American journal of Psychiatry, 159*(8), 1284-1293.

Steinhausen, H.-C. (2009). Outcome of eating disorders. *Child and Adolescent Psychiatric Clinics of North America, 18*(1), 225–242.

Stice, E., Shaw, H., & Marti, C. N. (2007). A meta-analytic review of eating disorder prevention programs: encouraging findings. *Annu Rev Clin Psychol, 3*, 207–231. doi: 10.1146/annurev.clinpsy.3.022806.091447

Stice, E., Marti, C. N., Spoor, S., Presnell, K., & Shaw, H. (2008). Dissonance and healthy weight eating disorder prevention programs: Long-term effects from a randomized efficacy trial. *Journal of Consulting and Clinical Psychology, 76*(2), 329–340.

Stiles-Shields, C., Hoste, R. R., Doyle, P. M., & Le Grange, D. (2012). A review of family-based treatment for adolescents with eating disorders. *Rev Recent Clin Trials, 7*(2), 133–140.

Striegel-Moore, R. H., Leslie, D., Petrill, S. A., Garvin, V., & Rosenheck, R. A. (2000). One-year use and cost of inpatient and outpatient services among female and male patients with an eating disorder: Evidence from a national database of health insurance claims. *Int J Eat Disord, 27*(4), 381–389.

Sullivan, P. F. (1995). Mortality in anorexia nervosa. *American Journal of Psychiatry, 152*, 1073–1074.

Swanson, S., Crow, S., Le Grange, D., Swendsen, J., & Merikangas, K. (2011). Prevalence and correlates of eating disorders in adolescents. Results from the national comorbidity survey replication adolescent supplement. *Archives of General Psychiatry, 68*, 714–723.

Swanson, S. A., Crow, S. J., Le Grange, D., Swendsen, J., & Merikangas, K. R. (2011). Prevalence and correlates of eating disorders in adolescents. Results from the national comorbidity survey replication adolescent supplement. *Archives of General Psychiatry, 68*(7), 714–723. doi: 10.1001/archgenpsychiatry.2011.22

Taylor, C. B., Bryson, S., Luce, K. H., Cunning, D., Doyle, A. C., Abascal, L. B., ... Wilfley, D. E. (2006). Prevention of eating disorders in at-risk college-age women. *Arch Gen Psychiatry, 63*(8), 881–888. doi: 63/8/881 [pii]10.1001/archpsyc.63.8.881

van Son, G., van hoeken, D., Aad, I., Bartelds, A., van Furth, E., & Hoek, H. (2006). Time trends in the incidence of eating disorders: A primary care study in the Netherlands. *Int J Eat Disord, 39*, 565–569.

Vandereycken, W., & Pieters, G. (1992). A large scale longitudinal follow-up study of patients with eating disorders: Methodological issues and preliminary results. In W. Herzog, H. C. Deter, & W. Vandereycken (Eds.), *The Course of Eating Disorders* (pp. 182–197). Heidelberg: Springer.

Viner, R., Bryant-Waugh, R., Nicholls, D., & Christie, D. (2000). Childhood obesity: Aim should be weight maintenance, not loss. *BMJ, 320*(7246), 1401.

Völker, U., Jacobi, C., Jones, M., Lock, J., & Taylor, C. B. (2013). Potential risk factors and early symptoms of anorexia nervosa: prevalence in 11–16-year-old girls. *Advances in Eating Disorders*(ahead-of-print), 1–12.

Wilfley, D. E., Agras, W. S., & Taylor, C. B. (2013). Reducing the burden of eating disorders: A model for population-based prevention and treatment for university and college campuses. *International Journal of Eating Disorders, 46*(5), 529–532. doi: 10.1002/eat.22117

Zipfel, S., Lowe, B., Deter, H. C., & Herzog, W. (2000). Long-term prognosis in anorexia nervosa: Lessons from a 21-year follow-up study. *Lancet, 355*, 721–722.

Chapter 19

Dissemination of Family-Based Treatment

Where Are We Now and Where Do We Go From Here?

Melissa S. Kimber and Jennifer L. Couturier

Despite the evidence for the efficacy of Family-Based Treatment (FBT) (Lock, Le Grange, Agras, & Dare, 2001) in treating children and adolescents diagnosed with Anorexia Nervosa (AN), many clinicians continue to use this model without fidelity in practice (Couturier, et al., 2013a). This paradox is not specific to FBT nor the eating disorder field. In fact, it can be argued that this paradox is one of the many examples of the notorious "research-practice" gap; that is, the disjuncture between research evidence and what is actually applied in routine clinical practice (McLennan, Wathen, MacMillan, & Lavis, 2006). This chapter begins by identifying the distinction between evidence-based practice and evidence-based treatment (EBT), as we believe that this distinction has important implications for the translation of FBT into the clinical practice realm. The chapter continues with a summary of the current state of the utilization of EBTs within the eating disorder field and, more specifically, the utilization of FBT. Next, we discuss the specific efforts that have been undertaken to understand the dissemination of FBT for the treatment of child and adolescent AN. We highlight the factors that have been identified to influence the dissemination and application of FBT with fidelity in practice, followed by the decision-making processes involved in these endeavors. We end with a discussion about how the implementation science literature can *and* will inform greater uptake and application of FBT, as well as other EBTs, into routine clinical practice.

Evidence-Based Treatment versus Evidence-Based Practice

One factor contributing to the research-practice gap is the common misconception that evidence-based practice is equivalent to evidence-based treatment. The latter refers to a specific form of intervention or technique that has empirical evidence—usually in the form of a randomized controlled trial—for its effectiveness in treating a particular ailment or illness within a specified patient population (Kazdin, 2008). However, evidence-based practice (EBP) consists of three interrelated actions aimed to identify the best possible approach to treatment: (1) consulting the research evidence for the most efficacious intervention(s); (2) identifying client values, preferences, and needs in relation to treatment; and (3) critically reflecting on how previous intervention experiences can inform the present treatment approach (i.e., using clinical expertise) (Kazdin, 2008; Sackett, Rosenberg, Gray, Haynes, & Richardson, 1996). In this regard, EBP encapsulates EBT. The dilemma, however, is the extent to which clinicians presume that a departure from the EBT model constitutes the continued utilization of the EBT. Herein lies one of the most hotly debated issues in the human health and social services; that is, the extent to which EBP requires fidelity to the EBT and the extent to which we can attribute outcomes—good or bad—to an EBT model if the model is not implemented with fidelity.

Evidence-Based Treatment Use in the Eating Disorder Treatment Field

Recent literature has begun to investigate the extent to which EBTs and treatment guidelines are implemented with patients diagnosed with eating disorders. Evidence suggests that fidelity to EBTs and clinical practice guidelines within the eating disorder treatment field is low (Couturier, Kimber, et al., 2013a; Fairburn & Wilson, 2013; Hughes et al., 2013; Kimber et al., 2013; Lilienfeld et al., 2013; Maine, McGilley, & Bunnell, 2010; Wallace & von Ranson, 2012). For example, a large-scale, cross-sectional survey of community physicians in London, England, indicated that only 3.8 percent of the 236 physicians reported following a published guideline or protocol when treating a patient with an eating disorder. Moreover, when physicians' treatment behaviors were compared to those recommended in the "best practice" guideline, their behaviors did not align with the empirically supported directions published within the guidelines (Currin et al., 2007).

Work focusing on the use of specific treatment models with eating disorder patients in practice shows similarly concerning results. For example, in their effort to assess the extent to which clinicians utilized cognitive-behavioral therapy (CBT) to treat individuals diagnosed with bulimia nervosa, Mussell et al. (2000) surveyed a randomly selected sample of 500 psychologists in the state of Minnesota. Among the 60 clinicians reporting a caseload of patients diagnosed with eating disorders, 38.8 percent of these individuals reported using CBT with their patients; with 28.3 percent of clinicians reporting the use of eclectic approaches, and the remaining 32.9 percent reporting other intervention techniques. Among the clinicians using CBT and its related principals, 78.3 percent indicated having never received training on manualized CBT models for the eating disorder patient population, and 83 percent wished to be notified of any upcoming training opportunity in the treatment of eating disorders.

A similar discrepancy in model use versus model training was found in the work by von Ranson and Robinson (2006) and von Ranson, Wallace, and Stevenson (2013). Recruiting a number of community professionals from a variety of disciplines within Calgary, Alberta, both studies asked clinicians to report on their most commonly used therapeutic approach when working with individuals diagnosed with eating disorders. In both reports, the clinicians indicated most often following an eclectic approach, followed by the use of CBT and addictions-based therapy techniques. Although clinicians reported having received some training in manualized models, very few of these individuals could actually articulate the name of the author(s) on whose work their training was based (von Ranson & Robinson, 2006), nor did they indicate any formal supervision in the new EBT model (von Ranson et al., 2013). Such results decrease our confidence in the extent to which clinicians are utilizing these manualized models with fidelity in practice.

In a recent cross-sectional survey among clinicians ($n = 80$) in the United Kingdom, fidelity to CBT practice among adults with eating disorders continued to be low. After explicitly reporting their use of CBT, participants were asked to report on their actual implementation of CBT techniques and strategies in practice. Unfortunately, use of techniques and strategies was far lower than what would be recommended by CBT practice guidelines (Waller, Stringer, & Meyer, 2012). In addition, there was a significant correlation between clinician age, anxiety level, and years of experience and actual implementation of CBT techniques. Specifically, clinicians who were anxious, older, or who had a greater number of years of experience in working with individuals diagnosed with eating disorders were less likely to employ the recommended number of CBT techniques with their patients. However, individuals who reported using an actual manual in their practice sessions were more likely to report a more appropriate level of CBT technique implementation. These results, in addition to those provided by von Ranson and Robinson (2006) and Mussell et al. (2000) suggest that clinician self-reported EBT use is not likely to be a reliable indicator of the extent to which the practice is actually being implemented. Even more concerning is the lack of confidence we can place on any claims about patient outcomes—whether good or bad—when assessed in relation to therapist self-report of EBT use.

Given clear indications that clinicians in the eating disorder field are not using EBTs with fidelity in practice, Tobin, Baker, Weisberg, and Bowers (2007) sought to understand what techniques clinicians are actually using—if not manualized EBTs—in the everyday clinical realm. To do so, the authors utilized international eating disorder conference venues and websites to survey 265 treatment professionals. Only a small number of respondents (6 percent) reported closely following a treatment manual in practice, with 21 percent reporting that they have never studied a treatment manual specific to patients with eating disorders. Principal components analysis revealed that clinicians were using therapeutic techniques that varied in relation to their evidence, with some techniques frequently used by clinicians having *no* empirical evidence for their support (ex. psychodynamic techniques). These findings map onto those of Thompson-Brenner and Westen (2005) who found that therapists (*n* = 100) use a range of intervention strategies and eclectic approaches with patients with eating disorders.

The implications of the previously mentioned literature are numerous. First, data suggest that despite empirical support for the use of certain EBT models for patients diagnosed with eating disorders, the models are rarely used with fidelity in practice. Second, few psychotherapists report being adequately trained in EBTs; a concern that compounds and contributes to low EBT utilization and fidelity. In addition, the literature focusing on EBT use among treatment professionals in the eating disorders field is fraught with its own limitations. Most of the studies are not specific with respect to age group; that is, the implementation of EBTs within the eating disordered population will vary as a function of patient age. For example, there is a limited evidence base for EBT effectiveness in treating symptoms of eating disorders among children and adolescents. The work by Waller et al. (2012), for example, only included clinician's treating adults with eating disorders. However, Mussell et al. (2000) and Tobin et al. (2007) did not ask clinicians to specify the age range of their participants, and von Ranson and Robinson (2006) did not report variations in EBT use across age-specific patient populations. The only study to report EBT use in relation to patient age was that of von Ranson et al. (2013). However, the authors did not report the specific EBT models under investigation. Finally, all of the present literature on EBT use among treatment professionals in the eating disorder field is cross-sectional in nature, and relies on recall, prohibiting our ability to adequately understand the extent of EBT use and fidelity over time. Thus, the eating disorder field stands to learn a great deal about EBT use and fidelity from programs of research devoted to understanding the process of EBT adoption, such as the field of implementation science.

Dissemination of Family-Based Treatment as a Case Study: Factors and Decision-Making Processes Influencing the Implementation of Family-Based Treatment

Despite the fact that a recent *Cochrane Review* (Fisher, Hetrick, & Rushford, 2010) and separate meta-analysis (Couturier, Kimber, & Szatmari, 2013) indicate that family approaches are superior to individual approaches in treating AN, and that FBT has the potential to reduce treatment costs by up to 70 percent through a reduction in hospitalizations (Lock, Couturier, & Agras, 2008), recent research indicates that few therapists treating children and adolescents diagnosed with eating disorders consistently use FBT with fidelity in practice (Couturier, Kimber, et al., 2013a). In an effort to understand the barriers and facilitators to implementing FBT into clinical practice, as well as identify knowledge translation strategies for increasing the use of FBT among clinicians practising in the eating disorders field, Couturier and colleagues (2013a, 2013b) analyzed qualitative interview data from 40 therapists providing psychotherapeutic intervention to children and adolescents diagnosed with AN. Content analysis revealed a number of specific barriers and facilitators affecting therapists' ability to implement FBT within their treatment programs; specifically those factors having to do with the characteristics of the intervention (i.e., FBT), the organization, patients and families, the clinician, the nature of the illness, and systemic issues inherent within the service delivery system (Couturier et al., 2013a). A number of these themes and their related concerns are similar to those that have already been identified in the literature, including clinician preferences and training (Aarons, 2004) and patient and family preferences (Karver, Handelsman, Fields, & Bickman, 2006).

However, participants did note some unique considerations that seem to be specific to the eating disorder field and FBT, in particular. The intensive nature of FBT, the lack of attention paid to the prevalence of comorbid diagnoses by the FBT model, and the need for intensive family involvement were all perceived to be barriers to routine FBT implementation within clinical practice. In addition, therapists were struggling to maintain fidelity to three aspects of the manual, the conduct of a family meal in the second session, omitting the dietician from the therapeutic process, and weighing the patient at the start of each therapeutic session. Only 10 of the 40 clinicians had ever implemented the family meal during a therapeutic session, with clinicians noting spatial constraints as often being the reason for its omission in practice. In addition, clinicians reported increased levels of interpersonal anxiety when conducting the family meal portion of the FBT model, as the process typically brings on increased familial conflict that can be difficult to manage in practice. Finally, the debate about the exclusion of the dietician from the therapeutic process appeared to be a salient concern among clinicians in this sample; with only six of the 40 clinicians indicating that they would be comfortable implementing FBT without a dietician. Five other clinicians reported that dietician involvement is necessary in *any* eating disorder treatment approach. The majority of clinicians indicated that dieticians would be responsible for weighing the patient prior to their sessions and providing guidance on caloric consumption, a component of treatment that a number of clinicians felt was outside their own scope of practice.

In addition to characteristics of the FBT intervention, clinicians also identified a number of organizational and systemic factors influencing their ability to implement FBT in their clinical practice. Perhaps most notably is that 100 percent of the clinicians acknowledged a seminal role for their administrator (also encompassing managers and directors, but referred to administrators going forward) in the adoption and implementation of EBTs within their organization. Specifically, 30 of the 40 participants indicated that their administrator's approval of the model would be required to implement FBT in practice; however, the remaining 10 therapists reported that if their program was going to adopt the FBT model as a designated intervention within their program, then the program administrator would have to approve this decision. In addition, 70 percent of participants indicated that team buy-in to the EBT model would play a key role in whether or not they adopted the therapeutic approach; alluding to the notion that team belief or conviction about a particular EBT may be more of a factor in EBT uptake and implementation than individual clinician preferences for practice.

Furthermore, a number of knowledge translation strategies that could be undertaken to effectively increase the uptake and implementation of FBT into routine clinical practice were identified (Couturier et al., 2013b). Couturier and colleagues (2013b) completed a secondary data analysis of the qualitative interview data to identify the five elements stipulated by Lavis et al. (2003) for successful transmission of research evidence into clinical practice, including the following: (1) identifying the knowledge needing to be transferred ("the message"), (2) identifying whom the knowledge should be transferred to ("the audience"), (3) assessing by whom should the knowledge be transferred ("the messenger"), (4) how the knowledge will be transferred ("knowledge transfer strategies and infrastructure"), and finally (5) the most appropriate method of demonstrating knowledge transfer ("evaluation"). Analysis revealed that FBT messaging should include both the provision of the research evidence supporting the models effectiveness but also the specific intervention components of the FBT manual. In addition, the "audience" for FBT messaging was identified as therapists, administrators, physicians, and community members working within the field of pediatric eating disorders; with the development and dissemination of clinical practice guidelines identified as one seminal strategy to ensure all audience members received consistent messaging.

Interestingly, therapists identified local FBT experts as an ideal source for FBT knowledge and training. Specifically, clinicians suggested that local experts in the FBT model could take on the challenge of training less experienced therapists to alleviate costs of traveling for intensive and specialized training. In addition, therapists recognized that protected time to learn, practice, and enhance their FBT skills would be necessary for successful implementation. Relatedly, clinicians acknowledged the importance of clinical supervision in learning a new EBT skill set. Participants reported that if a rollout of FBT was encouraged or mandated, then ongoing supervision and mentorship would be necessary to prevent fidelity drift, as well as an essential component of ongoing implementation and evaluation.

Thus far, the literature on FBT dissemination clearly indicates that both team and administrator buy-in has a central role to play in the uptake, implementation, and fidelity to FBT in clinical practice. However, what remained unclear was the specific decision-making processes involved in these endeavors. Kimber et al. (2013) completed a secondary data analysis of the interview data from the Couturier, Kimber et al. (2013a) study, as well as purposefully recruited and qualitatively interviewed the administrators of the programs from which the original 40 clinicians worked. The authors identified a multi-staged decision-making process for adopting and implementing any EBT, including FBT, into clinical practice. Respondents identified a seven-stage decision-making model for their uptake and implementation of EBTs in clinical practice, including the following: (1) individual exposure to the EBT; (2) team exposure to the EBT; (3) evaluating the EBT evidence; (4) determining program fit; (5) training in the EBT model; (6) using the EBT in practice with supervision; and (7) evaluating the EBT in their programs.

Although the first two stages appear to be intuitive, clinicians and administrators did acknowledge the potential for EBTs to go unnoticed, typically because clinicians and programs were overburdened with their caseloads and therefore prohibiting their ability to keep up to date on the relevant EBT literature. Thus, for an EBT to be adopted and implemented within their program, at least one clinician needed to be exposed in some way to the EBT model and then carry that information forward to other team members. In the third stage of the implementation process, clinicians and administrators indicated that their team would need to consult the evidence about the particular EBT in question and determine its rigor for improving outcomes of the patient population. Related to this concern is determining whether the model would fit within the clinical program given the current structure and compliment of program staff (stage 4). Administrators and clinicians were clear in that the extent to which staff needed training in the proposed EBT or whether the program had the structural space necessary to implement the EBT model would factor into the adoption and implementation of the model, particularly in relation to fidelity. Considerations of this nature would then determine whether the team moves to stage 5 of the implementation, that is, training staff on the new EBT model and providing supervision for staff to use the model in practice (stage 6). Both training and supervision were noted to have substantial influence on the decision to proceed for two reasons. First, clinicians and administrators acknowledge the importance of sound training and supervision in developing practice skills. And second, both training and supervision tend to require substantial fiscal resources that may or may not be available to the degree that is needed. Finally, clinicians and administrators acknowledged the importance of evaluating their use of the EBT model in relation to patient outcomes, acknowledging that doing so would provide justification for continuation, adaptation, or deletion of the model from program practices.

Inherent to the stages of decision making, the 51 respondents in Kimber et al. (2013) identified an "inclusive change culture" as a principal factor in the multi-staged decision-making process. Both clinicians and administrators identified as being reluctant to make decisions in isolation from one another, despite the fact that administrators had the power to do so. Both clinicians and their administrators identified this inclusiveness as an important way of working, insisting that making practice changes or adopting EBTs without the support of their team members or leaders would prove to be difficult. Working as a team for practice change, as well as moving through the successive stages of decision-making as a team, reinforced the notion that clinicians, administrators, and their programs would be making a strong case for practice change. Specifically, that advocating for practice change as a collective, and with support from the Academy of Eating Disorders or their local network of treatment professionals, would go a long way to garnishing approval for program shifts by higher decision-making authorities.

How Implementation Science Can Improve Dissemination of Family-Based Treatment

Disseminating and implementing EBTs is a critical step in making effective treatments available to patients outside the academic medical center (Novins, Green, Legha, & Aarons, 2013). Given the limited database supporting any EBT for adolescent eating disorders, it is not surprising that there are few studies examining dissemination or implementation and those that do exist focus on a single EBT, that is, FBT for adolescents with AN. Several preliminary studies are published that suggest that FBT can be utilized in settings beyond those of the primary research (Couturier, Isserlin, & Lock, 2010; Le Grange, Binford, & Loeb, 2005; Loeb et al., 2007; Tukiewicz, Pinzon, Lock, & Fleitlich-Bilyk, 2010; Wallis, Rhodes, Kohn, & Madden, 2007). For example, Loeb and colleagues (2007) report on a clinical case series of 20 patients and report low dropout (25 percent), end-of-treatment weight gain (from a mean of 82 percent at baseline to 94 percent), two-thirds of patients achieving normal menstruation and significantly improved scores on the Eating Disorder Examination measure. A Brazil-based study of 11 adolescents who were treated by therapists using the FBT manual and who underwent a two-day training in FBT (Tukiewicz, Pinzon, Lock, & Fleitlich-Bilyk, 2010) found that 82 percent of patients and families found the FBT treatment model to be acceptable; with most patients having a normalized body mass index (BMI) and improved eating related psychopathology at the end of treatment. A third study by Couturier and colleagues (2010) in Canada found that 13 adolescents who were treated by four therapists using manualized FBT had similar clinical improvements with respect to weight and eating disorder symptoms to those patients in the work by Loeb (2007) and Tukiewicz (2010); however, Couturier and colleagues (2010) also evaluated the fidelity of the clinicians to the manualized intervention. Using a standardized fidelity measure for FBT, the researchers found that therapists demonstrated relatively good fidelity to the first phase of FBT (72 percent with good ratings) but that fidelity lessened in the second (47 percent with good ratings) and third (54 percent with good ratings) phases, suggesting that appropriate implementation of the FBT model may require additional support during the latter phases of treatment. Finally, two institutional "case histories" describing the implementation challenges related to using FBT in Australia have been published. The first of these describes the impact of FBT on decreasing readmission rates at a children's hospital in Sydney by about 50 percent over the implementation period (Wallis et al., 2007). The second study also documents substantial changes in use of hospitalization since FBT was implemented systemwide at a children's hospital in Melbourne, including a 56 percent decrease in admission, a 75 percent decrease in readmissions, and a 51 percent decrease in overall hospital days (Hughes et al., 2013). In addition, 83 percent of families treated with FBT completed it and 97 percent of those completions achieved greater than 90 percent of expected body weight (Hughes et al., 2013). However, challenges to the uptake of FBT were identified and included concerns about the change in professional roles for pediatricians, dieticians, and therapists (Katzman, Peebles, Sawyer, Lock, & Le Grange, 2013). These limited data suggest that it is likely possible to disseminate FBT, but fidelity to the treatment is largely unexplored and its impact on outcome almost unknown.

The knowledge translation strategies, processes, barriers, and facilitators identified to affect FBT implementation map onto those discussed in the general child and youth mental health literature but also add to our understanding about the unique implementation needs of therapists and decision-makers working in the pediatric eating disorder treatment field. For example, the FBT decision-making processes highlighted by Kimber et al. (2013) are similar to those stipulated by the National Implementation Research Network's (NIRN) model of implementation. Meant to characterize the overarching process of implementing a single EBT within an organization, the NIRN model posits that successful implementation hinges on the consideration of five successive stages, including the following: (1) Exploration and Adoption, (2) Program Installation, (3) Initial Implementation, (4) Full Operation, and (5) Innovation. In addition, each implementation stage requires an ongoing consideration of EBT evaluation and sustainability (Fixsen, Naoom, Blase, Friedman, & Wallace, 2005). Concise descriptions of the NIRN implementation stages are available from Kimber, Barwick, and Fearing (2012) as well as Metz and Bartley (2012). Briefly, the *Exploration and Adoption* stage is the point at which the implementing program or organization considers the "fit" between the proposed EBT and the practice environment, paying particular attention to the resources needed to implement the EBT in the everyday setting and the resources currently available at the program. The goal of this phase is to make an informed decision about whether or not to proceed with implementing the chosen EBT model. During the second and third stages of implementation—*Program Installation and Initial Implementation*—the organization begins the actual adoption and implementation of the EBT model. The organization would identify the specific EBT training model and evaluation, identify the staff to participate in EBT training, and have the staff complete the training program. Finally, programs at this stage of implementation would put in place the needed resources for clinical supervision and EBT fidelity measurement. The fourth stage of implementation refers to *Full Operation*, where the actual EBT becomes ingrained in program operations and becomes a designated model of service delivery. Kimber et al. (2013) findings resonate with each of these stages in that clinicians and administrators reported a need to assess program fit prior to adopting FBT, seek out advanced training and supervision in the FBT model, try out FBT with their patient population, and determine the extent to which FBT and fidelity to the FBT improved patient outcomes.

The FBT dissemination research also speaks to a crucial component of NIRN implementation model; that is, the use of implementation teams. Specifically, results from Kimber et al. (2013) highlight the importance of inclusive leadership models in the adoption and implementation of EBTs, namely that clinicians and administrators were reluctant to make EBT decisions in isolation from the other. The importance of inclusive leadership models has been reported in other implementation literature and lends support for operationalizing an implementation team for EBT implementation endeavors (Aarons, 2006; Barwick, Kimber, & Fearing, 2011; Gershon, Stone, Bakken, & Larson, 2004; Metz, Blase, Bartley, Wilson, & Redmond, 2012).

The role of the implementation team is to oversee and monitor the implementation process and devise procedures and protocols to support the implementation of the EBT within everyday practice. According to the NIRN literature, an implementation team would consist of four or five individuals who represent core areas of the organization or program and are familiar with the EBT, as well as the program and organizational processes influencing the use of the EBT (Fixsen et al., 2005; Metz & Bartley, 2012). The implementation team has been identified as a seminal component to those change endeavours that have followed the NIRN stages of implementation (Barwick et al., 2011; Fearing, Barwick, & Kimber, 2013; Fixsen et al., 2005; Kimber et al., 2012; Rapp et al., 2008) and given the diversity of eating disorder treatment programs, it is likely that such a team who is charged with coordinating FBT implementation efforts would lend itself to the inclusive change and decision-making culture that is discussed earlier.

In addition to the necessity for a collegial approach, there are other elements of implementation that appear to be unique or of particular importance to the eating disorder field. For example, the express need to review all of the research evidence pertinent to the EBT prior to making an implementation decision, as well as having local FBT experts involved in the training and supervision of the FBT model. Damschroder et al. (2009) in their *Consolidated Framework for Implementation Research* (CFIR) would argue that each of these components of implementation are likely characteristic of the "inner setting" within which eating disorder professionals work, and thus, not addressing these components is likely to lead to implementation failure. Damschroder et al. (2009) reviewed 19 published theories pertaining to EBT implementation and, from this review, identified five overarching domains and their associated constructs that are relevant for successful EBT implementation. The five domains of implementation include the following: (1) intervention (EBT) characteristics, (2) the outer setting, (3) the inner setting, (4) clinician characteristics, and (5) the implementation process. In this regard the CFIR meta-theory offers specific suggestions about the characteristics of the organization, staff, and EBT that should be addressed throughout the NIRN implementation stages. For example, recent research suggests that involvement of EBT trainers on the implementation team is facilitative (Fearing et al., 2013), lending support for the notion that local FBT experts can play a role in assisting programs that are pursing FBT implementation.

While a number of theories and frameworks to guide the EBT implementation process have been published, many of these approaches and models have shown inadequate implementation effectiveness overall (Brownson, Colditz, & Proctor, 2012; Damschroder et al., 2009; Fixsen et al., 2005). The NIRN implementation model (Fixsen et al., 2005) and the CFIR meta-theory (Damschroder et al., 2009) have critically advanced our understanding for the need of a planful and supportive implementation approach when moving research evidence into the practice realm. Both have been used to inform the successful adoption and implementation of EBTs; with evidence for the applicability of the CFIR meta-theory and the NIRN implementation model for pediatric eating disorders coming from the general mental health and addictions fields (Damschroder & Hagedorn, 2011; Gordon et al., 2011; Lash, Timko, Curran, McKay, & Burden, 2011; Manuel, Hagedorn, & Finney, 2011; Ruffolo & Capobianco, 2012; Sorensen & Kosten, 2011; Williams et al., 2011). These settings mirror those of pediatric eating disorder treatment programs in their complex organizational structures, high and complex caseloads and the type of clinician education and skill set.

Conclusion

Evidence suggests that relying on clinicians to adopt evidence-based treatments into the clinical realm has led to their underutilization and in some cases, inappropriate use within frontline practice. Advances in implementation science suggest that active, purposeful and supportive implementation can result in 80 percent adoption of an EBT within three years of its initial dissemination (Fixsen, Blase, Timbers, & Wolf, 2001).

Sound qualitative data from FBT dissemination lend support for tailoring planful and facilitative implementation initiatives. More generally, the lack of FBT use with fidelity within the eating disorder treatment field, as well as the knowledge about the specific factors and processes important to treatment professionals in FBT uptake, lend support for the field testing of implementation models in the pediatric eating disorder treatment setting. Future work should focus on merging FBT dissemination findings into EBT implementation models that have been found to be successful in other human service areas; namely, the NIRN implementation model and the CFIR meta-theory. In addition, it is crucial for future dissemination work to identify the extent to which EBTs can be implemented within the real-world setting but not before identifying the active components of the EBT model, which are necessary to realize the model's effectiveness. Such investigations, in addition to those evaluating implementation of EBTs in eating disorder practice, will assist in ensuring that evidence-based and low-cost treatments that are shown to produce the best possible outcomes are effectively and efficiently translated into clinical practice.

References

Aarons, G. A. (2004). Mental health provider attitudes toward adoption of evidence-based practice: the Evidence-Based Practice Attitude Scale (EBPAS). *Ment Health Serv Res, 6*(2), 61–74.

Aarons, G. A. (2006). Transformational and transactional leadership: association with attitudes toward evidence-based practice. *Psychiatr Serv, 57*(8), 1162–1169. doi: 10.1176/appi.ps.57.8.1162

Barwick, M., Kimber, M., & Fearing, G. (2011). Shifting sands: A case study of process change in scaling up for evidence-based practice. *International Journal of Knowledge, Culture and Change Management, 10,* 97–114.

Brownson, R. C., Colditz, G. A., & Proctor, E. K. (Eds.). (2012). *Dissemination and implementation research in health: Translating science to practice.* New York: Oxford Unviersity Press.

Couturier, J., Isserlin, L., & Lock, J. (2010). Family-based treatment for adolescents with anorexia nervosa: a dissemination study. *Eat Disord, 18*(3), 199–209. doi: 10.1080/10640261003719443

Couturier, J., Kimber, M., Jack, S., Niccols, A., Van Blyderveen, S., & McVey, G. (2013a). Understanding the uptake of family-based treatment for adolescents with anorexia nervosa: therapist perspectives. *Int J Eat Disord, 46*(2), 177–188. doi: 10.1002/eat.22049

Couturier, J., Kimber, M., Jack, S., Niccols, A., Van Blyderveen, S., & McVey, G. (2013b). *Using a Knowledge Transfer Framework to Identify Factors Facilitating Implementation of Family-Based Treatment.*

Couturier, J., Kimber, M., & Szatmari, P. (2013). Efficacy of family-based treatment for adolescents with eating disorders: a systematic review and meta-analysis. *Int J Eat Disord, 46*(1), 3–11. doi: 10.1002/eat.22042

Currin, L., Waller, G., Treasure, J., Nodder, J., Stone, C., Yeomans, M., & Schmidt, U. (2007). The use of guidelines for dissemination of "best practice" in primary care of patients with eating disorders. *Int J Eat Disord, 40*(5), 476–479. doi: 10.1002/eat.20385

Damschroder, L. J., Aron, D. C., Keith, R. E., Kirsh, S. R., Alexander, J. A., & Lowery, J. C. (2009). Fostering implementation of health services research findings into practice: A consolidated framework for advancing implementation science. *Implement Sci, 4*, 50. doi: 10.1186/1748-5908-4-50

Damschroder, L. J., & Hagedorn, H. J. (2011). A guiding framework and approach for implementation research in substance use disorders treatment. *Psychol Addict Behav, 25*(2), 194–205. doi: 10.1037/a0022284

Fairburn, C. G., & Wilson, G. T. (2013). The dissemination and implementation of psychological treatments: problems and solutions. *Int J Eat Disord, 46*(5), 516–521. doi: 10.1002/eat.22110

Fearing, G., Barwick, M., & Kimber, M. (2013). Clinical transformation: Manager's Perspectives on implementation of evidence-based practice. *Adm Policy Ment Health.* doi: 10.1007/s10488-013-0481-9

Fisher, C. A., Hetrick, S. E., & Rushford, N. (2010). Family therapy for anorexia nervosa. *Cochrane Database Syst Rev*(4), CD004780. doi: 10.1002/14651858. CD004780.pub2

Fixsen, D. L., Blase, K. A., Timbers, G. D., & Wolf, M. M. (2001). In search of program implementation: 792 replications of the Teaching-Family Model. In G. A. Bernfeld, D. P. Farrington, & A. W. Leschied (Eds.), *Offender rehabilitation in practice: Implementing and evaluating effective programs.* (pp. 149–166). London, UK: Wiley.

Fixsen, D. L., Naoom, S. F., Blase, K. A., Friedman, R. M., & Wallace, F. (2005). *Implementation Research: A Synthesis of the Literature.* Tampa, FL: University of South Florida.

Gershon, R. R., Stone, P. W., Bakken, S., & Larson, E. (2004). Measurement of organizational culture and climate in healthcare. *J Nurs Adm, 34*(1), 33–40.

Gordon, A. J., Kavanagh, G., Krumm, M., Ramgopal, R., Paidisetty, S., Aghevli, M., ... Liberto, J. (2011). Facilitators and barriers in implementing buprenorphine in the Veterans Health Administration. *Psychol Addict Behav, 25*(2), 215–224. doi: 10.1037/a0022776

Hughes, E., Le Grange, D., Yeo, M., Whitelaw, M., Atkins, L., & Sawyer, S. (2013). Implementation of Family-Based Treatment for adolescents with anorexia nervosa. *Journal of Pediatric Health Care.* doi: doi.org/10.1016/j. pedhc.2013.07.012

Karver, M. S., Handelsman, J. B., Fields, S., & Bickman, L. (2006). Meta-analysis of therapeutic relationship variables in youth and family therapy: The evidence for different relationship variables in the child and adolescent treatment outcome literature. *Clin Psychol Rev, 26*(1), 50–65. doi: 10.1016/j.cpr.2005.09.001

Katzman, D., Peebles, R., Sawyer, S., Lock, J., & Le Grange, D. (2013). The role of the pediatrician in family-based treatment for adolescent eating disorders: Opportunities and challenges. *JAH, 53*(4), 433–440. doi: 10.1016/j.jadohealth.2013.07.011

Kazdin, A. E. (2008). Evidence-based treatment and practice: New opportunities to bridge clinical research and practice, enhance the knowledge base, and improve patient care. *Am Psychol, 63*(3), 146–159. doi: 10.1037/0003-066X.63.3.146

Kimber, M., Barwick, M., & Fearing, G. (2012). Becoming an evidence-based service provider: staff perceptions and experiences of organizational change. *J Behav Health Serv Res, 39*(3), 314–332. doi: 10.1007/s11414-012-9276-0

Kimber, M., Couturier, J., Jack, S., Niccols, A., Van Blyderveen, S., & McVey, G. (2013). Decision-making processes for the uptake and implementation of family-based therapy by eating disorder treatment teams: A qualitative study. *Int J Eat Disord.* doi: 10.1002/eat.22185

Lash, S. J., Timko, C., Curran, G. M., McKay, J. R., & Burden, J. L. (2011). Implementation of evidence-based substance use disorder continuing care interventions. *Psychol Addict Behav, 25*(2), 238–251. doi: 10.1037/a0022608.

Lavis, J. N., Robertson, D., Woodside, J. M., McLeod, C. B., Abelson, J., & Knowledge Transfer Study Group. (2003). How can research organizations more effectively transfer research knowledge to decision makers? *Milbank Q, 81*(2), 171–172.

Le Grange, D., Binford, R., & Loeb, K. (2005). Manualized family-based treatment for anorexia nervosa: A case series. *Journal of the American Academy of Child and Adoelscent Psychiatry, 44*(41), 41–46.

Lilienfeld, S. O., Ritschel, L. A., Lynn, S. J., Brown, A. P., Cautin, R. L., & Latzman, R. D. (2013). The research-practice gap: Bridging the schism between eating disorder researchers and practitioners. *Int J Eat Disord, 46*(5), 386–394. doi: 10.1002/eat.22090

Lock, J., Couturier, J., & Agras, W. S. (2008). Costs of remission and recovery using family therapy for adolescent anorexia nervosa: a descriptive report. *Eat Disord, 16*(4), 322–330. doi: 10.1080/10640260802115969

Lock, J., Le Grange, D., Agras, W. S., & Dare, C. (2001). *Treatment Manual for Anorexia Nervosa: A Family-Based Approach.* New York: Guilford Press.

Loeb, K., Walsh, B. T., Lock, J., Le Grange, D., Jones, J., Marcus, S., & Dobrow, I. (2007). Open trial of family-based treatment for adolescent anorexia nervosa: Evidence of successful dissemination. *Journal of the American Academy of Child and Adoelscent Psychiatry, 46,* 792–800.

Maine, M., McGilley, B., & Bunnell, D. W. (Eds.). (2010). *Treatment of eating disorders: Bridging the research-practice-gap.* (1st ed.). San Diego, CA: Elsevier Academic Press.

Manuel, J. K., Hagedorn, H. J., & Finney, J. W. (2011). Implementing evidence-based psychosocial treatment in specialty substance use disorder care. *Psychol Addict Behav, 25*(2), 225–237. doi: 10.1037/a0022398

McLennan, J. D., Wathen, C. N., MacMillan, H. L., & Lavis, J. N. (2006). Research-practice gaps in child mental health. *J Am Acad Child Adolesc Psychiatry, 45*(6), 658–665. doi: 10.1097/01.chi.0000215153.99517.80

Metz, A., & Bartley, L. (2012). Active implementation frameworks for program success: How to use implementation science to improve outcomes for children. *Zero to Three Journal, 32*(4), 11–18.

Metz, A., Blase, K. A., Bartley, L., Wilson, D., & Redmond, P. (2012). *Using implementation science to support and align practice and system change: A case study of the Catawba County Child Well-being Project*. Washington, DC: Child Trends.

Mussell, M. P., Crosby, R. D., Crow, S. J., Knopke, A. J., Peterson, C. B., Wonderlich, S., & Mitchell, J. E. (2000). Utilization of empirically supported psychotherapy treatments for individuals with eating disorders: A survey of psychologists. *Int J Eat Disord, 27*(2), 230–237.

Novins, D., Green, A., Legha, R., & Aarons, G. A. (2013). Dissemination and implementation of evidence-based practices for child and adolescent mental health: A systematic review. *Journal of the American Academy of Child and Adoelscent Psychiatry, 52*, 1009–1025.

Rapp, C. A., Etzel-Wise, D., Marty, D., Coffman, M., Carlson, L., Asher, D., ... Whitley, R. (2008). Evidence-based practice implementation strategies: Results of a qualitative study. *Community Ment Health J, 44*(3), 213–224; discussion 225–216. doi: 10.1007/s10597-007-9109-4

Ruffolo, M. C., & Capobianco, J. (2012). Moving an evidence-based intervention into routine mental health care: A multifaceted case example. *Soc Work Health Care, 51*(1), 77–87. doi: 10.1080/00981389.2011.622674

Sackett, D. L., Rosenberg, W. M., Gray, J. A., Haynes, R. B., & Richardson, W. S. (1996). Evidence based medicine: What it is and what it isn't. *BMJ, 312*(7023), 71–72.

Sorensen, J. L., & Kosten, T. (2011). Developing the tools of implementation science in substance use disorders treatment: applications of the consolidated framework for implementation research. *Psychol Addict Behav, 25*(2), 262–268. doi: 10.1037/a0022765.

Thompson-Brenner, H., & Westen, D. (2005). A naturalistic study of psychotherapy for bulimia nervosa, Part 2: Comorbidity and therapeutic outcome. *Journal of Nervous and Mental Disorders, 195*, 573–594.

Tobin, D. L., Baker, J. D., Weisberg, L., & Bowers, W. (2007). I know what you did last summer (and it was not CBT): A factor analytic model of international psychotherapeutic practice in the eating disorders. *Int J Eat Disord, 40*, 754–757.

Tukiewicz, G., Pinzon, V., Lock, J., & Fleitlich-Bilyk, B. (2010). Feasibility, acceptability, and effectiveness of family-based treatment for adolescent anorexia nervosa: An observational study conducted in Brazil. *Revista Brasileira de Psiguiatria, 32*, 169–172.

von Ranson, K. M., & Robinson, K. E. (2006). Who is providing what type of psychotherapy for eating disorder clients? A survey. *Int J Eat Disord, 39*(1), 27–34.

von Ranson, K. M., Wallace, L. M., & Stevenson, A. (2013). Psychotherapies provided for eating disorders by community clinicians: Infrequent use of evidence-based treatment. *Psychotherapy Research, 23*(3), 333–343.

Wallace, L. M., & von Ranson, K. M. (2012). Perceptions and use of empirically-supported psychotherapies among eating disorder professionals. *Behav Res Ther, 50*(3), 215–222. doi: 10.1016/j.brat.2011.12.006

Waller, G., Stringer, H., & Meyer, C. (2012). What cognitive-behavioral techniques do therapists report using when delivering cognitive-behavioral therapy for eating disorders? *Journal of Consulting and Clinical Psychology, 80*, 171–175.

Wallis, A., Rhodes, P., Kohn, M., & Madden, S. (2007). Five-years of family based treatment for anorexia nervosa: The Maudsley Model at the Children's Hospital at Westmead. *International Journal of Adolescent Medical Health, 19*, 277–283.

Williams, E. C., Johnson, M. L., Lapham, G. T., Caldeiro, R. M., Chew, L., Fletcher, G. S., ... Bradley, K. A. (2011). Strategies to implement alcohol screening and brief intervention in primary care settings: A structured literature review. *Psychol Addict Behav, 25*(2), 206–214. doi: 10.1037/a0022102

Chapter 20

Conceptualizing Fidelity in FBT as the Field Moves Forward

How Do We Know When We're Doing It Right?

Kathleen Kara Fitzpatrick, Erin C. Accurso, Vandana Aspen, Sarah E. Forsberg, Daniel Le Grange, and James Lock

This chapter presents a coding manual and rating scale for therapists' fidelity to the treatment model and techniques, specifically in the early sessions of family-based therapy (FBT), which are presumed to carry the majority of the active mechanisms of treatment. The measure's psychometric properties (reliability and validity) are being studied and established. We share the scale at this stage of development because it provides a face-valid elaboration of what is expected in FBT therapists' words and behaviors when implementing the major strategies of FBT. In this sense, this chapter functions as a companion piece to the FBT treatment manual for anorexia nervosa (AN) (Lock & Le Grange, 2012), making concepts and directions "come alive."

Fidelity to treatment is thought to encompass two important constructs: adherence ("How well am I 'sticking to' the manual, delivering what is prescribed, and avoiding what is proscribed?") and competence ("How skilled am I in delivering the intervention?") (Waltz, Addis, Koerner, & Jacobson, 1993). Managing fidelity in research studies is a challenge. Study therapists may come from different disciplines and training backgrounds, yielding variability in treatment delivery that goes beyond a stylistic level. When testing a treatment under controlled research conditions, it is imperative to be sure that the same "dose" of the same "agent" are being provided to all patients randomized to a particular study intervention. When it is disseminated in the real-world practice arena, after testing has demonstrated promise or worth as a treatment, fidelity challenges are amplified. Therapists often describe several clinical realities that pull for adherence drift, including coordinating care philosophy and delivery with other providers, demands to address comorbidities simultaneously when the best clinical algorithms are unclear, and slow patient response that may prompt premature requests for "more" treatment or alternate modalities.

Myths about fidelity also abound. One myth is that fidelity means strict adherence to the manual by the therapist, under all conditions and above all other clinical concerns. In fact, the competence aspect of fidelity requires flexibility on the part of the therapist to distinguish between the "letter of the law" and its spirit, or underlying principles. Excessive rigidity in manualized treatment delivery can compromise outcome (e.g., Castonguay, Boswell, Constantino, Goldfried, & Hill, 2010; Castonguay, Goldfried, Wiser, Raue, & Hayes, 1996; Gibbons, Crits-Christoph, Levinson, & Barber, 2003). Another myth is that fidelity is achieved at the expense of alliance. In the eating disorder (ED) literature, for example, better adherence is associated with enhanced alliance (Loeb et al., 2005). A third belief is that the relationship between adherence and symptom change is unidirectional. Adherence can also be influenced by prior symptom change (Loeb et al., 2005). Absence of treatment response might prompt either deviance from protocol on the part of the therapist or increased adherence in an attempt to deliver the most potent dose of the intervention. Finally, it is tempting to favor our "clinical judgment" as therapists over an approach proven efficacious in aggregate results from a controlled study. However, we owe it to our patients to first research supported interventions and then to deliver them well.

Fidelity coding can be a challenge, as families and therapists approach the tasks of FBT very differently. Further, tapes of sessions (the best documentation of what occurred) are rarely evaluated in order, which can make it challenging to understand the context of some of the behaviors or dialogue we are observing.

The rating format we employed was meant to accomplish two tasks— to rate the presence or absence of a desired therapist behavior and, if a task was implemented, to rate how well it was executed. A key part of fidelity ratings is to separate how well a task was implemented from its outcome. A therapist may have excellent fidelity to the model, but a family may struggle to understand or may require material to be repeated or restated for comprehension and behavior change. Our focus is on how well the therapist did at implementing these tasks and how faithful he/she was to the model. Outcome is rated separately in relation to fidelity. At times, however, if an implementation was not successful, the therapist may try a different approach and this can improve fidelity as the therapist is showing flexibility in implementation.

In Phase 1 many of the same techniques/goals are replicated, and thus there may be many efforts at externalization or parental alignment. Part of fidelity is in noticing when a family is not on target the way we expect (e.g., parents are not aligned) and taking the time in session to work toward this goal. Thus, there may be many opportunities to rate fidelity to these goals, even within a particular session. Most often we rate the fidelity by taking a summary of the techniques. This is particularly true in the case of "mixed messages," where a therapist may make a statement then either retract or attempt to buffer that statement, which makes it more confusing to the family.

Approaching Coding

There are multiple ways in which this coding system can be used, and they are not mutually exclusive. First, it can be used for an expert to evaluate and study therapist performance in the context of a treatment trial. Second, it can be used by supervisors or consultants for clinical training and feedback. Finally, a therapist may use it for self-assessment of fidelity to FBT. Across all these circumstances, videotaped sessions are the gold-standard source of what occurred in the sessions. Memory is fallible, notes only summarize, and as mentioned above, outcome is not always a marker of fidelity. It is important to give yourself time to code with the first few tapes, watching them all the way through, taking comprehensive notes, and then determining ratings. This process can be accelerated with training and established inter-rater reliability.

Common Challenges

In some cases it may be hard to see all family members on the tape or to know the relationships between members, especially because we often do not turn on the camera in the first session until we have made introductions and gained consent for taping verbally. If the therapist knows the names of family members or details about them, one can be relatively certain that they have made appropriate introductions.

Time with the patient is sometimes not recorded—at least at Stanford. We weigh the patients in a different room and often have some discussion in the weight room rather than being silent until we reach our offices. Sometimes clinical material may have been brought up that is not on tape. We can only rate based on what we see! However, with some techniques inferences can be made (e.g., "When we were talking, X said that she felt that you fed her more, Dad. Who else felt the same way?" can be coded for circular questioning in Phase 1). This is particularly true with circular questioning, remaining agnostic to the cause of the illness, engaging family members, and refocusing efforts on renourishment (which often are more subtle topic changes guided by the questioning of the therapist more than the therapist stating, "We need to get back on track here"). With some of these techniques, in particular agnosticism and refocusing on the eating disorder, fidelity may be as much about the absence of behavior on the part of the therapist (e.g., not engaging in a discussion of cause) as it is deliberately steering away from this (e.g., "We do not know the cause of AN, but like with cancer, we need to take responsibility for addressing these symptoms, more than we do in understanding how this illness arose in the first place"). Rating the absence of a behavior on the part of the therapist can still be considered fidelity but the effectiveness would likely garner a lower rating than when there are direct efforts to change or guide behaviors and attitudes.

Fidelity does not equate to how hard a therapist is working, only on the ability to deliver the treatment in a way that we would see as consistent with FBT. For example, some families bring really excellent family meals, of sufficient caloric density and nutrition, and plate them appropriately, and some patients are willing and able to eat and continue eating with little struggle. In such cases, provided the therapist is making certain parents are aligned in these behaviors and takes a history of these behaviors, fidelity would still be rated highly, even if there was not significant struggle to achieve these ends.

At other times, fidelity is really based on being quite direct and distinct in delivery—such as charging the family with the task of bringing a family meal to Session 2. This task really does require a fairly direct and measurable response on the part of the therapist, and fidelity may be lowered by explaining or providing too much information here.

Another important set of points refers to the activity level of the therapist. FBT is an active therapy, and particularly given the need to exhort action on the part of parents, higher fidelity ratings often go along with more active therapists. By active, however, we do not mean telling people what to do, but rather working to summarize, reframe, direct, and redirect treatment efforts.

Active therapists expand statements made by the family, introduce language (e.g., externalization), and reframe statements/issues in terms of the goals of treatment. They also tie concepts together and amplify points, with efforts to use issues or concerns identified by the family to make points in session. This can be considered a "bottom-up" strategy, in which what happens in session or is described by the family is used to illustrate a concept and then generalized for the family. It is important to note that active therapists do not prescribe ("You should feed her more butter") but rather draw from material in session ("It sounds like AN gets more activated when you butter the toast …"). Active therapists can jump in and redirect the focus of treatment, both directly ("I'm curious about something you just said, can we go back to that for a minute?") as well as indirectly, by the questions we choose to ask, the emotions that we want to amplify, and the events and issues that we spend time on in session. An active therapist is one who understands the integrated nature of many of the techniques used in FBT and pays attention to timing in sessions to introduce or expand these concepts. Practicing the skills we want families to use while they are in session is the best way we can teach and guide use of these skills. Active therapists are also adept at tolerating or managing emotions in the session, providing empathy or context for the challenges of renourishment rather than attempting to alleviate this distress. For example, reminding parents that the challenges they face in helping their child eat more are excellent examples of why they need to step in, as their child would not be able to manage these difficulties on his/her own. At other times, active therapists can also pre-empt concerns. For example, when sharing the weight, stating that the type of weight gain is "healthy and expected, exactly on target with our expectations" or by initiating a conversation about agnosticism by saying something such as, "We do not know what causes AN, just the way we do not know what causes most cancers, but that does not mean we do not treat both diseases aggressively and with treatments that we know to be effective in eliminating these diseases."

Passive therapists use their own language without shaping the language of the family. For example, in their own speech they may refer to "AN" or "ED," but when the family describes behaviors that could be externalized this way, the therapist does not actively reshape their language. They may also introduce a concept passively, as though checking a box that this is something they should introduce, without waiting for or expanding upon statements made by the family. There may be a reluctance to guide a conversation that is off-topic or to interrupt a family member who may be moving the session in a direction that is off-topic. In addition, they may never provide examples from the family concept to illustrate a point. Often this gives the entire session a fractured feel or as though there are many topics being run through without tying each of these back to efforts toward renourishment and the individualized details of the case history and current status. More passive therapists may nod encouragement for behaviors they see parents engaging in that are appropriate but do not provide direct feedback, "That sounds like an excellent way of managing that situation, what happened next?" or problem-solving with parents.

Ratings are made on a 7-point scale (see Appendix F, www.routledge .com/9780415714747). The rater should view a score of 4 as a "textbook implementation" of a concept or use of a skill, without expansion, generalization, or utility for the family. In contrast, fidelity ratings are boosted by application of these issues directly to challenges facing families. Lower scores are given when there are mixed messages, poor attempts at describing these behaviors, or failure to focus and direct conversations or issues raised in the session. Additional reasons for lowered scores include being off task, such as spending a long time in discussion of comorbidity, allowing or even engaging in criticism, or moving efforts away from parental empowerment toward empowerment of the patient either directly or indirectly.

Overall fidelity codes are made at the end of each session. These are also on a 7-point scale but should be rated considering the entire content of the session. In many cases, the whole is not equal to the sum of its parts—therapists may only adequately implement each skill, but overall their fidelity may be higher if they remained on task. Conversely, a therapist who is not connecting with the family may rate low on only one code, but the effect is that the family is unwilling or unable to engage in treatment. Additionally, many therapists seem to implement the skills as though they are separate points of engagement, when really they build upon one another. As Daniel Le Grange has described, a good session should build in intensity like Ravel's Bolero—where the skills build upon one another until the critical moment at which the parents are charged to take control of their child's renourishment. This is rated in overall fidelity, as the tenor of the session should be relatively focused, rather than fragmented, and should generally follow the skills described below in order (although this is not always possible) with the therapist working to orchestrate and guide the session.

Session 1

Greeting the Family in a Sincere but Grave Manner

This can be rated by the presence of a quieter more serious tone. Often the early part of Session 1 is spent making introductions, gathering informed consent, and orientation to treatment (check-ins, weekly appointments, etc.). Coding here should be guided by pacing as much as content: the therapist should speak in a lower tone, with slightly slower speech, and should keep these interactions simple. As such, good fidelity would be gathering information on people who are present, their names/relationships/types of work or grade in school. We want to have an idea of who these people are outside of AN, but this should be relatively brief.

Taking a History Engaging Each Member of the Family

The goal here is to have the therapist demonstrate the importance of each member of the family in treatment by directly asking for their input and observations. This is often done through circular questioning and can be rated for both. Often therapists make the mistake of focusing on parents for collection of information, which can also feel like unifying the parents. But it is also important to address the needs of the patient and siblings. Efforts to engage should be rated for fidelity, regardless of response, as many of our patients have difficulty engaging well in the early sessions of FBT. Stated differently, this is a place where attempts are rated rather than the outcome of those attempts. Another common dilemma is when therapists, especially those who are used to individual approaches, spend undue time engaging with the patient in an attempt to develop a stronger relationship with the patient or get "buy in" for the treatment. While efforts at developing relationships with our patients are critical, spending too much time here may reduce overall fidelity, as well as compromise time spent engaging the parents as the agents of change. It is also important to remember that these efforts overlap/continue with the efforts at gathering a history related to AN. Asking questions and engaging each member is important, and a good part of this assessment is engagement of siblings and the patient, as much as the parents.

Taking a History Focused on AN

There are two elements to this: the first is to keep a focus on eating disorder symptoms, rather than family conflict or family history, and the second is to keep more of a current focus: How is AN impacting dinners right now? Relationships right now? What has the family done to address these symptoms since they have become concerned? It is important to hear about comorbidity and other factors that may have led to heightened risk for development of ED symptoms, but assessment of these areas should be with a focus on learning sufficiently about family process around eating disorder symptoms and behaviors to guide renourishment. A good history tells us about how each of the family members has been impacted as well as the impact on domains of physical health, emotional health, and changes in behaviors at home or with others, including social relatedness. Better fidelity is achieved by clarifying or expanding on statements made by parents and patients, particularly when they are adept at providing history.

Externalization of Illness

This can also take many forms: Venn diagrams, metaphors, and illustrations, as well as use of the family's language to describe the disorder and make this distinct from the patient. In Session 1, direct efforts to externalize are considered the most effective and best examples of fidelity to this model (earning higher scores). In addition to direct coaching in externalization, the therapist's use of language to highlight the difference between the patient and AN ("It sounds like AN is very strong when just one parent is involved") can be considered examples of externalization but earn higher fidelity ratings in later sessions, where reinforcement of externalization is the goal, than they do in Session 1. Sessions in which the therapist provided an understanding of why we externalize, assisting the family in these efforts through use of metaphors or Venn diagrams and then utilized the family's language ("the beast" or "ED" or "AN") or shaped use of such a language are rated as having the highest fidelity.

Orchestrating an Intense Scene

This is one of the more challenging goals to code. This is because the goal of the intense scene is to create the anxiety necessary for a family to act. In some families, anxiety may already be quite high, and the orchestration may not reach the "fever pitch" necessary to engage other families. Additionally, families who have quite a bit of information about the illness may only require reiteration of points, rather than a longer, more detailed description. Ultimately, the critical points of this intervention are to facilitate an affective connection to the knowledge about the risks the adolescent with AN faces and to provide heightened drive to engage in the renourishment process. The rater has to judge if this was done appropriately to rate fidelity.

Reducing Guilt and Blame

The extent to which this is necessary depends upon the family expression of guilt and blame for the illness. The therapist can be proactive, reassuring the family that they are not responsible for the illness and pointing out the ways in which their efforts have been directed toward restoring health rather than perpetuating the illness. For some families this may mean a more active approach to reducing these emotions, through externalization, emphasis on parental strength, or returning to the steps they have taken to assist their child and their willingness to pursue the current course of treatment. Empathy is also an important component here. Acknowledging for parents that they typically did not see this disorder coming and may have engaged in behaviors that they now realize may have unwittingly supported the illness is an important way to reshape guilt. A core component of this is also keeping a present moment focus, such that the therapist works to direct family efforts on the now and the upcoming, rather than spending undue time on mistakes or missteps they may feel they have taken in the past.

Therapist Agnosticism

This is one code that also tends to be as much about the absence of behavior as the presence. It is both about not assuming a cause as it is redirecting parents away from exploring causal theories and back toward current renourishment efforts. Redirecting the family can take many forms: Reminding them that they were successful in nourishing their ill child/other children in the family until the illness appeared as well as reshaping specific statements made by the patient or the parents. Efforts can also be pre-emptive ("We do not know the cause of this illness, though we know many factors can contribute …"). Lower ratings are given to therapists who simply ignore causal statements made by family members, while higher ratings are given when the therapist directly addresses these concerns or identifies them for the family ("It sounds like you might be worried that you do not know what your daughter needs, but remember, parents do not cause this illness, and you have many skills …"). In Session 1, the therapist needs to bring up the concept of agnosticism directly to achieve fidelity.

Modification of Parent or Sibling Criticism

Efforts here should be active—directly shaping this behavior. Criticism can be managed by reframing, restating, or redirecting these statements. This code is rated for criticism originating from parents and siblings; although criticism from the patient may be present in a session, it is not coded. There are several things that may fall here: helping develop skills in selective ignoring (not attending to or responding to behaviors that distract from the task at hand or redirect the session), helping parents manage their frustration or upset (such as teaching specific skills in managing their own distress at these statements or reframing them—most often this is done when efforts at avoiding nourishment result in personal attacks on parents), and helping the family as a whole identify ED behaviors.

In Session 1, criticism is largely managed through psychoeducation and externalization. Efforts may be slightly more subtle, as the therapist may not know the family very well or may be evaluating statements in the context of family communication. Generally speaking however, criticism in Session 1 should mostly be managed by redirecting family concerns by helping the family understand the disorder. This may also include externalization techniques, if these are used in direct response to criticism. Overtly harsh or unnecessary criticism should be shaped directly, by redirecting or restating the critical comment. In the most extreme circumstances this could include reminding families of the "rules" of appropriate, compassionate communication in treatment.

Charge with the Task of Refeeding

The entire session should build to this point—the most important of part of the coding rests on the injunction to bring a family meal. This should be coded as several aspects: placing the responsibility on the parent(s) to supply the meal and stating that this should be what they feel will contribute to renourishment of their ill child. Typically, the therapist could use the direct statement, "I want (the two of) you to choose/provide a meal that *you* feel will renourish your starving child." In this sense, intonation and the specificity and gravity of the delivery can also be considered for fidelity. Like the sincere but grave manner, this should be delivered with sincerity and specificity. To rate for highest fidelity, the meal injunction must be specifically directed toward parents, should encourage them to work together to solve the problem, and must include that the meal should be sufficient for weight gain/renourishment/physical healing. The presence of statements during therapy sessions, such as "Feeding her is your job" can contribute to the fidelity of this code, but without a specific meal injunction these would be considered insufficient to meet fidelity.

Session 2

The focus in Session 2 is on renourishment efforts in the truest sense of the present moment—with the goal being to utilize the family meal itself to promote these efforts. Session 2 is the most behaviorally active and directive session for the therapist, who can and should provide more direct guidance for parental behavior and actively work to shape skills and problem-solving. As such, greater direction can be provided in these sessions and using specific examples from the family's experiences is essential.

When thinking about this session, it can be useful to think about therapists who approach these tasks in a "bottom-up" versus a "top-down" process. In bottom-up, the therapist uses materials, examples, even food items that are present in the session to reinforce a point, then helps the family generalize these. The use of these concrete and specific examples from the session or family report are given higher ratings because these are often the easiest for families to understand and to use to expand. In contrast, when therapists use more general statements and do not integrate these into the learning within the session, they miss the opportunity to help a family learn more efficiently.

Providing Feedback to the Family Regarding Weight

This should occur at the outset of the session and is used to guide the direction of renourishment efforts. There are several ways therapists may go about this, but the most typical involve sharing specific weights ("100 pounds") or specifics around weight gain ("an increase of two pounds"). Some families have asked that specifics not be shared, and in these instances, raters should listen carefully for clear feedback that provides guidance to parents. For example, in one session viewed, the therapist provided pros and cons to knowing a specific weight before sharing a chart that showed the increase without specific numbers. In addition to showing the weight chart, the gain was placed in perspective, "This is considered healthy weight gain and exactly what we would expect and what would be considered appropriate at this stage of treatment." This would be given high ratings as the therapist both took efforts to provide appropriate feedback and to provide this in a context that was of the most use to families. Fidelity ratings are lowered when therapists attempt to "explain away" weight changes, particularly weight loss, or provide feedback that is challenging to interpret (e.g., "Weight was up a bit").

Take a History of the Family Patterns around Food Prep, Serving and Discussion around Eating

This is a good example of a place where a bottom-up strategy may be most beneficial. The goals here are to understand not only the specifics of what a family brought for the current meal: who selected the meal, observations of how they serve it, what/how much is served to each family member, caloric density of the meal, as well as how typical this meal is for the family in general. By the end of the session, the therapist should have a solid idea of the way meals go in this family, see where there are obstacles to renourishment, and have an understanding of the ways these issues may contribute to maintaining (or overcoming) the illness. It should be noted that gathering this information does not mean that the therapist needs to act on it, only that this is the information that should be gathered here.

Assist the Family in Understanding Nutritional Needs of the Patient

The focus of this intervention should be on assisting parents in understanding the need for increased frequency of meals, increased portions, and/or increased caloric density. For some families, this may also include specific guidance on adding back foods that are avoided, although this is not necessary. This is another area in which a bottom-up strategy can be the most effective, using items brought to the family meal to provide specific instruction that parents can then generalize to meals at home. A good example of this in one session was the therapist "noticing" that there was still gravy on the table and using this as an opportunity to discuss that this is a higher calorie density food and encouraging parents to use this. Parents were then able to generalize this food to others of similar density (oils, butters, nuts) to understand calorically dense foods. Specific discussions around calories are not necessarily rated lower, but highest ratings are given when the therapist uses the language and skills of the parents to guide these interventions. Specific areas for discussion should include direct discussion of the frequency of meals/snacks, increased portion sizes for meals, and discussions of caloric density. Helping parents reorient to what the patient liked or enjoyed before AN would also be counted here. Additionally, the focus should be on these discussions with parents, and ratings are decreased if the focus of these discussions is with the patient.

Align Parents in Efforts to Work Together in Renourishment

This code focuses on alignment of parents and should include efforts to get parents to agree on the amount and type of food being served to the patient as well as focus efforts to help the patient eat more. Additionally, it can include elements of aligning parents around the seriousness of the illness or the behaviors that constitute AN. Ultimately, parental agreement on the need for monitoring, increasing intake, decreasing physical activity, and compliance with therapy all fall under this code.

One More Mouthful

Although this appears to be fairly straightforward, this can be challenging to code if the patient eats easily. The goal is one bite more than the patient intended, and in the case of relative ease of eating, fidelity is associated with the ability to present a paradoxical intervention and to continue to challenge the parents in adding to the meal or creating more challenge within this meal. Parental efforts to increase their child's intake should be rated here, even if the therapist does not respond to these efforts (this would lower fidelity). For example, if a parent asks the ill child if he/she wants something more to eat and the patient refuses, the therapist should use this to help parents gain compliance with this request. Failure to do so would be considered missing a critical opportunity in this session. In rare cases when there is not sufficient food to help a patient eat one more mouthful, hypothetical examples can be used by the therapist.

In many sessions, therapists are reluctant to step in to help families with renourishment efforts. It is important that this session have a specific focus on understanding how to help families with how to work as a team to increase their child's nourishment. The first order of business is to ensure that the family has provided sufficient nourishment. If a family plates an insufficient amount of food, it is critical that the therapist act relatively quickly to help the family plate sufficient food. Waiting until the end of the meal to help provide additional food is not helpful to the family. It is most helpful to work with the family from the time they plate the food and history has been gathered. In other words, once the food is plated, providing direct feedback on amounts and types of food is ideal. Guiding parents on direct renourishment is coded elsewhere, but it is critical that the family is guided in providing sufficient food. This, in and of itself, is often sufficient to help incite AN in the patient and help parents see the challenges facing them.

Another critical goal in this session is to move parents away from the notion that eating "anything" is sufficient. In fact, it is confronting AN that is the goal. In most sessions, this means helping parents realize that compliance does not imply that the patient eats with no struggle. The struggle is an important part of helping their child, and this should be a significant part of the session. Many therapists tend to wait until the end to coax parents to help their child eat more, but this injunction should be introduced as soon as it is evident that the meal that parents agreed on has been plated and the patient has stopped eating. If the patient is eating compliantly, paradoxical injunctions should be made: asking them to eat only if they want to; pointing out the challenging aspects of their meal ("it is so good to see you eating something like cheese; that is a great calorie dense food with fats and protein ..."). If necessary, help parents by asking them how this meal is the same as or different from meals at home and help them create a meal that is more similar to what happens at home (in emotional tenor).

Setting Parents on Their Way to Work Out among Themselves How to Renourish Their Child

This code comprises two aspects: parental empowerment and problem-solving efforts toward renourishment. In parental empowerment, the focus should be on aligning parents with one another and empowering them to manage renourishment. This may mean discouraging discussions with the patient around food and eating and encouraging communication between parents around meals to be served. There is the element of problem-solving to this conversation which may include helping parents choose a target for intervention (e.g., if they state they cannot tackle all ED symptoms, the therapist may help guide them toward specific areas for intervention—increasing caloric density before tackling annoying, but not intake limiting, behaviors). There are continued efforts to empower parents, by pointing out their strengths, decreasing guilt/blame, and encouraging them to rely on their own skills for renourishment.

Modifying Parental and Sibling Criticism

Efforts here are fairly direct. Criticism can be managed by reframing, restating, or redirecting these statements. This code is rated for criticism originating from parents and siblings. Although criticism from the patient may be present in a session, it is not coded.

Externalization of Illness

This can also take many forms within Session 2, but it is most effectively delivered when examples in the session are directly tied to behaviors in the session. In particular, in instances where there is disruptive behavior around efforts to consume the meal in session, these can be actively externalized by the therapist. The therapist's use of language to highlight the difference between the patient and the AN is appropriate here.

Align Patient with Siblings for Support

This represents efforts to move the patient into the sibling subsystem by encouraging the sibling to take an active role in distracting the patient or providing emotional support. This can include efforts to reduce anger and upset in a sibling as well as direct efforts toward engaging the sibling for support.

Keeping Focus on AN and Eating Disorder Behavior

The bulk of Session 2 should focus on direct eating behaviors and efforts of parents to increase intake. Discussions around other issues decrease fidelity. One way to think about rating here is that increasing the percentage of time spent in focus directly on the meal is correlated with higher fidelity.

Agnosticism

See information for coding in Session 1, as all apply here. In Session 2, agnosticism involves the redirection toward current eating behaviors and renourishment efforts as well as avoids discussions regarding causality. For maximum effectiveness, therapists should continue to be overt in efforts to address causal concerns raised by family members (including patients). This code can be rated as "not applicable."

Session 3 and the Remainder of Phase 1

The focus in Session 3 (and the remainder of Phase 1) is on consolidating knowledge and redirecting efforts toward increased intake and weight gain. Because families move at different paces, these sessions may vary somewhat widely in their presentation across Phase 1. As such, the focus may be on specific renourishment efforts (e.g., increasing caloric density, providing sufficient calories for weight gain), parental alignment, and empowerment to face challenges presented by AN (e.g., conflict management). Session 3 is directed by challenges faced by the family and is an introduction to the ways in which treatment will progress from this point forward. However, in Session 3, setting up a structure for the remainder of Phase 1 is important, and this begins with discussing and sharing weight and then keeping a focus on familial efforts toward disrupting the patterns that maintain the illness. In addition, while Sessions 1 and 2 have very specific foci, the remainder of Phase 1 sessions are more interactive and directed by the needs of the family in tackling the challenges of renourishment. Where the therapist places his/her attention and focus, the questions they ask, and the ways in which they guide the sessions are important to rate for overall fidelity, even if the family does not necessarily follow the therapist's lead. In some instances, this may mean employing more overt strategies to guide the conversation, including interrupting and refocusing the conversation, provided that these are in service of the goal of improving renourishment efforts.

Providing Feedback to the Family Regarding Weight

This should occur at the outset of the session and is used to guide the direction of renourishment efforts. See Session 2 for additional information. In Session 3 and beyond, there is the ability to track a trajectory rather than single data points, which typically means the weight chart is more useful in gauging parental efforts. This is also the point in time that parents and/or patients may become more resistant to weigh-ins or other problems may arise. Therapists should listen to parental concerns regarding weigh-ins and ultimately must proceed based on their clinical judgment regarding the manner in which they provide this information. Sharing specific information (a specific weight, a description of increases/decreases, and/or sharing of a weight graph) are critical components.

A common challenge to this goal, arising in later sessions, is when patients manipulate their weight by waterloading, weigh down themselves with weighted items, or scream/yell/tantrum around weigh-ins. These typically arise at Session 3 or later when patients learn the "rules" of treatment and have not developed strategies for responding. For the first two issues, a key goal is to take a weight that represents as close to a "true" weight as possible. This means doing clinic weights with relatively minimal clothing (t-shirts and pants; no shoes, sweaters, sweatshirts, hats, heavy jewelry, or belts, etc.). If a weight seems unusual, such as a rapid increase in weight, take a weight again after making certain there are no scale abnormalities. Following that, when the weight is shared, ask parents directly if weight changes are in line with their expectations. If they are, but you suspect weight manipulation, you can wonder about that with the family ("Sometimes in an effort to show weight gain, some kids drink or eat just before session ... did you see anything like that before this session?"). If the patient uses the restroom during the session, taking a second weight to see weight changes after urination can be important. There is a difference between kids being able to wait an entire session before using the restroom and kids needing to use a restroom during a session. The former is not quite as concerning as the latter. Parents are often unaware of waterloading behaviors and should be informed about these. This can be particularly helpful in continuing to raise parental anxiety, as waterloading can cause acute heart failure. This can often be addressed by noting, "It can be important to watch for waterloading behaviors, including eating salty foods and drinking water before session, because these behaviors are quite dangerous and can cause death through heart failure. The kinds of things we look for are drinking water before sessions in order to fill up, and there are even things online that can guide these behaviors, without acknowledging how dangerous they are. Have you seen anything that would make you think this is going on in your family?" If yes, ask them more about it; if it is not, encourage them to observe or monitor.

Another challenge exists when patients weight themselves to inflate the numbers on the scale. With nongowned weigh-ins, it can be quite challenging to catch. Removing all excess clothing (apart from the minimum that can be worn to be considered a clothed weight) is important. Additionally, make certain shoes (and sometimes socks as well), hats, scarves, phones, etc., are all removed.

Helping parents see the reasons behind weigh-ins can also be a challenge. Many parents see their child being distressed following a weigh-in and seek to avoid this. It is important to frame the importance of weigh-ins under several conditions: providing direction and exposure and provocation.

Providing direction refers to the importance of knowing, understanding, and analyzing weight changes to focus the session and guide parents. It is not essential for patients to know their weight (more on that later), but it is critical that the therapist and the parents know the weight.

Having a weight taken at consistent times and on a consistent scale is indispensable to this treatment. It is important to help parents understand that a medical weight answers different questions than our therapy weights—our weigh-ins are not used to determine medical stability but are used to guide the current treatment session. Spacing weigh-ins means we may miss behaviors or changes in weight that are important in evaluating overall efforts. Using a weight from another source also means we do not have opportunities to discuss things such as waterloading or weight loss. In addition, parents often feel like there is a big focus on weight at the outset of treatment, and they need to be reassured that this is one measure, albeit a very important one, of overall health, and hence the focus. Finally, while patients are often weighed frequently at the start of sessions, when they are likely having more frequent medical follow-up, medical appointments are often spaced differently than therapy visits. What appears efficient at the outset can later become cumbersome or unrealistic (for instance, using a weight from the doctor a week before the session or not having a weight at each session). Knowing the potential pitfalls can help guide decision making. The manual also provides other areas of support for weigh-ins at the start of session, including reminding parents that measures such as this keep us "on target" and help us focus our aim and not be swayed by AN.

Exposure and provocation are also important concepts in FBT. Although many parents feel their child becomes unduly upset when they know their weight, most patients already know their weight and most are quite obsessed with these numbers. Rather than avoiding the numbers, however, it can be useful to reframe for parents that seeing the weight on a consistent basis, in the face of AN thinking, can also help to alleviate goals. Rather, the goal is to help patients see that the amounts that they are eating are translating into slow, steady weight gain. One might also use this to highlight differences between AN expectations ("I gained 10 pounds this week! My parents fed me like a pig!") and reality, which is often substantially less weight gain than expected by the patient. Further, patients think that weight gain is going to be exponential when in reality it is highest at the outset of treatment and drops off. This helps reinforce the trajectory and expectations of treatment as well. (Phase 1 focuses on weight gain and stabilization, Phase 2 is less about weight gain and more around flexibility and expansion of eating behaviors, and Phase 3 is not about weight or weight gain at all.) Finally, the notion of provocation is an important one to review. In many treatment modalities, the goal is often to better regulate the emotions and symptoms of the patient. However, in FBT we want to help parents engage with AN directly, and taking weight can often invite the "anorexic fog" into the room. This provides opportunities to coach parents in how to manage AN directly and with specific examples (see use of bottom-up opportunities to shape behaviors from Session 2). This can be disconcerting to families, and sometimes to novice therapists, who prefer that therapy remain a calm and controlled environment. The drawbacks of this are that we cannot coach parents in managing more challenging behaviors, in tolerating distress, and in achieving a sense of ecological validity to our sessions. The goal is not, of course, to unnecessarily distress our patients, but we must also assume that the healthy part of our patients is present (albeit usually silent) in these early sessions and that the ability to train parents in managing the worst of the AN—both by our own modeling as well as development of specific techniques to shape the disorder maintaining behaviors.

Did the Therapist Direct, Redirect, and Focus Therapeutic Discussion on Food and Eating Behaviors and Their Management until Food, Eating and Weight Behaviors/Concerns Were Relieved?

The main movement here is from the meal the family has presented in the family meal session to gathering history regarding meal preparation, delivery, and intake following the family session. This means gathering information on the types, frequencies, and portioning of meals; efforts to manage meal disrupting behaviors; and keeping focus on ways to improve these aspects without being distracted by issues of comorbidity, causality, or conflict. This is similar to Session 2 where we might consider the percent of time in session focused on issues related to AN. In Session 3, a considerable portion of the session should be spent in focus on food and eating concerns with only minimal time spent on niceties, scheduling, and transitional topics of discussion. Discussions of comorbid conditions or causal factors should generally be minimized and redirected. The only exception to this is if the family has made excellent weight progress and has fewer challenges. In these cases, it can be considered acceptable to focus on topics such as expected developmental progress or ways the family may have felt that the patient was never on a "typical" developmental trajectory. However, this type of conversation will generally not lower fidelity if the therapist has duly reviewed efforts toward renourishment and joining parents.

Did the Therapist Discuss, Support, and Help the Parental Dyad's Efforts at Refeeding?

The focus of this intervention should be on assisting parents in improving their communication to maintain a consistent front. This might best be embodied by the "on the same line, on the same letter, on the same dot," and this is how many therapists describe this to parents. However, for some families it may mean continuing efforts to get them to agree on the need for treatment or the focus of this treatment. Parents may also express concerns related to the family meal, and the presentation of these concerns can serve to unify parents. In ideal situations, parents enter Session 3 focused on working together with the therapist. In some situations, however, the family may present aligned against the therapist. In this case, taking time to understand parental concerns and finding areas for common ground are important. In other families, parents may present not aligned with one another, and whether this is a new onset or a continuation from previous sessions, efforts should be made at aligning parents with the goal of renourishment. Simply, if parents are not aligned either with the treatment or with each other, efforts should focus here.

As in Session 2, this may also include specific guidance on caloric density, increasing frequency of meals, and managing eating disorder behaviors, such as excessive exercise. The specific focus will depend on the challenges facing the family. In most cases there are many areas the family could focus on, and fidelity can be rated for helping the family focus on specific goals. This is not to say that the therapist should tell parents where to focus, but skillful implementation requires the therapist to problem-solve with the family in the areas in which their intervention and energy will yield the most effective outcomes. Generally speaking, this means focusing on increasing nutrition/nourishment rather than focusing on reducing agitation or unusual, but not obstructive, eating habits (cutting food into small bites). Another way of saying this is that no one will gain weight if they continue restricting but reduce exercise—increasing intake is a critical and foremost goal. (Note: This is not to discourage efforts at reducing exercise and calorie-burning activities but only to state that one cannot really "outrun bad nourishment.")

Throughout the remainder of Phase 1, a strong strategy is to work with the family to identify the areas where they are on the same page, specify goals in that area, and then work out how to solve these challenges. For example, some families may identify breakfast as an area in which they are having more challenges achieving nutritional goals. If parents agree upon this, then problem-solve ways to accomplish this. If they are not on the same page, however, it is important to find out if there is a place where they do agree on an intervention and, if not, the therapist should work with them to get them on the same page. Thus efforts at alignment are rated here (where these codes were separate in previous measures; discussed more in the next paragraph). Specific discussions around calories are not necessarily rated lower, but highest ratings are given when the therapist uses the language and skills of the parents to guide these interventions and direct the session. Specific areas for discussion may include direct discussion of the frequency of meals/snacks, increased portion sizes for meals, and discussions of caloric density, as well as following medical advice around exercise, including schooling, disrupting exercise, and calorie-burning activities (e.g., remaining unnecessarily chilled to burn more calories). Strategies may include:

- Identifying for parents the areas in which they are concerned about "pushing more" and how you might help with this reluctance
- Identifying previously enjoyed snacks/food items—usually those that are higher calorie—and assisting them in adding back in these feared foods
- Continuing psychoeducation around the ways in which AN symptoms may change as a result of renourishment efforts—such as new concerns being stated, upset and threats from the child directed at one or both parents, etc.

These should be reframed for the family where possible and placed in the context of the disorder.

Efforts toward alignment of parents are included here and refer to efforts to get parents to agree on the amount/type of food being served to the patient as well as focused efforts to help the patient eat more. Additionally, it can include elements of aligning parents around the seriousness of the illness or the behaviors that constitute AN. Ultimately, parental agreement on the need for monitoring, increasing intake, decreasing physical activity, and compliance with therapy all fall under this code. More often, however, behaviors coded here are specific goals such as identifying weight disrupting behaviors and targeting those. Thus, a focus here may be on understanding parental communication styles, behaviors they observe, and helping them observe or communicate more around these meals. Some strategies may be working with parents specifically to develop ways of talking with one another (using a Google doc to list meals or reactions, finding time to speak each evening or morning to identify challenges, etc.). Other strategies, however, may focus more on reducing upset between parents, which may be a result of long-standing conflicts in the marriage or disagreements on the illness itself. In these cases, the therapist should avoid marital conflict issues (or refer to an outside therapist as necessary). Reminding the family that their other agreements may co-exist with their desire to save their child's life and that these other disagreements or conflicts are minor compared to the challenges facing them with AN can help guide these interactions.

Another common issue that arises and which is coded here is the changing nature of the symptoms of AN. Most therapists are familiar enough to realize that, with greater pressure on the illness, other behaviors may arise as AN becomes more desperate to maintain a foothold of illness in the face of parental efforts. These may include development of other ED behaviors—purging behaviors, redoubled efforts at restriction, increases in exercise, including nighttime exercise, or restless/agitated behaviors (e.g., walking or standing while doing homework or during meals). Reframing this as success in an effort to put pressure on AN can help some parents but may also require the therapist to introduce strategies or thinking around ways to disrupt these behaviors (e.g., injunctions to monitor after meals to reduce purging).

One way that this can be stated is as "Outwit, Outlast, Outplay"—stolen from the show *Survivor* and adapted to FBT. *Outwit* means that parents will always be one step behind the AN. They may find that the more pressure they put on eating dinner, the harder it is to get breakfast in regularly, or that the more they are nourishing their child, the more there are attempts to exercise. It is critical to reframe this as progress, rather than the creation of more problems through treatment. These new behaviors are a response to parental pressure to overcome the disorder. *Outlast* is much as it sounds: families are busy and have many tasks, challenges, and activities. Few families can easily take the time to monitor all meals without making some sacrifices. Placing critical importance on early steps and accommodations to assist with renourishment is important to help families realize that little is as important in early treatment as taking the time to get meals in. "Outlasting" AN—including temper outbursts and upset—is often a key goal in renourishment efforts. *Outplay* refers to behaviors that distract from nourishment efforts: swearing, pitting parents against one another, raising issues of "fairness," or calling attention to the behavior of parents or siblings in efforts to distract from AN are all areas in which parents "are being played" by AN. These behaviors benefit from therapist redirection to the symptoms that are presenting the greatest challenge.

Modifying Parental and Sibling Criticism

Efforts here are fairly direct; criticism can be managed by reframing, restating, or redirecting these statements. This code is rated for criticism originating from parents and siblings; although criticism from the patient may be present in a session, it is not coded. There are several things that may fall here: helping develop skills in selective ignoring (not attending to or responding to behaviors that distract from the task at hand or redirect the session), helping parents manage their frustration or upset (such as teaching specific skills in managing their own distress at these statements or reframing them—most often this is done when efforts at avoiding nourishment result in personal attacks on parents), and helping the family as a whole identify ED behaviors.

Externalization of Illness

In Sessions 3–10 this may mean a slightly different focus than in Sessions 1 and 2. When efforts are more abstract/educational (Session 1) and tied to specific behaviors (Session 2), they become increasingly focused on interpreting the behaviors described by the family outside of session and should be used to amplify the message of a nonblaming stance as well as education on the nature of the disorder. One way to do this is to help the family understand the ways in which AN moves the patient away from his/her own goals. For example, in a patient who longs to return to exercise but refuses most nourishment, pointing out to parents that behaviors are in direct conflict with stated desires can help highlight the ways AN interferes with their child's healthy and expected behaviors. Unlike the previous sessions, this can, albeit briefly, also be directed at the patient to help him/her understand the difference between himself/herself and the AN. Patient-directed externalization of the illness should be brief and only provided when "speaking to the healthy part of the patient" rather than devolving into "AN arguments" between the therapist and the patient. For example, if a patient states that he or she no longer likes chocolate ice cream, a previously favored food, it may be helpful to note to the family that one challenge with AN is that it has the tendency to obscure what one likes with what one is afraid of. The patient may be afraid of the calories and richness of ice cream, but it is unlikely that they no longer like the food itself. Helping the family externalize with specific examples and challenges is most beneficial in this early stage of treatment.

Agnosticism

Read information for coding in Sessions 1 and 2, as all apply here. In Session 3, agnosticism involves the redirection toward current eating behaviors and renourishment efforts as well as avoiding discussions regarding causality. For maximum effectiveness, therapists should continue to be overt in their efforts to address causal concerns raised by family members (including patients). Assessing comorbidity by itself is not a move away from agnosticism but can be coded as such if the therapist uses these efforts as a means of explaining why the disorder developed to the family. Assessment of comorbidity is NOT coded here when the therapist is working with the family to identify if a current comorbid illness is present and interfering with efforts at parental renourishment. This code can be rated as "not applicable."

Distinguishing between Adolescent Patient and His/Her Interests versus AN

This is the first time this is coded in these sessions and refers to attempts to amplify differences between AN and the goals, ideals, and patient characteristics that defined him/her prior to the onset of the illness. This is often an extension of externalization (which targets parents) but is directed toward the patient. This includes demonstrating the ways in which AN leads to behaviors and ideas that are counter to what the patient may claim to want. For example, if there is a desire to exercise, pointing out the ways in which increased nutrition can help speed return to those goals is a way of demonstrating the differences between the patient and the interests of AN. Some of this occurs during time spent alone with the patient; at other times it occurs during the family session. There is less focus on the development of insight but rather on simple observations of the differences between the patient and AN. Other examples include wanting to be more social, difficulties concentrating due to malnourishment, interference with excessive exercise, and academics or other personal goals.

References

Castonguay, L. G., Boswell, J. F., Constantino, M. J., Goldfried, M. R., & Hill, C. E. (2010). Training implications of harmful effects of psychological treatments. *American Psychologist, 65*(1), 34–49.

Castonguay, L. G., Goldfried, M. R., Wiser, S., Raue, P. J., & Hayes, A. M. (1996). Predicting the effect of cognitive therapy for depression: A study of unique and common factors. *Journal of Consulting and Clinical Psychology, 64*(3), 497–504.

Gibbons, M., Crits-Christoph, P., Levinson, J., & Barber, J. (2003). Flexibility in manual-based psychotherapies: Predictors of therapist interventions in interpersonal and cognitive-behavioral therapy. *Psychotherapy Research, 13*(2), 169–185.

Lock, J., & Le Grange, D. (2012). *Treatment manual for anorexia nervosa: A family-based approach*, 2nd Ed. New York: Guilford Press.

Loeb, K. L., Wilson, G. T., Pratt, E. M., Hayaki, J., Labouvie, E., Walsh, B. T., Agras, W. S., & Fairburn, C. G. (2005). Therapeutic alliance and treatment adherence in two interventions for bulimia nervosa: A study of process and outcome. *Journal of Consulting and Clinical Psychology, 73*, 1097–1107.

Waltz, J., Addis, M. E., Koerner, K., & Jacobson, N. S. (1993). Testing the integrity of a psychotherapy protocol: Assessment of adherence and competence. *Journal of Consulting and Clinical Psychology, 61*, 620–630.

Index

case management as part of intensive
family treatment program (IFT) 89
"chaining" flavors of food 268, 275
"challenge" food 102
chat rooms 148–9
Child and Adolescent Eating Disorders
Service (CAEDS) 110, 132, 134
child as a helpless victim 9–10
childhood obesity. *See* pediatric obesity
Children's Hospital at Westmead 24
circular questioning 420, 423
Cleveland Center for Eating Disorders
(CCED) FBT-DBT treatment model
316–24
clinical director as part of intensive
family treatment program 73
clinical guidance with family
therapy 147
Clinical Practice Guidelines (CPG) 282
clinician: in family-based treatment
for transition age youth with
anorexia nervosa (FBT-TAY) 240;
implementing family-based therapy
406–8
coaching strategies to handle the
family meal 53–56
coding system for fidelity to family-based
therapy 419–39; session 1, 423–6;
session 2, 427–30; session 3, 431–9
"Coffee Breaks," 147
cognitive aspects of eating disorders
treated with family-based therapy in
a specialty practice setting 381
cognitive-behavioral therapy (CBT)
20, 93, 132, 234, 270, 306, 381;
for bulimia nervosa 403; for eating
disorders 403–5
cognitive change as an emotion
regulation strategy 347–50
cognitive dissonance 349–50
cognitive factors inhibiting diagnosing
eating disorders 161–2
cognitive model of anorexia nervosa 93
cognitive restructuring techniques 23
Colborn, Danielle 3
collaboration: in family-based therapy
for pediatric overweight (FBT-PO)
207, 213–14; increasing in dialetical
behavior therapy (DBT) 312;
between youth and parents in
family-based treatment for transition
age youth with anorexia nervosa
(FBT-TAY) 237, 244–5

Collins, L. 142
co-morbidities: addressed in dialetical
behavior therapy (DBT) 309–10;
addressed in family-based therapy
for adolescent weight loss surgery
(FBT-WLS) 287–8; addressed in
family-based therapy for avoidant
restrictive food intake disorder
(ARFID-FBT) 270; addressed in
family-based therapy in a specialty
practice setting 379–80; mental
health issues in transition age youth
with anorexia nervosa (FBT-TAY)
244; in young adults with anorexia
nervosa 234
conflict avoidance 10, 14; in situation
modification 342–4
conjoint family therapy (CFT) 13,
59–61; benefits and challenges
59–61; differences and similarities
with parent-focused treatment 63
consensus building to implement
family-based therapy 363–4
*Consolidated Framework for
Implementation Research
(CFIR)* 412
constructivist theory of family
therapy 8
"consultation-to-the-client"
approach 321
counseling, family 61
Crane, A. 150
criticism 13, 14, 141; modification
of parent or sibling 426,
430, 437
cybernetic principles of family
therapy 7

Damschroder, L. J. 401
Darwin, Charles 329
day programs utilizing multi-family
therapy (MFT) 131–2
death risk increase after weight-loss
surgery 294
decision-making in complex settings
362–3
development level of child impacting
family-based therapy for pediatric
overweight 184–92
Diagnostic and Statistical Manual of
Mental Disorders. *See* DSM
diagnostic criteria for eating disorders
158–61